(Continued on back endsheets)

Dictionary of Literary Biography
Yearbook: 1990

Dictionary of Literary Biography
Yearbook: 1990

Edited by
James W. Hipp

6522

A Bruccoli Clark Layman Book
Gale Research Inc.
Detroit, London

Printed in the United States of America

Published simultaneously in the United Kingdom
by Gale Research International Limited
(An affiliated company of Gale Research Inc.)

The paper used in this publication meets the minimum requirements
of American National Standard for Information Sciences—Permanence
Paper for Printed Library Materials, ANSI Z39.48-1984.   ∞™

Library of Congress Catalog Card Number 82-645187
ISSN 0731-7867
ISBN 0-8103-4570-6

Contents

Plan of the Series

. . . Almost the most prodigious asset of a country, and perhaps its most precious possession, is its native literary product—when that product is fine and noble and enduring.

Mark Twain*

The advisory board, the editors, and the publisher of the *Dictionary of Literary Biography* are joined in endorsing Mark Twain's declaration. The literature of a nation provides an inexhaustible resource of permanent worth. We intend to make literature and its creators better understood and more accessible to students and the reading public, while satisfying the standards of teachers and scholars.

To meet these requirements, *literary biography* has been construed in terms of the author's achievement. The most important thing about a writer is his writing. Accordingly, the entries in *DLB* are career biographies, tracing the development of the author's canon and the evolution of his reputation.

The purpose of *DLB* is not only to provide reliable information in a convenient format but also to place the figures in the larger perspective of literary history and to offer appraisals of their accomplishments by qualified scholars.

The publication plan for *DLB* resulted from two years of preparation. The project was proposed to Bruccoli Clark by Frederick G. Ruffner, president of the Gale Research Company, in November 1975. After specimen entries were prepared and typeset, an advisory board was formed to refine the entry format and develop the series rationale. In meetings held during 1976, the publisher, series editors, and advisory board approved the scheme for a comprehensive biographical dictionary of persons who contributed to North American literature. Editorial work on the first volume began in January 1977, and it was published in 1978. In order to make *DLB* more than a reference tool and to compile volumes that individually have claim to status as literary history, it was decided to organize volumes by topic, period, or genre. Each of these freestanding volumes provides a biographical-bibliographical guide and overview for a particular area of literature. We are convinced that this organization—as opposed to a single alphabet method—constitutes a valuable innovation in the presentation of reference material. The volume plan necessarily requires many decisions for the placement and treatment of authors who might properly be included in two or three volumes. In some instances a major figure will be included in separate volumes, but with different entries emphasizing the aspect of his career appropriate to each volume. Ernest Hemingway, for example, is represented in *American Writers in Paris, 1920-1939* by an entry focusing on his expatriate apprenticeship; he is also in *American Novelists, 1910-1945* with an entry surveying his entire career. Each volume includes a cumulative index of subject authors and articles. Comprehensive indexes to the entire series are planned.

With volume ten in 1982 it was decided to enlarge the scope of *DLB*. By the end of 1986 twenty-one volumes treating British literature had been published, and volumes for Commonwealth and Modern European literature were in progress. The series has been further augmented by the *DLB Yearbooks* (since 1981) which update published entries and add new entries to keep the *DLB* current with contemporary activity. There have also been *DLB Documentary Series* volumes which provide biographical and critical source materials for figures whose work is judged to have particular interest for students. One of these companion volumes is entirely devoted to Tennessee Williams.

We define literature as the *intellectual commerce of a nation:* not merely as belles lettres but as that ample and complex process by which ideas are generated, shaped, and transmitted. *DLB* entries are not limited to "creative writers" but extend to other figures who in their time and in their way influenced the mind of a people. Thus the series encompasses historians, journalists, publishers, and screenwriters. By this means readers of *DLB* may be aided to perceive litera-

*From an unpublished section of Mark Twain's autobiography, copyright © by the Mark Twain Company.

ture not as cult scripture in the keeping of intellectual high priests but firmly positioned at the center of a nation's life.

DLB includes the major writers appropriate to each volume and those standing in the ranks immediately behind them. Scholarly and critical counsel has been sought in deciding which minor figures to include and how full their entries should be. Wherever possible, useful references are made to figures who do not warrant separate entries.

Each *DLB* volume has a volume editor responsible for planning the volume, selecting the figures for inclusion, and assigning the entries. Volume editors are also responsible for preparing, where appropriate, appendices surveying the major periodicals and literary and intellectual movements for their volumes, as well as lists of further readings. Work on the series as a whole is coordinated at the Bruccoli Clark Layman editorial center in Columbia, South Carolina, where the editorial staff is responsible for accuracy of the published volumes.

One feature that distinguishes *DLB* is the illustration policy–its concern with the iconography of literature. Just as an author is influenced by his surroundings, so is the reader's understanding of the author enhanced by a knowledge of his environment. Therefore *DLB* volumes include not only drawings, paintings, and photographs of authors, often depicting them at various stages in their careers, but also illustrations of their families and places where they lived. Title pages are regularly reproduced in facsimile along with dust jackets for modern authors. The dust jackets are a special feature of *DLB* because they often document better than anything else the way in which an author's work was perceived in its own time. Specimens of the writers' manuscripts are included when feasible.

Samuel Johnson rightly decreed that "The chief glory of every people arises from its authors." The purpose of the *Dictionary of Literary Biography* is to compile literary history in the surest way available to us–by accurate and comprehensive treatment of the lives and work of those who contributed to it.

　　　　　　　　　　　　　　　The *DLB* Advisory Board

Foreword

The *Dictionary of Literary Biography Yearbook* is guided by the same principles that have provided the basic rationale for the entire *DLB* series: 1) the literature of a nation represents an inexhaustible resource of permanent worth; 2) the surest way to trace the outlines of literary history is by a comprehensive treatment of the lives and works of those who contributed to it; and 3) the greatest service the series can provide is to make literary achievement better understood and more accessible to students and the literate public, while serving the needs of scholars. In keeping with those principles, the *Yearbook* has been planned to augment *DLB* by reflecting the vitality of contemporary literature and summarizing current literary activity. The librarian, scholar, or student attempting to stay informed of literary developments is faced with an endless task. The purpose of *DLB Yearbook* is to serve these readers while at the same time enlarging the scope of *DLB*.

The *Yearbook* is divided into two sections: articles about the past year's literary events or topics; and obituaries and tributes. The updates and new author entries previously included as supplements to published *DLB* volumes have been omitted. (These essays will appear in future *DLB* volumes.) Included in the articles section are a symposium discussing the scholarly and teaching use of facsimiles of literary manuscripts, inter-

views with Russell Hoban and rare book dealer Glenn Horowitz, reproductions of readers' reports from the Bobbs-Merrill Archives at The Lilly Library, Indiana University, and extended discussions of the year's work in fiction, poetry, drama, and literary biography. The *Yearbook* continues two surveys begun in 1987, an overview of new literary journals, and an in-depth examination of the practice of book reviewing in America. In addition, the *Yearbook* features an article on the recipient of the 1990 Nobel Prize in Literature, Octavio Paz, including Paz's Nobel lecture.

The death of a literary figure prompts an assessment of his achievements and reputation. The obituaries section marks the passing of Lawrence Durrell, Walker Percy, and Samuel Beckett, who died too late in 1989 to be included in last year's *Yearbook*.

Each *Yearbook* includes a list of literary prizes and awards, a necrology, and a checklist of books about literary history and biography published during the year. This year, the *Yearbook* includes a section covering international literary events.

From the outset, the *DLB* series has undertaken to compile literary history as it is revealed in the lives and works of authors. The *Yearbook* supports that commitment, providing a useful and necessary current record.

Acknowledgments

This book was produced by Bruccoli Clark Layman, Inc. Karen L. Rood is senior editor for the *Dictionary of Literary Biography* series.

Systems manager is Charles D. Brower. Photography editors are Edward Scott and Timothy Lundy. Permissions editor is Jean W. Ross. Layout and graphics supervisor is Penney L. Haughton. Copyediting supervisor is Bill Adams. Typesetting supervisor is Kathleen M. Flanagan. Information systems analyst is George F. Dodge. Charles Lee Egleston is editorial associate. The production staff includes Rowena Betts, Polly Brown, Reginald A. Bullock, Teresa Chaney, Patricia Coate, Sarah A. Estes, Robert Fowler, Mary L. Goodwin, Ellen McCracken, Kathy Lawler Merlette, Laura Garren Moore, John Myrick, Pamela D. Norton, Cathy J. Reese, Laurrè Sinckler-Reeder, Maxine K. Smalls, and Betsy L. Weinberg.

Walter W. Ross and Timothy D. Tebalt did the library research at the Thomas Cooper Library of the University of South Carolina with the assistance of the following librarians: Gwen Baxter, Daniel Boice, Faye Chadwell, Jo Cottingham, Cathy Eckman, Rhonda Felder, Gary Geer, David L. Haggard, Jens Holley, Jackie Kinder, Thomas Marcil, Laurie Preston, Jean Rhyne, Carol Tobin, Virginia Weathers, and Connie Widney.

Dictionary of Literary Biography
Yearbook: 1990

Dictionary of Literary Biography

The 1990 Nobel Prize in Literature
Octavio Paz
(31 March 1914 -   )

Ann B. González
University of North Carolina at Charlotte

BOOKS: *Luna silvestre* (Mexico City: Fábula, 1933);
¡No pasarán! (Mexico City: Simbad, 1936);
Raíz del hombre (Mexico City: Simbad, 1937);
Bajo tu clara sombra y otros poemas sobre España (Valencia: Españolas, 1937; revised edition, Valencia: Tierra Nueva, 1941);
Entre la piedra y la flor (Mexico City: Nueva Voz, 1941);
A la orilla del mundo y Primer día; Bajo tu clara sombra; Raíz del hombre; Noche de Resurrecciones (Mexico City: ARS, 1942);
Libertad bajo palabra (Mexico City: Tezontle, 1949);
El laberinto de la soledad (Mexico City: Cuadernos Americanos, 1950; revised edition, Mexico City: Fondo de Cultura Económica, 1959); translated by Lysander Kemp as *The Labyrinth of Solitude: Life and Thought in Mexico* (New York: Grove, 1961);
¿Aguila o sol? (Mexico City: Tezontle, 1951); published in a bilingual edition, translated by Eliot Weinberger as *¿Aguila o sol?/Eagle or Sun?* (New York: October House, 1970; revised edition, New York: New Directions, 1976);
Semillas para un himno (Mexico City: Tezontle, 1954);

Note: Translations in the text are by Professor Gonzáles, except those marked by an asterisk, which are from *The Collected Poems of Octavio Paz: Bilingual Edition*, translated by Eliot Weinberger (New York: New Directions, 1987).

Octavio Paz (© The Nobel Foundation)

El arco y la lira: El poema; La revelación poética; Poesía e historia (Mexico City: Fondo de Cultura Económica, 1956); translated by Ruth L. C.

3

Simms as *The Bow and the Lyre: The Poem, the Poetic Revelation, Poetry and History* (Austin: University of Texas Press, 1973);

Las peras del olmo (Mexico City: Universidad Nacional Autónoma de México, 1957; revised edition, Barcelona: Seix Barral, 1971);

Piedra de sol (Mexico City: Tezontle, 1957); published in a bilingual edition, translated by Muriel Rukeyser as *Sun Stone/Piedra de sol* (New York: New Directions, 1963); translated by Peter Miller as *Sun-Stone* (Toronto: Contact, 1963); translated by Donald Gardner as *Piedra de sol: The Sun Stone* (New York: Cosmos, 1969);

La estación violenta (Mexico City: Fondo de Cultura Económica, 1958);

Agua y viento (Bogata: Ediciones Mito, 1959);

Tamayo en la pintura mexicana (Mexico City: Universidad Nacional Autónoma de México, 1959);

Libertad bajo palabra: Obra poética, 1935-1958 (Mexico City: Fondo de Cultura Económica, 1960; revised, 1968);

Salamandra (1958-1961) (Mexico City: Mortiz, 1962);

Selected Poems of Octavio Paz (bilingual edition), translated by Rukeyser (Bloomington: Indiana University Press, 1963);

Cuadrivo: Darío, Lopez Velarde, Pessoa, Cernuda (Mexico City: Mortiz, 1965);

Los signos en rotación (Buenos Aires: Sur, 1965);

Puertas al campo (Mexico City: Universidad Nacional Autónoma de México, 1966);

Blanco (Mexico City: Mortiz, 1967); translated by Weinberger as *Blanco* (New York: The Press, 1974);

Claude Lévi-Strauss; o, El nuevo festín de Esopo (Mexico City: Mortiz, 1967); translated by J. S. and Maxine Bernstein as *Claude Lévi-Strauss: An Introduction* (Ithaca: Cornell University Press, 1970) and *On Lévi-Strauss* (London: Cape, 1970);

Corriente alterna (Mexico City: Siglo Veintiuno Editores, 1967), translated by Helen R. Lane as *Alternating Current* (New York: Viking, 1973);

Disco visuales (Mexico City: Era, 1968);

Marcel Duchamp; o, El castillo de la pureza (Mexico City: Era, 1968); translated by Gardner as *Marcel Duchamp; or, The Castle of Purity* (New York: Grossman, 1970; London: Cape Goliard Press, 1970);

Conjunciones y disyunciones (Mexico City: Mortiz, 1969); translated by Lane as *Conjunctions and Disjunctions* (New York: Viking, 1974);

La centena (Poemas: 1935-1968) (Barcelona: Seix Barral, 1969);

Ladera este (1962-1968) (Mexico City: Mortiz, 1969);

México: La última década (Austin: Institute of Latin American Studies, University of Texas, 1969);

Posdata (Mexico City: Siglo Veintiuno, 1970); translated by Kemp as *The Other Mexico: Critique of the Pyramid* (New York: Grove, 1972);

Las cosas en el sitio: Sobre la literatura española del siglo XX, by Paz and Juan Marichal (Mexico City: Finisterre, 1971);

Los signos en rotación y otros ensayos, edited by Carlos Fuentes (Madrid: Alianza, 1971);

Topoemas (Mexico City: Era, 1971);

Traducción: Literatura y literalidad (Barcelona: Tusquets, 1971);

Vuelta (Mexico City: El Mendrugo, 1971);

Configurations, translated by G. Aroul and others (New York: New Directions, 1971)—contains *Piedra de sol/Sun Stone*, *Blanco*, and selections from *Salamandra* and *Ladera este*;

Renga, by Paz, Jacques Roubaud, Eduardo Sanguinetti, and Charles Tomlinson (Mexico City: Mortiz, 1972); translated by Tomlinson as *Renga: A Chain of Poems* (New York: Braziller, 1972);

Aparencia desnuda: La obra de Marcel Duchamp (Mexico City: Era, 1973; enlarged, 1979); translated by Gardner and Rachel Phillips as *Marcel Duchamp: Appearance Stripped Bare* (New York: Viking, 1978);

Early Poems: 1935-1955, translations by Rukeyser and others (New York: New Directions, 1973);

El signo y el garabato (Mexico City: Mortiz, 1973);

Solo a dos voces, by Paz and Julián Riós (Barcelona: Lumen, 1973);

La búsqueda del comienzo: Escritos sobre el surrealismo (Madrid: Fundamentos, 1974);

El mono gramático (Barcelona: Seix Barral, 1974); translated by Lane as *The Monkey Grammarian* (New York: Seaver, 1981);

Los hijos del limo: Del romanticismo o la vanguardia (Barcelona: Seix Barral, 1974); translated by Phillips as *Children of the Mire: Poetry from Romanticism to the Avant-Garde* (Cambridge: Harvard University Press, 1974);

Pasado en claro (Mexico City: Fondo de Cultura Económica, 1975; revised, 1978);

Vuelta (Barcelona: Seix Barral, 1976);

The Siren and the Seashell, and Other Essays on Poets and Poetry, translated by Kemp and Margaret Sayers Peden (Austin: University of Texas Press, 1976);

Xavier Villaurrutia en persona y en obra (Mexico City: Fondo de Cultura Económica, 1978);

Air Born/Hijos del aire, by Paz and Tomlinson (Mexico City: Pescador, 1979);

El ogro filantrópico: Historia y política, 1971-1978 (Mexico City: Mortiz, 1979);

In/mediaciones (Barcelona: Seix Barral, 1979);

México en la obra de Octavio Paz, edited by Luis Mario Schneider (Mexico City: Promexa, 1979);

A Draft of Shadows and Other Poems, translated by Elizabeth Bishop, Mark Strand, and Weinberger (New York: New Directions, 1979);

Poemas (1935-1975) (Barcelona: Seix Barral, 1979);

Selected Poems, bilingual edition, translated by Tomlinson and others (New York: Penguin, 1979);

El laberinto de la soledad; Posdata; Vuelta a El laberinto de la soledad (Mexico City: Fondo de Cultura Económica, 1981);

Rufino Tamayo, by Paz and Jacques Lassaigne (Barcelona: Ediciones Poligrafia, 1982); translated by Kenneth Lyons (New York: Rizzoli, 1982);

Sor Juana Inés de la Cruz; o, Las trampas de la fe (Barcelona: Seix Barral, 1982); translated by Peden as *Sor Juana; or, The Traps of Faith* (Cambridge: Harvard University Press, 1988);

Guenther Gerzo (Neuchâtel, Switzerland: Griffon, 1983);

Sombras de obras: Arte y literatura (Barcelona: Seix Barral, 1983);

Hombres en su siglo y otros ensayos (Barcelona: Seix Barral, 1984); translated by Michael Schmidt as *On Poets and Others* (New York: Seaver, 1987);

Selected Poems, edited by Weinberger, translations by Aroul and others (New York: New Directions, 1984);

Tiempo nublado (Barcelona: Seix Barral, 1984); translated by Lane and expanded as *One Earth, Four or Five Worlds: Reflections on Contemporary History* (San Diego: Harcourt Brace Jovanovich, 1985);

Cuadro chopos/The Four Poplars, bilingual edition, translated by Weinberger (Purchase, N.Y.: Center for Edition Works, 1985);

The Labyrinth of Solitude, The Other Mexico, Return to the Labyrinth of Solitude, Mexico and the United States, The Philanthropic Ogre, translated by

Kemp, Yara Milos, and Rachel Phillips Belash (New York: Grove, 1985);

On Poets and Others, translated by Schmidt (New York: Seaver, 1986);

Arbol adentro (Barcelona: Seix Barral, 1987); translated by Weinberger as *A Tree Within* (New York: New Directions, 1988);

The Collected Poems, 1957-1987: Bilingual Edition, edited by Weinberger (New York: New Directions, 1987);

Convergences: Essays on Art and Literature, translated by Lane (San Diego: Harcourt Brace Jovanovich, 1987);

Sor Juana; Or, the Traps of Faith, translated by Peden (Cambridge, Mass.: Harvard University Press, 1988);

One Word to the Other (Mansfield, Tex.: Latitudes Press, 1991).

If it is at all possible to sum up the multifaceted work of Octavio Paz, it would be to insist on his fundamental search for the role of poetry and the place of the poet in a world which ignores art and marginalizes its artists. In his acceptance speech for the Nobel Prize given in Sweden last December, he calls his work both a "pilgrimage" and a "quest" for what he calls "modernity," that is the moment, outside history, to which the poet speaks. He concludes that modernity is not to be found at the end of linear time, but rather in the present, which he often calls the "instant" ("*ser eterno un instante*"/to be eternal one instant), the poetic moment which re-creates order and clarity in the midst of confusion and uncertainty. These epiphanous instants allow the poet to forge a place for himself in relation to a world which has lost the certainty, comfort, and optimism of order and progress and is instead beset by accident, catastrophe, multiplicity, and "*capricho*" (whim).

Octavio Paz Lozano, born in Mexico City in the middle of the Mexican revolution in 1914, remembers growing up in Mixcoac, a small town now part of the capital, in an old house with a classics-filled library and a tree-filled garden. His mother, Josefina Lozano, an unmarried aunt, and his paternal grandfather raised him, while his father, Octavio Paz, a journalist and lawyer who was active in Mexican politics after the revolution, was generally absent. He remembers playing with his cousins in the garden and long solitary hours reading in the library, all the while being strangely isolated from the political chaos following the Mexican revolution. At age seventeen he published his first poem and founded *Barandal*, a literary review. Before he turned twenty, he published his first book of poems, *Luna silvestre* (1933), a collection of lyrical poems which Paz never chose to reedit, and founded another literary magazine, *Cuadernos del Valle de Mexico*. His serious career as a poet began around 1935, or so it would seem from his 1979 book *Poemas (1935-1975)*, in which Paz collected and revised his best work and eliminated most of his youthful poems. The few pre-1935 compositions included employ images which Paz continues to develop throughout his career: night, dream, stars, sea, shadow, rock, bird, silence. His feel for the sound and rhythm of language in these early works is apparent: the poems roll and crash like the surf he describes, making his work difficult to translate; to preserve their meaning is to lose their form.

These early poems celebrate life and nature and mark the beginning of Paz's search for how poetry can define our relationship with the world. One of his repeated images is the ocean, which serves as a metaphor for the world and for all of nature, for the beginning and end of time, for the order and power of the natural world. Sometimes poetry can be found in between the extremes of the crests, sometimes on the pinnacle of the wave, and in his lyric "Frente al Mar" (Facing the Sea), poetry is synonymous with the entire movement of the wave itself rather than with any of its parts: *"Su movimiento es su forma"* (Its movement is its form). Another of his repeated images is the starry sky, which signifies the order and vastness of the universe. It is an image to which he refers again in his Nobel banquet speech when he recounts the experience of simultaneously staring up into the night sky and hearing the sounds of a tiny cricket. Opposites and extremes set the boundaries within which Paz searches for his place and his role as poet, his roots as a Mexican, his relationship to the world and to the "other," and the point at which opposites converge.

In 1937 he quit his university studies and began to write *Entre la piedra y la flor* (finally published in 1941). He also married Elena Garro (whom he divorced in 1959) and attended the Second Congress of the International Association of Writers in Republican Spain at the special invitation of Pablo Neruda. He was impressed by the political idealism of the times, and his poems from this period often reflect his admiration for comradeship and fraternity in defense of love and lib-

erty. In 1938, back in Mexico, Paz founded *Taller* (1938-1941), a literary review, and continued to support at an intellectual level the fight against fascism. His poetry of this period, however, begins to wean itself from the concrete world of politics to continue the search for origins:

> En ese olvido sin edad ni fondo
> labios, besos, amor, todo, renace:
> las estrellas son hijas de la noche.
>
> (In this oblivion without age or end
> lips, kisses, love, all, is reborn:
> the stars are daughters of the night.)

During this time Paz also began his prolific essays which explore in prose the issues he confronts in his poetry. In 1940 Paz began to move away from his earlier belief in political revolution, and in 1941, disillusioned by the Hitler-Stalin pact, he broke openly with Neruda, who symbolized for him the poet bound by an ideological position which Paz could no longer sustain. His 1942 collection of poems, *A la orilla del mundo*, continued his move away from politics and toward the belief that poetry is central in a world gone mad. Paz looked inward at the poet (*solo, desnudo, despojado*/alone, naked, wretched), at poetry's origins, and at poetry's possibilities to effect a mental rather than a political revolution:

> Eres tan sólo un sueño,
> pero en ti sueña el mundo
> y su mudez habla con tus palabras.
>
> (You are only a dream,
> but in your dream the world
> and its silence speaks with your words.)

In 1943 Paz went to the United States on a Guggenheim Fellowship, founded and edited *El hijo pródigo* (1943-1945), a literary review which translated major contemporary poets from around the world into Spanish and, in Jason Wilson's words, "strengthened his belief in the efficacy and importance of poetry in a world set on eradicating it as a value." In 1945 he went to Paris, and from 1946-1951 he served as the Mexican cultural attaché there. In Paris, Paz found, in his friendship with André Breton and his surrealist group, the alternative to politics and ideology he had been seeking. Paz's poetry of this period reflects the strong influence of surrealism's essential values, which he recalls in *Las peras del olmo* (1957) as love, liberty, and poetry. During this pe-

Dust jacket for the 1985 American edition of Paz's collection of essays

riod Paz published three collections: *Libertad bajo palabra* (1949), poetry which looks at the transformational role of poetry on the poet; *El laberinto de la soledad* (1950; translated as *The Labyrinth of Solitude*, 1961), essays which probe the character and soul of being Mexican; and *¿Aguila o sol?* (1951; translated as *¿Aguila o sol? / Eagle or Sun?*, 1970), prose poems verging on short stories which continue his search into his Mexican roots and identity. In addition, he wrote poems later collected and organized in *La estación violenta* (1958) which reflect his travels to Italy, India, Japan, and back to Mexico. They also concern his continued and often frustrated and disillusioned search for how poetry might provoke not only the inner transformation of the poet but also external transformations; that is, how poetry might instigate political action (not to be confused with ideologically promoted action): "*Hay que dormir con los ojos abiertos, hay que soñar con las manos*" (One must sleep with eyes opened, one must dream with one's hands).

After Paz's return to Mexico in 1953, he published *Semillas para un himno* (1954), a collection of poems, and *El arco y la lira* (1956; translated as *The Bow and the Lyre*, 1973), a collection of essays, neither of which was well received by Mexican critics, who charged that Paz had been overly influenced by European surrealism and that he was not ideologically committed or engaged. Paz, however, was attempting to look behind Mexican nationalism and ideological revolution to the possibilities of a new society founded on the liberating vision of language; that is, he was beginning to see poetry itself as a subversive force. In 1956 he wrote a play based on Nathaniel Hawthorne's short story "Rappaccini's Daughter" (1844) that was performed as part of a cycle of plays by various writers called *Poesia en voz alta*, which was, on the one hand, criticized as being too surrealistic, but, on the other hand, acclaimed for bringing poetry to the Mexican stage.

Paz's international career, however, was launched with the publication in 1957 of *Piedra de sol* (translated as *Sun Stone*, 1963), a long, circular poem using Mexican and Aztec motifs, originally included in his 1960 collection *Libertad bajo palabra* (the title of one of his earlier books) and reissued as the starting point for his latest dual language collection, *The Collected Poems, 1957-1987: Bilingual Edition*. The poem has received five English translations and one French as well as numerous readings, interpretations, and critical responses. Both thematically and structurally, the poem insists that the poet's search must continually, repeatedly, and inevitably lead him back to origins, to roots, in a nonstop spiral where the end hearkens back to the beginning. This search through time and history for the poet, the poem, and ultimately the word itself underscores Paz's work from this point on in his career, the search for what Paz himself calls, in his Nobel Prize acceptance speech, "the meeting place for the three directions of time."

In 1959 Paz went to Paris as part of Mexico's foreign service and he served from 1962 to 1968, when he resigned as Mexico's ambassador to India in protest over the Mexican government's massacre of students prior to the Olympic games. During the 1960s he began to collect what he had written in prose on a variety of topics and about various people into several books: *Los signos en rotación* (1965), *Puertas al campo* (1966), *Corriente alterna* (1967; translated as *Alternating Current*, 1973), *Conjunciones y disyunciones* (1969; translated as *Conjunctions and Disjunctions*,

1974), as well as to publish monographs on Claude Lévi-Strauss (1967), and Marcel Duchamp (1968). In 1962 he published *Salamandra*, which critics have referred to as a transitional work, since Paz begins to experiment with the form of the poem on the page, the use of shorter lines, isolated words, and blank, white spaces, that is, silence. His goal was to purify language, to rid it of its contamination and distortion by history, and to endow it with transparency so that people can once again see what their present alienation will not allow:

> un pescado volaba
> Cambió el semáforo hacia el verde
> Se preguntó al cruzar la calle
> en qué estaba pensando.
>
> (a fish flew
> The light turned green
> As he crossed the street he wondered
> what he'd been thinking).*

The title of the collection itself recalls the Aztec fascination with the axolotl, a type of salamander (see Julio Cortazar's short story "Axolotl," (1964) in which the narrator simultaneously becomes the axolotl and remains himself), and suggests the idea of the divided self, the two in one, the movement from one to the other, in short, the notion of transformation which recurs in Paz: transformation of self, transformation of society, transformation of language itself.

In 1963 Paz was awarded the International Poetry Prize of Brussels. In 1964 he was married, this time to Marie-Jose Tramini. Both his unconventional poem *Blanco* (1967) and his collection of poems *Ladera este* (1969) celebrate his love for his new wife, sometimes in the form of the "other," sometimes as his muse, sometimes as the body of "woman," while continuing the effort to liberate language from its historical and cultural bondage. He fuses the words for *woman* with the feminine *word* "*la palabra*" and experiments with the sight and the sound of the poem like the notes of music on a page.

Along with poetry, he continued to write prose which defended poetry. His attack on Levi-Strauss (1967), for example, for ignoring poetry in his study of myth was translated into French (1970) and English (1970). Both Paz's poetry and prose of the 1960s are infused with his experience of living for six years in India. He examines the cultural confrontations between Mexico, Europe, and Asia and reaffirms his belief in the pres-

ent, the now, the "*instante*" of poetry rather than the transcendence and eternity of either religion or ideology.

In the 1970s Paz taught at various universities: Cambridge, where he occupied the Simón Bolívar Chair; the University of Texas; and Harvard, where he was Charles Eliot Norton Professor. In addition, he founded *Plural*, a monthly cultural and political supplement to the Mexican newspaper *Excélsior*. After the government takeover of the paper in 1976, he founded *Vuelta*, which he continues to edit and which is one of the leading literary reviews in Latin America. He also published seven books of essays on a myriad of topics; an anthology of the writings of Charles Fourier; a collection of his translations of poetry from six languages; *Posdata* (1970; translated as *The Other Mexico*, 1972), a best-seller with fourteen editions by 1980; *Renga* (1972), a collaborative chain of poems and their translations by Charles Tomlinson, Jacques Roubaud and Eduardo Sanguinetti, and Paz; *Los hijos del limo* (1974; translated as *Children of the Mire*, 1974), his Harvard lectures; *El mono gramático* (1974; translated as *The Monkey Grammarian*, 1981), a prose poem on language and one of his most critically acclaimed works; *Pasado en claro* (1975), a long, partly autobiographical poem on time and memory; *Vuelta* (1976), a collection of his poems from 1968 to 1975 (also the name of his literary review); and his definitive 1979 collection of *Poemas (1935-1975)*. Both his poetry and prose of this period argue more openly for democracy; that is, poetic action within a democratic framework. He severely criticized Cuba and Nicaragua, and was, in turn, attacked as a neoconservative by his critics.

In the 1980s Paz continued to lecture and travel around the world, appear on Mexican television, edit and translate, in addition to publishing a complex critical study on *Sor Juana Inés de la Cruz o las trampas de la fe* (1982; translated as *Sor Juana; or, The Traps of Faith*, 1988), three books of essays, and *Tiempo nublado* (1984; translated as *One Earth, Four or Five Worlds: Reflections on Contemporary History*, 1985). In 1987 Paz published *Arbol adentro*, his first collection of poetry in eleven years. The translation was included in the 1987 *Collected Poems of Octavio Paz (1957-1987)*.

International recognition of Paz's contribution to Spanish American letters has been steady: the Jerusalem Prize (1977), the Golden Eagle Prize, Nice (1979), the Olin Yoliztli Prize, Mexico, and an honorary degree from Harvard (1980), the Cervantes Prize, Madrid (1981), the Neustadt

Prize, University of Oklahoma (1982), the Peace Prize, Frankfurt (1984), and finally, of course, the Nobel Prize for Literature in 1990. As Ivar Ivask affirmed in 1973, "it is too early for a definitive scholarly monograph on a writer who does not cease to astonish and surprise friends of literature from one year to the next." Paz has not disappointed. Almost twenty years later it may still be too early.

References:

Ivar Ivask, *The Perpetual Present: The Poetry and Prose of Octavio Paz* (Norman: University of Oklahoma Press, 1973);

Jason Wilson, *Octavio Paz* (Boston: Twayne, 1986).

NOBEL BANQUET SPEECH
Octavio Paz

Translated from the Spanish
by Anthony Stanton

Your Majesties, Ladies and Gentlemen,

I shall be brief—but, since time is elastic, I am afraid you are going to hear me for one hundred and eighty very long seconds.

We are witnessing not only the end of a century but the end of a historical period. What will arise from the collapse of ideology?

Is this the dawn of an era of universal concord and freedom for all or will there be a resurgence of tribal idolatry and religious fanaticism, unleashing discord and tyranny? Will the powerful democracies that have achieved freedom and abundance become less selfish and show more understanding towards the deprived nations? Will the latter learn to distrust the preachers of doctrinaire violence who have led them to failure? And in my own part of the world, in Latin America, and especially in Mexico, my native land, will we finally achieve true modernity, which is not just political democracy, economic prosperity and social justice but also reconciliation with our tradition and with ourselves? It is impossible to know. The recent past has taught us that no-one holds the keys to history. The century ends with a throng of questions.

Yet we can be certain of one thing: life on our planet is endangered. Our unthinking cult of progress together with the very advances in our

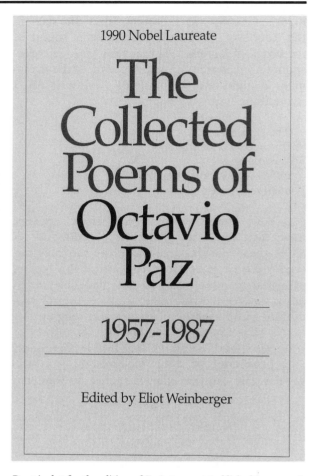

1990 Nobel Laureate

The Collected Poems of Octavio Paz

1957-1987

Edited by Eliot Weinberger

Dust jacket for the edition of Paz's poems republished in recognition of the Nobel Prize

struggle to exploit nature have turned into a suicidal race. Just as we are beginning to unravel the secrets of the galaxies and the atomic particle, as we explore the enigmas of molecular biology and the origins of life, we have wounded the very heart of nature. This is why the most immediate and most urgent question is the survival of the environment, regardless of whatever forms of social and political organization nations may choose. The defence of nature is the defence of mankind.

At the close of this century we have discovered that we are part of a vast system (or network of systems) ranging from plants and animals to cells, molecules, atoms and stars. We are a link in "the great chain of being," as the philosophers of antiquity used to call the universe. One of man's oldest gestures, repeated daily from the beginning of time, is to look up and marvel at the starry sky. This act of contemplation frequently ends in a feeling of fraternal identification with the universe. In the countryside one night, years ago, as I contemplated the stars in the cloudless sky, I heard the metallic sound of the elytra of a cricket. There was a strange correspondence between the reverberation of the firmament at night and the music of the tiny insect. I wrote these lines:

The sky's big.
Up there, worlds scatter.
Persistent,
unfazed by so much night,
a cricket: brace and bit.

Stars, hills, clouds, trees, birds, crickets, men: each has its world, each is a world, and yet all of these worlds correspond. We can only defend life if we experience a revival of this feeling of solidarity with nature. It is not impossible: *fraternity* is a word that belongs to the traditions of Liberalism and Socialism, of science and religion.

I raise my glass—another ancient gesture of fraternity—and drink to the health, happiness and prosperity of Your Majesties and to the great, noble and peace-loving people of Sweden.

NOBEL LECTURE 1990
Octavio Paz

Translated from the Spanish by
Anthony Stanton

IN SEARCH OF THE PRESENT

I begin with two words that all men have uttered since the dawn of humanity: thank you. Grace is gratuitous; it is a gift. The person who receives it, the favored one, is grateful for it, and if he is not base, he expresses gratitude. That is what I do now, at this moment, with these weightless words. I hope my emotion compensates for their weightlessness. If each of my words were a drop of water, you would see through them and glimpse what I feel: gratitude, acknowledgment, and also an indefinable mixture of fear, respect, and surprise at finding myself here before you, in this place that is the home of both Swedish learning and world literature.

Languages are vast realities that transcend the political and historical entities that we call nations. The European languages that we speak in the Americas illustrate this. The special position of our literatures, when compared with the litera-

tures of England, Spain, Portugal, and France, depends precisely on this fundamental fact: they are written in transplanted tongues. Languages are born in, and grow from, the native soil; they are nourished by a common history. Some of the European languages were rooted out from their native soil and their own tradition, however, and planted in an unknown and unnamed world. They took root in the new lands, and as they grew within the societies of America, they were transformed. They are the same plant, and yet a different one. Our literatures did not passively accept the changing fortunes of the transplanted languages; they participated in the process, even accelerated it. Soon they ceased to be merely trans-Atlantic reflections. At times, our literatures have been the negation of the literatures of Europe. More often, they have been a reply.

In spite of these oscillations, however, the link has never been broken. My classics are those of my language, and I consider myself a descendant of Lope de Vega and Quevedo, as any Spanish writer would. Yet I am not a Spaniard. I think that most writers of Spanish America, as well as those from the United States, Brazil, and Canada, would say the same about the English, Portuguese, and French traditions. To understand more clearly the special position of writers in the Americas, we might recall the dialogue that has been conducted by Japanese, Chinese, or Arabic writers with the different literatures of Europe. It is a dialogue that cuts across multiple languages and civilizations. Our dialogue, on the other hand, takes place within the same language. We are Europeans, yet we are not Europeans. What are we, then?

It is difficult to define what we are, but our works speak for us. In the field of literature, the great novelty of the present century has been the appearance of the American literatures. The first to appear was the English-speaking one, and then, in the second half of the twentieth century, the Latin American literature in its two great branches, Spanish America and Brazil. Although they are very different, these three literatures have a common feature: the conflict, which is more ideological than literary, between cosmopolitanism and nativism, between Europeanism and Americanism.

What is the legacy of this dispute? The polemics have disappeared; the works remain. Apart from this general resemblance, the differences between the three literatures are many and profound. One of them belongs more to history than to literature: the development of Anglo-American literature coincided with the rise of the United States as a world power, whereas the rise of our literature coincides with our political and social misfortune, with the upheavals of our nations. This proves, once again, the limitations of social and historical determinism: the decline of empires and social disturbances sometimes coincide with moments of artistic and literary splendor. Li-Po and Tu Fu witnessed the fall of the Tang dynasty; Velázquez painted for Felipe IV; Seneca and Lucan were contemporaries and also victims of Nero.

The other differences are of a literary nature. They apply more to particular works than to the character of each literature. But can we say that literatures have a character? Do they possess a set of shared features that distinguish them from other literatures? I doubt it. A literature is not defined by some fanciful, intangible character; it is a society of unique works, which is united by relations of opposition and affinity.

The first fundamental difference between Latin-American literature and Anglo-American literatures lies in the diversity of their origins. Both began as projections of Europe—in the case of North America, the projection of an island; in our case, the projection of a peninsula. The two regions are geographically, historically, and culturally eccentric. The origins of North America are in England and the Reformation; ours are in Spain, Portugal, and the Counter-Reformation. About the case of Spanish America, I should briefly mention what distinguishes Spain from other European countries, giving it a particularly original historical identity. Spain is no less eccentric than England, but its eccentricity is of a different kind. The eccentricity of the English is insular, and is characterized by isolation: it is an eccentricity that excludes. Hispanic eccentricity is peninsular, by contrast, and consists of the coexistence of different civilizations and different pasts. It is an inclusive eccentricity. In what would later be Catholic Spain, the Visigoths professed the heresy of Arianism, and we might note also the centuries of domination by Arabic civilization, the influence of Jewish culture, the Reconquest, and other characteristic features of Spanish history.

Hispanic eccentricity was reproduced and multiplied in America, especially in countries such as Mexico and Peru, where ancient and splendid civilizations had existed. In Mexico the Spaniards encountered history as well as geography.

That history is still alive; it is a present rather than a past. The temples and gods of pre-Columbian Mexico are a pile of ruins, but the spirit that breathed life into that world has not disappeared. It speaks to us in the hermetic language of myth, legend, forms of social coexistence, popular art, customs. Being a Mexican writer means listening to the voice of that present, that presence. Listening to it, speaking with it, deciphering it, expressing it.

Perhaps we may now perceive more clearly the peculiar relation that binds us to, and separates us from, the European tradition. This consciousness of being separate is a constant feature of our spiritual history. Separation is sometimes experienced as a wound that marks an internal division, as an anguished awareness that invites self-examination. At other times it is a challenge, a spur that incites us to action, to go forth and encounter others and the outside world.

It is true that the feeling of separation is universal, not peculiar to Spanish Americans. It is born at the moment of our birth: as we are wrenched from the Whole, we fall into an alien land. This experience becomes a wound that never heals. It is the unfathomable depth of every man; all our ventures and exploits, all our acts and dreams, are bridges designed to overcome the separation and reunite us with the world and our fellow beings. Each man's life, and the collective history of mankind, can be seen as an attempt to reconstruct the original situation. An unfinished and endless cure for our divided condition. But it is not my intention to provide yet another description of this feeling. I wish simply to stress that for us this existential condition expresses itself in historical terms. It becomes an awareness of our history.

How and when does this feeling appear, and how is it transformed into consciousness? The reply to this double-edged question can be given in the form of theory or in the form of personal testimony. I prefer the latter: there are many theories, and none is entirely convincing. The feeling of separation is bound up with the oldest and vaguest of my memories: the first cry, the first scare. Like every child, I built emotional bridges in the imagination to link me to the world and to other people. I lived in a town on the outskirts of Mexico City, in an old dilapidated house that had a jungle-like garden and a great room full of books. First games and first lessons. The garden soon became the center of my world; the library, an enchanted cave. I used to read and play with my cousins and schoolmates. There was a fig tree, a temple of vegetation; and four pine trees, three ash trees, a nightshade, a pomegranate tree, wild grass, and prickly plants that produced purple grazes. Adobe walls. Time was elastic, space was a spinning wheel.

All time, past or future, real or imaginary, was pure presence. Space transformed itself ceaselessly. The beyond was here, all was here: a valley, a mountain, a distant country, the neighbors' patio. Books with pictures, especially history books, eagerly leafed through, supplied images of deserts and jungles, palaces and hovels, warriors and princesses, beggars and kings. We were shipwrecked with Sinbad and Crusoe, we fought with D'Artagnan, we took Valencia with the Cid. How I would have liked to stay forever on the Isle of Calypso! In summer the green branches of the fig tree would sway like the sails of a caravel or a pirate ship. High up on the mast, swept by the wind, I could make out islands and continents, lands that vanished as soon as they became tangible. The world was limitless, yet it was always within reach; time was a pliable substance that weaved an unbroken present.

When was the spell broken? Gradually, rather than suddenly. It is hard to accept that a friend has betrayed you, that a woman you love has deceived you, that the idea of freedom is the mask of a tyrant. What we call "finding out" is a slow and tricky process, because we ourselves are the accomplices of our errors and our deceptions. Still, I can remember rather clearly an incident that was the first sign, though it was quickly forgotten. I must have been about six when one of my cousins, who was a little older, showed me a North American magazine with a photograph of soldiers marching along a huge avenue, probably in New York. "They've returned from the war," she said. This handful of words disturbed me, as if they foreshadowed the end of the world, or the Second Coming of Christ. I vaguely knew that somewhere far away a war had ended a few years earlier, and that the soldiers were marching to celebrate their victory. That war had taken place, however, in another place and in another time, not here and now. The photograph refuted me. I felt literally dislodged from the present.

From that moment, time began to fracture. And there appeared a plurality of spaces. The experience repeated itself more and more frequently. Any piece of news, a harmless phrase, a headline in a newspaper: everything proved the outside world's existence, and my own unreality. I felt that the world was splitting, that I did not inhabit the present. Real time was elsewhere. My time, the time of the garden; the fig tree, the games with friends, the drowsiness among the plants under the afternoon sun, a fig torn open (black and red like a live coal, but sweet and fresh): this was a fictitious time. In spite of what my senses told me, the time from over there, that belonged to the others, was the real one, the time of the real present. I accepted the inevitable. I became an adult.

That was how my expulsion from the present began. It may seem paradoxical to say that we have been expelled from the present, but it is a feeling we have all known. Some of us experienced it first as a punishment that we later transformed into consciousness and action. The search for the present is the pursuit neither of an earthly paradise nor of a timeless eternity; it is the search for a real reality. For us, as Spanish Americans, the real present was not in our own countries. It was the time lived by others, by the English, the French, the Germans. It was the time of New York, Paris, London. We had to go and look for it and bring it back home. Those were the years of my discovery of literature.

I began to write poems. I did not know what made me write them; I was moved by an inner need that is difficult to define. Only now have I understood that there was a secret relationship between my expulsion from the present and my writing of poetry. Poetry is in love with the instant, and seeks to relive it in the poem. Thus it separates the instant from sequential time and transforms it into a fixed present. In those years, though, I wrote without wondering why I was doing it. I was searching for the gateway to the present; I wanted to belong to my time and to my century. A little later this obsession became a fixed idea: I wanted to be a modern poet. My search for modernity had begun.

Modernity is an ambiguous term. There are as many types of modernity as there are societies. Each has its own. The word's meaning is uncertain and arbitrary, like the name of the period that preceded it, the Middle Ages. If we are modern compared with medieval times, are we the Middle Ages of a future modernity? Is a name that changes with time a real name? Modernity is a word in search of its meaning. Is it an idea, a mirage, or a moment of history? Are we the children of modernity or its creators? Nobody knows for sure. It doesn't matter much: we follow it, we pursue it. For me, in those early years as a writer, modernity was fused with the present, or rather produced it: the present was its final supreme flower.

My case was not exceptional. Since the Symbolist period, modern poets have chased after that magnetic and elusive figure that fascinates them. Baudelaire was the first. He was also the first to touch her, to discover that she is nothing but time that crumbles in one's hands. I am not going to relate my adventures in pursuit of modernity; they are not very different from those of other twentieth-century poets. Modernity has been a universal passion. Since 1850 she has been our goddess and our demoness. In recent years there has been an attempt to exorcise her with talk of "postmodernism." But what is postmodernism, if not a more modern modernity?

For us, as Latin Americans, the search for poetic modernity runs historically parallel to the repeated attempts to modernize our countries. This tendency began at the end of the eighteenth century, and it included Spain, too. The United States was born into modernity, and by 1830 it was already, as Tocqueville observed, the womb of the future; but we were born at a moment when Spain and Portugal were moving away from modernity. That is why there was frequent talk of "Europeanizing" our countries: the modern was outside, it had to be imported.

In Mexican history, this process began just before the War of Independence. Later it became a great ideological and political debate that passionately divided Mexican society throughout the nineteenth century. One event was to call into question not the legitimacy of the reform movement, but the way in which it had been implemented: the Mexican Revolution. Unlike its twentieth-century counterparts, the Mexican Revolution was not really the expression of a vaguely utopian ideology. It was, rather, the explosion of a reality that had been historically and psychologically repressed. It was not the work of a group of ideologists intent on introducing principles derived from a political theory, but a popular uprising that unmasked what was hidden. For this reason, it was more of a revelation than a revolution. Mexico was searching for the present outside only to find it within, buried but alive. The search for modernity led us to discover our antiquity, the hidden face of the nation. I am not sure that this unexpected historical lesson has been learned by all—that between tradition and modernity there is a bridge. When they are mutually iso-

lated, tradition stagnates and modernity vaporizes. When they are joined, modernity breathes life into tradition, while the latter responds with depth and gravity.

The search for poetic modernity was a Quest, in the allegorical and chivalric sense that this word had in the twelfth century. I did not find any Grail, although I did cross several wastelands, visiting castles of mirrors and camping among ghostly tribes. Still, I discovered the modern tradition. For modernity is not a poetic school, it is a lineage, a family dispersed over several continents, which for two centuries has survived many changes and misfortunes: indifference, isolation, and tribunals in the name of religious, political, academic, and sexual orthodoxy. Because it is a tradition and not a doctrine, it has been able to survive and to change at the same time. This is also why it is so diverse: each poetic adventure is distinct, each poet has sown a different plant in the miraculous forest of speaking trees.

If the works are diverse and each route is distinct, what is it that unites all these poets? Not an aesthetic, but a search. My own search was not fanciful, even though the idea of modernity is a mirage, a bundle of reflections. One day I discovered that I was returning to the starting point instead of advancing, that the search for modernity was a descent to the origins. Modernity led me to the source of my beginning, to my antiquity. Separation became reconciliation. Thus I discovered that the poet is a pulse in the rhythmic flow of generations.

The idea of modernity is a byproduct of our conception of history as a unique and linear process of succession. The origins of this conception are in the Judeo-Christian tradition, but it breaks with Christian doctrine. In Christianity, the cyclical time of pagan cultures is supplanted by unrepeatable history, which has a beginning and will have an end. Sequential time was the profane time of history, an arena for the actions of fallen men, yet still governed by a sacred time that had neither a beginning nor an end. And after Judgment Day, there will be no future either in heaven or in hell. In the realm of eternity there is no succession, because everything *is*. Being triumphs over becoming.

The new time, our concept of time, is linear like that of Christianity, but it is open to infinity, it makes no reference to Eternity. Ours is the time of profane history, an irreversible and perpetually unfinished time that marches toward the future and not toward its end. History's sun is the future. Progress is the name of this movement toward the future.

Christians see the world, or what used to be called the *seculum* or worldly life, as a place of trial: in this world, souls can be lost or saved. In the new conception, by contrast, the historical subject is not the individual soul but the human race, sometimes viewed as a whole and sometimes through a chosen group that represents it: the developed nations of the West, the proletariat, the white race, or some other entity. The pagan and Christian philosophical tradition had exalted Being as changeless perfection overflowing with plentitude, but we adore change; it is the motor of progress and the model for our societies. Change articulates itself in two ways, as evolution and revolution. The trot and the leap. Modernity is the spearhead of historical movement, the incarnation of evolution or revolution, the two faces of progress. And progress takes place by means of the dual action of science and technology, applied to the realm of nature and to the use of her immense resources.

Modern man has defined himself as a historical being. Other societies chose to define themselves in terms of values and ideas different from change: the Greeks venerated the *polis* and the circle, yet they were unaware of progress. Like all the Stoics, Seneca was much exercised by the eternal return; St. Augustine believed that the end of the world was imminent; St. Thomas constructed a scale of being, linking the smallest creature to the Creator; and so on. One after the other, these ideas and beliefs were abandoned. It seems to me that the same decline is beginning to affect our idea of Progress—and, as a result, our vision of time, of history, of ourselves. We are witnessing the twilight of the future.

The decline of the idea of modernity, and the popularity of a notion as dubious as "postmodernism," are phenomena that affect not only literature and the arts. We are experiencing the crisis of the essential ideas and beliefs that have guided mankind for over two centuries. First, the concept of a process open to infinity and synonymous with endless progress has been called into question. I need hardly mention what everybody knows: that the resources of nature are finite and will run out one day. We have inflicted what may be irreparable damage on the natural environment and our own species is endangered. Science and technology, the instruments of progress, have shown with alarming clarity that they

can easily become destructive forces. The existence of nuclear weapons is a refutation of the idea that progress is inherent in history—a refutation that can only be called devastating.

Second, we must reckon with the fate of the historical subject, mankind, in the twentieth century. Seldom have nations or individuals suffered so much: two world wars, tyrannies spread over five continents, the atom bomb, the proliferation of one of the cruelest and most lethal institutions known to man: the concentration camp. Modern technology has provided countless benefits, to be sure, but it is impossible to close our eyes to slaughter, torture, humiliation, degradation, and all the other wrongs inflicted on millions of innocent people in our century.

And third, the belief in the necessity of progress has been shaken. For our grandparents and our parents, the ruins of history—the spectacle of corpses, desolate battlefields, devastated cities—did not invalidate the underlying goodness of the historical process. The scaffolds and tyrannies, the conflicts and savage civil wars, were the price to be paid for progress, the blood money to be offered to the god of history. A god? Yes, reason itself deified and was prodigal in cruel acts of cunning, according to Hegel. But now the alleged rationality of history was vanished. And in the very domain of order, regularity, and coherence (in pure sciences like physics), the old notions of accident and catastrophe have reappeared. This disturbing resurrection reminds me of the terrors that marked the advent of the millennium, of the anguish of the Aztecs at the end of each cosmic cycle.

The last in this hasty enumeration of the elements of our crisis marks the collapse of all the philosophical and historical hypotheses that claimed to reveal the laws governing the course of history. The believers, confident that they held the keys to history, erected powerful states over pyramids of corpses. These arrogant constructions, destined in theory to liberate men, were quickly transformed into gigantic prisons. Today we have seen them fall, overthrown not by their ideological enemies, but by the impatience and the desire for freedom of the new generations. Is this the end of all utopias? It is, more precisely, the end of the idea of history as a phenomenon whose outcome can be known in advance. Historical determinism has been a costly and bloodstained fantasy. History is unpredictable, because its agent, mankind, is the personification of indeterminacy.

Thus we are very probably at the end of one historical period and at the beginning of another. The end of the Modern Age, or just a mutation? It is difficult to tell. In any case, the collapse of utopian schemes has left a great void, not in the countries where this ideology has been proved to have failed, but in those countries where many embraced it with enthusiasm and hope. For the first time in history, mankind lives in a sort of spiritual wilderness, no longer in the shadow of the religious and political systems that consoled us even as they oppressed us. All societies are historical, but every society has lived under the guidance and the inspiration of a set of metahistorical beliefs and ideas. Ours is the first age that is ready to live without a metahistorical doctrine.

Whether they be religious or philosophical, moral or aesthetic, our absolutes are not collective, they are private. This is a dangerous experience. It is also impossible to know whether the tensions and the conflicts unleashed in this privatization of ideas, practices, and beliefs that belonged traditionally to the public domain will end up destroying the social fabric. Men could become possessed once more by ancient religious fury or by fanatical nationalism. It would be terrible if the fall of the abstract idol of ideology were to foreshadow the resurrection of the buried passions of tribes, sects, and churches. The signs, unfortunately, are disturbing.

The decline of the ideologists whom I have called metahistorical, by which I mean those that assign to history a goal and a direction, implies a tacit abandonment of global solutions. With good sense, we tend more and more toward limited remedies for concrete problems. It is prudent to abstain from legislating about the future. Still, the present requires much more than attention to its immediate needs. It demands a more rigorous global reflection. For a long time I have firmly believed that the twilight of the future heralds the advent of the now. And to think about the now requires, first of all, a recovery of critical vision. For example: the triumph of the market economy (a triumph that is owed to its adversary's default) cannot be only a cause for joy. As a mechanism the market is efficient, but like all mechanisms it lacks conscience and compassion. We must find a way of integrating it into society so that it expresses the social contract and becomes an instrument of justice and fairness. The advanced democratic societies have reached an enviable level of prosperity, but at the same time they

are islands of abundance in the ocean of universal misery.

The question of the market is intricately related to the deterioration of the environment. Pollution affects not only the air, the rivers, and the forests, it also affects our souls. A society possessed by the frantic need to produce more in order to consume more tends to reduce ideas, feelings, art, love, friendship, and people themselves to consumer products. Everything becomes a thing to be bought, used, and thrown on the rubbish heap. No other society has produced so much waste, material and moral, as ours.

Reflecting on the now does not imply relinquishing the future or forgetting the past: the present is the meeting place for the three directions of time. Neither can it be confused with facile hedonism. The tree of pleasure does not grow in the past or in the future, but at this very moment. Yet death is also a fruit of the present. It cannot be denied, for it, too, is a part of life. Living well implies dying well. We have to learn to look death in the face. The present is alternately luminous and somber, like a sphere that unites the two halves of action and contemplation. Thus, just as we have had philosophies of the past and of the future, of eternity and of the void, we shall have a philosophy of the present. The poetic experience could be one of its foundations. What do we know about the present? Nothing, or almost nothing. Yet the poets do know at least one thing: that the present is the source of presences.

In my pilgrimage in search of modernity, I lost my way in many places, only to find myself again. I returned to the source and discovered that modernity is not outside us, but within us. It is today and the most ancient antiquity; it is tomorrow and the beginning of the world; it is a thousand years old and newborn. It speaks in Nahuatl, draws Chinese ideograms from the ninth century, appears on the television screen. This intact present, recently unearthed, shakes off the dust of centuries, smiles, and suddenly starts to fly, disappearing through the window. A simultaneous plurality of time and presence: modernity breaks with the immediate past only to recover an age-old past, and to transform a tiny fertility figure from the Neolithic age into our contemporary.

We pursue modernity in her incessant metamorphoses, but we never trap her. She always escapes; each encounter ends in flight. We embrace her, and she disappears immediately: it was just a little air. It is the instant, that bird that is everywhere and nowhere. We want to capture it alive, but it flaps its wings and vanishes in the form of a handful of syllables. We are left empty-handed.

And then the doors of perception open slightly and the other time appears, the real time, the one that we were searching for without knowing it: the present, the presence.

The Year in the Novel

David R. Slavitt
University of Pennsylvania

So many books; so little time.

Well, yes, but where in all that plethora, that appalling spate, were the good books, the important or even amusing books? What kind of list can one contrive that represents anything more than a peculiar and partial glance at the dismaying number of novels that came out during the year? The notion that there might be, in the mind of God, some ideal list we can pretend to approximate would be mortifying if it were at all plausible. My guess however, is that God, busy with other things, doesn't read novels much, preferring, let us suppose, poetry and the theater. Besides, the writers and publishers of novels already have enough on their consciences without our attributing to them the possibility of having offended—or merely having bored—the Deity.

The year in fiction is whatever you happened to read in 1990 that you liked or found interesting or in some fortuitous way memorable. Not even the busiest reviewer could have had a chance to sample a tenth of the novels that came out during the year. That ritual I remember and still sometimes reenact of an arbitrary culling from the always messy table or bookcase where some clerical helper has arranged the review copies by date is . . . unpleasant. One feels bad at being turned for the moment into a mini-Mengele, deciding which shall live in the light of public attention and which shall be left to languish and perish. The promptings of these flighty moments are frivolous, and publishers know this, which is why they have bright dust jackets, strident flap copy, insanely enthusiastic blurbs, peppy releases, and all the tawdry blandishments and tricks of the business that would put most streetwalkers to shame.

Let me confess at once, then, to having paid insufficient attention and having missed much. Like any other reasonable reader, I had other things to do, even other books to read, some old, many in other genres, and a fair number by Europeans or Asians. My year in fiction was much taken up by the work of Cees Nooteboom, the extraordinary Dutch novelist (also poet, but his poetry hasn't been translated yet), and that of Thomas Bernhard, the late Austrian novelist and dramatist. And I've been reading Yasunari Kawabata. And some of the stories of Chekhov I hadn't encountered before. This was hardly a waste of time, but it made my sampling of the American novels of 1990 even more finical than it might have been.

There is a further disclaimer—if not actual apology—that may be appropriate. Even those judgments among all those books that we make with less than absolute whimsicality or bad faith are unreliable. We look to authors we have liked before and avoid those we have found pompous, tiresome, tendentious or stupid. I don't read Vonnegut any more, so I haven't the vaguest notion what *Hocus Pocus* (Putnam's) is like. (The reviews said it was much the same as most of the earlier books, so if you liked them or could stand them, you'll be able to like or stand this too.) I don't read Pynchon and can't imagine why anyone would, so *Vineland* (Little, Brown) is simply not on the table for comment. Arrogant? Well, perhaps. But does it make it better or worse if I confess to having glanced in a bookstore at the opening line and having decided that my prejudices were sound? ("Later than usual one summer morning in 1984, Zoyd Wheeler . . ." *Zoyd?* More hermetic word games? More arrant foolishness? Thank you, no!)

Unfair, perhaps, but it is more than most authors can count on, and all that previous accomplishment—or previous egregious success—will get you in this unfair arena. God, remember, is elsewhere.

The year, nevertheless, can be crudely characterized, even by a not especially acute observer, as one in which various cycles completed themselves. I notice John Updike's Rabbit series, George Garrett's Elizabethan trilogy, Ivan Doig's Montana trilogy, and Gore Vidal's American history series all seem to have concluded, while in England D. M. Thomas's five-volume "Russian Nights" series that began with *The White Hotel* wound down rather lamely with *Lying Together* (Viking). Vidal may continue his highly profitable and quite entertaining roman-fleuve (his advances are said to be up in the seven-figure range), but these other novelists have declared themselves to have been, at last, freed of this particular embrace of what is surely the burliest of the muses. Perhaps there was something odd in the air as we lurched into the last decade of the millennium?

More likely, there is some sort of reaction to the highfalutin ambitions of modernist aesthetics, a yearning for the more modest but perhaps more solid accomplishments of those novelists who flourished before World War I. One thinks of John Trollope first of all, but also Anthony Galsworthy or even Roger Martin Du Gard. There is no upper limit to the accomplishment of such huge undertakings, as witness the fact that these panoramic works presently before us are all, in a sense, the protégés of Marcel Proust. One of the concerns of these multivolume enterprises is inevitably the passage of time, the way in which the solidity of the world changes and, to some degree, betrays us. In one volume, there can be an achievement of a kind of stasis; the series allows for that stasis to evolve and develop, grow and decay. And there can be no question but that Vidal, for all his bright and impish wit, is moved at some deeper level by a nostalgia for old-fashioned virtues that he sees as fallen away, as we hurtle through ever lower circles of hell in his elegant handbasket. *Hollywood* (Random House) is the fifth installment of his "American chronicle" as the publisher is billing it; the other volumes are

Burr (1973), *Lincoln* (1984), *1876* (1976), *Empire* (1987), and *Washington, D.C.* (1976).

What seems at first glance to be the unfashionable aspect of all these undertakings is that they are, in one sense or another, historical novels—a genre that is, if one takes the professors at all seriously, almost a stepchild of contemporary fiction. Still, Vidal, Garrett, Doig, Updike in his way, and recently Thomas Flanagan (*The Year of the French* in 1979 and *The Tenants of Time* in 1988) have all voted the other way. The theoretical and abstract novel, the collapsing novel, the intellectual construction that doesn't deign to dirty its hands in the tawdriness of things of everyday life may lend itself to classroom performances and further campus careers, but there is a kind of bloodlessness to such fiction. These novelists have refused to be constricted or intimidated by the theoreticians. The only question is how long it will take the news to penetrate through the ivy that has all but obscured the view from the academic towers.

Vidal is fun—which is okay, actually, in a work of literature. He is witty, civilized, epigrammatic, entertaining. I open the volume at random to find a demonstration of this and see at the start of a chapter a typically triste trope: "For Caroline, love had always meant—if anything—separation." The gesture within those dashes is almost of Jamesian aplomb. *Empire* was about the yellow press, William Randolph Hearst, and the invention of mass journalism with its inevitable impact on the politics and the taste of the republic; *Hollywood* takes this investigation to its next logical step, the extension of the mass media beyond the restrictions of print, with the result that every illiterate could be persuaded that he or she was actually thinking (and had a right, therefore, for those thoughts to be heard and attended to). It may not have turned out quite like what Jefferson had in mind, but it is interesting and awkward, outrageous and absurd. And Vidal has the right kind of patrician credentials to allow the best possible combination of ruefulness and amusement that gives these books their considerable charm. He can say here, as an entertainer, what he has been saying for many years in his higher-brow essays for a considerably smaller audience.

Updike's tetralogy—*Rabbit, Run* (1960), *Rabbit Redux* (1971), *Rabbit Is Rich* (1981), and *Rabbit at Rest* (Knopf)—is quite different, sociologically. Updike isn't at all a patrician, but has risen, through merit, to a dizzying eminence. Not merely Harvard and the *New Yorker*, but a kind of success that keeps other writers slaving away in the hope that, at least now and then, virtue can find some extrinsic rewards. It seems to be Updike's function in the world to serve as the exception that proves the rule. Every other *New Yorker* writer of fiction of any consequence has left the magazine in one form or another of rage or madness. Irwin Shaw and John O'Hara both despised the magazine to which they had contributed; John Cheever, as his daughter's memoirs demonstrate, was turned into a quivering psychic jelly and helpless drunk by the manipulative and condescending treatment he got at the magazine; Salinger retreated into a semi-mystic silence that is difficult to read but hardly encouraging. Only Updike has been sending them his stories and book reviews over many decades without obvious discomfort—except that his politics are to the right of theirs, and he can't write their lead "Talk of the Town" pieces anymore. His novels are lapidary and painstaking, elegant, the kind of thing that one might expect to be off-putting to any sizeable audience. And yet with the Rabbit series he has managed to find a vein that has a deep and broad appeal. My guess is that the vein is his fear of falling. Having ascended, he feels a kind of psychic vertigo that is the dark side of meritocratic societies and a peculiarity of the American experience. Rabbit Angstrom is what Updike might well have been, had he not been blessed with extraordinary talents.

That vertigo is but one of many themes that hold things together. The series is a kind of running encounter with the times, each of the books having been written at a different address and having appeared in a different decade. Rabbit is not the object of Updike's condescension but, on the contrary, is an alter ego into which he has lavished a scrutiny and attention that are impossible without respect and even love. Surely this is what enlivens these forays and what Updike's audiences have responded to—even to the point where they are willing to overlook his elegance as a maker of sentences. One can see that close identification with Rabbit at odd moments in Updike's extraordinary and frequently moving memoir, *Self-Consciousness*, which was published by Knopf in 1989. He says, for instance, "The drive home from the restaurant, the unseasonable sleet, and my entire life all rankle in me. I have come here from some Midwestern university where I read and talked into a microphone and was gracious to the local rich, the English faculty and college

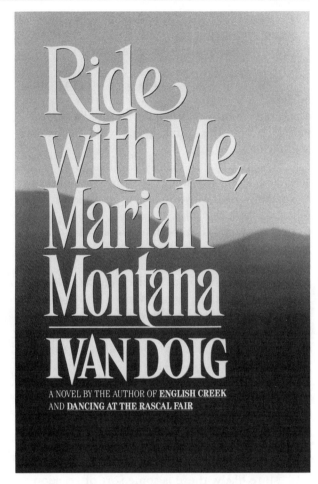

Dust jacket for the final volume of Doig's McCaskill family trilogy

president, and the students with their clear skins and shining eyes and inviting innocence, like a blank surface one wishes to scribble obscenities on. I need these excursions, evidently: they reassure me that I don't stutter, or stutter too much. They leave me feeling dirty and disturbed, as though I have wasted this time away from my desk, posing as an author instead of being one, and it is hard to get back from the academic unreality and ponderous flattery into my own skin." It is hardly the kind of confession one expects from a Harvard man who ought to be able to maintain his poise at any "Midwestern university." There is the Shillington boy peeping out through the famous author's eyes, however, and seeing these things quite differently. Updike therefore can invite a much more general identification on the part of readers than he would otherwise be able to summon. It is no exaggeration to suggest that these books of his are core drillings into the bedrock of the nation and that what they offer is as reasonable and as flattering a portrayal of the country's spirit during the second half of this century as we have any right to expect. Some of the reviewers have grumbled and carped—Garry Wills's attack in the *New York Review of Books* comes immediately to mind—but they have been criticizing the novels less than Updike's politics. Or perhaps it is the vision of the country that arises from the books with which they are uncomfortable; indeed, it could even be the country itself that makes them unhappy, and what they can't stand is that Updike's vision is fairly accurate and persuasive.

There were other multivolume productions to come to completion during 1990, less well known but no less interesting for that. Ivan Doig's new volume, *Ride with Me, Mariah Montana* (Atheneum) completes the cycle about the McCaskill family and their Two Medicine country, the first two of which were *English Creek* (1984) and *Dancing at the Rascal Fair* (1987). This is a grand celebration of place—which is one of prose fiction's persistent concerns. As Eudora Welty has remarked somewhere, place is that crossroad of time and character that watches over "the racing hand of fiction." Doig's sense of the country around Dupuyer, Montana, is uncanny and scrupulous, and he traces his family's fortunes over the course of a century or so with an admirable sweep and no little affection. If his plotting is somewhat old-fashioned, this is probably more a matter of temperament and preference than any want on his part of imagination or intelligence. I am reminded, not by the details but by the fictional techniques, of the late Paul Scott's books about India that became popular only after Scott died (because of the PBS series, "Jewel in the Crown"). One reads Doig, at any rate, more for the prose and for his sense of pride in the hardiness of those people in Montana than for the mere story—which is what any intelligent reader has been doing, anyway, since junior high school.

Finally, there was my favorite among these vast multivolume structures, George Garrett's remarkable Elizabethan trilogy, which includes *Death of the Fox* (1971), *The Succession: A Novel of Elizabeth and James* (1983), and, this year, *Entered from the Sun* (Doubleday). The last of these is—at least on one level—a detective story about the death of Christopher Marlowe, but the appearance at the climactic moment of Sir Walter Raleigh works in the most wonderfully old-fashioned way to give us a sense of momentous res-

Dust jacket for the final volume of Garrett's Elizabethan trilogy

olution that has little to do with the actual plotting. These are gestures of the kind that Sir Walter Scott devised and that Georg Lukács has discussed. The historical novel, a century ago, was a serious mode of discussion of the tragic necessities of life, and the great figures that came in at the end to make their token appearances were numinous with Hegelian if not actually Marxist importance. Garrett is hardly a Marxist, but he has put these old tricks and tropes to a quite novel and poetic application, which is the revival of—and, impliedly, an appeal to—a better time than ours in the language and culture.

His trilogy is, preeminently, a dazzling display of language. Shakespeare and the King James Bible established the most fundamental expectations in all our minds about how English ought to resonate. Those expectations and standards are still very much in effect, and from first to last, these books are a performance of the odd lilt Garrett has worked out to suggest the speech patterns of that golden time. Only a poet could have attempted such a feat, but then only a poet would have thought it worth doing. What is striking with all that show of cadence and melody is the unsentimental view of that rowdy age that all the linguistic virtuosity finally comes from and tends toward. Garrett comes out at the end, in propria persona, in an "Author's Farewell," to say, "Well now. Here we are at the end of it. I have been happy for a time, living among the Elizabethans. Happier, I do believe, than I could have been living only in our own century. Our bitter shiny century. I like to think that since I was no more than a visitor to theirs (though I visited, off and on, for many years, a persistent kind of tourist you might say), I am even entitled to prefer their time to ours. If I care to. Entitled to imagine, if I feel like it, that, by and large and in many ways, they were more interesting than we are. Of course—and it is an enormous fact—I never had to live there all the time. That might have changed my tune. I am not, never have been, and never will be a proper scholar of those times. Nevertheless, how greatly I admire them, one and all, the scholars, living and dead, who have so carefully performed their duty and service of hard labor, against huge and discouraging odds, often in the face of no little indifference and even less reward from and respect of others, to preserve our past, to keep that lost past time available for us, accessible to us. We are, each and all, debtors and creditors of each other. Like it or not."

Surely the appetite for such performances is keen—as public television demonstrates over and over, with its expensive and expansive series ("The Jewel in the Crown," "Upstairs, Downstairs," or, for that matter, "The Civil War"—which resulted in a spurt of sales for Shelby Foote's narrative history of the Civil War of something like ninety-thousand volumes!). Vidal, Updike, Doig, and Garrett have all discovered the same thing, for curiously none of them set out to write a multi-volume historical work: in each instance, there was a book that begat upon its begetter further books. And what it was that they found, in their various ways and given their quite different tastes and temperaments, were versions of the truth that Lukács announced about Scott (in *The Historical Novel*) that, "by bringing to life those objective poetic principles which really underlie the poetry of popular life and history, [he] became the great poet of past ages, the really popular portrayer of history. Heine clearly understood this quality and saw, too, that the strength

of Scott's writing lay precisely in this presentation of popular life, in the fact that the official big events and great historical figures were not given a central place. . . . The important historians and philosophers of history of this period, Thierry and Hegel, aspire to a similar interpretation of history. But with them it goes no further than a demand, a theoretical pronouncement of this necessity."

There were other, ordinary single-volume novels that were published during the year, a few good ones, a lot of mediocre ones, and a great many dreadful books that sat like fat toads on the best-seller lists, mocking the democracy of the marketplace over which they so predictably preside. The difference is not one of high- , middle- , and lowbrow. There are always books that may be short on pretension but are lively and deft, genre exercises that, with a real moral fervor and an accuracy of vision and hearing, seem to suggest a more general impression of what life is like. There are a few old reliable practitioners of this kind, two of whom produced better than average (for them) books: George V. Higgins's *Victories* (Holt) and Elmore Leonard's *Get Shorty* (Delacorte) were both agreeable entertainments. Higgins's ear for the patois of the Boston underworld is remarkable and always fun, no matter how slight the plot (which is, at any rate, always conveyed through dialogue). Leonard also has a great sense of which words to omit to suggest the patterns of street speech, and to this he also brings an appalling vision of really twisted, evil people, one or two of whom show up with predictably dire results in each of his books. His yarns are generally similar in their construction, but they don't seem—so far—to be mere self-imitations.

There were several reliable writers who came through with more serious and ambitious works. The indefatigable Joyce Carol Oates, of course, has a new book, or actually new books. One is a kind of mystery story—or at least misery story—of miscegenation and intolerance—*Because It Is Bitter, And Because It Is My Heart* (Dutton). The other, published later in the year, was a ninety-page novella, similar in tone and theme, called *I Locked My Door Upon Myself* (Ecco). The novella was apparently part of a set exercise in which writers were invited to take works of art—in this instance, an 1891 portrait by the Belgian painter Fernard Khnopff—and turn it into a work of fiction. One imagines her writing with a couple of word processors going at once, like one

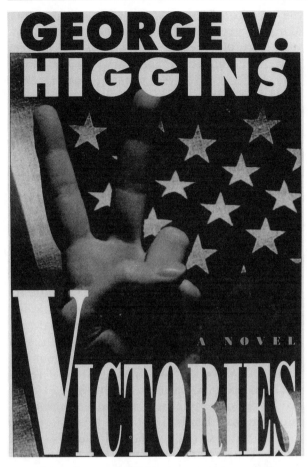

Dust jacket for Higgins's novel about a former baseball player who runs for Congress in New England

of those women in bars who play both piano and organ, while singing along to their own accompaniment. Still, the level of her achievement is very high and remarkably even. Vance Bourjaily's new book, *Old Soldier* (Donald Fine), may not have been the very best of his work, but then the standard of excellence set by *The Violated* and *Now Playing at Canterbury* is stratospheric, and one can't reasonably expect such heights every time. The new novel involves a sixty-year-old ex-top sergeant who takes off for a fishing trip in the Maine woods where he can demonstrate character, competence, and the usual evidences of harmony with nature, which is Bourjaily's (and also Hemingway's) way of suggesting a state of grace. Even knowing all the tricks, though, wise to them from earlier encounters, the reader finds that their effectiveness is undiminished, and is all the more impressive for that. What makes the equation work is the accuracy of the observation, the painstakingness of the prose, the modesty—which are literary equivalents of those very quali-

ties that Bourjaily is celebrating in his eponymous hero. The AIDS business—there's a homosexual brother who shows up, has the disease, and becomes the target of rage and fear of a bunch of inept nearby campers—is mostly a plot gimmick here, and the pretext for a sermon on tolerance and decency. The AIDS novel of the year was probably the elegant but obviously deeply felt work of Paul Monette, *Afterlife* (Crown), about three AIDS "widowers" trying to rebuild their lives after the deaths of their lovers.

Philip Roth's *Deception* (Simon and Schuster) was good enough so that even coming to it with a chip on my shoulder (having grown exceedingly weary of his complaints about celebrity and its burdens), I found myself at first admiring and then delighting in his elegant games-playing account of the duplicities and fictions involved in an affair. Witty, shrewd, this rather French exercise—it's a *recit*, really—is rueful at its heart, but it keeps that mostly hidden, as good manners and good artistic practice would both prompt.

Richard Ford's *Wildlife* (Atlantic Monthly) was more or less what one would expect from him—another demonstration of how the Big Sky Country can be turned into a psychic slum by sleazy people, all of which is demonstrated through the eyes of a bruised child. This kind of subject becomes, after enough repetitions, a bit whiny, and it wears less well in the length required of a novel than in the short stories. Still, there were no passages or pages to which one could point and say—aha, there's where he made his mistake, his gaffe, committed his fatal bêtise. But to recognize that one is unhappy, that one is looking for such a justification for one's dissatisfaction, one's fatigue . . . is a necessary if uncomfortable admission honesty compels.

Who else among the known and mostly reliable writers produced reasonable and solid books this year? Ann Beattie gave us *Picturing Will* (Random House); Frederick Busch offered *Harry and Catherine* (Knopf); Larry McMurtry brought out *Buffalo Girls* (Simon and Schuster); Josh Greenfield produced *What Happened Was This* (Carroll and Graf); Peter Matthiesen did *Killing Mr. Watson* (Random House); and Reynolds Price came out with *The Tongues of Angels* (Atheneum). These were all solid achievements and all welcome.

Among the less well established writers who have emerged in recent years, there were various interesting and lively books. Lawrence Thornton, who made an impressive debut with *Imagining Argentina* shows the same kind of moral and politi-

Dust jacket for Boyle's seventh novel, which concerns a Japanese sailor who escapes to America only to face mounting indignities, culminating in exposure to a writers' colony

cal fervor in his second novel, *Under the Gypsy Moon* (Doubleday), which is about the European experience during World War II and, particularly, the death of Federico García Lorca. Literary death seemed almost modish this year, between Thornton's book and the new novel by Jay Parini, *The Last Station* (Holt), about the death of Leo Tolstoy whose wife and disciples are struggling for his soul—in which the novelist also maintained a certain interest. There was, from England, a third book of this odd genre, Martin Booth's *Dreaming of Samarkand* (Morrow), about T. E. Lawrence, the poet James Elroy Flecker, and Hellé, Flecker's Greek wife, and while the novels of non-Americans are beyond my purview (there's quite enough on the plate already, thank you), the coincidence deserves mention, especially in that all three of these books are intelligent and appealing.

T. Coraghessan Boyle's *East Is East* (Viking) is a boisterous, extravagant book that relies on a hyperbole that may have something to do with the practice of those South American novelists, Marquez among others, who were modish a few years ago. Wherever it comes from, the manner is lively and attractive, and can make for a brisk read. *East Is East*, Boyle's seventh novel, is about one Hiro Tanaka, a Japanese sailor who jumps ship off the coast of Georgia to seek the American dream, but instead of any dreamland Big Apple he encounters swamps, leeches, mosquitoes, sinister Crackers, immigration agents, and, best and worst of all, a writers' colony—full of such desperate crazies as to make him flee back to the more congenial swamps. Paul Auster's *Music of Chance* (Viking) is another of these extravagances, show-off-ish and exuberant, about gambling, enthrallment, and other such self-consciously mythic matters. Henry James's remark that "less is more" seems to have had little appeal for Boyle or Auster, and while the first impression of this kind of book may be exhilaration and approval of the sheer dazzle, there is a danger of diminishing return, a suspension of our suspension of disbelief, and finally a kind of revulsion. One certainly wouldn't want to read these two books, one right after the other. More modest, or at least less bullying, and therefore more to my taste was Lawrence Naumoff's *Rootie Kazootie* (Farrar, Straus, & and Giroux), which continues the same odd mixture of high farce and deep sadness about love under duress that he displayed in *The Night of the Weeping Women*.

Pop and schlock figures showed up in titles—not for their shock value, I think, but as a part of an effort on the part of some novelists to encompass the discontinuities and contrarieties of an all but incoherent culture. Kelly Cherry's *My Life and Dr. Joyce Brothers* (Algonquin) is about being a woman in modern America, with maybe an occasional flash of the memory of incest which isn't so much Gothic as merely domestic. Cherry is bright and sassy, but the busy surface for her is never an end in itself. She rather allows her characters to emerge from behind the glitz, and the reader's sympathies are engaged as he or she intuits what is going on beyond and behind all the cheery Nora Ephron-like patter. I also liked, for roughly similar reasons, Tommy "Tip" Paine's *Gordon Liddy Is My Muse* (Linden); MacDonald Harris's *Hemingway's Suitcase* (Simon and Schuster); and Michael Herr's *Walter Winchell* (Knopf).

A couple of first novels got some attention during the year: Timothy O'Grady's *Motherland* (Holt) about Ireland during the last eight hundred years, and Jessica Hagedorn's *Dogeaters* (Pantheon), about Marcos-era street life in the Philippines, which was on the short list for the National Book Award, and which was rather better, I thought, than the winner—Charles Johnson's *Middle Passage* (Atheneum), which was yet another demonstration in fiction that slavery was bad.

Madison Smartt Bell's *Doctor Sleep* (Harcourt Brace Jovanovich) is technically a 1991 book, but it comes close enough to the cusp to be included. It was a part of my 1990, at any rate. Energetic in the manner of an Auster or a Boyle, it has an insomniac hypnotherapist who is careering around the unattractive underbelly of London and the fringes of hallucination, sorting out a tangled love life, and doing some private-eye work for Scotland Yard. Bell's work has varied considerably in quality, from the splendid *The Year of Silence* to the rather slapdash *Straight Cut*, but the general trend is upward as he learns how to discipline his very considerable talent. This time, he has a firm grip on the horses of his gift, and he contrives an ending that is at the same time stylishly dazzling and also deeply satisfying. He is surely one to watch.

Finally, as if the world knew I needed a kind of envoi, there was a little flurry of excitement at the end of the year that was suggestive of the state of American fiction and American publishing, when Simon and Schuster decided not to publish Bret Easton Ellis's *American Psycho* for which they had reportedly paid an advance of $300,000. The grounds for their demurral were the book's alleged tastelessness and violence, but, as the *New York Times* pointed out, the parent company of Simon & Schuster also owns the movie studio that has been making and distributing the *Friday the Thirteenth* series, in which Jason, the loony, behaves more or less the way Ellis's madman does—but more vividly, being on screen, after all.

The announcement was made that Vintage, which is owned by Knopf, and therefore Random House, would go ahead with the publication of the paperback edition. Censorship is not the issue, then. And any publisher obviously has the right to publish or not to publish whatever he likes or hates. What struck me in this, and what failed, so far as I have been able to tell, to draw any particular comment (let alone outrage or even derisive laughter) was the curious disclosures about the practices of publishing houses that were made, by the bye—that Simon and Schuster should pay $300,000 for a book that Richard Snyder, the C.E.O., hadn't looked at, let alone read, seems to be perfectly normal. Of course, reading is the donkey work for which kids fresh out of Harvard can be hired and drastically underpaid. There were excerpts of the Ellis novel that *Spy* magazine got hold of, and ran, and only then, forced by these rude disclosures, did Snyder feel impelled to take a look at what he'd paid a third of a million dollars to acquire. And out of finical distaste—or so it was announced—he elected to forgo the money and wash his hands of the whole sorry affair. As if S&S had higher standards than Knopf!

To make perfect the season of peace on earth and goodwill toward men, the California branch of the National Organization of Women decided to announce a boycott of all Random House, Knopf, and Vintage books. Asked on National Public Radio whether they were serious, whether they really wanted to discourage people from going out to buy paperback copies of, say, Ralph Ellison's *Invisible Man*, the N.O.W. spokeswoman made it clear that this was just what she intended and that if anyone absolutely needed to consult the Ellison text, there were public libraries.

It's Nancy Reagan's unsuccessful antidrug campaign reborn—"Just Say No" to books. And if the results are anywhere near similar, there will be teenage runners and desperado Columbian gangs selling copies of Ralph Ellison, William Faulkner, and other Random House authors on street corners. For the really poor people, poetry may be the drug of choice, offering as it does a quick hit, like crack, that may give you an exquisite high but then, only a few minutes later, leaves you restless and yearning for more.

The Year in the Short Story

George Garrett
University of Virginia

I don't care what they say, those large commercial publishers and the so-called slicks, about their love of literature and the life of the mind. I know why they're in business and what they love, and so do you. Profit. Dividends. Increase. Is Rupert Murdoch interested in contemporary American literature? Does Paramount Entertainment care about the integrity of language? Does S. I. Newhouse think Pantheon's list is crucial to our intellectual life? Or that our intellectual life is crucial to our culture? Of course not.

—Russell Banks, "Introduction" to *The Pushcart Prize 1990-1991*

In *Prize Stories 1990: The O. Henry Awards* (Doubleday), the seventieth in the annual series, William Abrahams presented twenty good stories and, in his "Introduction," an enthusiastic sense of the new decade—"blazing new trails, new paths, and aiming toward new destinations." Abrahams surprises by more than his excitement about the present state of the story and its foreseeable future. At a time when almost everybody else is (almost reflexively) taking the opposite tack, he makes a point of praising the blooming creative-writing programs: "Despite the occasional carping of critics (myself included), I think it has to be acknowledged that the effect of these programs and courses has been significantly to the good." And he likewise indicates that the little magazines and quarterlies have gradually become the principal sources for his prizewinning stories, a trend that is clear to anyone who has been following his editorial choices over the years. This year three-fourths, fifteen of the twenty stories, come from the literary magazines rather than "magazines of large circulation," a reversal of the figures for a decade ago. A point made by the table of contents is that the prizewinning stories by some of the better-known writers—for instance Alice Adams and T. Coraghessan Boyle and Joyce Carol Oates—were found in the pages of literary magazines. Abrahams's selection, which includes Peter Matthiessen's superb new story, "Lumumba Lives,"

seems more various than usual and offers the work of a goodly number of talented newcomers.

Editor Shannon Ravenel and guest-editor Richard Ford, in *The Best American Short Stories 1990* (Houghton Mifflin), offer a gathering of twenty stories equally divided in their original publication between literary magazines and others (six come from the *New Yorker*, a predominance not seen in the O. Henry collections in many years). The "little" magazines tend to be the best known. There are more "name" writers here than in the O. Henry—Lorrie Moore, Joy Williams, Elizabeth Tallent, Alice Munro, Steven Millhauser, Padget Powell, and others; and two writers enjoy the rare distinction of having two stories selected for the anthology—Alice Munro and Richard Bausch. But there are outstanding stories in the collection, including the two by Richard Bausch, Christopher Tilghmann's "In a Father's Place," and Madison Smartt Bell's "Finding Natasha." Richard Ford contributes a lively and mildly provocative "Introduction."

Shannon Ravenel appears (without benefit of any guest-editor) as editor of two other anthologies—*The Best American Short Stories of the Eighties* (Houghton Mifflin) and *New Stories from the South: The Year's Best, 1990* (Algonquin). The former title, marking the seventy-fifth anniversary of the *Best American Short Stories* series, and the thirteenth year of Shannon Ravenel's editorship of it, allows Ravenel to review the editorship of her predecessors Edward O'Brien and Martha Foley and to write, in her "Introduction," about the decade during which she has managed the anthology ("And I believe the 1980's will be known as another golden age, though for reasons very different from those which led to the story's great popularity in the teens and twenties, when writers could live off their work in a way that today's practitioners cannot."). Her choices for the best of the *Best* for the past decade, admittedly given the extra edge of brilliant hindsight, are excellent, a gathering of worthy and highly honored names. There are no surprises, really; but the publisher writes: "The names of the contributors are

Shannon Ravenel, editor of three short-story anthologies in 1990: The Best American Short Stories 1990 *(Houghton Mifflin);* The Best American Short Stories of the Eighties *(Houghton Mifflin); and* New Stories from the South: The Year's Best, 1990 *(Algonquin) (photograph by Mark Katzman)*

the best testament to the quality of this collection." *New Stories from the South*, with a different emphasis, offers a significant number of newer, younger names; and all but one of these stories—Richard Bausch's "Letter to the Lady of the House," which appeared in the *New Yorker*—are taken from the little magazines and quarterlies. As in the earlier volumes of this series, Ravenel devotes her "Preface" to an attempt at an ongoing definition of the South and the tricky problem of what constitutes southern literature. This is lively and interesting stuff, though it is marred by one serious mistake of fact. Trying to establish workable criteria for her evolving definition, she dismisses place of birth, arguing that under such a rubric Richard Bausch's story "might not qualify." Richard Bausch was born in Georgia and makes his home in Broad Run, Virginia.

There were, as ever, a variety of other anthologies of short fiction, based upon prizes or selected as the best or most representative work from a particular source. *The Pushcart Prize*

1990-1991 (Pushcart) is in its fifteenth year, now firmly and clearly part of the literary establishment it once modestly sought to challenge and modify. And, establishment organ or not, the *Pushcart Prize* volume is firmly based on a simple fact, itself firmly stated by Russell Banks in his "Introduction" to this volume: "Increasingly, then, if we want to know what's worth reading of contemporary American letters, we must look to our small presses, and our home-grown *Samizdat*. These are the poems, stories and essays that have been shut out by the official press—shut out by economics, by timidity, and by legislation." Of course, it is hard to maintain a genuinely revolutionary fervor while working closely, over the years, "with the assistance of over 150 *distinguished* Contributing Editors [my italics]," but *Pushcart* does fairly well. *Pushcart* publishes poems, essays, and stories, but there are enough stories (twenty-five by my count, made a little tricky by the absence of some thirty or forty pages in my hardcover edition) to make a full anthology. Although there are solidly establishment types on board, people such as Padgett Powell and Leonard Michaels, Carol Bly and Lydia Davis, there are two "first published" stories—by Kim Herzinger and Wally Lamb—there are stories by exciting newer talents like Josip Novakovich and Robin Hemley, and there are contributions by top-flight story writers such as Kent Nelson, Sarah Glasscock, Rick Bass, and Molly Best Tinsley, whose "Zoe," first published in *Shenandoah*, also appears in *New Stories from the South* and the "100 Other Distinguished Stories of 1989," in *The Best American Short Stories 1990*. Even though the distinguished editors of *Pushcart* do seem to favor the slicker and more upscale among the literary magazines, places such as *Antaeus, Paris Review*, the *Quarterly, Grand Street, Boulevard*, and other, smaller places (*Shenandoah, Crazyhorse, Carolina Quarterly, Gettysburg Review, Ploughshares, Agni Review*) are well represented. Another gathering of prizewinning stories, these from a particular competition, is *The Luxury of Tears: Winning Stories from the National Society of Arts and Letters Competition* (August House). Here are twelve stories, none previously published in magazines; and at least one of them, "Dragon Lady and the Ponytail Plant," by Laura Leigh Hancock, is good enough for a place in any of the anthologies mentioned here.

It has been a year for magazines to bring together their own best or most representative short fiction. C. Michael Curtis, celebrated senior editor of the *Atlantic Monthly*, edited *American*

Stories: Fiction from the Atlantic Monthly (Atlantic Monthly), nineteen impressive stories, "a selection of the magazine's distinguished modern fiction," from Eudora Welty and James Jones through Ann Beattie and Raymond Carver and John Updike, to people such as Charles Baxter, Tobias Wolff, and Jane Smiley. It is an impressive, if idiosyncratic (many first-rate writers who appear in the modern *Atlantic* do not appear here) collection, perhaps most important to writers as well as readers for some of the things it tells us about Curtis and his editorial cohorts. Writing in the "Introduction," Curtis says: "What we look for, in short, are indications of a literate and controlled imagination, the sorts of insights and observations that make us pay rather more than the usual attention to a dinner companion or a reliable friend." Well, nobody, except for Mark Twain, ever called the people at the *Atlantic . . . uncivilized.*

Probably the largest and fattest among the magazine anthologies (close to six hundred pages), a veritable and varied program of top names among contemporary short-story writers, some forty-seven of them, and many of them well and widely known, is *Fiction of the Eighties: A Decade of Stories from TriQuarterly* (TriQuarterly). Editors Reginald Gibbons and Susan Hahn take considerable and justified pride in the accomplishments, and the variety, of their magazine during the past decade: "While *TriQuarterly* cannot claim to have brought together the full range of fictional strategies of the decade just ended (for that wasn't our purpose as we went along), we can hope that the works we selected for publication during the decade, and especially those selected in a further refinement of judgment for this volume, do give a view of the short story, and of the purposes to which it has been turned, that effectively characterizes the decade artistically." The assertion may or may not be the case, but any anthology offering the work of writers of the highest caliber and distinction, people such as the late William Goyen and Fred Chappell, Grace Paley and Joyce Carol Oates, John Sayles and Leslie Marman Silko, can take pride in its accomplishment. *The American Story: The Best of Story Quarterly* (Cane Hill) has seventeen stories, including ones by writers of reputation such as Ann Beattie, Janet Burroway, Daniel Curley, Stephen Dixon, and Leon Rooke, as well as interviews (the newest fictive form?) by Ann Beattie, John Cheever, Grace Paley, Richard Stern, and Gordon Lish, who invokes the highest seriousness

to explain his art: "Art is a way to manage our death. I think we die more easily, or less horribly, to the extent that we have done our work. The crudest being is competent to summon for himself some kind of magic for managing his mortality."

Another of the year's anthologies taken from the pages of literary magazines is "*Eric Clapton's Lover" and Other Stories from the Virginia Quarterly Review* (University Press of Virginia), which claims only to be representative of the kind and forms of fiction published in that magazine in the past quarter of a century. It is a various gathering, including a diversity of well-known writers (Peter Taylor, Nancy Hale, William Hoffman, Ward Just, Ann Beattie, David Stacton) with stories by a variety of energetic newer talents—Ellen Wilbur, Alyson Hagy, Kelly Cherry, Peter LaSalle and Hilary Masters and Kent Nelson, among others. There are twenty-one stories in this anthology. Also worthy of note this year is *The Paris Review Anthology* (Norton), which boasts a full complement of distinguished contributors and is surely worth its price for the sake of one story alone—Dallas Wiebe's "Night Flight to Stockholm."

Other anthologies followed more or less conventional guidelines. For example, ethnic and national groupings. Among these, attention was earned by *The Singing Spirit: Early Short Stories by North American Indians* (University of Arizona Press), a gathering of nineteenth- and early-twentieth-century stories, selected by the Swiss scholar Bernd C. Peyer. Terry McMillan edited *Breaking Ice* (Viking), an anthology of 57 African-American writers chosen from among 300 submissions. Another anthology devoted to the work of African-American writers is *Talk That Talk* (Simon and Schuster), which brings together more than 100 examples of traditional African-American story-telling. Others, among the year's examples of anthologies based upon ethnic or racial considerations, include *Northern Tales: Traditional Stories of Eskimo and Indian People* (Pantheon), offering 116 folktales, many of them animal fables; *America And I: Short Stories by American Jewish Women Writers* (Beacon), consisting of 23 entries from four generations of writers, from the turn of the century to the present, including contemporary writers such as Tillie Olsen, Cynthia Ozick, Lynne Sharon Schwartz, and Hortense Calisher. More books of more or less national limits include *Winter's Tales* (St. Martin's), fifth in the second series of this annual roundup, 12 stories this time including work by A. L. Barker and Muriel Spark, and Graham Greene's "The Moment of Truth"; *Names and Tears and Other Stories* (Graywolf), 26 stories from the past forty years of Italian writing, including early stories by Italo Calvino and Natalia Ginzburg and newcomers (to the American scene) such as Gesualdo Bufalino, Luigi Malerba, and Giuseppe Pontiggia; Canadians are the authors of the 50 stories, from the 1930s to the present, found in *From Ink Lake* (Viking).

Similarly there are other significant nationally organized anthologies. *Forgiveness* (Four Walls Eight Windows) consists of twenty-five contemporary Irish stories and includes prominent writers such as John Banville, Aisling Maguire, William Trevor, Joseph O'Connor, and Edna O'Brien, who wrote the title story. Translator Norman Thomas de Giovanni edited *Celeste Goes Dancing* (North Point), bringing together fourteen stories by outstanding contemporary Argentine writers, among them Adolfo Bioy-Casares, Silvina Ocampo, Fernando Sanchez-Sorondo, Alberto Castillo, Fernando Sorrentino, and Santiago Sylvester. *New Italian Women* (Italica), edited by Martha King, presents some well-known Italian story writers such as Elsa Morante and Natalia Ginzburg as well as others (for example Frabrizia Romondino and Maria Occhipinti) not yet widely known in literary circles in America. The complexities and contradictions of life in the Soviet Union, just as *glasnost* began to break down walls and habits, were evident in the work of fourteen contemporary Russian women writers represented in *Balancing Acts* (Indiana University Press). Giles Gordon and David Hughes brought out their fifth edition of English-language stories, published in America as *Best English Short Stories II* (Norton), consisting of twenty-five stories, including one, "The Man with the Dagger," by the expatriate American Russell Hoban. Many of the writers—for example Nadine Gordimer, Elizabeth Jolley, Desmond Hogan, William Boyd, Alice Munro, Frederic Raphael—are well known in America. Others are quite new. "We have made our discoveries—we offer first publication in book form by at least three writers," the editors write, "but most of the best finds tend to be by authors of established voice."

Another kind of perennial and popular anthology is the one built around some common theme or subject. *Fathers and Daughters* (NAL) is what it announces itself to be, being "23 rich and stirring stories about the profound relationship between fathers and their daughters." The range here is from old-timers Budd Schulberg and Joyce Cary, E. M. Forster and F. Scott Fitzgerald to contemporaries such as John Updike, Raymond Carver, Larry Woiwode, and Harold Brodkey. Two especially fine examples of the theme—Peter Taylor's "*Je Suis Perdu*" and "A Father's Story" by André Dubus—greatly enhance the collection. Two large-scale anthologies of stories about dogs received considerable attention from reviewers. *The Literary Dog: Great Contemporary Dog Stories* (Atlantic Monthly), edited by Jeanne Schinto, is a very handsome book that has thirty-four stories of all kinds about all kinds of dogs. There are excellent stories by Madison Smartt Bell ("Black and Tan"), Pinckney Benedict ("Dog"), Mary Hood ("How Far She Went"), and Wright Morris ("Victrola"); likewise, unusual juxtapositions—David and John Updike, son and father, each represented; a genuine oddity, Mark Strand's "Dog Life"; a rarity, "The English and Their Dogs," by the seldom-anthologized Jerry Bumpus. Meanwhile Michael J. Rosen's *The Company of Dogs* (Doubleday) has some fifty-five dog stories, all published within the past ten years, of which only half a dozen happen to appear in both anthologies. Another popular anthology of the same kind is *The Dick Francis Treasury of Great Racing Stories* (Norton), edited by John Welcome and the former jockey, now a best-selling author, Dick Francis. Both editors have a horse-racing story among the fourteen stories here collected. Among the other dozen are such writers as Sherwood Anderson, J. P. Marquand, A. Conan Doyle, and John Galsworthy. Among the special surprises are Beryl Markham's "The Splendid Outcast" and "The Major" by Colin Davy, former cavalryman and jockey and novelist and, according to the editors, author of "one of the best of all racing autobiographies"—*Ups and Downs* (1939).

Other well-received anthologies were constructed on a thematic foundation. Jon Mukand, who earlier and successfully edited an anthology of contemporary poetry about medicine—*Sutured Words* (1987)—produced *Vital Lines: Contemporary Fiction About Medicine* (St. Martin's). This is a large-scale collection of fifty-six stories by an equal number of contemporary story writers, some well known (Joyce Carol Oates, T. C. Boyle, Gail Godwin, Raymond Carver, Margaret Atwood, Lynne Sharon Schwartz), others of equal merit and accomplishment but less often "discovered" and included in anthologies—poets Robert Watson and

Robert Hass, for example; Mary Peterson and Susan Dodd, David Shields and David Huddle. Physician-writers John Stone and Richard Selzer also contributed stories to this collection. Richard N. Albert gathered and edited *From Blues to Bop: A Collection of Jazz Fiction* (Louisiana State University Press). Dedicated to the memory of the late John Clellon Holmes, whose novel *The Horn*, the editor writes, "inspired my interest in jazz fiction," *Blues to Bop* is historical in concern and chronological in progression, presenting nineteen stories and two excerpts from novels (from *Young Man With a Horn*, 1938, by Dorothy Baker and from Evan Hunter's *The Streets of Gold*, 1974), from Langston Hughes's "Dance" and Eudora Welty's "Powerhouse" to work by Pamela Painter, William Manus, and Beth Brown. Writers as various and distinguished as J. F. Powers, Jack Kerouac, James Baldwin, and John Clellon Holmes are represented; and it is graced by the presence of Shelby Foote's novella "Ride Out," which has been out of print and inaccessible. This year saw the appearance of a variety of genre anthologies. Among those receiving national reviews and attention were two anthologies of horror stories: *Best New Horror Stories* (Carroll and Graf), edited by Stephen Jones and Ramsey Campbell; and *Lovecraft's Legacy* (Tor/Doherty), with fourteen stories by contemporary writers in homage to the great H. P. Lovecraft. Among the writers on board are Robert Bloch, Gene Wolfe, and Hugh B. Cave.

Other anthologies have other intents and purposes, sometimes uniquely so, as in the case of *Delphinium Blossoms: An Anthology*, coming from a brand-new publisher, Delphinium Books, and evidently conceived of and created as a kind of advertisement and an exemplum of the literary variety and quality aspired to by the publisher. Some prominent writers contributed original work to this collection of seventeen stories, including Lee K. Abbot, Russell Banks, E. L. Doctorow, and Grace Paley. These stars rub shoulders with people well known for reasons other than the writing of short fiction: for example Vernon Jordan, Jr. ("Our Children, Our Peers"), longtime president and chief executive officer of the Urban League; Eve Babitz ("Slumming at the Bistro Garden"), Los Angeles gossip columnist and regular contributor to *Smart* magazine; Lori Anne Hackel ("Mucho About the Nada"), who has been singled out by some reviewers for her role, under another name, as the wife of a prominent financier.

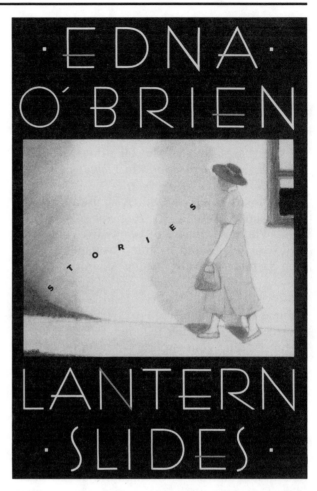

Dust jacket for O'Brien's sixth book of short stories, which won the Los Angeles Times *1990 Book Prize for Fiction*

Interest, on the part of both publishers and readers, in the short fiction of writers from other countries and traditions seemed undiminished in 1990. Latin-American writers continued to publish influential work: Gabriel García Márquez, whose new novel, *The General in His Labyrinth* (HarperCollins), received maximum attention, also published in one volume, and more quietly, *Collected Novellas* (Harper), composed of *Leaf Storm* (1955), *No One Writes to the Colonel* (1961), and the celebrated *Chronicle of a Death Foretold* (1983), all previously available separately. Mexico's Carlos Fuentes brought out *Constancia and Other Stories for Virgins* (Farrar, Straus), five short novels. These are complex works, often "projects of the bizarre and the uncanny," as Denis Donoghue wrote in the *New York Times Book Review*, adding: "One's interest is not limited to the true and the probable." Images out of, and allusions to, the work of the great Spanish painter Goya link the stories subtly together. Things surreal and magical happen as a matter of course. Argentine by birth, Chilean by citizenship, and by profession a teacher at Duke University, Ariel Dorfman published his fourth work of fiction, a collection of eleven short stories—*My House Is On Fire* (Viking). These are hard-nosed, tough stories about families and individuals trying to endure in a climate of political and social oppression. One of the more powerfully ironic stories, "Consultation," tells of an interrogator seeking medical advice from a physician he is torturing. Reviewing the book in the *New York Times Book Review*, young American novelist Jim Shepard praised the power of the stories which, he argued, derives from "the intensity of the political commitment behind them: the intensity of the understanding and the intensity of the caring." Dorfman fled Chile in 1973 after the revolution which overturned the regime of Salvador Allende Gossens. Cuban writer Antonio Benitez Rojo, a 1980 defector from Castro's Cuba now teaching at Amherst, produced *The Magic Dog* (Ediciones del Norte), a collection of twelve stories taken from four collections previously published in Spanish, dealing chiefly with voodoo, spirits, and kinds of enchantment. From Brazil, originally in Portuguese, came *Soulstorm* (New Directions) by the late Clarice Lispector, twenty-nine stories and sketches (*cronicas*), mostly about women and mostly experimental in form though solidly "real" in substance. Lispector died in 1977. George Szanto, an Irishman who splits his life between Montreal and Mexico, writes about life in a Mexican village in *The Underside of Stones* (HarperCollins). Reviewing the collection for the *Washington Post*, Tom Miller chided the author for "self-conscious posturing," but nevertheless allowed that the book contains some "immensely likable vignettes." Another anthology of interest, *Landscapes of a New Land* (White Pine Press), edited by Marjorie Agosin, is composed of twenty-two stories by women of ten Latin-American countries. Noteworthy among them are Maria Luisa Bombal (Chile), Elvira Orphee (Argentina), Nelida Pinon (Brazil), and Christina Peri Rossi (Uruguay).

Books of stories by English-speaking writers from foreign countries continued to have a significant impact on the American scene. Edna O'Brien's *Lantern Slides* (Farrar, Straus and Giroux), her seventeenth book and her sixth collection of stories, which includes twelve stories, most of them rooted or set in a village in Ireland of the present or near past, won the *Los Angeles Times* distinguished 1990 Book Prize for Fiction. Writing about that award ("On Edna O'Brien's 'Lantern Slides,'" *Los Angeles Times*, 4 November 1990), Thomas Cahill stated: "The fictional Irish village she returns to again and again is her village and your village." He concluded that "Edna O'Brien writes about love and death, the only two things that can ever matter to a great writer. She tells the truth." Describing these stories as "little tragedies of passion, stupidity, or stubbornness," the editors of the *New York Times Book Review* (2 December 1990) selected *Lantern Slides* as one of the "Notable Books of the Year." Another collection by an Irish writer which earned wide attention and respectful notice was *Family Sins* (Viking), twelve recent stories by William Trevor. Author of ten novels and six previous collections of stories (on the jacket his publisher carelessly credits him with only five volumes of stories), Trevor is a well-known writer in America, and, in fact, eight of the stories in *Family Sins* were first published here—four in *Grand Street* and four in the *New Yorker*. In a review for the *New York Times Book Review* (3 June 1990), Joel Conarroe, president of the Guggenheim Foundation, pinpointed the rhetorical effect of Trevor's work on the attentive and sensitive reader. "Mr. Trevor's obsession with injustice, his sense that no good life goes unpunished," he wrote, "now and then puts the reader in the position of a somewhat reluctant voyeur, transfixed by the fascination of the abomination."

From Scotland's John Murray came *The Masked Fisherman* (David and Charles), a collection of twenty-one tales, most of them set or centered in the Orkney Islands. From neighboring Canada we were given the extraordinary gift of ten new stories by Alice Munro—*Friend of My Youth* (Knopf). Munro, who has published a novel and five previous story collections, is one of the most highly regarded story writers alive. "She is our Chekhov," Cynthia Ozick has written, "and is going to outlast most of her contemporaries." These stories, set in Canada, in Scotland, and in one case on an outgoing ocean liner, manage to re-create the history of whole lifetimes, gracefully, and without seeming at all minimal, in the limited space the story form allows. In a rave review of the collection for the daily *New York Times*, Michiko Kakutani wrote: "It is a collection that attests, once again, to Ms. Munro's complete fluency in the short-story form, her emergence as one of the most eloquent and gifted writers of contemporary fiction." *Friend of My*

Youth was listed among the five finalists for the *Los Angeles Times* 1990 Book Award for Fiction.

Views of another kind of rural life, coming from another kind of place, are to be found in the twenty stories of *The Home Girls* (Norton). Australian writer Olga Masters originally published in 1943 this book concerning poverty and family life in her country. She is especially good at developing the characters of children. An odd collection coming from New Zealand is *Dear Miss Mansfield* (Viking) by Witi Ishimaera, a male New Zealander whose whole collection is directly addressed to Katherine Mansfield (1888-1923). *Advance, Retreat* (St. Martin's) offered a selection of stories from the past thirty years by the late South African writer Richard Rive, whom the *New York Times Book Review* praised, in "Notable Books of the Year," as "one of the first to explore the meaning of mixed race in a rigid, dualistic society." *Mercy, Pity, Peace and Love* (Morrow) has two poems and thirteen stories by Rumer and Jon Godden, eleven by the former and four by the latter, who died in 1984. These are stories of India set in Bengal, Calcutta, Kashmir, from the memories and experiences of the sisters. Rumer Godden writes, in an "Afterword," that she is concerned with a timeless India and not with specifics of history. "It was the same when I was a child and will be the same when I am long gone but, then, the Hindi word for yesterday and tomorrow is the same." A celebrated Indian writer whose life seems most unlikely to be the same as it was or is, Salman Rushdie produced his first book-length work since he went into hiding to escape the official wrath of Moslems mortally offended by what they took to be blasphemy and ridicule in *The Satanic Verses* (1989)—in a collection of fantastic tales, *Haroun and the Sea of Stories* (Granta/Viking). It is called a novel and was announced and publicized as a book for children, both of which it may well be; but it is also a book of stories and, inevitably, weighted with implications and insinuations. Lee Lescaze, in a highly favorable review in the *Wall Street Journal* (27 November 1990), wrote that it is "a new fairy tale for a new age, but it encapsulates traditions from 'The Arabian Nights' to 'The Wizard of Oz.' It awakens memories in adults and opens doors to new worlds for children." It is (in part) the story of the world's greatest storyteller, the Shah of Blah, who loses his power to make up and tell stories, and of Haroun, his son who goes on a magical quest to try to restore his father's powers. There are fun and

games with a variety of allegorical possibilities and things come, appropriately, to a happy ending. The worldwide writing community has ralᴊflied around the somewhat beleaguered Rushdie. There are urgent blurbs on the book jacket from Doris Lessing, Mario Vargas Llosa, Nadine Gordimer, Graham Greene, Oscar Hijuelos, and Stephen King. Shortly after the book's publication in Britain, Rushdie emerged briefly from his hidey-hole and, heavily guarded, dropped in on some pleased and astonished bookstores to autograph copies of *Haroun*.

An assortment of story collections from European writers appeared. From Sweden's Torgny Lindren came *Merab's Beauty* (HarperCollins), described by Indian-American writer A. G. Mojtabai as a "beautiful, disturbing, God-haunted book." Lindren's early novel, *Bathsheba* (1988), was well received here. From Italy came a new collection of earlier stories, mostly written in the 1960s, by the late Primo Levi—*The Sixth Day* (Summit). These twenty-five stories are mostly fables, *what-if* stories, and science fiction, concerned with the possibilities of modern technology. Another Italian writer of growing international reputation, Natalia Ginzburg, brought out *The Road to the City: Two Novellas* (Arcade/Little, Brown). Both these spare and evocative stories concern death, in both cases a kind of murder, and are brooded over by "the vast multitude of the dead." *MS* magazine has compared Ginzburg's fiction to "wonderfully composed photographs of a bombed-out city. . . ."

German-language writing is represented by collections of three prominent contemporary writers. *Masquerade* (Johns Hopkins University Press) is a selection of stories by the powerfully influential Robert Walser (1878-1956; he strongly affected Hermann Hesse, Robert Musil, and Franz Kafka). *Circe's Mountain* (Milkweed), selected and translated by the American poet Lisel Mueller, is made up of twelve stories by Marie Luise Kaschnitz, taken from three volumes of stories published between 1952 and 1966. Roughly half of them are set in Rome, where Kaschnitz lived for years with her husband at the German Archeological Institute. Novelist, poet, critic, biographer, radio dramatist, and travel writer, Kaschnitz was also a wonderful story writer. Describing her concerns, Lisel Mueller writes: "Kaschnitz is concerned with the interior lives of her characters; she explores—or lets them explore—guilt, grief, transformation, sexuality, the effect of severe emotional trauma, and the connection between the living and the dead." Born in 1926 and widely considered to be among Germany's greatest writers, a peer to Günter Grass and Heinrich Boll, Siegfried Lenz has not until now had a representative or comprehensive selection of his short fiction published in English. *The Selected Stories of Siegfried Lenz* (New Directions) consists of twenty-six stories, about a third of his complete work, so far, in the story form. The collection is divided into three parts—"Tales of Our Times," which are worldwide in setting and contemporary in concerns; "Tales from the Village," rural stories of days gone by, before World II; and "German Lessons," which, self-evidently, deals with people and events on the stage of modern German history. Speaking at the acceptance of the 1988 Friedenpreis of the German Book Trade, Lenz argued: "Anyone can locate historical documents, but the spirit of an age can only be grasped by someone who does not turn aside from his own inner self." In a "Translator's Afterword," Breon Mitchell (of Indiana University) praises Lenz for technical mastery and versatility, but adds that the essence of Lenz's power is more than that. "What shines through these stories," he writes, "is a decency and humanity which reverberates deeply in the reader."

Also writing in German, but most often regarded as a Czech writer, Leo Perutz, who died in 1957, was born and grew up in Prague. *By Night Under the Stone Bridge* (Arcade), a collection of fourteen closely related stories but also classified as a novel, is set in sixteenth-century Prague. Among the extraordinary cast of characters are King Rudolf II; the financier Mordechai Meisl; the Great Rabbi and his beautiful wife, Esther; Johannes Kepler; the Jewish musicians Jackele-the-fool and Koppel-the-bear; and Asael, an angel. On the jacket his publisher accurately describes Perutz's art as blending "in varying degrees history, legend, suspense and the fantastic to form a kind of magic realism *avant la lettre.* . . . " Translated from the Czech is Josef Skvorecky's *The End of Lieutenant Boruvka* (Norton), six interrelated stories about a homicide detective in Prague during 1968. Polish writer Alecksander Wat (1900-1967), a cofounder of Polish futurism whose work is often named as part of the tradition of Edgar Allan Poe, Jorge Luis Borges, and Italo Calvino, is represented by a gathering of his fables—*Lucifer Unemployed* (Northwestern University Press). Stories are much a part of *The Complete Fiction of Bruno Schulz* (Walker). The literary impact of his discovery and translation into

English—*The Street of Crocodiles* (1977) and *Sanatorium Under the Sign of the Hourglass* (1979)—has been profound. Gustaw Herling, a Polish writer now living in Italy, writes freely back and forth between the seventeenth and eighteenth centuries and the present in the long stories of *The Island* (Peter Owen/Dufour).

From Russia this year came two novellas by Boris Vakhtin, who died in 1981: *The Sheepskin Coat & An Absolutely Happy Village* (Ardis). Both of these stories are examples of Soviet satire. "The Sheepskin Coat" is also boldly allusive, being an updated and rewritten version of Gogol's well-known story "The Overcoat." The reviewer for the *New York Times Book Review* (18 March 90) summarized the two novellas as follows: "Both speak, as do the works of Gogol and Kafka, to those illogical laws of modern life, made by persons powerful and unknown, that the average man only learns of after he's broken them."

We round off this brief notice of foreign short-story collections published this year with four excellent Asiatic examples. From Korea we have Hwang Sun-Won's *Shadows of a Sound* (Mercury House), taken from five decades of this artist's work from the furtive days of the Japanese occupation (when writing in the Korean language was banned) to the present. Three collections, each of them involving long stories (novellas), were translated from Japanese. *The Phoenix Tree* (Kodansha) by Satoko Kizaki is composed of four long stories, of international concern, dealing with contemporary Japanese in a variety of settings: "Barefoot," "The Flame Trees," "Mei Hwa Lu," and "The Phoenix Tree." Kizaki is regarded as one of the leading women writers of Japan. Another prominent writer is Chinatsu Nakayama, who has been an actress on television and on stage and has also served as a member of the Japanese Diet. The three novellas which make up *Behind the Waterfall* (Atheneum) represent the first work of hers to be translated into English. Her fictional world comes out of her own, the Japan of here and now. For example, the setting and situation of the longest of the three stories, "Good Afternoon, Ladies," arise out of an afternoon television show and involve cast, crew, audience, and studio executives. *Rain in the Wind* (Kodansha) has two short stories and two novellas, one of which, "Tree Shadows," won the 1988 Kawabata Prize for author Saiichi Maruya. Maruya (fortunate in having as his translator the master, Donald Keene) taught English literature and translated contemporary English novels; and he has said that what probably affected and influenced him most as a writer "was the way that the modern English novel could be serious in a light, entertaining manner." His situations are clearly serious enough, yet he also manages to evoke the comic, in style as well as substance.

This year has been a season for collections by major American masters of the short story. The form is often thought of as being ideally suited, as is the lyric poem, for the young writer, a point made straightforwardly by the American master Wallace Stegner in the "Foreword" to the large *Collected Stories of Wallace Stegner* (Random House). Writing about the short story, he says: "It seems to me a young writer's form, made for discoveries and nuances and epiphanies and superbly adapted for trial syntheses. Increasingly, in my own writing, the novel has tended to swallow and absorb potential stories." Nevertheless he has managed to bring together thirty-one stories, of varying length and wonderfully various in time, setting, and situations, occupying 525 pages. All of the stories are good to excellent and a few stand alone, masterpieces of the form, among them the novella "Genesis," which is surely one of the finest stories ever written about the life of real cowboys. The same general praise could be lavished upon *Collected Stories* (University of Arkansas Press) by R. V. Cassill. The thirty-nine stories (642 pages) represent a lifetime of writing, encompassing twenty-two novels and four collections of stories, and of teaching writing, for years at the Iowa Writers Workshop and then at Brown. Cassill also serves as editor for the *Norton Anthology of Short Fiction* and the *Norton Anthology of Contemporary Fiction*. Cassill's stories have even more variety than Stegner's, including a greater range of technique and experimentation; a few move beyond excellence to as much immortality as a short story can provide. Another master and a master teacher was Caroline Gordon; and Louisiana State University has brought out *The Collected Stories of Caroline Gordon* in a handsome new paperback edition. Although this volume contains the stories that earlier appeared in two collections by her, *The Forest of the South* (1945) and *Old Red* (1963), together with several previously uncollected stories, it is smaller (350 pages) than Cassill's or Stegner's books, in part because Gordon's singular strength lay in the rules of a strict form of her own choice, if not devising. The result was, in the words of Robert Penn Warren in the "Introduction," "a disci-

plined style as unpretentious and clear as running water, but shot through with glints of wit, humor, pity, and poetry." Gordon put her own experience and her artistic rigor to work when she with her husband, Allen Tate, compiled that highly influential textbook anthology, *The House of Fiction*. Another master of the form, though she is more often recognized as a poet, is Josephine Jacobsen. Her *On the Island: New & Selected Stories* (Ontario Review) consists of twenty stories, some newly collected, others taken from her earlier collections, *A Walk With Raschid* (1978) and *Adios, Mr. Moxley* (1986). Various in settings—Baltimore, the Caribbean, the Guatemalan jungle—and in method, these are stories, in the words of William Abrahams, "of uncommon excellence." Over the years seven of her stories have appeared in Abrahams's O. Henry Prize anthologies. A couple of other books of short fiction by writers much better known for their poetry came along this year: Louis Zufkosky's *Collected Fiction* (Dalkey Archive), four stories and a long novel; and *Septuagenarian Stew* (Black Sparrow), by that wildman and author of forty-five books since 1960, Charles Bukowski. Another writer most often mentioned as a poet, Charles Edward Eaton, is represented by *New and Selected Stories 1959-1989* (Cornwall). Assembled from three earlier collections and including several new stories, this latest volume was described, in terms of subject matter and tone, in the *New York Times Book Review*: "these 24 sardonic still lifes mock the mores of America's social and intellectual upper crust."

Although it is his twenty-fourth book with the same publisher (Knopf), John Hersey's collection of eleven short stories, *Fling*, is his first story collection. The eleven stories included were first published from 1950 to 1989, though the majority of them date from the late 1980s. They are as various as the magazines wherein they first appeared: the *Atlantic* and *Esquire*, *Shenandoah* and the *Yale Review*, and one credit any writer would enjoy; "The Captain" first appeared in the *Yacht*. *Fling* received mixed notices, and clearly the short story has not been a form which has deeply engaged Hersey's interest or imagination. Nevertheless these are, each and all, well made, and his publisher's modest claim that "his eleven tales will delight all who love a good short story" is well founded. Hersey and novelist Ward Just have real things in common. Both have been very successful journalists and both are at ease and at home in the corridors of power. The book jacket of *Fling* says of its author: "He divides his time between Key West and Martha's Vineyard." The jacket copy of Ward Just's *Twenty-One: Selected Stories* (Houghton Mifflin) announces: "He and his wife divide their time between Paris and Martha's Vineyard." Small world for the few who do better than the many. Anyway, Just has managed to bring his journalistic knowledge and experience, in many others the essence of nonfiction, pertinently to bear in his fiction. As is evident in his novels, most recently in *Jack Gance* (1989), Just can write fiction about various kinds of public people and events which has (in the accurate words of his publisher) "the flawless ring of authenticity." These stories, published from 1972 to 1989 in a variety of prominent magazines, both "large circulation" (*Gentlemen's Quarterly*) and literary (the *Virginia Quarterly Review*), cover our times and places—Europe and Washington, D.C., the Midwest (chiefly the North Shore of Chicago) and Vietnam. Describing his own interests and art in the "Introduction," Just writes: "The working life, the war, politics, love affairs, and marriage seem to be the waters on which my boats set sail, men and women glaring at their compasses and navigating home—or anyway a port of convenience, some consoling anchorage, someplace *else*." Another writer who fully lived a double life, as a successful lawyer as well as a writer, John William Corrington (1932-1988) is remembered with *The Collected Stories of John William Corrington* (University of Missouri Press). This contains work from three previously published collections, together with several new and uncollected stories.

While speaking of veterans and old-timers, one must take note of the late Roald Dahl's *Ah, Sweet Mystery of Life*, seven stories written in the 1940s, published in magazines in the 1950s, and collected for the first time. They are stories set in one village and sharing a lively cast of characters throughout and riddled, in the words of Dahl's "Preface," "with acute nostalgia and with vivid memories of those sweet days many years ago." No account of old masters of the form would be complete without mention of Henry Clune's *Souvenir* (James Brunner), celebrated in the *Los Angeles Times* (11 November 1990): "The Oldest Living Novelist Tells All." Clune, 101 years old, has been writing and publishing fiction since 1937 when his first novel, *The Good Die Poor*, appeared. *Souvenir* consists of seven stories, mostly involving his hometown of Rochester ("I liked London but it was no Rochester."). Summing up his career in

a recent interview, Clune said: "If I had ten years more, I might do pretty well."

Teacher and critic as well as writer, and, since the death of Ray B. West years ago, the principal advocate and defender of the American short story, William Peden had not published a collection of stories since *Night in Funland* (1968). His reappearance on the scene this year with *Fragments & Fictions* (Watermark) is as exciting as it is surprising; Peden, always a solid craftsman, has produced a highly experimental and demanding book, yet with all the delight and energy that are appropriate to a celebration of creativity. The first unit, close to a hundred pages, "Fragments from the Workbook of an Obscure Writer," is what it professes to be—apparently random and chaotic notes on one subject or observation and another, some odd and enigmatic, others clearly interesting in and of themselves. Part II is titled "Fictions" and includes fifteen short stories, most of them originally published in literary magazines—*Texas Review, New Letters, Greensboro Review*, and others. All are spare, refined, minimal. The payoff of the "Fragments" section is double. We see where many of the stories come from, how the original experience or impulse, the notes, are transformed (sometimes radically) into something that has a shape and a life of its own. Secondly, by the time we finish "Fragments" we know something about the character and interests of the author (himself a kind of fictional persona also) who makes the stories. His presence is more than a shadow in the clean, bright world of the stories. All in all a brilliant performance by an elder statesman, who may well have had that in mind in a one-sentence notation near the end of "Fragments": "Don't try to tell grandpa how to suck turkey eggs." It is also worth noting that Peden's publisher, a small press, has produced what surely must be the most handsomely made book of stories in many years.

Two other collections by highly regarded writers deal almost exclusively with the tricky subject of writers and the creative process. Leonard Michael's *Shuffle* (Farrar, Straus and Giroux) is described accurately by the publisher as an "autobiographical fiction in the form of confession, memoir, journal, essay, and short story." *Shuffle* opens with the seventy-five-page "Journal," which is followed by five personal stories, and ends with a novella-length memoir, "Sylvia," an account of Michael's first marriage and the suicide of his wife Sylvia. Michael, who had earned the highest critical praise for his earlier collections of stories—

Going Places (1969) and *I Would Have Saved Them If I Could* (1975)—as well as his novel, *The Men's Club* (1981), received widespread attention for *Shuffle*, most of it mixed, some of it strongly negative. In the *New York Times Book Review* Anatole Broyard called it "a shockingly bad book for a man of Mr. Michael's stature." Other, more sympathetic reviewers felt the arrangement, the sequence of presenting the author as central character, is wrong; that the tragic story of his marriage should have come first rather than last, for it engages reader interest and sympathy too late and could, as well, have served to justify some aspects of Michael's style and stance—a little numb and distant and cold. Unlike the author-character in Peden's book, the author-character in *Shuffle* is often short on charm and long on arrogance. Yet the documentary aspects of Michael's method, arising in part from those very weaknesses of the central character, crackle with a kind of bitter nostalgia:

> In those days R. D. Laing and others sang praises to the condition of being nuts, and French intellectuals argued for allegiance to Stalin and the Marquis de Sade. Diane Arbus looked hard at freaks, searching maybe for a reservoir of innocence in this world. Lenny Bruce, at the Village Vanguard, a few blocks northwest of MacDougal Street, was doing hilarious self-immolating numbers. A few blocks east, at the Five Spot, Ornette Coleman eviscerated jazz essence through a raucous plastic sax. In salient forms of life and art, people exceeded themselves—or the self; our dashing President, John F. Kennedy, was screwing movie actresses. Everything dazzled.

Nicholas Delbanco's *The Writers' Trade* (Morrow) is more subtle, more ambitious, and more successful overall. He has nine stories, each with a writer as its central character, but these are nine different writers ranging from very young to elderly: Mark Fusco, protagonist of the title story, is twenty-two; Martin of the final story, "Everything," is seventy. Author of nine novels, two works of nonfiction, and an acclaimed earlier collection of stories, *About My Table* (1983), Delbanco is also a teacher (University of Michigan) and critic of distinction. He is coeditor of the forthcoming *Writers and Their Craft: Short Stories and Essays on the Narrative* (Wayne State University Press, February 1991). With the stories in *The Writers Trade*, he has managed to avoid the chief curses of the writer-as-protagonist, solitude and passivity.

Here, quite accurately, writing is seen as an occupation and the contemporary American writer's life is shown to be as intricately entangled with the lives of others, friends and enemies, lovers and families, as that of any other line of work.

Several collections of short fiction, rediscovered or revived, appeared in 1990. Reputed to be an authorized edition with definitive texts was the 832-page *The Short Stories of Jack London* (Macmillan). English novelist Anita Brookner selected and edited *The Stories of Edith Wharton* (Carroll and Graf), while Cynthia Griffin Wolff edited the more official version, *Edith Wharton: Novellas & Other Writings* (Library of America), a work which includes "Ethan Frome," "Summer," and the autobiographical fragment "Life and I." *Ronald Firbank: Complete Short Stories* (Dalkey Archive) was edited by Steven Moore. Firbank's nine novels, determinedly decadent and delightfully amusing, were greatly influential. Michael Dirda, writing in *Washington Post Book World*, boldly claims that Firbank "should be honored as a great master of 20th-century literature, one whose books taught narrative economy, lightness of touch and speed to a generation of writers, among them Evelyn Waugh, Henry Green and Anthony Powell." Firbank's short fiction, however, is mostly juvenilia, originally marked "Not to be published," and of serious interest only to Firbank's dedicated admirers. More recent revivals include such items as Philip Wylie's *Crunch & Des* (Lyons and Burford), tales of a pair of fishermen and their cruiser, *Poseidon*, originally published in *Saturday Evening Post* during 1939-1954. Also from Lyons and Burford is a handsome edition, illustrated by John Groth, of *The Last Running* by John Graves, a celebrated story set in 1923 and featuring a Texas rancher named Tom Bird and a Comanche chief called Starlight; another handsome edition is the twenty-fifth anniversary edition of Robert Drake's story collection, *Amazing Grace*, eighteen related stories set in a small west Tennessee town and highly praised by the late Robert Penn Warren: "Making no pretensions, the book accomplishes its own small, but authentic miracle."

Eighteen of the books under "Fiction" in the *New York Times Book Review* "Notable Books of the Year" are collections of short stories. Some are by newcomers and some are by established writers at various stages of productive careers. Among these latter are such genuinely outstanding and original works as Madison Smartt Bell's *Barking Man* (Ticknor and Fields), Richard

Dust jacket for Bell's second collection of stories, which was named a Notable Book of the Year by the New York Times Book Review

Bausch's *The Fireman's Wife* (Simon and Schuster), and *Me and My Baby View the Eclipse* (Putnam's) by Lee Smith. *Barking Man* is the second collection of stories by Bell, a greatly gifted and productive young writer (he had published five novels and a collection of stories before his thirtieth birthday) who has as much (or more) variety and originality in the story form as anyone writing at this time. He is equally at home and ease with gritty urban and rural settings. He can tell a straightforward tale ("Customs of the Country," which was chosen for *Best American Short Stories 1989*) or an off-the-wall fable—"Holding Together," which is told from the point of view of a white mouse. Reviewing Bell's gathering of ten stories for the *Los Angeles Times*, Paul D. McCarthy wrote (30 September 1990): "Bell's profound compassion and his wise, forgiving vision that avoids contempt and harsh judgment but is never blind to the world's ugliness are given wonderfully varied and eloquent expression in the stories." *The Fireman's Wife* is also a second collection, following upon the much-praised *Spirits* (1987). Richard Bausch

is also the author of four novels. The ten stories here, though various in form, are firmly "realistic" and unified by their deep concern for family and for the faces and guises of love. Noting the connections between these various stories of quite different characters, Bette Pesetsky wrote in the *New York Times Book Review* (10 August 1990): "Are these stories linked? In a way, for they are all about relationship; they are all about redemption through understanding." The stories in *The Fireman's Wife* appeared first in the *New Yorker, Atlantic Monthly*, and *Wig Wag*. "When you get too old to be cute, honey, you got to be eccentric," says Cherry Oxendine in "Intensive Care," one of the nine stories in *Me and My Baby View the Eclipse*. In seven previous novels and an earlier collection of stories, *Cakewalk* (1981), Lee Smith has written about a large crowd of characters who are often both cute and eccentric, but who are also full of surprises and whose sufferings and sadnesses and dreams are as vivid as can be imagined. Sooner or later the engaged reader shares, following the ups and downs of Lee Smith's dimensional characters, the feeling of Raymond toward Sharon in the title story—"You're an endless mystery to me, baby." These three writers are all southerners-in-good-standing.

Other southern writers of distinction and reputation who published story collections in 1990 include Larry Brown, whose second collection, *Big Bad Love* (Algonquin), has nine first-person stories thematically linked; and Kelly Cherry, whose *My Life and Dr. Joyce Brothers: A Novel In Stories* is closely structured around the life of a single character, Nina Bryant, whose life closely parallels the author's own. Here the autobiographical elements are explicitly evoked to form a kind of shadow dance behind the story line. Praised by writers such as Alison Lurie and André Dubus, this book received wide attention nationally. Somewhat less widely and favorably noticed was *I Cannot Get You Close Enough* (Little, Brown), by Ellen Gilchrist, who has earlier enjoyed the limelight of literary celebrity. This latest is composed of three interconnected novellas, involving characters who have appeared in earlier works by her. James W. Hall, author of four books of poetry and two successful thrillers—*Under Cover of Daylight* (1987) and *Tropical Freeze* (1989)—has nine stories, all from literary magazines, gathered in *Paper Products* (Norton). Variety is the keynote here in form and substance, but they are nonetheless strongly linked by the author's idiosyncratic sensibility, his wit and satirical

Richard Bausch, author of The Fireman's Wife, *his second collection of stories*

point of view. Genuinely funny stories are rare in any season. Hall can make the reader laugh out loud. Surely "The Electric Poet" and "Poetic Devices" are the most amusing and stringent American literary satire in years. Another southern writer of genuine distinction is Starkey Flythe, Jr., whose *Lent: The Slow Fast* (University of Iowa Press) is a first collection and winner of the Iowa Short Fiction Award for 1989. Reviewing it for the *New York Times Book Review*, Judith Freeman called it "a sumptuous little collection." Flythe was editor of the *Saturday Evening Post* from 1970 to 1980. Not southern by birth, though several times included in anthologies of southern writers, novelist and critic (National Public Radio) Alan Cheuse brought out his second collection of stories, *The Tennessee Waltz* (Peregrine Smith), fourteen varied stories which have appeared in literary (*Quarterly West, Blue Ox Review*) and commercial (the *New Yorker*) magazines. Three stories are carried over from his first collection, *Candace* (1980). Widely reviewed and praised, Cheuse's stories are various in setting—the South, the West, Latin America—and deal with a variety of characters. Several of these stories are effectively told from a woman's point of view. Another highly respected story writer, Charles Baxter, published his third collection, *A Relative Stranger* (Nor-

ton), thirteen stories, as various as Cheuse's and, like his, linked with common concerns. Baxter's publisher accurately explains: "Most of the stories are love stories, but it is love tinged with fear, even danger." Two of the stories in the collection appeared in *Best American Short Stories*. Reviewing *A Relative Stranger* for the daily *New York Times*, Michiko Kakutani praised "Mr. Baxter's ability to orchestrate the details of mundane day-to-day reality into surprising patterns of grace and revelation, his gentle but persuasive knack for finding and describing the fleeting moments that indelibly define a life." Poet and novelist and author of a previous collection of novellas, *Legends of the Fall* (1980), Jim Harrison brings together three novellas, one of which appeared in the *New Yorker* and another in *Smart* magazine, in *The Woman Lit by Fireflies* (Houghton Mifflin/Seymour Lawrence). Harrison tells three very different stories, alike only in the imaginative originality of his focus and a great energy that is transformed into authority. In *Washington Post Book World* (2 September 1990) Arthur Krystal wrote: "Harrison has a narrative voice that fairly defies the reader to ignore it."

Poet, novelist, story writer, former priest, and former director of the creative-writing program at Stanford, John L'Heureux collected in *Co-*

medians (Viking) four stories, one ("Brief Lives") composed of nine separate but related stories, all of them concerned one way and another with the lives (and deaths) of saints and artists, a collection which, in the words of *Publishers Weekly*, "explores the possibility of faith and redemption in a secular age." Terrible, often unspeakable things take place, but the book ends with the vision and visionary words of a woman ("Maria Luz Buenvida") who has been raped and mutilated and left to die on a lonely hilltop—"And at the last it will be well."

For years North Dakota writer Larry Woiwode has been working on fiction about the immigrant Neumiller family, who are the subjects of his celebrated novel, *Beyond the Bedroom Wall* (1974). Between 1964 and 1974 Woiwode worked with *New Yorker* fiction editor William Maxwell on a series of ten stories which now appear in their original form for the first time, together with three newer, uncollected stories, in *The Neumiller Stories* (Farrar, Straus and Giroux). Anne Tyler has described his special quality as "a grave, direct, deliberate voice that gives a sense of nothing held back, no issues evaded." Among other outstanding collections by male writers in midcareer is *The Things They Carried* (Houghton Mifflin/Seymour Lawrence) by Tim O'Brien. O'Brien, who had earlier written about Vietnam in *If I Die in a Combat Zone* (1973) and *Going After Cacciato* (1978, National Book Award 1979), returns to the subject with a collection of twenty-two fictive recollections in some of which the author appears as a remembered self. *The Things They Carried* was selected by the *New York Times Book Review* as one of the fourteen books comprising the annual list—"Editors' Choice: The Best Books of 1990."

The prolific Stephen Dixon, author of eight collections of stories since 1976, and, according to book-jacket copy, "about three hundred" stories in magazines, published two collections of stories in 1990—*Love and Will* (Paris Review) and *All Gone* (Johns Hopkins University Press). Describing the eighteen stories of *All Gone* for the *New York Times Book Review* (1 July 1990), Steve Erickson called it "an act of literary terrorism" and "an almanac of incidents in which life's semblance of fairness goes haywire." A more significant talent than most of the writers mentioned and listed here is Chicago-born Stuart Dybek, whose first collection of stories, *Childhood and Other Neighborhoods* (1980), had a major impact on the American scene and whose second gather-

ing is *The Coast of Chicago* (Knopf). The fourteen stories of this handsomely made little book, all set in the ethnic neighborhoods of Chicago, are quite accurately defined by the jacket copy: "Dybek's wonderful book is unified by a sense of place, by overarching themes and recurrent motifs and by a striking, original prose style." Of the latter, the best critics have been able to do is to describe a blending of, perhaps, Nelson Algren and Saul Bellow with Franz Kafka and Italo Calvino. Somewhat odder, though it is more a matter of subject than style, is Steven Millhauser, whose latest, *The Barnum Museum* (Poseidon), has ten stories of the surreal and supernatural and was widely reviewed though earning mixed responses. Praised by Jay Cantor in the *New York Times Book Review*, it was bombed in *Publishers Weekly* ("repetitious, oppressively belletristic") and described as probably belonging to "the genre of science fiction, which Millhauser flirts with and never quite embraces," by Aram Saroyan in the *Los Angeles Times* (30 September 1990). Surgeon-author Richard Selzer flirts with fantasy and, perhaps, science fiction in *Imagine a Woman* (Random House), six stories which, for the first time, are not primarily involved with medicine and surgery. It received mixed notices, as did John Calvin Batchelor's *Gordon Liddy Is My Muse, By Tommy "Tip" Paine* (Linden), a sequence of stories about the search for heroes at home and abroad, told by "Tip" Paine, a best-selling author, a "Sci-Fi/Spy Guy," who sees himself as "a travelling salesman of make believe." Another writer who received mixed signals from critics on the value of his latest collection of stories, *A Place I've Never Been* (Viking), is David Leavitt. His collection of ten stories, all but two mainly concerned with gay life and loves, was honored by some, shrugged off by others, and savaged by a few. In what may well stand as the outstanding hatchet-job of the year, Donna Rifkind writes for "Book Life" of the *Washington Times* ("Leavitt's tales plumb the shallows of despair!") an examination of the book in some detail, story by story, ending with this summation: "The mood of depression, malaise, boredom and grief that hangs uniformly over this author's work is nothing more than a retreat, a bad habit." Another quite different kind of book (described in the *Los Angeles Times* as "stylistically rich, philosophically speculative, structurally adventurous"), dealing mainly with the vicissitudes of gay experiences, is Guy Davenport's *The Drummer of the Eleventh North Devonshire Fusiliers* (North Point), four short stories and the novella

"Wo Es War, Soll Ich Werden." Davenport, an elegantly experimental writer and an intelligent and knowledgeable critic, is a master of this limited subject matter. "This intimacy thing is highly overrated," says a student in Allen Barnett's *The Body and Its Dangers* (St. Martin's), offering up six stories of gay and lesbian love, AIDS, cancer, and complex ambiguous sexual histories.

Two Italian-American writers, both of whom have written chiefly for the *New Yorker* and both of whom have chiefly written autobiographical stories, published collections this year. Nicolo Tucci's *The Rain Came Last* (New Directions) is a selection of fourteen autobiographical stories written between the 1940s and the 1960s, linked by a concern with the aristocracy in a changing world. *The Tales of Arturo Vivante* (Sheep Meadow Press) has thirty-five short narratives, most of them set in and against the Sienese countryside. Reviewing it for the *New York Times Book Review* (23 December 1990), Beverly Fields emphasized the autobiographical center: "The variously named protagonists, like the first-person narrators, appear to be avatars of the author, remembering and touching up significant places in his life." Ethnicity in several forms shapes the collections of several African-American writers. Dionne Brand's stories in *Sans Souce* (Firebrand) deal with contemporary black life in the Caribbean and in Canada. A former student and protégé of both Raymond Carver and Frederick Barthelme, John Holman, in *Squabble* (Ticknor and Fields), uses original ways and means to deal with the "slightly surreal lives of blacks in the New South." In these strong stories there is a good deal of good humor as reality collides with stereotypes. Reality collides head-on with the conventions of postmodern metafiction in poet and novelist Clarence Major's *Fun & Games: Short Fictions* (Holy Cow!), nineteen "prose pieces," imaginative and freewheeling, and including both "real" and fictional characters. Some of the "real" people who appear in these stories are Flannery O'Connor, Adolf Hitler, Edgar Allan Poe, and Zora Neale Hurston, not to mention a familiar pair from another work and kind of fiction—Hansel and Gretel. Among the influences traced in Major's prose style are Chester Himes, Oscar Wilde, and Calvino.

Women writers now actively in midcareer contributed interesting and sometimes important story collections to the year's bountiful harvest. Some of these come from writers who have established themselves as trendsetters; others come from writers not known so widely. Several from among the former category received considerable review attention coast-to-coast. Trendy Atlantic Monthly Press brought out *Escapes* by veteran Joy Williams. Forms of pain and sorrow are her subjects. As an old lady says in one of these tales, "If things cry, they got souls. If they don't, they don't." Writer Patrick McGrath, writing in *Washington Post Book World*, argued that Williams has only one basic method of constructing a story. "The set up is generally gloomy—a drinking problem, a failing relationship, a terminal disease—which is then transformed, not by a Carveresque 'a small good thing,' but rather by a small weird thing. From out of the gloom appears a magic show, a boa constrictor, a rabid bat—or a black T-bird with a dead man behind the wheel." Something of the same consistency of tone and mood was evoked by Rand Richards Cooper (*New York Times Book Review*, 21 January 1990), who called the book "an exercise in dread," adding that "*Escapes* is by no means a funny book. Its laughs are all bright birds that at the slightest sound flap away into a black and empty sky." Another, though funnier, celebrant of the bleakly enigmatic is novelist A. M. Homes, whose *The Safety of Objects* (Norton) engaged much critical attention. Writing about Homes and her work and these ten stories, Stacey D'Erasmo opined in *Village Voice Literary Supplement* ("The Wizard of Odd," November 1990): "If you took the entire cast of *Thirtysomething* and put them on crack, you might get something close to the twists and turns of *The Safety of Objects*." Not atypical is "A Real Doll," in which a man has a relationship with a talking Barbie Doll, her voice described by Homes as "a cross between the squeal when you let the air out of a balloon and a smoke alarm with weak batteries." Equally eccentric and original, if decidedly different, is Amy Hempel, whose first collection, *Reasons To Live*, was roundly praised for its chic minimalism and a quick and clever style. The sixteen brisk little stories (the longest is twelve pages) of *At the Gates of the Animal Kingdom* (Knopf) earned the book a place on the *New York Times Book Review* annual "Notable Books of the Year." Something of her technique and strategy is exemplified by this sentence from "The Day I Had Everything": "Jean said she thought she might still hear from Larry but that hoping he would call was like the praying you do after the bowling ball has left your hand." Another of the kind and the era, if not that ilk, is Lorrie Moore, whose earlier collection, *Self-Help*, was admired. Her latest, the eight stories forming *Like Life* (Knopf), also appears on the "Notable Books of the Year" list. Writing about the collection in the *New York Times Book Review* (20 May 1990), Stephen McCauley saw distinct artistic development, arguing that the new stories are "less capricious and far more capacious." Somewhat less generous was Merle Rubin for the *Washington Post* (3 June 1990), who described Moore's work as "a kind of Lean Cuisine for street-smart urban sophisticates who like to read and run," adding that Moore is "a writer with a wry, skittish sense of humor and enough verbal glibness to provide material for all the stand-up comics in Los Angeles, but with very little ability to create convincing characters or tell stories that invite us to suspend our disbelief as we read them or to brood upon them after they've been read." A story from this collection, "You're Ugly, Too," which was first published in the *New Yorker*, was chosen by Richard Ford for *The Best American Short Stories 1990*. An altogether different kind of story is characteristic of Susan Dodd, whose first collection won the 1984 Iowa Short Fiction Award and whose latest, *Hell-Bent Men and Their Cities* (Viking), is on the "Notable Books of the Year" list. The fifteen stories are widely different in form, alike in their solid grounding in character and with deeply moving moments which can obviate the need for clever irony; as, for example, here in "Bifocals," where Phil, a mortician, is starting to prepare the body of an old friend—"The scars seemed to Phil like stories written in an ancient and secret tongue. Sacred mysteries, he thought, the things I will never know." Kate Braverman is a poet and novelist of enviable reputation on her native West Coast and altogether deserving of much more attention in the eastern literary establishment. *Squandering the Blue* (Ballantine) is her first collection of short stories, twelve pieces organized regionally and around thematic concerns and, essentially, a cycle of events involving two principal characters, poet Diana Barrington and her best friend, Carlotta McKay, and others. Another outstanding regional writer is the southerner Martha Lacy Hall, whose nine stories, brought together in *The Apple-Green Triumph* (Louisiana State University Press), all appeared between 1986 and the present in southern quarterlies. Her work here and in two previous collections of stories—*Call It Living* (1981) and *Music Lesson* (1984)—has been compared to that of Eudora Welty. Not as well known, yet, as she should be, is Valerie Miner, novelist, international feminist, and political activist,

who has lived in Britain, Africa, Canada, Australia, and Latin America and writes about these places and others in the sixteen stories of *Trespassing* (Crossing Press). Poet Constance Urdang, who has earned praise for her novellas, again has published together a pair of short novels—*The Woman Who Read Novels* and *Peacetime* (Coffee House), the first more or less straightforward, the second dealing with three women friends and a search for "peace," a somewhat experimental collage. The two major experimental collections of the year are by women. Ursule Molinaro's *A Full Moon of Women* (Coffee House), subtitled "29 Word Portraits of Notable Women From Different Times and Places," delivers what it promises, experimental versions of the lives of real and imaginary women from the twelfth century B.C. to our own time. Among the characters treated are the likes of Charlotte Corday, Cassandra, Madame Blavatsky, and (of course!) Snow White. The inimitable Kathy Acker followed her most recent novel, *Empire of the Senseless* (1989), with *In Memoriam To Identity* (Grove Weidenfeld), which can be essentially, if simplistically, described as an interweaving of elements of four short novels—"Rimbaud," "Airplane," "Capitol," and "The Wild Palms," being based (loosely) on the contrapuntal narrative interchange found in Faulkner's *The Wild Palms* (1939). Some sense of it can be gleaned from two sentences of the (desperately seeking common sense) book-jacket prose—"Rimbaud is in love with revolution: he hates school, militarism, and his mother. Even the leader of the motorcycle gang can't recruit him." Acker is a major talent among the few dedicated adventurers of the avant-garde.

Among the other noteworthy collections by women writers of some established reputation: *Reliable Light* (Rutgers University Press), by Meredith Steinbach; the mostly lesbian stories of Jane Rule in *Theme For Diverse Instruments* (Naiad); Sheila Kohler's stories of affluent and dangerous people in Africa and Europe in *Miracles in America* (Knopf); Mary Clearman Blew's *Runaway* (Confluence), powerful, gritty stories of Montana ranch life half a century and more ago; Carol Shields's *The Orange Fish* (Viking); another Viking book, Laura Kalpakian's traditionally crafted tales (six of them) in *Dark Continent*; a novella and four stories set in west Florida and Cajun country from Shylah Boyd's *A Real Man* (British American).

This annual report is not much concerned with genre fiction, but it is nevertheless appropri-

Dust jacket for Hempel's second collection of short stories

sults of this development are complex and space-consuming and often debatable. But one thing is certain—there are many excellent first books of stories, collections of the highest literary quality, published each year. And this year is no exception to that new rule. Some always stand well above the others, and here are some of the best and best-received first books published this year. Two which found places among the *New York Times Book Review* "Notable Books of the Year" were Christopher Tilghman's *In a Father's Place* (Farrar, Straus) and Richard Spilman's *Hot Fudge* (Poseidon). Few first books of any kind have received the attention and the honor, justly deserved, accorded to Tilghman's book of seven stories (which individually earned honor and attention in the *Sewanee Review, Virginia Quarterly Review, Ploughshares*, and the *New Yorker*). The settings are various—the Eastern Shore, Montana, the highways and byways of the West; but the voice, "strong, resonant and unexpected," above all, ample and unhurried, remains the same and is worth listening to. Praised by a surprising range of writers—Carolyn Chute, Joseph Heller, Madison Smartt Bell, among others—the six stories of *Hot Fudge* are more a matter of diverse voices; for Spilman has an impeccable understanding of the words we speak and the ways we speak them. Variety is his way—characters of all kinds, young and old, settings all over America. And fully realized characterization is his greatest strength. "The characters churn in our imagination," R. V. Cassill writes, "beckoning and alluring us in the fascinating labyrinths of their destinies."

Some first collections were highly promoted and advertised, though whether or not these books succeeded with reviewers and in the bookstores seemed somewhat beyond the control of publishers. Scott Bradfield, whose first novel, *The History of Lumunious Motion* (1989), was much praised, ran into some flak with a baker's dozen of stories in *Dream of the Wolf* (Knopf). Steven G. Kellman in the *New York Times Book Review* announced that "Mr. Bradfield is a bully who controls the channel changer." Stephanie Vaughn's *Sweet Talk* (Random House), on the other hand, was massively promoted and well received. The ten stories here follow a central character, Gemma, an Army brat, from adolescence into middle age. One of the strongest and most memorable of the stories is "Kid Macarthur," about Gemma's brother who served in Vietnam. Equally promoted was Walter Kirn's *My Hard Bargain*

ate and necessary to call attention to three worthy collections of short fiction which are essentially genre rather than "mainstream." Brian W. Aldiss has gathered a group of his own fantasy stories published from 1960 to 1989 in *A Romance of the Equator* (Atheneum). *House Without Doors* (Dutton), thirteen horror stories by Peter Straub, was praised in *Publishers Weekly* as "playfully postmodern." And genre-master Stephen King produced four horror novellas for *Four Past Midnight* (Viking). This reviewer's two favorites are "The Sun Dog," where a Polaroid camera, no matter where pointed, only takes pictures of a huge, ugly, and very mean dog; and "The Library Policeman," wherein a middle-aged man with a bunch of overdue books discovers the hard way that the librarian is a monster.

One aspect of the so-called renaissance of the American short story has been the verifiable fact that more and more writers of prose fiction are introduced to readers with story collections rather than first novels. The reasons for and re-

(Knopf), thirteen traditional stories told in a variety of voices. Kirn's book as well as Vaughn's appear on the *New York Times Book Review* "Notable Books of the Year" list. Writing for the *Los Angeles Times* (11 November 1990), Michael Harris particularly praised Kirn's tact as a writer, adding: "You have to have tact to write a story about masturbation without embarrassing your readers." Some of Kirn's stories concern the lives and problems of contemporary Mormons.

There were, as always, first collections of the highest quality, as good as any mentioned in this roundup, which, though favorably reviewed, for one reason or another did not receive the full attention and appreciation they richly deserve. My special favorites among first collections published in 1990 include among others: Stephen Dunning's *To the Beautiful Women* (Samuel Russell), nine quirky, edgy, unsentimental, and often very funny stories; Januce Eidus, *Vito Loves Geraldine* (City Lights), eighteen slightly off-the-wall little stories by a writer who, in the words of Paul West, "makes marginality poignant and nervousness a gift." Edward Falco, who also published a novel, *Winter in Florida* (Soho), this year and who has won prizes for his individual stories, brought out *Plato at Scratch Daniel's* (University of Arkansas Press). Strong accounts of hard lives and wounded people, these stories were described by R. H. W. Dillard as "powerful tales of painful discoveries and unexpected losses." Well-known photographer Bernard Gotfryd has put together twenty-one spare, powerful, and personal stories of the Holocaust and its ongoing impact, in *Anton the Dove Fancier* (Washington Square). The ten stories of Lisa Koger's *Farlanburg Stories* (Norton), all concerning small-town southern life in rural Farlanburg, have seized the attention and evoked the praise of some of the best and brightest among our writers, including Lee Smith, Madison Smartt Bell, Judith Freeman, and the popular Anne Rivers Siddons. Koger is aptly called "a natural storyteller with the power to stun and delight" by Jill McCorkle. The world of the small town—in this case the fictional Union, Ohio—is the world of the seventeen stories in Lynn Lauber's *White Girls* (Norton). These linked stories follow the life of young Loretta Dardio, who is herself narrator of fifteen of the tales, and deal mainly with an interracial love affair between Loretta and a young black man, Luther Biggs. In the final story, "Homecoming," Luther gets her pregnant, then leaves her for the town's first black high school homecoming

queen. One of the finest books of the year, one which would be among the few and finest in any given year, is Ralph Lombreglia's *Men Under Water* (Doubleday), consisting of nine very original and moving stories from some of the very best places—the *Atlantic*, the *New Yorker, Best American Short Stories* (twice). His publisher understood that Lombreglia is "one of the most original and entertaining short story writers at work today." But nevertheless they somehow failed to promote this book adequately enough to reach many readers or reviewers. Fred Chappell calls *The Rat Becomes Light* (HarperCollins), by Donald Secreast, "one of the best books of stories I ever read." And that should raise eyebrows and expectations. These are fourteen tales out of a small Appalachian town, Boehm, North Carolina, and most of them concern a group of characters who work at the Chalfant Furniture Factory there. Superlatives are likewise in order and have been earned by Steve Yarbrough's *Family Men* (Louisiana State University Press). Again, the setting and general subject is mostly small-town southern life, in this case the world of Yarbrough's native Mississippi Delta; but as a writer Yarbrough has a wide vision; and at least one story not included in the collection, "The Formula" (*Virginia Quarterly Review*), is set in contemporary Poland and its central characters are Poles. Finally there is *Economics of the Heart* by Christopher Zenowich (HarperCollins), the ten stories of which are, indeed, a kind of "novel-in-stories," closely focused on the life of young Bob Bodewicz, who was the central character in Zenowich's first novel—*The Cost of Living*. His publisher is perfectly truthful calling these stories "a compelling picture of growing up poor and determined."

Other first collections which deserve honorable attention and which, in a quieter year, might easily have stood out among the very best, include the annual prizewinners: *Limbo River* (University of Pittsburgh Press), winner of the 1990 Drew Heinz Literature Prize; three winners of the Flannery O'Connor Award for Short Fiction (University of Georgia Press)—*The People I Know* by Nancy Zafris, Debra Monroe's *The Source of Trouble*, and *The Expendables* by Antonya Nelson; *The Effigy* (University of Missouri Press), winner of the 1990 Breakthrough Award, by Joan Millman; *A Hole in the Language* (University of Iowa Press) by Marly Swick, winner of the 1990 Iowa Short Fiction Award; and the newly created William Goyen Prize for Fiction, awarded to a first collection of stories—*Earthly Justice* (TriQuarterly), by E. S. Goldman.

There are two more examples of that new and ambiguous label, the "novel-in-stories," both from Milkweed, Sheila O'Connor's *Tokens of Grace* and Susan Straight's *Aquaboogie*. Straight's volume, concerned with the life of an all-black California community, was the winner of the Milkweed National Fiction Prize. Well deserving of being listed among the outstanding first collections of 1990: *The Power of Horses* (Arcade/Little, Brown), by Elizabeth Cook-Lynn, fifteen stories about Sioux Indians in this century; Rachel Simon's *Little Nightmares, Little Dreams* (Houghton Mifflin); Lauri Anderson's *Hunting Hemingway's Trout* (Atheneum), a series of stories and sketches about Hemingway and a variety of fictional characters; *Pretending To Say No* (Plume), by Bruce Benderson, eleven stories and a novella, all but one about the New York City drug scene; Mary Bush's *A Place of Light* (Morrow), concerning hard lives in upstate New York; Mary Caponegro's *The Star Cafe* (Scribners), blurbed by John Hawkes and Robert Coover, four longish stories not surprisingly described (by Richard Eder in the *Los Angeles Times*) as "surreal eruptions"; *Life After Death* (Faber and Faber) by Susan Compo, devoted to the postpunk subculture; *Dancers & the Dance* (Coffee House) by Summer Brenner, a dozen stories about dancers and performers by a dancer and performer; *The Wars of Heaven* (Houghton Mifflin/Seymour Lawrence), six stories and a novella about rural West Virginia fifty years ago, by Richard Currey; *Karankawa County* (Texas A & M University Press), by rancher Neal Morgan, linked tales of the county of the title; John Morrel Adler's *The Hunt Out of the Thicket* (Algonquin), stories of hunting and fishing in the Georgia and South Carolina Lowcountry; *Interim in the Desert* (Texas Christian University Press), a dozen stories of the rural Southwest, by Roland Sodowsky; Chris Spain's *Praying for Rain* (Capra), twelve minimalist stories, four of them set in mental institutions and one, "Entrepreneurs," winner of a Pushcart Prize in 1988. The range of age and background among the authors of first collections is as wide and various as the form and substance of the stories. Eleanor Devine, author of *You're Standing in My Light* (Beacon), is a seventy-five-year-old former feature writer for the *Chicago Sun-Times* and the *Chicago Tribune*; not surprisingly, her stories are set in the suburbs of Chicago. Marjorie Sandor is young enough to have appeared in the anthology *Twenty Under Thirty* and *A Night of Music* is simply announced as "astounding" by her trendy publisher, Ecco Press. Californian by birth, Melissa Lentricchia is on the faculty, and a faculty wife, at Duke. Her book, *No Guarantees* (Morrow), is described by her publisher as "a lyrical collage of styles, tones, and characters." Variety among male authors seems no less. Poet and playwright Frank Manley—*Within the Ribbons* (North Point)—is a middle-aged professor of English at Emory. David Lipsky, on the other hand, whose *Three Thousand Dollars* (Summit) arrived hull down with a rich cargo of praise (John Barth, Raymond Carver, Nicholas Delbanco, Meg Wolitzer, Bob Shacochis; Blurb King for 1990?), is a recent graduate of Brown. Small presses continue to publish some of the finest fiction; so it is no surprise that Greg Johnson's highly praised *Distant Friends* comes from Ontario Review Press. Similarly, the university presses continue to publish collections of stories. Rutgers University Press joined the others, initiating a new series with a first collection—*Life in the Temperate Zone* by Robert Wexelblatt.

The American publishing grapevine had it that 1990 would be, then was, the peak year for the publication of collections of short stories, that the economy and other factors would bring to an end the decade-long boom for short fiction. Time will tell if this rumor has any validity. But meanwhile, already, bound galleys of many more new collections are in circulation and early assessments and advance reviews are coming in. Just for the record, here are a few 1991 collections already gaining attention, arousing interest: Alyson Hagy's *Hardware River* (Poseidon); *White People* (Knopf) by Allan Gurganus; *The Voice of America* (Norton), by Rick DeMarinis; John Dufresne's *The Way That Water Enters Stone* (Norton); Fred Chappell's *More Shades Than One* (St. Martin's); and, appropriately titled, *Short Stories Are Not Real Life* (Louisiana State University Press), by David Slavitt.

The Year in Poetry

R. S. Gwynn
Lamar University

A controversy surfaced early in 1990 over the choice of Charles Simic's *The World Doesn't End* (Harcourt Brace Jovanovich) as winner of the Pulitzer Prize for Poetry. In the past, Simic has received awards from the American Academy of Arts and Letters and the Poetry Society of America, so few readers would deny that he is an important figure in contemporary American poetry. Nevertheless, *The World Doesn't End* is in the main a collection of prose poems, with only five short pieces, in all totaling twenty-one lines, written as verse. This in itself is unremarkable, for prose poetry has been around since the middle of the nineteenth century and many contemporary American poets—Russell Edson, John Ashbery, Mark Strand among them—have experimented with it with some degree of success. What the members of the jury—Helen Vendler, Garrett Hongo, and Charles Wright—either accidentally overlooked or willfully chose to ignore is that the official provisions of the Pulitzer Prize committee, as verified by administrator Robert C. Christopher, stipulate that the award shall go "for a distinguished volume of *verse* [italics mine] by an American author."

The fact did not escape Louis Simpson, a former winner of the prize who has served on the Pulitzer jury in the past. In an open letter to the Pulitzer Prize board that was reprinted in the June issue of the *New Criterion*, Simpson raises valid questions of integrity, responsibility, and professional competence. The letter is worth quoting in full:

> This year a Pulitzer Prize was awarded for a book of "prose poems." No award was made for verse. Does not a rule of the Pulitzer Prizes state that the prize for poetry is to be awarded for a book of verse? Has the rule been changed? If so, readers and writers of verse would like to know why. If it has not been changed, the Board appears to have been irresponsible.
>
> Have you thought of the consequence of awarding the prize for verse to a book of prose? If in the future a publisher submits a book of short stories for the prize in poetry, a book of essays, a "po-

etic" biography or history, on what grounds will you say that it is ineligible?

> There are several Pulitzer Prizes for prose. You have taken the one prize that was open to writers of verse and awarded that also to a book of prose. You have, in fact, eliminated the prize for verse.
>
> Why?

In response, Mr. Christopher admitted that Simpson was correct, rather lamely offering, according to the *New Criterion*'s summary of his letter, that "it has been the practice of the Pulitzer board to describe the award as one for poetry rather than for verse, and that 'prose poems' have long been a 'recognized form.'" With unconcealed sarcasm the editors of the *New Criterion* add, "Presumably, Mr. Christopher does not go so far as to claim that prose poems are a recognized form of verse," going further to assert that "what has been described in these pages [by Brad Leithauser in a 1980 essay] as 'metrical illiteracy' has long made a good deal of what passes for American poetry a literary wasteland. That this phenomenon of metrical illiteracy has been tolerated and even encouraged by university writing programs is also well known. By lending its weight to the destructive side of this debate about poetic form, the Pulitzer board has not only subverted the provisions of its award for verse but has done considerable harm to the art of poetry."

Those who are thoroughly confused at this point would do well to attend to some basic matters of definition, as explained by Lewis Turco in *The New Book of Forms: A Handbook of Poetics* (1986):

> There are only two modes in which any genre can be written, *prose* and *verse*. Prose is *unmetered* language; verse is *metered* language. Any of the genres can be written in either of the modes; that is, ... there are *prose poems* and *verse poems*.... Poetry is a genre, and verse is a mode.... Prose poems are sometimes mislabeled "free verse," but this misnomer is a contradiction in

terms, as we have seen, for there are only two modes of language—prose and verse. Either language is metered, or it is not metered; it cannot be both simultaneously.

By "metered" we usually mean a line that is *measured in length* according to some system. This system may be arrived at by counting traditional units in the line like syllables, strong stresses, or metrical feet—what, for lack of a better term, might be labeled formal verse; or by breaking the line according to some personal system based on cadenced phrases or clauses, "breath units," "variable feet," or even visual units—all of which, though they actually may have little in common, have come to be known as free verse. Whatever the system, verse is distinguished from prose by virtue of the integrity of individual lines and the "turn" (from the Latin *vertere*) from line to line. The unit of verse is the line. The unit of prose is the sentence. The popular belief that all verse has to follow an obvious rhythmical pattern (and be rhymed as well) is as false as the notion that the term "verse" implies a lesser degree of ambition and achievement (as in "occasional verse" or "light verse") than "true" poetry.

Perhaps stung more by the *New Criterion*'s assignment of blame to creative-writing programs than by any exception to Simpson's original point, D. W. Fenza, editor of *AWP Chronicle*, the official publication of the Associated Writing Programs, responded in the September issue of his own magazine:

> While we weary of hearing blame being automatically heaped upon creative writing programs for everything that's wrong with contemporary letters, the controversy over the prize does raise interesting questions? [*sic*] Can prose be poetry? How much can verse appropriate the rhetoric of prose?

It is immediately apparent that Fenza himself misconstrues the distinction between verse and poetry, and, thus, his final question seems not only irrelevant to the point being addressed, but absurd to boot. Students of classical rhetoric know that most of the linguistic schemes (largely matters of syntax, placement, and repetition of sounds and words in sentences) and tropes (figures of speech) are shared by both poetry and prose and that only a few of them (syncope and other forms of rhythmical elision are the main examples) are unique to the verse mode. It is perhaps true that much of the poetry of this century has

tended to avoid the excessive flourishes of the Victorian era, but the same could be said, in general, for modernist prose when it is compared with that of the nineteenth century. The belief that the language of poetry should aspire both to the economy of prose (Ezra Pound's "Poetry ought to be as well written as prose") and speech (Robert Frost's notion of "the sound of sense") has become an article of faith for most poets of this century. Nevertheless, they have continued to write, for the most part, in the verse mode.

Fenza goes on to cite numerous examples to support his shaky case—Whitman's borrowing of "sweeping, parallel sentence structures from the Bible," Dickinson's appropriation of hymnal stanzas to add "fragmentary impositions of consciousness—the segues between repression and expression," even Sharon Olds's and Adrienne Rich's "political invectives that are expository, confessional, lyrical, and dramatic"—but he climbs on so high a soapbox that the rarified air seems to have left him light-headed:

> The boundaries between poetry and prose necessarily dissolved because poets came to realize that consciousness, even in its most exalted moments—or perhaps *especially* in its most exalted moments—is part song and part process, part verse and part prose. It turns upon itself to contain itself; it proceeds away from itself to extend its grasp, or to liberate itself. Because the new citizens of the New World dared to speak American rather than the King's English, because poetry succeeds by posing successive models of consciousness, poetry became a more inclusive genre.
>
> It seems Louis Simpson and the editors of the *New Criterion* feel that verse and prose should be segregated, that one should not dare to claim the dominions of the other. Such segregation is a kind of solution; by narrowly limiting what defines poetry, one can disregard much of this century's poetry.

Responding in the October/November issue of *AWP Chronicle*, Simpson took close aim at this statement:

> This is misrepresentation. Neither I nor the editors of the *New Criterion* have attempted to define poetry. The word poetry is vague and can be made to mean almost anything, from a sunset to a book of verse. But the word verse has a specific meaning, and the regulations of the Pulitzer Prize state clearly that a prize is to be given for a book of verse. In awarding the prize to a book

of prose poems the Pulitzer Board subverted the intentions of those who designed the prize.

If a prize intended for playing the violin were awarded to a trumpet player, everyone would see immediately how absurd and unacceptable this was. The Pulitzer Board has done something just as absurd and unacceptable.

As for Fenza's statement that to award a prize intended for verse only to verse would "disregard most of this century's poetry," I can only suppose that Fenza has not read much poetry. Most of what has been called poetry in this century is written in verse.

You have titled Fenza's column "Totally Miffed about the Pulitzer." I would like my answer to be titled "Totally Ignorant of the Issues at Stake."

One is tempted to add nothing to so elegant a rejoinder, but several other matters are worth considering and will perhaps perplex future Pulitzer selection juries. First, is the jury at liberty to decide what books are eligible for the prize, in spite of what the original prize guidelines stipulate? And is the prize committee bound to follow the recommendations of the jury? Simpson, in a letter on a related topic (the selection of the 1979 Pulitzer Prize, when he was chairman of the jury) published in the November issue of the *New Criterion*, notes that a book of prose poems by Mark Strand, the current poet laureate, was disqualified that year at his insistence, even though the two other members of the jury, John Ashbery and Nona Balakian, originally favored it for the prize. A second book of Strand's work published that year, a book of verse, was put forward, and the jury split 2-1 (in favor of Strand) between it and Robert Penn Warren's *Now and Then: Poems 1976-1978* (Random House). Apparently influenced by a letter in which Simpson dissented from the majority, the Pulitzer board declared Warren's book the winner.

Perhaps more troublesome are questions of degree. As I have noted, Simpson's book did contain a few verse passages, though it is preposterous to suppose that the jury made its recommendation on the basis of less than thirty lines. Would a book of poems such as Mark Strand's current *The Continuous Life* (Random House), which contains nineteen pages of prose out of sixty-three total pages, be eligible for the prize? Even Louis Simpson's own most recent book, *In the Room We Share* (Paragon House), concludes with a separate forty-page section of autobiography, though there is clearly no attempt to integrate what is clearly labeled as an "evocative extended prose

piece" with the book's 110 pages of verse. In light of this controversy and the apparently growing tendency of poets and their publishers to mix two modes within a single set of covers, it will be interesting to see how future Pulitzer juries deal with the question of eligibility of individual collections.

All of this has successfully avoided discussing the *merits* of Simic's prize-winning collection. Noting its publication last year, I remarked that the poems "begin with lines like 'We were so poor I had to take the place of the bait in the mousetrap' or 'In a forest of question marks you were no bigger than an asterisk.' This ground has already been staked out by Russell Edson, and Simic, for the most part, lacks Edson's saving grace, a bizarre sense of humor that teeters on the edge of sense." Rereading the book now, I find no reason to alter my original opinion. *The World Doesn't End* is a slight production by almost any standards, consisting of what seem to be inept verbal attempts to match the surrealistic wit of cartoonists such as the late B. Kliban or Gary Larson of *The Far Side*. Here is one example:

> The dog went to dancing school. The dog's owner sniffed vials of Viennese air. One day the two heard the new Master of the Universe pass their door with a heavy step. After that, the man exchanged clothes with his dog. It was a dog on two legs, wearing a tuxedo, that they led to the edge of the common grave. As for the man, blind and deaf as he came to be, he still wags his tail at the approach of a stranger.

As has happened too often in the past, the Pulitzer Prize here seems to have been awarded to recognize a lifetime achievement instead of the merits of a single book.

Simic's *Selected Poems 1963-1983*, in a revised and expanded edition, was published by George Braziller in 1990 and provides a good overview of the basis for his poetic reputation. In his early work he could be quite powerful, especially in the elemental qualities of his poems dealing with everyday objects. Here is the opening of "My Shoes":

> Shoes, secret face of my inner life:
> Two gaping toothless mouths,
> Two partly decomposed animal skins
> Smelling of mice-nests.

The poem concludes with what amounts to an existentialist's prayer to his own mortality:

I want to proclaim the religion
I have devised for your perfect humility
And the strange church I am building
With you as the altar.

Ascetic and maternal, you endure:
Kin to oxen, to Saints, to condemned men,
With your mute patience, forming
The only true likeness of myself.

At the beginning of 1991 it was announced that Simic's *The Book of Gods and Devils* (Harcourt Brace Jovanovich), which was not received for this survey, had been named one of five nominees for the National Book Critics Circle Award for poetry. *Wonderful Words, Silent Truth*, a collection of critical and autobiographical essays (yes, in *prose*), also appeared as part of the Poets on Poetry series from the University of Michigan Press.

Two other awards for books of poetry mentioned in these pages last year bear reporting. The National Book Critics Circle Award for poetry went to Rodney Jones for *Transparent Gestures* (Houghton Mifflin), his third collection. Jones, born in Alabama in 1950, shares with T. R. Hummer, Andrew Hudgins, David Bottoms, and Leon Stokesbury certain characteristics which bind together an important new generation of southern poets who came of age during the turbulent 1960s and who are redefining traditional concepts of regional poetry. Like his peers, he is a poet of strong narrative instincts, and his rhetorical inventiveness and obvious intelligence and wit consistently keep his poems slightly off center; a Jones poem is anything but predictable and can range from examinations of the inner lives of waitresses and shade tree mechanics to hyperboles comparing a hesitation to "the wait for a Campbellite / to accept Darwin and Galileo or for all Arkansas / to embrace a black Messiah." A poem titled "Winter Retreat: Homage to Martin Luther King, Jr." describes a government-sanctioned meeting of black and white educators at a posh Baltimore hotel. The picture Jones paints of self-conscious scholars of both races trying desperately to avoid the fatal faux pas or stereotypical response is at once deliciously parodic and ultimately touching:

> We extended ourselves
> with that sinuous motion of the tongue that is
>   half
> pain and almost eloquence. We black and white
> politely reprioritized the parameters of our
>   agenda

to impact equitably on the Seminole and the Eskimo.
We praised diversity and involvement, the sacrifices
of fathers and mothers. We praised the next white
Gwendolyn Brooks and the next black Robert Burns.
We deep made friends.

A black colleague of mine reports that he heard Jones read this poem at a racially mixed conference to a great wash of cleansing laughter and applause, exactly what Dr. King would have most desired from his efforts.

The Poets' Prize was established three years ago by Louis Simpson; Robert McDowell, publisher of Story Line Press; and Frederick Morgan, editor of the *Hudson Review*. It differs from other awards in that its winner is selected by a group of some thirty poets, who also put up the money for the prize out of their own pockets. Earlier winners were Julia Randall and Andrew Hudgins. This year's recipient is Miller Williams for *Living on the Surface* (Louisiana State University Press), a collection of new and selected poems published in 1989 and favorably reviewed here last year. Like Jones a southerner but hardly a regionalist, Williams, born in 1930, is a skillful master of tonal shifts, moving effortlessly from reflective love poetry and elegies to pieces of surreal humor. One of his best in the latter category is "Why God Permits Evil: For Answer to This Question of Interest to Many Write Bible Answers Dept. E-7" (titles are one of Williams's strong points). The poem takes off from an ad on a matchbook cover to imagine an office building housing the holy of holies:

> Some place on the south side of Chicago
> a lady with wrinkled hose and a small gray
>
> bun of hair sits straight with her knees together
> behind a teacher's desk on the third floor
>
> of an old shirt factory, bankrupt and abandoned
> except for this just cause, and on the door:
>
> Dept. E-7. She opens the letters
> asking why God permits it and sends a brown
>
> plain envelope to each return address.
> But she is not alone. All up and down
>
> the thin and creaking corridors are doors
> and desks behind them: E-6, E-5, 4, 3.
>
> A desk for every question, for how we rise
> blown up and burned, for how the will is free,

for when is Armageddon, for whether dogs
have souls or not and on and on.

The poem concludes with a bizarre image of
God that seems wholly appropriate for our be-
nighted age: a sort of cosmic Ann Landers frozen eternally between the *in* and *out* baskets. Reading through *Living on the Surface*, one quickly
comes to the remarkable conclusion that Williams
is still growing as a poet as he enters his seventh
decade.

Mark Strand was named Poet Laureate Consultant to the Library of Congress, succeeding
Howard Nemerov. Although one should not
place unreasonable expectations on any contemporary poet's relishing the ceremonial aspects of
the position (the thought of an American poet
cranking out odes in praise of the razing of Bagh-
dad is frightening to contemplate), all of the earlier honorees (Robert Penn Warren, Richard Wilbur, and Nemerov, respectively) had produced
infrequent pieces of public poetry; Nemerov,
whose lines on the *Challenger* crash provide an example of a sort of occasional poetry rarely seen
nowadays, perhaps best fit the public expectations of the role of national poet. To many
Strand must have seemed a surprising choice,
since his poetry reveals close affinities with European and South American surrealists (and to
American poets similarly influenced, such as
Charles Simic and Charles Wright) and rarely ad-
dresses issues of political or social importance, at
least in the direct manner, say, of Wilbur's "To
the Student Strikers," a poem urging dialogue
and prudence during campus protests of the Vietnam era. Strand's best work, it seems to me, is to
be found in the Kafkaesque narrative poems he
wrote in the late 1960s. One of the most memorable is "The Tunnel," in which the frightened
speaker, after describing a sinister man who "has
been standing / in front of my house / for days," decides to escape by tunneling out of his basement.
The poem concludes in a remarkable Borgesian
circle which illustrates how paranoia breeds on itself:

> I come out in front of a house
> and stand there too tired to
> move or even speak, hoping
> someone will help me.
> I feel I'm being watched
> and sometimes I hear
> a man's voice,
> but nothing is done
> and I have been waiting for days.

One wonders what the Poetry Appreciation
Society of Topeka will make of Strand's poems
when the members get together to discuss the laureate's new book, *The Continuous Life* (Knopf). By
comparison with his minimalist but finely etched
early work, much of Strand's recent poetry is reminiscent of the lackadaisical meandering of John
Ashbery:

> Like many brilliant notions—easy to understand
> But hard to believe—the one about our hating it
>   here
> Was put aside and then forgot. Those freakish
>   winds
> Over the flaming lake, bearing down, bringing a
>   bright
> Electrical dust, an ashen air crowded with leaves—
> Fallen, ghostly—shading the valley, filling it with
> A rushing sound, were not enough to drive us out.

As mentioned, the book contains several prose
poems, including an odd "prose sestina," and, surprisingly, a satirical ballad in the manner of
W. H. Auden, "The Couple," which is, to my
knowledge, the longest sustained piece of formal
verse Strand has produced. To mark his selection
as poet laureate, Strand's *Selected Poems* (1980)
has been reissued by the same publisher.

The major arts controversy of 1990, the
flap involving National Endowment for the Arts
(NEA) funding for controversial and sexually explicit works, also affected poetry to some degree.
Amid a great deal of heated rhetoric from one
side about homoeroticism, sadomasochism, and
even child pornography (the Mapplethorpe case)
and, from the other, dire warnings about "art
Nazis" and imminent book-burnings, only a few
voices arose to make the obvious point that if an
artist or institution feels unduly restricted by the
NEA's obscenity guidelines, he, she, or it should
simply reject the grant. It is difficult to see how
the nonaward of a sizable sum of money (twenty
thousand dollars in the case of the grants to creative writers) automatically constitutes censorship, especially when these grants often are used
to sponsor working leaves of absence from full-
time jobs. George Garrett has been eloquent for
over a decade now in taking the NEA to task for
the cronyism and regional bias that have marked
its grants procedures; if important federal contracts were discovered to have been awarded with
the same conflicts of interest that are standard in
the NEA, C-Span would have to expand to three
channels to carry the investigative hearings.

Dust jacket for the Poet Laureate's most recent book of poetry

Those whose voices were raised in protest against the award restrictions included poet and editor T. R. Hummer, who attacked the regulations in the *New England Review* after an innocuous short story by Ewing Campbell that had been published there was "flagged" by an NEA review panel as being in possible violation of anti-obscenity rules. The *Paris Review* rejected a sizable grant, as did the *Kenyon Review*. Marilyn Hacker, new editor of the *Kenyon Review*, noted that by "submitting to this restriction, we would agree to become censors-before-the-fact.... A grant to a literary magazine should express, as it has in the past, enough confidence in that magazine's editors, history, and intentions not to arrive dependent on the signature of a political/ sexual loyalty oath.... The *Kenyon Review* wants to continue that invaluable function into our second half-century. We cannot therefore accept the $7,500 grant awarded to us by NEA as long as it entails compliance with the new restrictions." As much as one applauds Hacker's common sense and editorial integrity, the *Kenyon Review* is primarily underwritten by Kenyon College; I would be very surprised to hear of any individual poet turning down a grant for similar reasons.

One of the major academic battles of the late 1980s and early 1990s, involving multiculturalism and the debate over the poetic canon, continued to be waged in the tables of contents of poetry textbooks and anthologies. In particular the *Heath Anthology of American Literature* came under attack from conservative critics and professors for its "equal-opportunity" approach to literary merit, which was fueled by publisher's hype: "109 women of all races, 25 individual Native American authors" and so on. Of course, any anthology makes some sort of political statement, but many recent ones, particularly those primarily published as college textbooks, seem little more than exploitative attempts to capitalize on current demands for what is "politically correct." The most recent edition of the *Norton Anthology of American Literature*, to cite only one example, contains no selections by any white male American poet born since 1930 or white female poet born since 1932; after Gary Snyder and Sylvia Plath, the seven poets whose work is included— Audre Lorde, Immamu Amiri Baraka, Michael Harper, Simon J. Ortiz, Rita Dove, Alberto Ríos, and Cathy Song—seem to have been chosen primarily to fill up a last-minute quota based on race, gender, and/or sexual preference. Recent specialized anthologies reviewed in these pages such as the 1988 *Gay and Lesbian Poetry of Our Time* (St. Martin's) at least display some honesty in making no claims to be "representative" of anything but their communities even if they contain much that is second-rate. On the other hand, a book such as last year's *An Ear to the Ground: An Anthology of Contemporary American Poetry* (University of Georgia Press), in a self-righteous attempt to supplant American literature's current bogeyman, Patriarchal Eurocentrism, ended up printing a great deal of poems so bad they seemed destined, to borrow a phrase from Dryden, to end up as "martyrs of pies, and reliques of the bum."

Those in search of the *most* traditional canon might care to consult Louis Phillips's *The Random House Treasury of Best-Loved Poems*. This little anthology, probably aimed at readers who rarely read contemporary poetry, represents an attempt to equal the success of such chestnut-laden baskets as *One Hundred and One Famous Poems* (Buccaneer), which is still in print after seventy-one years. Mr. Phillips, who is also a poet and humorist, deserves special credit as author of the year's funniest piece of literary criticism, "I Hear America Movieing: A Modest Deconstructive Introduction to the Poetic Oeuvre of Jimmy Stewart," which appeared in the fall issue of the *Poet*. Among Phillips's lighter observations about 1989's best-selling volume of verse was a dead serious slam at cynical publishers: "We have at last a poet for our times, a poet who, under the klieg lights, and far from the sophisticated martini settings of poetic careerism, gives us the score. It may not be a score in our favor, but it accurately reflects the reality of the game, as despicable and as mean as it is."

Of more serious interest for scholars and poets is William Harmon's *The Concise Columbia Book of Poetry* (Columbia University Press), which must establish some sort of record for requiring the least number of editorial decisions of any anthology ever published. Harmon relates, "These are the hundred poems in English that have been most anthologized, as calculated from the ninth edition of the *Columbia Granger's® Index to Poetry*. It is the best available record of the poems that have achieved the greatest success for the longest time with the largest number of readers." Some of Harmon's observations are quite revealing. For one, there are no poems by Chaucer, Pope, Burns, and Whitman, all of whom wrote either in dialect or longer forms that rarely are included in anthologies. Of the hundred poems, only one, Pound's "The River-Merchant's Wife: A Letter," is true free verse; the other ninety-nine are written in variations on the iambic line. Only eight either rhyme irregularly or do not rhyme at all. And, as Harmon notes, it is utterly mystifying that "the word 'darkling' should occur three times in these hundred poems . . . and practically nowhere else *in the language*." And the winners? Number one is Blake's "The Tyger," with "Sir Patrick Spens," Keats's "To Autumn," Shakespeare's Sonnet 73, Hopkins's "Pied Beauty," Frost's "Stopping by Woods on a Snowy Evening," Coleridge's "Kubla Khan," Arnold's "Dover Beach," Keats's "La Belle Dame sans Merci," and Herrick's "To the Virgins, to Make Much of Time" completing, respectively, the all-time top ten. The two youngest American poets represented are Randall Jarrell and Theodore Roethke. Surprisingly, Wallace Stevens, E. E. Cummings, and William Carlos Williams do not appear while Hart Crane's difficult "To Brooklyn Bridge" occupies seventy-fifth place. Harmon's witty and informative introductory notes to each poem provide some reasonable insights into what, exactly, makes a poem (in this case,

Tennyson's "The Eagle") a classic: "A brief and flawless heraldic realization of a creature in all the spikily tangible properties of his creatureliness."

Poet and critic J. D. McClatchy's *The Vintage Book of Contemporary American Poetry* is likely to arouse more yawns than controversy and, with stiff competition from *The Norton Anthology of Modern Poetry*, will probably disappear as quickly as Helen Vendler's *The Harvard Book of Contemporary Poetry* of 1985. McClatchy does not begin his introduction on the right foot, getting the facts wrong ("one of their chilly meetings in Key West") about a famous exchange of genial demurrals between Frost and Stevens, but, overall, his account of the generations of modernism and post-modernism tries to be evenhanded: "There is no need for any anthology to choose sides. No critic has to deploy our poets into opposing battle lines with names like Paleface and Redskin, or Academic and Avant-Garde." McClatchy thus wants to avoid the sort of partisanship that stimulated the so-called War of the Anthologies in the late 1950s and 1960s, when *New Poets of England and America* (1957) and *The New American Poets* (1960) offered tables of contents that mutually excluded each other's selections. Here, the editor's scheme of organization is mystifying: "I have begun this book with Robert Lowell and Elizabeth Bishop. They are placed slightly out of chronological order, and more generously represented than other poets. That is because I think they were— and remain—the strongest poets of their generation and have continued as towering models." Well and good perhaps, but McClatchy's haphazard ordering continues, with no further explanation, through the first one-fifth of the book; thus, Robert Penn Warren (1905-1989) comes *after* Theodore Roethke (1908-1963), John Berryman (1914-1972), and Randall Jarrell (1914-1965). Jean Garrigue (1914-1972) falls between Robert Hayden (1913-1980) and May Swenson (1919-1989); after Swenson, the poets are, for the most part, arranged chronologically by date of birth, though there are still odd exceptions such as Amy Clampitt (born in 1920), who shows up late in the book (perhaps because her first full-length collection was not published until she was in her sixties). I searched in vain for some editorial rationale but could find none. McClatchy's choices are, for the most part, fairly conservative, even timid; one might well wonder how an anthology claiming to represent "contemporary American poetry" can contain only four poets born

*Dust jacket for the anthology of war poems edited by
Leon Stokesbury*

since 1945—Edward Hirsch, Jorie Graham, Rita
Dove, and Gjertrud Schnackenberg. The anthologies of the 1950s and 1960s at least stirred up
some lively debate over their rival contents; this
one is likely to breed only indifference.

Graham is this year's editor of *The Best American Poetry: 1990* (Collier), the third volume of the
series, which is under the general editorship of
David Lehman. The poems were originally published in books and leading magazines; not listed
among the thirty-three periodicals from which
poems were selected are *Kenyon Review*, *New England Review*, and *Shenandoah*, to mention only
three, absences from the list that make me question the exhaustiveness of Graham's search. The
table of contents reads like the usual Who's Who,
though one is gratified to find poems by Tom
Disch and Yusef Komunyakaa; the latter's powerful "Facing It," a poem about the Vietnam Veterans Memorial, is hardly new, though, having ap-

peared in Leon Stokesbury's *The Made Thing: An
Anthology of Contemporary Southern Poetry* (University of Arkansas Press) four years ago.

Stokesbury contributes a wise and useful collection in *Articles of War: A Collection of American Poetry about World War II* (University of Arkansas
Press), nicely timed for the fiftieth anniversary of
Pearl Harbor and containing a introduction by
Paul Fussell, whose *The Great War and Modern Memory* (Oxford, 1975) and *Wartime* (Oxford, 1989)
have made him the leading critical authority on
the literature of modern war. Everyone knows
Richard Eberhart's "The Fury of Aerial Bombardment" and Randall Jarrell's "The Death of the
Ball Turret Gunner" (Jarrell, despite his reputation as a war poet, served in training commands
and never saw combat), but after them one often
forgets how much excellent war poetry was written by such soldier-poets as Louis Simpson, Richard Wilbur, Karl Shapiro, John Ciardi, and Howard Nemerov. Stokesbury has done an excellent
job of refreshing our memories, and deserves
credit for the labor of love that has resurrected
Phyllis McGinley's home front poems and Lincoln Kirstein's vigorous satirical ballads. He has
also printed two long bombing-raid narratives,
one by Richard Hugo and the other Edward
Field's harrowing account of a B-17's crew's Channel ditching, "World War II," as well as a generous selection of work by poets who are younger siblings and children of the war generation. Lucien
Stryk's "The Face" is one of the most memorable
short poems in the book, and it might well serve
as an appropriate epigraph for the whole anthology:

> Weekly at the start
> of the documentary
> on World War II
>
> a boy's face, doomed,
> sharply beautiful,
> floats in the screen,
> a dark balloon
> above a field of barbs,
> the stench of gas.
>
> Whoever holds the
> string
> will not let go.

Four other anthologies bear brief mention.
Also from the University of Arkansas Press
comes *The Best of Crazyhorse*, edited by David
Jauss. The magazine has had a peripatetic career,

beginning under Tom McGrath's editorship in Los Angeles in 1960 and literally crisscrossing the country (New York, North Dakota, Minnesota, Kentucky) before settling at the University of Arkansas at Little Rock in 1981. The book contains almost five hundred pages of poetry and fiction, the quality of which is as high, it seems to me, as that of a typical year's *Pushcart Prize* anthology.

As one who grew up in the South in the 1950s and 1960s I had to suspend my disbelief when I came across *Alabama Poets* (Livingston University Press); memories of the scowling face of George Wallace and other ugly scenes from those days have left me (and many others, I suspect) with a strong prejudice against a state that seemed primarily known for racism and football. Things have obviously changed a great deal since then. When Governor Wallace finally left office, he was hailed by both white and black as a champion of equal opportunity; Bear Bryant has gone on to the Great Endzone in the Sky; and the arts are flourishing among the state's residents. Edited by Ralph Hammond, the book is consistently good, filled with work by such accomplished poets as the much-honored Rodney Jones and Andrew Hudgins, Julie Suk, Jim Simmerman—whose excellent *Once Out of Nature* (Galileo) was applauded in these pages last year—former Yale Younger Poet John Bensko, Sonia Sanchez, and Gerald Barrax. I am particularly happy to become reacquainted with Andrew Hudgins's excellent long poem "Saints and Strangers," one section of which begins with the observation that "You teach a Baptist etiquette, she turns / Episcopalian."

80 on the 80s: A Decade's History in Verse (Ashland Poetry Press) is the third such anthology that editors Robert McGovern and Joan Baranow have assembled, and it provides proof that occasional poetry still thrives in America. Titles such as Elizabeth Patton's "Scripting James Brown," Barbara LaMorticella's "The Summer of Oliver North," and Harold Witt's "At the Anchors Aweigh: Chernobyl" will remind readers of the decade's trivia and tragedy. These lines are from a poem by Judson Jerome apostrophizing the Bakkers, Ronald Reagan, and Gary Hart:

> Go public. Tell us what we secretly know:
> that laws are nuisances, to be evaded.
> We get away with what we can. In school
> we are already wise—and jaded.

> How liberating it would be to hear

> words from on high to put our hearts at ease—
> that even presidents and preachers cheat
> when able. We're no worse than these.

Unaccountably, not a single poem on the *Challenger* disaster (there must have been hundreds, including one by the poet laureate) managed to make its way into the collection.

Working Classics: Poems on Industrial Life (University of Illinois) is edited by Peter Oresick and Nicholas Coles, who justify their book by noting that it contains "an unusual kind of poetry, largely absent from the standard poetry anthologies and introductions to literature used in most classrooms. In these textbooks, love, death, and nature appear as the proper subjects for 'literature.' If work appears there at all, it is usually somebody else's work, observed from a distance, as in the pastoral landscapes of classical oil painting." This is true only to some degree, for no poet more ably celebrates America at work than Whitman (I direct readers to the great catalogue in section 15 of "Song of Myself") and many of Frost's poems are drawn from the world of agricultural labor. Nevertheless, the editors are right in observing that the realities of the industrial workplace, even if they often do stimulate poems, are not often given status equal to the shepherd's pipe dreams of Arcadia. The book contains over 250 pages and the work of some seventy poets, the most prominent of whom include Philip Levine, Jim Daniels, and Tom Wayman. Despite the overall thoroughness of the editors, I am somewhat dismayed that nothing by Charles Bukowski is included and that a true workingman's classic, Alan Dugan's "On a Seven-Day Diary," does not appear. One old favorite I am happy to meet again is Kenneth Patchen's "The Orange Bears," which describes growing up in a coal town and how childhood innocence, symbolized in the stuffed animals of the title, is eventually crushed under the weight of a grim environment. Though he read Walt Whitman while he was growing up, Patchen asks:

> What did he know about
> Orange bears with their coats all stunk up with soft
>   coal
> And the National Guard coming over
> From Wheeling to stand in front of the millgates
> With drawn bayonets jeering at the strikers?

> I remember you could put daisies
> On the windowsill at night and in
> The morning they'd be so covered with soot

You couldn't tell what they were anymore.
A hell of a chance my orange bears had!

Many collected and selected editions by leading American poets were published in 1990, but Anthony Hecht's *Collected Earlier Poems* (Knopf) certainly leads the list as one volume essential to anyone's collection. If my own is any measure, many copies of *The Hard Hours* (Atheneum), winner of the 1968 Pulitzer Prize, are in danger of falling apart from overuse; Hecht's readers will be especially happy to replace them with the present volume, which also includes his two excellent collections from the 1970s, *Millions of Strange Shadows* (1977) and *The Venetian Vespers* (1979). Since 1954, when his first book, *A Summoning of Stones*, was published, Hecht has had the dubious distinction of being labeled an "Academic" poet who is invariably mentioned in the same breath as Richard Wilbur and James Merrill. True, he shares some traits with them—abundant formal expertise and an occasionally overornate way of spinning out a complex web of metaphors and allusions (particularly to the art and culture of the Quattrocento). Yet the true essence of his poetry lies in qualities which are uniquely his own—a belief that poetry has a moral function in an age when that stance has been unfashionable, a Jewish heritage that is invariably present as subtext to Hecht's elegiac subjects, and a wit that often explodes into uproarious satiric humor. Of his earlier poems I would single out "More Light! More Light!" and "It Out-Herods Herod. Pray You, Avoid It" as titles that exemplify the first two characteristics. The latter concludes with the poet's somber meditation on the messages his children learn from their television programs:

A hero comes to save
The poorman, beggarman, thief,
And make the world behave
And put an end to grief.

And that their sleep be sound
I say this childermas
Who could not, at one time,
Have saved them from the gas.

Hecht's lighter side shows up in such classic anthology pieces as "Samuel Sewall" and "The Dover Bitch." One of his best satiric poems is "The Ghost in the Martini," from *Millions of Strange Shadows*. The narrative concerns a middle-aged poet, attempting to pick up a much younger woman at a cocktail party and then angrily confronted with the spectral voice of his former self:

Her smile is meant to convey
How changed or modest I am, I can't tell which,
When suddenly I hear someone close to me say,
"You lousy son-of-a-bitch!"

A young man's voice, by the sound,
Coming, it seems, from the twist in the martini.
"You arrogant, elderly letch, you broken-down
Brother of Apeneck Sweeney!

Thought I was buried for good
Under six thick feet of mindless self-regard?
Dance on my grave, would you, you galliard stud,
Silenus in leotard?

Well, summon me you did,
And I come unwillingly, like Samuel's ghost.
'All things shall be revealed that have been hid.'
There's something for you to toast!"

This pose—social man in the grip of his own conscience yet eager to get on with the evening's allurements—is one of Hecht's most engaging and provides a neat counterpoint to the sexual fears expressed in "The End of the Weekend," one of his best early poems. Throughout his work, his technical control, displayed in a wide range of stanza patterns and occasional open-form poems, remains nothing short of astonishing.

Knopf also this year published *The Transparent Man*, a new collection of poems which indicates that Hecht's skills remain undiminished as he approaches his seventies. One of the most touching pieces here is "In Memory of David Kalstone," whose subject, we are told in an epigraph, died of AIDS. Though Hecht is moved by the loss of a friend and respected critic, his stance does not desert his characteristic irony:

Lime-and-mint mayonnaise and salsa verde
Accompanied poached fish that Helen made
For you and J.M. when you came to see us
Just at the salmon season. Now a shade,

A faint blurred absence who before had been
Funny, intelligent, kindness itself,
You leave behind, beside the shock of death,
Three of the finest books upon my shelf.

"Men die from time to time," said Rosalind,
"But not," she said, "for love." A lot she knew!
From the green world of Africa the plague
Wiped out the Forest of Arden, the whole crew

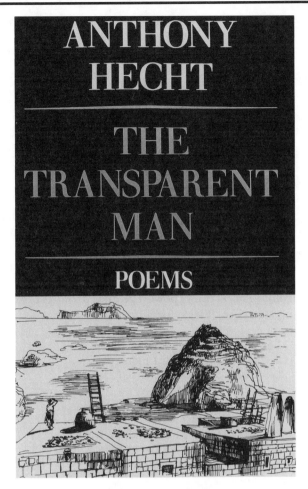

ANTHONY HECHT

THE TRANSPARENT MAN

POEMS

Dust jacket for Hecht's collection of new poems. His Collected Earlier Poems *was also published in 1990 by Knopf.*

Of innocents, of which, poor generous ghost,
You were among the liveliest.

The "J.M." of the first stanza is poet James Merrill, whose 1988 collection *The Inner Room* also contains two fine poems about Kalstone, including one which relates how Merrill spread his friend's ashes in Venetian waters. Here is Hecht's own version of the event, describing how the remains descend

Even to the bottom of that monstrous world
Or lap at marble steps and pass below
The little bridges, whirl and eddy through
A liquified Palazzo Barbaro.

That mirrored splendor briefly entertains
Your passing as the whole edifice trembles
Within the waters of the Grand Canal
And writhes and twists, wrinkles and reassembles.

Among his many other virtues, it is difficult to think of another living American poet who possesses anything approaching Hecht's tonal range; even Wilbur, the contemporary to whom he is most often compared, is rarely this moving.

Last year it was a pleasure to note Donald Hall's receipt of the National Book Critics Circle Award for *The One Day* (Ticknor and Fields) which was published in 1988. This year Hall's *Old and New Poems* (Ticknor and Fields) is another welcome guest and provides an overview of a career that began in 1947 and shows no sign of abating. It is only fair to say that Hall's poetry has been very uneven over the years; like many of his contemporaries he begins in the formalist manner and then moves on in the 1960s to experiment with a variety of other strategies, including the sort of Deep Image surrealism most often associated with his Harvard contemporary and friend, Robert Bly. There are some fairly grim stretches near the center of this collection; the poems written in the late 1960s and early 1970s display an uncommon degree of professional self-disgust. Here is the opening of the ironically titled "To a Waterfowl":

> Women with hats like the rear ends of pink ducks
> applauded you, my poems.
> These are the women whose husbands I meet on airplanes,
> who close their briefcases and ask, "What are *you* in?"
> I look in their eyes, I tell them I am in poetry,
>
> and their eyes fill with anxiety, and with little tears.
> "Oh, yeah?" they say, developing an interest in clouds.
> "My wife, she likes that sort of thing? Hah-hah?
> I guess maybe I'd better watch my grammar, huh?"

Leaving academia for a family farm in New Hampshire and a new marriage (to poet Jane Kenyon) revitalized Hall's career in the late 1970s, and his output of both poetry and prose in the last decade has been staggering in both quantity and quality. He has drawn strength from the New England landscape and its people, and, in his most recent work, has worked expertly with the dramatic monologue. "Cider 5¢ a Glass" is a newspaperman's account of a lifelong friendship with a lawyer, which ends in the latter's suicide. The poem's final section narrates a seemingly trivial incident from the friends' teenage years:

> ". . . As it turns dark,
> we head back toward school

on a shadowy gravel road;
    we are astonished
to see ahead (on a lane
    without cars in nineteen-
forty-four, as if an apparition
    conjured there
to conclude this day that fixed
    our friendship forever)
a small table with a pitcher
    on it, three glasses,
and a sign: CIDER 5¢
    A GLASS. A screendoor swings
open on the gray unpainted
    porch of a farmhouse,
and a woman (old, fat,
    and strong) walks down the dirt path
to pour us our cider.
    She takes our nickels and sells
us a second glass and then
    gives us a third. All day
today I keep tasting
    that Sunday's almost painful
detonation of cider sweet
    and harsh in my mouth."

The beautiful clarity and emotional force of much of Hall's late work is a joy to encounter. And he can still turn an epigram with considerable panache. This one, which many readers will find painfully familiar, is called "On a Teacher":

Chinless and slouched, gray-faced and slack of jaw,
Here plods depressed Professor Peckinpaugh,
Whose work J. Donald Adams found "exciting."
This fitted him to teach Creative Writing.

Hall has also provided an introduction to James Wright's *Above the River: The Complete Poems* (Farrar, Straus & Giroux/University Press of New England) that is insightful and touchingly personal. The volume is edited by Wright's widow, Anne Wright.

William Jay Smith, born in 1918, is older than both Hecht and Hall and has received his share of honors, including a term as Poetry Consultant to the Library of Congress from 1968 to 1970. His poetry, while widely respected (if one can accurately judge from the quotes from James Dickey, X. J. Kennedy, and Howard Nemerov that accompany his new collection), has not received the sort of serious critical attention lavished on other members of his generation. This is a shame, it seems to me, for there is much to like and admire in his *Collected Poems 1939-1989* (Scribners). "Epithalamium in Olive Drab," an early poem, describes the improvisational quali-

ties of a wartime wedding, wittily bringing off an affectionate parody of Tin Pan Alley:

O orange were her underclothes,
    her nails were hothouse pink,
when Rosalind, in jungle rose,
    was wed in a roller rink.

    The bell rings true: True-blue True-blue.
        She was cheery; he was chipper.
    They did not fly to Ho - no - lu - lu
        in the cabin of a clipper.

Over the years Smith has alternated between the tight meters and rhymes of poems like this and the unfettered long line that characterized *The Tin Can* (1966). He is most effective, it seems to me, when he strikes a balance between the two extremes, as in these powerful lines from the closing stanza of "Elegy for a Young Actor":

Lord, I know that the worst
is yet to come, but still I mourn
those who are doomed, cursed
from the start,
who can play but one part,
whose every conscious hour is bleak,
the alcoholic, the addict, and the freak,
the actor who makes it for one week.
I mourn their spooned-out lives, their hobbled
    youth.
And now while a light snow settles like oblivion
on the graveyard of a gray New England town,
I kneel to place,
in memory, one single-petaled, pink, wild rose
in that young actor's mouth.

The last line is a bleak allusion to the dead man's one brief triumph—one week playing the lead in a student production of *The Man with the Flower in His Mouth*.

Smith's autobiography, *Army Brat* (1980), an entertaining and poignant memoir describing what it was like growing up the son of a career noncommissioned officer at the Jefferson Barracks in St. Louis, is being reissued this year by Story Line Press. Smith also deserves notice for his work as editor and one of several translators in Nina Cassian's volume of selected poems *Life Sentence* (Norton), the seventh volume of translations in which he has played a major part. Cassian, a leading Romanian poet, has lived in the United States since 1985, and Smith has assembled a distinguished troupe of poet-translators—Richard Wilbur, Stanley Kunitz, Dana Gioia, Carolyn Kizer, among many others—to do justice to her

Collected Poems
1939–1989
William Jay Smith

"A most gifted and original poet
. . .One of the very few who cannot
be confused with anybody else."
—Richard Wilbur
Pulitzer Prize Winner for Poetry, 1989

Dust jacket for the complete collection of Smith's poems

lyrical skills. The collection occasionally, in the hands of several of the more skillful contributors, rises to brilliant levels. This stanza, translated by Smith, opens Cassian's ironic "Self-Portrait":

I was given at birth this odd triangular
face, the sugared cone that you see now,
the figurehead jutting from some pirate prow,
framed by trailing strands of moonlike hair.

The publication of Smith's own collected poems is a fitting tribute to fifty years of honorable service in the republic of letters.

The University of Arkansas Press continues its practice of releasing collected editions of poets whose work, for one reason or another, is difficult to find; in the past, collections by such poets as Ronald Koertge, John Ciardi, George Garrett, and Lewis Turco have appeared, and a selected edition of work by Frank Stanford, a remarkably talented young poet who died by his own hand in 1978, is scheduled for 1991 publication. In 1990 the press issued retrospec-

tive collections by Henri Coulette and Reed Whittemore. In Coulette's case, a bizarre professional tragedy is related by Donald Justice and Robert Mezey, co-editors of *The Collected Poems of Henri Coulette* (University of Arkansas Press): "He was to publish only two books during his lifetime, *The War of the Secret Agents* (1966) and *The Family Goldschmitt* (1971). The second, through an inexcusable error, was shredded in the publisher's warehouse before it could be properly distributed and was not reprinted. After this misfortune, public awareness of Coulette's poetry seems gradually to have receded." The editors go on to relate how Coulette composed only some fifty pages in the nearly two decades left to him before his death in 1988. However, his first book was a Lamont winner, and selections from it and the second were anthologized widely and remain influential today for a new generation interested in the possibilities of extended narratives and traditional form, both consistent concerns of Coulette.

The War of the Secret Agents is best known for its title poem, a sequence of some thirty pages in which various dramatic personae relate the collapse of a French spy network during World War II. It is a maddening, ultimately rewarding work, rather like the intricacies of a le Carré thriller funneled through the sensibility of Borges. The opening "Proem" describes how the efforts of these "gifted amateurs" at espionage are compromised from the outset:

They will appeal to lovers of the absurd:
there they were, bulging
with codes and automatics.
Like debutantes slumming on Skid Row,
they couldn't be missed—they advertised
and Death reads all the papers.

The story is framed by the research of a character named Jane Alabaster, a historian writing a book on wartime espionage who relates details of her research to her editor at Faber and Faber, T. S. Eliot. She sets up the poem's climax early, when she mentions that she is finally to meet with "Gilbert," a key figure in the spy network whom she suspects of having betrayed his comrades. When the confrontation occurs at the end of the poem, Gilbert opens the door to secrets darker even than those of Kieffer, the gestapo agent who captured the network, was aware of:

She was breathless now,
frightened by the innocence

that rode upon his smile. "Yes," he said,
"but I did only what London told me to—
I was London's instrument.

"There was an underground beneath the under-
    ground.
They protected it.
Kieffer never guessed the truth;
he was too busy counting the sheep
London let him have by way of sacrifice—
fifteen hundred little lambs!"

A narrative of this complexity, mated with sub-ject matter that possesses appeal to the general reader, is almost sui generis in contemporary American poetry, and it is heartening to have it once more available.

    Accounting for the relative obscurity of Coulette's poetic reputation, Justice and Mezey are correct in noting that his traditional formal-ism was unfashionable during his maturity; yet they also observe that while "his witty and ele-gant poetry is not at all like the poetry some read-ers will think of in connection with California—that is to say, not like Bukowski's or Fer-linghetti's—it reflects with no less truth as one of the many real Californias." As a young man Coulette worked in the publicity department of RKO Studios, and the mix of popular and "high" culture in his work is unusual, to say the least. At one time he spoke of writing poems "as real and vital as television, as soap opera, except in good language." Here are the closing lines of "The Aca-demic Poet," which offers a candid response to a typical student query:

        "The sestina—
can you use any six words?"
Well, yes, but they should define
a circle, which is the shape
I describe, chasing my tail
from class to class, the straight line
disguised, degree by degree.

Most of Coulette's acclaim may arrive posthu-mously, and Justice and Mezey should be saluted for their loyalty to a talented colleague whose work deserves to be remembered.

    When I mentioned to a friend that I had re-ceived a review copy of Reed Whittemore's *The Past, the Future, the Present: Poems Selected and New* (University of Arkansas Press), his immediate re-sponse was "Well, that's hardly what I'd call a *sus-tained* career." I had to agree, remembering how long it had been since I'd first admired the selec-tions of Whittemore's poetry in Donald Hall's

1962 Penguin anthology, *Contemporary American Po-etry*, particularly the delightful "A Day with the Foreign Legion":

And as they sat at the iron tables cursing the coun-
    try,
Cursing the food and the bugs, cursing the Legion,
Some Sergeant or other rushed in from The Fort
Gallantly bearing the news
From which all those the remorseless desert serves
Take their cues:
'Sir!'
        'What is it, Sergeant?'
                      'Sir, the hordes
March e'en now across the desert swards.'

Just like in the movies.

    Whittemore's best poetry has a sort of adoles-cent insouciance that is reminiscent of Kenneth Koch, with whom he shares space in the section on parody in poetry textbooks (Koch's hilarious send-up of Frost, "Mending Sump," is invariably accompanied by Whittemore's "The Fall of the House of Usher": "It was a big boxy wreck of a house / Owned by a classmate of mine named Rod Usher, / Who lived in the thing with his twin sister. / He was a louse and she was a souse."); how-ever, such high spirits are hard to maintain past middle age (Whittemore was born in 1919), and the recent work collected here often strikes the Ju-venalian public pose of his near-contemporary Howard Nemerov. These lines, taken from *The Fell of Rock* (1982), chronicle "The Destruction of Washington," as it might be pieced together from unearthed fragments by a future generation of "the world's Schliemanns":

Money of course they will miss,
Since money is spoke not at all on the plaques
    there,
Nor will they shovel up evidence
That the occupants of the chambers and cloak-
    rooms
Were strangers in town, protecting their deities else-
    where;

But sanctums they surely will guess at,
Where the real and true pieties were once ex-
    pressed.
If the Greeks had their Eleusinians,
Surely this tribe on the Potomac had mysteries too?

One more curious mystery surfaces regarding Whittemore's selections from his own work. One of his finest poems is "Tarantula," a dramatic monologue which first came to my attention through its appearance in Mark Strand's 1969 anthology, *The Contemporary American Poets*. It's a gentle little allegory in which the spider makes a still-timely plea for tolerance and understanding:

> Which brings me to my point here. You carry
> This image about of me that is at once libelous
> And discouraging, all because you, who should
>   know better,
> Find me ugly. So I am ugly. Does that mean that
>   you
> Should persecute me as you do? Read William
>   Blake.
> Read William Wordsworth.
> Read Williams in general, I'd say.

For some reason known but to William, God, and Mr. Whittemore it has not been reprinted here.

Three other collections of new and selected poems merit brief mention. Tom Disch's *Yes, Let's: New and Selected Poems* (Johns Hopkins University Press) was released late in 1989 and did not arrive in time for last year's survey. Disch—novelist, science-fiction writer, and theater critic (for the *Nation*)—lends a much-needed edge of outrageous humor to our often dull literary scene. Indeed, Disch provides the most entertaining table of contents of any poet on the current scene; titles such as "At the Grave of Amy Clampitt," "A Cow of Our Time," and "The Rapist's Villanelle" are typical of his fractured wit. Here he is in a somewhat more serious mood, in the opening lines of "At the Tomb of the Unknown President," a poem which invites the reader to pencil in presidential names in the margins:

> Here the virgins he could not devour
> In his lifetime are stacked like logs
> In the great cellblocks of his friendship:
> Each face wrapped in a famous silence,
> Each leal heart a lamp whose flame consumes
> The bonds of bankrupt cities. We have gathered
> Here today only to stare at, and restate
> Our faith in an innocence surpassing
> Mere event, more real than measurement.

The praise that Disch's work has garnered from British admirers such as Donald Davie ("It's a long time since I read . . . verse so consistently entertaining and intelligent.") and its relatively mild reception from this country's critics reveal a great deal about how little most American reviewers and readers value such brilliantly crafted satire as Disch provides.

Brendan Galvin's *Great Blue: New and Selected Poems* (University of Illinois Press) gives an overview of work from a poet whose central talents lie in descriptions of places and customs in his native region; his best poems evoke the atmosphere of villages in coastal New England—early morning chill and fog or, in this instance, the smell of neighbors' "Woodsmoke" mingling with the frozen air:

> It drifts out like
> the essence of a tree—
> a spirit tree is
> forking and branching
> across these fields,
>
> and I pull over on
> this moment of lemon
> dusk and new snow
> reducing the town
> to a huddle of cakes,
>
> and listen for the solitary
> plock of an axe
> beyond the wind-rattled
> hearts of weeds.

Galvin is as skillful in assimilating the materials of his own home turf as the late Richard Hugo was with landscapes on the other side of the continent. A poet who deeply desires connections with a less ignoble past, he describes an episode of not-so-petty larceny, explaining why he has stolen "A Double Ended Dory" that has been serving ingloriously as a flower box outside a seafood restaurant:

> You may never understand
> why I shoveled the zinnias out of her
> after closing time, looking over
> my shoulder for cops, if you've
> never put offshore
> in anything but a hull like tupperware.

Galvin's poetry is somewhat deficient in its intimate emotional content—his poems usually give the impression, like Hugo's, of being underpopulated—but within his self-chosen limits he remains an expert craftsman. Purely as a nature poet (Galvin was trained as a biologist; the book's title alludes to a type of heron) he strikes me as far superior to the much-overrated A. R. Ammons, who is often held up as our chief contemporary inheritor of the tradition of William Cullen Bryant.

Conrad Hilberry's *Sorting the Smoke: New and Selected Poems* (University of Iowa Press) collects poems from six earlier collections dating back to 1968. Hilberry's work is not easily characterized; he has tried many formal strategies, and his subjects have ranged from meditations on friendship to sequences on foreign locales he has visited (Greece and Mexico most prominently). These lines from "North and South," one of the new poems appearing here, explain the basis of one side of a form/content, reason/emotion duality that the poet seems to feel lies at the heart of his aesthetic:

We sons of German mothers honor
small perfections: a well-cooked flan,
the soundless turning of a wheel,
A mitred corner, the polish on

an auto grill. The philodendron
answers the thrown curve of its pot.
Poised for verse, we ask if rhyme
would be appropriate or not.

As for landscapes, we assume
that well-hedged fields will fall into
a satisfactory pattern—and
of course they do, they do.

The second half of the poem describes a wilder, southern landscape where "heat, recklessness, and sloth somehow / are granted cypresses and sea." It is no small measure of Hilberry's technical expertise that he chooses suitably broken rhymes (*olives / gives, sunlight / right*) for the stanzas that deal with this more slovenly side of the poet's psyche. Three sections of the book include illustrations: "Housemarks" is a sequence based on ancient signs used by peasants to identify their property; "Mexican Poems" uses Mexican clay stamps of fantastic monkeys and toads; and "The Lagoon" matches poetry with Takeshi Takahara's wood engravings of insects.

Among individual collections published in 1990 by members of the senior generation of American poets, one of the most impressive is William Everson's *The Engendering Flood* (Black Sparrow Press), which consists of the first four cantos of *Dust Shall Be the Serpent's Food*, a projected autobiographical epic. Everson, who also lived and wrote for some years as the Dominican Brother Antoninus, has published nearly forty individual collections, dating back to 1935, and he possesses an imposing reputation in many circles, particularly on the West Coast. I have generally found both his apocalyptic vision, largely derived from his much-admired Robinson Jeffers, and his spiritual wrestlings, most evident in the Brother Antoninus poems, to be forbidding and not very pleasant reading. But his best poems do possess undeniable power. Like his longtime friend and fellow World War II conscientious objector William Stafford, he is a prolific poet, but, unlike Stafford's modulated stanzas, Everson's poems are all too often prolix and awkward. It is easy to see why he found favor among the San Francisco Renaissance poets of the late 1950s, who generally favored, to borrow a phrase from Robert Lowell, the "raw" over the "cooked." That said, I must eat some of my own cooked words and confess that *The Engendering Flood* is a totally engaging poem suffused with wisdom and the calm voice of age (Everson was born in 1912). To summarize briefly, the four cantos begin, "In Medias Res," at his father's funeral in 1945, then back up to narrate, respectively, his father's immigration to America from Norway, the seemingly hopeless romance between the poet's divorced father and his Catholic mother, and their eventual marriage and permanent settlement in southern California. Canto 2, "Skald," describes the father's Atlantic crossing, as the title indicates, in alliterative lines reminiscent of Norse and Anglo-Saxon sea poetry:

And a strange
Voyage they had of it. The great ship surged forward,
Shearing the deceptively flaccid sea. At summer solstice
A black storm broke, a howling tornado, its waterspout
Twisting and writhing, a monstrous phallus
Sucked down by the uterine sea. Driven off course,
Lay in doldrums with a broken rudder
Till rescue reached them—ignominiously towed
Into New York harbor by a scrawny little tug,
Triumphantly tooting.

It may well be argued that Everson's idiom lacks polish and that his Freudianism tends to get in the frame too often; nevertheless, this is one of the most *readable* books of the year, and I eagerly await its continuation. The fourth canto concludes with Everson's meditation on the intricate workings of fate that lead to our existence:

As I write, my feeling is one of awesome destiny,
But fearsome mischance as well:
One could so easily not have been born!
You tentatively feel of yourself,

Just to make sure you are really here,
That you do exist, the events of your life
Did actually happen, arriving at terminus
Ineluctably confirmed in the eschatological
Reckoning of who you are, to leave in your passing
As hidden increment, like quartz of the sea
On the glimmering strand, the pure distillate
Of the engendering flood.

All of Everson's obvious faults as a writer are clearly in evidence here, yet the passage has a rhetorical grandeur, sustained by the sheer power of feeling, that few contemporaries can approach.

Louis Simpson's *In the Room We Share* (Paragon House) follows by only two years his *Collected Poems* (1988), from the same publisher. Over the years the idiom of Simpson's poetry has become as spare and deliberate as Everson's is luxuriant, but he shares with him a fascination with his own origins. As I mentioned in my introduction, the present volume contains "Villa Selene," a prose journal chronicling a trip the poet and his wife made to Italy during summer 1988 to visit his convalescing mother, who died late in 1990. Simpson admits that his remarkable Rosalind, who became successful and wealthy as the South American distributor of Helena Rubenstein cosmetics, was never a stickler for accuracy when discussing her age: "She is ninety-two or -three. Up to now she has been able to take twenty years off her age, but now she is in pain and looks very old." Those who cherish, as I do, Simpson's autobiography *North from Jamaica* and his many poems dealing with his Jamaican childhood ("My Father in the Night Commanding No" is a classic anthology piece) will greatly enjoy "Villa Selene," which ends, like Everson's poem, with a meditation on the strangeness of circumstances that led his parents to meet. His mother's sojourn from Russia to New York and thence to Jamaica as a member of the Annette Kellerman bathing beauties, where she married the poet's lawyer father, is, Simpson concludes, a fit subject for romance: "If I were a novelist I would write about my mother's life. You would have to concentrate on certain episodes otherwise the thing would spread out in every direction. Where to begin?" His concluding paragraph recalls her in her prime, walking the fairways of the Liguanea Club in Kingston: "She strode on ahead, the caddy following with the bag. The golf course was close to the hills. You could see them clearly with gullies running down their sides. A breeze had sprung up, rustling the leaves. It came from the sea and all the places in the world."

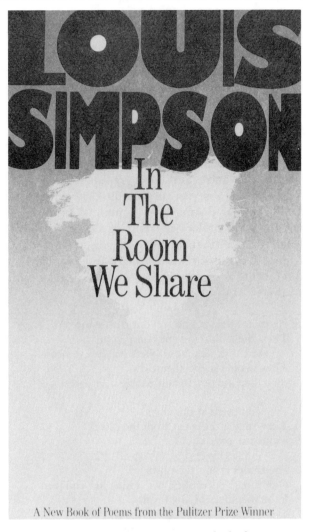

Dust jacket for Simpson's most recent book of poems

As in his *Collected Poems*, Simpson here orders his poems with the stages of his own life, beginning with "Neptune's Daughter," an account of his mother's youth, and proceeding through his own coming to New York and almost immediate enlistment as an infantryman. As *Wartime* (1989), Paul Fussell's account of the literary legacy of World War II, reminds us, Simpson is perhaps the finest American soldier-poet of his generation. As I write this, surrounded by the martial cadenzas of war in the Middle East, it seems appropriate to quote from "Volksgrenadiers," which details the grisly effects of an artillery barrage on entrenched German infantry:

When night falls and the moon
glimmers in leaves and branches
the Volksgrenadiers sit up.

One gathers his intestines . . .
they're slippery and keep escaping.
The other with his one hand

feels in the dirt around him.
"Meinen Arm . . . Er hat eine Tätowierung
mit zwei Herzen . . . 'Fritz und Elsa.' "

Which is to say a tattoo with two hearts, containing names that could be of any nationality.

Other poems in the book's two later sections further advance Simpson's reputation as our most astute observer of middle-class suburban life. "Another Boring Story" opens by summarizing the plot, or lack thereof, of the eponymous Chekhov tale, then turns to an observation of a friend, a professor whose marriage has survived, though not very prettily, a scandalous episode of adultery:

He mixes drinks, she lays out cheese-dip.
Then the children come running in,
streaked with dirt from wherever they've been.
They make for the cheese-dip,
stick their fingers in and dabble.

I've seen them at the table.
They snatch the meat from the plate
with their hands.

She smiles at her little savages.
One thing's sure: she's not raising her children
to be members of any faculty.

Simpson's deliberately low-key idiom and rhythms may surprise those who have not looked at his poetry in the twenty-odd years since his first volume of selected poems, but it seems undeniable that he has found a voice appropriate to his chosen subjects. Dick Allen, reviewing *In the Room We Share* in the *Hudson Review*, makes a fitting analogy: "A number of years ago, after looking at a small charcoal sketch by Giacometti, I tried to draw something similar. It seemed an easy task: a few lines, balance, a face and thin legs. But dozens of crumpled drawings later, I'd relearned the lesson of deceptive simplicity." Those who think that there is anything easy about Simpson's method are advised to attempt a few similar exercises in imitating him. They will be dismayed by how far they miss the mark.

Mona Van Duyn's *Near Changes* (Knopf) is the seventh collection from a poet who has won almost every major award for poetry (the Pulitzer Prize is the lone exception), and it follows *Letters from a Father, and Other Poems* (1982), which on the strength of its title poem alone should stand as one of the strongest collections of the last decade. There is nothing that quite comes up to that level in *Near Changes*, though some of Van Duyn's observations on long marriage and senior-citizen love display her customary pungency: she notes how love "flames up fierce / and wild whenever I forget that we live / in double rooms whose temperature's controlled / by matrimony's turned-down thermostat." Rhyme appears frequently in Van Duyn's poetry, but in many cases its effectiveness is compromised by her slack meters:

On the streets of New York I've seen them rummaging, the grizzled,
the torn, grimed and scabbed by the world, their mouths muzzled,

misers of crust and Coke bottle, whatever is valued or needed.
My unhelpful heart glints out at them, but is unheeded.

Despite an admirable attempt to invest the tragicomedy of suburban living with high seriousness, Van Duyn too often falls victim to her two major faults, lack of compression and sentimentality. Many of the poems seem much longer than the slightness of the subject matter can support, and the climax of "Cotton Wagons," to cite but one example, seems bathetic. The poet has just described attempting to pass a truck which appears from a distance to be loaded with cotton but which is actually, on closer inspection, filled with "White chickens . . . mashed together in layered pens":

A wagonload of suffering,
silent as cotton. "Drive faster, get away!"
The wagon passes us. Again a snow
of ripped-off feathers. "Pass it, I can't stand it!"
We crash the speed limit and leave it behind,
but can't leave behind the rocketing hearts,
the pain of the wind, the red-flecked white silence.
I think of the fryer in my freezer, my recipe
for mixing five-spice powder and soya in a paste.
I rub the paste on the cold skin with my fingers.

As Charles Bukowski enters his seventies his energies seem undiminished, if one is to judge from the 375 pages that make up *Septuagenarian Stew: Stories & Poems* (Black Sparrow). I doubt if anyone familiar with Bukowski's massive body of work expects to find anything new in these further exploits of his alter ego, Henry Chinaski, but, as always, Bukowski somehow manages to make poetry out of the grubbiest set of environments—skid-row bar, flophouse, race-track betting window—that any poet has ever chosen to inhabit. Here is a characteristically unflattering self-portrait:

> I was always a natural slob
> I liked to lay upon the bed
> in undershirt (stained, of
> course) (and with cigarette
> holes)
> shoes off
> beerbottle in hand
> trying to shake off a
> difficult night, say with a
> woman still around
> walking the floor
> complaining about this and
> that,
> and I'd work up a
> belch and say, "HEY, YOU DON'T
> LIKE IT? THEN GET YOUR ASS
> OUT OF HERE!"

Bukowski defies the usual academic analysis (and that defiance is part of his poetic strategy), and, if the reader isn't immediately put off by this sleeveless-undershirt, unshaven demeanor, he has a great deal to offer. In these late poems he often openly gives thanks for the good fortune that has brought him this far:

> always, this late at night, I
> come down to the last drink and
> look at it with a special
> fondness.
> usually I've had some luck at the
> machine and
> I reserve the last drink
> as
> a toast to the gods
> who allow me the
> luck.

At the opposite end of the poetic spectrum is John Nims, whose *Zany in Denim* (University of Arkansas Press) is the model of classical wit and compression. Reminiscent of his 1967 book, *Of Flesh and Bone*, the present collection is comprised for the most part of epigrams, the longest of which does not exceed a sonnet's fourteen lines. Some of these exercises, like "Cynic," are true Bennett Cerf-style groaners: "Better perhaps smile wryly, if you smile, / In a world where guys and gals are guise and guile." Others, such as "Watching the Planes Come in at La Guardia"

successfully negotiate a full-fledged metaphysical leap:

> Joan's kiss
>   —it pancakes—
>   a flat smack.
>
>   But Jeanne!
>
> The delicate approach, slow tilt and lean.
> All hovering danger and delight.
>   As when
> Home, over mountain, sea, and chancy weather,
> Plane and its shadow
>   thrill
>   and touch together.

A revised and enlarged edition of Nims's collected translations, *Sappho to Valéry*, originally published in 1971, was also issued by Arkansas in 1990. The title is actually misleading, since the new sections include versions of poems by 1990 Nobel Prize-winner Octavio Paz and José Emilio Pachecho, who was born in 1939. Nims's insistence on following the formal patterns of his originals presents a clear challenge to the fashionable multitudes, unfortunately in the majority these days, who would pass off what are essentially prose paraphrases as serious examples of the translator's craft.

John Haines's *New Poems: 1980-88* (Story Line Press) is the winner of the 1990 Western States Book Awards. Dana Gioia's excellent introduction provides a reminder that Haines's first book, *Winter News* (1966), was published when he was forty-two years old and had already weathered nearly two decades as an Alaskan homesteader, hunting and running trap lines for his livelihood. Though he is associated in my mind with a younger generation, he is actually the contemporary of poets such as Simpson, Nemerov, and Hecht. Gioia points out that "there was little precedent in mainstream American poetry of the Forties and Fifties for the work Haines hoped to do," that is, writing a poetry simultaneously *in*, *of*, and *about* the Alaskan wilderness that demands to be read as more than regional writing, one in which the *spiritual* landscape is as important as the literal one. "Rain Country," a six-part poem which originally appeared in the *New England Review* and which subsequently won a Pushcart Prize, strikes me as one of Haines's finest. Recently I heard a young fiction writer who lives in a remote Montana valley comment (I forget whom he was quoting) that all great literature is about one subject: loss. Haines's meditation on the Alaska where he was once a tenderfoot and is now a stranger contains some beautiful passages on the inexorable movements of time and memory:

> It was thirty-one years ago
> this rainy autumn.
>
> Of the fire we built to warm us,
> and the singing heart
> driven to darkness
> on the time-bitten earth—
>
> only a forest rumor
> whispers through broken straw
> and trodden leaves
> how late in a far summer
> three friends came home,
> walking the soaked ground
> of an ancient love.

Interestingly, all of the poems in this collection are dated to show their time of composition, in this case, 1979-1983.

Galway Kinnell's new collection, *When One Has Lived a Long Time Alone* (Knopf), is dedicated to Sharon Olds, which seems curious indeed when we compare Olds's angst-filled rants against her parents with Kinnell's benign "Memories of My Father":

> Those we love from the first
> can't be put aside or forgotten,
> after they die they still must be cried
> out of existence, tears must make
> their erratic runs down the face,
> over the fullnesses, into
> the craters, confirming,
> the absent will not be present,
> ever again.

The surrealistic narratives in the book's middle section resemble parts of Kinnell's 1971 collection, *The Book of Nightmares*, but his more recent dreams have tended toward comic absurdism rather than horror. The long-lined "Oatmeal" describes breakfast with an imagined John Keats:

> Even if eating oatmeal with an imaginary companion is not as wholesome as Keats claims, still, you can learn something from it.
> Yesterday morning, for instance, Keats told me about writing the "Ode to a Nightingale."
> He had a heck of a time finishing it—those

were his words—"Oi 'ad a 'eck of a toime," he said, more or less,
speaking through his porridge.

The poem ends with the poet planning to eat a leftover baked potato for supper: "and therefore I'm going to invite Patrick Kavanagh to join me." Humor is not something I would usually associate with Kinnell; neither that nor the intimate tenderness that comes at the end of "The Perch," where he describes a woman friend's eyes:

> the blue
> of her eyes shone out of the black
> and white of bark and snow, as lovers
> who are walking on a freezing day
> touch icy cheek to icy cheek,
> kiss, then shudder to discover
> the heat waiting inside their mouths.

The book's final section is a challenging sequence of eleven fourteen-line poems, all beginning and concluding with the same line, which is also the book's title. The poem works through a Thoreau-like section of meditations on nature to a final desire "to live again among men and women, / to return to that place where one's ties with the human / broke, where the disquiet of death and now also / of history glimmers its firelight on faces . . . . " Since the dust jacket note mentions that Kinnell is both state poet of Vermont and a professor at New York University, both seemingly public activities, one wonders when he has found time for such extended periods of isolation as this poem describes.

Brief mention should be made of two collections by established poets now in their sixties. Philip Booth's *Selves* (Viking) contains several memorable poems about "Farview Home," where the aged residents "still hold on for what used to be called dear life." In many ways Booth is the epitome of the successful contemporary professor-poet; his poems never make egregious mistakes, and they appear only in the best periodicals. But his neat-appearing stanzas, unrelieved plainness of idiom, and rather anonymous voice seem to me somewhat less than praiseworthy, the marks of a professional blandness from which any real vitality has ebbed. The opposite could be said of Edward Dorn, whose *Abhorrences* (Black Sparrow) is a countercultural tour of the 1980s, with dated poems that often have their starting point in a newspaper headline or media quote. This is "sound-bite" poetry, in this case a 1986 quote from singer Cyndi Lauper:

"We didn't really
realize what was
going on in Europe
until we went to Japan
and Australia."

Dorn's politics consist, for the most part, of simple-minded Reagan-baiting, and almost everything, it seems, provides an occasion for his rage, even an innocuous chain of clothing stores:

But I will go down
to Banana Republic
and I will take hostages
among the customers, only
the fat ones perhaps,
but no! The thin ones—
there are more of them.
And I'll ship off
the whole lot with on their belts
to chilly North Dakota.

More often than not, Dorn resembles the town crank, firing off interminable pages of spleen to the editor of a local newspaper.

I hope I may be excused for proceeding with the remainder of this essay in a somewhat haphazard manner, discussing other individual collections of some measure of importance published during 1990. The reader should not take too seriously any attempts to link several books together, for he or she can rest assured that what follows these scattered islands of organization will fall pretty much according to whim.

Since Rita Dove won the Pulitzer Prize in 1987 for *Thomas and Beulah*, the number of books by black women poets seems to have increased each succeeding year, with several noteworthy individual collections appearing in 1990. Marilyn Nelson Waniek's *The Homeplace* (Louisiana State University Press) seems to me one of the strongest books of the year, one that should receive serious consideration when the year's major prizes are judged. Wanieck's focus on family history will invite comparisons between her work and Dove's—the two co-authored an essay on modern African-American poetry in *Poetry After Modernism* (Story Line)—a recent anthology of critical essays, but for many reasons—formal variety, narrative coherence, range of subject—*The Homeplace* owes its success only to Waniek's abundant talent. The family tree begins with the poet's great-great-grandmother, Diverne, a slave who bears two children by one John Tyler, a white man. But this is not the usual evil-Massa mis-

Dust jacket for Waniek's book of poems focusing on family history

cegenation story. As Waniek describes the night of her great-grandfather Pomp's conception, ". . . it wasn't rape. / In spite of her raw terror. And his whip." When Tyler meets the mother of his son briefly while on leave from fighting with General Nathan Bedford Forrest's Confederate cavalry, he tries to do the right thing:

He whispered promises—
a house, their freedom—
trying to expiate
in tenderness
what he'd seen and done.

Eventually Tyler sees that Diverne moves into town and into a house. Her son Pomp grows up, and prospers selling land and coal. When, in the early years of the century, Pomp is asked to run for alderman on the Republican ticket, he receives a surprising visit:

Two white men came to call
a few days later at his store,
younger than he, but tall
like he was. They told Pomp he was their brother:
It ain't your fault you had a nigra mother.
They said they'd stand behind him if he ran.

Even with this support Pomp knows that running for office in the segregated South is tantamount to suicide, and he withdraws.

The other poems in the collection—which include well-turned examples of the ballad, sonnet, and villanelle—bring the story to its conclusion in the meeting of her parents during World War II. The final section of the book, "Wings," consists of several fine narrative poems about the famed "Tuskegee Airmen," the black combat pilots who set many precedents, racial and otherwise, during the war: "The only outfit / in the American Air Corps / to sink a destroyer / with fighter planes." One of these fliers describes how he inherits the property of a fellow pilot with whom he has jokingly traded his leaking air mattress while his friend was on a mission:

I found his chocolate,
three eggs, and a full fifth
of his hoarded-up whiskey.
I used his mattress
for the rest of my tour.
It still bothers me, sometimes:
I was sleeping
on his breath.

As far as I know, the only other literary treatment of this remarkable military subject is a single short story, "Flying Home," by Ralph Ellison.

Two other collections by black women poets of the younger generation merit notice. Thylias Moss's *At Redbones* (Cleveland State University Poetry Center) is her third collection. Moss's tone cuts more sharply than Waniek's, and her poems, for the most part lyric improvisations, flirt with surrealism:

The white women my mother cleaned
for didn't notice she had changed. I guess
it was a small event, a resurrected African
jumping out the gap in her front teeth. I
guess it looked like a cockroach; that's
what she was supposed to have, not dignity.

Many of Moss's poems have a religious subtext that implies a lapsed Christianity; the book opens with these lines: "One day your place in line will mean the / Eucharist has run out. All because

you waited / your turn. Christ's body can be cut into only / so many pieces." The final poem in the collection describes how "At St. Paul's, the cracked walls testify / that a growing holiness is splitting the seams. / The lone dollar in the collection plate lacks a means / to amplify its testimony."

Elizabeth Alexander's *The Venus Hottentot* (University Press of Virginia) is a first book published as part of the Callaloo Poetry Series. Alexander plays with Caribbean-sounding syncopated rhythms, perhaps a legacy from her teacher at Boston University, Derek Walcott. These two stanzas open "Who I Think You Are":

Empty out your pockets nighttime, Daddy.
Keys and pennies, pocket watch, a favored
photograph of Ma, and orange-flavored
sucker-candies, in the dresser caddy.

Grandpa leaves his silver in his trousers,
potions for catarrh set on the bureau,
and his Castile soap. "All Pure." Oh,
those oval, olive cakes for early rousers!

The book's title poem refers to a grotesquely endowed African woman exhibited in English freak shows during the early nineteenth century; she describes herself as "a black cutout against / a captive blue sky, pivoting / nude so the paying audience / can view my naked buttocks." After this impressive opening poem, Alexander's collection seems a bit thin on material (only forty-two pages of poetry), but she does seem to have already developed a range of technique broad enough to deal with many different kinds of subjects.

Sadly, almost nothing positive can be said of *I Shall Not Be Moved* (Random House) by Maya Angelou; even the title promises a self-congratulatory, cliché-ridden stance. Twenty years ago, when Angelou published her autobiography, *I Know Why the Caged Bird Sings* (1970), she was hailed as an emerging major talent, but she has since become one of those people who are chiefly famous for being famous, a public performer who can command a five-figure sum for an evening of recitations. As a poet she can certainly no longer be taken seriously. One may applaud Ms. Angelou for her humanitarian efforts and for her skills on the stage, but it is hard to be charitable to a poet who would allow doggerel like "These Yet To Be United States" to get into print:

You control the human lives
in Rome and Timbuktu.

Lonely nomads wandering
owe Telstar to you.
Seas shift at your bidding,
your mushrooms fill the sky.
Why are you unhappy?
Why do your children cry?

This sort of pandering to an undemanding audience has also proved to be the undoing of Nikki Giovanni, who was once ranked as one of the most important younger black poets but who was recently dropped unceremoniously from the second edition of the *Norton Anthology of Modern Poetry* (1988).

Fate (Houghton Mifflin) by Ai should perhaps be mentioned here, though Ai's mixed racial heritage (her *Contemporary Authors* statement claims black, Native American, and Oriental blood), southwestern background, and exclusive focus on the dramatic monologue make her difficult to categorize. It is undeniable that most African-American poets share certain affinities of idiom and subject matter, as do many Native American writers. Ai's affinities to them seem tenuous at best. She so effectively submerges her own voice that a reader would have no clue to her ethnic identity or to her gender; even her name is a conundrum: is it "I" or a scream of pain? In many of these poems she forsakes her usual personae, the hopeless, beaten-down men and women of the great American underclass, for the voices of the famous dead. As she says in her author's note, "*Fate* is about eroticism, politics, religion, and show business as tragicomedy, performed by women and men banished to the bare stage of their obsessions." The dramatis personae include Mary Jo Kopechne, General George Armstrong Custer, and Jimmy Hoffa—and the overall effect is, well, rather like something out of a supermarket tabloid. These lines are from "The Resurrection of Elvis":

The Colonel tied a string around my neck
and led me anywhere he wanted.
I was his teddy bear
and yours and yours and yours.
But did I whine, did I complain about it?
Like a greased pig,
I slid through everybody's hands
till I got caught between the undertaker's sheets.

Ai's work should provide an alternative to those tired of a steady diet of confessional I-poetry; even if her work does not exactly extend the boundaries of the dramatic form, it does manage to hold the reader's interest, if only through pop-culture morbidity.

Southern poets, both male and female, were prominent during the year. Dabney Stuart's new collection, *Narcissus Dreaming* (Louisiana State University Press), is his strongest book since his first, *The Diving Bell*, which was published almost twenty-five years ago, in 1966. In the title poem Narcissus's desire to be rid of a world where everything is overlaid with his own image sounds like the poet's own farewell to the introspection that has marked much of his work in the past:

Bob, line,
sinker, hook return
to him, bringing
his reflection off the water
as if it were a laid-out suit
of clothes lifted
by its center. He lowers
it into the boat, takes
it upon himself,
drenched, obscene,
a perfectly imperfect fit,
leaving the water
imageless, opaque,
other.

The poems here for the most part deal with encounters with what lies outside one's own "perfectly imperfect" skin, many of them descriptive pieces in the third person. "Gospel Singer" provides one good example:

Everything
rides on his bringing
his mouth down to the mike,
almost into it. It is more
than intimate. He delivers
his part
with such control
you hear nothing
but music, as if
he were breathing
song.

Satirical poems are also prominent in the collection. *Narcissus Dreaming* contains several witty bits of insider's knowledge about palace intrigues in the world of poetry. "The Blurb Writer," totaling up the overkill of his name's appearance in "one year on the back / of 26 books . . . / under paragraphs he rarely / remembered writing," begins to see himself as the literary equivalent of J. Robert Oppenheimer: "*This is death* he thought. *I have / created death*, and he saw / his blurbs rising like mushroom / clouds, carrying their sickness / into the atmosphere forever." A selected edition of this fine poet's work is long overdue.

From the same publisher comes Catharine Savage Brosman's *Journeying from Canyon de Chelly*, a book, as the title indicates, filled with poems of travel and landscape. The pleasure readers derive will be in direct proportion to their familiarity with the locales. Brosman's eye for picturesque detail is exact enough ("wisps of foam toboggan on the waves"; "the streaking sky ignites, then / breaks toward storm and strafes a ridge"; "windmills, mushroom-brown, / at work like egrets in the saline marsh"), but it is essentially a *tourist's* eye, and I miss the inner tension that might invest the places with something beyond precise description. Occasionally, the poems have this quality; "Ash Lawn" is a bleak and ironic description of the restored homeplace of President Monroe:

> Without
> fires burning, sheets under the counterpane,
> there is no reality to the beds,
> no virtue in the sideboard tureens;
> nothing lives except intruders' breath
> and, outside, the boxwood,
> slow, seasonless green.
> Might not one remain at home, warmer,
> and know just as well there the loneliness
> of things abandoned?

Brosman has the twin virtues of formal precision and obvious seriousness, and one wishes that her poems would more often glory in simple moments of sheer physical delight. These lines on "Strawberries" demonstrate a talent for evocation that many will envy:

> Now, juice from these domestic berries stains
> the bowl, as slices fall under the knife,
> and leaves and stems become discarded stars.
> Their breeding rounded firm in ruddiness,
>
> these are the tastiest, surely, of their kind,
> crushed between spoon and palate. Let us eat
> such fruits, beauty in glass—but I recall
> the nestling plants, sunlight at play on leaves,
> that feast of fire in the wilderness.

A moment like this is worth savoring and returning to.

The exact basis for the hushed tones of admiration with which Dave Smith is invariably mentioned has always eluded me, but I suspect that

Dust jacket for Brosman's book of poems concerning travel and landscape

the deference is due less to his skills as a poet than to awe at his successful pursuit of a literary career; he served as coeditor of *The Morrow Anthology of Younger American Poets* (1985) and currently is editor of the *Southern Review*. There are, to be sure, a few fine narrative and descriptive pieces about the fishermen and landscapes of the Virginia Tidewater, but Smith's predilection for the purple patch exceeds even that of James Dickey, the southern poet of the older generation he most resembles, and the late Richard Hugo, whose western landscapes bear evidence of lives of not-so-quiet desperation. Here is a passage from "Cumberland Station," one of Smith's most anthologized poems, conflating an adult's description of a decrepit railway station with a child's memories of the same scene:

> Churning through the inner space of this godfor-
> saken

wayside, I feel the ground try to upchuck and I dig
my fingers in my temples to bury a child
diced on a cowcatcher, a woman smelling
alkaline from washing out the soot.
Where I stood in that hopeless, hateful room
will not leave me. The scarf of smoke I saw
over a man's shoulder runs through me
like the sored Potomac River.

Does the poet really want us to compare a child
hit by a train with produce run through a Veg-O-
Matic? Does the woman smell alkaline or smell *of*
alkaline? And what, pray tell, is a "sored" river?

Solecisms like these, which occur all too frequently in Smith's earlier poetry, are evident on almost every page of his new book, *Cuba Night* (William Morrow), and cannot be explained away by
claims that the poet's earnest attempts to recap-
ture some essential moment of his childhood
force him into an appropriate incoherence—what
I. A. Richards called the imitative fallacy. I am indebted to Tom Clark, reviewing the book in the
San Francisco Chronicle, for singling out such gems
as "we lie in gore dreams"; "to fist / the sky with
anger"; and "the past's untranslated / beasts, the
present's tongue-tied selves." Here is one of my favorite similes:

I want to lie down and dream of God counting
my sins until in anger he sounds sexual
as a Peterbilt diesel in a fishing scow.

And this overwritten passage, as nearly as I can
tell, describes the poet switching on an outside
floodlight when he hears an animal in the middle of the night:

                    It is
no decent hour but I ease from my bed's cool,
step down the blind corridor
with my nakedness swaying, then
paw for the switch. Harms I might do rise
like a fester of wings when I throw
the light of revelation over our backyards,
into bedrooms. What makes me
heave it as indifferently as a hunting sun?

Mercifully, I am not the only person confused by Smith's poetry; I read the book's longest poem, the 230-line narrative "To Isle of
Wight," as a dramatic poem whose persona,
drunkenly driving home from visiting his
brother, is involved in what appears to be a fatal
car wreck:

                    My face floats through
a woman's face planted on my windshield,

wanders into the sheared cries of a world
that pumps breath in my mouth. I'm down in clay
kissed by moons of teeth. A man says "Gon die."
Oh God, I hear them humming gospels, flashed
red light scorching me under him. I'm pinned
to a spruce, tasting blood.

According to Morrow's publicity release, "The volume begins with 'To Isle of Wight,' an accomplished longer poem in which the poet travels by
car through his native eastern Virginia, observing
its people and commenting on the poet's attempt
to sing." Deconstruction, anyone?

The talents of the current generation of
southern women poets—I am thinking primarily
of writers such as Ellen Bryant Voight, Margaret
Gibson, Julia Randall, and the estimable Betty
Adcock—would be significant by any measure,
and Susan Ludvigson is certainly one of the best.
I did not particularly like her 1987 collection,
The Beautiful Noon of No Shadow (Louisiana State
University Press), where it seemed as though the
heavy hand of Rilke had managed to overshadow
her flair for bizarre humor. European influences
abound, to be sure, in *To Find the Gold*, from the
same publisher; the book's first section is a sequence of nineteen poems, many of them epistolary monologues, about Camille Claudel, the
sculptor who was both mistress and protégé of
Rodin and recently the subject an award-winning
film. Here, as her paranoia deepens, she writes
to her estranged lover, demanding that he break
his marriage:

Don't look for me. I want no
letters, no word from you at all,
unless it's to tell me Rose is dead,
and you poisoned her! Or that you're publishing
a confessions listing all your crimes
against me. Too late for anything else.
Everything you've said has turned to salt,
it penetrates the cracks in my skin,
so that I work all day with a sense
that my whole body's burning.

Ludvigson is usually an open-form poet; it's interesting to observe that the letter that comes from
the depths of Claudel's insanity, written from an
insane asylum, is cast in a loose version of
Dante's terza rima.

Other poems in the collection range widely—
landscapes, a descriptive sequence on Scandi-
navian paintings, a narrative which conflates
Ludvigson's childhood memories of World War

II with the story of Albert Camus's involvement with the French underground, and autobiographical lyrics; "After Thirty Octobers" displays, in the midst of some rather lulling nostalgia, one of those unexpected turns that lift Ludvigson's poetry out of the ordinary:

> Dinner's ready,
> Mother's heaping pork chops onto a platter.
> The grapefruit tree in the corner has spread
> its leaves to the steam wafting out from the kitchen,
> is fuller and greener than it will be
> again. When the phone rings it's the boy
> I'll marry, who's on his way, innocent
> as the Siamese cat who suddenly drags
> used Kotex all over the house. I run room
> to room, scooping up bloody pads. Sun streams
> into the cage of the new canary, who's just
> stopped singing.

The curiously titled *Sigodlin* (Wesleyan University Press) is Robert Morgan's eighth collection. The title poem, an ode in praise of honest craftsmanship, explains the word as carpenters' slang for "out of plumb." The conclusion, reaching back for the word's origins, strikes me as especially fine:

> And what they fitted
> and nailed or mortised into place, downright
> and upstanding, straight up and down and flat
> as water, established the coordinates
> forever of their place in creation's
> fabric, in a word learned perhaps from
> masons who heard it in masonic rites
> drawn from ancient rosicrucians who
> had the term from the Greek mysteries'
> love of geometry's power to say,
> while everything in the real may lean just
> the slightest bit sigodlin or oblique,
> the power whose center is everywhere.

The poems in the second half of the book, descriptive and narrative pieces about the poet's native North Carolina mountains, will most cheer those who have enjoyed his work in the past. One of them, "Sidney Lanier Dies at Tryon 1881," invites comparison with Andrew Hudgins's treatment of the same subject in his award-winning *After the Lost War* (1988).

Come now four survivors of the 1960s, all looking somewhat worse for wear and displaying poetic strategies that summon up smoke-filled dorm rooms with black-light posters and a stereo booming Jim Morrison (whose poems—I use the term advisedly—keep creeping back into print,

persistent as an exotic fungal infection). At least Ron Padgett's *Great Balls of Fire* (Coffee House Press) cannot be accused of merely fashionable retro-ism since it is a reissue of the 1969 collection that put him in the front rank of the younger generation of the New York School (Koch, Ashbery, Schuler, and O'Hara were their elder mentors). Why, exactly, anyone would want to bring out a "revised edition" of a book that prided itself on its slapdash, improvisational quality is beyond me, but, whatever the case, it's a pleasure to have the book back in print, if only to be reminded of one's distance from his own youth. Rereading Padgett is like opening a time capsule from the Age of Warhol; here are all of the era's experimental techniques, from Dada ("Nothing in that Drawer" merely repeats its title fourteen times) to outright theft (Padgett prints Stephen Crane's "A Man Saw a Ball of Gold" without credit to the author—a somewhat extreme case of the sincerest form of flattery). For reasons that I am at a loss either to explain or justify, I have always enjoyed such wacked-out rambles as "Joe Brainard's Painting *Bingo*," which begins by stating, "I suffer when I sit next to Joe Brainard's painting *Bingo*," and, after a few goofy observations ("I don't know anything about hemorrhoids / Such as if it hurts to sit when you have them"), concludes:

> In fact I didn't originally say
> I suffer when I sit next to Joe Brainard's painting
> *Bingo*
> My wife said it
> In response to something I had said
> About another painting of his
> She had misunderstood what I had said

A collection of new poems by Padgett, *The Big Something* (The Figures), was also published during the year. The book contains several poems about his friend and fellow Tulsan, the late Ted Berrigan.

Tom Clark, who served as poetry editor for the *Paris Review* during the same period, checks in with *Fractured Karma* (Black Sparrow), 164 pages, the majority of which are more than half blank with many containing only two or three lines, which must rate it as the least ecologically conscious production of the year—one hopes the publisher is using recycled paper. It takes a great deal of patience to find something to admire here. These lines on poet-as-performance-artist from "Self Portrait: The Artist As Personality" are fairly typical of Clark's nontechnique:

I tossed my hair like a salad until it met my boa flying around from the back inducing fission
Chanting through my Laurie Anderson voicebox
modulator in my best imitation of Spalding Gray
I noticed the critics reacting as though I were drag-
ging chalk down a blackboard the wrong way
At the University of Southern Nowhere I drew an audience
of one dog plus one professor who was doing a thesis on me

A new collection of Clark's book reviews from
the 1980s, *The Poetry Beat* (University of Michigan
Press), displays a levelheaded critical sensibility
with tastes somewhat more catholic than his poetry indicates; that he can praise formalist Timothy Steele equally with Ed Sanders indicates that
Clark is not narrowly doctrinaire in his poetics.

The late Lucille Ball, before her television
fame, was affectionately known as "Queen of the
B Movies"; Lin Lifshin's publicity release refers
to her unabashedly as "The Queen of the Small
Press," noting that there is virtually no "small
press magazine in America that has not published at least some of her poetry." *The Doctor
Poems* (Applezaba Press) once more demonstrates
that almost anything—rectal thermometers, new
contacts, cabbage—is grist for Lifshin's unceasing
mill. The book is framed by two sequences about
doctors, medical and professorial respectively,
which are filled with Lifshin's characteristic eroticism. This one is called "Doctors of English 4":

Geoffrey couldn't hold his booze   everyone knew it
he
hung out over his belt   wondered about other people's
women. He pretended to snarl but really he was a
pussy
over coffee i could feel him   imagine pulling off he
called
them my black (over white lace panti hose) de sade
boots

James Tate's *Distance from Loved Ones* (Wesleyan University Press) is somewhat more sophisticated than the three contemporaries with whom
he is discussed here, and his career has followed
the conventional academic route to a professor-
ship at the University of Massachusetts. Tate's
brand of surrealism has always seemed to me a pe-
culiarly homegrown variant; if he resembles any
past writers, it is not Bréton or Eluard but Americans such as James Thurber and Robert Bench-
ley. "Bewitched" tries to trace the random nature
of mental associations:

I was standing in the lobby,

some irritant in my eye,
thinking back on a soloist
I once heard in Venezuela,
and then, for some reason,
on a crate of oranges recently
arrived from a friend in Florida,
and then this colleague came up to me
and asked me what time it was,
and I don't know what came over me
but I was certain that I was standing there naked
and I was certain she could see my thoughts,
so I tried to hide them quickly. . . .

Tate's poems seem to vanish from memory almost as quickly as the pages are turned; his
brand of flip humor, engaging enough at first, ultimately has a way of making the people and
events in his poems seem inconsequential and,
thus, forgettable. This might be excusable, even
charming, in a poet in his twenties, but Tate has
reached the age when we might reasonably expect some evidence of mature thought in his
work.

Trivia Time! What do the following lines
have in common?

It's a year exactly since my father died.

In our family, everyone loves flowers.

I'll tell you something: every day
people are dying.

I have a friend who still believes in heaven.

I grew up in a village: now
it's almost a city.

If you answered correctly, that they are all opening lines from poems in Louise Glück's *Ararat*
(Ecco), you win first prize, a 1974 Ford Pinto. In
the whole book by this vastly overrated poet
there is nothing as arresting as the first sentence
on the dust jacket: "If Freud had, at the last, col-
laborated with instead of repudiating Jung—if
Freud's revelatory case studies, bristling with
particulars, had fused with Jung's paradigmatic
model—perhaps Louise Glück would not have
needed to write these poems." Wishful thinking,
I'd say. Speaking of her father, she says,

What he wanted
was to lie on the couch
with the *Times*
over his face,
so that death, when it came,
wouldn't seem a significant change.

A sentiment, it seems to me, that could be applied to the experience of reading *Ararat*.

There seems little urgency behind the poems in *The Want Bone* (Ecco), Robert Pinsky's fourth collection. Reading the book, one gets the impression of the poet, having selected a promising topic, sitting at his desk several evenings in a row, dutifully hammering the thing out like a freshman completing an assigned theme. The results are never disgraceful, but the reader is likely to wonder what, precisely, is the point of "Visions of Daniel," a four-page retelling of a familiar Bible story, or "Jesus and Isolt," a long prose parable in which Jesus returns, in the form of a "ciclogriff," an animal that sounds like a cross between a raccoon and a bat, to observe and perhaps attempt to save a famous pair of courtly adulterers. The tale bogs down in its own turgid self-analysis: "The Jewish soul of Jesus, pragmatic, ethical, logical, found in the passionate and self-defeating codes of romantic love and knightly combat some of what he lacked in the jeweled pavilions of Heaven." "Shirt," while not exactly riveting, is a typical Pinsky meditation:

> Wonderful how the pattern matches perfectly
> Across the placket and over the twin bar-tacked
>
> Corners of both pockets, like a strict rhyme
> Or a major chord. Prints, plaids, checks,
> Houndstooth, Tattersall, Madras.

The poem meanders on to discuss the famous Triangle Factory fire; "Hart Crane's Bedlamite," 'shrill shirt ballooning'; the capitalist origins of Scottish tartans, and the unexpected revelation of "George Herbert, your descendant is a Black / Lady in South Carolina, her name is Irma / And she inspected my shirt." Speculations of this sort perhaps belong more properly to the genre of the whimsical personal essay; I wonder if Pinsky is deliberately trying to become a postmodern version of Charles Lamb's Elia.

Brad Leithauser's *The Mail from Anywhere* (Knopf) is the third collection from a poet whose name is automatically invoked whenever the New Formalists are discussed. Over the years Leithauser has taken his lumps (one wag referred to his work as "lite verse") for his outspoken views on his contemporaries' lack of basic skills (he originated the phrase "metrical illiteracy") and for writing poems about giving summer tennis lessons and working for a law firm.

Dust jacket for the new book of poems by the most famous of the New Formalists

Leithauser is neither as good as Helen Vendler has claimed nor as disreputable as, say, the blue-collar Iowa critics find him; true, he writes too many facile poems in syllabic stanzas purchased at Miss Moore's estate sale, but he can also occasionally rise to considerable heights, especially when he stays close to his roots. Here, I admire "Uncle Grant," a character study of a crackpot relative who fancies himself the next Alexander Graham Bell:

> Which was—or was if one can tell
> By results alone—the purest folly. His
> Dream was of a kind of workbench El
> Dorado, where the gold of free
> Fancy, mined systematically
> At last, would sift itself out.
> Not a thing came of his labors
> in the end, excepting some
> Dubious family tales and—no doubt—
> Much laughter for and from the neighbors.

Equally impressive is "The Caller," a long meditation in twelve-line stanzas on a dour great-aunt, a spinsterish Michigan schoolteacher about whom the poet's grandmother muses: *"What a man never seems to realize / Is that even the stoniest / Looking woman may be broken hearted, / And for the first and only time I saw / A sort of soupy look come into her eyes."* The irritating flippancies (a "post-coital" sonnet in monosyllabic lines, lame epigrams of the nudge-nudge, wink-wink school) that have marred Leithauser's work in the past are for the most part absent from this collection. Leithauser, it is worth mentioning, is the husband of Mary Jo Salter, whose *Unfinished Painting* was last year's Lamont Poetry Selection.

Another poet much praised in New Formalist circles is Vikram Seth, whose verse-novel *The Golden Gate* found surprising commercial success in 1986. Seth was lauded for his deft handling of Pushkin's fourteen-line *Eugene Onegin* stanza to tell a contemporary tale of the intertwined love and friendships of a group of young San Francisco professionals. Those who have eagerly awaited a new collection of lyrics will be happy, at first sight, to have *All You Who Sleep Tonight* (Random House), but they will also, I fear, be let down hard by the sing-song rhythms and predictable rhymes of "Round and Round," the book's opening poem:

> After a long and wretched flight
> That stretched from daylight into night,
> Where babies wept and tempers shattered
> And the plane lurched and whiskey splattered
> Over my plastic food, I came
> To claim my bags from Baggage Claim.

A short poem, "Across," compounds the fault with inexpert usage and awkward syntax:

> Across these miles I wish you well.
> May nothing haunt your heart but sleep.
> May you not sense what I don't tell.
> May you not dream, or doubt, or weep.
>
> May what my pen this peaceless day
> Writes on this page not reach your view
> Till its deferred print lets you say
> It speaks to someone else than you.

"Someone else than you" does not strike my ear as idiomatic, and this is especially troublesome in a poem's final line. The book's second section, "In Other Voices," includes "Soon," a dramatic monologue in which the speaker is apparently dying of AIDS:

> How am I to go on—
> How will I bear this taste,

> My throat cased in white spawn—
> These hands that shake and waste?
>
> Stay by my steel ward bed
> And hold me where I lie.
> Love me when I am dead
> And do not let me die.

Seth's humanitarian concern may be sincere, but, subject matter aside, the level of versification he attains here seems more appropriate to the studios of Nashville than the slopes of Parnassus.

The title poem of Sydney Lea's *Prayer for the Little City* (Scribners) describes a motley collection of shacks occupied by ice fishermen during the dead of a New England winter. As one who has been accused of fishing in a bathtub when no other waters are available, I can identify with

> the care with which   all night men linger,
>
> as if in prayer for a novel fish, or a novel way
> by which to address   some thing they're feeling
>   Surely this is
> part of what holds us under crude ceil-
>   ings beaded with pitch,
>
> amid this fetor with speechless friends. Surely,
>   surely
> a sense that early, before the dawn (or sooner,
>   or later)
> our flags will all at once, together, tremble and
>   shimmy.

Lea's poetry has always exhibited a great deal of formal variety, and the poems gathered here range from nine-line stanzas turning on single slant rhymes to blank verse. Occasionally his stanza patterns, elaborately spaced, centered, or indented, are too pretty for their own good, and they can weary the reader's eye. In this instance, I can only speculate at the reason for these three-stage lines; perhaps Lea is paying homage to the variable foot of William Carlos Williams, that earlier master of "local conditions." Like him, Lea has drawn his own boundary lines precisely— New Hampshire's streams and woods, church ("Six Sundays Toward a Seventh" is a sequence taking place over Lent), neighbors, and family—and it seems clear that he has no second thoughts about being labeled a regional writer. I like him best at his plainest, as in these slant-rhymed couplets from the end of "Winter Tournament," a father's description of his daughter and her team-mates playing basketball in a drafty gym:

> I speculate
> As we collect our children. Those defeats—
> Goals rejected, miscues, slips and fouls—
> May work their disenchantment on our girls.
> Yet I daresay that we imagine beauties
> Are at their truest when they're so ungainly.
> We cling to daughters, and to that surmise,
> As carefully we tiptoe over ice
>
> —Clownish in the dark—to heating cars.
> At least in awkwardness they are mostly ours.

Lea's New England, like Frost's, is often violent and lonely, but he takes it in with a wholeness and health rarely encountered in contemporary poetry.

Jane Kenyon is another New Hampshire resident (she is married to Donald Hall), and her poems in *Let Evening Come* (Graywolf) are firmly grounded in a sense of place, punctuated from time to time with trips to Barbados or Maui. At home, Kenyon goes over the same lyric ground too many times—how many gardening poems, replete with bone meal and mulch, or church fairs ("We made less than usual on the Church Fair supper, / held this year in the Blazing Star Grange, / because of rain.") or references to the poet's reading habits ("I have been reading *War and Peace*"; "I begin Gogol's story / about a painter whose love of luxury / destroys his art"; "At dinner I laughed with the rest, / but in truth I prefer the sound / of pages turning . . .") can one book bear? Kenyon's level of craftsmanship in individual poems is generally high, but when they are read in quantity her lack of variety comes to the surface. At her best, she has a Dickinson-like way of springing small surprises, as in these lines about a housefly that wakes in midwinter:

> Then it lurched into the paper clips.
> The morning passed, and I forgot about
> my guest, except when the buzz rose
> and quieted, rose and quieted—tires
> spinning on ice, chainsaw far away,
> someone carrying on alone. . . .

While I am making comparisons to Dickinson it is appropriate to mention the two books published in 1990 by Wendy Barker, whose study of that poet's patterns of imagery, *Lunacy of Light*, has been widely admired. Her first collection of poems, *Winter Chickens* (Corona Publishing) draws effectively on family, marriage, and parent-

hood for subjects. In "Disappearing Acts" her son's delight at a magic show ("the woman / in the shower vanished!") is sobered by thoughts of a newspaper story about "the girl they'd found dead, / months had gone by, / no one had claimed her. / Who could disappear like that?" In another poem she whimsically describes Cub Scouts who have "earned / their transformations into bears, / . . . into wolves," noting that "the boys have not grown fur, only / tufts of hair that poke / and tangle under their caps." Among many distinct moments of pleasure, "Needle-point" stands out as one of the best. Barker describes a handmade bookmark stitched by her mother: "soft, curling yarn, / spiralling over and / over the blue / and the green, / she has sewn, / so that I / won't lose / my place." *Let the Ice Speak* (Ithaca House) is an even stronger collection, and contains one narrative poem, "Identifying Things," that speaks to parents' darkest fears. Learning from her teenage son that he has been jabbed by a needle that his friend has picked up on the street, Barker describes how she and her husband play a frightening game of "find the needle, / bring in that needle, make sure those boys / find that needle." Weaving in and out of this plot line is another, the poet's inability to name the new sort of bird gathering at her feeder. At the poem's climax the needle is found and declared harmless, and the two line of metaphor intersect:

> And the new birds
> are pine siskins, yes, they are,
> just a little yellow on the wings and tail,
> it helps, it always helps when you know
> what things are.

Barker's way of combining disparate elements into a seamless whole hearkens back to the lyric manner of the English metaphysical poets, but in building her conceits she does not neglect the strong narrative elements that make her poems succeed.

The centerpiece of poet-critic Jonathan Holden's *Against Paradise* (University of Utah Press) is "Son of Babbitt," a Browningesque dramatic monologue of about three hundred lines. The speaker named in the title is a wealthy advertising executive who changed his name to Babcock during the 1960s to avoid the stigma of being singled out as, yes, the grandson of Sinclair Lewis's fictional creation. Babcock is a complex and fully conscious monster, a former Harvard English major who understands irony as something that helps "when you have to eat crow every day" and who is aware that "all stereotypes contain a grain of truth," even the one he is fulfilling as he speaks. Reveling in Nixon's 1972 election triumph, he reassumes his true identity:

> Suddenly, I remembered what
> it means to be Republican. I thought:
> "I am going to change my name back to what
> it always should have been—to "George Babbitt!"
> *George Babbitt.* That night I knew, just *knew*
> who I am, and what I had to do.

The poem concludes with Babbitt triumphantly planning an ad campaign "to put a decent face / on certain facts involving toxic waste." This is, of course, a wide-screen, Technicolor, paranoid cartoon for liberals, but the voice that Holden creates, speaking in nicely modulated blank verse, is compelling and holds the reader captive in its spell. Holden, with mixed emotions of awe and disgust, has created a contemporary version of Milton's Satan. In the other poems in the collection, for the most part lyrics and personal narratives, Holden's apparent disaffection with almost all aspects of his life—love, sex, taxes, plumbing, even the American heartland of rural Kansas—may be too sour for most readers; he is beginning to sound crankier than Alan Dugan, if such were possible. Yet to those who have had too much sweetness and light he will speak most eloquently.

Both Richard Howard ("a new Orpheus among us, in seersucker shorts and eager to be riven by the Thracian Women") and J. D. McClatchy ("an elixir of perfumed fantasies and sweaty secrets") wax rapturous in their dust jacket notes for Wayne Koestenbaum's *Ode to Anna Moffo and Other Poems* (Persea). "Mired in low culture, / I was aching to reach the high," writes Koestenbaum in the title poem, a long meditation that conflates memories of obsessive fandom for the celebrated diva with vignettes of the poet's adolescence in Santa Cruz ("I adored / the shy rehearsal pianist / whose sideburns intimated future movements, / son of a busty / dwarf who drank and drove and taught him / rudiments of musicianship." Koestenbaum displays some skill in evoking teenage sexual squeamishness and uncertainty, but his work is absolutely without compression; even one of his "epigrams" stretches to over twenty lines. His attempts at traditional verse forms such as the Spenserian are, for the most part, embarrassing:

for November '59, when your "Amami, Alfredo!"

moved cognoscenti. I heard you once, live, late:
you sang "Tacea la notte," hair coiled, alfresco
in Baltimore's Melody Tent, tugboat lights
and popcorn smell clotting the wharf-soft night.
Before your entrance, I saw you adjust the chopstick
in your bun for a *South Pacific*, pulled tight.
That was '81. Your trills, oil slicks,
mercilessly miked, showed rich ore in the derrick

There is neither linear nor stanzaic integrity here and, thus, no real justification for the form beyond the poet's misguided attempts to display his virtuosity.

It is difficult to understand the reasoning behind the critical hosannas welcoming Amy Gerstler's *Bitter Angel* (North Point Press), which arrives with a typically meaningless blurb from the ubiquitous Jorie Graham ("a music more perfectly capable of driving narrative into the extended slow-motion conflagration of postmodern lyricism") and a nomination for the National Book Critics Circle Award. The other nominees were John Haines, Anthony Hecht, Charles Simic, and Frank Bidart, whose *In the Western Night* (Farrar Straus & Giroux) was not received for this survey. About a third of this collection is prose poetry, and the rest ranges from the outright silliness of "A Love Poem" ("Me fork, you can opener. / You sweetmeat, me bean-cake. / Me zilch, you nada.") to competent, if unsingular, lyricism. This catalogue of apostrophes, from "the Soul Looks Down on the Body," summons up the voices of the American Puritan-poets, Anne Bradstreet and Edward Taylor:

> Dung heap. Poor cooled shell.
> Orange peel. Husk, crust, bark.
> Armor my meat rode beneath—
> stink-mobile with me asleep
> at the wheel. Fleas' breeding
> ground. Rigamarole of gristle
> and digits. Pain parlor.

Nothing else in the book quite comes up to the level of purely *sonic* interest that these lines generate.

Space does not permit more than the merest mention of other worthwhile books arriving from poets whose reputations range from established to emerging. David McKain's *Spirit Bodies* (Ithaca House) contains "In Soviet Georgia," a descriptive poem I selected as winner of the first James Boatwright III Poetry Prize, named after the late editor of *Shenandoah*. The poem describes the expert slaughter of animals in the marketplace: "The last lamb slides its jaw back / and forth chewing on the sweet grass, / the spray of its blood a surprise— / the men jump back as if someone had thrown / a flat rock in the water." McKain's other work was unknown to me at the time, so I am glad to have this collection, which displays a consistently accurate eye for detail. Harry Humes displays similar skills in his scenes of the Pennsylvania coal country in *The Way Winter Works* (University of Arkansas Press). Humes's poems, as always, are filled with intimate knowledge of sinkholes and abandoned deep mines, of the pheasant fields and trout streams of his rural demesne. He can even make snapping turtle soup sound delicious when he recalls a neighbor who would "carry liver and heart and white meat / back to the pot in the kitchen. / One day each year would go rich / with spices and onions, / her fine dress, small yellow crackers, / the bottle of sherry." Wayne Dodd's *Echoes of the Unspoken* (University of Georgia Press), though called "an extended meditation on the presences and processes of nature," smells less of the landscape than of the lamp, with references to "dense, syllabic woods," nature's green described "as clear // and certain as the mind's / syntax will utter," and pathetic fallacies that would have amused Mr. Ruskin: "The oak sapling waves / its small arms / for balance / in the wind. . . ." On one hand Dodd alludes to the lessons of the Imagist master (*"Make it new* / Pound said and we answer // *Make it true"*) but on the other he does exactly the sort of thing Pound railed against: "The small wild horses / of the mind wheel / and rear among the bushes. . . ."

Both Alvin Greenburg's *Why We Live with Animals* (Coffee House Press) and Richard Grossman's *The Animals* (Graywolf) come during a year when animal rights activists spray-painted the fur coats of affluent Christmas shoppers. Greenburg, in a sequence of sixty sonnets (I use the term advisedly since Greenburg has no ear for meter and rhymes very loosely), deals mostly with domestic animals. Here, in a representative passage, he describes a dog proudly bearing home a scavenged deer leg: "you see that delicate hoof / between his jaws, the whole thing terribly uncouth, / tattered and dry, long dead, but he won't let go / and even growls a little at your grab, your 'no!' / —you know you're caught in the teeth of a larger truth." In an earlier era, verse like this might have found a home in the back pages of *Grit*. Grossman's collection, an even five hundred pages long, is billed as a "pastoral," attempting the give-and-take form of the eclogue by setting poems with titles such as "Shame" in the book's opening 150 pages against the rest, which make up a contemporary bestiary. The "Bedbug" notes, "Above our dorm, / everybody is expected to perform, / dream, // or at best totally / rest." On the basis of its length alone, *The Animals* is something of an anomaly, and I suspect, not intending to patronize Grossman's considerable achievement, that it will be read mostly by those who would not ordinarily buy collections of contemporary verse.

Tom Sleigh's *Waking* (University of Chicago Press) is part of editor Robert von Hallberg's Phoenix Poets series. The book opens with "Ending," a twenty-page monologue spoken by a man who has learned that he is terminally ill, and the book seems overburdened with poems located in cancer wards, operating theaters, and delivery rooms where "The umbilicus strangling / Like a whip around my neck" destroys the brain of one poem's persona. "The Physical" is a good piece of narrative reporting in which the poet recalls a Vietnam War-era medical examination and a grossly overweight inductee who becomes hysterical when he is rejected: "why should he weep, *weep* / To be rejected by the War?" Memories of Vietnam form the sole subject of Mark Kessinger's *The Book of Joe* (Cleveland State University Press), a sequence of short poems about the life of the typical veteran of that war, still suffering and embittered (the title puns on "Job" and alludes to "G.I. Joe"). "If," according to Kessinger, "you took all the soldiers / who have fallen on their swords / since the end of the war / you could bury the Vietnam memorial / in Washington DeeCee. // With just the swords." *Simonides in Vietnam* (John Daniel) is a chapbook in which R. L. Barth, one of the ablest poets of the Vietnam War, captures the pitch and pith of the Greek Anthology. Among his epigrams is "A Brief History of the Vietnam War," which perhaps alludes to the military service, or nonservice, of a famous politician: "The essence was economy: / How wealthy was your family?" "Movie Stars" is particularly pungent: "Bob Hope, John Wayne, and Martha Raye / Were dupes who knew no other way; / Jane Fonda, too, whose Hanoi hitch / Epitomized protester kitsch." We can only hope that Barth will soon turn his cold eye on the current wave of post-Iraq chest thumping.

I earlier mentioned the anthology *Working Classics*. Jim Daniels is prominently represented there and in *Punching Out* (Wayne State University Press), a book-length sequence about a young man named Digger who works in a car factory. The labor is numbing, joyless, occasionally dangerous. "Small Catch" relates one day's high point: "The ambulance races up / they toss the bleeding finger in / with the man and race off. / Everyone looks for a second / then goes back to work: / a finger." Like many works in the mainstream of American naturalism, this one has difficulty rising above Digger's limited consciousness; eventually the flat idiom and downbeat observations, repeated like the routine of the assembly line that wears down the characters, defeats the reader as well. Somewhat more miscellaneous are the poems in *Definitions* (West End Press) by Peter Oresick, who is the coeditor of *Working Classics* and a knowledgeable observer of the effects of what he calls the "Deindustrialization of America." Describing the workingmen's bars in Ford City, Pennsylvania, he recites a litany of names— "Kijowski, Valasek, and Dietz / gulping beer like air"—and laments, "For God's sake, let's sit on these stools // and tell sad stories / of the deaths of common men."

Former Lamont-winner Stephen Dobyns's *Body Traffic* (Viking) is a collection in search of unity; sonnet-length poems about Cézanne, obviously composed as a sequence, are scattered haphazardly throughout the book, and none of them is quite strong enough to make an impression when isolated from the others. "Inappropriate Gestures," like several other poems in the book, calls to mind the absurdism of the late Donald Barthelme's short stories: "We are surrounded by inappropriate gestures. / The house is on fire. Quick, grab a tomato! / Bobby fell in the well. Hurry, play the trombone!" David Slavitt's *Eight Longer Poems* (Louisiana State University Press) is fairly literary stuff—a meditation on *La vida es sueño;* "The Wound," which connects Achilles' spear to the caduceus of mythic healing; "Vlad," a sequence about the original of the Dracula legend. W. S. Di Piero's *The Dog Star* (University of Massachusetts Press) evokes neither the rage nor madness to which its title perhaps alludes: Pope's "The Dog Star rages! nay, 'tis past a doubt / All Bedlam, or Parnassus, is let out." "Walt, the Wounded" quotes from Whitman's letters to the families of Civil War wounded, "Our roughed-up beauties dead or dying." In his lyrical poems Di Piero's overly ornate idiom becomes a burden: "I stepped down / first, ramming the pool's / flexions, scattering the waterbug's shade, / fouling

middle clarities / with surfed bottom silt." *The Drowned River* (Houghton Mifflin) by Thomas Lux also contains a poem about Whitman, "Walt Whitman's Brain Dropped on Laboratory Floor," which provides Lux with the occasion for some easy moralizing: "That our nation // does not care does not matter, much. / That his modest federal job was taken from him, / and thus his pension, does not matter at all. / And that his brain was dropped and shattered, a cosmos, / on the floor, matters even less." A poet who admits that he gives "a honk / for Wallace Stevens" each time he drives through Hartford and apostrophizes his unborn child as "Tadpole" is leaving himself wide open to charges of sentimentality. One wants to be generous to Lux's positive thinking; still, it is pretty difficult to excuse a poem about the tomb of Herbert Hoover (a *villanelle*, of all things) that concludes with this couplet: "On the prairie's edge they buried the president. / Still— so many people can't pay their rent."

Many readers will remember Joy Harjo from the Bill Moyers television series "The Power of the Word." Her new book, *In Mad Love and War* (Wesleyan University Press), invokes both Native American animal spirits ("When Rabbit doubted the miracle of creation. . . ") and the intricacies of revolution, as expressed by an argumentative male: "*What we are dealing with here are ideological / differences, political power*, he says to / impress a woman who is gorgeously intelligent / and who reminds me of the soft talc desert / of my lover's cheek." Harjo covers so many political, sexual, and ethnic bases that reading her is like taking a crash course in political correctness. Carol Potter's *Before We Were Born* (alicejamesbooks) is unfortunately typical of much contemporary gay women's poetry, full of overripe erotic content ("you tongue this / nest of hair making my skin swell from the wet V / of my thighs") and a sort of amniotic cosmic-consciousness ("When the waters broke, a tremendous dark river burst from inside me.") that is fast becoming a cliché. Barbara Goldberg's *Cautionary Tales* (Dryad Press) is a deliciously wicked collection with sharp edges like Jules Feiffer's cartoons. One wife, in a small revolt, cuts a small hole, "the loss of perfect / fabric," in her husband's prized hunting jacket. Another allows her husband to tie her up for his fortieth birthday present; he does so, then goes off to the hospital where his mother lies in a coma: " 'The story of our lives,' / she snarls. 'Your mother has always come first.' " The husband, remembering his days in the Boy Scouts, is "astonished the knots he has tied still hold." Nancy Vieria Couto's *The Face in the Water* (University of Pittsburgh Press) is a nicely balanced collection with some interesting poems about growing up in the 1950s. "You Bet Your Life" imagines an unexpected epiphany: "I guess I must say something right / under my breath, / because the ceiling divides / and the duck / comes down and gives me a hundred dollars." "Tea Party" remembers the texture of "macaroons / crumbling from the saucer that you balance / with kid gloves." Alice Fulton's *Powers of Congress* (David R. Godine) contains at least one moment of parodic brilliance, a poststructuralist's nightmare called "Point of Purchase." The poem itself is a representative post-modernist hodgepodge, starting from "How God and billiards originated / no one knows," and going on to discuss the statues on Easter Island, Mother Theresa, and the speaker's Catholic childhood, among *many* other subjects. What makes the poem succeed, though, are the marginal comments, in at least four different hands, which purport to be from fellow members of a poetry workshop. One complains of a word that sounds like "a deconstructionist's neologism" while another is fixated on the wisdom of her sister: " 'Don't get me started on that,' she used to say. 'When I get started I'm like a raccoon washing a sugarcube till there's nothing left.' I wish I could send her this poem." "Why don't you buy her a Hallmark!" another "critic" adds.

With Fulton in mind, it is distressing to note how many recent collections seem cut to the cloth of the latest fads in critical theory. Scott Cairns's *The Translation of Babel* (University of Georgia Press) calls on a couple of the fashionable icons—Borges, Calvino—and goes them one better by inventing "the greatest postmodern poet writing in Portuguese," one Raimundo Luz of Brazil, "devoted family man, a fan of American rhythm and blues, an accomplished cook, and a fiction." If Senhor Luz had anything significant to say, this would be a fascinating conceit; unfortunately, he is a rather tedious fellow, given to ungrammatical observations such as "I am careful to avoid things German, / in particular the food. As for English , / I leave that now to whomever [*sic*] needs it. / I never look north from Florianopolis." Donald Revell's *New Dark Ages* (Wesleyan University Press) is that poet's third collection in eight years, each one growing progressively more artificial. There is not much one can do with warmed-over Ashbery like these lines

from "Against Pluralism": "And it's a wise child who can understand / that the mothers and fathers on the trains / see only the receding pastorals / the lamplit villages of other angels / and that his suffering is only one pinpoint / on a lithic hoarding of departures / each passenger reads like an advertisement of heaven." At least Susan Howe breaks some new ground as far as experimentalism is concerned. Her *The Europe of Trusts* (Sun and Moon) literally cuts and pastes lines from a chosen "text," rearranging and sometimes even overprinting words and phrases. One section, a closet drama called "God's Spies," has three characters—Stella, Cordelia, and The Ghost of Jonathan Swift—and mixes passages of Swift's verse with fragmented elements of *King Lear*. One tries in vain to imagine a reader who has the patience to wade through this book's 218 pages. Presumably that brave soul will be first in line to purchase a copy of *Singularities* (Wesleyan University Press), another collection of Howe's pellucid wit and wisdom, of which these four lines can stand as synecdoche: "Still we call bitterly bitterly / Stern norse terse ethical pathos // Archaic presentiment of rupture / Voicing desire no more from here."

Richard Katrovas's third collection, *The Public Mirror* (Wesleyan University Press), has the year's best cover photograph (credited by Robert Dois Neus), a shot from the rear of six elementary school youngsters standing at a public urinal; one of them (the poet receiving the blessings of the muse?) unaccountably has a white pigeon perched on his head! None of the poems quite comes up to this level of weirdness though Katrovas's garrulous personal narratives capture something of the ambience of New Orleans, where revelers's "companionable joy / rocks the muted city stars / and convenes the Parliament of Shadows." *Days of Summer Gone* (Galileo) by Joe Bolton also has an unusual cover photograph (by John C. Runnels): a naked woman carrying two suitcases emerging from the back of a tractor-trailer with the Manhattan skyline looming in the distance. Bolton committed suicide in 1990 at age twenty-nine; his career seems to have been on track and had already included an NEA grant and a verse-novella, *Breckinridge County Suite*, published by Cummington Press in 1989. The newer book's middle section contains poems about Bolton's native Kentucky and other parts of the South of his childhood, which now has begun to "sprout suburbs and shopping malls like tubercles." The poems allude to losses in love and a good deal of solitary drinking, and the poet's personal tragedy makes his references to his unhappiness take on greater significance: "I've tried to learn to love only so far / As that love is specific and precise, / And to leave when I feel it becoming otherwise."

The Same Water (Wesleyan University Press) is a first book by Joan Murray, unusual in that it consists of only ten poems. Murray's best poems are the narratives about growing up in New York City; "Coming of Age on the Harlem" describes the poet swimming as "sister / to half-filled soda cans floating / vertically home from a picnic, and to condoms / that look like mama doll socks." Mark Jarman, coeditor (with Robert McDowell) of the journal *The Reaper*, is another strong advocate of poetic story-telling. *The Black Riviera* (Wesleyan University Press) has several fairly long blank verse narratives; the book's title poem, one of the shorter pieces, recalls a drug dealer's "long car / A god himself could steal a girl in, / Clothing its metal sheen in the spectrum / of bars and discos and restaurants."

Three other first books, chiefly lyrical, are worth singling out. *The Dogwood Tree* (University of Alabama Press) by Jennifer Atkinson has several fine poems, led perhaps by "Expecting Fear," in which the poet, "to prove myself," leaps into an open grave. The two men with her, "a man I loved / and his friend whom I later married," pretend to leave, moving "out of sight to scare me, and it worked." At the end of the poem the husband-to-be is the one who returns to lift her out. From the same publisher comes Chard deNiord's *Asleep in the Fire*, poems marked by a strong ethical slant that reflect the poet's background as a psychotherapist and teacher of religion and philosophy. "The Suet Feeder," visited only by a few starlings, moves the poet to a transcendentalist's prayer: "I would give up my telephone and car / to see one pretty bird at the suet. / I would fall asleep at my altar / to lure one godly bird from her nest in the sky." Del Marie Rogers's *Close to the Ground* (Corona Publishing Company) displays the sort of Deep Image surrealism that Robert Bly practiced in the 1960s: "A wild bush near my shoulders burns white, / tangle of bones, fingers, storm in dry sun. / Winter draws shadows tight in its wires." When Rogers moves to more familiar ground her poetry can be quite likeable, particularly in several poems with southwestern locales.

Leading the year's prize-winning collections is Daniel Hall's *Hermit with Landscape* (Yale Univer-

sity Press), latest volume in the Yale Younger Poets Series. In his foreword, series editor James Merrill praises Hall by mentioning literary works in which "we appreciate how much is foreshortened or left out." In Hall's case, though, the sins of omission are too great; the poems consistently work around the edges of situations without quite engaging either their subjects or readers's attention. Some of Hall's quatrain poems, such as "Love-Letter-Burning," bring Merrill's own voice to mind: "The archivist in us shudders at such cold- / blooded destruction of the word, but since / we're only human, we commit our sins / to the flames. Sauve qui peut; fear makes us bold." It is simply amazing how bland the Yale winners have been in recent years, a fault that must surely be laid at the feet of the editors of the series.

Martha Hollander won the 1989 Walt Whitman Award for *The Game of Statues* (Atlantic Monthly Press), which was selected by W. S. Merwin. The poems are double-spaced, lending a deceptive heft to the book. This seems competent enough apprentice work but somewhat detached and lacking in emotional conviction. "Accidents" describes a pair of car wrecks suffered by two people (their exact relationship is not made clear). In the aftermath, Hollander speculates on the workings of fate: "Today / let our anniversary be smitten / with a little fear and knowledge, just as the cars / and pale New England roads are mauled and dirtied." Too often, though, the poems waste away in a stream of uninspired verbiage: "When energy arises from nothing, / from its own lack, it dies on the first wind. / My initial sweep of vigor at the / idea of us as companions here / was cut short as it left my fingertips. . . ."

Chris Semansky's *Death, But at a Good Price* (Story Line Press) is this year's winner of the Nicholas Roerich Poetry Prize, an award which in the past several years has swung from the excellence of David Dooley's *The Volcano Inside* to the misfires of Jane Reavill Ransom's *Without Asking*. This collection falls somewhere between those two poles—rather dated surrealism that ends up sounding sophomoric: "a crippled stallion limped in / saddled with a puckish dwarf in velcro shorts / and a brassiere fit for a cow." When a collection is framed, at the beginning, by yet another "remembering the 1960s" poem ("The day after television broke / new [sic] of the Tet Offensive, I protested / going to school in the leather pants / and wide tie Mother bought me to keep / her son in step with the times.") and, at the end, by a second-person prose poem ("In the morning you will wake to the sound of your heart again, as it beats against your chest like a caged ape screaming to be released. You are old.") there's little occasion for celebration or enthusiasm.

Two winners of the National Poetry Series arrived for review. *Stubborn* (University of Illinois Press) by Roland Flint was selected by Dave Smith. The title poem narrates how the poet finds a small boy in the street and how returning him to his searching parents stirs up some painful connections: "I don't want to say more, and I'm afraid I'll start crying / but I have to, to make it clearer: / I tell him my son was killed in the street like this." Flint's language rarely rises above the level of competent prose, but he possesses abundant emotional force. Tom Andrews's *The Brother's Country* (Persea Books) was selected by Charles Wright. The book, which consists of experimental work of the dreariest sort, concludes with "A Language of Hemophilia," a meditation on the fear of AIDS. These deathless lines are typical: "Clotting time—40 minutes (normal 5 to 10 minutes) / Clotting retraction—good / Prothrombin consumption—15.5 seconds (normal over 20 seconds)." And so on. One shudders at the thought of being trapped in a stuffy lecture hall and having to listen to Andrews read from this collection—the Poetry Reading from Hell. The year's other winners were *Terra Firma* (Copper Canyon Press) by Thomas Centolella, selected by Denise Levertov; *Blessings in Disguise* (E. P. Dutton) by David Clewell, selected by Quincy Troupe; and *Artist and Model* (Atlantic Monthly Press) by Carol Snow, selected by Robert Hass. None of these books was received for review.

Three other prizewinners are *Refuge* (University of Pittsburgh Press) by Belle Waring and *Second Wind* (Texas Tech University Press) by Davis Graham, both winners of the AWP Award Series in Poetry, and *Level Green* (University of Wisconsin Press) by Judith Vollmer, winner of the Brittingham Prize in Poetry. Waring is lively and displays a good ear for the street; Graham alludes to jazz and writes several poems on music with titles beginning with "planxty," a term I am not familiar with; Vollmer covers the pop culture landscape with references to "the greatest woman rock guitarist in the world" and the death of John Belushi. All three collections have work of some merit.

Chapbooks allow established poets to release new material between collections and give many newcomers their first exposure. In the former category I should mention *Some Atrocities*

(Bits Press) by former Poet Laureate Richard Wilbur, a collection of puns that would have curled the hair of Louis Untermeyer. X. J. Kennedy's *Distant Thunder* (Robert L. Barth) contains miscellaneous new poems by another contemporary master of form and wit. Barth, whose chapbook series survives despite my premature obituary last year, also released collections by Jeffrey Akard and Dick David, both English, and an anthology in honor of Charles Gullans's sixtieth birthday, edited by Timothy Steele. Bruce Bennett's *The Garden & Other Abridged Versions* (Bellflower Press) contains four-line "digests" of well-known poems such as "Xanadu." Lewis Turco's *A Family Album* (Silverfish Review) recently won a chapbook prize from *Poet* magazine. Craig Watson's *Unsuspended Animation*, Spencer Selby's *Barricade*, and Jena Osman's *Underwater Dive* continue Paradigm Press's longstanding tradition of publishing highly experimental work which often combines graphics with poetry. Thomas Carper's *Musicians* (Aralia Press) is a selection of skillful sonnets on musical themes. Evelyn Corry Appelbee's and Violette Newton's *Letters from Two Women* (Harp & Quill Press) is a touching exchange between two longtime friends on aging and widowhood. Suzanne Rhodenbaugh's *A Gold Rain at Lonelyfarm* (Heatherstone Press) showcases work by a talented poet who has recently appeared in the *Hudson Review* and the *New England Review*. Gary Fincke's *Handing the Self Back* (GreenTower Press) collects new selections from a poet whom David Citino calls "one of American poetry's best-kept secrets." All of these collections provide delightful examples of the diversity of the printer's and book designer's craft.

Having come to the end of another year's survey, I find that "I am overtired / Of the great harvest I myself desired." Yet I would be remiss if I did not note the arrival of several prose works of more than passing interest to poets and readers. *Missing Measures* (University of Arkansas Press) is a history of modern poetry's revolt against meter by Timothy Steele, one of the most dexterous of all contemporary metricists. By the very nature of its subject, the book is highly speculative, since it attempts to account for the reasons why this century, and no earlier one, has made free verse the norm rather than the exception. Steele's responsible scholarship, which displays wide acquaintance with authorities ancient and modern, is impressive, particularly in his historical accounts of the experimentalism of the first generation of modernists, and lends considerable weight to his conclusions. *Poetry After Modernism* (Story Line Press) is edited by Robert McDowell and provides essays on just about every aspect of today's poetry, from feminism and race to poetry's relationship to politics and business. It is a mixed collection, with particularly good contributions by Dana Gioia, Frederick Pollack, and Bruce Bawer. This book is a good companion volume to last year's *Expansive Poetry*, from the same publisher, a collection of essays on the new formalism and new narrative in contemporary poetry. Robert DeMaria's *The College Handbook of Creative Writing* (Harcourt Brace Jovanovich) is geared mainly to fiction writers but does contain a section on poetic meter and form that may be useful to beginning creative-writing classes. *Directory of Poetry Publishers* (Dustbooks), edited by Len Fulton, is the sixth edition of that reference book, which will invite comparison with Judson Jerome's *Poet's Market* (Writer's Digest Books), now also in its sixth edition. Jerome's book is somewhat easier to use and con-

tains appendices giving advice to fledgling poets; Fulton's volume is more utilitarian in look but seems slightly more detailed in the individual entries. One plus is that Fulton includes a list, formed on the basis of responses from over six thousand editors, of the ten poets most often mentioned as having been published recently. It should come as no surprise that Lin Lifshin leads her nearest competitors, William Stafford and Charles Bukowski, by a wide margin. Fulton makes an offer that will appeal to the vanity of many poets who read his volume: "If you would like a count for any given poet write to me and I will be happy to provide it."

As long as vanity is the closing topic, I should mention that a chapbook-length section of my own poems, *Body Bags*, appeared in *Texas Poets in Concert: A Quartet* (University of North Texas Press), which also includes substantial selections of new work by Jan Epton Seale, Naomi Shihab Nye, and William Virgil Davis.

The Year in Drama

Howard Kissel
New York Daily News

Normally a survey of the year in drama focuses on texts, on the assumption that the history of the theater is essentially a history of texts. We do not know much about street entertainers in ancient Athens. We do know about the plays of Sophocles. We have scanty information about the bear-baiting pits in Elizabethan London, which competed for business with such enterprises as the Globe Theater. We do know about what was presented in the Globe.

In trying to understand why theater texts are becoming of increasingly little interest, it is perhaps useful to look at the competition, the contemporary equivalent of bearbaiting. Nowadays this means not simply television or the movies, which attract considerably greater attention and audiences than the stage, but also the "alternative" theater, which for some time has rebelled against what it perceives as the tyranny of the word.

A useful illustration of the "alternative" theater, which prides itself on its daring and iconoclasm, was the production of Shakespeare's "King Lear" by the venerable Mabou Mines company, a mainstay of the Off-Off Broadway movement for more than twenty years.

In Lee Breuer's production, the play's title was abbreviated to *Lear* and all its genders reversed. Set in the American South during the 1950s, *Lear* became the saga of the matriarch of a white trash family, two of whose sons abuse her after she divides her estate between them. The gender reversal illuminated nothing. The cruel torture of an aging knight like Gloucester is shocking. When, however, Gloucester is a feeble old black lady, as she is here, her mauling by Lear's shiftless sons is not just an affront to chivalry. It is also gratuitous, sick, and ultimately meaningless.

Nor did setting the play in a more recent time clarify any of the issues Shakespeare raises. Authority in the rural South, after all, whether matriarchal or patriarchal, has nothing to do with Shakespeare's monarchical or theological concerns. (The concept wasn't even true to itself—in Lee Breuer's Georgia of the 1950s blacks and

Program cover for the Lincoln Center Theater production of John Guare's play about racial guilt and manipulation

poor whites are bosom friends. Moreover it doesn't make much sense to have the Fool played as a drag queen since there probably weren't a lot of them in rural Georgia in the Eisenhower years.)

Reducing the mythic, poetic scale of Shakespeare to crude naturalism trivialized the play. The visual effects compounded the trivialization. Lear and her sons drive around in miniature, flashy cars from the Age of the Tailfin, giving the play a Disney aura.

Though such theater presents itself as a counterbalance to the commercial theater, it is instructive to see how it is financed. The commercial theater, of course, in its vulgarity, supports itself through ticket sales. The noncommercial theater, like Mabou Mines, finances itself through corporate subsidies, from such apparently noncommercial entities as the AT & T Foundation, Philip Morris, the Readers Digest/Wallace Funds, and the Rockefeller Foundation. *Lear* was also funded by the National Endowment for the Arts as well as the arts councils of the states of New York and Massachusetts.

One of the things that made *Lear* attractive to corporate sponsors was that it was "politically correct." That it questioned the nature of gender, for example, made it a statement of consequences—at least among the funders—regardless of whether it yielded any answers (and, of course, regardless of whether it shed any light on the Shakespeare play). Thus Mabou Mines, by accepting money from cigarette manufacturers or the publishers of Reader's Digest, grants these enterprises cultural cachet, not to mention a certain measure of absolution from the politically incorrect ways in which they have amassed their wealth.

The comic socio-economic backdrop of this dramatically inept *Lear* suggests a culture in comic disarray. Happily there is some evidence that the theater—of all things, the commercial theater—is cognizant of this sort of cultural dislocation.

The most deservedly praised of the plays that opened in 1990 was John Guare's *Six Degrees of Separation*, which was presented by the Theater of Lincoln Center. Guare's play was based on an actual incident in which a young black man insinuated his way into the homes of several wealthy, prominent New Yorkers (one of them being Osborne Elliot, the former editor of *Newsweek*), not for anything as base or old-fashioned as stealing their silverware, but rather for the odd pleasure of participating in their lives.

The title refers to the theory that any two people on this planet can be linked by six others. In this case, Paul, a young man from the lower rungs of society, wills his way onto the higher rungs, playing on both the guilt and the sense of emptiness of his social "superiors." The fact that he is black—but well-spoken and seemingly of good family—makes them eager to help him. They can extend the hand of liberal generosity without fear of getting mussed up in the process.

Paul pretends to be a school friend of their children. In the case of the couple with whom he becomes most closely involved—an art dealer and his wife, Flanders and Louisa, known to their friends as Flan and Ouisa—Paul tells them he has just been mugged in Central Park and has come to their Fifth Avenue apartment because he knows, from everything their children have told him, they would take him in. Moreover, he tells them he is the son of Sidney Poitier, who will arrive in New York the next day to begin directing a film of the musical *Cats*. Paul speaks quite elegantly of the contemporary impoverishment of the imagination, but he has taken the measure of his hosts: he knows that their own imaginations are stimulated by the possibility of getting bit parts in *Cats*.

The speech about the imagination is the most dazzling sequence in the play. It begins with Paul's acute analysis of the dangerous implications of the book all his friends adore—J. D. Salinger's *Catcher in the Rye* (1951). He asserts that the book "mirrors like a fun house mirror and amplifies like a distorted speaker one of the great tragedies of our times—the death of the imagination. . . . The imagination has been so debased that imagination—being imaginative—rather than being the lynchpin of our existence now stands as a synonym for something outside ourselves like science fiction or some new use for tangerine slices on raw pork chops—what an imaginative summer recipe—and *Star Wars!* So imaginative! And *Star Trek*—so imaginative! . . .

Why has imagination become a synonym for style? I believe that the imagination is the passport we create to take us into the real world . . . To face ourselves. That's the hard thing. The imagination. That's God's gift to make the act of self-examination bearable."

In fact Paul is a hustler. He has gained information about the families he "invades" from a young man who desperately wants his sexual services. The young man tutors him on how to speak, how to behave. We later learn that the speech on Salinger was a commencement address at Groton a few years earlier. It doesn't matter if Paul learned it from his mentor. He has appropriated it. He believes it. He is clearly using his imagination, his hustling skills to create a new identity for himself, even to help his benefactors create more interesting identities for themselves.

In a sense *Six Degrees* is an update on some of the ideas Tom Wolfe advanced in "Radical Chic" twenty years ago. Writing about the party

Program cover for the Playwrights Horizons production of Martin Sherman's play about Isadora Duncan

Leonard and Felicia Bernstein threw to introduce *le tout New York* to the Black Panthers, Wolfe noted that among wealthy liberals, dwelling in a world of unreal luxury, there was a deep yearning for the grubby, real world of their forebears. This yearning stemmed partly from feelings of guilt about their money. In Guare's play the guilt takes odd, self-destructive forms, as when a white South African declares, "One has to stay there to educate the black workers, and we'll know we've been successful when they kill us."

One of the amusing things about Guare's wealthy characters is that they have conveyed to their children how intensely they are disgusted with themselves. Their children despise them, and articulate their scorn frequently, vehemently and hilariously. Paul, on the other hand, genuinely seems to enjoy the company of Flan and Ouisa, or at least that of Ouisa, the only character who can take time out from self-involvement to exhibit concern for him.

By sharing his ideas with Flan and Ouisa and their friends, Paul assuages their guilt almost as effectively as the Panthers did by accepting the Bernsteins's canapes.

At one point, in an earnest conversation with Ouisa, Paul reminds her that Donald Barthelme declared collage "the art form of the twentieth century." The play itself is an artful narrative that resembles collage since Paul, in the constant exercise of his hustling skills and his imaginative powers, draws seemingly disparate people into the composition. Every scene, every character captures the bizarre, self-destructive mood of New York today.

Most impressive, Guare has transformed a jumble of confused, frenetic voices into a kind of music. The children's whining, their parents' calculated archness, Paul's chameleonlike responses to their moods and needs—Guare shapes these voices so precisely that the play has the irresistible momentum of musical theater. In a stunning production directed by Jerry Zaks—with a particularly arresting performance by Stockard Channing as Ouisa—the play transcends social satire to become something Paul might admire, a celebration of the human imagination.

Peter Shaffer's *Lettice and Lovage* constituted a similar celebration. The play, written in 1987 as a vehicle for Maggie Smith, finally made its way across the Atlantic with its great star this year. On the surface Shaffer's play seemed slight, more than a little contrived. Conceivably, with a lesser actress in the lead role, its artifices would outweigh its virtues. But with Smith, the play seemed a veritable feast of the actor's art.

Smith played Lettice Douffet, a tour guide assigned to the most boring castle in England. Lettice, she tells us, is drawn from Laetitia, the Latin word for gladness. ("As a vegetable it is obviously one of God's mistakes—but as a name it passes, I think.") Lovage, we learn, is an herb, its name drawn from "love" and "ache," which was the medieval name for parsley. Lovage is one of the ingredients in quaff, a medieval drink Lettice prepares, which also contains mead, vodka, and sugar. As her name and her obsession with the past suggest, Lettice is of unusual parentage. Her father was a Free French soldier quartered in London during the war. He married her mother and, shortly after siring Lettice, abandoned her. A resourceful woman, Lettice's mother founded an all-girl troupe which performed Shakespeare in French throughout rural France. Mama's motto was "Enlarge! Enliven! Enlighten!"

Lettice puts this motto into practice in her work as a tour guide at Fustian House, the dullest of the stately homes of England. We see her give her tour of Fustian House, first giving no more than the meager facts that constitute its actual story. Then, with each successive tour, she embroiders its history, turning a black and white documentary into an MGM Technicolor musical. For this she is fired. But we soon find that her superior, who first seems so severe, shares Lettice's sense of the drabness of modern England: "I cannot accept *merely*," Douffet declares. "We live in a country now that wants only the *mere*."

The supervisor, Lotte Schoen, is the daughter of a German refugee who never ceased mourning the death of his native Dresden, destroyed by Allied bombs. She says of her father, "He believed anybody born after 1940 has no real idea what visual civilization means—and never can have. 'There used to be such a thing as the Communal eye,' he'd say. 'It has been put out in our lifetime . . . The disgusting world we live in now could simply not have been built when that eye was open. The planners would have been torn limb from limb—not given knighthoods.'"

Lotte herself says she is an idolator: "If I could save a great Baroque city or its people I would choose the city every time. People come again: cities never."

Out of this shared obsession with the past they forge a friendship, then a plan to waken their fellow citizens to the dreariness of the architecture around them (using methods, however, that might not gain them the patronage of their fellow architecture critic, Prince Charles). One of the remarks Shaffer gives Lotte resembles the thinking of Paul in Guare's play. Looking at the Shell Building, a banal skyscraper that went up in London in the early 1960s, Lotte declares, "The people who put this up should be hanged in public for debauching the public imagination."

A tour de force for Maggie Smith and Margaret Tyzack, *Lettice and Lovage* is a more solid edifice than it first appears. The delights of Shaffer's conceits, of course, were magnified by the performances.

Yet another celebration of the imagination enjoyed a brief run at Playwrights Horizons. It was *When She Danced*, by the American Martin Sherman, best known as the author of "Bent." Sherman lives and works in England, where *When She Danced* had two productions, one in Guildford in 1985 starring Pauline Collins as Isadora Duncan, another in London in 1988, di-

Program cover for the Walter Kerr Theatre production of August Wilson's 1990 Pulitzer Prize-winning play

rected by Tim Luscombe, who directed the limited New York engagement, which featured Elizabeth Ashley as Isadora.

When She Danced is set in 1923, when Isadora, broke, has set herself up in a house in Paris with her husband, Gergei Yessenine, the Russian poet. Their entourage includes a delicate Jewish refugee from Bolshevik Russia, who translates for the fractious couple, neither of whom speaks the other's language. They are also visited by a young Greek pianist, a prodigy named for Isadora because his mother was so profoundly moved by seeing her perform shortly before he was born.

Throughout the play the characters try to explain the phenomenon of what it was to see Isadora dance. The interpreter, heartbreakingly played by Marcia-Jean Kurtz, comes closest, but even she cannot account for what Isadora did to her: "I do not know exactly *what* it was—I think perhaps she simply walked from one side of the stage to another—and then it was hard for me to see, because my eyes were burning—that is what happens when I cry—but I do not know why I was crying. I thought I saw children dancing, but there were no children. I thought I saw the face of my mother as she lay dying. I thought I remembered the rabbi's words. I thought I was kissing my child before they took him away from me . . . and all she was doing on the stage was walking, just a few steps up, a few steps down, but this walk of hers, it was like a comet shooting through my body—and then, suddenly, she stopped—and that was it—it was over. . . ."

At the end of the play the young Greek recalls asking his mother on her deathbed what it was like to see Isadora dance. "Tell me, Mama. My mother smile. She is remembering. And she look at me. And she take my hand. And she press my hand. And she kiss my hand. And she say, 'O youmou'—'Oh, my son.' 'Then mboro na to exiyi so'—'I can not explain.' " As he spoke the words Robert Sean Leonard, as the pianist, smiled in a way that suggested the comic dimension in our continuing quest for the "meaning" of art.

Much of what Isadora herself says is silly, but some of it is deeply poetic, as when she says of her violent lover, "Sergei Alexandrovich is a disaster in the real world, but a creature of infinite beauty in the only world, the *only* world worth living in—the imagination."

Sherman creates a Chekhovian sense of absurdity in his portrait of Isadora and her circle, impoverished, living on ideas, fantasies, and money borrowed from useful if uninspiring bourgeois patrons. The constant explosions between Isadora and her husband; the poignant interjections of the interpreter, who seems the very essence of the displaced person; and the innocent, wondering exclamations of the pianist—farce and sadness are carefully ground lenses through which one can put into perspective, if only fitfully, the beauty and mystery of art.

Steve Tesich treated the perils of the imagination in *Square One*, a quirky, poignant comedy set in a totalitarian country. Even the fall of the Berlin wall, which preceded the production by only a few months, did not make the play seem "dated." For its portrayal of love and egos in a bureaucratic regime had a sense of irony with universal reverberations.

A young woman named Dianne is picked up by a swaggering fellow named Adam, who is a little miffed that she does not recognize him. He is, after all, a television star, appearing on the prime time Patriotic Variety House. He is a "state artist third class," she reads on his identity card. He tells her, with some pride, "I've been certified as a General Entertainer with a speciality in singing," to which she exclaims, "A performance artist!"

She assures him he will rise some day. "Do you know how hard it is to become a second class artist?" he asks her. She senses he has what it takes: "I don't know if I have any faith in you at all, but I do know where you belong. Second class." The play, which describes their tense, brief marriage and his rise to second class artist, is full of this melancholy, painful kind of humor.

What makes the play more than an acutely observed study of the bleak perspectives Marxism imposed on the already Kafka-esque sensibilities of Eastern Europe is its understanding of how desperate modern people are to dramatize themselves, which gives the play validity despite the fall of the Soviet world. As Adam declares, "Everybody thinks they can be an entertainer these days . . . . To be an entertainer these days, a state certified entertainer, a licensed professional, to have that be my bread and butter is to compete in a world that's laughing at its own material. So don't tell me about terror."

There are constant references to elderly people screaming. They are horrified at the way the state operates. "The old ones tend to scream," Adam explains. "They probably remember the bad old days before Reconstruction. Once they're gone, once that generation is gone, there'll be no more screaming. I believe in progress." It is Dianne's elderly relatives, in fact, that keep her from watching the Patriotic Variety Hour: "They think the show's a nightmare they're having and they start to scream, trying to wake themselves up, only they can't."

Late in the play Dianne has a particularly chilling vision: "Jesus Christ returns to earth. For whatever reason, call it faulty navigation, he makes a big mistake and lands on a continent inhabited by cannibals. Religious cannibals. Christian cannibals. And in their fervor they proceed to eat His flesh and drink His blood and poof . . . He's all gone. All I'm saying is this: You wouldn't call that a Holy communion. Nor would you call them insincere."

Tesich incorporated such bleak assessments into an oddly cool, yet genuinely dramatic narrative about the vicissitudes of the young couple.

Wendy Makkena, Joan Copeland, and D. W. Moffett in a scene from the Manhattan Theatre Club production of Richard Greenberg's The American Plan

Square One describes a system in which one's options decrease even when one's horizons seem to be expanding, which may be true even outside the Eastern bloc. In *Square One* the whimsicality, freshness, and pathos one frequently encounters in Tesich's plays attain and sustain a lofty level quite unexpected from his earlier works. The play was superbly performed by Dianne Wiest and Richard Thomas, directed by Jerry Zaks, whose gifts for bizarre comedy were revealed both by this and by Guare's play.

The Pulitzer Prize for 1990 and the New York Drama Critics Circle Award for Best Play were given to August Wilson's *The Piano Lesson*. Part of his decade by decade depiction of black life in America, *Piano Lesson* is set during the Great Depression. It concerns a family quarrel between a brother and sister, Boy Willie and Berniece, over whether to sell a piano their great-grandfather carved into a piece of sculpture during slavery days. In his carvings he expressed his love for his wife, who had been bartered for the piano.

The instrument's history reflects the family's tortured history. For this reason Berniece does not want to sell it, even though she never plays it any more. Boy Willie (whom she calls "nothin' but a whole lotta mouth") sees the piano not as a monument to the past but as a way to alter the future, to redeem historic suffering. If he sells the piano he can use his share of the profits to buy some land on which their grandparents worked in bondage. (I am not well enough acquainted with Southern social history to know if the poor whites descended from the slave-owning family would have been quite so eager to sell their land to the descendants of their former property.)

Throughout the long play Boy Willie's and Berniece's positions are reiterated but not really developed. Ultimately we learn more about the piano than we do about the two siblings fighting over it. The play is full of enchanting interludes—a little romance between Lymon, Boy Willie's sidekick, and a beautiful young woman he meets up North; an elegant speech by his uncle, a former railroad conductor, poeticizing the stops the train makes as it goes through Mississippi; a vaudevillian scene in which Lymon is sold a chartreuse suit.

But when all is said and done there must be some resolution of the argument between brother and sister, and here the play falters. Wilson does not want to leave either of them disappointed. So he introduces an element of the supernatural, which leaves the ending quite unsatisfactory. As in *Joe Turner's Come and Gone*, Wilson wants to incorporate black mysticism into an otherwise realistic and sometimes poetic style. The attempt seems valid and potentially important, but so far the results have been disappointing.

Charles S. Dutton, who has appeared in several of Wilson's plays, could not have made Boy Willie more charming, and S. Epatha Merkerson had great dignity as Berniece. Rocky Carroll made a vivid impression as Lymon, and Carl Gordon captured the elegiac quality of the conductor's evocation of the railroad traversing Mississippi. The overall impression the play made was musical, but, as has often happened in Wilson's plays, the ending seemed a way of avoiding the genuine pain that underlies American black life.

One of the surprises of 1990 was that rarest of plays, an American comedy of manners. Several decades ago S. N. Behrman observed that "there are no drawing rooms in America. There are living rooms, parlors, dens, romp rooms, snuggeries but no drawing rooms. For the matter of fact, there are very few manners left either...."

Richard Nelson, a playwright whose work has often been of a cerebral, deliberately difficult sort, has had the wit to recognize that if Americans lack drawing rooms in which to jockey for social position, they abandon any pretense of equality and exhibit all their latent snobbism when they go to Europe.

In *Some Americans Abroad*, he focuses on a class especially prone to such jockeying— academics. His play is a witty, painfully accurate study of the pathetic triumphs intellectuals score against one another during an arduous course of playgoing in London and Stratford. Nelson captures the pettiness, the cruelty, the deviousness of academic politics superbly. Even the placement of trays on a small cafeteria table has its drama, though the main contest focuses on a more important issue, the denial of tenure to a man who, despite his intelligence, good will, and his skills as a teacher, had the bad taste to graduate from the "wrong" school and thus cannot hope for advancement.

Among the valuable imports from London was Andrew Davies's *Prin*, another look at the claustrophobic world of academia, this time a British private school presided over by the domineering title character, admirably played by Eileen Atkins. "Why should anyone of intelligence pursue a career in education?" Prin asks.

Prin prides herself on having been a leftist intellectual at Oxford, but there is a poignant irony in the fact that her subsequent revolutionary activities have been confined to some reforms in the teaching of movement in physical education. Her elitism seems increasingly pathetic in view of our growing awareness of the mess she has made of her own life. Her constant harping on "the extraordinary" seems little more than a relentless, ugly snobbishness. She is also a lesbian and regards her students in a frankly sexual way that also undermines her hoity-toity manner. What makes *Prin* more than an unsettling character study is our sense that from time to time—as when she inveighs against "a nation that expresses its feelings about the future through a falling birthrate and newspaper Bingo"—Prin does understand what is happening both in her disintegrating personal life and in contemporary England.

A curious import from London was the work of one of the major British playwrights seldom heard from in the last decade, David Storey. His earlier plays, like *Home*, *The Contractor*, and *The Changing Room* suggested he was as powerful

a playwright as Pinter and Osborne, but in recent years he has not written for the theater at all, concentrating instead on fiction. *The March on Russia*, like another early play, *Celebration*, is a rueful look at a family reunion. The parents whose sixtieth anniversary is being celebrated have settled into a routine of backbiting and bickering that seems like a ritual the celebrants practice without much emotional commitment. The arrival of their grown-up children, however, somehow gives new vitality to their ancient animosities.

The children have their own problems, especially their son, a successful author who finds himself subject to unaccountable mental paralysis. Storey projects the rhythms of family reunions, their tensions, the burdens of what people are willing to voice and of all they leave unexpressed. The play does not seem as assured as Storey's earlier work, but his is a talent always refreshing to encounter.

William Nicholson's *Shadowlands* is a tepid account of the relationship between the British writer and scholar C. S. Lewis and the American poet Joy Davidman. The two met when he was in his mid fifties, a lifelong bachelor who lived with his older brother, leading a scholarly, eccentric, apparently sexually neutral life. She had written him fan letters from New York before she met him. She and her younger son moved to Oxford during the 1950s to be near him. He, however, seems to have regarded her mainly as a friend, though he married her secretly in a civil ceremony to grant her British citizenship. A few years later, when she develops terminal cancer, they have a proper religious ceremony in the hospital. Only when she dies does he understand the depth of his love for her.

Occasionally Lewis makes trenchant comments about his situation. "It's all love and sex these days," he observes at one point. "Friendship is almost as quaint and outdated as chastity." You sense that Nicholson has been very careful about the words he puts in Lewis's mouth, and that much of it has probably been culled from Lewis's own writing. Nicholson originally wrote *Shadowlands* for British television, and the stage version seems a padding of the teleplay. Despite the literary personages it treats, despite the many interesting questions their relationship raises, the play never has the size or power of theater.

New York's debt to London is so great that even a dramatization of John Steinbeck's *The Grapes of Wrath* came from London, though the play originated in Chicago. It was a venture of the celebrated Steppenwolf Company, under the direction of Frank Galati. Originally presented in Chicago in 1988, it was produced later that year in Los Angeles; then, in summer 1989, it created a sensation in London, where it was deemed commercial enough to be brought to New York, where it won the 1990 Tony for Best Play.

Although the play condensed the sprawling novel intelligently, the performance by the Steppenwolf Company rarely, at least in this minority view, had the scope or passion of the novel (or even the memorable film). Also it relied on stage gimmickry—actual fires, actual rain, a pool deep enough for a naked young man to jump into—more than so earnest a story ought to.

A modest but satisfying play was Douglas Scott's *Mountain*, a portrait of Supreme Court Justice William O. Douglas. Scott's attempts to understand Douglas's complicated life occasionally made the play unnecessarily simplistic, but since much of the dialogue was from Douglas's own writing, the evening was one of uncommon eloquence and passion. As Douglas, Len Cariou gave a masterly performance, lunging into the character with the same gusto with which Douglas tackled his own life.

Richard Greenberg, whose "Eastern Standard" created some interest a seasons ago, produced a more solid play in *The American Plan*. Though it showed a greater understanding of character than *Eastern Standard*, this play also made clear Greenberg's limitations, his predilection for making statements over exploring characters and situations.

The title implies a criticism of American life, a suggestion that it is necessarily a constricting, blighting experience. In order to justify the title most of the action is set in the Catskills, near a resort that might offer the American Plan. The focal character, however, is a young woman whose mother is a German Jewish matron, whom others have nicknamed The Czarina, a woman whose snobbishness is so intense she would never, never build a country house—as Greenberg has her do—near a vulgar Jewish resort. (But without the nearby resort, there goes the title.)

Her daughter is courted by a young WASP who has come to the resort with another Jewish girl. (Since the play is set in 1960, a period when social classes were more rigidly defined that they are now, his presence near the vulgar Jewish resort is even more inexplicable than The Czari-

na's.) We soon learn, however, that he is gay and that he has been followed to the Catskills by his former lover. Eventually he settles with neither the wealthy Czarina's daughter nor the young man who still desires him. The reason for his denying himself either of these choices is unclear, just as we feel unsatisfied by his decision to become a high school math teacher in the Midwest. All this seems designed by Greenberg to justify his ironic title. It's as if he worked backward, fitting his characters into preconceived molds rather than letting them develop on their own, which is an unfair to his own talent as it is to American life.

Whatever its faults, the play was beautifully acted, especially by Joan Copeland as the Czarina. Asked if she would like demitasse coffee, she refuses because the proper spoons were left behind in Germany. "How can you have demitasse when the spoons are elsewhere?" she asks, in her elegant accent and weary tone, making it sound like Rilke as he might have been translated by Eliot.

Craig Lucas, one of the most heralded of the younger playwrights (for such works as *Reckless* and *Blue Window*) wrote a sort of Yuppie fairy tale, *Prelude to a Kiss*. In it an old man who attends the wedding of a young couple, gives the bride an intense kiss during which, we learn late in the second act, he has managed to switch bodies with her. How he has achieved this is never explained, but we do learn why. He is terminally ill and wanted to reexperience the joys of health and youth. (That he apparently also wanted to experience the life of the opposite sex is not examined.)

In the hands of James M. Barrie, such a play might have been amusing, even moving. In the hands of Lucas, it is haphazard and merely baffling. Thinking back over the play, for example, you realize that all the old man did with his regained youth was to behave boorishly and buy himself a vulgar, expensive bracelet. Does the play thus reduce itself to a statement about the power of materialism? If so it is as much a missed opportunity as the old man's fling at renewed youth.

The style of the play varies with virtually every scene. The courtship of the young couple has a hip, absurdist tone. A scene with the young woman's parents is a most conventional satire of bourgeois life. On top of its inconsistencies, the play has a repellent glibness, as when the old man defines luck as not being born "in Calcutta, Colombia, or the U.S. without money."

Aaron Sorkin, whose gifts for banter and structure were ably demonstrated in his 1989 *A Few Good Men*, was represented by *Making Movies*, an unsuccessful attempt to satirize the Hollywood mentality. *A Few Good Men* seemed a stronger play as its cast changed—by the end of its run, when the roles originally played by Thomas Hulce and Stephen Lang had been assumed by Bradley Whitford and Perry King, it was no longer a confrontation between a virtuous young attorney and an evil, egotistical, fundamentalist commanding officer, but rather an uneasy examination of the unhappy consequences of blind obedience to a code, even if the code is honorable.

More experienced authors than Sorkin also turned out work of less interest than usual. Jules Feiffer's *Elliot Loves* began with a stunning monologue that established a tone of wit, irony, and wry melancholy. Elliot, superbly played by Anthony Heald, tells us about the woman he loves, his first lucky break in a lifetime of amorous and sexual confusion. We see at once that he has peculiar notions. "The distance between what I need and what I'm getting—is love," he says. He also confides that "sex without guilt is garbage—it has no moral dimension." Alas, the play that followed rarely fulfilled the promise of this witty speech.

Similarly Beth Henley, trying to go beyond the bizarre small town domestic comedies for which she is best known (*Crimes of the Heart, The Miss Firecracker Contest*), wrote a piece about women on the frontier, *Abundance*, which had no depth. Another historical exercise that lacked historical understanding was *Burner's Frolic*, by Charles Fuller, the author of *A Soldier's Play*. *Burner's Frolic* is part of an ongoing series of plays about blacks in the wake of the Civil War, but it shows a distressing lack of complexity about the issues that confronted both races. Nor do Fuller's characters or situations have enough interest of their own to sustain a play.

Michael Weller, best known for his low-key studies of contemporary young people, from *Moonchildren* to *Loose Ends*, ventured into more poetic territory with *Lake No Bottom*, which concerned a confrontation between a wealthy critic and a talented young novelist whose career he has helped. Weller occasionally gives his characters some witty self-understanding, as when the critic says, "I'm rich and a critic, a man who knows from two directions what it means to be useless," but much of the play seems to strive unsuccessfully for grand gestures and achieves only

rhetoric, though Weller has created a grandly theatrical "duel" in the second act.

John Patrick Shanley, the author of the film *Moonstruck* and numerous works for the stage, attempted a comedy of ideas in *The Big Funk*, which was theoretically about the decline in the level of public discourse. The play was an excellent illustration of the situation it bemoaned. None of the rhetoric about moral decay was convincing. The only memorable part of the play is a scene where one man slathers Vaseline all over the face and hair of a young woman and another man takes her home, gives her a bath, then dusts off her naked body with an oversize powder puff.

The number of stupid plays presented by reputable institutions increased in 1990. Circle Rep, for example, did *Imagining Brad*, a play in which a young woman speaks glowingly of her husband, a mute with neither arms nor legs, who lies, vegetablelike, in a baby crib—what makes him the ideal husband is that he cannot abuse her. WPA did *Twenty Fingers, Twenty Toes*, a musical about Siamese twins in vaudeville.

A great disappointment was the first New York production of a 1926 play by the Soviet satirist Mikhail Bulgakov, *Zoya's Apartment*, a wonderfully comic portrait of life in Moscow just after the Civil War. But the production by Circle in the Square, directed by a Soviet whose understanding of his own history seemed slim, bungled the play completely. There are, for example, frequent references to the color of shoes the KGB men wear in the play's somber final sequence. This relates to the fact that in the early Soviet period you could always tell foreigners in Moscow by the quality of their shoes. The natives wore cheap, unsubstantial shoes of a hideous orange color. In this production the shoes were painted a trendy yellow, as if this were a bizarre fairy tale, which made no sense.

Lastly we come full circle to the Mabou Mines company, which, in addition to the horrendous *Lear* mentioned earlier, revived *Through the Leaves*, by the prominent young German playwright Franz Xavier Kroetz. This seventy-minute piece studies the relationship between a charmless, dumpy, middle-aged woman who runs a butcher shop and her equally charmless, callous, bullying middle-aged lover.

Their lives are entirely joyless. Neither is capable of anything resembling intimacy, and their life together seems little more than the result of a sense of obligation to simulate companionship.

Even their sex, of which we see more than at least I wanted to, is essentially lifeless, a mechanical necessity that must be gotten through.

Throughout these grim proceedings the butcheress makes jottings in her diary, such as, "If I *was* good-looking, I wouldn't be as independent as I am." We are to take this portrait of these petit bourgeois lives as symptomatic of all modern relationships—arid, manipulative, insensitive. But it seems easier to accept this bleak relationship as symbolic of the smugness and contempt of the author and his hip audience toward working-class people.

Though there were a handful of plays aware that the theater needs to set its imaginative sights beyond the barren terrain of the popular culture, much of the theater New York saw in 1990 was firmly, proudly entrenched on that barren terrain, unaware it should attempt to soar above it.

The Year in Literary Biography

Mark A. Heberle
University of Hawaii at Manoa

Life writing in 1990 was marked by a movement away from standard biographies of canonical male literary masters toward a wide variety of group biographies, autobiographical testimonies, and works dealing with women authors as well as nonfiction writers who might have been considered nonliterary ten or twenty years ago. This relative slighting of conventionally significant figures follows naturally from the academic need to publish on previously neglected subjects, but it may also reflect general changes within the profession of literature over the last decade. These changes include the discovery and celebration of alternative literary voices, the breakdown and dispersal of the traditional literary canon, and the redefinition of literature as rhetorically significant discourse, often within a particular cultural and historical context, and not simply as "great" poems, plays, and novels.

Judged by this year's titles, the history of English literature is becoming more contemporary, and less English. The last three years have seen new lives of Geoffrey Chaucer, Ben Jonson, William Shakespeare, William Davenant, John Dryden, Daniel Defoe, Edward Gibbon, and William Wordsworth; except for Henry Fielding, however, all the subjects of literary biographies initially published in 1990 are post-Romantics, and the great majority are mid-twentieth-century writers. For the first time ever, perhaps, more books were published on American than English writers—even when "English" is loosely enough defined to include Irish and Scottish men and women as well as third world authors who write in English. The first full biographies of half a dozen major American and English modernist poets may be symptomatic of the ending of an old literary order—or the beginning of a new. In a lesser way, life writing concerning foreign authors reflects these trends as well. Though several works extend the canonization of continental giants to an English-speaking readership, this year's publications also include studies and memoirs of lesser known third world writers and a meticulous biography of the founding mother of French feminism.

Of course, the old giants are still worth exploring, as Martin and Ruthe Battestin's *Henry Fielding: A Life* (Routledge) attests. The product of fifteen years of exhaustive research by the authors, it gives us the first detailed, reliable life of the previously shadowy novelist and magistrate. Richard Holmes has added splendidly to his previous excursions into Romantic biography with *Coleridge: Early Visions* (Viking), the first of two volumes on the Romantic poet and theorist; and Katherine Frank has produced *A Chainless Soul: A Life of Emily Brontë* (Houghton Mifflin), the

*Dust jacket for the English edition of the first volume of
Holmes's life of the Romantic poet and critic*

first full-length life of Emily Brontë in twenty
years, one that finds in anorexia nervosa a key to
the writer's creative genius and pathology. Victorian masters are represented by Ina Taylor's *A
Woman of Contradictions: The Life of George Eliot*
(Morrow), Wolfgang Kemp's *The Desire of My
Eyes: The Life and Work of John Ruskin* (Farrar,
Straus & Giroux; translated from the German),
and Frederick Kirchhoff 's *William Morris: The Construction of a Male Self, 1856-1872* (Ohio University Press), a critical study rather than a biography proper of the first seventeen years of
Morris's literary career. England's involvement in
Arabia is represented by J. M. Wilson's *Lawrence
of Arabia: The Authorized Biography of T. E. Lawrence* (Atheneum), the longest work of the year,
and Edward Rice's fascinating *Captain Sir Richard
Francis Burton: The Secret Agent Who Made the Pilgrimage to Mecca, Discovered the Kama Sutra, and
Brought the Arabian Nights to the West* (Scribners),
the one with the longest title. And among the
more controversial books of the year is Martin

Seymour-Smith's *Rudyard Kipling* (St. Martin's),
which celebrates the writer while exposing the purported failings of the man.

Turning to modernist writers, the prolific Jeffrey Meyers has provided another fine biography, this time *D. H. Lawrence* (Knopf); Robert Calder has written *Willie: The Life of W. Somerset
Maugham* (St. Martin's), drawing on the testimony
of Maugham's secretary and friend Alan Searle
that explicitly corrects Ted Morgan's hostile life
of 1980; and Richard P. Graves completed *Robert
Graves: The Years with Laura, 1926-1940* (Viking),
the second of his three-volume life of his uncle
Robert. Like his iconoclastic *Tolstoy: A Biography*
(Norton, 1988), A. N. Wilson's *C. S. Lewis: A Biography* (Norton) is both controversial and engaging. Less significant is his *Eminent Victorians: The
Clash of Absolutes* (Norton), a late-twentieth-
century counterpart to Lytton Strachey's study of
prominent Victorians, which includes essays on
Charlotte Brontë and John Henry Newman
among its six portraits. Alan Bold has given us
MacDiarmid: A Critical Biography (University of
Massachusetts), the first full-length biography of
Hugh MacDiarmid (Christopher Murray Grieve),
the Scottish poet whose letters he edited in 1985.
Among the lives of popular writers are *No Laugh-
ing Matter: The Life and Times of Flann O'Brien*
(Grafton), by Anthony Cronin; *A. A. Milne: The
Man Behind Winnie-the-Pooh* (Random House), by
Ann Thwaite; *Agatha Christie: The Woman and Her
Mysteries* (Free Press), by Gillian Gill; and *The Re-
markable Case of Dorothy L. Sayers* (Kent State Uni-
versity), by Catherine Kenney. W. J. Weatherby,
in *Salman Rushdie: Sentenced to Death* (Carroll &
Graf), has produced the fullest biographical
study yet of the *Satanic Verses* (Viking, 1989) af-
fair. Revised biographies of Yeats, *W. B. Yeats: A
New Biography* (Farrar, Straus & Giroux), by A.
Norman Jeffares; Synge, *J. M. Synge, A Biography*
(New York University), by David H. Greene and
Edward M. Stephens; and Nancy Cardozo's
Maud Gonne (New Amsterdam), a reprint of
Lucky Eyes and a High Heart (Bobbs-Merrill,
1979), review the Irish Renaissance.

Besides Wilson's *Eminent Victorians*, English
group biographies include Humphrey Carpenter's *The Brideshead Generation: Evelyn Waugh and
His Friends* (Houghton Mifflin) and Mary Ann
Caws's *Women of Bloomsbury* (Routledge), a portrait of Virginia Woolf, Vanessa Bell, and Dora
Carrington. The scholar and critic Denis
Donoghue has written *Warrenpoint* (Knopf), an
evocative, erudite memoir of his youth, and re-

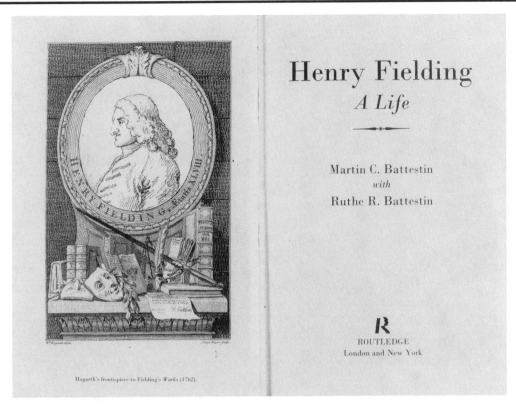

Title page and frontispiece for the Battestins' life of the eighteenth-century novelist

printed autobiographies include those of Edwin Muir, the Scottish translator and poet, and Nirad Chaudhuri's *A Passage to England* (Random Century), an account of his movement from Asia to England. Further autobiographical revelations are found in a new edition of *The Oxford Diaries of Arthur Hugh Clough* (Oxford), a one-volume abridgment of Virginia Woolf's diaries, and a collection of material from the earlier entries. Olga Kenyon's *Women Writers Talk* (Carroll & Graf), a series of interviews with ten contemporary English women writers (e.g., Margaret Drabble, Fay Weldon, Iris Murdoch), explores "how women write, why they write, and how they read other women." Collections of letters include the first volume of George Gissing's correspondence (Ohio University) as well as the selected letters of John Clare (Oxford). Finally (out of chronological order), Norman Page adds a Samuel Johnson chronology to Macmillan's and G. K. Hall's ongoing series.

Among American writers, Mark Twain and Tennessee Williams were the most prominent in 1990, with three books on each. Margaret Sanborn provides a detailed study of Twain's bachelorhood (Doubleday), while John Lauber, author of a previous account of Twain's early years,

has written a brief complete life (Hill & Wang) that concentrates upon the writing and reception of *Huckleberry Finn* and the 1880s. Twain's comments about himself are edited by Michael Kiskis. David Stuart's long-delayed *O. Henry: A Biography of William Sydney Porter* (Scarborough) appeared this year, together with the final volume of Richard Lingeman's splendid *Theodore Dreiser* (Putnam's). Biographies of feminist precursors include Emily Toth's exhaustive *Kate Chopin* (Morrow) and Ann Lane's *To "Herland and Beyond": The Life and Work of Charlotte Perkins Gilman* (Pantheon); in addition, Gilman's *The Living of Charlotte Perkins Gilman: An Autobiography* (University of Wisconsin) was published this year, with an introduction by Lane. The Indiana writer and naturalist Gene Stratton-Porter is treated by Judith Rerck Long in *Gene Stratton-Porter: Novelist and Naturalist* (Indiana University).

Among more modern American writers, Ernest Hemingway continues to be a common subject. Following just in the footsteps of Michael Reynolds, Peter Griffin has published *Less Than a Treason: Hemingway in Paris* (Oxford), the second volume of his biographical study of the writer—this year's book, like Reynolds's 1989 volume, deals with the Paris years, 1921-1928. Carl

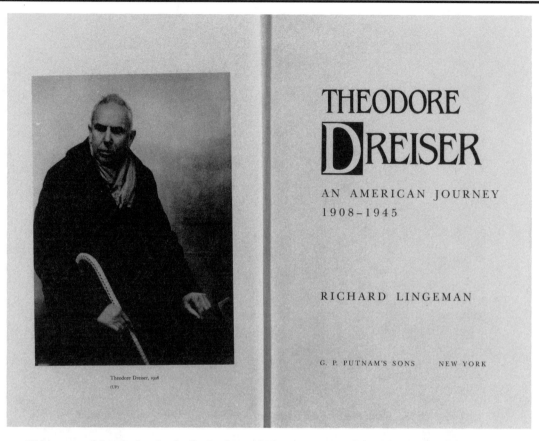

THEODORE

DREISER

AN AMERICAN JOURNEY
1908–1945

RICHARD LINGEMAN

G. P. PUTNAM'S SONS   NEW YORK

Theodore Dreiser, 1928
(UP)

Title page and frontispiece for the final volume of Lingeman's two-volume life of the American novelist

Rollyson, the biographer of Marilyn Monroe as well as Lillian Hellman, provided the first life of the elusive Martha Gellhorn, Hemingway's third wife, in *Nothing Ever Happens to the Brave* (St. Martin's). Jean Stafford, whose tragic life was movingly detailed for the first time by David Roberts in 1988, is the subject of *Jean Stafford: The Savage Heart* (University of Texas), a fine biography by Charlotte Margolis Goodman. Philip Kurth's engrossing, impressively researched *American Cassandra: The Life of Dorothy Thompson* (Little, Brown) provides a portrait of this tireless, unforgettable American journalist who was unhappily married to Sinclair Lewis. William MacAdams wrote *Ben Hecht: The Man Behind the Legend* (Scribners), an anecdotal life of the Hollywood screenwriter. Important biographies of major mid-century American poets include Paul Mariani's *Dream Song: The Life of John Berryman* (Morrow), Charles Molesworth's *Marianne Moore* (Atheneum), and Barry Silesky's *Ferlinghetti* (Warner). The first volume of Lyle Leverich's authorized life of Tennessee Williams, *Tom: The Young Tennessee Williams* (Grove Weidenfeld), was issued, while Bruce Smith, publicist and friend, provided an intimate and sympa-

thetic view of the aging playwright's final years in *Costly Performances: Tennessee Williams: The Last Stage* (Paragon). Williams's letters to another friend, Maria St. Just, are collected in *Five O'Clock Angel* (Knopf), which includes commentary by the correspondent herself. In a work that combines biography and excerpts from personal papers with literary criticism of the works, Ruth Miller's *Saul Bellow: A Biography of the Imagination* (St. Martin's) gives us an admiring portrait of Bellow, her teacher and friend. One year after Donald Miller's superb biography of Lewis Mumford, Thomas and Agatha Hughes examine the ideas of this prophet against modernity in *Lewis Mumford: Public Intellectual* (Oxford), in a collection of his final lectures. Gale Christianson's *Fox at the Wood's Edge: A Biography of Loren Eiseley* (Holt) portrays the life of a lesser American intellectual who also wrote for a popular audience. Revised or reprinted American biographies include Candace Falk's new edition of *Love, Anarchy, and Emma Goldman* (Rutgers) and Mark Harris's republished, romantic *City of Discontent* (Second Chance), his 1952 account of the life of Vachel Lindsay.

Beyond standard authors' lives, a rich gathering of group biographies marks life writing on American subjects in 1990. The most engrossing of these are Patricia O'Toole's *Five of Hearts* (Crown), a study of the Henry Adams circle, Wendy Smith's *Real Life Drama* (Random House), a portrait of the Group Theatre of the 1930s, and Carolyn Cassady's *Off the Road* (Morrow), a memoir of the Beat Generation. Shaun O'Connell provides in *Imagining Boston* (Beacon) a recreation of the writers of Boston, the city that produced Edith Wharton, Jack Kerouac, Henry James, and Malcolm X, among others. Ian Hamilton's *Writers in Hollywood, 1915-1951* (HarperCollins), a study of early Hollywood screenwriters, extends to the HUAC hearings of 1951. And Charles Scribner III provides an editor's-eye view of American writers in *In the Company of Writers* (Scribners). Autobiographies include *Reports of My Death* (Algonquin), the second volume of Karl Shapiro's life; memoirs of mental illness by William Styron and Kate Millett, *Darkness Visible* (Random House) and *The Loony-Bin Trip* (Simon & Schuster); and *Fragments and Fictions: Workbooks of an Obscure Writer* (Watermark), reflections cum reminiscences of writers by William Peden, a Kansas academic. Alan Ansen provides excerpts from extensive, previously unpublished conversations with W. H. Auden between 1946 and 1948 in *The Table Talk of W. H. Auden* (Ontario Review Press), and "Conversations" with John Gardner, Richard Wilbur, and Tom Wolfe are the latest additions to this University of Mississippi series. In *Inter/View: Talks with America's Writing Women* (University Press of Kentucky), Mickey Pearlman and Katherine Usher Henderson provide mini-essays, drawn from more extensive, intimate interviews, on twenty-eight contemporary American women writers from Alison Lurie to Nancy Willard. Finally, three important collections of American letters were published in 1990, including the *Letters of Katherine Anne Porter* (Atlantic Monthly Press); *Henry James and Edith Wharton: Letters, 1900-1915* (Scribners); and *In Love, In Sorrow: The Complete Correspondence of Charles Olson and Edward Dahlberg* (Paragon).

Vladimir Nabokov: The Russian Years (Princeton), the first volume of Brian Boyd's biography, presents a subject who was a foreign writer before he became an American one. This year's biographies of other non-English writers include translations of Jean Canavaggio's *Cervantes* (1986) and Claude Pichois's *Baudelaire* (1967—slightly abridged), the only reliable life of the poet. An-

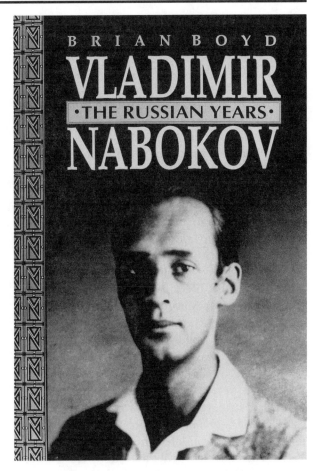

Dust jacket for the first volume of Boyd's authorized life of Nabokov

other translated life is Peter Jungk's *Franz Werfel* (Grove Weidenfeld), an account of his years in America after his flight from Hitler's Austria in 1938. With this year's *Proust: A Biography* (HarperCollins), Ronald Hayman adds another distinguished, readable biography to his previous studies of Friedrich Nietzsche, Franz Kafka, and Jean-Paul Sartre. Biographies of two great Frenchwomen, David McLellan's *Simone Weil: Utopian Pessimist* (Simon & Schuster) and Deirdre Bair's *Simone de Beauvoir* (Summit), are among the best of this year's biographies. McLellan, who has written extensively on Marx and modern ideology, provides a bristling intellectual life of the Christian activist; Bair, whose revelatory 1980 *Samuel Beckett* (Summit) was based on numerous intensive interviews with the writer, has used the same method to produce an exhaustive study of de Beauvoir's works and life. Ray Monk's *Ludwig Wittgenstein: The Duty of Genius* (Free Press), which brings together the man and the philosopher and was written with the full cooperation of

Wittgenstein's literary executors, may be one of the finest intellectual biographies ever written. Peter Bien completed *Kazantzakis: Politics of the Spirit* (Princeton), the first of his own two-part intellectual biography of the Greek writer, taking us to the 1938 *Odyssey*, prior to the popular novels and the writer's active political involvement.

In addition to these full-scale biographies, Oscar Mandel produced *August von Katzebue* (Penn State University), a study of the theater of the nineteenth-century dramatist; and Gene Bell-Villada included a biographical sketch and some personal details in his *García Marquez: The Man and His Work* (University of North Carolina). Autobiographical writing includes Heberto Padilla's *Self-Portrait of the Other* (Farrar, Straus & Giroux), a memoir of his life as a writer in Castro's Cuba from 1959-1981; Marguerite Duras's *Practicalities* (Grove Widenfeld), reflections on her alcoholism, her travels, and political events, drawn from conversations; Fadwa Tuqan's *A Mountainous Journey* (Graywolf), memoirs of her life as a woman poet, born to a traditional Arab family, who has witnessed fifty years of upheaval in the Middle East; and *Disturbing the Peace* (Knopf), a collection of talks, translated into English, between Vaclav Havel, Czech writer and newly elected president, and Karel Hvizdala, exiled Czech journalist, that took place in 1985-1986. Only one collection of a foreign writer's letters was published in 1990, but it is extremely significant: *The Letters of Thomas Mann* (University of California) includes correspondence with André Gide, Sigmund Freud, Bertolt Brecht, and Theodor Adorno among others, as well as letters to members of his own family. Finally, in a highly readable collection of essays on literary biography itself, Park Honan, biographer of Jane Austen, Matthew Arnold, and (partially) Robert Browning, discusses procedures, problems, and pleasures of life writing in *Authors' Lives: On Literary Biography and the Arts of Language* (St. Martin's).

Literary Biography in 1990: A Checklist

Alan Ansen, *The Table Talk of W. H. Auden*, edited by Nicholas Jenkins (Princeton, N.J.: Ontario Review Press, 1990);

Deirdre Bair, *Simone de Beauvoir: A Biography* (New York: Summit, 1990);

Martin C. Battestin, with Ruthe R. Battestin, *Henry Fielding: A Life* (London: Routledge, 1989; New York: Routledge, 1990);

Gene H. Bell-Villada, *García Marquez: The Man and His Work* (Chapel Hill: University of North Carolina Press, 1990);

Peter Bien, *Kazantzakis: Politics of the Spirit* (Princeton, N.J.: Princeton University Press, 1990);

Alan Bold, *MacDiarmid: A Critical Biography* (Amherst: University of Massachusetts Press, 1990);

Brian Boyd, *Vladimir Nabokov: The Russian Years* (Princeton, N.J.: Princeton University Press, 1990);

Robert Calder, *Willie: The Life of W. Somerset Maugham* (New York: St. Martin's, 1990);

Jean Canavaggio, *Cervantes*, translated by Joseph R. Jones (New York: Norton, 1990);

Nancy Cardozo, *Maud Gonne* (New York: New Amsterdam, 1990);

Humphrey Carpenter, *The Brideshead Generation: Evelyn Waugh and His Friends* (Boston: Houghton Mifflin, 1990);

Carolyn Cassady, *Off the Road: My Years with Cassady, Kerouac, and Ginsberg* (New York: Morrow, 1990);

Mary Ann Caws, *Women of Bloomsbury: Virginia, Vanessa, and Carrington* (New York: Routledge, 1990);

Nirad C. Chaudhuri, *A Passage to England* (North Pomfret, Ver.: Random Century, 1990);

Gail E. Christianson, *Fox at the Wood's Edge: A Biography of Loren Eiseley* (New York: Holt, 1990);

John Clare, *Selected Letters*, edited by Mark Story (New York: Oxford University Press, 1988);

Arthur Hugh Clough, *The Oxford Diaries of Arthur Hugh Clough*, edited by Anthony Kenny (New York: Oxford University Press, 1989);

Anthony Cronin, *No Laughing Matter: The Life and Times of Flann O'Brien* (London: Grafton, 1989);

Denis Donoghue, *Warrenpoint* (New York: Knopf, 1990);

Marguerite Duras, *Practicalities* (New York: Grove Weidenfeld, 1990);

Candace Falk, *Love, Anarchy, and Emma Goldman: A Biography*, revised edition (New Brunswick, N.J.: Rutgers University Press, 1990);

Katherine Frank, *A Chainless Soul: A Life of Emily Brontë* (Boston: Houghton Mifflin, 1990);

John Gardner, *Conversations*, edited by Allan Chavkin (Jackson: University Press of Mississippi, 1990);

Gillian C. Gill, *Agatha Christie: The Woman and Her Mysteries* (New York: Free Press, 1990);

George Gissing, *The Collected Letters, Volume 1: 1863-1880*, edited by Paul F. Matthessen, Arthur C. Young, and Pierre Coustillas (Athens: Ohio University Press, 1990);

Charlotte Margolis Goodman, *Jean Stafford: The Savage Heart* (Austin: University of Texas Press, 1990);

Richard P. Graves, *Robert Graves: The Years with Laura, 1926-1940* (New York: Viking, 1990);

David H. Greene and Edward M. Stephens, *J. M. Synge, A Biography*, revised edition (New York: New York University Press, 1989);

Peter Griffin, *Less Than a Treason: Hemingway in Paris* (New York: Oxford University Press, 1990);

Ian Hamilton, *Writers in Hollywood, 1915-1951* (New York: HarperCollins, 1990);

Mark Harris, *City of Discontent: An Interpretive Biography of Vachel Lindsay* (Sag Harbor, N.Y.: Second Chance, 1990);

Vaclav Havel, *Disturbing the Peace*, translated, with an introduction, by Paul Wilson (New York: Knopf, 1990);

Ronald Hayman, *Proust: A Biography* (New York: HarperCollins, 1990);

Richard Holmes, *Coleridge: Early Visions* (New York: Viking, 1990);

Park Honan, *Authors' Lives: On Literary Biography and the Arts of Language* (New York: St. Martin's, 1990);

Thomas P. and Agatha C. Hughes, eds., *Lewis Mumford: Public Intellectual* (New York: Oxford University Press, 1990);

Henry James and Edith Wharton, *Henry James and Edith Wharton: Letters 1900-1915*, edited by Lyall H. Powers (New York: Scribners, 1990);

A. Norman Jeffares, *W. B. Yeats: A New Biography* (New York: Farrar, Straus & Giroux, 1989);

Peter Stephan Jungk, *Franz Werfel: A Life in Prague, Vienna, and Hollywood*, translated by Anselm Hollo (New York: Grove Weidenfeld, 1990);

Wolfgang Kemp, *The Desire of My Eyes: The Life and Work of John Ruskin*, translated by Jan van Heurck (New York: Farrar, Straus & Giroux, 1989);

Catherine Kenney, *The Remarkable Case of Dorothy L. Sayers* (Kent, Ohio: Kent State University Press, 1990);

Olga Kenyon, ed., *Women Writers Talk* (New York: Carroll & Graf, 1990);

Frederick Kirchhoff, *William Morris: The Construction of a Male Self, 1856-1872* (Athens: Ohio University Press, 1990);

Peter Kurth, *American Cassandra: The Life of Dorothy Thompson* (Boston: Little, Brown, 1990);

Ann J. Lane, *To "Herland and Beyond": The Life and Work of Charlotte Perkins Gilman* (New York: Pantheon, 1990);

John Lauber, *The Inventions of Mark Twain* (New York: Hill & Wang, 1990);

Lyle Leverich, *Tom: The Young Tennessee Williams* (New York: Grove Weidenfeld, 1990);

Richard Lingeman, *Theodore Dreiser, Volume II: An American Journey, 1908-1945* (New York: Putnam's, 1990);

Judith Rerck Long, *Gene Stratton-Porter: Novelist and Naturalist* (Bloomington: Indiana University Press, 1990);

William MacAdams, *Ben Hecht: The Man Behind the Legend* (New York: Scribners, 1990);

Oscar Mandel, *August von Katzebue: The Comedy, The Man* (University Park: Pennsylvania State University Press, 1990);

Thomas Mann, *The Letters of Thomas Mann, 1889-1945*, edited and translated by Richard and Clara Winston (Berkeley: University of California Press, 1990);

Paul Mariani, *Dream Song: The Life of John Berryman* (New York: Morrow, 1990);

David McLellan, *Simone Weil: Utopian Pessimist* (New York: Simon & Schuster, 1990);

Jeffrey Meyers, *D. H. Lawrence* (New York: Knopf, 1990);

Ruth Miller, *Saul Bellow: A Biography of the Imagination* (New York: St. Martin's, 1990);

Kate Millett, *The Loony-Bin Trip* (New York: Simon & Schuster, 1990);

Charles Molesworth, *Marianne Moore: A Literary Life* (New York: Atheneum, 1990);

Ray Monk, *Ludwig Wittgenstein: The Duty of Genius* (New York: Free Press, 1990);

Edwin Muir, *An Autobiography* (St. Paul, Minn.: Graywolf, 1990);

Shaun O'Connell, *Imagining Boston: A Literary Landscape* (Boston: Beacon, 1990);

Charles Olson and Edward Dahlberg, *In Love, In Sorrow: The Complete Correspondence of Charles Olson and Edward Dahlberg*, edited, with an introduction, by Paul Christensen (New York: Paragon, 1990);

Patricia O'Toole, *The Five of Hearts: An Intimate Portrait of Henry Adams and His Friends, 1880-1918* (New York: Crown, 1990);

Heberto Padilla, *Self-Portrait of the Other: A Memoir*, translated by Alexander Coleman (New York: Farrar, Straus & Giroux, 1990);

Norman Page, ed., *A Dr. Johnson Chronology* (Boston: G. K. Hall, 1990);

Mickey Pearlman and Katherine Usher Henderson, *Inter/View: Talks with America's Writing Women* (Lexington: University Press of Kentucky, 1990);

William Peden, *Fragments and Fictions: Workbooks of an Obscure Writer* (Wichita, Kans.: Watermark, 1990);

Olga Anastasia Pelensky, *Isak Dinesen: The Life and Imagination of a Seducer* (Athens: Ohio University Press, 1990);

Claude Pichois, *Baudelaire*, translated by Graham Robb (New York: Viking, 1990);

Katherine Anne Porter, *Letters of Katherine Anne Porter*, selected and edited by Isabel Bayley (New York: Atlantic Monthly Press, 1990);

William H. Pritchard, *Randall Jarrell: A Literary Life* (New York: Di Capua, 1990);

Edward Rice, *Captain Sir Richard Francis Burton: The Secret Agent Who Made the Pilgrimage to Mecca, Discovered the Kama Sutra, and Brought the Arabian Nights to the West* (New York: Scribners, 1990);

Carl E. Rollyson, *Nothing Ever Happens to the Brave: The Story of Martha Gellhorn* (New York: St. Martin's, 1990);

Margaret Sanborn, *Mark Twain—The Bachelor Years: A Biography* (New York: Doubleday, 1990);

Charles Scribner III, *In the Company of Writers* (New York: Scribners, 1990);

Martin Seymour-Smith, *Rudyard Kipling* (New York: St. Martin's, 1990);

Karl Shapiro, *Reports of My Death* (Chapel Hill, N.C.: Algonquin, 1990);

Barry Silesky, *Ferlinghetti: The Artist in His Time* (New York: Warner, 1990);

Bruce Smith, *Costly Performances: Tennessee Williams: The Last Stage* (New York: Paragon, 1990);

Wendy Smith, *Real Life Drama: The Group Theatre and America, 1931-1940* (New York: Random House, 1990);

David Stuart, *O. Henry: A Biography of William Sydney Porter* (Chelsea, Mich.: Scarborough, 1990);

William Styron, *Darkness Visible: A Memoir of Madness* (New York: Random House, 1990);

Ina Taylor, *A Woman of Contradictions: The Life of George Eliot* (New York: Morrow, 1990);

Ann Thwaite, *A. A. Milne: The Man Behind Winnie-the-Pooh* (New York: Random House, 1990);

Emily Toth, *Kate Chopin* (New York: Morrow, 1990);

Fadwa Tuqan, *A Mountainous Journey: A Poet's Autobiography* (St. Paul, Minn.: Graywolf, 1990);

Mark Twain, *Mark Twain's Own Autobiography: The Chapters from the North American Review*, edited by Michael J. Kiskis (Madison: University of Wisconsin Press, 1990);

W. J. Weatherby, *Salman Rushdie: Sentenced to Death* (New York: Carroll & Graf, 1990);

Richard Wilbur, *Conversations with Richard Wilbur*, edited by William Butts (Jackson: University Press of Mississippi, 1990);

Tennessee Williams, *Five O'Clock Angel: Letters of Tennessee Williams to Maria St. Just, 1948-1982*, commentary by Maria St. Just and Kit Harvey, preface by Elia Kazan (New York: Knopf, 1990);

A. N. Wilson, *C. S. Lewis: A Biography* (New York: Norton, 1990);

Wilson, *Eminent Victorians: The Clash of Absolutes* (New York: Norton, 1990);

J. M. Wilson, *Lawrence of Arabia: The Authorized Biography of T. E. Lawrence* (New York: Atheneum, 1990);

Tom Wolfe, *Conversations with Tom Wolfe*, edited by Dorothy Scura (Jackson: University Press of Mississippi, 1990);

Virginia Woolf, *A Moment's Liberty: The Shorter Diary*, abridged and edited by Anne Olivier Bell, with an introduction by Quentin Bell (San Diego: Harcourt Brace Jovanovich, 1990);

Woolf, *A Passionate Apprentice: The Early Journals, 1897-1909*, edited by Mitchell A. Leaska (San Diego: Harcourt Brace Jovanovich, 1990).

Book Reviewing in America: IV

George Garrett
University of Virginia

I

Book reviewing is the prime means of selling books, and there are very few reviewers now who could make somebody want to buy a book. Book reviewing seems to me to be at its nadir.

—Herman Gollob, Editor-at-large,
Bantam, Doubleday, Dell

A portion of this essay appeared in the March 1991 issue of *Chronicles: A Magazine of Culture*

The state of book reviewing in America, together with a reiterated basic explanation of how the system works, or is supposed to work, are more and more the topics of public forum and discussion. There are more and more feature stories on the subject, more and more panel discussions of the general topic. *Mānoa: A Pacific Journal of International Writing*, originating from the University of Hawaii, is assembling a "symposium," scheduled for early 1991 publication, of responses by writers and critics to "The Situation of Reviewing," a piece by the National Public Radio book critic Alan Cheuse. *Mānoa*'s editor, Robert Shapard, in a letter sent out to potential contributors, asks pertinent questions: "Is it as bad—or as good—as it's ever been for readers, authors, and publishers? Who pays attention and why? Who wins and who loses in the current situation? If there is any hope for American letters, how should things be done differently?" Cheuse's article is deliberately provocative. Exemplary of what he calls a "moral mud slide in publishing," he writes: "In the last few decades the atmosphere of reviewing in the United States seems to have worsened even more, and lately entertainment has dissolved into something resembling pure publicity." As a positive note he cites the fact that the industry has begun to find "more and more reviewers among the fiction writers and poets themselves. While this can lead to back-slapping and (sometimes) back-stabbing, more often again than not the artist serving as critic even for the brief length of a review allows the general reader a more sympathetic approach to a novel or story collection than your average critic can produce." Cheuse's purpose is to raise observations and opinions; and so he asks some pertinent questions also: "Do reviews have any effect at all on sales? Has there been in recent years an inflation of praise at the expense of judgment in reviewing? Has the publishing world begun to succumb to the celebrity culture of the society at large?"

Cheuse, himself, was in large part responsible for, and acted as moderator of, an important public discussion of the ways and means of book reviewing, a well-attended session at the Miami Book Fair (Saturday, 17 November 1990) entitled "The Reviewer's Art: A Discussion of Book Reviewing." Here were enough important figures from the book reviewing business to arouse the notion (if not a suspicion) that there is, indeed, an immediate problem, a certain amount of damage control to be practiced these days as a routine part of the book editor's job and function.

Moderated by Cheuse, the panel consisted of George Core, editor of the *Sewanee Review*; William Robertson of the *Miami Herald*; Richard Flaste of the *New York Times Book Review*; Nina King, editor of "Book World" for the *Washington Post*; Stanley Crouch of the *Village Voice*; and John Leonard, one-time editor of the *New York Times Book Review* and now, among other things, a reviewer for CBS's "Sunday Morning" program and the *Nation*. As is evident in the simple listing of panelists, the predominant emphasis was journalistic (only George Core represented those critics and publications whose concern is not primarily the reporting of literary news) and, though varied in constituency, mostly out of one region, the New York-Washington, D.C., axis, representing the region's attitudes and problems. In a brief opening statement Cheuse argued that book reviewing is more important than ever, in part because of "the decline and decadence of literary criticism in the academies" and because of the increasing difficulty of keeping "American readership in touch with the evolving values and

97

aspects of our culture." To the audience he argued that the chief goal of the committed book reviewer is "to help you find what is important to your reading life."

George Core spoke first, describing book reviewing as "one of the most essential activities of the literary magazine and the scholarly journal." Using his own experience at the *Sewanee* as an example, he showed that there was a steady increase in the number of titles reviewed, from twenty-five books reviewed in the calendar year 1973 to the current level of forty to fifty books reviewed in each of his four issues. "Sometimes as many as 250 books have been reviewed," he said, "with another 250 noticed." He singled out several quarterlies for special notice and praise in terms of reviewing.

"Such departments as the 'Bookmarks' section in the back of the *Georgia Review*, 'Notes on Current Books' in the front of the *Virginia Quarterly*, and 'Current Books in Review,' including my own column 'Procrustes' Bed,' in the opening pages of the *Sewanee Review* are all means of having many more books reviewed than can be considered in essay-reviews alone. Joseph Epstein, one of this country's best editors, publishes both short reviews and longer essay-reviews in the *American Scholar*. My taste and judgment tell me that any literary magazine or scholarly journal should have a combination of both forms, as do—to cite a few more examples—*Prairie Schooner*, the *New England Quarterly*, the *Hudson Review*."

Although the best of the literary reviews and quarterlies have an influence on the contemporary literary scene and, indeed, seek to do so, reviewing some commercially published books even within the rapidly shrinking limits of their brief "shelf life," Core maintained that the reviewing purposes of the quarterlies are less linked to consumers and consumption than to the creation of a body of serious literary criticism. "What we editors are chiefly trying to accomplish," he said, "is to make reviewing a department of criticism."

Speaking of the kinds of writers he looks to, both as regulars and irregulars, for his book reviewing, Core indicated that skill, even in short notices, is crucial. "The reviewer who says to me that he cannot review a book in nine-hundred to one-thousand words is usually telling me—unintentionally, of course—that he is windy, meandering, self-indulgent." Praising the exemplary work of his regular reviewers Sam Pickering and George Woodcock, he likewise listed some of the negative qualities in potential reviewers he must

be ever alert to: "We don't want bitter failed poets, historians, biographers and so forth—the kind of people Coleridge, himself a better critic than poet, inveighed against. Nor do we want desperate academic and academical types. The reviewer proves himself or herself with each book encountered. We should always remember Lichtenberg's law: 'A book is a mirror; if an ass peers into it, you can't expect an apostle to look out.'"

Core was followed by Richard Flaste, who pictured the *New York Times Book Review* as "the gatekeeper" of contemporary literature, organizer of a system of judgment and reviewing "that really is awe-inspiring."

"Not unaware that lives and careers are at stake," he said, "the *New York Times* tries somehow to do right." He added that, although mistakes are inevitably made, "what happens happens fairly and without bias." Having made a case for the integrity of his mission, he added that it must be accomplished in a lively and entertaining fashion: "If you don't have a little bit of showmanship in you, you might as well give up."

The *Miami Herald*'s Bill Robertson, who in addition to editing the book pages also writes a once-a-week column of nine-hundred-to-one-thousand words, took off from Flaste's comment on showmanship, throwing down a kind of challenge to his fellow journalistic book editors. He argued that it is clearly not the role of the newspaper book critic to support writers. Nor is it his job to serve a consumer function. In an era of conglomerate ownership of newspapers and of shrinking book pages, likewise an era when it can be safely assumed that "more people will be reading the book review than will ever actually read the book," it becomes the primary aim of the book editor "to entertain the readers of my newspaper." "The critic's chief obligation is to entertain readers," he continued. "Even fairness doesn't have much to do with it."

Unfortunately the other journalistic book critics ignored the ironic challenge Robertson presented, not denying a certain irrefutable validity to his position, but not denying, themselves, either, the advantage of a more serious goal. Nina King of the *Washington Post*, whose eighteen hundred titles reviewed annually make her "Book World" second in numbers only to the *New York Times Book Review*, allowed that newspaper reviewing is complex and often ambiguous. "We are concerned with reviewing books that are the best of their kind," she said, "but are also of concern to a wide newspaper audience." She allowed that a certain element of the newspaper reviewer's program was "consumer advice." For Ms. King, however, the biggest problem lies not in the necessarily complex goals and objectives of popular journalism, but in the endless and important difficulty of "matching the book and the reviewer." She defined the ideal reviewer as knowledgeable and fair and possessed of "a sexy byline—a John Updike or a Robert Redford." Serving as a matchmaker for good books and good reviewers has its rewards. "It's not easy," she said. "But it's a lot of fun."

The *Village Voice*'s Stanley Crouch, one of the nation's most influential African-American critics, took a different and more critical stance. Arguing that recent American fiction "has largely failed the task that is set before it by American reality," Crouch criticized the writers who, working safely out of self-contained and largely self-imposed "segregated worlds," failed to deal with or to convey "the excitement and dismay of our culture." He blamed critical "cowardice" for the encouragement of the acceptance of strict inhibitions of subject and point of view and of limits of artistic imagination. Crouch took a moral position, arguing that it is the critic's duty to encourage those literary materials which attempt to advance our imaginative understanding of the diversity and complexity of contemporary American society and culture.

"My job is to perform an act of seduction," said John Leonard. Leonard, who reviews some ninety books a year, said that since "I believe in author gods," he conceives of himself more as a "missionary" than critic. "Books save our lives," he said. "Books have changed the way I felt about the world." Returning to his original analogy, Leonard said that he views his obligation as "how best can I seduce the reader to feel what I did." The job of the critic is "to create effectively in the reader your own process of discovery." According to Leonard, "the real problem is that the reviewer is lazy." Few do their required homework and research.

An intense question-and-answer period gave some clues to the kinds of things which concern writers and readers. There was a good deal of talk about regionalism, about why a strip of the eastern seaboard of the United States had acquired and managed to maintain a national power while preserving a regional point of view. There were questions, some of them angry, arising from the critique presented by Stanley

Crouch. Mainly these questions related to the editorial habit of assigning books for review to the same special group about which the author has written or from which the author comes, i.e. gay book to gay reviewers; African-American to African-American; feminist to feminist, etc. In neither case did the answers and explanations of the journalists on the panel seem to satisfy their interrogators. George Core was spared from these matters, though he did volunteer information indicating that the *Sewanee Review* is not, by any means, regional in bias or interests.

Other subjects of interest to the Book Fair audience included the much-publicized fate of *American Psycho* by Bret Easton Ellis and the perennial problem of the reviewing of poetry. John Leonard allowed that poetry reviewing had been a special headache for him in his days at the *New York Times Book Review* in part because the poets were the worst offenders in matters of conflict of interest, general and personal puffery, malice, and self-promotion. Richard Flaste calmed the questioners with the news that the *New York Times* has already embarked upon a program of more extensive and thorough review coverage of contemporary poetry. This, in fact, seems to be the case although, so far, the reviews coming from this new policy seem to be, as might be expected, written by establishment poets about other establishment poets, not yet daring or able to come to terms either with the diversity of contemporary American poetry or the exciting and varied talents of many of our excellent, if lesser known, poets. It is clear enough that the poetry establishment in America is not seriously interested in "discovery" outside of its own networking or in the recognition of talents other than their own, no matter how original or worthwhile.

Interviewed in Charlottesville, Virginia, David Streitfeld, a prominent literary journalist for the *Washington Post* who did not attend the Book Fair, seemed more pessimistic than his fellow critics and reviewers, as much about the fate and future of book pages as about the decline of interest in serious literary art. He, like Robertson of the *Miami Herald*, spoke of conglomerate ownership of newspapers (and many magazines) nationwide and of the "bottom-line" mentality of management, leading, inevitably, to loss of space allowed for reviewing books and covering things of primarily literary interest. On the other hand, Streitfeld suggested that a new system for exposure has developed which can compensate for the lost power of book reviews to identify and to offer criticism of literary books, which, in the absence of significant advertising and promotion, can easily fade from sight. More and more of those books, mildly profitable midlist books at best, are declared by their publishers to be "review driven." Which means they are more or less unsupported by their publishers except for filling of orders coming from bookstores.

(Here a parenthetical point is in order. Thanks to technology and improved efficiency, together with the growing importance of a middleman, the book distributor, independent book stores—which are a modest growth industry, compared to the chain stores and the discount stores, which deal almost exclusively with established blockbusters—are able to order and to receive books promptly. The result is that the independent store can quickly respond to a local demand, a demand arising, for example, from a local book review. Most major publishers, at least those able to react to this situation, are much better at distribution than they were as recently as a decade ago, depending more and more, of course, on the distributors and less and less on the individual sales representative who had a territory to cover and, ideally, a direct, personal relationship with booksellers. In 1990 Doubleday, for example, long noted for the size and ability of its sales force, fired most of its sales representatives.)

In any case, Streitfeld seems to be among the very few critics and observers of the scene to notice that, quietly and steadily, a new system for exposure, "visibility," of literary writers has developed and is already becoming influential. While the authors of blockbusters and best-sellers, real and imaginary, are involved with author tours involving book signings, radio and television appearances, etc., scrambling against each other for maximum media attention, writers of literary fiction—poetry, short stories, serious novels—are organizing reading tours which send them to colleges and universities, with often a good independent bookstore in the same community, to read aloud from their work, and to sell some books. Measured against the sales of the successful blockbuster, these sales are small beer at best. But, as Streitfeld persuasively argues, this sort of literary tour can serve the writer well, especially if that writer is reasonably interesting and attractive in person and is able to give a good public reading.

"Of course," I tell him, veteran and victim of several such homemade tours myself, "that

can really help a published book reach an audience. The only trouble is that during all that time the writer is not doing what he is supposed to do and presumably does best—writing. You come off these tours punchdrunk from airplanes and airports, weary of the whole thing and with your new work still waiting to be done."

"Exactly," he says. "And I have written some columns about just that. When does the writer have a chance to write?"

II

The Quarterlies: Two Interviews On The Book Reviewing Panel

I think that one of the most important functions of any literary magazine is to try to do as many book reviews as they can work in without creating an imbalance. So many of us refer to ourselves as reviews, and yet we don't review a whole lot.

—Paul Ruffin, editor of the Texas Review

Shortly following his appearance at the annual Miami Book Fair, this interview with George Core took place in a fifteenth-story hotel room high above downtown Miami, its boarded up store fronts and decay, its winos and druggies mercifully out of sight. A quiet, light-filled room with a view of Biscayne Bay and Miami Beach beyond that. An occasional jet gliding toward Miami International Airport. Oddest and seemingly most incongruous of all, flocks of buzzards soaring on the air high above downtown Miami. What brings them here? Neither of us, George Core or myself, has ever seen buzzards in an urban setting, though we have both read about them as a fact of life in the cities of the Third World.

It's all of it, high and low, a far cry from Sewanee, Tennessee, the lightly populated, ten-thousand-acre domain of the University of the South, isolated and beautiful atop a mountain, where in a gray gothic-style building the *Sewanee Review* has its offices.

We are still talking about the themes of the panel on book reviewing and the news of the day.

"Isn't that a chilling story about that Bret Easton Ellis?" Core asks. "Reading between the lines, I think that it sounds absolutely repulsive. Yet what comes across in the press is that the wife of the CEO of the company that owns

Simon & Schuster is another Mrs. Doubleday suppressing a work as great as *Sister Carrie*, which is nonsense, of course. This latter-day Mrs. Doubleday tried to carry out a public service—but at great expense to Simon & Schuster; but her efforts were immediately thwarted by Random House, which to its immense discredit and obvious greed is now publishing this wretched book, which might make the Marquis de Sade blush with shame.

"We are faced with the fact that reading is a dying art. I mean, people read this kind of trash, this new novel, *American Psycho*, that certainly is worthy of being suppressed if anything ever has been. We are going to be in bad shape if Jesse Helms starts deciding the artistic taste of the country. I also think we're going to be in bad shape if work as bad as this Brett Ellis novel, work that bad, *isn't* suppressed occasionally. It's not really being suppressed, of course, it's being rejected. Everybody has the right to reject a manuscript. But what happens is that the word 'censorship' comes up and a great many people get exercised. You should not censor art. But if you couldn't censor it in some form and at some stage, then everything would see print in one form or another. The book reviewer ought to be prepared to say that something is rubbish. George Woodcock once said about some very bad book he reviewed for me that it was a waste of good trees to publish the book."

Speaking of the earlier panel discussion, he says: "The operative word in all that conversation was 'entertainment.' I would have been happier if they talked about being lively and entertaining, but not about simply providing entertainment for their readers. And the news value of a book, from their standpoint, is not one that you and I would agree to. In other words, we would quote Ezra Pound and say that a good book is the news that stays news. They were talking about reviewing books that are newsworthy at the moment. What a lot of these people don't understand (a point I tried to make today, but which was certainly lost in this case), is that book reviewing ought to be a department of criticism. It shouldn't be entertainment or news or something which is ephemeral by definition.

"I think a lot of people start reading quarterlies by reading the book reviews; then they go on and read the fiction and the essays and the poetry. Some of the quarterly editors haven't figured out how important the book review is in the economy of the magazine—if for no other reason

than that they have to get ads. And they have to keep getting review copies."

A native of Lexington, Kentucky, George Core was educated at Transylvania College, Vanderbilt, and Chapel Hill. He served as an officer for four years (1960-1964) in the U.S. Marine Corps. He is editor or coeditor of some five scholarly and critical books dealing largely with American literature. Forthcoming are *The Literalists of the Imagination: Southern Letters and the New Criticism* (LSU), a study of the criticism of Ransom, Tate, Brooks and Warren, and other New Critics; and, together with novelist and critic Walter Sullivan, he has co-edited *Writing from the Inside* (Norton), a textbook on composition. Core reviews for the *New York Times Book Review*, the *New Republic*, *Baltimore Sun*, *Washington Post Book World*, *Washington Times*, and the *Hudson Review*, the *Virginia Quarterly Review*, and his own magazine. He was senior editor of the University of Georgia Press from 1968 to 1973, when he began editing the *Sewanee Review*.

"The experience I had at the University of Georgia Press was enormously helpful in terms of editing the magazine. I picked up a fair amount of information about design and production on the one hand and, on the other, promotion. But it seems to me that these are matters that everybody has to be constantly learning about. I don't pretend to be an expert. For instance, when the copyright law changed in 1978, I think we handled the matter pretty intelligently. We went to the Library of Congress and I talked to a lawyer there who actually called me up. I found out what was going on, how to make up the copyright forms, and how to protect our authors and protect the magazine. Other magazines, like the *Yale Review* and the *New Yorker*, kept doing what they had always done as if the copyright law had never changed.

"I don't pretend to be an expert on a lot of things. And I've certainly been very dismal at promoting the *Sewanee Review*. I think it's extremely important that an editor promote his magazine intelligently, and I'm afraid I haven't done as good a job as I should have. On the other hand, I think some editors are better promoters than they are editors. Ronald Sharp and Frederick Turner were great at promoting the new *Kenyon Review*. But they got out a very bad magazine.

"My greatest frustration since I have been editor of the *Sewanee Review* is that we can't seem to get more subscribers. We are between three- and four-thousand; and the only comparable quarterlies which do better are the *Virginia Quarterly Review* and the *Hudson Review*. The *Hudson* has done well in the recent past, with maybe four thousand. They were at twenty-five hundred at one point in the recent past and now have about four-thousand subscribers. The Morgans have been very resourceful at pushing up their subscriptions. On the other hand, there's the *Partisan Review*, which doesn't do much better through the mail, but has a very good sale on the newstands.

"The fact is," Core continues, "we are now living in an age of the specialized magazine. I talked to one guy who has done all this body work—not on me, but on my automobile and my children's automobiles. He does antique cars on the side. I talked about doing a piece about him, and he told me there are three antique automobile magazines. And there are all these other magazines about gourmet cooking and everything else. The literary quarterly is taking it on the chin. The heyday of the quarterlies was probably the late 1950s. And there's really nothing anybody can do culturally to create issues and make them important for the informed general reader. The thing that keeps staring me in the face is that the informed general reader is going to be as dead as the dodo in the near future."

We are soon talking about the individual quarterlies, those he admires and those he does not and, as well, features of this quarterly or another which he can praise or criticize. For example, he singles out the "Bookmarks" section of the *Georgia Review* as "a good idea," adding that "the problem is they are not reviewing enough books." He argues that the *Georgia Review* has done well in recent years, in part "because they have held down the subscription rate. It's a big fat magazine selling for a modest amount of money."

He adds: "the *Southern Review* is comparable, but the *Southern*, it seems to me, is becoming more and more academic. Unless Dave Smith turns it around, it is not going to be a literary quarterly any more. But I want to give James Olney great credit for his work during a time of great change and disruption.

"The ones who do what, say, Peter Stitt is doing at the *Gettysburg Review*, running only essay-reviews, are making another kind of mistake. I think you need as much review coverage as you can possibly get."

About the others, to use Mailer's phrase, the other talent in the room:

Joseph Epstein, editor of the American Scholar

"My judgment is that the *American Scholar* is a wonderfully edited quarterly and that Joseph Epstein—who is a very good short-story writer and one of our best essayists, not only personal, but a critical essayist, as well—does a first-rate job. Everybody in the country who edits a quarterly is envious of his situation. He has forty- or fifty-thousand people, the membership of Phi Beta Kappa, taking the *American Scholar*. As Malcolm Cowley said to Allen Tate about 1930, we no longer wear our Phi Beta Kappa keys. What he might have gone on to say is that we subscribe to the *American Scholar* and we put it on the coffee table whether we read it or not.

"I doubt, frankly, that he has many more careful readers than the rest of the quarterlies; but he's got an ideal situation and he's done a superb job.

"I think we might devote a little consideration to the demise of the *Yale Review*. The *Yale Review* proved that it was not essential to literary life in this country under the editorship of Kai Erikson, who could not bear to bring it out on time. As a result it was six to nine months late, and he finally had to give up altogether putting the season on the cover of the magazine. So you had to look inside and in tiny type it would say something like 'Vol. 79, no. 2, for Spring 1989, published January 1990.' That's the kind of thing that has gone on. And I'm afraid that Professor Erikson is largely responsible for the fact that the magazine has been closed down, not because he didn't do a fairly decent job editing it, but because it was not out in time. People just forgot about it.

"That's one side of it. And on the other hand you have got a president who is an attorney who has decided that instead of putting up the necessary money for the *Yale Review*—which is not much money for an institution that has a $3.5 billion endowment—that he will, instead, fund a lecture series or bring in a visiting writer or something of that kind. It seems to me that the basic problem there is that he and his advisors simply didn't know what a quarterly does for a university.

"It's astonishing, really that a little school like Sewanee has supported a magazine for almost one hundred years. Except for the very first few years when the magazine was funded privately (although by people who were with the university after all) the college has always supported it and put a lot of money into it."

The problems of the *Yale Review* lead, by a simple and direct segue, to what Core calls "a very complicated matter," the recent history of the *Kenyon Review*.

"T. R. Hummer edited the *Kenyon* for about a year after having been managing editor of the *New England Review* (*NER*)—*Bread Loaf Quarterly*. Then he decided he could go back to the *NER* and left them, at the *Kenyon*, high and dry."

Following the departure of Hummer, David Lynn was a kind of temporary editor.

"He was never given a chance to grow into the job," Core adds. "Just to hold it together until they could find somebody. Then—believe it or not—I was told that the three final candidates were all from Manhattan. I don't know who they voted for, whether it was Koch or Dinkins, but the fact is that there were plenty of people elsewhere in the country who would have been at least as good and maybe better.

"So now the editor they chose, Marilyn Hacker, says that she cannot bear to leave Manhattan until her child finishes school in the Bronx. Which to me is comparable to saying that you are enjoying having your house napalmed and so you will stay in it until it burns to the ground. The problem is, I don't think she can edit a magazine long distance from Manhattan. And her first issue certainly indicates that. In her initial editorial she is talking mainly about censorship and the NEA and about the fact that the *Kenyon* cannot possibly take a six- or seven- thousand dollar NEA grant if it means she will have to censor her authors. It seems to me that censorship is not the real issue and that it's simply a matter of terminology. It will be interesting to see what happens, but I don't think anybody can edit a magazine long distance for a lengthy period of time."

Core immediately thinks of an exception to his own rule, however, Joseph Epstein of the *American Scholar*, who has a very good staff working in Washington. He also notes that the *American Scholar* has always been edited in this way, that Hiram Hayden also edited the magazine from New York. "But this is the only exception I can think of. Every other editor is going to have to be on the ground most of the time in order to get his quarterly out."

I ask Core about some of the other directions taken by quarterlies, for instance the special issues, entirely built around a subject, published by the *Michigan Quarterly Review*.

"In theory the *Michigan Quarterly* idea might work, but in practice, when you see those special issues on the airplane and the automobile and things of that kind, although they could be good, they just don't work out. The issue on the automobile had one very brilliant little piece in it that was about two pages long, but the rest of it was almost a dead loss.

"One thing that goes on at a lot of quarterlies is that people think you can hoke up these ideas and bring in great editors who will be interested in following up on a subject. But the truth is every quarterly has to have an editor, a benevolent dictator (he may even have to be a savage dictator) and he can't just farm things out. He can't just pass his magazine around to everyone in the country and have him do a special issue.

"If you look at the history of literary quarterlies, beginning with Ford Madox Ford, you will see that the editor is the essential ingredient in these magazines and is in general a person who has been a benevolent tyrant."

Any exceptions to that observation?

"The one exception I can think of, of the idea that there should be one editor only, is the case of Brooks and Warren. Brooks and Warren working together were such an extraordinary team that they made up a third person. You can read their textbooks and you can't tell which one is writing. And yet, if you read the criticism of either man, there is a distinct difference in style in many respects."

Since Brooks and Warren are associated with the inception and the heyday of the *Southern Review*, this leads to some consideration of that venerable and once-influential quarterly.

"In general the way that the *Southern Review* has been edited since then bears out what I am talking about. I had Malcolm Cowley say to me one time in conversation, and not with any malice whatsoever, that the *Southern Review* was two different magazines. He was speaking, of course, of the two different editors—Lewis P. Simpson and Donald Stanford. I think the same thing is likely to be true now with Dave Smith and James Olney editing the magazine."

What about the regional situation, the place of the quarterlies, then and now, in southern letters?

"Well, for a long time there were two southern university presses and a few quarterlies that carried the whole southern literary establishment. There was the *Sewanee Review*; there was the *Southern Review*; there was that magazine that came out of New Orleans, the *Double Dealer*. The whole literary scene in the South used to depend on the quarterlies and two university presses— LSU and North Carolina. Now we have got a much better situation. We have got at least a half a dozen good university presses. And the South is probably characteristic of the rest of the country in that there are too damn many publications, too many magazines. We have really got too many magazines in the South and all the rest of the country. I would hate to see any of the good ones go. But, on the other hand, if somebody came to you or me and said what do we think about starting another quarterly, I hope we would say it is the most dismal idea we have ever heard of."

What *about* the future? What do the 1990s look like to this editor?

"Well, I would like to find some way of recharging our batteries, so to speak. I don't really know how to do this. I think that a magazine, when it tries to be different, is usually on the way out."

He cites the example of *Grand Street* which he sees as "now finished."

"It's got a new format; it's got a new editor; it's bloomed with illustrations. The writing looks much worse. It's got the first interview or two in the magazine's history. I think that it's very important for a quarterly to stick to what it has always done well. And I think literary quarterlies essentially ought to stick to literature. One of the big-

gest problems all of us have is that nobody reads with much intelligence. I don't know what to do about that. One of the essential aspects of the good quarterly is that your readers have got to know what you are going to do. You can have a lively magazine, but you also need to have a discernible program, one that your readers recognize and understand."

One West Range, the impeccable address in Charlottesville from which the *Virginia Quarterly Review* (*VQR*) is edited and at which this interview with its editor, Staige Blackford, took place, is a cluster of elegant high-ceilinged, early-nineteenth-century rooms, with fireplaces and with wide stained and waxed floorboards. It is part of Thomas Jefferson's original grounds, which is now a National Landmark. That the editor and his staff have to use the bathrooms over in Alderman Library, across a street and a good fifty yards away, only adds to the authentic ambiance. Blackford, a Rhodes Scholar and press secretary for Virginia's former governor Linwood Holton, took over the magazine following the retirement of Charlotte Kohler, who edited the *VQR* from 1942 through 1975. "I inherited from Charlotte one of our foremost intellectual beacons," he says. "And my job is to keep that beacon shining." He adds that the changes he has made are few. "I got rid of the Roman numerals and I've changed the covers a little bit." The precise shade of orange paper used for the covers ran out and is unavailable; so they have been using another shade of orange. About a year ago Blackford introduced photographs to the *VQR* cover, including some surprising faces—U. S. Grant, for example, or, for the Autumn 1990 issue, Abbie Hoffman, looking altogether shaggy-haired and ethnic and wearing a shirt made out of an American flag. "I wanted to jazz it up a little bit." Blackford says. "I wanted to appeal to a younger audience. That's one of my worries. People die off. One of my big concerns is what kind of an audience we are going to have ten years down the road. We have a lot of younger people, including graduate students, writing for us, partly because of the magazine's 'Notes on Current Books' section . . ."

From a huge stack of new books displayed on a large round oak table, faculty and graduate students may browse and select books, signing out to review them within a specified time limit. These reviews, published without attribution, appear in one of the eight sections of "Notes on Current Books" section: "History," "Literary Studies," "Lives and Letters," "Fiction," "National & International Affairs," "Poetry," and "General"; each section being composed of roughly fifteen reviews running from about 250 to 500 words apiece.

". . . But I also try to get young people writing regularly for us throughout the magazine, because I figure they are going to be the writers of tomorrow. And I have brought along any number of young writers in the magazine. In part, at least, it is an organ for younger writers.

"This is such a TV age," he adds. "But I think there is a future. We are trying to keep an ideal alive."

Other editors of quarterlies find Blackford in an enviable position. Although the 1989-1991 economic downturn has hurt the subscription lists of many literary publications and, in fact, has cut the numbers for the *VQR*, to something less than four thousand subscribers, he is still doing better in a bad time than almost any comparable magazine except the *American Scholar*. "What would I like to have right now that I don't have?" he asks. "Five thousand more subscribers."

He continues: "One thing I really don't have any idea of is what is the readership of this magazine; because forty percent of the subscribers are libraries. So you have no real idea who reads them or how many or when.

"The other day I got a letter from a guy in Hawaii, who has not only become a subscriber, but has given subscriptions to two friends for Christmas, because he was so taken by a story about Vietnam. He had been there. We do go fairly far afield, then. I know, for example, that the Quarterly is read at Queens College, Oxford, and it's read at the Atheneum club in London. Some of our regular contributors are from England and Ireland.

"I don't often get a lot of flak or reader response, mainly, I think, because we don't run a letters section. One thing, though, that I've gotten a lot of response about is a book review in the Autumn 1990 issue, written for me by a former World War II air force pilot, in which he took apart the women's air force."

The book in question, reviewed in the "Notes on Current Books" section of the Autumn 1990 issue, is *For God, Country and the Thrill of It: Women Air Force Service Pilots in World War II* (Texas A & M), by Anne Noggle. The words which most deeply offended seem to have been

the following: "From the very beginning when Jacqueline Cochran spread her political wings and brought this coterie of unneeded, out of place female fameseekers onto the public payroll, it was clear there would be costs in excess of results. The costs were not only in government property damaged and destroyed, the performance of missions which could have more appropriately been accomplished as training flights for combat-bound pilots, the lives of 38 of the women involved, but more importantly, in the morale of the combat pilots and air-crews whose job it was to fly into battle against the enemy. This coffee-table tome is distinguished by its photographic evidence that feminine youth and beauty are brutally evanescent. The contrast between the exciting comeliness of the girls who fill the wartime snapshots and the misshapen hags and scarecrows whose portraits adorn the latter half of the book should make any young man contemplating marriage pause and reflect."

. . . misshapen hags and scarecrows. . . !

"I have received letters from the women's air force," Blackford continues, more amused than distracted. "I have been castigated by the director of the Texas A & M Press. I heard this guy was getting ready to write a letter of protest to the AAUP, or somebody or other, demanding a formal investigation."

Then, after a pause for laughter: "I like controversy."

As edited by Blackford, the *Virginia Quarterly Review* reviews more titles per issue than any other quarterly in the nation. In addition to "Notes on Current Books" there is a large, back-of-the-book section of essay-length reviews—"Discussions of Recent Books." And within the main body of the magazine there are regularly literary essays and chronicle reviews which are essentially book reviews. For example, the Summer 1990 issue offered Peter Harris's essay "Forty Years of Richard Wilbur: The Loving Work of an Equilibrist." (The combination of essay reviewer of contemporary poetry at this time.) "Discussions of Recent Books" offered six essay reviews of nine books on a variety of subjects—literary, historical, political, biographical—including one more, "An Unacknowledged Poet" by Greg Johnson, on *The Time Traveller*, by Joyce Carol Oates. Other essays in the issue, for instance the lead essay, "Chinese Students and the Burden of the Past," by Hardy C. Wilcoxon, Jr., began in response and reaction to a variety of books on the general subject.

Staige Blackford, editor of the Virginia Quarterly Review

"Book reviewing has always been an essential part of this quarterly ever since it came into existence," Blackford allows. Faced with the fact that the shrinking shelf life of commercially published books is now reported to be down to a brisk and brief six weeks, Blackford has no illusions about having much influence on or relationship with the world of commercial publishing. "We do depend on publishers for advertising, but commercial publishers don't do as much as they used to. Otherwise, though, we are not in any way trying to sell books. I don't think our reviews are exactly 'reviews of record,' but you might call them, sometimes, a court of last resort.

"One of the reasons I don't as a rule have essay-reviews of books by, oh, say, John Updike and people like that is that you know their books are going to be reviewed to a fare-thee-well anyway. But sometimes there is a case where an author can bring a particular slant to a review, whether or not that book has already been widely reviewed. For example, take *The Diary of H. L. Mencken* (reviewed by Vincent Fitzpatrick, "After Such Knowledge, What Forgiveness?," Summer 1990). I got the book reviewed by a guy who works at the library there, the Enoch Pratt

Free Library of Baltimore. And the reason I did was that he disputes the fact that Mencken was anti-Semitic. He takes exception with the editor (Charles A. Fecher), who is a friend of his. I thought that was an interesting angle.

"But talking about the timing of book reviews, I've got one now on a book that came out in 1988 and the review will appear in 1991. The reasons I am running the review are (a) it's a very good review and (b) because I haven't seen any other reviews of the book. It's an encyclopedia of the French Revolution, published by Harper's."

Does he have any kind of agenda, personal or otherwise?

Not really. ("Well, it's probably personal, but, anyway, I just don't run any science fiction reviews.") It is true that most of his essay-reviews are assigned to likely reviewers. But he also has the regular services of people on the faculty of the large university who have a variety of interests and who write well and with style about books and subjects that interest them. "I've got a couple or three from the English Department, two from History, one in Government and so forth. I have got some good standbys." He would like to do more pieces, including reviews, in the fields of science and medicine. "We try to do more of that, but it's hard to get that kind of an article. We have had some people on our board from the medical faculty, and I would really like to have more material on health and medicine. I would also like to have something about religion. I can't recall that I have ever published anything about religion. That may have to do with my own agnostic tendencies. I don't know about contemporary philosophy . . ."

How about deconstruction?

"Literary theology? Good God, no! You know I was amazed to find myself agreeing with the *Wall Street Journal* in a recent editorial on being 'politically correct' in the universities. We have got some of those intellectual fascists around here, too."

Which among the quarterlies does Staige Blackford most enjoy and admire?

"We are supposed to have brotherhood," he says. "We don't usually say anything bad about each other. The rule is not to speak ill of the other quarterlies.

"Well . . . I admire the *Sewanee*, of course. And I like the *American Scholar*, a lot actually, and the *Hudson* and the *Michigan Quarterly*. Then there's what I call the uptown *Readers' Digest*—

Woodrow Wilson Quarterly. Which is a disappointment, it seems to me. It promised a lot more than it has performed. There's another one I used to admire—the *Yale Review.* I had forgotten about that one since it no longer exists. But I hear they are going to try to revive it."

What are his biggest problems at present?

"The thing that's overwhelming is the number of short stories we get every week. Look at that!"

He points to a huge stack of envelopes on a table.

"I am trying to run four short stories in every issue just to catch up a little. But even when I accept something I have to tell them it will probably be two years before I can publish it."

III:

Literary Journalism: Good News and Bad News

On Friday evening I am sitting in a luxurious hotel lounge knee-to-knee with Ivana Trump. So no one can say my life in journalism has been a total waste.
—David Brooks, "Schmoozing at the Frankfurt 'Buchmesse',"

Wall Street Journal

When a media phenomenon reaches a certain mass, criticism responds more to images and allegations than to the work itself.
—David Streitfeld, " 'Psycho' Analysis,"

Washington Post Book World (16 December 1990)

The subjects of literary journalism in 1990 followed the trends established in recent years, becoming more and more a matter of people and issues than books and texts, these latter being serviceable to literary journalists mainly as an occasion for the exploitation of the former. Similarly, outside the official boundaries of book pages, popular magazine and newspaper literary criticism often came disguised as a personality piece. For example, reviewer Jay Parini, finding *Fame* magazine as a home for his review of John Updike's latest novel *Rabbit at Rest* (Knopf)— "Hare Apparent," *Fame*, October—wraps an essay-review of the novel in the context of "an exclu-

sive interview" (which took place, briefly enough, in a Burger King!), rich with all the ritual gestures of the pop personality piece: "Updike enters the Burger King in chinos and a freshly pressed oxford shirt; he is, indeed, wearing Topsiders." "Freshly pressed" is a little sloppy. A witness can tell if a shirt has been pressed or not and whether it is clean and probably recently donned, but not, of course, if it has been just ironed. The irony of this, though, is that Parini's book review, though something of a puff piece, is a good and thorough treatment of this "final" novel in the four-part Rabbit series. Moreover, he sets himself another complex critical problem. Parini manages to argue that the new book proves that Updike is "politically correct," after all, in spite of various moderately conservative comments and observations he has made in interviews and essays. Parini argues that "a careful reading of the new book will prove that Updike, like so many writers, is smarter in his fiction than in 'real' life. As Rabbit Angstrom, in late middle age, is forced to deal with, for instance, his son's gay friend, Lyle, who has AIDS; with his son's addiction to drugs; with the general filthy mess that America, through greed and unbenign neglect, has become; one senses his growing political (and, of course, spiritual) awareness of things." The critic argues that Updike hates "the general filthy mess" that is contemporary America as much as any left-wing intellectual in good standing.

A doubtful proposition, but nonetheless significant in terms of one of the topics which was much discussed by journalists of all stripes—the importance of being demonstrably "politically correct," or, as it is abbreviated, without a ghost of irony, PC, in contemporary intellectual circles. Much of this problem first surfaced, at least for the general public, in public arguments among educators and critics about "quality" and "the canon." An important argument against too much thoughtless canon-bashing appeared near the end of the year, appropriately, in the *Chronicle of Higher Education* (December 5)—"Milton as Misogynist, Shakespeare as Elitist, Homer as Pornographer," by W. Robert Connor, director of the National Humanities Center. He argued that historical and social contexts are important, "but if the work is treated simply as a product of, or commentary on, such contexts, its distinctiveness is lost." A week later the *Chronicle* presented a front page story—"Academic Group Fighting the 'Politically Correct Left' Gains Momentum," by

Carolyn J. Mooney—which proved to be a report on the growing ranks of the National Association of Scholars (NAS). Complicating the situation for reflexive thinkers is the fact that some of the scholars in the organization, James David Barber of Duke, for example, are liberals of long standing and good repute. Barber served as chairman of Amnesty International U.S.A. Stanley Fish, chairman of the English department at Duke, wrote a letter to the student newspaper there arguing that the NAS is "widely known to be racist, sexist, and homophobic." There were plenty of hard feelings all around, and the battle spilled onto the editorial pages of national newspapers. The *Wall Street Journal* aroused a great deal of reaction with its 26 November editorial, "Politically Correct," and opened the new year with another shot at the subject (4 January 1991)—"PC at Hampshire College." Popular journalism quickly picked up on the topic. It became the cover story, the subject of a lengthy treatment, "A Gathering Storm Over the 'Politically Correct'," in *Newsweek* (24 December). The piece was nothing if not inconclusive, but, anyway, included a brief profile of Stanley Fish, who defended himself, and the inevitable confrontations resulting from strenuous efforts to police thought in universities, with a cheerful aphorism—"Disagreements can be fun."

How all of this will subsequently touch upon or even shape contemporary American writing remains to be seen. With so many American writers living and working in the colleges and universities, it seems bound to influence them and their art, one way or another. It seems more than likely to produce a "chilling effect" upon any literary work that might possibly be taken (never mind faint intention) as not PC. Meantime the Parini review of *Rabbit at Rest* demonstrates clearly (something we may already have guessed or at least inferred from the evidence at hand) that being PC may have more than a little to do with the success or failure of a new book and its author.

The Spring 1990 issue of the *Authors Guild Bulletin* led off with a proud statement of particular purpose and affiliation: "The Authors Guild has joined with Poets & Writers, PEN American Center (New York), PEN Center USA West (L.A.), Coordinating Council of Literary Magazines (CCLM), Associated Writing Programs, The Loft (Minneapolis), the Writer's Center (Bethesda, MD), and a number of small presses and magazines to head off any Congressional move to-

wards further restrictions of the National Endowment of the Arts [NEA]." A summer of noise and no little lobbying followed, though out of what necessity and to what avail no one has yet determined. At that point, with the matter not yet officially debated (or even much discussed except for the benefit of media) in Congress, it was unclear that the NEA, though somewhat pressured, was in any serious trouble. By early fall, modified by only one vague and cautionary phrase, the appropriations legislation had passed easily and the NEA was back in business as before. That phrase, created by Rep. Paul Henry (R-Mich) stated that the Endowment will fund projects of artistic excellence and merit that uphold "general standards of decency and respect for the diverse beliefs and values of the American public." Following which most people and institutions readily (if not always gratefully) accepted their tax-funded grants. Even before the issue was settled most grant recipients accepted awards made in 1990. For example, during that year the NEA awarded grants to thirty-six small presses. Thirty-four accepted their grants. Two—Four Walls Eight Windows (twenty-five thousand dollars) and the University of Iowa Press (twelve thousand dollars), the latter with much breast-beating and publicity—turned them down. At least for the time being. It seems likely, now that the problem has been more or less settled, that these two presses will now accept new grants. Will take the money and run. Quietly. It also seems likely that we, readers and interested taxpayers, will never know; for the media dropped the subject instantly when it was clear that the dramatic possibilities were now quite limited. The press did not completely ignore the story's end. At this writing there has been one more featured item in the national press, more in terms of a victory celebration than a fact piece, coinciding with the announcement that the Endowment, on 4 January 1991, announced grants of $47 million to some twelve hundred individual artists and arts organizations, "including" according to Judith Weintraub of the *Washington Post* ("NEA Approves Delayed Grants," 6 January) "the work of controversial performance artists Karen Finley and Holly Hughes." The *New York Times* ("Arts Endowment Reverses Stand," 5 January 1991) quoted performance artist Holly Hughes, who earlier identified herself as "openly lesbian," as saying of her funded project, "No Trace of the Blond": "I hope it will be everything that Jesse Helms fears."

But these matters were larger national concerns, not the specific and limited concern of literary journalism. Literary journalism, in all its aspects including book reviewing, is very much at the mercy of the ebb and flow of publicity. It tends to serve, at least in part (sometimes in large part), as the public relations wing of the publishing business and the literary establishment. One of the most significant articles published by *Publishers Weekly* during the year was Thomas Weyr's "Publicity's New Punch" (16 November). Basically, the piece described the many changes, mostly a matter of ever greater emphasis, which have taken place in the publicity departments of the publishers. Publicity has graduated from arranging publication parties to arranging and managing national tours—at least for some of their more important writers. Leigh Haber, publicity director for Harcourt Brace Jovanovich, is quoted with the aphorism that is the basic theme of Weyr's article: "Publicity used to be the icing on the cake. Now it is far more significant: it can make or break a book." Of course, what has happened is that the limited resources of the publishers' publicity departments are usually committed to the potential blockbusters, leaving the remainder of the trade list, estimated in this article as in excess of eighty percent, to be in the latest catch phrase—"review driven," which is defined as follows by Roger Cohen of the *New York Times* ("As Many Books Reach Print, The Interest Fizzles," 3 September): "Bewildered by the lack of advertising, the apparent inertia of publishers and the absence of their books in the stores, the authors get to know a euphemism widespread among publishing houses: they are told the book will be 'review driven'." Meaning next to no advertising, publicity, or promotion. Meaning sink or swim. Fly or die. Meaning that so-called serious or literary writers must manage to capture the wandering attention of literary journalists and book reviewers. Which, in turn and inevitably, means that, except for brand new and previously unknown writers, the literary press depends as much on "track record" (previous sales or prizes) as anybody else in the business. Meaning, finally, that the literary journalists are driven by their own contingencies and circumstances to support and maintain the literary establishment with its known hierarchies and established reputations. Meaning, finally, that with a six-week shelf life for most trade books (precious little time for the magic of "word of mouth" to work), the innocent and interested reader is more at the mercy of the literary journal-

ists than ever before and, therefore, unlikely to learn of anything new and different which might go against the grain of the literary establishment.

The increasing importance of publicity, and of a complex symbiotic relationship between literary press and publishers, has focused attention on the publishing business itself, its special problems and, in tune with these self-reflexive times, its view of itself. Both the *Wall Street Journal* and the *New York Times* regularly (and competitively) publish articles on the publishing business. Those in the *Times*, most often by Edwin McDowell, are addressed not to the industry, but to a more general reader. Inevitably, most McDowell pieces are educational, at least at the outset, telling this general and presumably interested reader basic things that may be taken for granted by people in the business. A pertinent example is a piece on the subject of sales conferences—"Companies Rally the Troops/To Incite Them to Sell Books," *New York Times*, 10 December—which opens with a brief and basic definition of a sales conference: "Employees of Macmillan Inc. and of Bantam Doubleday Dell are in Florida this week for that publishing ritual known as the sales conference. Part strategy session and part pep rally, its purpose is to introduce a company's sales force to the books the house hopes to turn into best sellers four to eight months from now." Not news to people in publishing or to regular readers of *Publishers Weekly*; nevertheless of some value to the often ignored general reader. A typical *Wall Street Journal* article, for example Meg Cox's "Blockbusters Give Fall Books a Needed Boost" (15 October), assumes somewhat more business acumen and sophistication (most *WSJ* readers know a little bit about buying and selling) and even some familiarity with publishing.

But contemporary journalism being what it is, it is the nifty combination of people and business that attracts the most attention. Gordon Lish, Knopf fiction editor and editor of the *Quarterly*, is a perennial source of copy, as in "Gordon Lish: A Man of Lofty Letters" ("Infamous writer and teacher Gordon Lish is in a snit, says a source . . ."), in *New York* magazine, 19 November. Something of the place of a bright young mover-and-shaker in contemporary publishing is illustrated by the general context ("The Three Divorces of John and Pat Kluge," "Hugh Hefner's Interview," "Gotti, Inc.: Portfolio of a Family Business") in the men's fashion magazine *M Inc.*, September, of a profile of poet and editor (Farrar, Straus and Giroux) Jonathan Galassi—"The

Burden of Profit." ("Sitting behind a desk in his office, four floors above Union Square, obscured by mountains of books and manuscripts, the 41-year-old Galassi fiddles nervously with a paper clip. He has thick, black hair and a slightly awkward, boyish posture; his horn-rimmed glasses make him look like a nerdy Romeo.") In New York City this kind of personal reviewing may help. Certainly the journalistic interest in publishing and especially publishers is at least tinted if not colored by regional social concerns and the fact that many journalists write books and need publishers for them. Galassi was also one of the featured figures in "Books & Bucks," (*Village Voice Literary Supplement*, May), where he is quoted expressing an appropriately cheerful, upbeat view of things: "In spite of all the trouble and trauma of recent months, it feels easier than ever to make a go of publishing serious books. The audience for them is broader, more willing, more adventurous, more widespread, hungrier for alternatives to the white bread of network culture." Another important piece on the business of publishing, rich with facts and numbers and soundbite quotes from agents, editors, writers, was Frank Kiernan's "The Great Publishing Crash of 1989," *7 Days*, 24 January 1990.

Except for being overtaken by other more urgent and unexpected events, the literary year of 1990 might have ended up being named the Year of Joni Evans. Carrying over (like a major best-seller) from 1989, the story of her divorce form her former boss, Richard Snyder, CEO at Simon and Schuster, was still deemed interesting enough to merit a full-scale article, well illustrated, in the June issue of *Manhattan, Inc.*, "The Cook, The Chief, His Wife and Her Career," by Philip Weiss: "It was the ultimate publishing marriage: he didn't read, she didn't cook." (The same issue contained another literary personality piece, Charles Kaiser's "Manhattan Ink," a mixed review of Bob Gottlieb's relatively new editorship at the *New Yorker*, arguing that "at Gottlieb's *New Yorker*, the more things change, the more they stay the same.") By late fall the headlines and articles about Joni Evans were more matters of business than domesticity as she was suddenly replaced as publisher at Random House by magazine and newspaper editor Harold Evans (unrelated). This story was taken as news by the *Times*, the *Wall Street Journal* and brought out the double-barreled journalistic gifts of Charles Trueheart and David Streitfeld of the *Washington Post* ("Management Shuffle at Random House," 31 October

1990). The national news magazines played the story also, most amusingly in *Newsweek* (12 November) under the headline "Manhattan Cannibals." See also *Time* magazine's 12 November piece "Random Taps a Tough Brit." *Publishers Weekly* came along with the most thorough and factual, as well as the most polite version of the events—"Harold Evans to Head Random House; Joni Evans to Form Own Imprint" (9 November).

With publicity more and more accepted as the premium fuel for literary success, and all the more so as most newspaper book pages shrink or barely hold onto their own turf, it is not surprising that other literary journalists took the route assumed by Jay Parini in his Updike review and used the occasion of book publication to create an indirect review in the context, camouflage, of an interview or profile. These are many and various. The *New York Times Magazine* became a regular publisher of this kind of piece. Noteworthy examples during the year, among others, were Mira Stout's "Martin Amis: Down London's Mean Streets" (4 February); Gerald Marzorati's "Rushdie in Hiding" (4 November); and Tad Friend's "Rolling Boyle: Novelist T. Coraghessan Boyle Hungers for the Respectability of William Faulkner and the Fame of Zsa Zsa Gabor" (9 December). True to itself and its own form, *Spy* (April 1990) published a cover story "McInerney Dearest," based on an interview with pop novelist Jay McInerney's wife, Merry, and advertised as an "Ultravoyeuristic Account of Her Doomed Marriage." Novelist Larry McMurtry received in *M Inc.* (December) somewhat the same sort of treatment, albeit kindhearted and, at the last, praising him highly, in "Lonesome Dude," by Cecil Cleveland, who is purported to be the original model for Jacy Farrow of *The Last Picture Show*: "The real-life Jacy Farrow deconstructs her childhood friend." As president of PEN American Center, McMurtry was also in the news concerning various internal squabbles in that volatile organization, and himself produced a piece for *Poets & Writers* (March/April) on the battle over the NEA— "Sex, Art and Jesse Helms," a cogent and amusing argument marred only by a minor misquotation of former Washington Redskins fullback John Riggins. Riggins told Sandra Day O'Connor to "lighten up," not to "loosen up." Incidentally, though in keeping with the theme of the regional (New York) domestication of writers, the "Evening Hours" section of the *New York Times* for Sunday, 8 April offered pictures of dancing writers (men in black tie) at the PEN-Mont Blanc Gala dinner at Roseland ballroom, including a cheerful photo of Pulitzer Prize-winner Annie Dillard "doing the jitterbug at the PEN dance." That happy PEN Gala may well prove to be the last of its kind, for a while, anyway. See "Socialite Cuts Ties to Writers," (*Washington Post*, 29 August 1990): "Mega-socialite and mighty fund-raiser Gayfryd Steinberg has severed her ties to the New York writers' organization [*sic*] PEN after *New York Daily News* columnist Ken Auletta called her husband, well-known corporate raider Saul Steinberg, 'sleazy' in a New York magazine gossip column."

There are, occasionally, happier uses of the literary publicity machines, sometimes for discovery or rediscovery. For example, when writer Charles Johnson won the National Book Award for his novel *Middle Passage*, an award somewhat marred by a burst of publicity about arguments and divisions among the judges, the press rushed forward to introduce this fine writer to readers (and themselves). Best coverage, overall: "The Author's Diverse Universe: Charles Johnson on Race and Writing," by Marjorie Williams (*Washington Post*, 4 December). Rediscovery, or, anyway, turning a spotlight on talent that has not been widely known or appreciated, is (strangely enough) a rare form of literary journalism. Representative of this exception to present practice is David Streitfeld's profile, "Maxwell the Smart" (*Fame*, Winter 1991), about the longtime (and very influential) *New Yorker* fiction editor William Maxwell.

One of the happiest, and most ironic, "rediscoveries" of the year, or many years, resulted from the appearance of novelist and historian Shelby Foote on the hugely popular public television documentary *The Civil War*. Suddenly, following the airing of that show, his name and picture were everywhere. He was, at seventy-three, an instant celebrity. There were pieces in the papers and the magazines. *USA Today* gave him most of a page ("Shelby Foote, Reflecting On His 'Civil War' Glory," 1 October). And because he is of age, Foote could be appropriately profiled in *AARP* (November) by William Thomas, "Shelby Foote's 'War': Civil War Chronicler Struggles Now For A Little Peace," the burden of which was simple enough. "All he wants to do now, says Foote, is ride out the publicity storm and hope that pop artist Andy Warhol was right when he said that fame lasts only 15 minutes."

Foote's time of fame seems likely to last at least through April 1991; for both he and Alex Haley are scheduled to be hosts and lecturers on a Mississippi River cruise of the celebrated *Delta Queen*, April 11-19.

Not all other working writers of 1990 seem to share Foote's ironic view of the pleasures and pains of publicity.

* * * * *

Much British tax money has been spent on safe houses, police guards and secure telephones. But now Mr. Rushdie has turned on his hosts and insulted their Faith. Hospitality is no longer the point. Britain no longer needs to shelter Mr. Rushdie. The next stop is obvious.
—*Raymond Sokolov, "Posturing in Vain for the Ayatollahs,"* Wall Street Journal *(9 January 1991)*

Salman Rushdie may or may not be a magic realist, a master of the novel form, a literary genius; but 1990 proved conclusively that he is a master magician at public relations and, considering the restrictive circumstances he has been faced with, all year spent more or less in hiding, albeit comfortable enough and well guarded, he has to be a genius at keeping his career actively alive. Of course, he had more than a little bit of help from his friends and especially his newfound friends, the literary journalists who knew an ever ready source of copy, gossip, and speculation when they saw one. Clark Blaise and Bharati Mukherjee, good friends and true, produced a major piece on Rushdie for *Mother Jones*—"After The Fatwa" (April/May 1990)—in which they pointed out the obvious; that once he had received the very large advance for *The Satanic Verses*, Rushdie was a clearcut subject for literary journalism waiting for something, anything, really, to happen. They wrote: "The advance ($850,000) helped transform Rushdie, already an undeniable literary superstar, but with limited sales potential, into a super-cruiserweight status, and virtually assured that the book would be treated as news, not literature." April was also the month when American writer Marianne Wiggins abruptly left her husband, Salman Rushdie, to move about more freely and ostensibly to promote her own 1989 novel, *John Dollar* (Harper and Row) which is, in her words ("The Stress of Being an Author and Being Married to Salman Rushdie," *New York Times*, 4 April 1990) "a book about imperialism and the United States as an empire, the empire of the dollar." On the same day the *Washington Post*'s "Style" section devoted its long lead story to her—"The Postponed

Life of Marianne Wiggins," by Paula Span. Essentially these, and others orchestrated at the same time, were domestic stories concerning an evidently happy marriage which was being subjected to unusual stress. There was no indication that the separation between Rushdie and Wiggins was a permanent condition until in a later cover story in the *New York Times Magazine* ("Rushdie In Hiding," by Gerald Marzorati, 4 November 1990) Rushdie made it seem plain enough: " 'I will tell you about my marriage in one sentence,' he said, and drew another cigarette from his pack. 'My marriage is over.' " Of course, one must remember, with the advantage of hindsight, that this is the same piece in which he is quoted as saying that he is not a Muslim, never has been a believer, but a "secular, pluralistic, eclectic man." And in the same interview he came out strongly in favor of the paperback publication of *The Satanic Verses*. Both of these things, and others, he would take a diametrically opposite position on within less than a month. According to *Newsweek* ("Rushdie Embraces the Faith," 7 January 1991), the same magazine in which Rushdie in an interview in February 1990 declared unequivocally, "I am not a Muslim," Rushdie met with some moderate Islamic leaders on Christmas Eve and "publicly asserted his belief that 'there is no God but Allah and that Muhammad is his last prophet.' " This conversion or reconversion ("Religion to me has always meant Islam") followed a series of television appearances and, in December, a sudden, unannounced, well-guarded appearance in some London bookstores to sign copies of his latest book, written while in hiding, *Haroun and the Sea of Stories* (Granta/Viking), all of the above widely covered by the press. "I feel a lot safer tonight than I felt yesterday." Rushdie was quoted in the *New York Times* in a front page story on Christmas Day. The press also, of course, reached out to fundamentalist Iran and reported the almost instantaneous response of Iran's spiritual leader—Ayatollah Ali Khamenei: "No Iranian Forgiveness for Rushdie" (*New York Times*); "Rushdie Still Must Die, Iranian Ayatollah Declares" (Reuters). Next day (28 December), Rushdie waved a polite white flag on the Op-Ed page of the *New York Times*: "Now I Can Say I Am A Muslim: New Threats From Iran Are Dismaying." "I appeal to all Muslims, and to Muslim organizations and governments everywhere, to join in the process of healing that we have begun." What will happen next remains to be seen, the only certainty being that whatever happens will be accompanied by a brass marching band of publicity. As for Rushdie's real motives, above and beyond publicity for its own sake and for the sake of selling, if possible, many more books, nobody is certain; or, more accurately, as the *Newsweek* story put it, "Only one person really knew what lay behind the avowal—and he was insisting on the act's authenticity." Authentic or not, whining ("I haven't been to a movie for a year, I can't walk down the street, I can't go to a bookshop.") or courageous, Rushdie's actions were all splendidly timed. But, then, as he told Clark Blaise and Bharati Mukherjee about his attempt to make "a two-part statement to the moderate Muslim community": "Timing's important. We plan to orchestrate it."

One of the best of the multitude of Rushdie articles published in 1990 was, in fact, a book review, "Shame," by Paul Berman, an essay review of three new books about Rushdie and two short pamphlets—"In Good Faith" and "Is Nothing Sacred?," both published by Granta—in the *New Republic* (8 October 1990). The occasion of the review offered Berman the opportunity to rehearse the whole story up to that point, as much of it as is or can be known, and to discuss critically the actions and reactions of those involved on all sides. The result is an extensive and intelligent essay, not without a firm and overt leftwing political bias, but by and large fair and persuasive. Except, perhaps, for one truly outrageous claim that he is neither: namely, that by some magic or other Rushdie and his famous book had something definite to do with the downfall of Eastern European totalitarianism. "The Rushdie affair," Berman writes, "as the first global event in that amazing year (1989), put the question of liberalism versus totalitarianism in a light so clear as to be dazzling, and in that manner helped prepare the tremendous victory that liberalism would shortly achieve in Europe and other regions."

Sounds a little like Jack Valenti on Lyndon Johnson. We can all sleep a lot better knowing that Salman Rushdie is out there, surrounded by young men of Scotland Yard's Special Branch, preparing the shining future for us all.

* * * * *

The cut-rate designer prose and mindless conversation are as obscene as this novel's sex crimes. Don't even crack the cover. (Complete review of American Psycho)

—*Cathleen Medwick,* Mirabbela *January 1991*

Whether or not Rushdie's moves, turns, and counterturns in the last part of 1990 were "orchestrated," part of an attempt to turn bad news into good publicity, he was strongly challenged for space and attention by a young newcomer, Bret Easton Ellis, whose latest novel, *American Psycho* (unpublished and unread in any form, except by a very few people, at this writing) stirred up an angry, noisy swarming in the literary hive. In a sometimes anguished reversal of roles from the lines drawn in the (shifting) sands of the NEA battle and the passionate defense of Salman Rushdie's apparently inalienable right to blaspheme or ridicule as he sees fit, many among the literary establishment found themselves awkwardly favoring at least a boycott of the publisher of *American Psycho*, if not the outright suppression of the book. Widely publicized in the national press, the events which led to the gusher of publicity were simple enough, if not entirely untouched by ambiguity. In the final weeks of November, with *American Psycho* ready for shipment to booksellers for its scheduled early January publication date, the ubiquitous Richard Snyder, according to his own version of things, took time off from his other plans and problems to read for the first time the Bret Ellis novel for which his company, Simon and Schuster, had paid a $300,000 advance. He was prompted to engage in this scholarship as a result of some brief mentions of the book and its contents in the press and the publication by *Spy* of an excerpt from the book. *Publishers Weekly* had already described the book, in its "Forecasts," as "a grisly, gritty gross-out." And in a thorough recapitulation of events, *Newsweek* ("The Killing of a Gory Novel," 26 November) referred to the novel's "gory dismemberings and vivid sexual perversities sprinkled through its 366 pages." By 30 November *Publishers Weekly*'s Maureen O'Brien could casually refer to *American Psycho* as "the graphically sadistic novel," and, soon after, Richard Bernstein of the *New York Times* could begin his summary of the situation ("*American Psycho*, Going So Far That Many Say It's Too Far," 10 December 1990) conceding the chief objections to the novel: "The few people who have actually read Bret Easton Ellis' novel *American Psycho*, which has yet to be published, agree on one thing at least: there are descriptions of murder and sadism so gruesome and grisly that Simon and Schuster's decision not to publish the book on the grounds of taste is understandable." After Snyder read the book, he canceled its publication by Simon and Schuster in

an admittedly belated exercise of taste. Ellis, by contract, kept the large advance and found an editor, Sonny Mehta of Knopf, and a publisher, Knopf's subsidiary Vintage, to do the book. Not all literary journalists accepted Snyder's version of the story, preferring the idea that Snyder only acted in response to the orders of his own boss, Martin Davis of Paramount Communications. This hypothesis, true or false, offered up a full serving of irony in any case; for Paramount itself had earned profits on some pretty grisly films, including the *Friday the 13th* series.

Soon enough all sorts of other people with a diversity of constituencies and interests jumped into the act and shared the publicity limelight with the original principals. Tammy Bruce, described by *Publishers Weekly* as "the charismatic 28-year-old president of the Los Angeles chapter of the National Organization for Women" called for a boycott of all titles by Random House (parent company of Knopf and Vintage) except books by feminists, and warned of "widespread demonstrations " when the book appears in bookstores. "Sonny Mehta made a capitalistic decision to buy the book," she was quoted as saying, "and he's going to pay the capitalistic consequences when he releases it to the public."

Soon the public battlefields, the pages of the national press, were heavily burdened with a cargo of opinions. Author Lorrie Moore, sometimes celebrated for her slightly spacey fiction and the wit therein of her ingenuous non sequiturs, wrote a piece, "Trashing Women, Trashing Books" (*New York Times*, 5 December 1990) which proved, if nothing else, that she can write spacey non sequiturs about real things and events, too: "We live in a country where we probably don't know what our censored books are, and where what we consider censored books become best sellers, even as they're still being called 'censored.' That is what's so amusing, so cute, 'so strange about America."

Say what?

This piece in turn evoked a rash of letters, some by prominent literary figures. Author Robert K. Massie, president of the Authors Guild, corrected Lorrie Moore ("We did not describe this as an act of censorship because it was not an act of censorship. It was a breach of contract" *New York Times*, 14 December). In the same batch of letters, novelist Anne Bernays took a position guaranteed, if not calculated, to focus some attention on herself: "What's all this fuss about violence toward women in a novel? It's worse in real life, it's

Salman Rushdie, in the wake of the controversy over The Satanic Verses, *embraced Islam in 1990 (photograph by Jerry Bauer)*

out there in appalling bloodiness and sorrow, and the situation is not improving. That Mr. Ellis managed to convey it so sickeningly is a tribute to his power as an author no matter what his motives or whether or not he actually knows why he wrote the book." In the "News of the Week" column of *Publishers Weekly* (30 November), Madalynne Reuter offered some inside information on the history and fate of *American Psycho* at Simon and Schuster, quoting an anonymous former editor about (among other things) the impact of publicity on the publisher's strategy: "There was a general feeling in-house that the book was going to lose money unless somehow the negative press backfired and it became an underground hit."

Not much chance of going or staying underground. Especially as, with the year's end in sight, various and sundry big gun feature writers joined the chorus of commentators. Probably the best piece, certainly massive in its wealth of information and wrath of argument, was "Snuff This Book! Will Bret Easton Ellis Get Away With Murder?" by *Life* columnist and essayist for "The MacNeil/Lehrer Newshour," Roger Rosenblatt (*New York Times Book Review*, 16 December 1990). Rosenblatt presented a clear and coherent account of the story to date, including a brief synop-

sis of the novel's basic story line and the introduction of its protagonist Patrick Bateman. The new wrinkles in Rosenblatt's scenario are the assigning of a full share of blame to Knopf's Sonny Mehta and his hirelings at Vintage ("The folks at Vintage seem to me to be the special scoundrels of our tale, whether they are being cynical and avaricious or merely tasteless and avaricious") and giving Bret Ellis the literary equivalent of the kind of thing that happened to many brief opponents of Joe Louis in days gone by. As in this sarcastic crack: "Whatever Melville knew about whaling, whatever Mark Twain knew about rivers are mere amateur stammerings compared with what Mr. Ellis knows about shampoo alone." Or this punch to the point of the jaw—"Someone has to look at Mr. Ellis's rat and call the exterminator."

David Streitfeld's new twist (" 'Psycho' Analysis," *Washington Post Book World*, 16 December 1990) was to bring in parallel and related material—the firing of senior editor Allen Peacock of Simon and Schuster and a letter from a group of Peacock's writers involved both Snyder and Martin Davis; and the denunciation of Doubleday by Cardinal John O'Connor ("Purveyors of hatred and scandal and malice and libel and calumny") concerning their publication of *Eunuchs for the Kingdom of Heaven* by Uta Ranke-Heinemann. Streitfeld took note that as a result of the Cardinal's statement Doubleday increased its original print order of sixty-five hundred copies by an additional twenty-five thousand. And he found an unblinking pragmatist in Doubleday editor Thomas Cahill, who seemed grateful to the cardinal ("We need one another, each in order to do his job properly") and the publicity value of his reaction. "You can be calculating," Cahill was quoted as admitting, "but there's no way to be sure that your calculations are going to come out."

Still, none of this late furor could match the Bret Ellis story; and both of these items were, at least briefly, blown off the pages by the sudden, wholly unexpected turn around and surrender of Salman Rushdie. It is unlikely that we shall ever have any valid evidence as to Rushdie's true feelings or motives, though his old friends Clark Blaise and Bharati Mukherjee in the *Mother Jones* article blithely claim for him certain qualities of character that most people, public and private, strive mightily to disguise, if not to suppress: "In his maneuvering for literary fame and riches, he has deserted many old friends, turned on others, and, as a consequence, been abandoned. It is perhaps only a shallow irony, for a man in his precarious position, that he threatens lawsuits against old friends and lovers, demanding alterations of potentially unflattering descriptions of himself. Hard feelings abound, but the solid front of public support remains."

IV

A Few Miscellaneous and Final Things

Thus the shelf life of a book, which has normally been somewhere between that of milk and yogurt, is getting closer to that of fresh flowers.
—Roger Cohen, *"As Many Books Reach Print, The Interest Fizzles,"* New York Times

On a positive note, Colin Walters, book editor for the *Washington Times* deserves double congratulations for 1990: first, he has managed to create a full-scale, separate book section, "Book Life," to replace the regular and conventional book pages; secondly, he has initiated "The Last Word," a series of one-thousand-word reviews by prominent writers and critics of older books they deem worthy of renewed attention. Changes, especially for the better, in newspaper book pages and sections are glacially slow. These new developments help place the *Washington Times* among the best of the newspapers, nationally, for book reviewing.

The year 1990 offered up more than the usual number of first-rate negative reviews, competitors for the Golden Hatchet Award. From many likely candidates, we have selected five. Two come from the *Washington Times*: Donna Rifkind's review of David Leavitt's *A Place I've*

Never Been (Viking)—"Leavitt's Tales Plumb the Shallows of Despair," (10 September) and " 'Rabbit' Hops into Oblivion with Tale Between Legs," an 8 October review of John Updike's *Rabbit At Rest* (Knopf), by Jeffrey Hart. Three were published in the *Wall Street Journal*: David Klinghoffer's "The Cut-and-Paste Novel," a review of Ann Beattie's *Picturing Will* (Random House), 31 January; "Ship of Fools," by Joe Queenan, a review of *The Death of Literature* (Yale) by Alvin Kernan; and Robert Schulman's "Boys Will Be Boys: Ode to the Old Days," a 19 December review of *Iron John* (Addison-Wesley) by Robert Bly. This last has what must be a strong contender for best wipe-out conclusion:

> Mr. Bly, who lives on a lake in Minnesota, appears to be suffering from a kind of intellectual cabin fever. He has been stuck inside his own head so long that he does not realize he is speaking in an idiosyncratic babble. His book will appeal mostly to the similarly preoccupied.
> Oh, boy.

A viable candidate for the worst all-around book review of 1990 is surely Jane O'Reilly's "Hemingway Was Her Greatest Mistake," a review of Carl Rollyson's biography of Martha Gellhorn, *Nothing Ever Happens to the Brave* (St. Martin's) in *New York Times Book Review*, 30 December. We learn more than we need to know about the reviewer—"Her grandmother, and my grandmother, were stalwart members of the Wednesday Club, a Progressive-era organization of women interested in the vote, good works and cultural enrichment." And, meanwhile, we learn next to nothing about the author, the subject, or his treatment of it. This review is unpersuasively negative, and it is shocking to find it published in the pages of the nation's premier book review.

An Interview with Russell Hoban

Alida Allison
San Diego State University

See also the Hoban entry in *DLB 52: American Writers for Children Since 1960: Fiction.*

Now in his fourth decade of being published, Russell Hoban is equally well respected as a writer of books both for children and adults. The sheer amount of Hoban's output is itself extraordinary: his work includes some sixty books for children, seven novels, many short stories and essays, plays, a libretto, and poetry. With few exceptions, reviewers have praised Hoban's books for children from the time his Frances books began appearing in 1961. His first novel, *The Mouse and His Child*, brought him broad notice in 1967, and critics in general have since admired his writing, taking it seriously even when, as with *The Medusa Frequency* (1987), some were not overwhelmed by a particular work. Two of his novels, *The Mouse and His Child* and *Riddley Walker* (1981), are regarded as masterpieces. Hoban has a loyal and literate readership, even amounting to something of a "cult" on some college campuses; and increasingly, his books are included in university courses, discussed at academic conferences, and covered in periodicals and books.

Hoban resides and writes in a quiet neighborhood in Southwest London. The ground-floor front room of the Hoban family's multistory home, its big front window facing a large common, runs the length of the house, large enough to accommodate Hoban's desk and computer, paintings and Punch and Judy puppets, files of newspaper articles, electronic equipment, ceiling-high rows of books with subjects such as mammal anatomy, fairy tales, physics, and Tarot. Ample room is left for several chairs, a sofa, and tables. Boxes of books fill the corners of the room, which still does not seem crowded, but rather cool and comfortable. Hoban's own books are readily at hand, as are galley proofs and mockups of upcoming books. Versions of work in progress are printed out on the yellow foolscap paper mentioned often in his novels.

Whether writing for adults or children, Hoban's depth and intelligence, his inventive use

Russell Hoban (photograph by Chris Steele-Perkins)

of forms, his painter's eye, his humor and copywriter's quickness with words, and his philosopher's alertness to the implications of language, the relationship among ideas and things, make him one of the most intriguing writers in the English language.

The *DLB* interviewed Hoban in California in fall 1990 during his lecture tour of four universities.

DLB: This is your first visit to California in over twenty years. In a general way, how does it all look to you?

HOBAN: It looks very alien to me because it just looks so relaxed, so horizontal; it looks so low, there is so much sky, and the people that I see don't look at all driven. Everything looks leisure oriented. That seems strange to me. At the same time I am an American, and the voices I hear are familiar ones, the accents are familiar, I find myself sounding like Americans as I speak here. It's strange, but pleasant.

DLB: You said something along the lines that if you lived in a place like California, you wouldn't want to write as much, you would just want to be.

HOBAN: It's a thought that has occurred to me. Whether it would actually be that way, I couldn't say. I think in a place where I would be in a closer contact with nature I would sort of drift into being more and writing less. I don't know, I think probably I can't live without writing so I would simply, if I found myself in a place where I wasn't writing, move back to where I could write.

DLB: And as things were changing in your own neighborhood in London, you moved your own writing situation back into the interior of your own house?

HOBAN: That happened a long time ago. I used to work at a desk that I built into the bay window where I could overlook the street. Then little by little I began to notice that the neighbors, as they passed by, didn't seem to like being looked at by me as I sat in my window, so I withdrew to another desk further into the room and that's where I work now.

DLB: Have the audiences that you've had so far on this rare reading tour of yours surprised you in any way? I know before you came over here you were wondering what an American audience, and American college audiences, would be like.

HOBAN: The audiences at San Diego State University exceeded my expectations. They were very responsive and very enthusiastic. At Cal State Long Beach there was a very nice group. At (the University of California) Riverside, as you said, they probably weren't familiar with my work, while at UCLA, the group was relatively small but seemed very familiar with my writing. But the first two readings at SDSU were especially nice.

DLB: At the first reading at SDSU, "Russell Hoban Reads Russell Hoban," you read from

works you had recently written, "Blighter's Rock," an essay about writer's block which begins, "You'll notice that I don't call it by its right name," and "The Raven," a short story about a man who goes to London Zoo and journeys with a raven to the heart of mystery and back. "Blighter's Rock" was published in one of your son's school magazines. In it, you mentioned that you do get stuck, even in the midst of your very rigorous writing schedule, and that you have certain things that you do when you get stuck.

HOBAN: Well, in "Blighter's Rock," the things that the hypothetical writer does are joke things, I mean like jogging and alcohol and snacks and so forth. When I get stuck I just sit there and take it and try to be as active as I can to get unstuck. I do whatever I can do, I make notes, I look at any reference books that might help me out. On the basis of past experience I figure that I'll get unstuck sometime, so that's what I do.

DLB: For all the talks you've given in California, you've brought out the actual mouse and his child. You've wound the toy up and let it circle and wind down while the audience laughs and sighs. Have you been surprised by the response this has gotten?

HOBAN: No, I'm not really surprised because there is something about a real tangible object that attracts most people. There is nothing theoretical about the mouse and his child. They are what they are, and everybody has played with clockwork toys at one time or another. And everybody, whether they've thought about it or not, has responded in one way or another to the pathos in clockwork toys. It's a thing that has familiarity in it for everyone who sees it.

DLB: In some of the interviews you have given in the past few years you've talked about the specific catalysts for works that you then developed into novels. For example, a stay in the hospital for *Kleinzeit* [1974], or a picture of the lion from Nineveh for *The Lion of Boaz-Jachin and Jachin-Boaz* [1973]. For *The Medusa Frequency* you said it was an olive tree you saw during a trip to Greece that looked like a goddess had just come out of it?

HOBAN: A particular olive tree, yes, on Paxos.

DLB: And the book that you're working on now?

HOBAN: Well, there wasn't one in particular, but in the very first draft the Kraken came into it, so the starting point for this one was *The Medusa Frequency*. I got stuck writing that and then I branched off into this science fiction thing and then, as I say, in the first draft the Kraken came into it. Then I put this aside and got back to *The Medusa Frequency*, finished it and used up the Kraken. Now I've come back to what I'm working on now and new things are growing out of it but without any external stimulus or catalyst . . . gee, I'm worried now that I think of it.

DLB: When you're working on something new you don't like to show it around, you don't like to talk about it?

HOBAN: I don't want to let any of the virtue drain out of it.

DLB: And is that sort of the same feeling as not reading a lot of other people's work?

HOBAN: Well, ever since I've been writing novels I've gone off reading other people, with some exceptions on holiday or sometimes a particular book will be put in my hands that will grab me and I'll read it. It's a little bit like I don't want anything leaking out and I don't want any influences coming in. I don't know why I picked up the Singer and the Jewish short stories and Malamud recently. I think I was looking into a logic for what I am working on now. I also looked at Martin Buber's *Tales of the Hasidim* [1947] and I drifted over into Singer for no particular reason. I have various currents of interest which are always running in my mind, and they might not be active for a long time but they are always there. And certain writers like Singer and Malamud are a part of that.

DLB: You mentioned as well that Dickens is someone you admire for the energy of the way he uses words, Conrad for the density of his thought.

HOBAN: I don't mean just the density of his thought, but the density of his writing, the density of his wordage. It's kind of like muscle fibers; it has layers over layers and often the layers are to keep you from getting too soon or too eas-

Dust jacket for Hoban's seventh novel, published in 1987

ily to the part that he wants you to get later. That's what I mean by density, the literary density.

DLB: In *The Medusa Frequency* the head of Orpheus is speaking. Orpheus has shown up in your writing for a long time. What is it about him in particular?

HOBAN: I suppose his connection with the idea of loss of beauty and the loss of love. And his connection of loss and his identity as a singer make me think of him as the essential poet, the essential writer.

DLB: In the familiar myth, Eurydice is cast as passive, the one who receives from Orpheus. Did you have in mind a recasting of that myth in having the modern character who corresponds in large measure to Eurydice in *The Medusa Frequency*, namely Luise, move out of Herman's life? She doesn't want to be Eurydice.

HOBAN: Both of the women, Luise and Melanie Falsepercy, leave Herman. Also in *The Medusa Frequency*, the story of Orpheus and Eurydice as told by Orpheus is that of Eurydice leaving Orpheus. She goes off with Aristaeus. So in all of the versions of the story in that novel, Eurydice is the one who leaves and Orpheus is the one who gets left.

DLB: You've recently written a libretto, *Some Episodes in the History of Miranda and Caliban*, parts of which were performed by the Gemini Ensemble in St. John Smith's Square. Helen Roe wrote the music. In that libretto, as well, there's a male and female who get along in some guises but not in other guises.

HOBAN: In their most essential state before they have names, when they're just male or female, they're happy in the dim green deep of unknowing. As soon as the unknowing drains away and as soon as they acquire names, they're on the way to losing each other, which in this case doesn't end up happily. They do manage to hang on to each other and they are together and they are together hoping to find their island in the end.

I think it's in my mind that all male/female stories are likely to end up unhappily unless the male and female find some way of preventing it. I guess it's a pessimistic view.

I was thinking about the male and female stories, and I sometimes am reminded of the fact that animals and birds have fairly complex mating rituals. Even insects. There is one kind of male spider who is much smaller than the female he wants to mate with and he is in constant danger of being killed or eaten by her. So when he comes courting he brings a present of a fly. He puts the fly where she can grab it with her mandibles while he goes around to the mating end and does what he can there. Sometimes when the fly isn't eaten, he takes the fly and goes away. And there are numerous birds and animals who have to go through a mating and bonding ritual to prevent the natural hostility between individuals from frustrating the effort. So it seems not to be in nature that males and females come through together. Among animals, nature programs them so that they have ways of getting around the difficulty; they have rituals, they have dances. There are geese and swans that have mating rituals where they run side by side during a display. There are all kinds of complicated things that make it possible for the male and female to demonstrate willingness to be together and procreate rather than parting in hostility. But men and women have nothing that they are programmed with; they have to sit down in bars and say "Do you come here often?," talk about their birth signs, what they do, all kind of pathetic things.

DLB: What was it about Caliban and *The Tempest* that appealed to you?

HOBAN: Just as I've always had thoughts about Orpheus and Eurydice, I've always had thoughts about Miranda and Caliban. To me, the most interesting character in the story is Caliban. He's the one that has the most potential; he's the one who seems to be bursting with possibilities that haven't been realized in the play. I mean, who am I to say that Shakespeare didn't realize possibilities, but nobody else is as interesting as Caliban. I think of possibilities between Caliban and Miranda. I'm not naturally analytical and I don't like to try; it's just that they live in my head and I wanted to have a go with them and see what happened.

DLB: You did an adaptation of *Riddley Walker* for the stage in 1985, which has been produced twice now, once in Manchester, England, and once in Long Beach, California. But that isn't the only play you've written, right?

HOBAN: I had *The Carrier Frequency*, which was done by the Impact Theatre Cooperative in 1985, but that isn't strictly a play. That is, it had people who spoke and people who did things but it wasn't straight dialogue like in a play. There was dialogue but it was set pieces, kind of like two people would be dialoguing, then it would change, and there'd be another person making a lyrical declaration, then there'd be action that didn't have any explanation or dialogue with it— it's called experimental theater. The set had a big plastic tank full of water that everybody sloshed around in and scaffolding with platforms that they climbed up onto. I liked it, but it wasn't what you'd call a play. It was the only other theater piece I've done. It was performed in London at the ICA [Institute of Contemporary Arts], then went on tour.

The way it developed was we had several meetings about things, then I wrote up a text that was accepted as the final and they took the text and went away and on their own they developed the movement to go with it, the way of presenting that text. So it was and it wasn't a collaboration.

DLB: And the play you're writing now? It has a lot of movement in it, there's a choreographer?

HOBAN: It was commissioned. My brief was to work up something in which the emphasis would be on music and movement, so I now have what I hope is a penultimate draft, but a lot of the words will have to be taken out and a lot of the tentative song words will have to be rewritten and a lot of things will have to be moved around when I get together with the choreographer and composer again.

DLB: What's it about?

HOBAN: Well, I don't want to say much, but it's called "Soonchild" and it's about an Eskimo kid who doesn't want to be born.

DLB: From *The Medusa Frequency* you read in a couple of places the part about fidelity, the paragraph on pages 70-71. It seems almost heartbreaking in being so true but so difficult.

HOBAN: In its impossibility, yes. It's something that exercises my mind a lot, the difficulty of fidelity, whether to a person or to an idea, or an ideal. I can do it in my writing; I can be utterly faithful to the idea that's on paper. I haven't been equally successful in my life.

DLB: Are you impatient sometimes when people read your work and analyze it and don't speak to what you think you are saying, to things that you want to have noticed?

HOBAN: Yes, I think a lot of critics will criticize anything that will hold still long enough, and simply bring the weight of the critical apparatus to bear on it, and often sidetrack the simple intuitive nonintellectual response which would be more appropriate.

DLB: What would such a response be like?

HOBAN: It would be to respond to the ineffable in it, to respond to that in the words that can't be put into words. You know I've known musicologists who couldn't listen to music; they could only listen to the "musicologic" of it. And I think there are people who kill literature for themselves that way. Part of the joy of reading is to think that good art hits you with the impact that comes from the way the words are put together. And if you try to analyze it, it pretty well kills it. I mean if you listen to a Schubert song cycle, I'm sure there are people who could analyze it and tell you that in musical technical terms that emotion is produced by a certain way of combining notes, by certain harmonics, by certain rhythms, by rising or falling tones. But that doesn't account for the beauty and the tragedy of the music, it's just a description.

DLB: That mystery is at the heart of a lot of what you've written. What you might call the significant action in your books occurs at those times your characters make themselves available to be lifted out of the mundane flow. You do that so easily, move your characters into supercharged reality so easily. And the mystery is not explained or analyzed.

HOBAN: No. It's just how things are.

DLB: But it's the most important thing. For example, in *Turtle Diary* [1975], there's never any explanation that either of the main characters makes about why they needed to do what they did. There is no dramatic change afterward; they simply feel complete about having done what they felt called upon to do.

HOBAN: The change afterward is not a dramatic one. But they are simply better able to go on with their own lives, better than they were before. They are willing to come out into the world a little bit more than they were before.

DLB: The Medusa Frequency too? Do you think Herman is better off? In the end he's made his choice, he's listened to what Orpheus had to say?

HOBAN: Orpheus is better off because he accepts the Medusa aspect of the female principle. And he's not looking for little dolls like he was before.

I'm not sure, but I doubt that in the female consciousness there is such a thing as an old man who corresponds to the female witch, or the female who having passed through the maiden and the wife phases is now something else, something that is magical and to be afraid of. I don't think there is a counterpart in the idea of a man. And I think the idea of the fearsome hag, the Medusa aspect, has to do with the female mysteries before which a man is weak and ineffectual. Men were not allowed to see the Eleusinian mysteries, and still I think there are pockets of fear in men about women; I mean the idea in many cultures that a menstruating woman is unclean or will prevent bread from rising. I think these are all manifestations of fear on the part of males.

DLB: Fear is an emotion that can fuel creativity, certainly.

HOBAN: That it has done.

DLB: Another characteristic of your writing is synaesthesia. For example, the kinds of colors that you use to express atmosphere in your writing. Does that come from the visual background you have with art?

HOBAN: Yes, I'm sure that the visual background that I have as an illustrator comes into it, but also I think it's just my way of thinking about things. When I'm describing it to myself or to anybody else I always run down the list of the senses and see what I can contribute to the thing that I'm describing. I mean, a certain place will have not only its own smell and its own look, but it will have a taste in your mind and so forth. I think, with me anyhow, the individual response is always in terms of all the senses.

DLB: This kind of blending together of all the senses corresponds to the profound experiences that a lot of your characters have of getting down as deep as one can go. The characters in your books aren't interested so much in the daily world of events.

HOBAN: I guess I'd say that all of my people in my stories are metaphysically aware. They're usually hooked up with ordinary, everyday activities in one way or another. Maybe at some point in the story they break out of it, like in *The Lion of Boaz-Jachin* the mapmaker leaves all that behind him, and Kleinzeit had a job in an advertising agency and he got canned. William and Neaera both make a living doing what they do; he works in a bookshop and she writes children's books and illustrates them. Riddley Walker had a calling: he was a connection man; that was his

work and his group. Pilgermann had some occupation. Herman is a not very successful writer. So they are all accounted for as to how they make a living and survive in the world. They are all hooked-up with the details of everyday to that extent.

DLB: Hooking-up is a term you use a lot, and in your books there are unusual connections made. The story will start from some sort of disruption of whatever their normal life may have been, like when the mapmaker leaves home, or when Kleinzeit becomes sick. They start from a loss; Riddley starts with a loss of his father.

HOBAN: Yes, they all start from being jolted out of the regular track of everyday in one way or another.

DLB: In your children's books, the ones you have written in the last fifteen years or so, that seems to be true as well. The characters don't come back home easily; the resolutions aren't as domestic as they used to be, as, say, in the Frances books.

HOBAN: The Frances books, which are still my most successful books commercially, all have their resolutions in the framework of the house, the domestic setup with mom and dad and everything coming out all right. When that kind of life ended for me, then that kind of book stopped happening. The books that I write now are like *Monsters* [1989], where the kid grows a monster that eats the psychotherapist. And some are anti-authority, like the one in which Tom defeats Captain Najork and he walks out on his Aunt Wonkham-Strong and puts an ad in the paper for a new aunt. But they all have to do with breaking out of the confines of the life that one was in. And whether you are a person given to breaking out or not, life has a way of lying in wait for you so that you fall into things that you didn't expect to fall into. I remember what I was thinking about when I was writing *Kleinzeit*, which happened after a stay in the hospital; I remember thinking that I had an image in my mind of a smooth facade like that smooth curving facade of housefronts on Regents Street. I think it's Jones, the architect for that, though I may be wrong; it might be Nash. But anyway, the smooth curving facade, and I was thinking that we hoped that we would just walk along the smooth facade of life, but there are always things waiting for us to crash through and into them. I mean the mad-house is always waiting, jail is waiting, the hospital is waiting. And at any moment the apparently smooth and solid facade may turn out to be tissue-paper thin and we just crash into something we weren't looking for, nor want. It's like that bumper sticker I saw the other day: Shit Happens.

DLB: In two of your recent books, *Monsters* and *Jim Hedgehog's Supernatural Christmas* [1989], the kids have a life very much of their own that the parents aren't aware of. Increasingly in your books the parents have gotten to be less wise. Frances's parents were understanding and wise and respectful, letting the child work out a resolution. But they were still there. In some of the later books, the parents are not much. You seem to be saying that this secret life of kids is something really worth reserving, that maybe very few adults can understand or respond to it.

HOBAN: Well, yes, I don't have a big rationale about this, but it used to be that the stories were about loving parents who made everything all right. And in my current children's stories, the parents, or the elders who are in place of parents, more often than not are baffled and frustrated by the kids. And sure, I believe that the inner life of children is a thing of worth and importance that is very often subverted by education, by society, by the simple fact of growing up.

DLB: Did you go to the movies a lot when you were growing up?

HOBAN: I used to go to the Saturday matinees as a kid. And I sometimes got taken to a theater in Philadelphia called the Europa, where they had European films, *Baker's Wife, The Blue Lights;* there were a lot of Russian and French films there. Also a couple of times we went to New York. I remember the *Barretts of Wimpole Street* [1934], *The Scarlet Empress* [1934].

DLB: Your story "The Man with the Dagger" is a story in which, among a lot of other things, there are confrontations with aspects in a person's past that haven't been faced yet. You read Jorge Luis Borges's "The South"—how did your story come to spin off from that one?

HOBAN: In the Borges story, a man who wasn't really looking for a fight is challenged to a

Dust jacket for Hoban's 1989 children's book

knife fight by a gaucho. He's in a strange mental state where once having been challenged and once having picked up the knife, he accepts the fact that if he had the choosing of the matter of his death, this is what he would choose: to go out into the sky of the South with a knife in his hand. This story is about the primal challenge, man to man—here's a stranger looking for trouble, here's the protagonist not looking for trouble, and he's forced to make up his mind. What's he going to do? And so it led into my own feelings about my own cowardice in the past—challenges that I've rejected.

DLB: And now it has been selected as one of Britain's ten best stories for 1990?

HOBAN: Well, it's not prize-giving ceremony or anything. The editors at Heinemann put out a book called *Ten Best Stories of the Year;* these guys decide that this collection contains, in their opinion, the ten best stories of the year.

DLB: The first short story you had published in some time was in 1985, "The Dream Maker." And then in 1989 and 1990 you published three more, "Dark Oliver," "Schwartz," and "The Man with the Dagger." Do the short stories get themselves written discretely or are they parts of things for something else that you didn't use?

HOBAN: "Dark Oliver" has in it the olive tree that was also involved in *The Medusa Frequency.* "Schwartz" I thought might even be the beginning of a novel, then I decided that it was better just as a concentrated thing for a short story. And "The Man with the Dagger" was just a short story idea. "The Raven" hasn't been published yet. I think I had in mind that would be a short story, although I used part of the same material in this play that I am writing.

DLB: Are you working on more short stories now?

HOBAN: I don't have any in mind, but the short stories sometimes come. I'll get an idea that I think I can do something with, then I put aside whatever I am doing and see how far I can get with it.

DLB: The mythological characters that appear so often in your work, are they convenient because there is so much meaning latched onto them already?

HOBAN: I guess. I don't think about thinking of it, but they are a part of my mental inventory. You know the way other guys have baseball players in their heads, I've got Hermes and people like that. I remember in junior high school in study period reading about Siegfried and so forth. I always went for mythology.

DLB: One critic said *The Medusa Frequency* was a book for academics. The implications seem to be that only an academic would enjoy the mental trip, or understand the allusions. Is there any accuracy in that?

HOBAN: I don't think about writing for a particular group of people, but I suppose I simply write for my own frame of reference and I assume that there are other people out there who are the same. Like I'll go to a film or I'll read a book or I'll know about a piece of music and I'll as-

sume that most of the people that I run into or spend time with are conversant with the same films and books and pieces of music and so forth. Sometimes they are, sometimes they aren't. Sometimes there's overlap and sometimes there are omissions, like my friend Leon doesn't listen to jazz, but we have a lot of other things to talk about. But everybody I know is familiar with mythology, maybe more than I, maybe less than I. It's part of their mental inventory.

DLB: You bring the old mythological characters into the everyday life. They pop up in unusual places in your books. Death, God, Hospital, or even Paper are sometimes characters. Does this ever really happen to you?

HOBAN: Well, it's metaphorical. I think one of the uses of mythology is that it takes a condition or a set of circumstances or a trend in the cosmos and it gives it a name and an identity so that you can refer to it that way and think about it that way. So that's why I think of Hermes as being the patron god of writing as he is of thieves and merchants and night journeys and all that. And I think it's a way for the mind to get a handle on things.

For example, like right now with the world being environmentally wasted. Like now [*driving toward Los Angeles*] we are looking at what I assume to be smog, air being polluted. If modern mythology were to give rise to a god or a demon called Mucko or Shitface or something that represented the demon who is constantly trying to drink up the good water and swallow the good air and leaving nothing but the bad water and air, then it would be a way of concentrating on the condition of people's minds, rather than talking about single issues. Instead of having to have one committee for saving the green belt and preventing overdevelopment in housing, and another committee for making sure that chemicals don't go into rivers, and another committee for watching for the ozone layer, having one big committee for anti-Mucko simplifies it. Mucko is eating the world: Stop Mucko.

DLB: A lot goes on in *The Medusa Frequency.* You gave an interview before the book came out where you talked about the male and female principles and their operation in that book. When the critics reviewed it, they focused on there being an author in it who needed shock therapy of some kind to get his creativity going again, and they commented on your style. They didn't really comment very much on what else you were saying. Do you think that happens a lot? You know, that people miss out on what you are saying?

HOBAN: Well no. Maybe what I was saying wasn't all that big and impactful. It was for me because in all of my books up to *The Medusa Frequency* I perhaps hadn't gone as far as I could in thinking about women relative to men and men relative to women. I mean what went on between them and my own life. I am in what can be described a contented state of marriage, but what I am saying is that I have never yet meant to a woman as I would want to, in the light of my present understanding. And that went into *The Medusa Frequency*.

DLB: Women in your books tend to come out pretty well. They're not major characters for the most part, except in *Turtle Diary*. But they're intelligent characters and they have a lot of integrity.

HOBAN: I like the women in my books.

DLB: They're also all fair and tall; there's Gretel from the Lion book, Sister from *Kleinzeit*, the princess from *La Corona and the Tin Frog* [1979], Sophia from *Pilgermann* [1984], Luise from *The Medusa Frequency*, even Bundlejoy

Cosysweet from *How Tom Beat Captain Najork and His Hired Sportsmen* [1974]. Have your women characters changed over time or are they all sort of the same woman?

HOBAN: They are all based on my wife Gundul.

DLB: Sometimes the catharsis for the people in your writing is a physical fight. In *Turtle Diary*, for example, William punches out the fellow with the seaweed and the dirty bathtub, but for the most part, your characters are civilized and educated. What do you think it is to be civilized?

HOBAN: Civilized people fight, too. Well, I guess the people in my books are pretty much the kind of person I am.

DLB: From traveling around Southern California university campuses with you this past week, I've seen that if you are asked a question, you answer it without hedging. I mean, it's not as if you lack niceties but it's been fascinating for the people who've come across you the past few days to find that the person who is writing the books isn't that different from the very honest person who is in them.

HOBAN: Oh yes, the voice in my books is my straight voice really.

The Uses of Facsimiles:
A Symposium

Facsimiles and the Research Library

William Cagle
The Lilly Library,
Indiana University

The published text of an author's work, if all has gone according to plan, is the version intended for the reader. Yet, as everyone who has written even a school essay knows, the finished work does not spring instantly from pen to paper. The creative process can be long and arduous and many a line may be written only to be discarded in favor of another. The evidence of this process does not show in the printed text. It may, however, in such of the author's drafts and working manuscripts as survive. To the student of literature, for whom the journey and not just the arrival matters, these revisions are of major importance.

How much insight a manuscript gives us into the mind of its author depends very much on the nature of the manuscript. A clean typescript, agreeing in all details with the published work, provides nothing significant, and a fair copy written out by the author without change after publication may appeal to the autograph collector but offers no new information to the scholar. A working manuscript, on the other hand, with revisions, insertions, and deletions, is quite another matter. Take T. S. Eliot's *The Waste Land* (1922) as a case in point.

On 19 July 1922 Eliot wrote to John Quinn, "I should like to present you the MSS of the Waste Land, if you would care to have it—when I say MSS, I mean that it is partly MSS and partly typescript, with Ezra's and my alterations scrawled all over it." Eliot had completed *The Waste Land* in Lausanne, Switzerland, while there on a rest cure and, on his way back to London, stopped in Paris to see Ezra Pound. Pound went over the manuscript and recommended numerous cuts and changes after which Eliot made further revisions of his own. Only in the manuscript is it possible to see the evolution of the final text, to see Pound's contributions and Eliot's fine tuning of one of the great poems in the English language. The manuscript, preserved among John Quinn's papers, is now in the Berg Collection in the New York Public Library where qualified scholars who are able to make the pilgrimage may consult it. A handsomely produced facsimile edition, edited by Valerie Eliot and published by Harcourt Brace Jovanovich in 1971, has made the manuscript much more widely available.

This edition of *The Waste Land* is a prime example of a well-made literary facsimile embodying three important criteria: (1) it reproduces the manuscript of a major work; (2) it facsimiles a working manuscript with extensive revisions varying from the published text; (3) it is produced in a clear and readable facsimile, in this instance enhanced with facing typeset transcriptions and notes to aid the reader. Both the selection of original materials and quality control during production are extremely important in this business. The principal market for literary facsimiles is research libraries, along with collections in the humanities and, perhaps, a few private collectors. To appeal to this market the manuscript chosen must have sufficient importance that it is likely to be studied, and it must offer something not already in the published text. There would be no point, for example, in producing a facsimile of the Lilly Library's manuscript of Edgar Lee Masters's *The Spoon River Anthology* (1916), one of several which Masters copied out and sold, long after the book had been published, when he wanted cash. It follows the published text exactly and offers nothing not in the printed book. By contrast, another Lilly Library manuscript, Arnold Bennett's *The Old Wives' Tale* (1911), reproduced in facsimile in 1927, is quite interesting in that almost every page contains the author's carefully inserted revisions. Literally, by reading between the lines, we can see Bennett's mind at work.

There are other manuscripts in the Lilly Library that may someday become candidates for facsimile editions, among them J. M. Synge's *The*

Playboy of the Western World (1907) and Ian Fleming's several James Bond novels. Both Synge and Fleming composed at the typewriter, turning out double-spaced copy that they then revised extensively, Synge using red ink and Fleming ballpoint, fountain pen, or pencil. Because of the variety of writing instruments Fleming used, it is possible to layer his revisions. If a facsimile edition of one of his manuscripts is undertaken it will be a challenge to see that the pencil and the various inks do not all look the same in a black-and-white reproduction. But Fleming's may be the last generation of writers for whom we will have to concern ourselves with these problems. The computer is eliminating the draft and the revised manuscript and with them the record of the creative process. Perhaps that is all the more reason to value the literary manuscripts we have and to seek new ways to make them more broadly available.

To do this, I have been asked, would the Lilly Library allow facsimiles to be made from manuscripts in its collections? Yes, with these provisos: photography for the facsimile edition must be able to be done without damage to the original; permission must be obtained from the owner of copyright; the Library reserves the right to exercise quality control to assure that the facsimile is of high standard. These points satisfied, as a public institution in part supported by tax dollars, it is our responsibility not only to collect and preserve manuscripts and books of value to scholars, but to make them available as widely as possible. If facsimiles of literary manuscripts in our collections will help to do this, we will be happy to work with publishers interested in producing them.

Facsimile Publishing

Leo Balk

*Vice-President, Garland
Publishing Company*

Garland has been active as a publisher of facsimiles for nearly two decades. Throughout this time our list has developed with the aim of making the resources of scholarship widely available in the humanities and social sciences. We began by reprinting large multivolume collections of books. These reprint sets presented comprehensive surveys of eighteenth-century English plays, Victorian novels, and other genres. We have al-

so issued bibliographical and research guides to the same literature. For us, facsimile publication seemed a natural outgrowth of this program. Our reprint program has made available rare or unobtainable editions of literary works. The facsimile program makes available the actual manuscript sources of major literary works. Both programs are designed to serve the scholar by bringing the objects of study from the library rare-book room into the main reference collection or even into the home.

An important part of the rationale for this facsimile program is our own view of the books as utilitarian. This utilitarian approach differs markedly from that of most other facsimile publishers. The facsimile has traditionally been seen as the finest product of the printer's art. Full-color manuscript facsimiles have generally been characterized by luxurious format, high price, and strict limitation. They have often been published with the most exacting four-color photography, on the rarest and most expensive stock, and with handsome bindings. In short, the aim has been to confer on the facsimile some of the aura of the original. This luxurious format works well for a small manuscript facsimile directed toward a market of bibliophiles. Publication costs are directly related to the number of pages involved. One notebook by Wordsworth is a candidate for this sort of publication, but the costs of paper, printing, and binding when multiplied out over the length of the facsimile sets we have published (twenty thousand manuscript pages by James Joyce, the same number by William Faulkner, ten thousand by F. Scott Fitzgerald, and comparable numbers for Byron, Keats, and Shelley) prohibit the use of such methods. A market of book collectors could not support luxury editions of such magnitude. Instead, we have concentrated on clear, legible, black-and-white photofacsimiles printed on acid-free paper and bound with library-standard bindings. Introductions by leading scholars have provided the basic bibliographical data needed to use the manuscripts. The books are designed to make more widely available the evidence in the documentary sources. In literature this evidence includes corrections, revisions, and discarded chapters or passages. Much of this material has never been published; and if it has been dealt with in scholarly editions, it is often noted in a summary manner.

To be sure, facsimiles must be used with some caution, and they never entirely replace the original. No scholar will base any argument

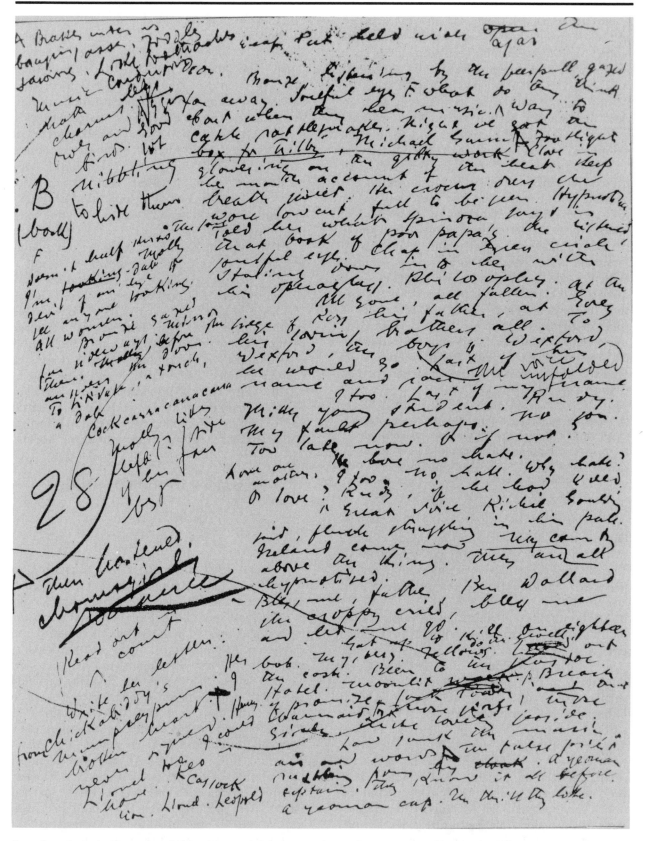

Page from James Joyce's manuscript for the "Sirens" section of Ulysses *from* Ulysses: A Facsimile of Manuscripts and Typescripts for Episodes 10-13, *prefaced and arranged by Michael Groden (New York: Garland, 1977)*

about the exact color, size, or physical structure of the original exclusively on the evidence of a facsimile. Such facts must be verified in the original manuscript, and any problematic passages must be checked in the original as well. Still, a facsimile of a primary source can permit students to understand nuances, become aware of textual ambiguities, and trace the creative growth and development of poetry and imaginative prose.

Another aspect of facsimile publication can be seen in Garland's music list. In music we concentrate not on publishing the sources of major, well-known musical masterworks but instead on making unavailable music available. For example, we have published two collections of manuscript facsimiles of seventeenth- and eighteenth-century Italian operas. Some eighty scores of opera—well-known in their day—were published for the first time by Garland. These works had never been issued in print and had not been performed in more than a century. In the essay for the brochure announcing our first Italian opera project, Howard Mayer Brown of the University of Chicago wrote:

> Were we to prepare full edition versions—with all variants noted and all manuscripts collated—of even a representative sample of seventeenth- and eighteenth-century operas we would need to wait several generations before we could attempt an overview of the Baroque and early classical opera.

Our music facsimile program has made available vast quantities of unknown or unavailable music. The study of large repertories need not await the necessarily laborious process that precedes a modern edition.

The difficulty of this kind of publication is that facsimiles of the eighteenth-century Italian operas or of manuscripts of Byron's *Don Juan*, Joyce's *Ulysses*, Fitzgerald's *Tender Is the Night*—all published by Garland—are directed at a very small public. The books do not appeal to bibliophiles; they are not luxury editions. They serve a scholarly audience. And, since the cost of these large sets of thousands of pages is high, sales are almost exclusively to libraries. This market, while small, has been dependable. Oddly enough, however, the American and British market alone has not been strong enough to support our publications. Even major American universities will pick up and choose from among our collections of Keats, Byron, and Shelley, and the purchase of large sets such as we have published on Joyce,

Faulkner, and Fitzgerald is often tied to special funding and specific and intensive use in classes. These books all seem to have a greater appeal in Japan. The Japanese, perhaps by virtue of their isolation from the centers of Western culture, have shown a voracious appetite for facsimile editions. Clearly they have a bias toward mastering the sources of literary works. This bias seems to show an intellectual interest emphasizing source studies and factual inquiry rather than purely critical endeavors. The Japanese alone cannot support our editions, but our publication of Faulkner and Fitzgerald manuscripts would not have been possible without them.

We hope to be able to continue our manuscript facsimile program. However, it is not a growing part of our list. Costs rise, and the purchasing power of library budgets declines. It has also become more and more difficult to assemble large facsimile sets. Some libraries, for whatever reasons, choose not to participate in facsimile projects, and the rights to the works of twentieth-century authors can be difficult and expensive to acquire. This type of publication grows difficult, but we remain committed to it. It forms a central part of our goal of making resources and information available for scholars throughout the world.

Facsimiles in the Classroom

Ron Fortune
Illinois State University

From 1987 through 1989, thirty-five to forty high school English teachers gathered each summer on the Illinois State University campus to participate in an NEH Summer Institute focusing on the uses of manuscript materials in the classroom. Although most of the 110 participants over the three-year duration of the Institute held at least master's degrees in English, virtually none had been exposed in their own studies to the material associated with the composition of the literary works they studied, and consequently none had attempted to incorporate these materials into their teaching. At the conclusion of one summer program, a participating teacher summed up the feelings of most of the participants when she wrote that she found the Institute to be "a once-in-a-lifetime experience" in part because she had the opportunity to work with "materials in writing and drafting that [she had] never seen before." The enthusiasm of the teachers for what amounted to a new approach to teaching English expressed itself in the visits of many teachers, following their experience in the NEH project, to libraries holding the manuscript materials of favorite authors or of authors figuring prominently in their curricula. The infectious nature of this interest in and enthusiasm for the uses of manuscript materials in the classroom can be seen in the efforts of colleagues of the project's participants who were not involved in the project themselves. As the participating teachers returned to their home schools and shared their ideas and materials with colleagues, these colleagues began to place as great a demand on the project's library of manuscript facsimiles as the project participants.

The responses of the teachers connected directly and indirectly with the NEH project are both surprising and not surprising. They are surprising in that, even though as English teachers the participants necessarily focus their instruction on what texts are, on how they are made, and on how they are read, the manuscript materials central to all of these issues have been ignored in their lessons. Nor are these teachers exceptions. Again and again, in the various regional and national forums through which the project's approach to using manuscript materials in the classroom has been discussed, teachers have readily acknowledged their ignorance of these materials and of their pedagogical utility. This state of affairs is not surprising in light of the absence of manuscript materials from the teachers' own undergraduate and graduate experiences. Typically, as teachers they emulate the teaching they experienced as students, and if this teaching excluded the composing materials associated with the works they studied, they were unlikely to discover the value of the materials themselves.

Helping teachers learn to value and use manuscript materials in literature and writing instruction focuses on three issues. First, teachers need to see the potential connection between manuscript materials and their teaching objectives. Second, they need to develop strategies for identifying and acquiring the specific materials most suited to these objectives. Finally, they must be able to bring together the objectives and materials in focused lesson plans that genuinely engage students in learning and develop their ability to read literature critically and to write effectively.

English teachers' objectives mostly focus on two primary activities: (1) helping students develop a critical appreciation of the literature they

read and (2) improving students' writing abilities. Exploring the composing materials associated with the literary texts students read can support both of these in ways that cannot be duplicated by any other means. In extending students' aesthetic appreciation of the literature they read, teachers typically focus on the published text exclusively, but much can be gained in aesthetic insight if students have the opportunity to witness as well the processes of creation through which the literary texts they read came into being. Samuel Johnson has expressed with characteristic succinctness the essential nature of the pleasure that derives from this perspective on a literary work: "It is pleasant to see great works in their seminal state pregnant with latent possibilities of excellence. Nor could there be any more delightful entertainment than to trace their gradual growth and expansion, and to observe how they are sometimes suddenly advanced by accidental hints, and sometimes slowly improved by steady meditation." The pleasure to which Johnson refers is not, as some might argue, contingent on an extensive exposure to literature but is available to any and all students when presented in accessible terms. Mostly, this means helping them to see concretely the drama inherent in acts of literary creation, and the most compelling way to do this is to make available to them the documents—an author's notebooks, manuscripts, typescripts, galley proofs—that reveal this drama most immediately. Simply seeing the fifty-seven leaves preserved from the draft manuscript of *The Red Badge of Courage*, for example, with its extensive crosshatched deletions of entire leaves, can begin to give students some sense of the exigencies, the disappointments and triumphs, of literary creation.

While many teachers can understand the value of opening students up to the kind of pleasure Johnson describes, they also argue that their first priority is to help students become more critically astute in their reading. This priority, however, does not preclude or even compete with an interest in exposing students to the dynamics of literary creation. Rather, both interests complement one another as studying the processes of creation can provide a unique means of articulating the issues that drive a reader's critical involvement with a literary work. Gerald Bruns's *Inventions: Writing, Textuality, and Understanding in Literary History* (1982) argues that a critical reading of any work is enriched substantially by an awareness of the work's compositional history. Bruns distinguishes a "manuscript culture" from a "book culture" and argues that the former allows readers to ask questions not available in the former. A manuscript culture, according to Bruns, is interested in all of the versions of a text as it progresses toward a final form that "succeeds into print." Such a culture is "open" in its disposition to texts because it highlights the fluidity and mutability of a text as it moves from version to version. A book culture concentrates on the version of the text that achieves printed form and is "closed" in that its attention is restricted to a single version of a work that only exhibits a single moment, though most would argue the most important moment, in a text's history.

This distinction between a manuscript culture and a book culture bears on the development of students' critical reading abilities because of the questions that the former allows but that are not available in the latter. Bruns argues that the questions possible in a manuscript culture but precluded in a book culture include "What does it mean to rewrite (or have different versions of) a finished poem? In what does the singleness (or finish) of any poem consist?" In practical terms, these questions mean allowing students to compare the manuscript and published versions of key passages in a work and, through the comparison, to explore why the author or editor judged one version to be better than the other and what being "better" means in relation to a particular work or a particular point in an author's life or a particular historical moment. Comparing the opening paragraphs of the manuscript of George Orwell's *1984* (1949), for example, with the opening paragraphs of the published book can get students involved in asking such questions as "Why is the character of the elevator operator prominent in the manuscript draft and almost invisible in the published text?" "Why is dialogue used extensively in the manuscript draft and almost not at all in the published novel?" "How do these changes alter the reader's experience of the novel's opening?" "Why would Orwell judge the manuscript opening to be an improvement on the published opening?" Comparing versions of the same work at different points in its development necessarily gets students involved in aesthetic judgments that form the foundation for their critical reasoning.

For teachers who place a great emphasis on writing in their courses, manuscript materials can play as critical a role in writing instruction as they do in literature instruction. A key source for many of the problems students have in their writing is that they do not understand the nature of the task in which they are involved. In what has become a classic study of the problems basic writers face in their efforts to learn to write and of the strategies their teachers can adopt to assist these students, Mina Shaughnessy recommends that teachers use Keats's manuscripts for "The Eve of St. Agnes." These manuscripts, and any manuscript for that matter, enable students to appreciate the messiness of writing and, in Shaughnessy's terms, to see maps of the writers' debates with themselves on the page. Students' inability to see writing as the messy process it is inhibits their getting to the next step, which is to develop strategies that enable them to manage and work their way through this messiness.

The argument here is not that students, through exposure to the composing materials of the authors they study, eventually will achieve a level of accomplishment comparable to that of these authors. Rather, students and these authors are working at the same kind of task, and students can benefit greatly merely from seeing how the published works they study, works that they often assume simply appeared in their published forms, developed through the same kinds of struggles they experience in their own writing. Often, specific passages in a manuscript or a revised typescript can be used to help students learn to work through some particular problem they are having in their own writing. In Shaughnessy's reference to using Keats's manuscripts in a basic writing class, she both recommends the practice because of what it communicates about the nature of writing in general and explains how these materials can specifically assist students with improving vocabulary in their writing. Teachers who use manuscripts in their writing courses quickly learn that these materials reflect the general and specific struggles of writing and any student sharing these struggles can learn something from them.

The present discussion of teachers' objectives and the role that manuscript materials can play in pursuing these objectives has reflected a common subdivision in most perceptions of the English curriculum. That is, in the ways English courses are structured and in individual teachers' approaches to their subjects, it is conventional to separate composition instruction from literature instruction. Recently, many have argued that this separation is counterproductive because it fragments the curriculum artificially and deprives teachers and students of the opportunity to ap-

Page from John Keats's manuscript for "The Eve of St. Agnes" from **John Keats: Poetry Manuscripts at Harvard;**
A Facsimile Edition, **edited by Jack Stillinger (Cambridge, Mass.: Harvard University Press, 1990)**

proach literature from the perspective of writing and writing from the perspective of literature. Bringing literary manuscripts into English courses provides teachers with a natural means of integrating literature and writing instruction. With these materials, teachers can help students learn about writing in their study of literature and learn about literature in their work as developing writers.

Building teachers' interest in using literary manuscripts to teach literature and writing carries with it an obligation to develop their command of the resources that will make it possible for them to get their hands on the materials needed to implement this approach. This is an especially important consideration because of the limited experience most teachers have with materials of this kind. The NEH project followed short-term and long-term strategies to address this issue.

The short-term strategy was designed to get teachers immediately involved in working with manuscripts. It followed two lines: (1) the daily class sessions in the Institute itself focused on manuscripts associated with the authors and works selected for study and (2) project funding permitted the development of a library of some 150 volumes, consisting mostly of manuscript facsimiles, put at the complete disposal of project participants. Institute faculty were selected because of their reputations for work with nineteenth-century Russian, nineteenth-century British, and twentieth-century American manuscripts. The daily sessions quickly expanded the teachers' awareness of what they would find in these materials and of how they could relate what they found to their reading and teaching of the works being studied. The project library complemented these sessions by providing the notebooks, letters, and manuscript and typescript facsimiles connected with these works as well as similar materials for other works in which the participants expressed a special interest. Having these materials readily available enabled the participants to develop ideas formulated in the daily sessions.

Even with the achievement of the short-term objectives, the project could not realize its ultimate goal if the participants left without having developed a command of the research tools needed to continue the work begun in the Institute. The long-term objectives, therefore, focused on giving teachers a command of these tools. One primary means of achieving this objective was a bibliographical essay appearing in each issue of *Literature and Writing*, the monthly Institute journal devoted to disseminating information and ideas related to the use of manuscripts in the classroom. Each month, the bibliographical essay contained discussion of resources focusing on the composition of a specific work. The works featured in these essays were taken from a list that the teachers themselves compiled, a list covering texts most commonly taught in the teachers' courses. Generally, the essays specified the surviving manuscript materials for the given work, identified the library or libraries possessing these materials, listed bibliographical information on published facsimiles of the manuscripts, and outlined what could be found in various scholarly and critical discussions concerning the composition of the work. Over the three-year duration of the journal, this information was provided for thirty-five different works, all of which figure prominently in English courses at the high school and college levels.

Giving teachers the ability to discover for themselves the kinds of information included in the monthly bibliographical essays required acquainting them with the bibliographical tools used by scholars in the field. These tools included everything from multivolume reference works (for example, *Dictionary of Literary Biography*) that contain biographical and bibliographical information bearing on the composition of individual literary works, including reproductions of selected pages from the manuscripts or the typescripts of a given work, to multivolume resources (for example, *Index of English Literary Manuscripts*) that provide information on the availability and location of manuscripts for a comprehensive range of texts. That the project teachers have learned to use these resources and have gone beyond the works covered in the Institute or discussed in *Literature and Writing* is suggested by the wide range of authors and works covered in the essays they have written for the project journal. In fact, most of the essays published in the journal show teachers adapting a manuscript approach to lessons on authors and works not covered anywhere else in the project.

The classroom lessons developed by teachers in the project suggest their degree of success in learning to make manuscripts work for them and their students. A common thread connecting the most successful applications is the close relationship between the purpose of a particular lesson and the manuscript materials used. When a clear sense of purpose drives a particular application, teachers and students are less likely to flounder in what can appear to be a morass of scribbles on a manuscript page. At the same time, manuscripts are so rich in the insights they provide that there are few purposes in an English course that they cannot accommodate. It is impossible to summarize here all of the applications teachers have developed, but a few examples can effectively suggest how well they have learned to use manuscripts in their lessons.

In one application, a teacher concerned with the passive responses of students to the texts they read decided to put them in the writer's place. By making them go through the same decision-making process as the writer, the teacher hoped to develop in them a sense of literary values that could provide the basis for critical judgment. Using the four extant stages of Keats's "The Eve of St. Agnes," the teacher subdivided the lesson into five parts, with the final part calling for students to write their own conclusions to the poem based on the critical reading developed through their work with the different drafts.

The four manuscript versions of the poem that provide the foundation for this lesson sequence show the stages of composition the poem underwent as it was prepared for publication. The first version of the poem is the holograph manuscript (now in the Harvard University Library), which is missing the first seven stanzas and exhibits cancellations of many false starts and frequent excisions of words and phrases. The second version, known as "the Woodhouse transcript," was made from Keats's holograph by his lifelong friend, Richard Woodhouse, and is important mainly because it restores the first seven stanzas missing from the holograph. The third version, the "Woodhouse second transcript," was copied from Keats's original manuscript but adds some stanzas and deletes others, reflecting changes Keats or his editors made in preparation for publication. Of this third copy, Woodhouse states, "This copy was taken from Keats' original MS. He afterwards altered it for publication, and added some stanzas and omitted others. His alterations are noticed here. The Published copy differs from both [versions] in a few particulars. Keats left it to his Publishers to adopt which they pleased, and to revise the whole." The fourth version was produced by Keats's brother, George, and it resembles very closely the second Woodhouse transcript with this transcript's corrections.

The teacher begins the lesson by having students work with the first omitted stanza, from which she has deleted key words. Without being told where the stanza is from or its place in the development of the poem from which it is taken, the students must complete the stanza by filling in the blanks with words they consider most appropriate. In the discussion that follows, students have the chance to compare their choices and to recognize the significance of choice in a literary work. After comparing their choices, they read the stanza as Keats wrote it, but they still are not told who wrote the lines, the poem from which the lines have been taken, or the placement of these lines in the poem's composition. This activity focuses attention on Keats's language and the likely reasons for his poetic decisions. Because they have made their own choices for selected parts of the stanza, they are more likely to be sensitive to the significance of Keats's choices than would be the case had they not gone through the initial exercise.

At this point, the students read "The Eve of St. Agnes" as it is printed in their textbook for the course. The discussion that follows focuses on clarifying the narrative, highlighting key motifs, and articulating the mood that dominates the poem as a whole. After this discussion, the students return to the omitted stanza they worked on initially. They are told that this stanza originally appeared between stanzas 3 and 4 of their textbook's version of the poem. They are again asked to evaluate the decision to delete the stanza from the poem: Is the stanza extraneous, or would the poem be better if the stanza had been left in place? How does leaving the stanza in change the poem?

Next, the students are given the second omitted stanza, again without being told anything about it, although they will immediately recognize it as being connected with the poem they have just read. The students are then asked to place the stanza in the poem and to discuss their reasons for placing it so. This discussion is followed by their being told that the stanza originally appeared between stanzas 6 and 7, and they are again asked to analyze the effect of its omission. Keats omitted the stanza under pressure from his publishers, even though it contained information that helps to prepare the reader for what is to follow in the poem. Students often elect to keep the stanza for this very reason, and in this, they agree with many critics who consider the poem weakened by the stanza's omission. From the perspective of this lesson's objective, students again have the opportunity to be-

Cayetano Ordoñez.
"Niño de la Palma"

FIESTA

I saw him for the first time in his room at the Hotel Quintana in Pamplona. Quintana We met Quintana on the stairs as Bill and I were coming up to the room to get the wine bag to take to the ~~corrida~~ bull fight. "Come on, said Quintana. Would you like to meet Niño de la Palma?" He was in room number eight, I knew what it was like inside, a gloomy room with the two beds separated by monastic partitions. Bill had lived in there ~~room~~ and gotten out to take a single room when the fiesta started. Quintana knocked and opened the door. He ~~introduced us.~~ The boy stood very straight and unsmiling, he was dressed in his white shirt and green pants all except his coat and his ~~hair~~ sash seeming far away had just been wound. He nodded and dignified when we shook hands. Quintana made a little speech about what great aficionados we were and how we wanted to wish him luck. Niño turned to me. He was the best looking kid I have ever seen, "You go to see the bull fight," he said in English

Page from Hemingway's manuscript for The Sun Also Rises *from* Archive of Literary Documents Volume II, Ernest Hemingway: The Sun Also Rises, *edited by Matthew J. Bruccoli (Detroit: Omnigraphics, 1990)*

come critically aware of the significance of choice in a literary work, in this case as it bears on the poem's structure.

The purpose of the next phase of the lesson is to give students a view of Keats in the act of composing. They are given both a holograph and a diplomatic proof for stanza 30. Seeing the many excisions, students can come to understand the literary work as a dynamic entity both in the writing and the reading, an entity that results from a complex network of choices, some brilliant but others regrettable. Their recognizing this dynamism is a necessary prerequisite to the development of their critical reading abilities because it effectively undermines the conviction with which they often approach a work: that everything is down in black and white and nothing remains for them to do. Concluding this sequence of activities by having students write their own "endings" to the poem (the poem itself vaguely suggests what happens to Madeline and Porphyro after the last stanza) reinforces in students an understanding that works of literature invite their critical involvement and that the pleasure of reading literature ultimately depends on it.

Using manuscripts in the classroom may seem to some a gratuitous addition to the curriculum that does not accomplish anything that could not be achieved through another means. As the sequence of lessons on "The Eve of St. Agnes" indicates, however, these materials are not gratuitous, and if they were deleted from the lesson, the development of the students' critical awareness of what texts are and of how writers and readers interact with them would suffer irrevocably.

In a lesson sequence designed to help students understand the critical role of revision in writing and to encourage them to revise in composing their own texts, a teacher incorporated F. Scott Fitzgerald's working draft and rewritten galley proofs for *The Great Gatsby* (1925) into his composition course. To maintain a clear focus, the lessons concentrate on Fitzgerald's efforts to develop the character of Jay Gatsby from the manuscript through the galley proofs. Specifically, the teaching unit shows the effects Fitzgerald achieved in the presentation of Jay Gatsby by moving two blocks of material in galley. After reading chapters 1 through 5 of the published text, students read chapter 6 as it originally appeared in the manuscript and outline in writing the action represented in this chapter. With the outline of the manuscript chapter 6 in hand, they read chapter 6 in the published novel and outline in writ-

ing the main action it documents. Their outlines should reveal that the published chapter differs from the manuscript chapter in two respects: it begins with an account of Gatsby's early years and it concludes with Gatsby telling Nick how he fell in love with Daisy. The ensuing class discussion comparing the two outlines helps students to see how much sharper Gatsby's character becomes through the addition of the opening and concluding passages.

The next part of the lesson sequence helps students to see what Fitzgerald did in his revisions to achieve the improved effect. This part begins by having students read and outline the manuscript material corresponding to chapter 7 of the published novel. They find in their outline the opening and concluding passages of the published version of chapter 6. This exercise helps students discover for themselves that the material added to the published version of chapter 6 to enhance the presentation of Gatsby's character was taken from the manuscript version of chapter 7. Most importantly, students can begin to understand the dramatic effect that moving blocks of material can have on the overall quality of a text.

Students also read at this point Maxwell Perkins's letter to Fitzgerald dated 20 November 1924 and Fitzgerald's reply of 1 December 1924. Allowing students to see the positive effects that an editor's comments had on an author's revision of a manuscript helps them better appreciate the peer editing they are required to do with each writing assignment they complete.

The lesson sequence concludes with students writing essays on ideas about *The Great Gatsby* developed through their study of Fitzgerald's revisions of the chapters highlighted in the lesson. As important as their insights into the novel, however, is their increased understanding of the writing process and especially of the critical role that revision plays in it. Therefore, as they write their essays, their experiences studying Fitzgerald's revisions inform the kinds of concerns they attend to in their own revisions. That is, in looking for opportunities to revise their own first drafts and in their peer editing of each other's drafts, they are instructed to be particularly sensitive to opportunities to rearrange blocks of material to sharpen the impact of their writing. Much recent research on revision processes has stressed the difficulty students have rearranging materials in their drafts. If working with Fitzgerald's manuscripts can begin to dissolve their resistance to this kind of revision, the

New York only recalls, and let you sleep at my
house. I'll get you some clothes and then we'll see
about getting you a job, so that you can make enough
to get back to your parents. How does that suit
you?"

"All right, indeed sir," Charley's ~~poture~~ voice ~~with~~
expressed the greatest relief. He would not have
to decide for himself what to do.

They went on for some time in silence;
Charley, tremendously excited by the speed and
the noise of the car, clutched the seat tightly. The
~~air~~ rushing of air nearly took his breath away, and
fluttered his torn shirt. Of a sudden, his companion
turned to him severely.

"Suppose, Charley, you can keep still about
things if you have to."

"Yes-sir," the boy answered with confidence.
At the same time he wondered vaguely whether everybody
around New York had so many secrets.

"Well, I don't want you to tell anyone
~~what can~~ where I picked up. You'd better not
say anything unless I'm around. There are several
things I don't want known." Charley felt
quite exhilarated by the confidence placed in him.
buildings By this time they were passing isolated
~~houses~~ of a new sort. It was fully dark now,
and the coarse light coming from rows of tumbledown
houses, more squalid than anything Charley had
ever seen before, streaked in little patches across the

Page from Dos Passos's manuscript for "Adventures about an Orchard" from Archive of Literary Documents Volume I, John Dos Passos: Afterglow and Other Undergraduate Writings, *edited by Richard Layman (Detroit: Omnigraphics, 1989)*

value of working with these materials as outlined in this lesson sequence cannot be overestimated.

Perhaps the final judges of the value of manuscript materials in English instruction must be the students who should benefit from the approach. Again and again, the students who have been enrolled in classes using this approach echo the enthusiasm of their teachers, emphasizing particularly how these materials enabled them to get around obstacles to the development of their reading and writing abilities. Student comments on the effects of manuscript study on their approach to literature consistently express their appreciation of the accessibility to the literature that working with manuscripts affords. After a lesson that drew on Blake's manuscripts for "The Tyger" and "The Poison Tree," one student wrote, "I enjoyed the lesson yesterday because I became interested in the poems. It was a new twist, instead of the boring study questions that don't really get the student involved. It's a tricky way to get a student to enjoy poetry." Students also regularly assert the value of manuscript work for their understanding of the writing process and of their efforts to improve their writing. A student in the same class as the one above found in the lesson using Blake's manuscripts an improved sense of herself as a writer: "Studying poetry using manuscripts makes it easier to accept yourself and your work; you know that not everyone can just sit down and write a 'perfect' poem." The very positive responses of both teachers and students to lessons incorporating manuscript work make it all the more surprising that manuscript materials have been so absent from the English classroom. As more and more teachers discover what a rich resource these materials provide, however, manuscripts will begin to occupy the central curricular position they deserve.

Facsimiles and Teaching

Joel Myerson
University of South Carolina

Facsimiles may be used as an important teaching aid in a variety of ways, all of which share the sense of immediacy that facsimiles alone can bring. You cannot get closer to a writer's thinking than by examining the ways in which he chooses and organizes his words in order to present his thoughts in written form.

First, facsimiles humanize a writer. Most readers are only familiar with an author's works as they are presented in a small-sized typeface printed on thin sheets of paper in an anthology. Facsimiles go beyond this to individualize a writer. They remind readers that each writer is unique in a way that is impossible to show in anthologies, with their formatted explanatory interchapters and standardized typefaces.

Second, facsimiles allow us to see writers create by showing the very process of creation. Words are chosen and discarded, inserted and crossed out, interlined and deleted. Blanks are left to be filled in later. Characters' names are changed. Whole sections of text are added, deleted, and shifted about. All this physical action is the result of considerable mental action, as the author's concept of his work is played out and changed. Genetic-text transcriptions—which use editorial symbols to represent textual changes—can hint at the complexity of the creative process, but only facsimiles can represent it in a pictorial fashion.

The problems Emily Dickinson's editors have had in editing her verse are graphically illustrated in the Harvard University Press edition of her manuscripts (1981), which reproduce her lack of standardized punctuation, failure to decide among alternate readings, and hard-to-decipher handwriting. The New York Public Library's facsimile of Walt Whitman's personal copy of the 1860 edition of *Leaves of Grass* (1968), used by him in preparing a new edition of the book, shows how Whitman never stopped revising, even when a poem was—by normal practices—declared "finished" by its having been published. In both cases, only the facsimile can convey a sense of artistic creation that approximates the original.

Finally, facsimiles show students that *all* writers—from famous authors to themselves—revise. Most students seem to believe that great works of literature were created ex nihilo, that the author's thoughts were somehow magically transferred to the printed page without an intermediate step. They then apply this principle to their own writing with disappointing results. Studying facsimiles shows that even the best writers agonized, revised, and fought with their works before declaring them complete. Students need to realize this and to apply the lesson to their own writing practices.

I regularly use facsimiles in two ways in teaching graduate courses. In my bibliography course,

I distribute to the class facsimiles of manuscript letters and ask them to transcribe them in such a way that all the characteristics of the manuscript are conveyed accurately. They can choose among any of the currently used systems, from clear-text with textual notes to genetic-text transcription. We then compare the transcriptions and discuss which method is most accurate and understandable. In my second exercise, which I use with literature classes, I hand out facsimiles of poetry manuscripts, and ask the class to discuss, in plain English, how the process of revision is carried out and how the meaning of the poem is affected during the writing process. Both cases clearly stress authorial intention and offer an attractive alternative to such critical readings as deconstruction.

Professor Myerson is preparing a facsimile edition of Whitman's Leaves of Grass *for Garland Publishing.*

Facsimiles and Student Research

Sarah Barnhill

My experience with facsimile manuscripts comes from doctoral research on the drafts of F. Scott Fitzgerald's fourth novel, *Tender Is the Night* (1934). Fitzgerald worked on the novel for nine years, from 1925 to 1934, leaving behind more steps of composition than do most novelists. My research focused on five separate and significant stages of *Tender* that have survived, including more than seven hundred pages of the original and complete manuscript. Because of the extant material remaining from the many layers of composition, *Tender Is the Night* offers a wealth of subject matter for the scholar—if, that is, the scholar has access to these numerous prepublication stages of development.

During the time I did all of my research of Fitzgerald's novel, a published facsimile of the *Tender* manuscript did not yet exist. Thanks, however, to the efforts of my dissertation direction, I had access to Xeroxes of the original manuscript as well as the setting copy, galleys, and numerous typescript galley inserts, all of which are part of the Fitzgerald collection at the Princeton University Library.

The greatest benefit of the facsimile manuscript for the graduate student is that a facsimile makes it possible for *any* student to do serious and significant textual work—not just those students at major research universities with large special collections in their libraries. In the broadest sense, therefore, facsimiles democratize literary research, granting access to original manuscripts—or the closest thing to them—to all students.

Work with facsimile manuscripts also introduces the student to an intimate scholarship that is as near as anyone can get to observing the creative process itself. The hand of the writer is never out of sight—literally, in Fitzgerald's case, for the margins of the setting copy and galleys are punctuated with his handwritten notes and caveats: "Beware Ernest" and "No italics!" With facsimiles, the student observes a writer's mistakes as well as his masterstrokes. Nowhere is this creative process more apparent than in the last chapter of *Tender Is the Night*. Throughout the composition of the novel, the envoi chapter goes through a process of shrinkage, until it is only 346 words. In its final form it is a highly compressed and understated coda to the story of the deterioration of Dick Diver, illustrating the narrative technique of what Fitzgerald called the "dying fall," or fadeout. Critics of the novel cite the ending as proof of Fitzgerald's own loss of energy or motivation. But a study of the prepublication layers of composition suggests just the opposite—that Fitzgerald was working carefully and deliberately to create a mood of formality and intentional distance. For example, "Certainly" becomes "almost certainly," "without" becomes "evidently without," and "a law suit" becomes "some law suit." Subtle though the changes are, their cumulative effect produces a mood of formal removal or emotional distance: as Fitzgerald adopts a narrative stance more and more removed from Dick, Dick himself slips farther and farther away. What a study of the facsimiles indicates is that the epilogue was the result of careful craft, not depleted energy.

Such scrutiny of a work-in-progress is of vital importance to the graduate student who is—or should be—in the process of becoming a specialist on a particular writer. It gives the apprentice scholar the grounds to speak with an authority that a study of published final texts alone will never give. Because of my own work on the *Tender* facsimiles, for example, I unearthed further evidence pointing to 1929 as the correct date for the novel's conclusion, and not 1930 as Malcolm Cowley argued. I also discovered several previously undetected errors in all published texts of the novel, discoveries that will help cre-

Page from Fitzgerald's manuscript for Tender Is the Night *from* F. Scott Fitzgerald Manuscripts, *edited by Matthew J. Bruccoli (New York: Garland, 1990-1991)*

ate a "pure text" of the novel. And, to silence further those who insist on seeing Fitzgerald as the alcoholic artist who allowed his drinking to interfere with his writing, I found only one instance in more than two thousand pages of material where Fitzgerald was writing in an alcoholic haze. The passage did not survive the next stage of revision.

Research based on a close study of facsimiles has two other benefits of no small consideration to the graduate student—namely, reductions of both cost and time of degree work. If published facsimiles do not exist, the expenses for Xeroxing the original manuscript and other stages of composition of a four-hundred-page novel are considerable. If cleaner copies are needed, copying and shipping charges imposed by the library holding the original material can be even higher. (For example, I requested from Princeton University Library recopies of three pages of material that was illegible on my own photocopies. The charge for the three pages was eighteen dollars.) Such costs become insignificant, however, when compared to the much greater costs of one or more research trips that could include not only travel expenses but also several weeks' worth of hotel and meal charges.

The availability of facsimiles means that the time required to finish a graduate degree diminishes. The National Research Council's latest findings (1989) in *Summary Report 1987: Doctorate Recipients From United States Universities* indicates that it takes longer to get a Ph.D. in the humanities than in any other field of study—an average of 8.4 years from baccalaureate to doctorate. Traditionally, humanities students spend more of this time on the dissertation than on course work or comprehensive preparation. Any way that facsimiles of original primary material can simplify the dissertation research process cuts this time appreciably. Using my own research as an example, I was able to complete both essential preliminary research and the dissertation itself in eighteen months. Had I not had facsimiles of the various stages of composition of *Tender Is the Night* sitting in five plastic milk crates on the floor of my study, the time needed for the dissertation would have doubled.

Use of facsimile manuscripts also introduces the graduate student to certain protocols of research with which all scholars should be familiar.

He learns a great deal about copyright, literary executors, publication permission, and all the workings of rare book and manuscript rooms.

Ultimately, work on and with facsimile manuscripts reassesses, for *all* students of literature, the importance of the text itself. Granted, such an approach runs counter to many current trends in literary criticism which frequently ignore the text and offer instead conjecture and "interpretation." What is often at issue in such approaches is not the failure or success of a writer, but the cleverness of the critic in making a work of literature fit the mold of a particular critical theory. Facsimile manuscripts, however, demand preeminence be given to *the thing written*, and not to the theory. In my case, the thousands of revisions Fitzgerald made to his novel, from one-word alterations to three-hundred word deletions, could not be dismissed or ignored. Honest scholarship will always deal with what a writer adds, removes, or alters during a novel's evolution. Facsimile manuscripts, therefore, provide the student of literature with both a test of truth as well as a text of truth.

Literary Facsimiles: A Checklist

The following is a preliminary survey of literary manuscripts and archives reproduced in facsimile on microfilm, microfiche, and hard copy in the last five years in the United States and the United Kingdom.

Chadwyck-Healey Inc.

Charles Dickens Research Collection Part 1: *The J. F. Dexter Collection at the British Library.* Part 2: *Selections from the Suzannet Collection at Dickens House Museum; from the holdings of the Bodleian Library, John Rylands University Library of Manchester; the Houghton Library, Harvard University; and other libraries in the United Kingdom and United States.* Editorial Board Chairman: Graham Storey. 102 microfilm reels. 1991. Cambridge, U.K. $10,400.

Records of the Stationers' Company, 1554-1920. Editor: Robin Myers. 115 microfilm reels. 1988. Cambridge, U.K. $9,900.

Garland Publishing, Inc.

F. Scott Fitzgerald Manuscripts: Facsimiles of the Novels, Short Stories, and Essays. General Editor: Matthew J. Bruccoli. 17 volumes. 1990-1991. New York. $3,300.

William Faulkner Manuscripts. Editors: Joseph Blotner, Thomas McHaney, Michael Millgate, Noel Polk, and James B. Meriwether. 44 volumes. 1987. New York. $6,245.

The Manuscripts of the Younger Romantics: Facsimile Editions, with Scholarly Introductions, Bibliographical Descriptions, and Annotations. General Editor: Donald H. Reiman. 20 volumes. 1986-1991. New York. $1,500.

The Bodleian Shelley Manuscripts: Facsimile Editions with Full Transcriptions and Scholarly Apparatus. General Editor: Donald H. Reiman. 16 volumes. 1985-1992. New York. $1,560.

The Tennyson Archive. Editors: Christopher Ricks and Aidan Day. 30 volumes. 1987-1991. New York. $3,000.

Jane Austen's Lady Susan: A Facsimile of the Manuscripts in the Pierpont Morgan Library and the 1925 Printed Edition. 1 volume. 1989. New York. $110.

The Later Poetic Manuscripts of Gerard Manley Hopkins from "The Wreck of the Deutschland" to the Final Dublin Sonnets in Facsimile. Editor: Norman H. Mackenzie. 1 volume. 1991. New York. $110.

The Early Poetic Manuscripts and Notebooks of Gerard Manley Hopkins in Facsimile. Editor: Norman H. Mackenzie. 1 volume. 1989. New York. $110.

The Victorian Muse: Selected Criticism and Parody of the Period. General Editors: William E. Fredeman, Ira Bruce Nadel, John F. Stasney. 32 volumes. 1986. New York. $1,849.

The Thomas Hardy Archive Series. Editor: Simon Gatrell. 2 volumes. 1986. New York. $250.

Harvard University Press

John Keats Poetry Manuscripts at Harvard: A Facsimile Edition. Editor: Jack Stillinger. 1 volume. 1990. Cambridge, Mass. $100.

Omnigraphics, Inc.

Archive of Literary Documents Volume I, John Dos Passos: Afterglow and Other Undergraduate Writings. Editor: Richard Layman. 1 volume. 1990. Detroit. $125.

Archive of Literary Documents Volume II, Ernest Hemingway: The Sun Also Rises. Editor: Matthew J. Bruccoli. 2 volumes. 1990. Detroit. $250.

Southern Illinois University Press

Jane Austen's Manuscript Letters in Facsimile: Reproductions of Every Known Extant Letter, Fragment, & Autograph Copy, with an Annotated List of All Known Letters. Editor: Jo Modert. 1 volume. 1989. Carbondale. $50.

The Bobbs-Merrill Archive at the Lilly Library, Indiana University

The papers of the Bobbs-Merrill Company were donated to Indiana University by Howard W. Sams in 1964. In 1958 Sams had acquired the firm which as Merrill, Meigs and Company began its "national prominence as literary publishers" in 1883 with James Whitcomb Riley's *The Old Swimmin' Hole and 'Leven More Poems*. In 1885 Merrill, Meigs and Company merged with Bowen, Stewart and Company to become Bowen-Merrill Company, which in turn became the Bobbs-Merrill Company in 1903.

The Merrill portion of the firm's name stems from Charles White Merrill (1861-1920), editor and part owner; his father, Samuel Merrill, Jr. (1831-1924); and his grandfather Samuel Merrill (1792-1855), treasurer of the state of Indiana, who moved the physical effects of the state from Corydon to the new capitol at Indianapolis—all of whom had been active in publishing and bookstore ventures bearing the Merrill name. William Conrad Bobbs (1861-1926), who had joined the Bowen-Merrill Company early in his career, served twenty-six years as president.

The earliest records in the company files (which are often incomplete) begin with the bound volume of the stockholders minutes for 1885, which report the merging of Merrill, Meigs and Company with Bowen, Stewart and Company in 1885, and continue to 1947. Other business materials include author ledgers, 1909-1918; board of directors minutes, 1913-1935; book store accounts, 1909-1958; drama and production rights, 1902-1922; dramatic and syndicate sales record, 1918; dramatic ledger, 1911; general ledgers, 1893-1915; newspaper story purchases, 1902-1924; record of educational publications, 1913-1917; record of publications, 1896-1906; royalty reports, 1898-1939; and salesmen's correspondence, 1925-1957. There is other correspondence related to business concerns for the period of 1907-1959.

The largest segment of material in the collection consists of the author files which range from 1898 to 1960. The materials include: biographical information such as the author's question-

D. Laurence Chambers, who joined Bobbs-Merrill in 1903 and was president of the firm from 1935 to 1958

naire (see *DLB Yearbook: 1985*) and photographs, clippings regarding activities, lecture tours, social notes, and clippings of articles by the author; collected correspondence in chronological order including interoffice memorandums and semiannual royalty reports; litigation papers (if any); writings arranged by title. The last include a variety of book makeup and promotional pieces—but not the manuscripts which appear to have been returned to the author or, by permission, destroyed. The archive also includes some of the following: readers' reports on the publishing viability of the manuscript; book jackets (designs, printed versions, and blurbs for flaps); illustrations (often in multiple formats); sales reports which were lengthy summaries for the use of the salesmen in promoting the book; advertising devices such as leaflets, postcard order forms, posters; bookstore promotional presentations; proofs of advertisements; reviews (newspaper, periodicals, statements from prominent figures); lists of newspapers to which review copies were sent. If the book were made into a movie, publicity for the event is to be found with the title of the book.

Among more than forty-five hundred authors represented in the collection are George Ade, Irving Bacheller, Bruce Barton, David Cecil, Irvin Cobb, James Oliver Curwood, Pietro di Donato, John Erskine, C. S. Forester, Alice Tisdale Hobart, Emerson Hough, Marquis James, Owen Johnson, Harold MacGrath, Vladimir Nabokov, Meredith Nicholson, Mary Roberts Rinehart, Kenneth Roberts, Channing Pollock, Carlo Sforza, C. P. Snow, William Styron, Brand Whitlock.

See Jack O'Bar, The Origins and History of the Bobbs-Merrill Company, (University of Illinois Graduate School of Library and Information Science Occasional Papers, *172 [December 1985])*, DLB Yearbook: 1985, DLB Yearbook: 1986, *and* DLB: 46, American Literary Publishing Houses, 1900-1980: Trade and Paperback.

—*Virginia Lowell Mauck*

Readers' Reports in the Bobbs-Merrill Archive

Readers' reports provide information about books that, in many cases, would not otherwise be available. The reports furnish details about the editing and publishing of books and answer questions about matters often obscured by the finished product. A well-written readers' report includes not only a plot synopsis but also a discussion of the editorial, literary, and commercial prospects for the manuscript. This discussion obviously benefits the publisher and editor. But the same information is also of benefit to the scholar. The reports provide documentary evidence of the condition of the manuscript when it was submitted; what changes in the text were recommended; and what prospects the publisher held for the title, both in terms of sales and in critical response. These reports can be useful in constructing the publishing history of a text and in providing clues to the source and motivation for editorial changes.

The following reports are reproduced with the generous cooperation of William Cagle, Director of the Lilly Library.

King—of the Khyber Rifles (1916)

Talbot Mundy's *King—of the Khyber Rifles* was published by Bobbs-Merrill in 1916. The novel, Mundy's third but his first published by Bobbs-Merrill, is his best-known work and has twice been filmed, first by John Ford in 1927 as *The Black Watch* and again in 1953 under its own name starring Tyrone Power. The publication of popular fiction was a staple for Bobbs-Merrill in the late nineteenth and early twentieth centuries, though by 1916 fiction sales had begun to decline. The report by M. A. Cleland reproduced here correctly identifies Mundy as an heir to the popular tradition of Kipling, though just at the time when that tradition of colonial race fiction was dying. The reader writes that *King—of the Khyber Rifles* "will be a sensation, and should be a gold mine to author and publisher alike." Bobbs-Merrill published twelve additional titles by Mundy during the next thirteen years.

The Joy of Cooking (1936)

Irma S. Rombauer's *The Joy of Cooking* was published by Bobbs-Merrill in 1936. The cookbook had been published privately in St. Louis in 1931 and was submitted to the company early in 1933. The two reports reproduced here hint at the appeal of the book to its millions of users. The first, signed by Nancy Poston, praises the recipes but questions the arrangement of the directions. This report also has the distinction of calling *The Joy of Cooking* "just another cookbook." The second report, signed only Jessica, is a memo to D. Laurence Chambers, then vice-president of the firm, which discusses reactions from several readers to the cookbook. One writer points out that her sister, because she was already an accomplished cook, disliked the arrangement of the directions and ingredients. The writer, on the other hand, was an amateur, and found the format easy to use. The book underwent refinement and revision before being published in 1936. It was a steady and, at times, prodigous seller; according to Hiram Haydn, New York editor during the early 1950s, children's books and *The Joy of Cooking* were the primary sources of profitability for the trade-book division. The book has been revised many times and each new edition has been successful. The 1953 edition reached the number six position on the *New York Times* bestseller list. The cookbook remains in print in 1991.

The Fountainhead (1943)

Ayn Rand's *The Fountainhead* was published by Bobbs-Merrill in 1943. Rand began planning in 1936 the novel that became *The Fountainhead* and began writing it in 1938. Under financial stress, Rand was desperately trying to parlay her nascent novel into a publishing contract with a healthy advance. Macmillan offered her $250, which she rejected as too little, and Knopf offered her $1200, but payable only upon completion of the novel. In all, eight publishers had opportunities to take the novel, but Rand was left without a contract or the much-needed advance. Rand submitted her manuscript, then titled "Second Hand Lives," to Bobbs-Merrill in late 1941. Archibald Ogden, Bobbs-Merrill's New York editor, was enthusiastic about the novel and wanted to sign a contract immediately. But Rand was still demanding a $1200 advance, an amount to which Ogden could not agree without approval from Indianapolis. He sent the manuscript and his own report to the corporate offices. The reports from the Indianapolis readers were greatly divided in opinion except in that "Second Hand Lives" was a very provocative piece of work. At Ogden's insistence, the novel was accepted, and a contract was signed in December 1941. Rand received a $1000 advance, and a deadline of 1 January 1943 was set for submission of a completed text. The first report reproduced here is that of Ogden, which accompanied the manuscript to Indianapolis. The second is a report signed by J. D., who suggests that the name be changed as it sounds "like a lending-library effusion on streetwalkers." The third is signed by Patricia Jones, who sees no chance for the book to become a financial success. The fourth is an editorial memo, signed Jessica, to Chambers recommending acceptance of the manuscript and a reduction of

the advance. *The Fountainhead* was published in May 1943 with a 7,500 copy print run. The novel's sales reached 18,000 copies by November and by 1948 had reached 400,000. The novel's success secured Rand's reputation and helped to legitimize her political views. It set the stage for her even greater success with *Atlas Shrugged*, which was published in 1957 by Random House. Bobbs-Merrill did not published another Rand title until 1982, when it issued *Philosophy: Who Needs It* after her death.

Lie Down in Darkness (1957)

William Styron's *Lie Down in Darkness* was published by Bobbs-Merrill in 1951. Styron began the novel in 1947 as a student in Hiram Haydn's fiction-writing seminar at the New School for Social Research in New York City. After Styron submitted a few short stories, Haydn convinced him to begin a novel. When Styron turned in the first twenty pages of what would become *Lie Down in Darkness*, Haydn, then an editor at Crown Publishing, took an option on the novel. Haydn worked with Styron on his novel for the next two years, developing a very close relationship with the novelist. When Haydn moved to Bobbs-Merrill in 1950, he brought Styron and his novel along with him. But Haydn had to convince Bobbs-Merrill of the importance of *Lie Down in Darkness* and sent the novel out to readers to do so. The unsigned reader's report reproduced here is lavish in its praise of the novel. It points out the strengths of the book, but, more important, it identifies the most serious editorial challenge that Styron's novel presented: Peyton's soliloquy. This concluding section of the novel was greatly changed during the editing process to soften its explicit sexual language. The report recommends the strict editing of the soliloquy so that the excellence of the novel not be obscured by the controversial portrayal of Peyton's decline. The publication of *Lie Down in Darkness* was a great success for Styron and Bobbs-Merrill, establishing the author's reputation and firming up for a time that of the company. Styron left Bobbs-Merrill for Random House when Haydn joined the latter firm in 1954.

—J. W. H.

KING, OF THE KHYBER RIFLES.

Andrew Lang, who once wrote a little verse about
a certain time coming in English literature which ended with
the lines—
" When the Rudyard's cease from Kipling,
And the Haggards ride no more;"
would surely think that that time had not arrived, should he
chance upon King, of the Khyber Rifles, for it is Kipling and
Haggard in one.   Think of that as a combination!
With the India of Kipling for a background, not,
however, the India of the luxurious bungalow, the ball-room,
the polo field, or the tennis court, but the India of the
teeming streets, the crowded railway stations with troops
entraining for the European War front, the stifling train
journeys, the India of the Hills and scorching plains, of the
British secret service and the native tribes, imagine a story
written with the imagination of a Haggard, with all of his
power in describing adventures in unknown lands, add the
mystery the thrill, and throw over it the elusive, intangible
spell of another She Who Must Be Obeyed, and you have an idea
of what this Mms. presents.
King, a member of the Indian Secret Service, is
sent by his general to prevent an uprising of the Hill tribes
who are planning a Holy War, hoping to rescue India from the
grasp of the English while her troops are at the Western
battle front.   A rumor is afloat that the mysterious "Heart
of the Hills" has come to life and is inflaming the natives.
King is detailed to discover, who or what this mystery is
and can only do so by penetrating into the Caves of Khinjan,
which no English has ever done and come out alive.   He is
told that he is to work with Yasmini, a woman he has never
seen but who has traveled up and down India winning the natives
everywhere by a wonderful witchery and who possesses a mysterious
power over them.   She is part Russian, the Widow, of a Rajah and
famed for her intelligence, her beauty and marvellous grace as
a dancer.
Ambitious, with the love of power and intrigue in
her blood, she has rendered aid to the Service more than once and
has promised to unearth the present plot with King's assistance.
The story of his journey to Khinjan, through the horrors of the
Khyber Pass, across the plains to that mysterious city of the
Himalayas, surrounded by treachery, in peril of his life at every
step, is one that thrills the reader at every sentence.
How he succeeds in entering the caves and in penetrating
to the very heart of the world, where he at last meets Yasmini and
finds, that she herself, as the natives believe is the reincarnation
of "The Heart of the Hills", and where by his unfailing bravery,
his ready wit and the proverbial luck of the British Army, he
circumvents her treacherous plans, accomplishes his mission and
finally escapes, is told in such a way as to form one of the most
amazing examples of imaginative writing that has been produced
for many decades.
The word gripping is very much overworked in speaking
of modern novels but there is no other which fitly describes this
Mms., for the reader is in the grip of strong emotions from start
to finish- admiration for its hero, amazement, wonder and horror
succeed one another as the story progresses.   At no point does the
interest lag, mystery after mystery developes until the final climax.
It is all thrilling, exciting, absorbing, for it is written with
the pen of an artist, Improbable as it is, it is made so real that
no thought of its improbability intrudes, as we read, to dull the edge
of our enjoyment.   The author has so used the mystery, the charm and
the superstition of the East as to make even the impossible seem
possible, and has exploited the treachery as well as the fidelity,

Reader's report for Talbot Mundy's 1916 novel

the cold-blooded cruelty as well as the tenderness of the native character with telling effect.

The English used is perfect, the style consistently maintained throughout, the descriptive passages so powerful that we read with the rush of mighty winds in our faces, the roar of the "Drink of the World" in our ears, we stumble through the dark over unknown ways with our nerves on edge, grope along ledges along bottomless depths with our hearts in our mouths, and live through all the perils seen and unseen which beset the hero.

It is not enough to say that the story if published will be a popular one- it will be a sensation, and should be a gold mine to author and publisher alike.

M. A. Cleland.

THE JOY OF COOKING

by Irma S. Rombauer

This is an anthology of favorite recipes compiled by the author, and as a whole it seems to me a very good one. Of course, it would be hard for me with only a practical experience of cooking and no knowledge of chemistry to pass on any particular recipe without trying it out. The collection does look interesting, varied and unusual, and perhaps more to the point, it appears to be practical. In reading through the various recipes I saw many I thought I'd like to try sometime or other.

Mrs. Rombauer employs a different form in writing her recipes that the one generally used. Instead of listing the ingredients and then giving directions underneath it goes like this:

Beat until very stiff.....................(2 egg whites
                                          (1/4 teaspoon salt

Fold in...................................(1 cup grated cheese

etc.

This is, I gather, supposed to be a more convenient way of putting the recipes. I found it irritating to read and though I might change my mind if working with it I feel now that I much prefer the other, more usual method. It seems both simpler and more logical to me to be able to glace through a list of ingredients at the top of a recipe to be sure that I have them and to collect them, and then to read a connected paragraph of directions. This is, of course, a purely personal reaction.

Another more or less unusual feature of the book is the "casual culinary chat" that runs through it. The author sometimes discusses the origin of a particular recipe and interpolates suggestions for changing them slightly under varying circumstances, and for combining them with other dishes to make interesting menus. This gives an attractive, informal note to the book, and should be particularly helpful to an inexperience cook.

There is a list of general rules, weights and measures, directions, hints, at the first of the book and as an appendix in the manuscript. In the different sections there are more specialized rules and hints regarding the particular food

Reader's report for one of the most famous American cookbooks

or type of recipe. These are very full and practical.

The appendices are an interesting aspect of the book. One deals with menus for every occasion: breakfast, luncheon, dinner supper, tea. Such menus are often helpful as sources of suggestion even if not followed in every detail. There is, in the book, a list of easily made favors for childrens parties. The section on using up left overs is arranged in an interesting way. It is arranged so that one can look up any particular food and find a list of suggestions for its use. For instance, under Sour Milk is listed Biscuits, Bran Muffins, Cottage Cheese, etc. There is a somewhat similar system under Lunnheon Menus, which would seem to me to make the chapter in the book entitled Luncheon and Supper dishes somewhat unnecessary, and I should think it would be better to have the recipes therein located under their respective chapters of sandwiches, fish, eggs, soups, and so on.

The chapter on Sandwiches and Canapès seemed to me especially good, and also the ones on soups, vegetable, salads. As a matter of fact, all the chapters have recipes that are both practical and unusual. Mrs. Rombauer not only gives basic recipes for basicfoods, but different ways of using the basic foods. She has simple recipes for boiling and steaming rice, and then has Milk Rice, Cheese Rice, talian Rice, Rice loaf, Spanish Rice, and many other rice recipes.

Another unusual feature--at least it is not in any cook book I have--is oxx a chapter on alcoholic beverages. There are directions for the making of the more usual cocktails and some of the more unusual. There are simple and very practical suggestions as to wines and their uses, and recipes given for several fruit wines and cordials.

All in all it is a very satisfactory cook book and one that any ardent collector of cookbooks would be glad to add to her collection. I should like to have it myself. But the question in my mind is whether it is not, in spite of all that can be said in its favor, just another cook book. I should never feel that it took the place of a standard manual such as the Boston Cook Book is. It isn't, as another cook book I own is, an ideal one for a bridge starting out with a limited income and limited experience in cooking. It doesn't have the special appeal of another Df Mine, entitled The Questing Cook, which contains a rather small collection of very delightful and unusual foreign recipes, written up in a manner which makes it

3.

fascinating reading. I'm afraid it is just another cook book, although it certainly

is ax nice one.

Nancy Boston

(Exclusively for Correspondence between Departments)

The Bobbs-Merrill Company, Publishers

Memorandum for   Subject   Editorial

Referred to   Date
       Mr. Chambers   1-28-33

My sister, Jean Wagoner, has not yet made her written
report on Mrs. Rombauer's THE JOY OF COOKING, but she
told me last night that it was awfully "tame" after
having Amiet's.   She is afraid that there isn't sufficient novelty or individuality about it to make it
stand out from other cookbooks. As regards the new
way of arranging and printing the recipes, she did
not think this any great advantage. I am inclined to
disagree with her on this point because I am more or
less an amateur and it generally takes me half a hour
to put in each ingredient and I think this arrangement
would help me to solve the process more rapidly. I
shall make a trial over the week end and see if it actually
does help. Jean is such an experienced cook that a
little thing like mixing ingredients doesn't bother her.
Perhaps this trick arrangement would only help amateurs.

I am writing you about this now in case you want to
discuss the situation with Mr. Olsen. You will remember
that we had the Home Economics teacher at Technical
Highschool read this book and while she thought the
menus and recipes were okay, she didn't seem to think
them outstanding or particularly attractive. Is there
any one you want me to have read the book when I get
it back from Jean?

                    Jessica

*Dear Jessie: this is your field
not mine. Do what you think
called for in the circumstances*
1-28-33

Reader's report for Irma Rombauer's cookbook

SECOND HAND LIVES
Ayn Rand

This is the first manuscript I have read in a long time so to hold my interest in the unfolding of its plot that I almost finished five hundred pages
before I was conscious of the exaggerated nature of its characters - or, at
least, before their incredibility bothered me slightly.   It is also the first
manuscript in a longer time with such power of expression that a too constant
reader's immediate reaction is: "Eureka! Here's someone who can write". God
knows she often writes too much, but her words carry you along with a rush, and
her facility of expression, her subtlety in psychological nuances, her bold conception of the story she wants to tell, impressed me from the start that hers is
an unusual talent and by no means an amateurish one.   The whole idea of this
book - and the way it is written - is entirely different from the current crop
of novels on the market - certainly from anything on our own list.

It is perhaps this very difference that is apt to put one off, at times
infuriate one, and certainly make difficult placing the book in a particular
category.   I only know that on putting it down I was pleased to feel that I had
at last come across a novel - and an author - I could wholeheartedly recommend
for publication.   By "wholeheartedly" I do not mean that the manuscript is
faultless. It isn't.   But it is provocative, challenging, ~~interesting~~ *interesting* and all
the other blurb-writer's cliches that should spell general interest and respect-
able sales.

The author has summarized (at length) the plot; so I won't repeat it.
Miss Rand feels she is writing the story of the triumph of the individual over
the forces of collectivism, and she wanted the book considered first by Bobbs-
Merrill because of our "courage in publishing THE RED DECADE, which is an attack on collectivism in non-fiction as her book is in fiction".   The political

Reader's report for The Fountainhead

-2-

implications of her book are, to me, irrelevant, as I believe they will be to all but the most politically minded readers. SECOND HAND LIVES should be read as an exciting and original story - not in any sense as propaganda. Her sadism - masochism theme as inherent in perfect physical love may irritate some people, but certain psychologists agree with her - and it <u>does</u> make for originality in this love story.

To me some of the best parts of the book deal with architecture - for architecture (it should be capitalized as Miss Rand considers it) is as much a character of the plot as Roark. She makes architecture seem vital, even to the layman; and she successfully accomplishes, I think, one of the most diffi-cult feats of fiction: she writes about art and makes it live. Rarely do you find a book about a composer where the author can convince you of the power and the beauty of his original compositions. This is true of books about mu-sicians, poets, novelists; but it's not true of Miss Rand's presentation of Roark and Architecture. You get the feel of his buildings and an almost intu-itive sense of what he is trying to achieve in architecture, and this without any technical knowledge necessary on the part of the reader. (Miss Rand spent a year, incidentally, working for nothing in an architect's office just to get the background material on this subject).

And now for what is at first disturbing about this novel - the exag-gerated nature of almost all the characters. If you grant the premise of the possibility of their existence, their behavior is always psychologically explicable (with the possible exception of Dominique, about whom we should know a good deal more before we can believe in her). We don't meet many such char-acters in life - life would be more upsetting than it is, if we did - but it <u>is</u> possible that we could meet such people; and we have all known a Keating, a Francon, even a Toohey and a Roark, or people who partake of the qualities

-3-

of these characters - qualities which for the purpose of her novel the author

has consciously carried to extremes.   My first thought - and it may be correct,

since I have not discussed this with Miss Rand - was that she visualized this

book as heroic in theme and in scope, and that she consciously created charac-

ters of heroic proportions, whether for good, or for evil, to carry the load of

her plot - something of the early classical idea of drama, in which only gods

and supermen were worthy to carry the theme, even though the theme itself might

be pertinent to the lives of ordinary mortals.   This still may be true of Miss

Rand's conception of her characters, even though I suddenly realized they are

all probably real people, or, in certain instances, a combination of the charac-

ters of two people.   Frank Lloyd Wright's life is very similar to Roark's.   For

almost thirty years he struggled for recognition of his functional design.   He

was jeered at by orthodox architects and critics, only the most daring and orig-

inal minds gave him occasional commissions, the first home he built was never

lived in by the owner's wife and the servants left because the servants of neigh-

bors made so much fun of them.   He studied under the man (I cannot remember his

real name) who is now recognized as the father of the modern sky-scraper, yet

who died a drunkard's death some years ago unrecognized or admired by anyone

other than Wright.   (Incidentally, Miss Rand is apt to let sentimentality get

the better of her ability in her scenes involving Cameron.)   I have no doubt

that Keating and Ffrancon have prototypes in reality, and I know the sculptor,

befriended by Roark, is based on a real person.   Toohey I could not place, al-

though there was a certain flickering of the early Heywood Broun in his makeup.

Broun was always organizing "intellectual" groups whom he could influence from

the background, or through whom he could influence the public (witness the Book-

of-the-Month Club for one of them).   In talking to Miss Rand I find Toohey is

-4-

indeed a combination of Broun and a "New Republic" critic whose name momentarily escapes me, but who holds in letters somewhat the position of Edmund Wilson. He often pontificates on modern architecture, painting, and books.

Wynand is all too obviously Hearst, and should be changed, I think - not for fear of libel, but in the cause of originality (Orson Welles has done enough with Mr. Hearst for the present.)

And so I came to feel that these characters aren't so incredible after all. It's just having such giants - and such pygmies - brought together in one novel that makes them temporarily difficult to swallow. That mental hurdle is I believe, made easier for us by the power and intensity of Miss Rand's writing, and by the compulsion of the plot.

This is not the place for points of specific criticism and suggestions of where judicious cutting might take place. Her manuscript is a first draft of hardly more than a third of what I feel sure will prove a big novel in every sense of the word. Mrs. Dettrick and I are compiling points to take up with the author, and doubtless Indianapolis reports will suggest additions to our list. At the moment I am interested only in infecting other readers with my enthusiasm for this project and this author. They don't come like either of them very often.

AGO.

1

SECOND-HAND LIVES

By Ayn Rand

Probably no more staggeringly original or infallibly controversial novel than this will ever cross an editorial threshold.
I have read it with absorption, anger and bafflement; I leave
it in the same fighting spirit and will take on all comers who
tell me that these specimens are two-legged humans, that this
Roark is of the stuff of heroes, that a man who feels no malice
will make destruction his passion, that a girl admitting a happy
childhood will for no reason be an ogress at nineteen, that this
too patly selected bevy of case-histories shape a novel of social
significance. I choke on unuttered expletives, epithets and oaths,
and shall do so until I rush out and find some one who has read
this amazing thing and can defend it against me or damn it with me,
and then I will urge it on others, to prolong the juicy fray.

This, in my opinion, is the sort of reader reaction that
sells books.

So there is no uncertainty in my mind as to whether I think
this phenomenon should be published. I do think it should be.
I am only torn between the two courses open to its publishers:
(1) to keep it in its present form (with drastic cuts) for just
such a response from readers as it has won from me, or (2) to
request of the author the rewrite that I see wholly feasible,
the remolding that will give the book the humanity it now lacks;
the leavening of plausibility which will let us understand and
pity these strange people instead of being more likely to hate

Reader's report for The Fountainhead

2

them.

It is a bold and dangerous thing for a writer, especially in a book of many characters, to deny his readers any single soul to love or to pull for -- for I think it safe to conclude that few readers, male or female, will share Miss Rand's fondness for her Roark. The persons for whom we are permitted to feel sympathy -- Keating's Catherine, Vesta Dunning -- are unimportant, and the best luck we can wish them, anyway, is to lose out on the men of their choice. But we _could_ feel sympathy for the central characters, and could accept as plausible the other main ones, if Miss Rand could be talked around to it. And in case our acceptance of this novel should turn out to stand or fall on the present unnaturalness of its characters (as I fear it may), I offer the following suggestions toward rewriting. They are at cross purposes with my own aforementioned hunch that controversy might make a big success of the book in its present pattern; but plenty of controversial matter will remain in any event, and so I pass along my proposed alternative to those who must decide (with a middle-course compromise likewise in mind). . . .

It all goes back to the old formula set forth in Hemingway's THE SUN ALSO RISES: "a little irony, a little pity." Miss Rand's novel is a veritable water-cure of irony; it is hosed down our throats. Where rare crumbs of pity allay the heroic dosage, they are too sweetish (the drooly Cameron), and are not administered when they would do the most good. Any pity our imagination contrives for characters toward whom we most need to feel pity is sneaked behind the author's back.

3

When I reached page 436, where Dominique reveals her frigidity, I felt the first faint semblance of pity's stirring that I
had felt thus far in the book, for I saw at last _my_ explanation
of the girl, the author notwithstanding. Dominique, thrown to
us a full-forged female cobra minus motivation or plausibility,
became to me a potential human in this important scene. Suppose
(in that admittedly happy childhood) a natural, romantic little
girl (left lonely, perhaps, by a fond but busy father) and an
·imaginative, sentimental adolescent had dreamed of love -- and
grown up to find it denied her? Suppose flashbacks were to show
us poignantly the shock, bewilderment and young despair at the
discovery of that (yes, ironic) frigidity that slammed the gates
to dreams? Might not a brilliant, dynamic, restless girl turn
bitter, even vicious? Wouldn't the old dreams linger subcon-
sciously in the very idealism which Dominique -- logically, now --
is doomed to mock and wound during the rest of her life? Logically,
for that "the right man," when he comes, should be the equally
warped Roark (q. v. below) is sheer tragedy. The fulfilment
which should have brought forth the normal woman can with him
only putrify the fruits of her original frustration. And if
we've been shown first that little girl dreaming and the young
girl stricken and confused, we will weep for her instead of
loathing her, and forgive her the fiercer bitterness that just
as sure as death and taxes must be her lot.

I felt pity again on page 461, where Roark waits for word
of his contract. Roark, the giant on a mountain top, the des-
piser of men, needing no man -- yet as heartbreakingly dependent
on men as this. "He told the rental agent . . . that there would

be a delay, which was all he knew how to do; but his knowledge
that he needed the delay, that he needed the alm from the rental
agent, that too much depended on it, had made it sound like
begging in his own mind. That was torture. . . . The telephone
bill was overdue for two months. He had received the final
warning. The telephone was to be disconnected in a few days.
. . . He sat, slumped across the desk, his face on his arms, his
fingers on the stand of the telephone. . . . The mail slot in the
door and the telephone -- there was nothing else left to him in
the world."

To me, here is Roark's pitiful motivation: that of a superior
man chained helplessly to the pettinesses, stupidities and foibles
of his species -- like a man locked in a dungeon with human stench
and filth. Roark's hardness is his defense, his sop to his own
pride; and his sadism, instead of a motiveless facet of an unexplained cold nature, is the bursting forth of pent hate for
his degraders, and if he hurts others because he almost cannot
bear their infliction of his debasement and his thwarts, we can
understand and pity him, and see both reason and tragedy in the
brutality of Dominique's rape. At this most bitter phase of
Roark's career, conveniently materializes a frail scapegoat whose
very strength of character and challenging antagonism symbolize
all the opposition he has been meeting in humankind. Weak physically, she is masterable, her futile resistance making his victory
the more savagely enjoyed.

Let him be humanized to the extent of feeling secret shame
afterwards, if the author can be persuaded to go that far. But

as I see it, this baseness to which he has sunk should be the
low-water mark of his character thus far. Miss Rand, too obsessed with arranging her set-up of abstracts, is too little
concerned with any change, any development, in her characters,
from their birth to us -- like babes in cabbages, with no pre-
natal history -- to their exit (as well as her outline lets me
judge). As I reweave the tale, Roark and Dominique could have
helped each other, could have gone far together, but their
pathetic false start (the result not of unexplained freak natures
but of well-motivated quirks) has rung the knell. Antagonism
must still be their portion, but with a difference from Miss
Rand's version. When Miss Rand's present Dominique gets revenge
by spiking Roark's chances for the Sutton contract, I cheer
loudly, and then wait avidly for Roark to get back at her. But
in my humanized version, when Dominique pulls her vicious coup,
the reader will want to beg her "Don't do it! Help him instead."

 We come to Toohey, who needs only plausibility, not sympathy,
for with this one ingredient added he's a villain of the first
water, on a colossus scale. That his is a failure's psychology,
that his motive is the only one possible to him -- envious hate
toward all superior to himself -- should be made clear by Miss
Rand. In her 644 pages so far written, Toohey is very baffling,
and he is more so in her outline, for there she states blandly
that he "glories" in his mediocrity and that this is why he tears
down true art.

 Keating comes the closest to normal. We can swallow most
of him, or could if he would "scream" less and be "frightened"
less. But one villain is enough when that one is of Toohey's

dimensions, and I would rather see Keating humanized as a sort
of pawn-like automaton, launched on life by his mother's cut-
throat religion of "Beat the other man." One does feel her influence, of course, but it could be stronger, with the flashbacks that this novel so badly needs. If Keating is the monster
that mother-love and a mother's pride have created, and who almost
helplessly marches on and on until he destroys himself, we can
feel sorry for him along his precipitous way and when that self-
destruction comes.

As for Wynand -- Heaven spare me from Miss Rand's wrath --
he seems excess baggage. We know him little, but page 8 of the
theme outline shows him (for all his complex motives) overlapping
upon and conflicting with Toohey's destructive machinations so
badly that he seems better ushered out. We do not need Mr. Hearst;
the book goes on so endlessly, with complexity piled on complexity.
I feel a simplified climax (capping the many other simplifications
the cuts will achieve) is greatly to be desired. Much of Wynand's
part is not convincing anyway, and we had better be rid of the
"romance" between Wynand and Roark. Though Wynand may have his
niche in Miss Rand's elaborate concept of abstracts, he confuses
the issue from the standpoint of a concise and readable plot.
By eliminating him we dilute the thesis which, as the book stands,
is a millstone around these people's necks. Toohey can take over
any functions of Wynand's that may seem to dangle. Let Dominique
be sent to Toohey to win a contract for her husband Keating, the
prospective awarder a new unimportant but unlovely character to
whom she sells herself. Keating gets the job, and rebounding to

self-annihilation Dominique marries <u>Toohey</u>; Roark rises to
success, and Dominique kills Toohey to keep him from destroying
Roark. That the victim is her husband makes the murder the
stronger. Let the author have her symbolism: Evil is dead;
Dominique and Roark find each other. Roark tries to shoulder
the crime, but Dominique stands her own trial, and is convicted,
as she would logically be. Roark is nearly dragged into the
muck, but she manages, in a soaring climax of her brilliance,
to keep him clear. And so the book ends in honest tragedy, for
Roark's and Dominique's walking hand in hand into the sunset is
a curious compromise with irony for Miss Rand to have made.
Keating might go back to Catherine, now that he has learned true
values, and so mitigate the starkness of the end. But it has
become Roark's and Dominique's story: an unusual love story,
less a thesis now than the drama of two warped and pitiable lives
that unwarp too late. The remaining characters (many minor ones
should be weeded out so that the woods may not obscure the trees)
will have been brought within the bounds of familiar human behavior, and toward this the cutting will contribute to an indes-
cribable degree, sweeping away the over-writing, the over-acting,
the landslides of weakening detail, the two fine shades of emotion
and reaction blueprinted by the author, the nuances within nuances,
the emotional and philosophical/gymnastics, and conversational the dragging-on of
scenes beyond their most effective ending, the straining in all
directions for the startling (so unnecessary with so original
a theme), the use of the same speech idiosyncracies by the
various characters, the cliches that are such shocking contrast

8

to Miss Rand's best.

Whether the tale is humanized or unleashed as it is for a
maelstrom of controversy, or a middle course struck, this drastic
cutting must be done, and with it the novel's great potentialities
and clouded power will spring to light. Take almost any page,
and a blue pencil, and see the clean bright gem emerge. There's
a pearl in this oyster, and it's up to the editor to remove the
oyster, without the author's help. A pearl regardless of which
of the three courses is followed, for I want to reiterate that I
do not mean my suggestions for rewriting to detract from the
substance of this report's first page, or to mislead as to my
belief in the sales possibilities of Miss Rand's story as she has
conceived it. I have offered my sketchy ideas only to show
that as extraordinarily gifted a writer as Miss Rand need not
be let slip through our fingers because this novel's unusual
type of character and the uncommon breadth of its canvas may
conceivably be called hazards. If SECOND-HAND LIVES should be
considered to have missed great stature as a social study, it
very definitely has not missed being a uniquely provocative,
brilliantly written piece of entertainment -- I stress again,
whichever form it takes. It can so certainly be that, and I
hope we will not give another publisher a chance to realize it.
. . . At the risk of seeming anticlimactic, I add that the
present title is attrocious. It sounds like a lending-library
effusion on street-walkers.

Critical Report

SECOND-HAND LIVES
by
Ayn Rand

This novel offers its readers a bewildering richness of material: a serious
philosophical theme, an original background of the profession of modern architecture, a lengthy study of a large group of characters, a dramatic plot filled
with incident, a sadist-masochist conflict, writing flavored with a nice irony.
It is a long and serious novel, inevitably demanding the reader's serious attention, as it unfolds the story of four men, who represent antithetic ideals and
practices.

The story traces first, the architectural careers of two young men, Howard
Roark and Peter Keating. Roark is a genius, a born architect, with a consuming
passion for his art. He makes no compromises, but pursues his chosen way totally
indifferent to opinion. Keating, on the other hand, is all things to all men- the
essence of compromise and compliancy. The two first met at architectural school,
from which Keating was graduated with all honors, and from which Roark was expelled
for his complete independence of thought and design. Keating goes to work for
Ffrancon and Heyer, a prominent firm, to which he soon becomes indispensable. He
shows a great ability in designing their characteristic pseudo-classic structures.
His carefully-laid plans soon work out, and he gradually usurps all the positions
to which he aspires, eventually becoming chief designer.

Roark, meanwhile, goes to work for Henry Cameron. Once New York's first architect, Cameron always refused to compromise with his clients. He built what and
as he wished, stressing functional design, and in Roark he recognizes a kindred
spirit. Although his office is rapidly failing, he takes Roark as a designer for
a few years, and relies on him until he has to close his office. Also paralleling
the boys' careers are emotional experiences. Keating is in love with Catherine
Halsey, but although he truly loves her, she fails to satisfy his necessary drive
toward fame and popularity. His love for her is his best quality; he refuses to
use her as he uses others, and even refuses to meet her uncle Ellsworth Toohey, the famous art critic

Reader's report for The Fountainhead

2

whose friendship he ardently desires. And Roark has met Vesta Dunning, an aspiring actress, who shares his feeling toward her chosen art. She loves Roark, but although he sleeps with her he is utterly indifferent to her. After appearing in a successful play, Vesta is ruined by popularity; she becomes reconciled to the cheapness of public opinion, and goes to Hollywood to achieve a more farflung popularity.

Thus far there is a parallelism in the boys' careers. But the closing of Cameron's office was a severe setback to Roark. Keating, who knows that Roark is a much better architect than himself, persuades Ffrancon to hire him as draftsman. By 1925 - the year that Toohey's sensational book on architecture is published - Keating is the respected chief designer, and Roark still a draftsman whose talents are utilized unscrupulously by Keating. Ffrancon once offers Roark a commission - a modified copy of one of Cameron's buildings; Roark flatly refuses, and is fired. Still unshaken in his conviction that each building is a complete, inviolate, and unapproachable expression of art, he calls on many architects, but finds no job until he is taken on by Snyte as "modernist" designer. There he can design freely although his finished plans are always modified by the office.

Keating finally meets Dominique Ffrancon, Guy's daughter, who writes a column on decoration for the great chain of Wynand newspapers - the same papers for which Toohey is a columnist. He is fascinated by her indifference to life and opinion, her perverse exhibitionism, and iconoclastic ideas. Ffrancon seems pleased at his interest, and encourages an affair between Keating and Dominique, hinting that marriage and a partnership will follow.

Roark meanwhile gets his first commission - a house for the prominent journalist Austen Heller. He loses his job with Snyte, fired for drawing over in his own way the first plans submitted to Heller. Heller likes Roark and admires his genius, and the house leads to a few more commissions.

Dominique is offered a better job on the paper, but refuses to take it. She wishes to care for nothing, to resist all desires, and she has a horror of being dependent on the common people for approbation. She writes architectural criticism

3

now, and wilfully ridicules her father's houses. Ffrancon still wants her to
marry Keating. Old Heyer, his partner, is ill, and he intends to make Keating his
partner. Catherine has begged Keating to marry her soon, for she senses that something will come between them, but Keating's ambitious mother persuades him to wait.

Roark, like Cameron, refuses to build unless clients accept his designs un-
conditionally. He turns down many clients, and his money is running low. Keating
finally comes to him and asks his advice on plans for a a great skyscraper contest
which he is entering. Roark works over the plans and Keating enters them as his
own. He is obsessed with fear that he will lose the contest and the partnership,
and his obsession leads him to force, by threatening blackmail, old Heyer to re-
tire. The old man has a stroke and dies, and Keating knows that he is almost a
murderer. His conscience hurts when he discovers that Heyer's will left everything
to him, but he forgets his conscience in the new partnership and in the publicity
attending his winning of the prize contest. Keating tries to give Roark a small
check but Roark refuses this charity.

He has refused several commissions, and at last has to close his office. He
gets work in the Ffrancon stone quarry in Connecticut, and tries to subordinate
his natural genius. Dominique, meanwhile, has gone to her father's Connecticut
house. She visits the quarry one day, and sees Roark. She knows at once that he
is the one man who could dominate her, as he knows she is the one woman he would
like to break. She gets him to her house on a pretext, and makes her strong physical awareness of him plain. A few nights later he comes and violates her brutally
and both are aware of sheer ecstasy in the act. But before Dominique can learn his
name, Roark is offered a commission for a big apartment house, and returns to New
York.

Keating finally meets Toohey, at Toohey's invitation. He senses that the
critic knows he did not design his prize building, but apparently he approves highly
of the young architect. A friendship springs up between them. But Toohey's mocking remarks about love and Catherine begin to disillusion Keating. He inexplicably

4

questions Keating closely about Roark, but disclaims acquaintance with him. He
sends Keating to an important new client, Lois Cook, a writer of the Gertrude
Stein school, and the weird house which Keating builds for her establishes his
reputation more firmly.

When Dominique returns to New York Keating senses that she endures his love-
making with loathing, and knows that he has a rival. Dominique and Roark finally
meet at an architectural salon to which Heller has dragged Roark, and they talk
impersonally. Toohey sees Dominique there and guesses at her secret as she guesses
his ultimate purposes. She soon writes a scathing column about Roark's new building
which costs him possible clients. Toohey outlines to her his malevolent plan for
torturing Roark, and they form an unacknowledged league to break him. Roark is
conscious of their antagonism, but is only amused.

Before attempting to criticize this novel I think it only fair to say that,
as a novel, I dislike the book; I think it fails, as writing of that kind, to reward the reader for the time and attention its length requires. Yet its very length
and profundity make a bid for serious attention, and the quality of the writing reinforces that claim. As the author sets forth in his analysis, and as the book
demonstrates, the novel is entirely abstract in conception. I am not capable of
judging the philosophical importance of the underscored theme, but I should hazard
a guess that the philosophy is a system of personal and oddly distorted concepts.
(Certainly it is odd today to find the individual championed in a "conflict of in-
dividualism and collectivism"!)

As the substance of fiction it requires lengthy and subtle development. It is
worked out, in an intricately dovetailed plot, with characters who are themselves
abstract generalizations. The main characters are presented at such length that
this abstractness is not, perhaps, as noticeable as it is in the minor characters
such as Mrs. Keating, the Dean, Vesta, etc., each one of whom is only a symbol of
some one thing. But in Howard, Peter, and Dominique more complexity is recognized.

5

The first part of the novel gives them a chance to appear as individuals; the second parts jerks them abruptly back to their abstract values. Altogether, they and the New York in which they live, seem to me to lack any convincing illusion of reality or vitality. They are too heroic in size, for one thing, and the child-ing symbolic value of their figures excludes any commonplace vitality. The author has attempted an overwhelming task in presenting so many characters on this strain-ed level, and his characters are too many and too big for one novel.

Of the main characters Keating and Roark are easy to comprehend, for there is a clean-cut antithesis between them as well as a simple integrity in their con-ception. They are comprehendable, if not knowable. I should guess that the same might be said of Wynand, though he promises to be more complex. Toohey, however, the most complex of the four, escaped me completely. The author's analysis helped slightly in clarifying the peculiar motivation, but at the end of Part II, Toohey is undeniably a puzzling figure. I doubt if any reader could realize him without the author's commentary, but he may gain in distinctness in the following parts. From what I have read, however, and probably from the whole, I feel sure that I could never fathom what the characte is intended to represent. All these char-acters spring full-fledged into the book - and so far there is little development of character. All are as mature in the beginning as they are about 10 years later. Of the characters, Guy Ffrancon and Lois Cook seem to me the most honest and dynamic, however unimportant. The names of the characters are, I think, admirably chosen -- they convey more precisely than pages of appearance the qualities of the characters.

The plot, is a trifle over-complex, is nicely detailed and offers seemingly in-exhaustible incident. The architectural background is also interesting, and I be-lieve, fairly novel. The author's evident preference for modern functional archi-tecture seems to me to be defended rather too vehemently. His writing of archi-tects and buildings, with its covert but cutting irony, is one of the best feastures of the book. The same irony is present in much of the novel - newspapers, colleges, films, advertising, social service, the man in the street, almost everything, in fact, falls under it. The criticism of 20th-century life, taste, and thought that emerges

6

from these pages is, to me, the strongest and best thing about the book.

In general, the book and the world it presents are viewed by the author in the light of dark profundity, ugliness, vast and ceaseless struggle on a Nietzschean scale. The heaviness of this view accentuates the weight of the book's theme. I feel strongly that the author has attempted too much for one novel. Four characters of the stature of these are overpowering - one of them, in fact, provides enough material for a detailed study of character. What has been written so far could scarcely be compressed into one book. And yet I doubt if the theme is strong enough to support the series of novels the manuscript could furnish.

Although there is much to be said for the book I doubt sincerely if it would ever become a popular book. It aspires to be a great novel, and I believe it fails in this. A novel of the importance to which this aspires should be readable more than once; I am frankly uncertain whether this novel could be read more than once. It impresses me as a luxury for its writer, which fails, with all its seem- ing profundity of purpose, to present anything of very great value for the reader today. Because of ~~its confused effect on me~~ my confused reaction to it as a whole, the difficulties of adapting the manuscript into adequate book form, and my conviction that it would not be a finan- cial success, I would not recommend the novel for publication.

Patricia Jones

(Exclusively for Correspondence between Departments)

The Bobbs-Merrill Company, Publishers

Memorandum for   Date 11/11/41

Referred to   Mr. Chambers   Subject

In general I feel that I am in accord with Archie
and Mrs. Deitrick about Ayn Rand's book. I felt the
same pull in it when I was reading it that they
do. And now that I've read their own reports on
the manuscript I do not feel that we are so far apart.
They see the same faults in the work that I do. Consequently I think they will be able to help the author
and prevent her from going to ridiculous extremes
in the final version. The symbolism, or the allegorical aspect of the main characters has never inter-
fered with my enjoyment of the novel. I found it
attractive. I liked the author's characterization
of Roark, Ffrancon, Keating, and Toohey. It was
the women who irritated me. Apparently Archie and
Mrs. Deitrick feel pretty much the same. (Incidentally the latter's suggestion that Wynand be
dropped is an excellent one.)

My recommendation is that we accept the manuscript
if Archie can reduce the terms of the advance. But
he should not approach her on the grounds he suggests
in his memo. It would be a dreadful mistake to say
that he was the one that pulled for the book and that
the rest of us were against it. He should put his
plea on the basis that the house as a whole wants to
gamble on the book and we hope she'll play along with
us. I would think $1,000 would be the limit of the
advance and that he should try for $750.00.

                                        Jessica

Reader's report for The Fountainhead

<u>critical</u>

LIE DOWN IN DARKNESS

by William Styron

Few books published this year will attract - or earn - more serious critical
attention than Mr. Styron's work. I believe it is quite possible, even probable,
that this novel marks the beginning of an important career. I found it one of the
most remarkable first novels I have ever read. It seemed to me a powerful and tragic
commentary on the inner lives of men and women. Its best moments, I think, comprehend
the tragic essence; the pity and terror they evoke effect true catharsis. I believe
there will be few who dispute the stature of the novel. Most of the adverse
criticism (aside from notice of faults from which no novel is free) will center in an
area where literary standards are not the sole criteria of judgment. The reasons for
this and its importance to the House must be developed in a full discussion of the novel.

It is a formidable book to summarize. For me the master theme found its best
expression in a speech by Peyton Loftis. Midway through the book she has run away from
the terrible tensions in her family. Her father, drunken, fearful and despairing,
has humiliated her. Her idiot sister lies dying. Her mother unjustly accuses Peyton
of responsibility for her death. What should have been a carefree football-dance
weekend in Charlottesville has become a horror. Peyton has run away with the college
boy who will now become her first lover. To him she says something like, "I'm sick of
hearing about my father's generation as the lost generation. They weren't lost. They
were losing us."

In Peyton's story and the story of her parents, Milton and Helen Loftis, William
Styron has shown the last of two generations (this is much more than the story of one
house) confronting old evil, old sickness of soul without the ancient resources against
it. He describes the search by the lost for the place of home, by the fugitive and
disinherited for the wise father, by the uncertain for the absolute principle, the
saving truth. For these people the rituals always fail. The ceremonies by which they

Reader's report for Styron's first novel

-2-

hope to exorcise evil and cure their sickness do not avail. The pretense that evil does not exist collapses. Evil is real and terrible - and it destroys them. There is no prospect of redemption. They have denied the principle of redemption.

This description is centered in the tragic division of the Loftis family, in the complex of love between father and daughter and the resultant antagonism of mother and daughter. It is a circumstance as old as man which has engaged the attention of great dramatists from Aeschylus and Sophocles to O'Neill. It is a first concern of contemporary psychiatry. To probe these areas is an undertaking for a fine artist, and Mr. Styron has been worthy of his undertaking. His insight is sometimes stunning; his craft as a dramatist is often superb. He shuns none of the implications of his subject. For most of his book he is frank, explicit without ever running the risk of imparting to the intelligent reader the sense of shock which might give one passage or another an unintended emphasis. For perhaps five-sixths of his book he holds faithfully the porportions he wishes. Then in the final one-sixth of the story he chooses to be as explicit in his description of erotic and phallic detail as was Joyce in the famous Molly Bloom soliliquy from Ulysses, a passage on which Mr. Styron's is closely modeled. There is no question that his choice was made with any but the best motives of a very talented artist. I think it was a mistaken choice which for most readers will destroy the author's plans and block real understanding of his book. The question, as well as other general criticism, can best be considered with the summary.

Mr. Styron writes in long, convolute sentences which pile image on image. They have a quality like Faulkner's (with overtones of Wolfe's) yet they are not imitative of either. The basic structure of many sentences is intricately modified and extended to establish both precise meaning and emotional value, to make the kind of poetry (the best term) the author wants to hear. In this poetry he uses very many words for their connotative values rather than for their precise meanings. His sentences have

-3-

a syntax of their own, the product of both their melody and meaning. Generally this style is very effective. There are sometimes (for my taste) excesses. Sometimes the use of favorite devices - the participial phrase, the nominative absolute, the parenthetical element - gets a little tedious. At its best (and there are many, many examples) the writing is deeply moving, tender, powerful, mordant, lively.

But Mr. Styron is at his best as dramatist, I think. His construction of scenes is beautiful. There is almost always a gradual bringing of the stage to full lighting. There is first the preliminary, subdued illumination of the subordinates - details of setting, an idea, the characters who will play the scene. Sharp focus comes slowly as the lights go slowly up. And at the climactic moment all is revealed brilliantly in the intended proportions, conveying the intended meaning. Once established in such a scene, no moment of dramatic climax is ever lost from the story. Again and again it will recur in after-scenes as an interpolated theme or a leitmotif.

The construction of the story is complex. It is not an original plan, but it is originally executed. It makes imposing literary architecture exept, I believe, for the exaggerations of the final segment, and this seems to me only distortion, not a flaw in planning. This is an anatomy of life and tragedy, made free of time, not ordered by chronology but by the artists judgment of values.

There is no prospect of my conveying either the scope or the effect of the action. I will be as brief as I can in the summary.

The story begins with the fact of tragedy; the opening scenes are built around the slow realization that Peyton Loftis is dead, a suicide at 22. The chief players are Milton Loftis, who on this day in August 1945 waits to receive the body of his daughter at the Port Warwick, Virginia, station; Helen, his estranged wife, and Dolly Bonner, Milton's mistress. From the station the hearse will take Peyton's body directly to the cemetery where a very short service will be held before immediate burial.

This - the journey of the hearse and the car carrying Milton and Dolly - from

-4-

the station to the cemetery is all the action in the book's present of 1945. In each
of the succeeding sections the progress of the pitiful cortege is noted. From this
point of time the reader goes into the past where all the contributing events with
all their meanings are accumulated for him. Sometimes the flashbacks (and the word
is inadequate to the complete recall of these scenes) cover hours of the day before,
or days of the month previous, or years in the past. The reader is usually led to
each flashback through the memory of a character but the focus of the scenes cannot
remain in the character's thoughts. The thoughts or memories blend with the author's
exposition until the scenes are being played as they happened.

At first the scenes concern only the days just before the tragedy. One understands (this required real skill) the enormous grief and terror of the father Milton.
To this is contrasted the dream-like isolation from the event of the mother Helen, not
so much in grief as in a fantasy of madness. Dolly is ordinary, platitudinous and
obviously fearful of how the tragedy may affect her standing with Milton, whom she is
to marry one day.

In these few scenes which begin, both the theme and the evidence of its truth are
clear. The lives of these people have no fix, no polar attraction by which they are
set in course, toward which they move with purpose and the expectation of reward.
The theme is enunciated by the remembered voice of Milton's father, detailing his
code, defining propriety, promising punishment for transgression. Here and hereafter
this voice is a kind of Greek chorus and its use is enormously effective. When the
preliminary scenes are over the reader knows that doom (the only word) has been
pronounced; the vessel has been shattered.

Again one sees the funeral cortege. Tragedy is made more poignant by contrast
with peripheral and transitory annoyances. A boy in the employ of the undertaker burns
his hand. The hearse will not run properly. There is a traffic jam. The slow
counterpoint defines pain.

-5-

The full plan becomes clear with the return to a spring morning in 1933, a Sunday when Milton begins drinking and refuses to go to church. Here is the first yielding to the pressures of a lifetime. Fearful of his own inadequacy, dreaming of what he might have been (and might yet become), resentful of Helen's possessiveness and her money on which he depends, Milton is a man who has lost life without dying. His realization that this is so grows slowly. His rebellion is tentative, his movement toward escape only a stirring in his prison. He drinks steadily and Helen is grimly patient or sweetly tolerant. He makes love to Dolly, who has come with her husband, or, really, only entertains the idea of making love. Peyton is there, the beautiful child, adored by her father. And the pitiful, malformed Maudie is there, somehow a reproach to Milton as she is instrument, shield and refuge for Helen. There are other details but here is the essence. And in this quiet day and evening, so briefly and so trivially disturbed, the author describes the imminence of tragedy. It is there now and there is no mistaking it. When Peyton abuses Maudie the dreadful antagonisms are instantly disclosed. The act is not the irresponsible, casual cruelty of a child. From this moment the end is inevitable; the proportions of dilemma and schism are fixed. The reader has seen the shattered vessel. He sees now the first line of flaw as it appeared and he has discovered all the lines of cleavage.

Each of these lines the author traces. Milton's rebellion of six years before is amplified, extended. At a country club dance for Peyton's sixteenth birthday in August 1939 he becomes Dolly's lover. Helen knows, and Peyton knows. She stands before the locked door of the room where her father and Dolly are and knows surely what has happened. She is a little drunk from liquor that her father has given her and she turns instantly to the boy with her, demanding to be held, to be comforted for loss. At the moment when Milton accomplishes his freedom he loses it. His infidelity is perfunctory; his yearning unsatisfied. He would turn back to something, go forward to something, but there is no escape from the moment and he takes the vapid Dolly. On

-6-

the terrace Helen exchanges bonalities with guests and nourishes hate.

Here there have been new indications, clear signs, and the reader understands thus
much more: the need of Milton for hope (and if not hope, any narcotic); the need of
Peyton for security (if not in her father then anywhere, in any arms); the need of
Helen for dominance (and if not dominance, hate).

So the novel grows with new power in every scene, with new insights always. In
each return to the funeral cortege making its way through the August afternoon in 1945
there is new understanding of the detail and meaning of this tragedy. The tragedy has
grown so that it is no longer an unhappiness to be viewed briefly with brief sympathy.
It has encompassed the reader. In this death he begins to understand the corruption
of beauty, the death of hope, the terrible fact of absolute loneliness.

As the hearse moves toward the cemetery the story moves forward in time. A few
weeks after the dance Helen visits Carey Carr, the androgynal Episcopal rector, proud
of his modern tolerance. To Carey Carr Helen discloses her jealousy, her dread, her
frustrated hope, the depth of her loneliness. She is hurt, and vindictive; confused,
and revengeful; seeking forgiveness and offering little. She looks back over her life
with Milton and selects the moments in which she believes its meaning has been
concentrated. And all moments have come to one moment of absolute hate. From a
window above the garden she has heard the voices of Peyton and Milton below, happy,
teasing, confident in their love for each other. And she has known then exclusion from
their love. Later in the garden, hearing the voices again, she has said, "I will not
yield to this." But, remembering Dolly, she has not been able to forgive, and the
time is passing when forgiveness is still possible.

Helen tells all this to Carey ("I just thought you might be able to help me.")
And while Helen talks she exposes the roots of her particular fanaticism. The reader
sees a girlhood in which the repression and prescribed form of the military have
concerted with the hearty and agressive Christianity of Helen's army-officer father.
Once again the father image becomes pre-eminently important as Helen, fanatic,

-7-

obsessed, already touched with madness, seeks some assurance that she will not be mad. Carey Carr can answer her only with platitudes. Helen's frustration is complete when she confronts Dolly and is cooly rebuffed by her.

Lie Down in Darkness is so fine that any criticism seems captious and trivial. Its excellence earns all kinds of indulgence for any shortcomings. But I did find these scenes with Carey Carr less satisfactory than most other episodes. The fault, I think, is in the character of Carr. Mr. Styron could not do a stereotyped character if he tried, but Carr is less a person and more a symbol than any other character in the book. His speeches, his attitude and his personality give the novel a momentary and unintended aspect of superficial criticism of church convention, criticism in terms of the obvious contrast of Carr's perfunctory piety to Helen's desperation. Of course the author must demonstrate the failure and emptiness of ritual in which not even the ritualist believes. But he has not, I think, shown here the inventiveness and understanding that give other episodes so much freshness and power. ("Power" seems my chief reliance. It is simply the most apt word.) Because of its somewhat conventional quality this passage seems too long. It handicaps the book further when Helen discusses with Milton the distance between them. All that she has to say has been rehearsed previously with Carey Carr and there is a repetition of tension without new value except as emphasis. Probably I have already written too much of this. It is not a serious flaw, just a passage a little below a superlative standard.

The years intensify division. There is a Christmas in 1941 - Peyton's last Christmas at home (she is now at Sweet Briar) which demonstrates the impossibility of reconciliation. Before Peyton's arrival Helen and Milton, for one intimate moment, come close to an intimacy lost so long ago that it has almost been forgotten. Then Peyton's voice in the hall below dissipates tenderness, shuts off memory. This is a Christmas-card holiday: snow, brilliant decorations, the visits of friends. All ceremony fails, fails with tragic and pathetic emphasis when (as if at a signal)

-3-

the family puts on party hats at Christmas dinner and the absurd festive touch
somehow turns them instantly to contemplate all the devastation of their lives.
(If this needs to be added, I will add it: this is a scene that stands with
the best I have ever read.)

By the fall of 1942 (of course the funeral cortege is progressing between
episodes) Milton has made Dolly Bonner his mistress, driven by Peyton's absence and
his need for her, by Helen's open detestation of Peyton and her contempt for him.
Dolly is surrogate and anodyne. One November evening he writes a letter to Peyton
while Dolly sits near. Helen is in Charlottesville with Maudie who is critically ill.
Milton remembers his father as an image of faith and security. All this his father
had foreseen. "We have lost our love words," his father had said. When Milton
sleeps with Dolly in Helen's bed he makes a gesture of defiance and it is only the
gesture of a lost boy.

Immediately Helen's dominance is re-asserted. Milton must drive to
Charlottesville where Maudie is dying. In the corridors of the hospital he struggles
to achieve a grief he cannot feel. He must bear Helen's censure. The impersonal,
formal, efficient dealing with death is insupportable. This is judgment, and he must
run away, must find Peyton who, he knows, is in Charlottesville for a football game
and a dance. His search is a journey back over all his life and a search for all he
has missed. Peyton is the object of all yearning, all desire, the promise of all
fulfillment. She eludes him always. He catches glimpses of her, misses her by a
moment or two here and there. Old friends offer him drinks and he is getting very
drunk. The memory of the first girl with whom he was intimate returns, and it seems
to him that she could have instructed him in the meaning of love. He meets Dolly's
ex-husband, who is serenely secure with a new and handsomer woman. When Loftis finds
Peyton he has been hurt in a fall. He has been abused, humiliated and reduced to
abject hopelessness. And he can say nothing to Peyton. She stands with her young

-9-

escort, Dick Cartwright, and she too is lost to Milton. They must yet see Helen who has kept the vigil at the hospital. Maudie will die soon of miliary tuberculosis, Maudie, the last object of Helen's love. "Neither of you knows what love means," Helen says. "I have waited for just one word to tell me loneliness was not in vain." In her prudent and dark life Helen has seen love once, and she recalls now this time: when a construction worker charmed Maudie with a display of slight of hand, producing colored balls between his fingers, when Helen watched, as a rain storm gathered and broke, and knew that Maudie found in this brilliance and mystery all the excitement, fascination and meaning of love. (I know no other scene in any novel at all like this. No one who reads it will ever forget it.)

In the reflected light of Maudie's love this family is for an instant made whole again. Then Helen in an access of hate accuses Peyton of responsibility for Maudie's death. (Three years before Peyton had let her slip on the stairs.) Peyton runs from Helen's madness. She goes with Dick Cartwright and allows him to make love to her. But she is not in love, and she cannot marry him. "Because I don't love you, and I can't love, and isn't that too bad."

Peyton does not return to Port Warwick until her wedding in 1943. She has gone to New York after Maudie's death. Milton and Helen have been in part reconciled after Maudie's death. To each other they say that there has always been love between them, and both believe this to be true. Yet Milton knows that only his self-abasement has freed Helen from grief and postponed madness. Helen has a new helpless object, and Milton has left Dolly.

Peyton is marrying a Jew, an artist and a gentle and real person. She has met him in New York where, she tells Milton, she gave up all restraint for a time. Harry's strength became then her reliance. "We weren't wrong, or wrongdoers, just aimless." (These passages of conversation between Milton and Peyton seemed to me the least successful in the novel. Once again, I do not want to magnify their importance.)

Peyton will not permit Milton his defence of order and restraint. She is

-10-

contemptuous of the uneasy peace in the household. And by not being part of the day which was to be Milton's spiritual vindication and atonement, Peyton destroys it for him. Milton begins drinking for the first time in months.

During the ceremony his love for Peyton resolves itself (for the first time in his mind) into the purely sexual. This has been implicit and obvious from the first. Now, as the ceremony is read, Milton is stripped to the basic hungers, basic needs. His impulses are primal and he cannot resist them. Images out of the accumulated longings of a lifetime flow into his mind. When he embraces Peyton after the ceremony he is making love to her. Loftis' act leaves naked the hatred between mother and daughter, the rivalry for male affection which is its cause.. Helen is irrational. She tells Carey Carr of her careful plans to restore her household, to hold Milton. Her compulsive need to dominate takes complete command. Her madness (she is mad, I think) flares and she recalls the phantasmagoria of her dreams in which all the symbols of her longing and desire have been expressed. Helen takes Peyton to a bedroom and Loftis listening outside knows a confusion of terror and guilt. "They should never have put the idea of love in the mind of an animal." It is over now, and Peyton on her honeymoon speaks to her new husband as Helen might speak to Milton. Helen's need has become hers, and Helen's madness is growing within her.

This scene accomplishes the climax. For the most part it is superbly done. It seemed to me there was one weakness in some of Helen's soliloquies. I thought it unlikely that she would think so honestly of her own ambitions and schemes. She thinks of herself as maintaining "the casual, collected air of a proud mother." Seemingly she has no illusions about herself. Her own estimate of her conduct here would accord with Peyton's. The passage is one of the few weak spots in the book.

I should begin writing of the final episode in the book by saying that it is conceived and executed with a depth of feeling and understanding beyond all but a very few writers. The criticisms are offered with a full realization of this and out

-11-

of a great admiration for the novel.

The episode begins with a description of Potter's Field in New York where Peyton has been buried after her suicide. It is a passage of apostrophe to the anonymous dead of every time, an invocation. Here Harry and his friend Lennie have gone to identify Peyton and here Harry looks into the open coffin and says, "It's her, son."

The rest is Peyton. Except for a few glimpses we have not seen her. We have known little of her heart and mind. Now in a single paragraph running 92 pages she is revealed as few characters in any novel have been revealed. The passage is done in the first person as stream of consciousness—perhaps interior monologue is the better term since the material is closely controlled. It is hopeless to try to represent in a summary anything of the quality of this passage. It is beautiful, wise, profoundly moving, and shocking. I am not here using "shock" to mean that there is an offense to the reader's sense of propriety. Parts of the passage will give that offense to many readers but discussion of that should come later. I mean shock that grows from watching a doomed girl walk to her death, from knowing how her death was ordained long ago in tragic circumstance, from feeling pity and real dread.

Peyton is mad (as we have known she must become) and the author shows every aspect of her madness. She has gone into darkness to find a new father, a new home. From Harry and his life (so different from what she has known) among esthetes and intellectuals she has gone to a succession of lovers. We see her with the last, a virile, stupid milkman, the complete male, the father-substitute. And from his bed we follow her last journey to find Harry who has left her months before, sick of infidelity, disorder, really sick of the disoriented soul. Peyton bears with her a clock, the symbol to her of order. She walks through memories of childhood and the hated mother, of finding men and discovering all men are one man for her – father. At each moment of excitement she hears—and sees—great wingless birds running toward

-12-

her, surrounding her. She is Ophelia the bereft daughter, Iphigenia the sacrificed daughter, Electra the loving daughter. She can find no understanding now. When she finds Harry at last she finds only a moment's solace--and then the clock is destroyed. Peyton commits suicide.

There is a final glimpse of Milton and Helen. In Port Warwick the funeral procession has reached the cemetary. Dolly sits in the car, knowing that Milton will never return. When Peyton has been buried Helen and Milton fade each other with all the ruin between them. Still Milton seeks one word from Helen of forgiveness or comfort. When Helen refuses, he leaps forward to choke her, to kill her. Before he can hurt Helen, Milton is torn away, and he runs from the cemetery crying, "Nothing, nothing."

There is a final word. On the day of Peyton's burial the Negroes of the Loftis household are attending a service conducted by Daddy Faith. With thousands of others they listen, with complete trust in fundamental faith, to the Negro revivalist: "De grass withereth, the flower fadeth. But the word of your God shall stand forever."

So it ends, and it is a magnificent book. In a long report I have used every adjective in the arsenal and they have fallen far short. And yet I think a few passages in Peyton's soliloquy can jeopardize the whole meaning and distort a work of art. They are as frank as anything I know in modern literature and any criticism of Lie Down in Darkness must give careful consideration to their effect. It is unnecessary to discuss in the abstract Mr. Styron's right as an artist to free expression. I do not question it; others will. I think our concern must be only with what these passages do to this novel.

It seems to me sure that most criticism and comment will focus on parts of Peyton's soliloquy. For these the book will be applauded or condemned. This in itself is unfortunate enough. It is the more unfortunate because, whatever form it takes, little of the criticism will have a literary basis. The passages will be applauded because they are "an example of what an honest artist dares to do," or they will be condemned as "the outpouring of a sewer." The fact that the author had in mind neither being courageous

-13-

nor (this most certainly) giving any reader a shock or vicarious sexual excitement will be lost in a discussion that will have a great deal more to do with propriety and convention than with literary judgment. The squabble over Edmund Wilson's Memoirs of Hecate County demonstrates that. Nothing more unfortunate could happen at the beginning of what might be a great career. Mr. Styron deserves fame based on real appreciation of his accomplishment, not notoriety. Joyce finally escaped; Faulkner now escapes. But Mr. Styron has not yet this kind of prestige.

There are more important points to be considered, bearing more directly on Mr. Styron's purpose as an artist. Most readers will not read Peyton's soliloquy without a sense of shock. I do not mean readers who protested Forever Amber. I mean intelligent readers of liberal attitudes who admit and defend realism in literature. The shock will be increased because nothing previous to Peyton's soliloquy has prepared them for the frankness of some of its details. The whole book has been shaped toward this revelation of Peyton. Its success as a work of art/in large measure contingent on a comprehension of her tragedy. This is the moment of catharsis, of full understanding and compassion. For most readers the element of shock will impair this moment. They are called on to make judgments—moral as well as literary—precisely when they should be concerned only with the action and meaning of the story. Some will decide that the author has used no materials he did not feel were justified by the rationale of his novel. Many will be baffled by the intricate play of symbol and, failing to appreciate the author's motives, resent parts of the soliloquy as gratuitous. The point is that judgments are called for and will be made. In making the lesser moral judgments, most readers will fail to understand Peyton as she must be understood here. They will fail to apprehend the large morality of the book, the powerful commentary on morality which is so great a part of its meaning.

I do not think anyone would suggest bowdlerizing Peyton's soliloquy. Peyton's aberration is sexual and sexual detail must be a part of its description. This criticism

-14-

refers only to those passages which clearly go beyond the bounds of the most liberal

convention, which distort in that part of the creation resting *with* the reader, the beautiful

proportions and real meaning of this novel.

Editing in the manuscript indicates the author has been willing to modify some

of Peyton's soliloquy. I believe his purpose would be better served if other elements

were modified, if the entire soliloquy were brought just within the limits of the most

liberal convention.

I can't end this report except with highest praise. I have read Lie Down in

Darkness with a sense of discovery very few novels have given me. I am convinced that

William Styron is a major talent.

Conversations with Rare Book Dealers I:
An Interview with Glenn Horowitz

Glenn Horowitz is a 1977 graduate of Bennington College. He worked at the Strand Bookstore in New York City after graduation until October 1979, when he founded Glenn Horowitz Bookseller, Inc. in New York City. This interview was conducted by phone by Matthew J. Bruccoli on 14 March 1991 and was subsequently edited by Mr. Horowitz.

DLB: The topics of this discussion are rare book dealers, antiquarian book dealers, as patrons of scholarship; the ways in which a rare book dealer helps build collections, the ways in which dealers work with librarians and curators, the influence they exert in placing materials at, say, Harvard instead of Princeton.

HOROWITZ: The answer is complex. It's also important, I think, to keep in mind that the dynamic you're describing is relatively new. Prior to World War II the number of American libraries with fully staffed special collections was modest; you could probably count them on both hands. Before then the contribution dealers made to scholarship was indirect, circuitous. We built the great private collections which became the foundation of the now-great research libraries.

DLB: For instance.

HOROWITZ: Numerous examples leap to mind: start with Henry Stevens in the nineteenth century building, grooming the Lenox collection, which became the principal building block of the research collection of the New York Public Library. The Morgan family turning the old man's library into a public institution. Widener (Harvard), Beinecke (Yale), Houghton (Harvard)—those names got carved into stone because the families bestowed large sums on the institutions but they also, at the same time, made gifts of enormously valuable and important book and manu-

Glenn Horowitz

script collections. Huntington, Clark (UCLA), Chapin (Williams)—a long, long list really.

Which is not to suggest that in the late 1940s the world was turned upside down and the great collectors went the way of the dinosaurs and up sprang full-blown research libraries which scoured the earth in search of rare books and manuscripts. Book dealers of course continued to build great collections that eventually wound up in institutions. Probably the best-known "collaboration" in the postwar decades was between C. Waller Barrett and John Kohn at the Seven Gables Bookshop. Barrett's American literature collection now serves as the nucleus of the great library at Virginia; but without Kohn, and his partner Michael Pappantonio, it couldn't have happened. Closer to hand is the collection being assembled in New York City by Carter Burden—an encyclopedic library of modern American literature that now totals more than one hundred thousand books and manuscripts and which Mr. Burden is intending, so it appears, to present someday to the New York Public Library. I say "closer to hand" since I've been instrumental in helping Burden assemble it, though Burden is also more promiscuous than Barrett and has bought heavily from other dealers, most especially, Peter Howard of Serendipity Books in California.

The biggest difference between now and 40 or 50 years ago is the number of independently funded special collection libraries that exist and regularly compete in the marketplace—the HRC at Texas, the Lilly at Indiana, the Berg at New York Public, the Beinecke at Yale—not one of them existed on V-J Day. And all have endowments of varying size that generate yearly acquisition budgets. They all, of course, work to raise additional funds, but each one of them can go into the marketplace, like a private buyer with a budget, and collect what a specific librarian feels merits preservation.

I do feel, however, that there is often a tension between rare book dealers and those special collection librarians, and that tension originates in their different attitudes toward money. The perception on the part of many librarians is that rare book dealers don't have the best interest of their institutions at heart, that we don't sympathize with the particular and specific vicissitudes of serious rare book librarianship being done on a limited budget and that in the end our allegiance lies more with well-heeled private collectors, buyers who will readily and unthinkingly pay up for an item—pay, that is, something much beyond a notional sense of a "correct" price. For instance, recently a librarian curating one of the best William Faulkner collections in the country called to ask me if I thought $1,750 was a fair price for him to pay for a fine first English edition in dust jacket of *The Sound and the Fury*. That means that after 30 years of collecting Faulkner that library lacked the second most interesting English-language printing of one of the great books of the twentieth century. The right answer to my friend's query is something a good dealer or private collector would know instinctively. In the end that's one significant reason why dealers gravitate to privates rather than institutions: they know what it is they're doing.

DLB: The message I'm getting from you is that you feel the great patrons of scholarship are the private collectors who eventually give or will their collections to the libraries because these collectors are less concerned about price than rare book curators who have either a fixed endowment or funds allotted every year from the institution.

HOROWITZ: It's a tough problem. The funds available to research libraries have not risen commensurately with the quality of their collections. And then there are institutions that might have two or three fine author or subject collections that should be fed and nurtured but don't have sufficient budget to do so. In those cases underpaid librarians with minimal funds try to figure out how to raise twenty grand to buy, say, *Vera* or a manuscript by Oscar Wilde. Not only can't they do it; they probably can't even begin to judge how the dealer affixed the price to the item in question. Big books cost big money and though it's true that a doctor doesn't have to suffer from a disease to know how best to treat it, it is useful for someone acquiring, or thinking of acquiring, expensive books to understand how the marketplace functions at the top end. I often suffer under the illusion librarians don't comprehend how rare book dealing works. I'll give you an example of why I feel that way: a few months back I purchased from the catalogue of a California dealer an uncommon secessionist pamphlet printed in Richmond in early 1861 advocating that Virginia follow South Carolina's lead and secede. The author, a minor political figure with equally minor literary value, a native of Virginia, happened to graduate from a small prestigious school in the North that collects the writing of their alumni. Apparently the curator of special collections at the school was the next person to order the pamphlet from my colleague, who kindly passed the information on to me. When I offered the pamphlet to the school for a modest advance of seventy-five dollars, the curator said that struck him as a reasonable mark-up and he'd buy it. That's frustrating. I could have sold that pamphlet for a larger profit to one of my private collectors of the Civil War or secession. My colleague missed the boat when he catalogued it; the curator still got a bargain, and I got a reminder why librarians and dealers don't co-exist entirely harmoniously.

DLB: I'm trying to persuade you that you are a benefactor, but you don't want that honor.

HOROWITZ: Patronage really doesn't manifest itself in dollars. It is measured in an awareness a dealer has of what distinguishes one institutional collection from another, and the ability to translate that awareness into deeds, and books and papers, for that institution. The best example I can provide happens to be a project I've been working on for some years now. A few years back a good friend in the United States introduced me to a good friend of his. The friend's friend lives in Switzerland and is the son of one of the great, magical names of modern literature—a name that means a helluva lot in twentieth-century letters. Due to the specifics of this writer's life, and the books he produced, a great mystique surrounds him. My friend told me that the writer's son needed help dealing with his father's archive. Now I'm no spring chicken—I knew full well that other dealers had tried to make a deal for the writer's son for his father's papers, and in all cases no deal was done. For many reasons. Some of the dealers were unsavory; a few unqualified; the sum of money asked for the papers was large, well beyond traditional funding avenues available to most institutions. But most importantly, the writer, in a gesture of thanks to his adopted country, had decades before made a gift to the Library of Congress of many of his papers, including manuscripts for books synonymous with his name. A part of me therefore was leery about getting involved, about flying at my own expense to central Europe to view a "broken" archive, only to find out that the seller wanted more than any buyer would pay (something I knew before hailing a taxi to JKF), and then having to return home frustrated. But the appeal of the name was too great. So what happened? Years later, many trips to Switzerland later, enormous credit card bills run up, I've not yet made a deal but I think I will.

DLB: How did you structure the deal?

HOROWITZ: What I did was first identify an institution that I thought could afford, spiritually and financially, to make the purchase if I could create a comfort zone for them to maneuver in. So I set out to act as an intermediary between committed seller and potential buyer and convince both parties that I would vigilantly stand guard over their respective interests. And I

think I've succeeded. I've been tenacious. At the institution I'm negotiating with I've watched what feels like legions of curators come and go—one who greatly moved the project along unfortunately died in mid-negotiation. But I managed to hold the framework of the deal together long enough to permit the institution to build up sufficient momentum to carry us to completion.

DLB: You're a broker and you're earning a fee. . . .

HOROWITZ: A good one, too, I believe, but in the time I've spent shuttling between Switzerland and New York, do keep in mind that I could've made, I suspect, a hell of a lot more money buying and selling rare books to private collectors than I'll realize on this project. Remember, this was the late 80s when even bond traders briefly thought it was fashionable to buy rare books.

DLB: So you're equating patronage and the furtherance of scholarship, not with money but with. . . .

HOROWITZ: With focused energy and a commitment to see things done properly and intelligently, even when we, rare book dealers, benefit materially. One could argue that the papers of the great writer in question are like energy that can't be destroyed and that eventually the papers would have wound up somewhere, in some archive. Maybe. But they're ending up in the right place, building on the existing strengths of the institution. Why do Kafka's manuscripts survive? Because Max Brod made damn sure they did. Somebody has to take responsibility. That's what rare book dealers do. I can list a dozen first-rate literary and historical archives in the United States and Europe that might not, given current ownership, survive, either intact or at all. It's not a drama with a consistently happy ending.

DLB: Can you think of other ways rare book dealers enhance scholarship?

HOROWITZ: There is a very direct way that *some* dealers make immediate contributions: they write consistently strong catalogues, replete with documentary and scholarly information.

DLB: Examples, please.

HOROWITZ: In London, one thinks of Bernard Quaritch, Maggs Brothers, Pickering and Chatto for antiquarian books. R. A. Gekoski, Bertram Rota, and Paul Rassam for modern books. In the States I find the catalogues written by Stephen Wiseman of Ximenes and those produced by the Reese Company in New Haven to be consistently first-rate and readable.

DLB: I would like to interject to say that the rare book dealer catalogues and the auction catalogues are under used as tools of scholarship.

HOROWITZ: No argument from me. My passion for dealer and auction catalogues is unbridled. My private collection of them runs into the thousands. Just recently I acquired over fifteen hundred nineteenth- and early twentieth-century auction catalogues in one purchase. I can't begin to suggest in few words the density and richness of bibliographical and biographical information they contain. It's amazing how often a bookseller's catalogue represents the sole reference to a major book or letter or manuscript that effectively seems to be lost. I recently was able to trace the existence of Wilkie Collins's unpublished first book through a mention of it in a 1900 catalogue by George D. Smith, the great rare book dealer. It helped me trace the provenance of the manuscript, which we are now offering for sale. I don't think it's an exaggeration for me to say that I spend more time reading catalogues than doing anything else except maybe talking on the telephone.

DLB: I would like to go back to your point about the great collectors who form collections specifically for a particular institution, and ask you to comment on the dealers' response to these endeavors.

HOROWITZ: A collector with a vision of what he is up to, a vision of what in a couple of decades his collection will look like, that sort of collector will invariably capture the imagination and affection of a dealer and in turn enjoy privileges the more casual, less committed collector never will. It does, of course, work both ways and one must never entirely lose sight of that. Rare book dealing is, finally, a commercial undertaking. We dealers adore clients who are in it for the long haul and on whom we can depend for repeat transactions. On the other hand, the collector with the staying power is the beneficiary of the dealer's

gratitude and he receives two tremendous advantages: first refusal on significant material and a crack at that stuff at a price somewhere south of what a regular buyer would be charged. I think the other important element in the dealer/collector relationship is that the dealer functions, to a large extent, as a conscience, as a vigilant voice reminding the buyer what he's up to. At its most sophisticated level, the sort we're talking about, book collecting is a tough, exacting discipline. It's easy for collectors to fall off the tightrope and that's precisely where a decades-long relationship becomes essential if a collector hopes to fulfill his final vision.

DLB: Don't dealers enjoy collaborating on building a major private collection that is destined for a library?

HOROWITZ: You're ascribing a touch too much altruism to dealers. There are practical elements involved in book dealing that can often interfere with the seamless equation you're hinting at.

DLB: Such as what?

HOROWITZ: Profits; cash flow; the ability a dealer has in a single transaction to satisfy both seller—if an object has been consigned, say—and buyer. For example, my best customer for Robert Lowell manuscripts can only make payments against his account two or three times a year. His Lowell collection is already a significant one, by any measure the best in private hands, and it is destined, as we speak, for an institution, one of Lowell's alma maters. I, as a dealer who loves Lowell and likes my customer, enjoy participating actively in this ongoing project. But I've also got a business to run with a weekly payroll to meet, monthly rent to pay, quarterly insurance premiums and yearly taxes. Somewhere I have to strike a balance between competing interests, and that's what I meant when I said that you might be portraying the dealer as a bit more of a philanthropist than reality warrants.

DLB: The dealer serves as a magnet for material. That is to say, people bring material to him.

HOROWITZ: The dealer is the clearinghouse, yes. We accumulate the material, assemble it, or break it down for easy inspection, and through running open shops and producing cata-

(1)

Chapter I

Iolani and Idia.

The last days of summer were near at hand, as one night, (while Tahiti was yet undiscovered by the voyagers of the North) the desolation ~~...~~ of the great lake Vahiria was brightened by the presence of two human beings — a man and woman who were listlessly wandering along its rugged and deserted shores.

It was a strange and, to most hearts, an unalluring place. Looking upward from the spot occupied on this particular occasion by the woman and her companion, the eye encountered a long and almost unbroken range of mountains, whose jagged sides, though occasionally chequered by a clump of dwarf trees, or a patch of parched, scanty verdure, were for the most part bare and precipitous in the extreme. The different masses that formed the chain, were generally but little distinguishable, the one from the other, ~~...~~ either in form or eleva=tion, but were relieved from absolute sameness, by the presence of the immense Orohena (the loftiest mountain in the island) that farther in the distance, rose like a beacon over the tops of the inferior ranges. Lower, between the mountains and the lake, stretched large, dense tracts of forest land; and beneath these again, lay in the utterest confusion, mass upon mass of basalt rock, wild and jagged in form and reaching down almost to the water side; while, the waves of the Lake, but partially lightened by the rays of the young moon and preserved ~~...~~ at most points from the wind by their natural guardians of forest and rock, looked wilder and gloomier than all beside, as they stretched forth dull and stagnant — here utterly lost in darkness, there faintly gleaming in the pale and fitful light. Truly, it was a desert and fearful spot. Hardly could the mind imagine from the appearance of those barren mountains, that their farther sides overlooked every variety that Nature could bestow — every charm that the seasons could dispense, and the blessed sunlight watch over and adorn.

Not a human habitation was to be seen on the borders of Vahiria. The natives generally, had a dread of the place and

---

✻ It may be necessary, perhaps, at the outset of our narrative, to inform the reader that the vowels of the Polynesian language are sounded in the same manner as in the Italian. Thus, the proper names at the head of the present chapter should be pronounced as if written — Eolahne and Edeah.

Page one of the manuscript of Wilkie Collins's unpublished first novel, "Iolani and Idia," recently acquired by Horowitz

logues we make it available, both to potential buyers and interested parties, including scholars.

DLB: Having assembled the material the dealer then exercises options of where to dispose of it. If he catalogues it, the catalogue becomes a bibliographical tool and record. If he sells it directly then he may be performing a scholarly act or an antischolarly act. Let us say that the dealer has a customer who's going to take this thing and lock it up in a vault, never make it available for examination, never lend it to a library for display, a speculator who's buying the thing for an investment. If the dealer sells the item to such a customer, he knows that he is performing an antischolarly act. On the other hand, if he offers it to a collector knowing that the collector will in time donate it to an institution then the dealer is helping in the formation of a body of research material.

HOROWITZ: There's a fault line in your logic, however. Institutional collections are going to grow regardless of dealer cooperation, either passive or aggressive, because they depend more upon gifts than purchases for the growth of their collections. There are few institutional collections in the United Sates that yearly add more to their collections by purchase than by gift. Those institutions—there may 75 to 100 now that are building scholarly rare book collections—are always going to be funded once a year. The funding may be modest; it may be middle-sized; it may be large; it may go up; it may go down; but they're still going to spend money on books and manuscripts that a librarian deems of importance to that collection. So between growth by gift and growth by slow but steady purchase the dealer's role is readily defined. Knowing that the majority of curators with whom he works regularly have very specific needs and interests, the dealer can direct his focus and energies accordingly. For example, I know that one of Harvard's interests is adding to the Kilgore collection of Russian literature, and I know that the Kilgore collection has a small endowment for acquisitions. Therefore when I return from East Europe with rare Russian poetry pamphlets I can telephone Harvard and say, "I'll work with you. I'll work within, or around, the realities of your budget to help you add this material to your collection." That's an agreeable and a positive act on the part of the dealer. But is it an act of a patron of scholarship?

At one level rare book dealers contribute daily to the increase in scholarly materials available to rare book libraries throughout the United States. The majority of rare book dealers that I'm intimate with are people who deeply and passionately care about books, about the history of books, about the transmission of texts. I would go so far as to say that the majority of them care more deeply about those life-and-death issues than do the majority of curators; maybe because of that dealers are acutely conscious and sensitive to the assistance they can provide rare book libraries.

DLB: You're saying dealers are better scholars than librarians.

HOROWITZ: Equivocally yes, but I want to qualify that statement. I think dealers are invariably better *bookmen* than librarians. There are few rare book librarians who I think could easily earn their way in the commercial give-and-take of rare books. But I believe numerous rare book dealers would make superb special collections librarians.

DLB: You're thinking of David Randall.

HOROWITZ: Yes—he was the first librarian of the Lilly Library at Indiana University. Before he went to Lilly—at the request of Mr. Lilly—Randall compiled a string of scholarly, imaginative, and enduring catalogues for Scribner's, in the days when they had a rare books business in their Fifth Avenue book store in New York. Randall is a fine example of that sort of a dealer—one who flourished as a librarian.

I'd like to add something that is jelling in my mind as we're talking, something I don't think I've thought about before. What happens with book dealers who are passionate about books—and I think that is what defines the best rare book dealers, not all of them but the large majority—is that they develop in the course of their careers intimate relationships with a handful of institutions. We become patrons, to use your word, of one or two libraries that we feel, for some reason, strongly about. Maybe we went to school there; maybe the curator is a friend, someone with similar intellectual and bibliophilic interests; maybe the library is just physically close. But long-term relations do develop and the book dealer ends up treating that particular library more like a private buyer than an institutional buyer, with the significant caveat that we're sensitive to the financial realities of our pet institutions. That's probably another very good and concrete way in which book dealers are patrons of scholarship—we tailor our expectations to fit the capacities of favorite libraries. Not all, but some. The sad side to this is that for every rare book librarian who has an intimate relationship with two or three dealers, there are dozens who don't even have casual relations with significant dealers. I think it fair to say that the project I alluded to earlier, the one that has me shuttling back and forth to Europe, is one that I wouldn't have remained committed to had it not been for my sense of affection for the potential purchasing institution.

DLB: How do these privileged relationships function?

HOROWITZ: Well before her death in 1990 I was quite close to Lola Szladits, curator of the monumental Berg Collection of American and English Literature at the New York Public Library. During the final five years of Lola's life we worked closely. Because I had, I think, a real idea of what she was looking to add to the Berg's holdings, and because I was able to wait patiently for funding to be available to her, she permitted me qualified carte blanche in acquiring materials that would wind up with her.

DLB: Stipulate.

HOROWITZ: Because of my friendship with Ed Mendelson, W. H. Auden's literary executor, biographer, and bibliographer, I've had extraordinary opportunities to buy major Auden letters and manuscripts. And Auden, of course, is one of the Berg's world-class archives and was one of Lola's passions. During the last half of the 80s I was on an Auden roll—I seemed to be constantly turning up material all over the world. It was great fun. Same thing, to a lesser degree, for Virginia Woolf, Vita Sackville-West, Henry Miller, Eliot, Faulkner, Conrad, even Arnold Bennett. I miss her very, very much, for many reasons.

DLB: Have you worked with a scholar on placing his research collection when he was finished with it?

HOROWITZ: Scholarly research collections can be tough nuts to crack in terms of institu-

tional sales. Libraries are searching for undigested research material; scholars do the digesting. One instance in which I devoted more time to a particular project than might have been warranted by the dollar dimensions but for which a proper resolution took place was the purchase by McGill University in Montreal of Leon Edel's archive in 1988. Leon graduated class of '28 from McGill and is perceived by many there as being one of the leading lights of the small Modernist movement that flourished in Montreal in the 1920s. After a long, protracted, slightly difficult negotiation that involved funding by the Canadian government, we managed to get the papers back where they belonged, to the great benefit of the University and the pleasure of the Montreal community at large.

DLB: Was the price made public?

HOROWITZ: No—McGill is a private institution with no obligation to reveal their business. Indeed, the transactions that take place with institutions that use publicly appropriated funds and are therefore required to reveal their activities are scarce. I can count on one hand such transactions that I've been involved in. There was only one of any real size in which numbers were disclosed. That was the sale of W. S. Merwin's papers to the University of Illinois in 1983 for $185,000, the funds for which were entirely supplied by the state—that is, no money came from private patrons.

DLB: Why the University of Illinois?

HOROWITZ: That's a good example of my putting my services at the behest of a university and working to see their goals met. In the case of Illinois I was initially approached by Bill Merwin, who had earlier that year been approached by the folks at the University about the possibility of a deal for his archive. I then visited Champaign-Urbana, where it quickly became apparent that at Illinois, and at two or three of the other major state universities in the Midwest, there was strong and maturing interest in doing textual and literary work on Merwin the poet, translator, man of letters. So the spur in that instance came from the University itself, from the literature department and from the library. After that I spent time traveling between Hawaii, where Merwin lived and his papers were, Champaign-Urbana, and New York, helping to craft what turned out

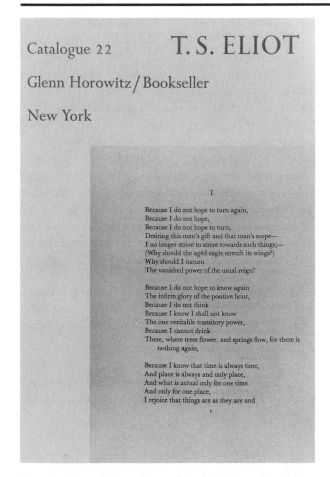

Catalogue 22 — T. S. ELIOT

Glenn Horowitz / Bookseller

New York

I

Because I do not hope to turn again,
Because I do not hope,
Because I do not hope to turn,
Desiring this man's gift and that man's scope—
I no longer strive to strive towards such things;—
(Why should the agèd eagle stretch its wings?)
Why should I mourn
The vanished power of the usual reign?

Because I do not hope to know again
The infirm glory of the positive hour,
Because I do not think
Because I know I shall not know
The one veritable transitory power,
Because I cannot drink
There, where trees flower, and springs flow, for there is
    nothing again,

Because I know that time is always time,
And place is always and only place,
And what is actual only for one time
And only for one place,
I rejoice that things are as they are and

*Cover for Horowitz's catalogue of works by the modernist poet
and critic*

to be a complex and lengthy transaction. In that instance I put my skills and staff to work for the buyer, the University, and the seller, Merwin.

DLB: Do graduate students or faculty members say to you "I understand that you have a certain Churchill item, or a certain Faulkner item, or a certain Virginia Woolf letter. It's out of the question for me to buy it. Will you let me look at it?"

HOROWITZ: Not as often as one might think, or as often as they should. There really isn't as close a relationship between the graduate faculty and the rare book librarians at major institutions, who are the conduits to the dealers, as there should be.

DLB: On average, how many times a year do you get a request from a student or a professor for help?

HOROWITZ: Probably a dozen, two dozen.

DLB: Do you have a policy on it?

HOROWITZ: We try to make available without restrictions anything that a scholar asks for access to.

DLB: Are you unusual in this respect? Many dealers say it diminishes value to let a scholar use a letter or manuscript before it's sold.

HOROWITZ: I think that's a wrongheaded position. At the highest dollar level at which we trade we are trading in letters and manuscripts that have fully matured, that have achieved a market value well beyond their scholarly value. A Fitzgerald letter that is worth ten thousand dollars is not worth ten thousand dollars because it's unpublished or published. It's worth ten thousand dollars because it's an F. Scott Fitzgerald letter and its value will not be reduced one iota by publication.

DLB: Is not a major unpublished letter worth more than a major published letter?

HOROWITZ: No.

DLB: When you're making a pitch to a customer and you are trying to explain why this thing is worth twenty thousand dollars . . .

HOROWITZ: I think I'm better off having the ammunition of publication in a collected edition rather than trying to explain how, miraculously, the letter has not existed up until this moment. The one instance in which I can think that unpublished material will lose monetary value once available or published is in the case of major archives by distinctly minor figures in which the only market for them is institutional. An example: say you have a fine run of Granville Hicks letters, but a decade back the previous owner had photocopied six sets of them and deposited them at six different research libraries. The commercial value of the originals is completely erased. Syracuse, the one legitimate Hicks archive in the United States, would never pay a nickel.

Now, suppose some book dealer manages to unearth five unknown, unpublished letters of Joyce to Hemingway. Those letters may be worth a quarter of a million bucks, but no institution is going to buy them. Or if by some miracle they do they're doing so not for their scholarly value but rather for their "trophy" value.

DLB: Elaborate, please.

HOROWITZ: If an institution is determined to own those letters they would have no choice but to get the funds to buy them from patrons. And the only way I think that a patron, or patrons, would fork over such a sum would be if they could be persuaded that their bequest was being used to acquire museum quality objects. You saw in the paper the other day about Sotheby's possibly auctioning off the newly resurfaced first draft of the first part of *Huckleberry Finn.* The value of the manuscript is not in its use to scholars. Scholars of course will use it. But at this point you're dealing with one of the great American literary manuscripts and if it goes to auction you're going to see it sell for a very large sum of money. Four or five wealthy people who are not buying it as scholars but as lovers of American literature will compete for it. And not because it's published or unpublished; nor is there any question that it will shortly after the auction see print somewhere. Anybody who competes for it at auction also knows that.

DLB: Can you sum up now?

HOROWITZ: I think the thing that most struck me in the course of our talk is the realization I came to about the reality of specific rare book dealers developing intimate relationships with a handful of institutions. In my bookselling life I have sold millions of dollars of books and manuscripts to American libraries. In the case of the overwhelming majority of the libraries we have dealt with we have developed good working relationships with particular curators. I think it's fair to say that most rare book dealers who are successful and handle quantities of important scholarly material have cultivated relationships with curators. But there are probably rare book curators throughout the United States who have no more than half a dozen encounters a year with rare book dealers and therefore the role in their orbit of the dealer as patron is an impossible one to establish since it requires the enthusiasm and the eagerness and the curiosity of the curator to engage the dealer. The dealer is finally a trader, and his role in life is to continue funding his business that keeps him afloat and alive because without that there will be one less galvanizing spirit in the book world.

DLB: What about the role of the rare book dealer as a scholar—that is, as bibliographer or historian?

HOROWITZ: My vision of myself as a rare book dealer is that when I shuttle off I will leave behind a series of 150 to 200 catalogues that will have something notable about them, something scholarly, something that will contribute to that long, long river of information that has always been the lifeblood of the rare book trade. I've also got planned two bibliographies—not sale catalogues—one of a publishing firm and one of early American baseball books.

New Approaches to Biography: Challenges from Critical Theory, USC Conference on Literary Studies, 1990

John Whalen-Bridge
University of Southern California

The conference "New Approaches to Biography: Challenges from Critical Theory," held at the University of Southern California on 19-21 October 1990 and organized by graduate students from the Department of English at USC, examined traditional approaches to literary biography and autobiography as they face challenges from feminism, deconstruction, New Historicism, and various other modes of recent critical theory. Papers such as William H. Epstein's "(Post) Modern Lives: Abducting the Biographical Subject" and Sidonie Smith's "Carnival, Pageantry, and the Politics of Universal Subject" offered the gauntlet to the factual narrative school of life-writing, but traditional biography occasionally returned the challenge, as it did in Jay Martin's "The Doing of John Dewey." From the first session to the closing panel, the papers led to animated debate on the political stakes, aesthetic aims, and economic foundations of contemporary biographical and autobiographical theory and practice.

In the first session, Ira B. Nadel of the University of British Columbia presented "Biography as Cultural Discourse," an exploration of genealogy á la Foucault and the anecdote á la New Historicism. Nadel argued that "a sustained theoretical discussion of biography incorporating some of the more probing and original speculations about language, structure, and discourse which have dominated post-structuralist thought" has so far been absent from the recent renaissance in biographical criticism; one possible new approach to biography, according to Nadel, would begin in the "anthropological concept that as we write our culture, we become what we have written." Nadel developed this point by looking at the place of the anecdote and the notion of origins in literary biography, turning then to one possible origin of the literary anecdote in Aubry's *Brief Lives*. Using Aubry as an example, he demonstrated that biography constitutes an appropriate vehicle for cultural criticism since biography, "given its traditions and paradigms . . . must incorporate conventional modes of discourse such as the family, law, social customs, the creative process, and textual composition, in addition to ethnographic and anthropological norms."

After Nadel's return to origins, Epstein of the University of Arizona investigated the primal scene of a postmodern work, Norman Mailer's "novel biography" *Marilyn* (1973). Mailer's biographical narrator is on stage in this scene when he remembers never being invited to Arthur Miller and Marilyn Monroe's home: " 'The playwright and the novelist had never been close. Nor could the novelist in conscience condemn the playwright for such avoidance of drama. The secret ambition, after all, had been to steal Marilyn.' " "(Post) Modern Lives: Abducting the Biographical Subject" took Mailer's local trope of abduction as an example of the way "a homosocial bonding between men (even, or especially, if they are rivals) . . . triangulates and victimizes women as it eroticizes, commodifies, and exchanges their bodies" in the institution of biography as in society in general. In recounting a lecture he gave on *Marilyn* that was crucial to his own tenure, Epstein turned the trope over once more to show how academics are abducted by their own professionalization. A vigorous debate on the assets and liabilities of critical theory's specialized discourse followed the first section when Professor Ronald Gottesman charged that writers such as Frederick Douglass had been instrumental to social change without using any jargon. Epstein responded that it is first essential to rework the master tropes that shape our discourse. No agreement here—but lines of division between the traditionalists and the critical theorists were clearly drawn in this dialogue.

The next section was organized around the problem of biography in the popular eye. As

Brian Finney of UCLA demonstrated in "Roth's Counterlife: Destabilizing the Facts," the fact of literary fame is as much of a problem for the writer as it is for any biographer. Roth's therapeutic self-demythologization in *The Facts* is not merely artful, it demonstrates that " 'Roth in person' is a fiction" no less than is Zuckerman in *The Counterlife*. Langdon Hammer of Yale University gave the second paper in this section, "Books, Lives and Merchandise: The Image of the Author in the Marketplace." Hammer examined the ideology of biographical and autobiographical writing with reference to Wordsworth to define a tension central to bourgeois conceptions of literary value. The writer must be singular and universal at once, a man speaking to men, and yet at once apart from other men. Hammer demonstrated the opposite faces of this coin with reference to the front page of the *New York Times Book Review* on two successive Sundays, the first featuring a review of Ann Beattie's *Picturing Will* (1990), the second reviewing Thomas Pynchon's *Vineland* (1990). Beattie's biographical presence and Pynchon's absence "restate the alternatives seen in Wordsworth, and they together specify the ideological horizon on which the modern practice of literary biography takes place."

The three papers in the next session critically approached the biographies of three writers, Stephen Crane, Joseph Conrad, and Mark Twain. John Clendenning of California State University, Northridge, began the session with "Rescue in Berryman's *Crane*." Berryman's attempted biographical rescue, *Stephen Crane* (New York: Sloane, 1950), was a doomed effort at self-rescue, "a detour that ended twenty-two years later on the Washington Avenue Bridge." Clendenning reviewed the ways in which Berryman seized on dubious elements in Crane's biography because they expressed his own primal scene, that of mother as femme fatal. Countertransference, properly understood and applied in a psychoanalytic framework, can be therapeutic, but Berryman's *Stephen Crane*, Clendenning suggested, may have been more a work of "irresponsible countertransference." Though it is often impossible to separate Crane's biography from Berryman's autobiography, Clendinning maintained that countertransference is an indispensable analytic tool "without which probably no worthwhile biography can be written. For Clendinning, the best biographies result not from the objectivity of the disinterested researcher, but rather from an essentially sympathetic approach to the life."

Leonard Orr of the University of Notre Dame resisted the tendency of conventional biography to use psychoanalytic methodologies to fill in the gaps in a writer's life in "Body and the Material Transduction: A Deleuzean Revision of Conrad Biography." Orr offered Deleuze and Guattari's concept of the rhizome—"an acentered, nonhierarchical, nonsignifying system"—as a way of avoiding the "achievement and decline" emplotments of Conrad's life, organizing fictions which do not respect Conrad's artistic deterritorialization. Laura Skandera of the State University of New York at Potsdam also spoke of the organizing fictions behind conventional biography in " 'The Mysterious Stranger': Absence of the Female in Mark Twain Biography." Concerned both with the absence of female Twain biographers and the absence of women as shaping forces within Twain biography, Skandera's feminist critique proposed a model for Twain biography that would respect Twain's genius for "joining different consciousnesses to forge an androgynous whole." The discussion after this session probed further into the matter of the biographer's empathy. A Berryman biographer, for example, could have empathy for Berryman and therefore describe his fear of the fatal woman with sympathy, or a different sort of biographer might have some identification with the demonized women that populated Berryman's dreams, *Dream Songs* (1969), and especially his *Stephen Crane*.

In "Biography and Narrative" Frederick R. Karl of New York University, author of biographies of Conrad, Faulkner, and Kafka, returned to problems raised in Orr's paper. What is the biographer to make of the modernist textual strategies that disguise more than they reveal? In what sense do modernist lacunae reveal the lives of modernist writers? Karl deployed Gerard Genette's distinctions among tense, mood, and voice to attack such problems and showed how the modernist tendency in which "structure devours substance" relates to the supposedly factual discourses of biography and history: as we abandon hope of narrative certainty in *Absalom, Absalom!* (1936), "we get glimpses of Faulkner's creative imagination, the deepest reaches of biographical act. With language problematic, we perceive that the elements language tries to define—race, history, memory, the past, personal feelings—are themselves uncertain events." Karl counseled the would-be biographer to attend the lessons of modernist textual strategies, to recognize in Faulkner's fiction his autobiographical disclosure that

New Approaches to Biography: Challenges from Critical Theory

FIRST ANNUAL CONFERENCE

USC Graduate Student Forum for Literary Studies

DEPARTMENT OF ENGLISH

October 19-21, 1990 University of Southern California

FRIDAY

1:00-1:45 Registration, Annenberg 205, Lobby
All Friday sessions are in ASC 205.

1:45-2:00 Welcome
Richard S. Ide, Chair, Department of English, USC
Barbara Solomon, Dean, The Graduate School, USC

2:00-3:30 Ira B. Nadel
University of British Columbia
"Biography as Cultural Discourse"

William H. Epstein
University of Arizona
"(Post)Modern Lives"

Moderator: John Whalen-Bridge

4:00-5:30 Biography in the Popular Eye

Brian Finney, University of California, Los Angeles
"Roth's Counterlife: Destabilizing the Facts"

Langdon Hammer, Yale University
"Books, Lives and Merchandise:
The Image of the Author in the Marketplace"

Catherine Schoen, University of Massachusetts, Amherst
"Invisible Narrators: Narrative Biography
and the Biographical Project"

Moderator: Andrea Ivanov

6:00 Reception, Taper Hall, Fourth Floor Lounge

SATURDAY

8:30-9:00 Registration, Coffee and Rolls
Annenberg, East Lobby
All Saturday and Sunday sessions are in ASC G21.

9:00-10:30 Psychoanalysis and the Nineteenth-Century Male Subject

John Clendenning, California State University, Northridge
"Rescue in Berryman's *Crane*"

Leonard Orr, University of Notre Dame
"Body and the Material Transduction:
A Deleuzean Revision of Conrad Biography"

Laura E. Skandera, State University of New York, Potsdam
"'The Mysterious Stranger':
Absence of the Female in Mark Twain Biography"

Moderator: Donald J. Newman

11:00-12:30 Frederick R. Karl
New York University
"Narrative Problems in Biography"

Sidonie Smith
State University of New York, Binghamton
"Autobiographical Practice and the Politics of Universalization"

Moderator: Jill Hall

12:45-2:00 Box Lunch, Annenberg East Lobby

2:15-3:45 Writing Among Others: Constructing a Conflicting Self

Deborah Martinson, University of Southern California
"Writing the Self--Deflecting the Other's Gaze:
Katherine Mansfield's *Journal*"

David Meng, University of Maryland
"Henry James's Autobiography:
Constructing the Self through Others"

Chizuko Yonamine, University of Oregon
"'Self' in a Tenth-Century Japanese Autobiography"

Moderator: Claire Marie-Peterson

4:00-5:30 Illness, Anxiety and Instability:
The Body Before the Text

G. Thomas Couser, Hofstra University
"Autopathography: Women, Illness, and Life-Writing"

Timothy C. Davis, University of South Florida
"*La Trappe*: Metaphor, Surplus Value,
and Sexual Anxiety in Nietzsche"

Allison Fraiberg, University of Washington
"Mothers of the Immaculate Contraction:
Gender, Ethnicity, and the Politics of 'Pediatric AIDS'"

Moderator: Phyllis Franzek

5:30-6:30 Cash Bar, Upper Commons

7:00-9:00 Dinner and Keynote Address, Upper Commons

George Simson
Director, Center for Biographical Research
University of Hawaii

"Whatever Happened to Truth
on the Way to Biography's House?
Or, How Credibility Ate Grandma Truth"

Introduction: John Whalen-Bridge

SUNDAY

8:30-9:00 Coffee and Rolls, Annenberg East Lobby

9:00-10:30 Genre Ambiguity and the Female Subject:
Fiction/Biography/Autobiography

C.L. Barney Dews, University of Minnesota
"Carson McCullers' Fiction and Lejeune's Autobiographical Pact:
When does Autobiographical Fiction become Autobiography?"

Merry Murdoch Pawlowski, California State Univ., Bakersfield
"Bodies into Text: Virginia Woolf's *Roger Fry: A Biography*
and 'A Sketch of the Past'"

Eleanor Salotto, Bryn Mawr College
"Inscriptions and Reinscriptions
in Elizabeth Gaskell's *The Life of Charlotte Bronte*"

Moderator: Jameela Lares

10:45-12:30 Jay Martin
University of Southern California
"The Doing of John Dewey"

Introduction: Joseph Raab

Conference Assessment

Moderator: Jay Martin

Panel Members:
William Epstein, Frederick R. Karl,
Ira B. Nadel, George Simson,
Sidonie Smith

Conference Organizers: John Whalen-Bridge (Director), Phyllis Franzek, Jill Hall, Andrea Ivanov, Jameela Lares, Donald J. Newman, Claire Peterson, Joseph Raab
With Funding from: USC Department of English, Division of Humanities, Association of English Graduate Students, The Graduate School, Graduate Program Board

The schedule of presentations at the conference intended to discuss the effects of critical theory on the practice of biography

"he was not a man whose life can be described as continuous or as part of a smoothly-running chronology."

Switching from the intricacies inherent in writing biography to those we confront as readers of autobiography, Sidonie Smith of the State University of New York at Binghamton sketched out the problem of "the universal subject" in "Carnival, Pageantry, and the Politics of the Universal Subject." Smith argued that "autobiographical writing has served to secure the hegemony of the 'universal subject,' what Gayatri Spivak has termed 'the white Western man of property.'" Using Mikhail Bakhtin's distinction between the pageant and the carnival (as modified by Peter Stallybrass and Allon White, and also by Terry Eagleton), Smith proposed that, as pageantry became passe as a cultural form, it "migrated imaginatively into other domains, including the domain of autobiography," where it becomes a reservoir of potential resistance to the hegemonic dominion entailed in the creation of the universal subject. Smith then turned to her two examples, Annie Dillard's *An American Childhood*, (1987), an interiorized pageant which universalizes Dillard's childhood and thus mutes the colorful and the carnivalesque, and Jo Spence's *Putting Myself in the Picture* (1988), a counterpageant ph/auto/biography that reveals differences in race, gender, and class in order to carnivalize the fictitious body of the supposedly universal subject.

Sidonie Smith's presentation prepared the way for the three papers in the next session, all of which dealt with the place of Others in the autobiographical text. Deborah Martinson of the University of Southern California presented "Writing the Self—Deflecting the Other's Gaze," in which she examined the effect of John Middleton Murry's gaze upon the writing of *The Journal of Katherine Mansfield* (1927) and described the ways in which Mansfield contrived to deflect the gaze of father and lovers, then of husband Murry. Using Mansfield as an example, Martinson submitted that "The diaries of women are especially vulnerable to the voyeuristic reader, both male and female, who want to know what it is to be woman, or to validate their own otherness against the portrait of the subject of the journal."

In his "Henry James's *Autobiography*: Constructing the Self through Others," David Meng of the University of Maryland does not position the Others as adversaries, but rather he shows how James's "center of consciousness technique," which has been so influential to the history of the novel, also applies to James's nonfictional self-portrait. In *Notes of a Son and Others* (1914) and *A Small Boy and Others* (1913), James is certainly present but is never center stage. Rather than expose himself, James reflects whatever of himself he chooses to reveal in his portrait of others, such as his brother William.

Chizuko Yonamine of the University of Oregon presented "'Self' in a Tenth-Century Japanese Autobiography." This presentation challenged the formulations of even the most critically sophisticated and politically correct literary theorists. It has become the habit of intellectuals educated in Europe and America to question the universality of the western white, male subject—without necessarily understanding the conditions or conventions governing non-Western subjectivity. The line of race has been carefully studied, as has that of gender, but less so that which separates the West from the rest of the world. Yonamine reviewed the problem of generic definitions of autobiography (which commonly assert that autobiography begins with an awareness of individuality) and then discussed the special problem of ascribing a "self" to the female author of a tenth-century "gossamer diary" entitled *Kagero Nikki*: "It is evident that women were not recognized as an autonomous presence but were seen always in association with male figures or with the places in which they lived. The writings by these nameless women seem to undermine the very presupposition that one needs to be aware of one's individuality in order to write an autobiography." In a conference including many prestigious authorities on contemporary approaches to lifewriting, this paper made a striking and much-needed contribution. Yonamine reminded us that we must not seize on differences between male and female without also attending to questions of cultural context.

The next panel concerned illness and anxiety in relation to both biography and autobiography. G. Thomas Couser of Hofstra University presented "Autopathography: Women, Illness, and Life-Writing," an account of "autobiographical narratives of disease or disability." Couser first came across the term "autopathography" in its clinical context, but was struck by Joyce Carol Oates's appropriation of the term to denigrate "'hagiography's diminished and often prurient twin, [whose] motifs are dysfunction and disaster....'" With reference to a wide variety of texts, Couser noted that autopathography, as a particular form of autobiography, forces us to confront the sometimes uncomfortable fact that physical, human bodies precede literary texts. Biographers have needed to be reminded of this point, and autobiographers have been generally silent as well: "unless illness threatens life, or ends it, biographers have tended to consider it as an interruption of the life that is their proper subject. Autobiographers are generally better equipped than biographers to report on the bodily lives of their subjects, but (ironically) they seem even less inclined to do so. Thus, illness has been as studiously ignored, or repressed, in life-writing as the body has been, and for the same reasons." Couser then considered texts that take up Virginia Woolf's call for a more sensual, bodily writing, Nancy Mairs's *Plaintext* (1986), *Remembering the Bone House* (1989), and *Carnal Acts* (1990), and Barbara Webster's *All of a Piece: A Life with Multiple Sclerosis* (1989). Couser presented these recent developments within autobiography as a "return of the repressed," and suggested that Mairs and Webster subject their cultures to a much-needed lay diagnosis.

Timothy C. Davis of the University of South Florida made connections between Nietzsche's formative years and his later use of yonic and ithyphallic imagery in *Thus Spake Zarathustra* (1883-1892) in "*La Trappe*: Metaphor, Surplus Value, and Life-Writing." Davis certainly captured the attention of his audience when he began his paper with this quotation from Derrida's *The Post Card*: " 'His friend told me one day . . . that a given, apparently rigorously theoretical text was written such that it gave him an erection whenever he read it.' " There was, unfortunately, no reader-response critic present to gauge the effect of Davis's text.

Allison Fraiberg of the University of Washington interrogated the ideological sources and political effects of the new category "pediatric AIDS" in "Mothers of the Immaculate Contraction: Gender, Race, Ethnicity and the Politics of 'Pediatric AIDS.' " Fraiberg demonstrated that, due to the spread of AIDS beyond the traditional "guilty" sources, there was an ideological need to distinguish and protect from narratives of blame the "innocent victims." This line between innocence and guilt is a hegemonic device. With the category of "pediatric AIDS," even Ronald Reagan—who was silent about AIDS during his administration—can appear to have compassion with AIDS victims. In the popular press, the mainstream news media, and in the scholarly medical discourse, representations of HIV-positive people

have supported, according to Fraiberg's analysis, white, middle-class hegemony: "Living with HIV, for mothers within the narrative context of Pediatric AIDS, does not depend as much on opportunistic infection or elitist medical care, but rather on association with certain behaviors: the guilty mothers who are associated with drug use—almost always represented as women of color—succumb to disease while the immaculate contractors—almost always represented as white, middle-class women in nuclear families—continue the fight for children." Fraiberg presented a striking challenge to those who hold that "the body" or "the life" or "the facts" precede the interpretive schemes of those who would write about them.

George Simson of the University of Hawaii and editor of *biography* marshaled arguments against the notion that words ending in "y"— dialogicity, narrativity, transitivity, or periodicity, to name a few from Simson's list—should distract us from the fact that biography begins with a baby's birth: "Even Alexander was a baby once." Simson's main example was near at hand, as he referred on several occasions to a certain Thomas Josiah Whalen-Bridge, aged two months. If the main impetus of Simson's talk was against critical theory and in favor of common sense, he willingly conceded to the academic revolution of the last quarter-century a few of its gains: "in the mid-sixties along came the serious intellectual obsessions, which I think were caused by a rotten job market. There was the new and in my opinion justified impetus in Europe and America to smash up the WASP consensus. A new holy trinity emerged: race, gender, and class. The husserlian phenomenology was the instrument for these premises. Autobiography in its various forms married memory with desire. James Olney led the theorists, but the brilliant and skilled Maxine Hong Kingston really showed how it could be done, using a hologrammatic of autobiographical fact, legend, and fiction that created a manifesto out of a phrase: 'the woman warrior.' " Simson closed with half-a-dozen practical new approaches for biographical criticism and then, after telling a room full of budding theorists that they owed their discourse to a rotten job market and that the fiction writers had gotten there first anyway— asked that he be allowed to eat dessert rather than answer questions. Though he closed with Wittgenstein's notion that "What we cannot speak about, we must pass over in silence," his desire for dessert met with loud applause.

In a panel dedicated to genre ambiguity in texts written by women, C. L. Barney Dews of the University of Minnesota presented "Carson McCullers' Fiction and Lejeune's Autobiographical Pact: When does autobiographical fiction become autobiography? or ~~Carson McCullers' Fiction and LeJeune's Autobiographical Pact: When does autobiographical fiction become autobiography.~~" The repeated title under erasure signifies the basic theoretical site of struggle within the argument. Dews became concerned, when writing an early draft of his call to read McCullers as an autobiographer, with the repressive structure of such taxonomic literary operations. Also reading in this panel was Merry Pawlowski of California State University, Bakersfield. In "Bodies into Text: Virginia Woolf's *Roger Fry: A Biography* (1940) and 'A Sketch of the Past'" Pawlowski intelligently apprehended "the space of an interval between her self-perception and her recreation of Roger Fry, a space filled with autobiographical remembrance." Woolf attempted to reproduce the artistic rhythms of Fry's work (that of art and that of life) in her biography in order to create "moments of being" that would transcend the linearity of narrative art, and in so doing came to interrogate "the very nature of biography and autobiography as generic forms." Forced by the pressure she felt from Fry's own aesthetic into a dissatisfaction with conventional biography, "Woolf insisted on crossing the grain of conventional biography with the textures of narrative artistry."

Jay Martin of the University of Southern California, biographer of Nathanael West and Henry Miller, gave the final formal presentation when he read "The Doing of John Dewey: Some Thoughts Concerning Sabino." In reading this section from his work in progress, Martin gave a masterful rendition of the traditional biographical approach. How was it that one of John Dewey's children, all of whom have traditional Anglo-American names, came to be named "Sabino"? In a moving narrative with several surprising turns, Martin revealed how a seemingly marginal detail, an out-of-place name, can develop into a central psychological pattern. Sabino, it turns out, was a "replacement child" for a favorite Dewey child who died in youth, leaving Dewey shattered. The

adoption of the Italian boy Sabino filled this void in Dewey's life. Martin then returned to Dewey's own early years to reveal that Dewey was himself a replacement child, and this revelation in Martin's narrative precipitated an inquiry into the psychological burdens and pressures upon the replacement child. The first question presented to Martin after his formal presentation concerned his privileging of Dewey's subject-position in constructing his narrative. Sidonie Smith and William Epstein pointed out that Martin's biographical empathy for John Dewey obscured Sabino Dewey's origins. What of Sabino's Italian family? Smith suggested that this unexamined empathy parallels colonial practices. Martin responded that he hoped his empathy for Sabino registered clearly, but that John Dewey was his biographical subject. He agreed that one could write a different sort of biography, one in which the biographical subject shifts from moment to moment, but that he preferred not to. Frederick Karl concurred with Martin's pragmatic approach and added that those who *read* biographies do not always wish for the same sort of books as those who *write* them.

Since the conference was dedicated to an open-ended exploration of the place of "life-writing" in contemporary literary studies, it included an impressive variety of approaches to biography. Although there could be no consensus at such a meeting about what did (or did not) constitute "biography," the study of life-writing has most certainly been invigorated by all the strands of continental philosophy, psychoanalytic practice, and feminist intervention that have renovated literary studies in the last twenty-five years. As William Epstein suggested in his paper, new biographies are being written that do not follow the traditional emplotments. And, as Jay Martin demonstrated, reports of traditional biography's death have been greatly exaggerated. Balanced appraisals aside, "New Approaches to Biography: Challenges from Critical Theory" demonstrated beyond a theoretician's doubt that students of life-writing, old school or new, will do well to receive hospitably (though never uncritically) the innovative biographies, autobiographies, autobiographical fictions, and perhaps even libelous biographies that are presently going to press.

New Literary Periodicals: A Report for 1990

Richard R. Centing
Ohio State University

The following report on new literary periodicals, the fourth in a series of annual reports scheduled to appear in the *Dictionary of Literary Biography Yearbook*, documents scholarly journals, annuals, newsletters, and reviews launched in 1990, along with some 1989 titles that had not come to our attention by press time last year. Any 1990 titles that we missed will be covered in the 1991 *Yearbook*. These descriptions are not meant to be evaluative, although we do stress the importance of a few titles. By highlighting outstanding facts of each serial, our intention is to bring them to the attention of librarians and scholars for purposes of collection development, scholarly submission, and to alert indexing services of the need for the inclusion of new titles in their core lists. Please contact the author with any comments on the report for 1990 or suggestions for inclusion in the 1991 report.

Syllecta Classica (University of Iowa, Department of Classics, 112 Schaeffer Hall, Iowa City, Iowa 52242) began in 1989 as a refereed outlet for interdisciplinary research on the classics, with particular emphasis on the scholarship of younger scholars. The first annual includes essays on the Fabullus poem of Catullus, the galliambic meter in Catullus, two epigrams of the *Greek Anthology* that refer to Menippus, Euripides' *Medea*, Xenophon's *Cynegeticus*, and two discussions of Aristotle. Betty Rose Nagle, Indiana University Department of Classics, contributed "Ovid's Metamorphoses: A Narratological Catalogue," a twenty-nine-page analysis of the embedded tales in Ovid's *Metamorphoses*. A section devoted to "Work in Progress" includes reports on recently completed and in-progress dissertations at four American universities. The editors include a call for scholars and students to submit brief accounts of work in progress for inclusion in future issues. This issue includes a report on Greek paleography research at the University of Iowa, presumably an example of the type of report they are seeking. This issue is dedicated to Archie Bush (1940-1989), who formulated the original plans for the journal. At the time of his

Cover for the first issue of the annual coedited by Helena R. Dettmer and Erling B. Holtsmark

death he was acting chairman of the Iowa classics department. The journal is now coedited by Helena R. Dettmer and Erling B. Holtsmark.

William Shakespeare (1564-1616) is served by numerous journals in many languages, including *Shakespeare-Jahrbuch* (1865-), *Shakespeare Survey* (1948-), *Shakespeare Quarterly* (1950-), and *Shakespeare Studies* (1965-). Margaret C. Patterson's *Author Newsletters and Journals* (Gale Research Company, 1979) located fifty-seven Shakespearean titles worldwide. The latest entry is *Shakespeare Yearbook: An Interdisciplinary Annual* (Edwin

Mellen Press, P. O. Box 450, Lewiston, New York 14092), first issued Spring 1990. The annual intends to deal "with all influences on the Shakespearean corpus and culture." The general editor is listed as Linda Kay Hoff (Edwin Mellen Press). Other editors are Joan Hartwig (University of Kentucky), who is the liaison to the International Congress on Medieval Studies (Shakespeare section), and Ronald Bryden, director, Graduate Centre for the Study of Drama, University of Toronto, who is to edit the section of theater reviews (with emphasis on productions at the Canadian Stratford festival). The bulk of the publication is taken up with nine scholarly essays contributed by North American academics on aspects of Shakespeare's plays, with one essay on Thomas Kyd's *The Spanish Tragedy* as "an apocalyptic revenge tragedy" that reflects the political and religious conflicts between Spain and England. *Shakespeare Yearbook* concludes with five book reviews and a "Books Received" column.

Laurence Sterne (1713-1768), author of the immortal *Tristram Shandy* (1760-1767), now has an annual volume devoted to the historical investigation of his life and work. Taking its title from his most famous work and from Shandy Hall (a cottage he once occupied and that he named), *The Shandean* (The Laurence Sterne Trust, Shandy Hall, Coxwold, York, England Y06 4AD) is a richly illustrated, finely printed, and impeccably edited repository of Sterneiana. Launched in November 1989, the editorial policy of the annual announces that it will shun "interpretative debate" and focus more on facts and the publication of primary material. The editorial board is headed by Peter J. de Voogd, General Editor (Rijksuniversiteit te Utrecht). The first volume contains thirteen articles, covering such subjects as the *Catalogue* of Sterne's library, the Oates Collection of Sterne at Cambridge University Library, the *Politicks*, and even an architectural discussion of the chimneypiece into which Sterne was supposed to have flung the manuscript of *Tristram Shandy* when his friends fell asleep during a reading. The primary material includes some new Sterne letters. The making of a German television documentary on Sterne is also noted. The annual concludes with excellent book reviews.

A Scottish poet and novelist, James Hogg (1770-1835) is the subject of *Studies in Hogg and His World* (University of Stirling, Department of English, Stirling, Scotland FK9 4LA), an annual published by the James Hogg Society beginning in 1990. Edited by Gillian H. Hughes, the first

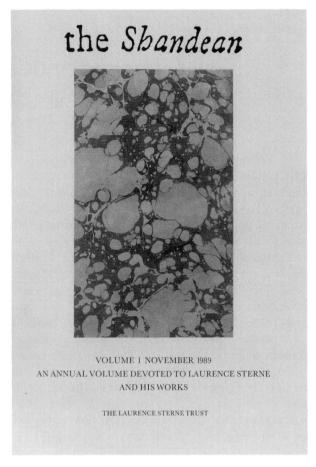

VOLUME 1 NOVEMBER 1989
AN ANNUAL VOLUME DEVOTED TO LAURENCE STERNE
AND HIS WORKS

THE LAURENCE STERNE TRUST

Cover of the first issue of the annual edited by Peter J. de Voogd

issue includes eleven scholarly articles and three notes covering such topics as Hogg's reputation, satire, songwriting, and membership in a debating society called the Forum. The influence of the witchcraft tradition on Hogg is documented, and Hogg's neglected plays are reassessed. A newly edited sketch by Hogg, "Odd Characters," is published with textual and bibliographic notes by Elaine Petrie. There are five book reviews. A review of *The History of Scottish Literature: Volume 3, Nineteenth Century* (Aberdeen University Press, 1988) evaluates the Hogg essay by Thomas Crawford in that volume as "the best essay-length introduction to Hogg to have appeared so far."

Emily Brontë (1818-1848) and Charlotte Brontë (1816-1855), and other members of the Brontë family, are the subjects of the *Brontë Society Gazette* (Brontë Society, Brontë Parsonage, Haworth, Keighley, West Yorkshire, England BD22 8DR), an irregular newsletter begun in May 1990. There is no editor listed, although the "Introduction" is signed by Chris Sumner, chairman of the Membership Committee, who states that the Brontë Society Council has decided to "put out two or three newsletters on an experimental basis" at the request of the membership. The *Gazette* lists upcoming events, has a picture of members attending a literary luncheon at Wellington, Shropshire, includes short notes on various facts concerning the Brontës, explains the movement of a bronze statue of the Brontë sisters, and has an interesting piece on the first lost silent film version of *Wuthering Heights* (1847), made at Haworth in 1920. The Brontë family has also been studied in the more scholarly *Brontë Society Transactions* (1895-), and the United States-based *Brontë Newsletter* (The Brontë Society, 335 Grove Street, Oradell, New Jersey 07649), issued annually since 1982.

Scholars of James Joyce (1882-1941) currently have seven publications devoted to his life and work: *James Joyce Quarterly* (1963-); *James Joyce Broadsheet* (1980-); *A Finnegans Wake Circular* (1985- : formerly *A Wake Newslitter*, 1962-1980); *James Joyce Literary Supplement* (1987-); and *James Joyce Newestlatter* (1989- : formerly *James Joyce Foundation Newsletter*, 1969-1989); and the two latest publications covered in this year's survey, *European Joyce Studies* (1989-) and *Joyce Studies Annual* (1990-).

European Joyce Studies (Editions Rodopi, 233 Peachtree Street, N.E., Suite 404, Atlanta, Georgia 30303) is an annual that began in 1989 with a theme issue, "Joyce, Modernity, and its Mediation." The general editor of the series is Fritz Senn (Director, James Joyce Foundation, Zürich, Switzerland), although this special issue was edited by Christine van Boheemen (University of Leiden). As Christine van Boheemen-Saaf she is known for her *Novel as Family Romance: Language, Gender, and Authority from Fielding to Joyce* (Cornell University Press, 1987). The annual is published by Editions Rodopi in Amsterdam, The Netherlands, and by calling this series "European" it reflects not only its geographic origin but its aim to stress "European concerns" such as language and continental critical theory. The first annual includes fourteen scholarly essays: one on *Exiles* (1918), six on *Ulysses* (1922), one on *Finnegans Wake* (1939), and six touching on more general topics. *European Joyce Studies* will not publish book reviews or news items. Forthcoming for 1990 is a theme issue on *Finnegans Wake*.

Joyce Studies Annual (University of Texas Press, Journals Department, P. O. Box 7819, Austin, Texas 78713) is an important annual that

Table of contents for the first issue of the annual edited by Thomas F. Staley

began in 1990. The editor, Thomas F. Staley, is director of the Harry Ransom Humanities Research Center and professor of English, University of Texas at Austin. The editorial board includes leading Joyceans such as Morris Beja, Bernard Benstock, and Clive Hart. The attractively printed, hardbound annual features nine lengthy essays, but no book reviews. The first contribution, "Selections From the Paris Diary of Stuart Gilbert, 1929-1934," publishes for the first time excerpts from Gilbert's diary that record his association with Joyce. The Humanities Research Center acquired the Stuart Gilbert library and literary archive in 1989. The excerpts are illustrated with three photographs of Gilbert and Joyce. Some of the other subjects covered include Italian translations of *Finnegans Wake*, the politics of childhood in "The Mime of Mick, Nick, and the Maggies," and the "Cyclops" episode of *Ulysses*. The volume concludes with the "Annual James Joyce Checklist: 1989," a fifty-page bibliography of new primary and secondary material, including references to musical settings, motion pictures, and other miscellaneous items.

Literary reference collections have been enhanced by the annual *British Theatre Yearbook* (Christopher Helm Ltd., Imperial House, 21-25 North Street, Bromley, Kent, England BR1 1SD), begun in 1989 as an illustrated record of British professional theater. The annual contains six major sections: London West End; Royal Shakespeare Company; National Theatre; Outer London, Fringe, and Club Theatres; Provincial Theatres; and Touring Companies. Each section provides theater-by-theater information on all the plays given in the calendar year (the 1989 volume covers 1988). The information provided varies from brief to very full, depending on the response to letters sent by the editor to every theater and production company in Britain. Each entry generally includes the author, title, translator or adaptor, cast, director and technical staff, and dates of the run. New plays and revivals are both covered. There are annotations for many plays, ranging in length from a few sentences to longer expositions that serve as mini-reviews. The annotations have important comments that deserve attention, often discussing the locale of the plot, the literary work on which it is based, or previous productions. The editor, David Lemmon, is an authority on cricket, with professional theater experience.

The *Journal of American Drama and Theatre* (Center for Advanced Study in Theatre Arts, CUNY Graduate School, 33 West 42nd Street, New York, New York 10036) first appeared Spring 1989 and is scheduled to be published three times a year. It is coedited by Walter J. Meserve and Vera Mowry Roberts. The contributors are mostly U.S. academics from departments of English or theater. All periods in American dramatic history will be covered from the Colonial to the present. Noted theater historian Don B. Wilmeth contributes a checklist of Indian plays of North and South America. Richard Wattenberg (University of California at Riverside) compares the work of Robert Sherwood and William Saroyan. James A. Robinson (University of Maryland) discusses parental authority in Arthur Miller's *All My Sons* (1946). Rock poetry in the plays of Sam Shepard is analyzed, and a history of French language drama in New Orleans is provided. T. S. Eliot, Edward Albee, and other important playwrights are treated in each ninety-page issue.

Marvin Carlson, Sidney E. Cohn Professor of Theatre at the City University Graduate Center in Manhattan, has authored many articles and books on the theory and history of dramatic literature, including the recent *The Play's the Thing: An Introduction to Theatre* (Longman, 1990). He is the editor of the new semiannual theater journal *Western European Stages* (Center for Advanced Study in Theatre Arts, CUNY Graduate School, 33 West 42nd Street, New York, New York 10036). The first issue (Fall 1989) includes nine informal articles that stress reportage of current performance in European theater. They are illustrated with black-and-white photographs of production, but do not include bibliographic references. Jane House, director of the Theatre Project at Columbia University's Institute on Western Europe, interviews Dacia Maraini, an Italian playwright and novelist. Another piece discusses Maraini's work as a contribution to feminist theater. Marvin Carlson contributes two reports on theater in France. A historical overview of various productions of Wagner's *Der Ring des Nibelungen* at Bayreuth is included, as well as general comments on theater in London.

First issued December 1989, the informal four-page *Newsletter* of the newly established American Literature Association (Alfred Bendixen, Executive Director, Department of English, California State University, Los Angeles, California 90032) carries the "Statement of Purpose" of this coalition of major societies devoted to American authors. It also announces their first annual conference, held in San Diego, 31 May - 3 June 1990. The irregular newsletter publishes information on new author societies and their journals, but does not publish scholarship or reviews.

The *James Fenimore Cooper Society Newsletter* (Hugh C. MacDougall, Secretary-Treasurer, Cooper Society, 32 Elm Street, Cooperstown, New York 13326) serves as a place of record for the affairs of the Cooper Society, founded on the bicentennial of Cooper's birth, 15 September 1989. The six page, semiannual newsletter was first issued Spring 1990. The newsletter cites all the celebrations of the two-hundredth anniversary of the birth of Cooper, documents scholarly works-in-progress, announces conferences, and includes other short historical notes. The editor is George A. Test (SUNY-Oneonta), who contributed "The Bicentennial of James Fenimore Cooper: An International Celebration" to the *Dictionary of Literary Biography Yearbook: 1989*.

Henry David Thoreau (1817-1862) is the subject of the *Thoreau Research Newsletter* (Bradley P. Dean, Editor, Route 2, Box 36, Ayden, North Carolina 28513), an independent quarterly whose first issue was dated January 1990 and whose second issue was dated April 1990. Each newsletter runs eight pages. No article is longer than one page, with most entries being much shorter, covering specific facets of Thoreau studies: the manuscript of Thoreau's lecture on walking; a biographical sketch of Daniel Foster (1816-1864), an antislavery activist known to Thoreau; and an anonymous report on the dedication of the North Bridge Monument, 4 July 1837. The tone of the newsletter is very personalized, with lists of individual subscribers and notes on "interested persons," along with encouragement of interaction among readers. The *Thoreau Society Bulletin* (1941-), edited by Walter Harding, a major Thoreau scholar, remains the seminal publication (it published *Bulletin* no. 193, Fall 1990). The Thoreau Society has also issued the semiannual *Concord Saunterer* (Thoreau Lyceum, 156 Belknap Street, Concord, Massachusetts 01742) since 1966.

The American novelist Willa Cather (1873-1947) has been the subject of a small newsletter issued since Summer 1957 by the Willa Cather Pioneer Memorial of Red Cloud, Nebraska. *Cather Studies* (University of Nebraska Press, 327 Nebraska Hall, 901 N. 17th Street, Lincoln, Nebraska 68588), scheduled to be issued every two years, is a hardbound compilation that is comprised of twelve long critical articles. The articles cover such topics as the influence of the Russian literary tradition on Cather, the use of Dante in her work, her dislike of publicity, and her style. Cather's friendship with Dorothy Canfield Fisher is also chronicled. The authors are mainly American academics. Each article concludes with a useful bibliography of works cited. The first volume (1990) also has a detailed subject index that enhances its accessibility. The editor is Susan J. Rosowski, author of *The Voyage Perilous: Willa Cather's Romanticism* (University of Nebraska Press, 1986) and editor of *Approaches to Teaching My Antonia* (MLA, 1989).

The *Henry Miller Memorial Library Newsletter* (Jerry Kamstra, Highway One, Big Sur, California 93920) is a fanzine devoted to Henry Miller (1891-1980), author of *Tropic of Cancer* (1934). The editor, Jerry Kamstra, is also the director of the Henry Miller Memorial Library, whose house and collection are the legacy of Emil White (1901-1989), a literary associate of Miller dating back to 1942. Kamstra is a novelist, (*The Frisco Kid* [Harper & Row, 1975]), and nonfiction writer (*Weed: Adventures of a Dope Smuggler* [Harper & Row, 1974]). The first issue of the semiannual newsletter is dated 28 April 1990 and contains sixteen pages. The contents are a ragbag of news clips, poetry, graphics, informal recollections, and information on local environmental concerns at Big Sur.

American Writing (Alexandra Grilikhes, 4343 Manayunk Avenue, Philadelphia, Pennsylvania 19128) is an independent, semiannual poetry/fiction/essay outlet that publishes contributions from a nationwide roster of novelists, artists, and poets. The first issue was bibliographically identified as Number 1 (1990) and ran seventy-seven pages. The style of the contributions is innovative, sometimes exhibiting surrealist playfulness. Ivan Argüelles, an active California poet, contributed three poems: "Texts of Smoke and Plumes," "Burning Water," and "Eyeballing the Truth." One piece is an interview with the photographer, Becky Young, that lacks any reproductions of her work. Alexandra Grilikhes is the editor.

An annual literary review that began in 1989, *Calypso* (175 E. Washington, Apt. C, El Cajon, California 92020) is an independent "journal of narrative poetry and poetic fiction." It is published and edited by Susan and Frances Richardson. The first sixty-five-page issue includes eighteen poems, seven fictional pieces, and a short essay. The contributors are widely published in both small press publications and national markets, and they employ a wide variety of styles. The poets include Andrew J. Grossman, John Bradley, and Sandy Meek Henson. The fiction is by Paul Milenski, David Hopes, and Lu Vickers. Eve Shelnutt, a professor of writing at Ohio University, who has published three story collections with Black Sparrow Press and two poetry collections with Carnegie-Mellon Press, contributed the sole essay, "Finding the Story Through Language and Form," combining autobiographical confession and her theories about the "tension between language and form."

The semiannual *Carbuncle* (Thumbscrew Press, 1331 26th Avenue, San Francisco, California 94122) is a small poetry journal edited by the poet William Talcott. The first thirty-two-page issue appeared late in 1989. The second issue (Spring 1990) expanded to eighty pages. It includes attractive artwork, along with the work of over twenty poets. The *Small Press Review* (Octo-

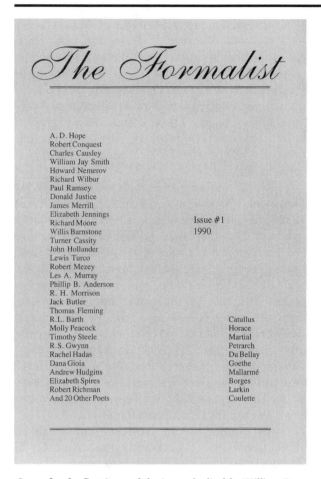

Cover for the first issue of the journal edited by William Baer

ber 1990) called it "one of the best little mags." The poets included are Ann Elliot Shermann, Victor Contoski, August Kleinzahler, Betsy Ford, Anselm Hollo, Walt Franklin, and others.

Crazy River (Central Ohio Technical College, University Drive, Newark, Ohio 43055) is a literary review that is published twice a year. The first issue (Spring 1990) contains three works of fiction and poetry from thirty-one poets. The majority of the contributors have midwestern connections such as the poet/editor David Citino of the Ohio State University English department. Some contributors are students. An experimental piece of fiction, "Mumbo-Jumbo," is the contribution of George Myers, Jr., book critic for the *Columbus Dispatch*. The poetic subjects range from the music of Ray Charles to the ordinariness of Newark, Ohio. Innocuous photographs of river beds, trees, farms, and weathervanes illustrate this journal edited by Roy Bentley, who is known for his poetry collection, *Boy in a Boat* (University of Alabama Press, 1986). Robert Fox, Ohio Arts Council, is the fiction editor.

The press release for *The Formalist* (The Formalist, 525 S. Rotherwood Avenue, Evansville, Indiana 47714) contains blurbs from the likes of Arthur Miller, Anthony Hecht, and Alfred Dorn attesting to the need for a journal dedicated to publishing poetry in traditional forms and meters. Yeats, Frost, and Auden are cited by the editor, William Baer, as the models for the "metrical poetry" that he feels constitutes "the mainstream of English-language verse." The names published in the first 122-page, semiannual issue for 1990 are impressive, including luminaries such as A. D. Hope, Howard Nemerov, Richard Wilbur, James Merrill, Elizabeth Spires, and John Hollander. Translations of golden formalists such as Catullus, Petrarch, Horace, and Goethe are also encouraged. Famous statements of formalist critical thought are also reprinted, such as Philip Larkin's essay "The Pleasure Principle." Other essays cast poets like Walt Whitman and Ezra Pound as the enemy of the formalist tradition.

La Bête (MiamiArtwords, Inc., P. O. Box 24-8782, Coral Gables, Florida 33124) is a South Florida quarterly of poetry, fiction, artwork, and critical writing that began with the "Premier Issue" (Winter 1990/91). The editor, Gene Ray, says that the title ("The Beast") refers to the "mysterious, instinctual, irrational aspects of our human nature" which are best expressed in art and literature. The art includes numerous photographs, etchings, oil on linen and acrylics all reproduced in black-and-white. Some of these reproductions illustrate a critical article on the paintings of two Miamians, Adriano Lambe (born Buenos Aires, 1949) and Julio Antonio (born Havana, 1950). This article is by Ricardo Pau-Llosa, Miami-Dade Community College English department, a scholar of Cuban émigré art. The fiction includes an excerpt from a novel-in-progress by Hiram Pérez. The first "Poet Interview" is with Judith Berke, author of *White Morning* (Wesleyan University Press, 1989), a lucid discussion that also touches on her radio acting career (she studied with Lee Strasberg). The poetry is contributed by both students and teachers, and includes translations of Pier Paolo Pasolini (Italian) and Félix Morisseau-Leroy (Haitian Creole). The essays examine the cinema of Luis Buñuel, the concept of multiculturalism, and Peter Greenaway's "The Cook, the Thief, His Wife and Her Lover." *La Bête*, although publishing contributors from the region of South Florida, exhibits an international range of sensibilities, mixing academic insights with first appearances of independent artists and writers.

The genesis of *New Myths/MSS* (State University of New York at Binghamton, P. O. Box 6000, Binghamton, New York 13902) began with *MSS*, a magazine edited by the American novelist John Gardner (1933-1982) at Chico State College (1961-1964). A retrospective anthology of the best work from the original *MSS*, edited by John Gardner and L. M. Rosenberg, was issued by New London Press (Dallas, 1980). Gardner then resurrected *MSS* at SUNY-Binghamton in Spring 1981 just prior to his death in a motorcycle accident, 14 September 1982. *MSS* was continued by his coeditor, L. M. Rosenberg, through 1989. *MSS* then evolved into a monographic series called "MSS Paper Book," the first publication of which was a collection of poems by Milton Kessler, *The Grand Concourse* (1990). This complicated genealogy preceded the late 1990 creation of the new, awkwardly titled, semiannual *New Myths/MSS*, edited by Robert Mooney, dedicated to "publishing the best work of established writers alongside that of the best new writers and artists." Devoted to stories, poems, and essays, it is a traditional literary review including established names like David Ignatow and Joyce Carol Oates, and newcomers like Jeff Shiff.

The semiannual *Prospect Review* (Peter A. Koufos, Editor/Publisher, 557 10th Street, Apt 3, Brooklyn, New York 11215) first appeared Fall 1990. Privately funded, the review publishes only poetry and fiction. The editorial statement indicates that some of the contributors are bricklayers. Richard Burgin, the editor of the literary journal *Boulevard*, contributed a short story. The beat poet Arthur Winfield Knight contributed a poem, "The In-Laws." The style is decidedly nontraditional, with one poem merely printing the word "shish-kabab" twenty-seven times along with four printings of the numerical term "100%."

LIT: Literature, Interpretation, Theory (Gordon and Breach Science Publishers S.A., Marketing Department, P.O. Box 786 Cooper Station, New York, New York 10276) is a quarterly that publishes "theoretical and critical essays that center on literature and culture." Essays are accepted on all historical periods and from any critical school including Marxist, structuralist, formalist, semiotic, and hermeneutic. The editors, Lee A. Jacobus and Regina Barreca (University of Connecticut Department of English), also welcome studies on feminist and gender issues, and ethnic criticism. The "Preview Issue" (vol. 1, nos. 1-2) was re-

leased December 1989. This first issue includes Donald B. Gibson (Rutgers) on Toni Morrison's *The Bluest Eye* (1970), Gerhard Joseph (Lehman College and the Graduate Center of CUNY) on "Hegel, Derrida, George Eliot, and the Novel," and Alice Hall Petry (Rhode Island School of Design) on Zelda Fitzgerald. The biographical reassessment of Zelda Fitzgerald includes an excellent color plate of her painting *Ballerinas*. The March 1990 issue (vol. 1, no. 3) begins with Robert Tracy (an advisory editor of *LIT* and professor of English and Celtic Studies, University of California, Berkeley) on James Joyce's subversive attack on the English language as a promotion of Irish culture. Other essays examine Ezra Pound with the assumption that sexism is "an ingrained element of the dominant Euro-American aesthetic," translations of Ecclesiastes, the trickster in Ralph Ellison's *Invisible Man* (1952), and the preoccupation with textuality in Bram Stoker's *Dracula* (1897). The editorial board includes well-known scholars such as Sacvan Bercovitch, Mary Ann Caws, and Henry Louis Gates.

The second series of the semiannual *Literature and History* (Mrs. M. Read, King Alfred's College, English Department, Winchester, England SO22 4NR) began with volume 1, number 1 (Spring 1990) and volume 1, number 2 (Autumn 1990). It continues *Literature and History* (1975-1989) with new editorial members and financial assistance from King Alfred's College. The new editors are: John King (Ohio State University), Philip Martin (King Alfred's College), Roger Richardson (King Alfred's College), and David Underdown (Yale University). The journal's coverage extends from the fourteenth century to the twentieth century, ranging from articles on Chaucer to Paul de Man. The arrangement of the journal begins with five long interdisciplinary articles, followed by a few review articles (basically group reviews of four or five related books), and concluding with a major section of signed book reviews (nineteen in the first issue, thirty-six in the second issue). The editors are aware that *Literature and History* exhibits an "anglocentric imbalance" and welcome articles on other literatures. The subjects of the first two issues, however, are established canonical writers such as John Milton, Charles Dickens, and Virginia Woolf. A woman of the new canon, Sylvia Plath, is discussed in relation to her years at Cambridge circa 1956.

Australian and New Zealand literature is the focus of *Australian & New Zealand Studies in Canada* (University of Western Ontario, Department of English, London, Ontario, Canada N6A 3K7), a semiannual that began Spring 1989. The editor is Thomas E. Tausky (University of Western Ontario). He is assisted by an editorial board of Canadian academics. One article in *ANZSC* discusses the controversy surrounding Keri Hulme's New Zealand novel *The Bone People* (1984) and the question of minority group identification. Another piece transcribes interviews with four Australian writers originally broadcast by the Canadian Broadcasting Corporation in early 1988.

Original poetry is also included, with a selection of poems called "Such Far-Off Dominions" by Elizabeth Brewster, a Canadian poet and novelist. There is no explanation in the journal as to why a Canadian poet is being published in a specialty journal on Australia and New Zealand. The poems apparently reflect New Zealand themes. Robert Ross, the editor of *Antipodes* (a journal of Australian literature), offers "The Recurring Conflicts of Australian Literary Criticism since 1945."

Samuel Beckett
(13 April 1906 - 22 December 1989)

Andrea G. Bell
Hunter College

See also the Beckett entries in *DLB 13: British Dramatists Since World War II* and *DLB 15: British Novelists, 1930-1959*.

BOOKS: *Whoroscope* (Paris: Hours Press, 1930);
Proust (London: Chatto & Windus, 1931; New York: Grove, 1957);
More Pricks than Kicks (London: Chatto & Windus, 1934);
Echo's Bones and Other Precipitates (Paris: Europa Press, 1935);
Murphy (London: Routledge, 1938; New York: Grove, 1957); French translation by Beckett (Paris: Bordas, 1947);
Molloy (Paris: Editions de Minuit, 1951); English translation by Beckett and Patrick Bowles (Paris: Olympia Press, 1955; New York: Grove, 1955; London: Calder & Boyars, 1966);
Malone meurt (Paris: Editions de Minuit, 1951); published in English as *Malone Dies*, translation by Beckett (New York: Grove, 1956; London: Calder, 1958);
En attendant Godot (Paris: Editions de Minuit, 1952); published in English as *Waiting for Godot*, translation by Beckett (New York: Grove, 1954; London: Faber & Faber, 1956);

L'Innommable (Paris: Editions de Minuit, 1953); published in English as *The Unnamable*, translation by Beckett (New York: Grove, 1958; London: Calder & Boyars, 1975);
Watt (Paris: Olympia Press, 1953; New York: Grove, 1959; London: Calder, 1963); French translation by Beckett, Ludovic Janvier, and Agnes Janvier (Paris: Editions de Minuit, 1968);
Nouvelles et Textes pour rien (Paris: Editions de Minuit, 1955); published in English as *Stories and Texts for Nothing*, translation by Beckett (New York: Grove, 1967);
Fin de partie, suivi de Acte sans paroles [I] (Paris: Editions de Minuit, 1957); published in English as *Endgame, Followed by Act Without Words* [I], translation by Beckett (New York: Grove, 1958; London: Faber & Faber, 1958);
All That Fall (New York: Grove, 1957; London: Faber & Faber, 1957); published in French as *Tous ceux qui tombent*, translation by Beckett and Robert Pinget (Paris: Editions de Minuit, 1957);
From an Abandoned Work (London: Faber & Faber, 1958); published in French as *D'un ouvrage abandonné*, translation by Beckett and Ludovic Janvier (Paris: Editions de Minuit, 1967);

Samuel Beckett (photograph by Jerry Bauer)

Waiting for Godot, All That Fall, Endgame, From An Abandoned Work, Krapp's Last Tape, and Embers (London: Faber & Faber, 1959);

La Dernière Bande, suivi de Cendres, French versions of *Krapp's Last Tape* and *Embers*, translation by Beckett and Pierre Leyris (Paris: Editions de Minuit, 1960);

Krapp's Last Tape and Other Dramatic Pieces (New York: Grove, 1960)—includes *Krapp's Last Tape, All That Fall, Embers, Act Without Words I*, and *Act Without Words II*;

Comment c'est (Paris: Editions de Minuit, 1961); published in English as *How It Is*, translation by Beckett (New York: Grove, 1964; London: Calder, 1964);

Happy Days (New York: Grove, 1961; London: Faber & Faber, 1962); published in French as *Oh les beaux jours*, translation by Beckett (Paris: Editions de Minuit, 1963);

Poems in English (London: Calder, 1961; New York: Grove, 1963);

Play and Two Short Pieces for Radio (London: Faber & Faber, 1964)—includes *Play, Words and Music*, and *Cascando*;

Imagination morte imaginez (Paris: Editions de Minuit, 1965); published in English as *Imagination Dead Imagine*, translation by Beckett (London: Calder & Boyars, 1965);

Assez (Paris: Editions de Minuit, 1966);

Bing (Paris: Editions de Minuit, 1966);

Comedie et actes divers, French translations by Beckett (Paris: Editions de Minuit, 1966)—includes *Comédie, Va et Vient (Come and Go), Parole et Music (Words and Music), Dis Joe (Eh Joe)*, and *Acte sans paroles II (Act Without Words II)*;

Eh Joe and Other Writings (London: Faber & Faber, 1967)—includes *Eh Joe, Act Without Words II*, and *Film*;

Come and Go (London: Calder & Boyars, 1967);

No's Knife: Collected Shorter Prose 1945-1966 (London: Calder & Boyars, 1967);

Poèmes (Paris: Editions de Minuit, 1968);

Cascando and Other Short Dramatic Pieces (New York: Grove, 1969)—includes *Cascando, Words and Music, Eh Joe, Play, Come and Go*, and *Film*;

Sans (Paris: Editions de Minuit, 1969); published in English as *Lessness*, translation by Beckett (London: Calder & Boyars, 1970);

Le Dépeupleur (Paris: Editions de Minuit, 1970); published in English as *The Lost Ones*, translation by Beckett (London: Calder & Boyars, 1972; New York: Grove, 1972);

Mercier et Camier (Paris: Editions de Minuit, 1970); published in English as *Mercier and Camier*, translation by Beckett (London: Calder & Boyars, 1974; New York: Grove, 1975);

Premier amour (Paris: Editions de Minuit, 1970); published in English as *First Love*, translation by Beckett (London: Calder & Boyars, 1973);

Breath and Other Shorts (London: Faber & Faber, 1972)—includes *Breath, Come and Go, Act Without Words I, Act Without Words II*, and *From an Abandoned Work*;

Film, suivi de Souffle, translation by Beckett (Paris: Editions de Minuit, 1972);

Not I (London: Faber & Faber, 1973);

First Love and Other Shorts (New York: Grove, 1974)—includes *First Love, From an Abandoned Work, Enough, Imagination Dead Imagine, Ping, Not I*, and *Breath*;

Oh les beaux jours, suivi de Pas moi, translation by Beckett (Paris: Editions de Minuit, 1975);

I Can't Go On, I'll Go On: A Selection from Samuel Beckett's Work, edited by Richard W. Seaver (New York: Grove, 1976);

That Time (London: Faber & Faber, 1976);

Fizzles (New York: Grove, 1976);

Foirade: Fizzles, bilingual edition, with French translations by Beckett (London & New York: Petersburg/Paris: Fequet & Baudier, 1976);

Footfalls (London: Faber & Faber, 1976);

Pour finir encore et autres foirades, translation by Beckett (Paris: Editions de Minuit, 1976);

Ends and Odds (New York: Grove, 1976)—includes *Not I, That Time, Footfalls, Ghost Trio, Theatre I, Theatre II, Radio I and Radio II*;

Companie (Paris: Editions de Minuit, 1979); published in English as *Company,* translation by Beckett (New York: Grove, 1980);

Rockaby and Other Short Pieces (New York: Grove, 1981)—includes *Rockaby, Ohio Impromptu, All Strange Away,* and *A Piece of Monologue*;

Three Plays by Samuel Beckett: What Where, Catastrophe, Ohio Impromptu (New York: Grove, 1983);

Worstward Ho (New York: Grove, 1983);

Collected Poems 1930-1978 (London: John Calder, 1984);

Collected Shorter Prose (London: John Calder, 1984);

Collected Shorter Plays of Samuel Beckett (New York: Grove, 1984).

COLLECTION: *The Collected Works of Samuel Beckett,* 19 volumes (New York: Grove, 1971).

Samuel Beckett's death on 22 December 1989, at the age of eighty-three, ended the career of one of the twentieth century's most influential writers. Beckett captured in his work the terrifying forces of tyranny and brutality, the apocalyptic horror, and the profound sense of futility and despair that have characterized life in a century ravaged by two world wars. The people who populate his work live in a world stripped of meaning; they are without homes, without the promise of release or salvation, without futures, and with pasts that weigh heavily but from which they are irrevocably divorced. And yet Beckett holds out hope for humanity in his evocative portrayals of solitary survivors, who suffer mercilessly and yet somehow persevere, with their immense sadness and their sorrow; with their mordant, self-deprecating humor; and with their caustic and savage wit.

According to his own testimony, Samuel Barclay Beckett was born on Good Friday, 13 April 1906, in the Dublin district of Stillorgan. His birth certificate, however, gives 13 May 1906 as his date of birth. As Deirdre Bair points out in her biography of Beckett, *Samuel Beckett: A Biography* (1978, revised 1990), the matter of Beckett's birthdate cannot be definitively settled: since the custom in Ireland was to record births after the infant had survived the first month of life, and Beckett's birth was officially entered on 14 June, the May date seems the more plausible. Though the controversy surrounding the actual date of Beckett's birth seems insignificant (13 April is now generally accepted as the correct date, in deference to the author's version of his life), it alludes to the importance of Beckett's personal history to the quests of his fictional and dramatic antiheroes, the solitary wanderers doomed to failure from the very outset as they search for a stable, identifiable self. The uncertainty surrounding Beckett's date of birth is perfectly in keeping with the major preoccupations of his plays and fiction: the problematic question of identity and the impossible search for self. Much of the humor of Beckett's play *En attendant Godot* (1952; translated as *Waiting for Godot,* 1954), for example, derives from the inability of its central figures to establish with any certainty even the most fundamental details of their experience. Even the very fact of their existence is uncertain: "We always find something, eh Didi, to give us the impression that we exist?"

Son of William Frank "Bill" Beckett, Jr., a wealthy Protestant quantity surveyor, and Mary Jones "May" Roe, a nurse prior to her marriage, Samuel Barclay Beckett was born four years after his brother and only sibling, Frank, in the fashionable Dublin suburb of Foxrock. Cooldinragh, the family home where Beckett spent his childhood years and to which he returned for annual visits throughout his adulthood after settling permanently in Paris in 1937, was a three-story Tudor house with acres of garden, croquet lawns, and a tennis court.

In an interview with Alec Reid in 1969, Beckett described his childhood as ". . . uneventful. You might say I had a happy childhood . . . although I had little talent for happiness. My parents did everything they could to make a child happy. But I was often lonely. We were brought up like Quakers. My father did not beat me, nor did my mother run away from home." This telling, if somewhat cryptic, assessment of his childhood is marked by Beckett's elusive stance toward autobiographical revelation. The internal tensions of Beckett's claims suggest a childhood that was, in fact, far from idyllic, a notion that is reinforced by the facts of Beckett's early years and by the images of parental tyranny and childhood terror in Beckett's writing. In *Fin de partie, suivis de Acte sans paroles* [I] (1957; translated by Beckett as *Endgame, Followed by Act Without Words* [I], 1958), Beckett voices the feelings of childhood loneliness in Hamm's lines: "Then babble, babble, words, like the solitary child who turns himself into children, two, three, so as to be together, and whisper together, in the dark."

Although Bill Beckett did not beat his son, he was often away from home; Beckett's genuine feelings of love and affection for his father seem to have had ample room to flourish during Bill Beckett's frequent absences from the house. Beckett's tenderness for his father endured throughout Beckett's lifetime. For Beckett, the symbol of that tenderness was the hat his father had given him as a child, hats later becoming a recurring motif in his work.

Of the lifelong anguish Beckett suffered as a result of his troubled relationship with his mother there can be no doubt. May Beckett's mercurial temperament, deep depressions, and "thundering rages," were a constant source of tension in the Beckett household. Her mood could become dark and tempestuous without provocation or warning. Although, as Beckett claimed, his mother did not run away from home, she did, in fact, beat her son, frequently and sometimes severely. May's determination to dominate and control her son's life and Beckett's struggle to escape her tyranny began when Beckett was a young child and continued until his mother's death in 1950. The struggle found expression in Beckett's writing and gave to some of his finest work much of its savage humor and wrenching pathos. The dark humor of *Molloy* (1951), for example, derives in part form Beckett's treatment of Molloy's quest for his mother, "whom I called Mag, when I had to call her something . . . because for me, without knowing why, the letter g abolished the syllable Ma, and as it were spat on it, better than any other letter would have done. And at the same time I satisfied a deep and doubtless unacknowledged need to have a Ma, that is a mother, and to proclaim it audibly."

The impact of Beckett's childhood and adolescence on his writing can be seen in the harsh depictions of family life that emerge in his work. *Endgame* has as its center a multi-generational "family romance" played out against the backdrop of a nuclear holocaust; the tyranny and terror at the center of this and many of Beckett's other works are informed as much by Beckett's early childhood memories as by his experiences during World War II, perhaps the two most important influences on Beckett's literary development.

At the age of seventeen, in 1923, Beckett entered Trinity College, Dublin, after having attended the Portora Royal School in Northern Ireland where he distinguished himself as a fine athlete. Though somewhat withdrawn and reclusive even as an adolescent, Beckett's talent as an athlete earned him the recognition and respect of his classmates. During his third year at Trinity Beckett began to blossom intellectually, thanks in part to the influence of his professor of French, Thomas B. Rudmose-Brown. Beckett graduated from Trinity in 1927 with a B.A.; he was first in his class in modern languages. His years at Trinity changed significantly Beckett's relation to the members of his family. He had become increasingly removed from their lives, maintaining distance, separateness, and independence.

While at Trinity Beckett developed a taste for the theater of Luigi Pirandello and Sean O'Casey, his fascination with slapstick and vaudeville, and a love of the films of Laurel and Hardy, Charlie Chaplin, and the Marx Brothers. These would all become strong influences on his work. Toward the end of his time at Trinity he also exhibited an intellectual promise which earned him the respect of Rudmose-Brown, who secured for Beckett a two-year teaching appointment at the Ecole Normale Superieure in Paris, to begin in 1928, with the intention of grooming Beckett for a future position at Trinity College. At the Ecole Normale, he was first drawn into the intellectual and literary life of Paris, and most important, into an association with James Joyce, whose relationship with Beckett was crucial to his development as a writer.

While at the Ecole Normale Beckett met Thomas McGreevy, ten years Beckett's elder, who became Beckett's closest friend. A central member of the Joyce circle, it was McGreevy who introduced Beckett to Joyce. Richard Aldington, a friend of McGreevy and himself a member of the Joyce coterie, described Beckett during this time as ". . . the splendidly mad Irishman . . .

who wanted to commit suicide, a fate he nearly imposed on half the faculty of the Ecole by playing the flute—an instrument of which he was far from being a master—every night from midnight to dawn."

When Beckett met Joyce in 1928, he had already read *Ulysses* (1922), was impressed by its technique, and recognized it as an important and influential work. Beckett was in awe of Joyce; Joyce, in return, was intrigued with Beckett and recognized his artistic promise. Beckett's reverence for Joyce found expression in imitation; he adapted Joyce's habits, mannerisms, and even his style of dress. Although literary lore has it that Beckett was Joyce's paid secretary, Beckett has tried to dispel this myth: "I was never Joyce's secretary, but, like all his friends, I helped him. He was greatly handicapped because of his eyes. I did odd jobs for him, marking passages for him, or reading to him, but I never wrote any of his letters." Richard Ellman described the meetings between the two men in his *James Joyce* (1959): "Both men were prone to long silences," and their conversations were suffused with "sadness, Beckett mostly for the world, Joyce for himself."

In 1929 Beckett began working on an article which Joyce had asked him to write for *Our Examination Round His Factification for Incamination of Work in Progress* (1929), a volume edited by Sylvia Beach and assembled to respond to critics of Joyce's *Work in Progress*, the work that would become *Finnegans Wake* (1939). Beckett's essay, "Dante . . . Bruno . Vico . . Joyce," appeared first in that volume. It was also published, along with "Assumption," an early short story, in the June 1929 issue of *transition*, the influential literary journal of Eugene and Marie Jolas. Like most of the work Beckett produced during the early years of his association with Joyce, "Assumption" relies heavily on imitation of Joyce's style. It is clearly a juvenile work characterized by an almost unbearably strained syntax; it does, however, introduce many of the themes that subtly dominate Beckett's later writing—the association of birth and death, the terror of violence, the yearning for silence and death, and the simultaneous longing for and terror of sexual love. The arrogance and pretension of Beckett's essay on Joyce's *Work in Progress* is also characteristic of the earliest work of promising young writers. Yet what seems most striking about Beckett's praise for Joyce's writing is that it is expressed in terms that apply with remarkable accuracy to the work that Beckett himself produced in the years following

World War II: "Here form is content, content is form. You complain that this stuff is not written in English. It is not written at all. It is not to be read, or rather it is not to be only read. It is to be looked at or listened to. His writing is *not about something: it is that something itself*. . . . When the sense is sleep, the words go to sleep. When the sense is dance, the words dance" (Beckett's emphasis). The self-reflexivity of Joyce's work that Beckett so admires, the essential oneness of its medium and message, is the defining feature of Beckett's postwar writing.

After working in an early style imitative of Joyce, Beckett worked on developing his own voice and on what he would call "a form to accommodate the mess." Whereas Joyce was striving to make his work all-inclusive, Beckett was paring down his materials to their barest essentials. In a 1956 interview with Israel Shenker in the *New York Times*, Beckett explained his aesthetic differences with Joyce: "[Joyce is] tending toward omniscience and omnipotence as an artist, I'm working with impotence, ignorance. I don't think impotence has been exploited in the past. . . . My little exploration is that whole zone of being that has always been set aside by artists as something unusable—as something by definition incompatible with art." Still, the works of Joyce and Beckett share one defining feature: a conviction that it is the minutest particulars wherein is to be found the universal.

Throughout his literary career Beckett wrote poetry, much of it during his early years in Paris. His first separately published work was *Whoroscope*, a poem influenced by René Descartes, which was submitted for and won a contest on the subject of "time" sponsored by Nancy Cunard and her Hours Press. This led to Beckett's being commissioned to write a critical essay on the work of Proust (*Proust*, 1931), a volume which provides invaluable insight into the themes which dominate Beckett's own work—the impossibility of love, the limits of subjectivism, the deadening effects of habit, the individual's imprisonment in time, and the role of memory. Moreover, in his art Beckett adheres with remarkable consistency to the aesthetic credo he announces in *Proust*: ". . . the only possible spiritual development is in the sense of depth. The artistic tendency is not expansive, but a contraction. Art is the apotheosis of solitude . . . the only fertile research is excavatory, immersive, a descent. The artist is active, but negatively, shrinking from the world of extracir-

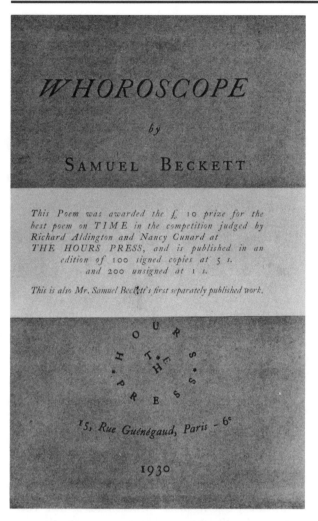

Cover for Beckett's first published work

cumferential phenomena, drawn into the core of the eddy."

After completing his fellowship at the Ecole Normale, Beckett returned to Dublin to a three-year appointment as a lecturer at Trinity College. His introspection and self-critical attitude were already strong, and were quickly being known as an essential part of his personality. An oft-told story from this time is of Beckett walking home from a cricket match with friends. All were in high spirits and one turned happily to Beckett and said: "Glorious spring weather, the trees are blooming, and our team won. It's the kind of day that makes you glad to be alive, Sam." "Well," Beckett replied, "I wouldn't go that far."

Beckett was becoming increasingly depressed, and his mental anguish was causing terrible physical pain. To numb the pain he drank excessively, often having to travel to Cooldinragh to recuperate. When there, he remained bedridden

for long periods of time, frustrated by a growing inability to write, instead immersing himself in the work of Arthur Schopenhauer, whom he later described as "one of the ones that mattered most to me." Relations between Beckett and his mother grew increasingly strained. Realizing that he was unable to control his explosive rage or the physical symptoms it caused, Beckett decided in 1934 to travel to London to enter psychoanalysis at the Tavistock Clinic. In 1935 Beckett attended a lecture at the clinic given by Carl Jung that permanently altered his perspective on his suffering and particularly on his tormented relationship with his mother. As related by Bair, during a question and answer period with the audience "Jung mentioned a ten-year-old girl who had been brought to him with what he called amazing mythological dreams. He could not tell the father what the dreams signified because he sensed they contained an uncanny premonition of her early death. Indeed, she did die a year later. 'She had never been born entirely,' Jung concluded." Jung's remark was a revelation; Beckett embraced the idea that he himself had "not been born entirely" and used it to explain some of his own deeply troubling tendencies—his obsessive need to return to his mother, his womb fixation, and his preoccupation with death and with suicide. Jung's remark itself turned up in Beckett's 1957 radio play *All That Fall*.

Most of the writing Beckett produced during the early 1930s shows him still under the influence of Joyce. His first substantial fiction was the unpublished novel, "Dream of Fair to Middling Women," which many regard as an earlier version of *More Pricks than Kicks*, a collection of short stories published in 1934. Both works show the influence of Dante on Beckett; the hero of each is named Belacqua, after Dante's Florentine lutemaker. The materials of the novel are taken directly from Beckett's life; in *More Pricks than Kicks* Beckett's emphasis is on technique, often at the expense of substance.

In 1934, while in London, Beckett began a short story which would eventually become *Murphy* (1938), a carefully crafted novel which took longer to write than any of Beckett's subsequent novels and which was rejected by forty-two publishers before Routledge agreed in 1937 to publish it. Although Murphy, as John Fletcher has claimed, is "Beckett's last citizen of this world," he is hardly a conventional hero. The novel itself is highly original and innovative, although it is the most conventional of Beckett's novels. Much of the novel takes place inside the mind of Murphy, who works in a mental institution, and whose only form of solace is to strip himself naked, strap himself to a rocking chair, and rock himself into a trance. *Murphy* is heavily influenced by the philosophical principles Beckett was exploring at the time, particularly the Cartesian principle of duality of mind and body. Much of the novel deals with Murphy's ambivalence about his relationship with Celia Kelly, a streetwalker with whom he is living: "The part of him that he hated craved for Celia, the part that he loved shrivelled up at the thought of her." In *Murphy* Beckett finally produces work independent from Joyce's influence. Its style is much simpler and more refined than that of any of his previous works. Thus it occupies an important place in Beckett's development as a writer, marking the transition from a prose style based on imitation of Joyce to the distilled style that he would perfect in the interior monologues of his postwar fiction.

In 1937 Beckett made the decision to settle permanently in Paris. On 7 January 1938 Beckett was stabbed in the chest on a Paris street by a pimp whom he had refused to give money. While in the hospital Beckett was visited by a piano student, Suzanne Descheuvaux-Dumesnil, who became his lifetime companion, and, in 1961, after they had lived together for twenty-three years, his wife. Eight years older than Beckett, Suzanne had a quiet strength that was a source of great comfort for him. Both Suzanne and Beckett were intensely private individuals, she even more than he. Their relationship seemed based in part on a mutual respect for privacy and, for Suzanne, on a single-minded devotion to Beckett's artistic career. Without Suzanne's tenaciousness and the time and energy she devoted to her Beckett's career, it is likely that some of Beckett's books would never have been published.

Beckett and Suzanne had little time to grow accustomed to a life together in Paris. When the Germans invaded Poland in September 1939 Beckett was in Ireland visiting his mother. He returned to Paris, claiming years later that "I preferred France during war to Ireland at peace." Soon after the war began, Beckett and Suzanne were working underground for a French Resistance group. "I was so outraged by the Nazis," Beckett later claimed, "particularly by their treatment of the Jews, that I could not remain inactive." Their lives in constant danger and turmoil,

Beckett and Suzanne survived terrifying narrow escapes from the Nazis. Eventually the Resistance group was broken by the Nazis, and Beckett and Suzanne were forced to become vagabonds, wandering the French countryside for months to escape capture, until they came to the French village of Rousillon where they remained in hiding for two-and-a-half years. For Beckett, life at Rousillon was psychologically devastating. While there, he wrote the novel *Watt* to ward off psychic dissolution. With scenes taken directly from his life, the novel's schizophrenic quality bespeaks of Beckett's anguished mental state. After the end of the war, Beckett was awarded the Croix de Guerre with a gold star and was given a citation signed by Charles de Gaulle in recognition of his resistance activities.

On a visit to Dublin in 1945 Beckett had a vision that resulted in his tremendous productivity over the next few years. Wildly drunk, during a winter storm, Beckett found himself by the sea at the end of a jetty when it struck him that "the dark that he had struggled to keep under" was, in fact, the source of his creative power. Beckett included part of this vision in his 1959 play *Krapp's Last Tape*. During the years following the war Beckett's productivity reached its height, resulting in the work which earned him the reputation as one of the century's finest writers. The themes treated in Beckett's postwar writing did not differ significantly from those which had always concerned him. Yet the war brought a dramatic shift in Beckett's handling of these materials. The war seems to have provided a validation that the demons that had haunted him throughout the whole of his life were real, that the terror of violence and tyranny which had been instilled in Beckett during his childhood was an appropriate response to the capacity for brutality and destruction which the war had proven to be unmistakably human.

After the war Beckett began writing exclusively in French, then translating his work into English. He chose to write in French, he said, "parce qu'en francais c'est plus facile d'ecrire sans style [because in French it is easier to write without style]." From the mid 1940s to the early 1950s Beckett wrote the novel *Mercier et Camier*, (1970), whose vaudevillian couple are often regarded as precursors of *En attendant Godot*'s Vladimir and Estragon; the (still unpublished) play, "Eleutheria"; and the plays *Godot* and *Fin de partie*. He also wrote the short stories "The Expelled," "The Calmative," and "First Love," the protagonists of which are solitary figures existing on the fringes of a society from which they have been expelled. The voices of the stories are marked by an ironic, self-deprecating humor and by a keen and savage wit that also characterize the voices in each of Beckett's trilogy of novels, *Molloy* (1951), *Malone meurt* (1951; translated by Beckett as *Malone Dies*, 1956) and *L'Innommable* (1953; translated by Beckett as *The Unnameable*, 1958), all written in the late 1940s.

Molloy, the first novel of the trilogy, is divided into two sections. Part 1 concerns Molloy, who is in his mother's bed, from where he writes the narrative which comprises all but the section's first paragraph. That narrative is the story of Molloy's mishaps and "adventures" as he wanders the countryside in search of his mother. Most of the novel's first part is an exploration of the mind of Molloy, a familiar Beckettian antihero, an outcast without a home, bound to the earth, a stranger to the social world with which his periodic conflicts are occasions for much of the laughter the novel generates. Although Molloy's story is suffused with pain and sadness, it is quite often hilarious. The second half of *Molloy* concerns Jacques Moran, a bourgeois, hypocritical, church-going tyrant of a father, and his son. Moran has been sent on a mission, for reasons unknown, to find Molloy. The tension of the novel is created by the relationship between its two parts and by the mysterious transformation and gradual dissolution of Moran when in "Molloy Country." *Molloy* has been widely acknowledged as a brilliant novel, revolutionary in form as well as in content. The second and third of Beckett's trilogy of novels trace the progressive dissolution of their solitary narrators until one is left in *L'Innommable* with a dying voice, "rotting with solitude and neglect," crying out in anguish and terror. Beckett would say of the fiction he wrote in the years following the war that he "was doomed to spend the rest of my days digging up the detritus of my life and vomiting it out over and over again."

Although Beckett considered his prose his important work, it is his drama for which he is more widely known. Beckett claimed in 1972 that he "turned to writing drama to relieve myself of the awful depression that the prose led me into. . . . Life at the time was too demanding, too terrible, and I thought theater would be a diversion." *En attendant Godot* in particular was begun "as a relaxation, to get away from the awful prose I was writing at the time," as an escape

from "the wildness and rulelessness of the novels." Although Beckett considered *Godot* a "bad play," it is the work which launched him into the public arena. In the first review of the French premiere of the play in 1953, Beckett was hailed as "one of the world's best playwrights." The play's greatness, however, was not universally acknowledged. Its opening in London in 1955 was met with hostility and outrage until London's two leading theater critics, Kenneth Tynan and Harold Hobson, reversed public opinion, the latter claiming that the play would "securely lodge in a corner of your mind for as long as you live." The American premiere in 1956 at the Coconut Grove Playhouse in Miami was a complete disaster. Misguidedly billed as "the laugh sensation of two continents," most of the audience left soon after the curtain had risen and lined up at the box office early the next morning demanding refunds. It was not until it opened in New York on Broadway that *Godot*'s success in America was assured.

En attendant Godot is now regarded as a landmark of contemporary theater, revolutionary in its impact on dramatic form and content. It has been translated into twenty languages and performed in more than forty-two countries throughout the world. A play that had baffled and outraged its early audiences is now recognized as one of this century's most evocative representations of the plight of humanity in the modern age.

In *En attendant Godot*, Beckett's vision of the inhabitant of the postwar world is that of a solitary wanderer, adrift in a world without meaning, divorced from others and from oneself, a stranger in a once familiar landscape. Beckett was not the only postwar writer to explore the sense of alienation and anguish that defined the postwar experience. The works of the French existentialists Jean-Paul Sartre and Albert Camus treated similar themes. Yet, as Martin Esslin has pointed out in *The Theater of the Absurd* (1969), unlike Sartre and Camus, Beckett treated the "sense of metaphysical anguish at the absurdity of the human condition" not in rational, logical forms of discourse, "but by the open abandonment of rational devices and discursive thought." The most striking feature of *En attendant Godot* is its self-reflexivity, the essential oneness of its medium and message, the effects and implications of which are quite profound. Like Vladimir and Estragon, the play's main characters, the audience is confronted with a world (the stage) which

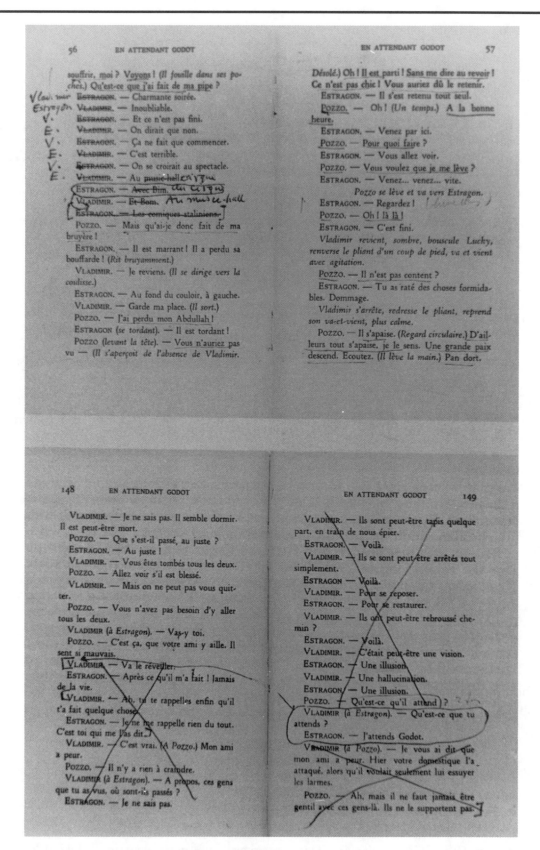

Pages from Beckett's working rehearsal copy for the first performance of En Attendant Godot *in Paris, 1953. Many of Beckett's revi-sions, some shown here, were incorporated into the second published edition of the play, which is the standard text (Sotheby's, 13 December 1990)*

it cannot understand; like Vladimir and Estragon, the audience attempts to endow with significance a world from which it feels divorced and distant, a world in which it is constantly reminded of its ignorance, impotence, and insignificance. As Vladimir and Estragon devise games to play to pass the time while they wait in vain for the arrival of Godot, the audience realizes that it is watching itself conduct the tedious business of living. When language fails them and habit breaks down, Vladimir and Estragon have only each other to help them confront the true horror of their existence. At such moments they enter into the "perilous zones" Beckett described in *Proust*, ". . . dangerous, precarious, painful, mysterious and fertile, when for a moment the boredom of living is replaced by the suffering of being."

In the 1950s and 1960s Beckett continued to write primarily in French. Most of the prose works from this period were short fragments, including *Nouvelles et Textes pour rien* (1955; translated by Beckett as *Stories and Texts for Nothing*, 1967) which contains some of Beckett's most piercing and evocative lines and which reads more like prose poems than narratives. Among the dramatic works he wrote during these years were the radio plays *All That Fall* (1957), *Embers* (1959), *Words and Music* (1964), and *Cascando* (1964); *Eh Joe* (1966), a play for television; and the stage plays *Krapp's Last Tape* (1959) and *Happy Days* (1961). In 1964 Beckett made his only visit to the United States when he came to New York for the making of *Film*, his movie starring Buster Keaton. Beckett proved himself a master in each medium for which he wrote; his work for radio, film, and television expanded the boundaries of those mediums as radically as his stage plays continued to redefine the limits of that genre.

His most acclaimed stage play of the period is *Krapp's Last Tape*, the main character of which is the emotionally and physically constipated Krapp, an embittered and drunken old man who sits before us on stage with his bananas and his tape recorder. When the play opens, Krapp is about to embark on a "new retrospective," an annual birthday recording of the previous year's events. First, however, he replays recordings from two earlier years, one of himself at age thirty-nine, the other at approximately twenty-nine. As Krapp reacts with contempt and bitter regret to these earlier versions of himself, the impression is one of immense sadness and waste. The play shows that Krapp is doomed to failure in his at-

tempt to piece together a coherent identity from the fragmentary voices that make up his life.

Winnie, the main character in *Happy Days*, is buried up to her waist in a mound of dirt when the play opens and up to her neck by act 2. Winnie talks almost unceasingly to avoid confronting the horror of her condition. Her husband Willie is also on stage; his presence, however unresponsive to her he may be, convinces Winnie that she is alive because, she reasons, he is listening to her. The play is a brilliant rendering of a concept that recurs throughout Beckett's work: Esse est percepi—To be is to be perceived.

Among the works Beckett wrote during the 1970s was the harrowing play, *Not I* (1973), featuring a disembodied, heavily lipsticked mouth spewing forth an uncontrolled torrent of words after having been silenced for the first sixty years of its existence. The role of mouth was originally played by Billie Whitelaw, for whom Beckett wrote many of his most important female roles. Whitelaw also played the lead in *Rockaby* (1981), which concerns an old woman who rocks herself to death.

Beckett received numerous awards during his lifetime, including in 1959 an honorary doctorate of letters from Trinity College. In 1961, the year of his marriage to Suzanne, Beckett received word that he had been named to share the annual Prix International des Editeurs with Jorge Luis Borges. And on 23 October 1969 word came that the Swedish Academy had awarded Beckett the 1969 Nobel Prize for Literature for "a body of work that, in new forms of fiction and the theater, has transmuted the destitution of modern man into his exaltation." Beckett accepted the award graciously, though he regarded as absurd the choice of himself as recipient, claiming that the award was intended to go to elevating work. "Mine is hardly elevating," he said.

In keeping with the vision which prompted him to trust the forces of darkness within himself as the source of his creative inspiration, Beckett transformed his most deeply felt experiences into art. In so doing he touched something very profound in readers and audiences throughout the world. For the anguished voices of Beckett's fiction and drama have come to be recognized as our voices; we have come to see in the nightmarish images and desolate Beckettian landscapes reflections of our own psychic geography.

A year prior to his death, Beckett was moved to a nursing home after falling in his apartment. When Suzanne died on 17 July 1989, Beck-

1.4

MOUTH:
(contd)

... realized ... words were coming ... words were coming ... a voice she did not recognize ... at first ... so long since it had sounded ... then finally had to admit ... could be none other ... than her own ... certain vowel sounds ... she had never heard ... elsewhere ... so that people would stare ... the rare occasions ... once or twice a year ... always winter some strange reason ... stare at her uncomprehending ... and now this stream ... steady stream ... she who had never ... on the contrary ... practically speechless ... all her days ... how she survived! ... even shopping ... busy shopping centre ... supermart ... just handed in the list ... with the bag ... old black shopping bag ... then stood there waiting ... any length of time ... middle of the throng ... motionless ... staring into space ... mouth half open as usual ... till it was back in her hand ... the bag back in her hand ... then pay and go ... not as much as goodbye ... how she survived! ... and now this stream ... not catching the half of it ... not the quarter ... no idea ... what she was saying ... imagine! ... no idea what she was saying ... till she began trying to ... delude herself ... it was not hers at all ... not her voice at all ... and would have no doubt ... vital she should ... was on the point ... after long efforts ... when suddenly she felt ... gradually the felt ... her lips moving ... imagine! ... her lips moving! ... as of course till then she had not ... and not alone the lips ... the cheeks ... the jaws ... the whole face ... all those - ... what? ... the tongue? ... yes ... the tongue in the mouth ... all those contortions without which ... no speech possible ... and yet in the ordinary way ... not felt at all ... so intent one is ... on what one is saying ... the whole being ... hanging on its words ... so that not only she had ... had she ... not only had she ... to give up ... admit hers alone ... her voice alone ... but this other awful thought ... sudden flash ... oh long after ... even more awful if possible ... that feeling was coming back ... feeling was coming back! ... starting at the top ... then working down ... the whole machine ... but no ... spared that ... the mouth alone ... so far ... ha! ... so far ... then thinking ... oh long after ... sudden flash ... it can't go on ... all this ... all that ... steady stream ... straining to hear ... make something of it ... and her own thoughts ... make something of them ... all - ... What? ... the buzzing?

Page from Beckett's proofs, with corrections of Not I *(1973). Beckett made significant corrections, revisions, and deletions at the proof stage (*No Symbols Where None Intended, *1984)*

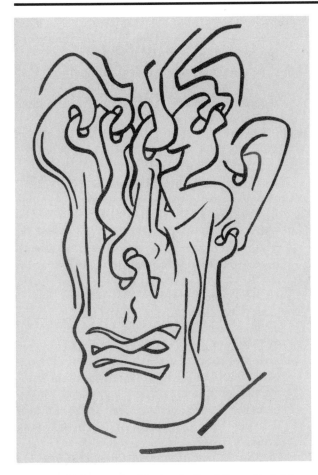

Pen and ink portrait of Beckett by Sorel Etrog (Sotheby's, 13 December 1990)

ett left the nursing home to attend her funeral. He lived his last year in a sparsely furnished room with a television, on which he watched tennis and soccer. He kept a few books, including his boyhood copy of Dante's *Divine Comedy* in Italian. Beckett's last work to be published in his lifetime was a short prose piece, "Stirrings Still," a meditation on aging. Beckett often insisted that "I couldn't have done it otherwise. Gone on, I mean. I could not have gone through the awful wretched mess of life without having left a stain upon the silence." Throughout his life Beckett vigorously maintained that his life was "without interest," that "nothing matters but the writing. There has been nothing else worthwhile." Even when he was convinced that there was "nothing to express, nothing with which to express, no power to express, [and] no desire to express," Beckett was compelled to write by "an obligation to express," and for that his readers and audiences are deeply indebted.

Bibliography:

Robin J. Davis, *Samuel Beckett; Checklist and Index of his Published Works, 1967-1976* (Stirling: The Compiler, 1979).

Biography:

Deirdre Bair, *Samuel Beckett: A Biography* (New York: Harcourt Brace Jovanovich, 1978; revised edition, New York: Summit, 1990).

References:

Ḥ. Porter Abbott, *The Fiction of Samuel Beckett: Form and Effect* (Berkeley; University of California Press, 1973);

James Acheson and Kateryna Arthur, eds. *Beckett's Later Fiction and Drama: Texts for Company* (New York: St. Martin's, 1987);

Alfred Alvarez, *Samuel Beckett* (New York: Viking, 1973);

Cathleen Culotta Andonian, *Samuel Beckett: A Reference Guide* (Boston: G. K. Hall, 1989);

Morris Beja, S. E. Gontarski, and Pierre Astier, eds. *Samuel Beckett: Humanistic Perspectives* (Columbus: Ohio State University Press, 1982);

Linda Ben-Zvi, *Samuel Beckett* (Boston: Twayne, 1986);

Harold Bloom, ed. *Samuel Beckett: Modern Critical Views* (New York: Chelsea, 1985);

Enoch Brater, ed. *Beckett at 80/Beckett in Context* (New York: Oxford University Press, 1986);

Brater, *Beyond Minimalism: Beckett's Late Style in the Theater* (New York: Oxford University Press, 1987);

Susan D. Brienza, *Samuel Beckett's New Worlds: Styles of Metafiction* (Norman: University of Oklahoma Press, 1987);

John Calder, ed., *As No Other Dare Fail: For Samuel Beckett on His 80th Birthday by His Friends and Admirers* (London: Calder, 1976);

Calder, ed. *Beckett at Sixty: A Festschrift* (London: Calder, 1976);

Bell Gale Chvigny, ed. *Twentieth Century Interpretations of Endgame: A Collection of Critical Essays* (Englewood Cliffs, N.J.: Prentice-Hall, 1969);

Richard N. Coe, *Samuel Beckett* (New York: Grove Press, 1970);

Ruby Cohn, *Back to Beckett* (Princeton: Princeton University Press, 1973);

Cohn, "A Checklist of Beckett Criticism," *Perspective*, 11 (Autumn 1959), 193-196;

Cohn, *Samuel Beckett: The Comic Gamut* (New Brunswick, N.J.: Rutgers University Press, 1962);

Cohn, ed., *Samuel Beckett: A Collection of Critical Essays* (New York: McGraw-Hill, 1975);

Cohn, ed., *Waiting for Godot: A Casebook* (London: Macmillan, 1987);

Steven Connor, *Samuel Beckett: Repetition, Theory, and Text* (London: Blackwell, 1988);

Thomas J. Cousineau, *Waiting for Godot: Form in Movement* (Boston: Twayne, 1990);

Colin Duckworth, *Angels of Darkness: Dramatic Effect in Samuel Beckett With Special Reference to Eugene Ionesco* (New York: Barnes and Noble, 1972);

Martin Esslin, *The Theater of the Absurd*, revised edition (New York: Doubleday, 1969);

Esslin, ed., *Samuel Beckett: A Collection of Critical Essays* (Englewood Cliffs, N.J.: Prentice-Hall, 1969);

Raymond Federman, *Journey to Chaos: Samuel Beckett's Early Fiction* (Berkeley: University of California Press, 1965);

Federman and John Fletcher, *Samuel Beckett: His Works and His Critics* (Berkeley: University of California Press, 1970);

Brian Finney, *Since 'How It Is': A Study of Samuel Beckett's Later Fiction* (London: Covent Gardens, 1970);

John Fletcher, *The Novels of Samuel Beckett*, second edition (New York: Barnes and Noble Press, 1970);

Fletcher and Beryl S. Fletcher, *A Student's Guide to the Plays of Samuel Beckett*, revised edition (London: Faber and Faber, 1985);

Alan Warren Friedman, Charles Rossman, and Dina Sherzer, eds. *Beckett Translating/Translating Beckett* (University Park: Penn State University Press, 1987);

Melvin J. Friedman, ed., *Samuel Beckett Now: Critical Approaches to His Novels, Poetry, and Plays* (Chicago: University of Chicago Press, 1970);

S. E. Gontarski, *The Intent of Undoing in Samuel Beckett's Dramatic Texts* (Bloomington: Indiana University Press, 1985);

Gontarski, ed., *On Beckett: Essays and Criticism* (New York: Grove Press, 1986);

Lawrence Graver and Raymond Federman, eds., *Samuel Beckett: The Critical Heritage* (London and Boston: Routledge, 1979);

Ihab Hassan, *The Literature of Silence: Henry Miller and Samuel Beckett* (New York: Knopf, 1967);

David Hesla, *The Shape of Chaos: An Interpretation of the Art of Samuel Beckett* (Minneapolis: University of Minnesota Press, 1971);

Frederick J. Hoffman, *Samuel Beckett: The Language of Self* (Carbondale: University of Southern Illinois Press, 1962);

Sighle Kennedy, *Murphy's Bed: A Study of Real Sources and Surreal Associations in Samuel Beckett's First Novel* (Lewisberg, Pa.: Bucknell University Press, 1971);

Hugh Kenner, *A Reader's Guide to Samuel Beckett* (New York: Farrar, 1973);

Kenner, *Samuel Beckett: A Critical Study* (Berkeley: University of California Press, 1968);

Kenner, *The Stoic Comedians: Flaubert, Joyce, and Beckett* (Boston: Beacon, 1962);

James Knowlson and John Pilling, *Frescoes of the Skull: The Later Prose and Drama of Samuel Beckett* (New York: Grove Press, 1979);

Charles R. Lyons, *Samuel Beckett* (New York: Grove Press, 1984);

Vivien Mercier, *Beckett/Beckett: The Truth of Contradiction* (New York: Oxford University Press, 1977);

Edouard Morot-Sir, Howard Harper, and Dougald McMillan III, eds., North Carolina Studies in the Romance Languages and Literatures 5, *Samuel Beckett: The Art of Rhetoric* (Chapel Hill: University of North Carolina Press, 1976);

Kristen Morrison, *Canters and Chronicles: The Use of Narrative in the Plays of Samuel Beckett and Harold Pinter* (Chicago: University of Chicago Press, 1983);

J. D. O'Hara, ed., *Twentieth Century Views of Molloy, Malone Dies, and The Unnamable* (Englewood Cliffs, N.J.: Prentice-Hall, 1980);

John Pilling, *Samuel Beckett* (London: Routledge, 1976);

Rubin Rabinovitz, *The Development of Samuel Beckett's Fiction* (Urbana: University of Illinois Press, 1984);

Alan Schneider, *Entrances: An American Director's Journey* (New York: Viking, 1986);

Nathan A. Scott, Jr., *Samuel Beckett* (Hewlett, New York: Hillary House, 1965);

Bennett Simon, *Tragic Drama and the Family: Psychoanalytic Studies from Aeschylus to Beckett* (New Haven: Yale University Press, 1968);

Bert O. States, *The Shape of Paradox: An Essay on Waiting for Godot* (Berkeley: University of California Press, 1978);

James T. F. Tanner and J. Don Vann *Samuel Beckett: A Checklist of Criticism* (Kent, Ohio: Kent State University Press, 1969);

Eugene Webb, *The Plays of Samuel Beckett* (Seattle: University of Washington Press, 1972);

Katherine Worth, *Revolutions in Modern English Drama* (London: G. Bell, 1972);

Worth, ed., *Beckett the Shape Changer: A Symposium* (London: Routledge, 1975).

Papers:

Portions of Beckett's papers are housed in the Harry A. Ransom Humanities Research Center, University of Texas at Austin; Baker Library of Dartmouth College; Ohio State University Libraries, Columbus; the Beineke Library of Yale University; in private collections in the United States and Canada. In England, there is a Samuel Beckett Archive at the University of Reading. A small number of partial manuscripts are in Trinity College, Dublin.

Lawrence Durrell
(27 February 1912 - 7 November 1990)

Carol Peirce
University of Baltimore

See also the Durrell entries in *DLB 15: British Novelists, 1930-1959* and *DLB 27: Poets of Great Britain and Ireland, 1945-1960.*

BOOKS: *Pied Piper Of Lovers* (London: Cassell, 1935);

Panic Spring: A Romance, as Charles Norden (London: Faber & Faber, 1937);

The Black Book: An Agon (Paris: The Obelisk Press, 1938; New York: Dutton, 1960);

A Private Country (London: Faber & Faber, 1943);

Prospero's Cell: A Guide to the Landscape and Manners of the Island of Corcyra (London: Faber & Faber, 1945); republished with *Reflections on a Marine Venus* (New York: Dutton, 1960);

Cities, Plains and People (London: Faber & Faber, 1946);

Cefalû: A Novel (London: Editions Poetry London, 1947); republished as *The Dark Labyrinth* (London: Ace, 1957; New York: Dutton, 1962);

On Seeming To Presume (London: Faber & Faber, 1948);

Sappho: A Play in Verse (London: Faber & Faber, 1950; New York: Dutton, 1958);

Key to Modern Poetry (London: Peter Nevill, 1952);

Reflections on a Marine Venus: A Companion to the Landscape of Rhodes (London: Faber & Faber, 1953); republished with *Prospero's Cell* (New York: Dutton, 1960);

The Tree of Idleness And Other Poems (London: Faber & Faber, 1955);

Selected Poems (London: Faber & Faber, 1956; New York: Grove, 1956);

Bitter Lemons (London: Faber & Faber, 1957; New York: Dutton, 1958);

Esprit De Corps: Sketches from Diplomatic Life (London: Faber & Faber, 1957; New York: Dutton, 1968);

Justine: A Novel (London: Faber & Faber, 1957; New York: Dutton, 1957);

White Eagles Over Serbia (London: Faber & Faber, 1957; New York: Criterion, 1957);

Balthazar: A Novel (London: Faber & Faber, 1958; New York: Dutton, 1958);

Mountolive: A Novel (London: Faber & Faber, 1958; New York: Dutton, 1958);

Stiff Upper Lip: Life Among the Diplomats (London: Faber & Faber, 1958; New York: Dutton, 1961);

Art and Outrage: A Correspondence about Henry Miller between Alfred Perlès and Lawrence Durrell (London: Putnam, 1959; New York: Dutton, 1961);

Clea: A Novel (London: Faber & Faber, 1960; New York: Dutton, 1960);

Collected Poems (London: Faber & Faber, 1960);

The Poetry of Lawrence Durrell (New York: Dutton, 1962);

Lawrence Durrell

The Alexandria Quartet: Justine, Balthazar, Mount-olive, Clea (London: Faber & Faber, 1962; New York: Dutton, 1962);

Lawrence Durrell and Henry Miller: A Private Correspondence, edited by George Wickes (New York: Dutton, 1963; London: Faber & Faber, 1963);

An Irish Faustus: A Morality in Nine Scenes (London: Faber & Faber, 1963; New York: Dutton, 1964);

Acte: A Play (London: Faber & Faber, 1964; New York: Dutton, 1965);

Sauve Qui Peut (London: Faber & Faber, 1966; New York: Dutton, 1967);

The Ikons and Other Poems (London: Faber & Faber, 1966; New York: Dutton, 1967);

Tunc: A Novel (London: Faber & Faber, 1968; New York: Dutton, 1968);

Spirit of Place: Letters and Essays on Travel, edited by Alan G. Thomas (London: Faber & Faber, 1969; New York: Dutton, 1969);

Nunquam: A Novel (London: Faber & Faber, 1970; New York: Dutton, 1970);

Le Grand Suppositoire: Entretiens Avec Marc Alyn (Paris: Pierre Belfond, 1972); translated by Francine Barker as *The Big Supposer: A Dialogue with Marc Alyn* (London: Abelard-Schuman, 1973; New York: Grove, 1975);

Vega and Other Poems (London: Faber & Faber, 1973; Woodstock, N.Y.: The Overlook Press, 1973);

The Revolt of Aphrodite (London: Faber & Faber, 1974);

Monsieur, or the Prince of Darkness (London: Faber & Faber, 1974; New York: Viking, 1975);

The Best of Antrobus (London: Faber & Faber, 1974);

Sicilian Carousel (London: Faber & Faber, 1977; New York: Viking, 1977);

The Greek Islands (London: Faber & Faber, 1978);

Livia, or Buried Alive (London: Faber & Faber, 1978; New York: Viking, 1979);

Collected Poems, 1931-1974, edited by James A. Brigham (London: Faber & Faber, 1980; New York: Viking, 1980);

A Smile In The Mind's Eye (London: Wildwood House, 1980; New York: Universe, 1982);

Literary Lifelines: The Richard Aldington-Lawrence Durrell Correspondence, edited by Ian S. MacNiven and Harry T. Moore (London: Faber & Faber, 1981; New York: Viking, 1981);

Constance, or Solitary Practices (London: Faber & Faber, 1982; New York: Viking, 1982);

Sebastian, or Ruling Passions (London: Faber & Faber, 1983; New York: Viking, 1983);

Quinx, or The Ripper's Tale (London: Faber & Faber, 1985; New York: Viking, 1985);

Antrobus Complete (London: Faber & Faber, 1985);

The Durrell-Miller Letters, 1935-80, edited by Ian S. MacNiven (London: Faber & Faber, 1988; New York: New Directions, 1988);

Lawrence Durrell: Letters to Jean Fanchette, 1958-1963 (Paris: Two Cities, 1988);

Caesar's Vast Ghost: Aspects of Provence (London: Faber & Faber, 1990).

So now all time is winding down to die
In soft lampoons of earthly grace set free.
Caesar's Vast Ghost (1990)

In *The Alexandria Quartet* (1962) Lawrence Durrell writes of the death of the great novelist, Pursewarden: "we talked of him like people anxious to capture and fix the human memory before it quite shaded into the growing myth." So one might strive to catch the essence of Durrell himself, now that he has died, before he, too, moves into myth.

In a way Durrell had already in life become a legend, living mostly in worlds apart from England—India, Greece, Egypt, and southern France—weaving his brilliant tapestry of language and imagination. "There is a point where sunlight and inner light meet," he said to Marc Alyn in 1972 in one of the interviews of *Le Grand Suppositoire* (1972; translated by Francine Barker as *The Big Supposer*, 1973). He was speaking of Greece, but the phrase describes him too, with his outer laughter and warmth and his inner intellect and sadness. Alyn, describing him, says, "I struggled hard not to yield to the fascination—a very real fascination—that this extraordinary man exerts over all who come near him." In an obituary in *The Independent* David Gascoyne writes: "he never allowed fame and success to affect his spontaneously generous and questing disposition.... Among his friends and all who knew him, Larry Durrell's loyalty and generosity must long have been legendary." Gascoyne adds, however, "though his was probably one of the most sophisticated intelligences of his generation, he was from the start concerned above all with the spiritual condition of nihilistically-inclined twentieth-century man." These poles of sensuality and intellect, described in the *Quartet* as elemental to the syncretism of Alexandria, characterized Durrell himself.

If one were to have visited Durrell sometime in the past ten years in his old manor house in Sommières, one would undoubtedly have found him on his closed sun porch, windowed partly with colored glass, either typing at his workplace at one end of the room, drinking wine at his oil-clothed table bright with flowers at the other, or comfortably practicing yoga on the floor somewhere in between. Books piled high, as well as letters and photographs from all over the world, would be neatly stacked about, while on the wall his own paintings gleamed. Just to the side from the small kitchen, redolent with local herbs and exotic spices, if one were lucky, would later come a feast prepared by Larry himself of gingered chicken, fresh salad, and a bottle of Provence wine. And then talk, witty and wise, into the night.

This is the world to which he invited prospective renters for August 1976, who called the

Dust jacket for Durrell's 1960 novel, the final volume in The Alexandria Quartet

phone number in the *Herald Tribune*: "Madam, you must come then, for the plums will be falling into the pool, the swallows will be darting through the garden, and the white owls will hoot from the stone tower late into the night." It was a magical month.

Durrell came to the United States in 1986 at the invitation of Pennsylvania State University to speak at the International Durrell Conference. Professing amazement that such a conference should exist, he nevertheless came. And he attended every session, listened to every paper, complimented many of the speakers, especially the young, and talked at length genuinely and generously about his work. The following week in New York it was with the greatest reluctance that he was persuaded to attend a glittering function in his honor hosted by his publishers.

Mary Mollo, an old and dear friend, recalls in *Twentieth-Century Literature* a 1946 meeting: "We faced each other—the suntanned little blond man, the dark slim shy girl—a long look. I felt I was drowning in the blueness of the bluest of eyes. They sparkled, those eyes, like sunshine on the Aegean; they were deep, they were humourous, they held laughter and tears, they were piercing, friendly, and altogether compelling. 'The blueness of the old man' he might have written later. The 'old man' was thirty-four but seemed a lot younger."

And Henry Miller's recollection of Larry in the 1930s, collected in *The World of Lawrence Durrell* (1962), concurs: "*Always merry and bright!* Always coming toward you with countenance a-gleam, the *heraldic* (his favorite word then) gleam of the blazoned escutcheon. The golden boy. Or a water sprite. Anyway youth incarnate."

Joie de vivre was certainly his; yet, as with the palimpsest that he used to describe his *Quartet*, layer on layer lay beneath. He was both a romantic and a modern, who in his later works advanced into the postmodern, seeking new forms, breaking old ones, moving in his writing from his first love, poetry, to work in many genres. He became famous for his novels, his volumes of travel or evocations of "place," and his poetry; but he also wrote popular humorous stories, poetic plays, a critical book, many articles, and volumes of correspondence.

A truly professional "man of letters," a consummate stylist, he was often seen by the British as a romantic adventurer, an expatriate, an exotic inhabitant of strange places, who had somehow almost betrayed his "homeland." But to Durrell, England was never really home except through its literary legacy. He went to school and came of age in England; but he lived his last thirty years in France, his young manhood and middle years in Greece and the eastern Mediterranean, and his childhood in India. As he grew older, though he never returned, his realization of his heritage from India became more and more clear and poignant.

Durrell said in his talk at Pennsylvania State University, "I was born, as you know, in India, and I lived there until I was eleven." He added, reflecting, "I had not been at all conscious, being so British, that India had rubbed off on me at all, until I became about fifty years old." But it had. Though his father, Lawrence Samuel Durrell, was British and his mother, born Louisa Florence Dixie, was Irish, neither had been to England. Indeed, speaking the varied languages, they considered themselves truly "Indian." Larry's own first language was Hindi. Since his father was a civil engineer, helping to build the growing railway system, they lived throughout India. Durrell described his background in his Centre Pompidou lecture, "From the Elephant's

Back": "One part of me has remained a part of the jungle, ever mindful of the various small initiations which an Indian childhood imposes. I had seen the Rope Trick when I was ten, and distinctly felt the hypnotic power of the conjuror over us as we sat round him in a circle. I have been followed from tree-top to tree-top by sportive monkeys. . . . I have seen the peak of Everest from the foot of my bed." In a poem written in the 1970s, "Last Heard Of," he remembers the river ". . . black Brahmaputra / Where I was born and never went back again / To stars printed in shining tar."

His whole family enjoyed reading, literature, and the current of ideas. He very early grew to love Kipling's *Kim* (1901), "the only great poem," of "that strange world." Although they were Protestant, he went to a Jesuit school; but he really lived closest to the Buddhist world, practiced yoga as a child, and vividly remembered "all that smiling silence where the lamas walked": "Often in my dreams I hear the squeak of their little prayer wheels."

Visiting an uncle, he learned to ride Sadu, a young elephant, and longed for one of his own. At the same time, and from the age of eight, he had been writing poetry and "had decided early on to become a poet." His father thought both aims were fine as dreams but was absolutely convinced that he should attend school in England and go on to Oxford, returning to a top civil position in India. His mother thought he was too young to leave home. But his father prevailed. For Christmas he asked for an elephant and a typewriter. The elephant he never achieved, but he received the typewriter and a complete collection of Shakespeare. Thus at eleven he left for England, or "Pudding Island," as he called it. Although he excelled at sports and got on at school, the shock of the change was enormous. "The juxtaposition of the two types of consciousness was extraordinary and created, I think, an ambivalence of vision which was to both help and hinder me as a writer," he said in the Pompidou lecture.

Durrell failed his examinations for university several times. In retrospect he tied this to his love of his mother and India and to a determination not to accede to the "constricted world" of English values. In fact, he told Alyn that when he was seriously beginning to write and to love D. H. Lawrence, he was struck by one of Lawrence's essays on how England treated its writers:

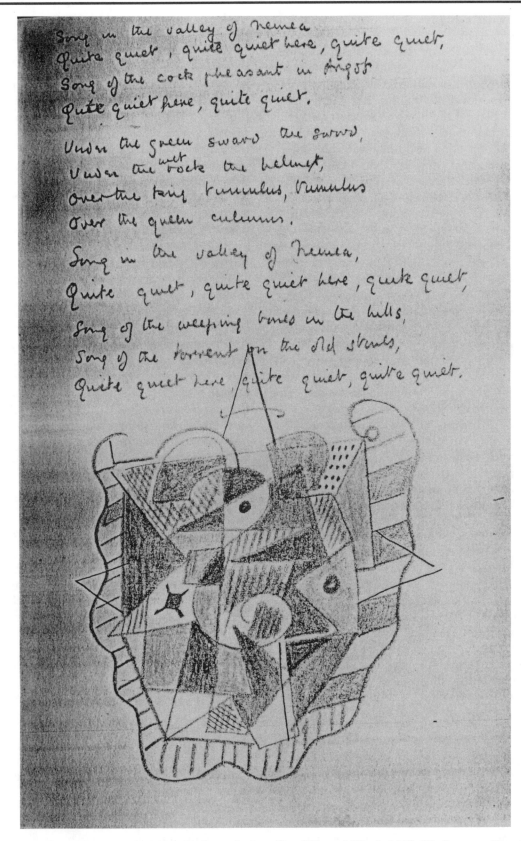

Page from Durrell's notebook "Book of Travels," begun by Durrell and Henry Miller in 1939 (The Lawrence Durrell Papers Accession II, Special Collections, Morris Library, Southern Illinois University at Carbondale, by permission of the Durrell estate)

"That was what made me resolve always to swim against the current."

The year 1935 was an important one for Larry. He married Nancy Isobel Myers, an art student at the Slade, moved to Greece, and published his first novel. Working in jazz clubs, composing, and playing the piano to support himself, he had also begun to publish his poetry. But in that year he persuaded his family (with his father dead, his mother, two brothers Leslie and Gerald, and sister Margaret were in England) to all go with him and Nancy to Greece, which he hoped would prove more congenial to writing. The acceptance of his first very conventional novel, *Pied Piper of Lovers* (1935), coincided with the move. The family's experience in Corfu is chronicled by brother Gerald in the wonderfully comic book, *My Family and Other Animals* (1956).

For twenty years Durrell's world was primarily Greece and the eastern Mediterranean, "Where mythology walks in a wave / And the islands are." "All our religions founder, you / remain, small sunburnt *deus loci* / safe in your natal shrine, / landscape of the precocious southern heart," he writes in tribute in "Deus Loci."

Indeed, Durrell's love and delineation of the "Greek sea's curly head" is a lasting part of his memory. At the time he went to Greece, it seemed incredibly remote. For the last thirty years, however, thousands of visitors, especially students, have gone there, carrying copies of his island books—*Prospero's Cell* (1945), *Reflections on a Marine Venus* (1953), *Bitter Lemons* (1957), *The Greek Islands* (1978). In the opening of the first of these, he invites: "Other countries may offer you discoveries in manners or lore or landscape; Greece offers you something harder—the discovery of yourself." "World," he writes evocatively, "of black cherries, sails, dust, arbutus, fishes and letters from home."

One of his most haunting descriptions is of a Corfu cove and small shrine above it. There he and Nancy dropped cherries and dived for them into "two fathoms of blue water, and a floor of clean pebbles." "Once," as he tells it, "after a storm an ikon of the good Saint Arsenius was found here by a fisherman named Manoli, and he built the shrine out of red plaster as a house for it. The little lamp is always full of sweet oil now, for St. Arsenius guards our bathing." Years later he brought oil from France to rekindle the light. Today, tourist guides, hustling their boats into the harbor of Kalami, shout over loudspeakers and point to Durrell's "White House"

where he spent so much enriching and maturing time.

He told Alyn that "before you can understand me, you must first appreciate Greece." In an essay in *Spirit of Place* (1969) he writes, "writers each seem to have a personal landscape of the heart which beckons them." And he expresses it as a philosophy in the *Quartet*: "We are the children of our landscape; it dictates behaviour and even thought in the measure to which we are responsive to it."

From his youth in England, Durrell continued to read widely and voraciously in works of contemporary thought. He studied Sigmund Freud and Carl Jung and read Sir James G. Frazer's *Golden Bough* (1911-1915), as well as experiencing Greek myth at first hand. Exploring psychology further, he was influenced by Georg Groddeck and Otto Rank; in science he was fascinated by Albert Einstein and the new concepts of physics. And in literature, moving from his "beloved Elizabethans," he concentrated on the moderns: "One had to have studied Proust and Joyce and then forgotten them," he told Alyn. In Greece too he became acquainted with other writers, such as Katsimbalis and George Seferis. Later he would love the poetry of the Alexandrian C. P. Cavafy. Most important of all he came to read and personally to know Henry Miller and T. S. Eliot—"godfathers" he called them.

Durrell discovered Miller's *Tropic of Cancer* (1934) in Corfu while writing his own second novel, *Panic Spring* (1937). The novel was published under the pseudonym of Charles Norden by Faber and Faber, his primary publisher for the rest of his life. Although he always considered this book a second apprentice attempt, it was actually more; in it for the first time he attempted to work on the planes of both past and present and to push the novel out from the center—methods that would characterize his greatest work.

Tropic of Cancer came like a revelation to him; there were new and freer ways of writing. He was already dissatisfied with his own work and ready for change. In a letter to Alan Thomas included in *Spirit of Place*, he exploded: "My God! talking of epics. Have you read a book called *Tropic of Cancer* by Henry Miller? . . . There isn't a word with which to express its excellence. Of course, like all works of genius it's strong fruit and you'd have to be careful about getting it into England." His response was a book of his own, *The Black Book* (1938), where "I first heard the sound of my own voice, lame and halting perhaps, but nevertheless my very own." He also attracted the attention of T. S. Eliot, who called it, "the first piece of work by a new English writer to give me any hope for the future of prose fiction." He was learning from his "godfathers." Durrell decided against publishing a watered-down version with Faber and Faber, but Eliot became, and remained until he retired, Durrell's editor there, strong and careful in his criticism. *The Black Book* was finally published in Paris, where Durrell had come on the invitation of Miller and where he became one of a remarkable group of writers and artists gathered at the Villa Seurat under the leadership of Miller and Anaïs Nin. "Henry Miller," Durrell told Alyn, "inspired me with his feeling for life, Eliot with his feeling for thought."

Returning to Greece from this heady triumph just in time for World War II, he sped before it with Nancy and his small daughter, Penelope Berengaria, first to Crete and then, in one of the last boats out, to Egypt. There he spent the war years, working for the British Information Office. His marriage did not survive, however; and after the war, now a Public Information Officer in Rhodes, he married an Alexandrian, Eve "Gypsy" Cohen. While in Rhodes, too, he published three books that were really odes to Greece: *Prospero's Cell*; *Cities, Plains and People* (1946), a book of poetry; and *Cefalû* (1947), a novel. A fast-written potboiler on one plane, *Cefalû* more deeply pursues a mystic quest and ends on a mountain-top beyond time in a sort of "Heraldic Universe"—a work of fabulation presaging things to come.

After serving stints for the British in Argentina and Yugoslavia, continuing to write poetry now being collected in anthologies, and completing *Reflections on a Marine Venus*, Durrell decided he had accumulated enough money to write for a year in Cyprus. For a long time he had contemplated a work he called "The Book of the Dead." But Eve had a nervous breakdown, and Durrell made his way to Cyprus with his two-year old daughter, Sappho Jane, only to find the marriage itself dissolving. His money gave out, and he both taught and became a British Press Officer again, working into the night and rising in the dark to write. Unfortunately, Cyprus itself erupted in a tragic struggle to join Greece, and, as the feelings of his Greek friends became more and more bitter against the English, he sorrowfully left the island. But with him went Claude Marie

Vincendon, a beautiful Alexandrian he had met there, a novelist herself, and the woman who became the deepest love of his life. In England, he swiftly wrote his greatest island book, *Bitter Lemons*, winner of the Duff Cooper Memorial Prize. And with him he carried the manuscript of the first volume of his long-planned "Book of the Dead."

In one miraculous year, 1957, Durrell published four books: *Esprit de Corps*, one of his parodies of the British foreign service; *White Eagles Over Serbia*; a boy's adventure story, the award-winning *Bitter Lemons*; and *Justine*, the first volume of *The Alexandria Quartet*. Durrell's first claim to fame beyond his poetry—though that may in its growing power prove to be just as exciting—is *The Alexandria Quartet*. Written rapidly in four years, it was, nevertheless, the product of many years of thought, mentioned as early as 1937. This was Durrell's writing method—a long pondering and maturing in his mind and then a swift and intensive transfer to paper.

With the *Quartet* he was recognized around the world. Reed Way Dasenbrock, in *Twentieth Century Literature*, describes its amazing success in America: "in the 1960s when I was growing up in a small town in Ohio, even our family doctor had read *The Alexandria Quartet* and was deeply engrossed by it." Young people still feel its amazing power, especially as a spiritual quest, and often respond to it in college courses as a book that affects their lives.

Durrell said in an interview with Bruce Cook in the *Philadelphia Inquirer* of 29 July 1982, "It was one of those turning points in my life. Cavafy puts it somewhere that in every man's life there comes a time when he must give a big yes or a big no. . . . Up to then I had little confidence in my power to grow as a writer. I knew I was industrious, but I had yet to make what Camus calls the 'mystical jump.'" With the *Quartet*, Durrell not only made a leap within himself but traced through the four volumes the evolution of a young writer to that "mystical jump" into the "Heraldic Universe." On the surface an "investigation of modern love" and a poetic portrait of Alexandria, it is beneath that a search for both truth and mystic understanding. In many ways it is closest of all to Eliot's *Waste Land* (1922) in its quest for a modern Grail.

Twenty years earlier in *Panic Spring* Durrell had groped for a method; in *The Alexandria Quartet* he again attempted to spread out in space and to work in depth on many planes of being and

Henry Miller, Alfred Perles, and Durrell, 1959, drawing by Eve Miller

time. But now he had mastered his art. Durrell explained to Alyn, "The thing was, I wanted to produce something that would be readable on a superficial level, while at the same time giving the reader—to the extent that he was touched by the more enigmatic aspects—the opportunity to attempt the second layer, and so on. . . . Just like a house-painter; he puts on three, four coats. And then it starts to rain, and you see the second coat coming through. A sort of palimpsest."

Told principally by young Darley, but containing many voices speaking from various points of view, the *Quartet* is a kaleidoscope in its changing perspective and style. The characters too are ever shifting. Like D. H. Lawrence, Durrell believed that the day of the "discrete ego" was over, that Freud had changed our understanding of people forever. Thus he created his personae prismatically, always attempting to reach the inner mystic essence. His people are, as he says in *Mountolive* (1958), "living on several different levels at once."

Space-time is a central concept behind the *Quartet*: "I have turned to science," he writes in the "Note" to *Balthazar*, (1958), "and am trying to complete a four-decker novel whose form is based on the relativity proposition." Einstein and modern physics, as well as the relationship of science to eastern metaphysics, were never far from his mind. The circle of Jung's mandala seemed to him to symbolize the unity of the Indian prayer wheel with the curvature of space, the four sides of the rectangle to connect ancient knowledge with Einstein's four dimensions. *The Alexandria Quartet* symbolically unites senses and intellect, the humane and the scientific.

Durrell wanted to show, as he expresses it in *Justine*, "the spiritual city underlying the temporal one"—and the mystic city beneath that. "Alexandria, the capital of Memory," he muses near the end. As much as a novel, and a major one, the *Quartet* is a prose poem to this capital of history and of the heart. The language constantly changes color as Darley moves from romantic apprenticeship to chastened master of his craft, the great novelist, Pursewarden, mentoring him from beyond the grave. In *Clea*, Pursewarden and Durrell speak as one: "a novel should be an act of divination by entrails, not a careful record of a game of pat-ball on some vicarage lawn!"

The *Quartet* has been denigrated by its realist critics for its foreign setting and jeweled prose. But the setting is foreign only to those not resident in the eastern Mediterranean; to Durrell, living in the region for twenty years, it was home. And Durrell wrote a prose as resplendent and varied as if it were Elizabethan; he hoped to help return the language to some of its Renaissance beauty and power. Summing up the whole, it is a vast achievement—as Jane Pinchin called it, "a masterpiece of size."

After the tremendous reception of the *Quartet*, there was excitement about how Durrell might follow it up. But he did not want to continue so much as to do something new. He had in mind a work combining the richness of Elizabethan bawdry with the Pop Art of contemporary postmodernism—a satiric sort of novel taking a tongue-in-cheek swipe at the computerized world of the megalith corporation. Most who had admired *The Alexandria Quartet* were not prepared for *Tunc* (1968) and *Nunquam* (1970). Those who had not admired it found only more to dislike. It was as if he wanted to play a joke on the world now that he held it in the palm of his hand. The critics responded rudely, and Durrell's downward cycle began.

Perhaps some of his black humor came from the sudden, early death of Claude from cancer in 1967. Asked by Alyn if he had been happy early in the Sommières years, Durrell responded, "Infinitely. Sideways, lengthways, in every way." In fact he never quite got over her death. Even in 1980, in *A Smile in the Mind's Eye*, he wrote about Claude: "To have been loved—I suddenly realized what a great compliment it was! Yet amazingly enough so often we had not been aware whether we had actually *made* love or not—so rapt had been the insight, so dense the communion of presence and touch." Later, in 1973, he would marry Ghislaine de Boysson; but the marriage did not last.

In January 1971, Durrell wrote Miller that he had "started a queer sort of novel about the gnostic heresies, the Templars etc etc. It's still all very fragile and may well jolt to a stop before I finish it." In May he reported, "I am firming up a version of what may well be my best novel if only I can get it the way I want it." The novel was *Monsieur* (1974), the first of five volumes of *The Avignon Quintet* (1974-1985), his strongest novel series after the *Quartet* and according to some few critics his greatest work. A wonderfully wise

book, it attempts to bridge his worlds of east and west.

Set mainly in southern France during and after World War II, its central characters are mainly western, though it glances at Egypt and Egyptians. But its spirit is eastern. For a long time Durrell called it "My *Indian Quintet*"; as he rethought and relived his life in age, he was becoming more deeply attached to the Taoist philosophy and the Buddhism of his childhood. He was delighted that a group of Buddhist monks had settled in Provence; he grew to know them and felt that they helped him "recreate his soul." And in an interview in *La Stampa* on *Sebastian* (1983), he explained, "But the *Quartet* is Western, and now I am trying to achieve a type of novel that I call Indian, one that reflects an Asian concept of the psyche. . . . Some part of India has always been at the core of my being." He attempted, he said, to infuse one of the five compartments of the Indian concept of personality into each volume. The result is a book of which, writes Ian S. MacNiven in *The Modernists*, "The treasure—Templar, psychological, spiritual, intellectual—is there for us to find, if we seek it in the proper frame of mind."

Very few critics or readers understood what he was attempting, but Nicholas Shrimpton wrote in the London *Sunday Times* (6 November, 1983), "Lawrence Durrell now seems to be four-fifths of the way through one of the great novels of our time." The last volume, Shrimpton felt, however, did not live up to the first four. Indeed, *Quinx* (1985), affirming the final peace of Nirvana or his "Heraldic Universe," begins with the challenging epigraph: ". . . must itself create the taste by which it is to be judged . . . Wordsworth *dixit*." The ending proclaims the coming of the Heraldic future and all the changes lying ahead for the novel itself: "It was at this precise moment that reality prime rushed to the aid of fiction and the totally unpredictable began to take place!" If any novel is a work ahead of and beyond its time, this is it.

After completing the *Quintet*, Durrell paused. He had just one more project, to write a last poetic evocation of place for his beloved Provence. A week before he died on 7 November 1990, *Caesar's Vast Ghost* was published and in his hands. It is a beautiful book, brilliant in its coloring and containing, mixed with the prose, some of his finest poetry. In Erica Jong's words, "It is a hard book to describe—part travel-book, part poetry, part mythology, part autobiography, part valediction forbidding mourning." It is most fitting that his last work evokes the "deus loci" of southern France and is filled with poetry. For Provence was his final home in life; poetry was always his home in literature.

Most of all Durrell wanted to be a good poet. When asked by Alyn what form meant the most to him, he answered, "My poetry, naturally." About it he said that he had always tried to combine "sensuality and intellectual acuity." That mixing "is what produces the surface, at the same time strong and fragile, hermetic and luminous. The shell knitted to the body." These, of course, represent the same combination of qualities that informs *The Alexandria Quartet* and his life—the mixture of the sensual and the intellectual. He so very much wanted to be "a poet," an enduring one. He thought he had "missed the boat" and said sadly, "To achieve great poetry, you must give up everything. Personally, I have been over-greedy about life." Perhaps he underestimated himself though. Both Eliot and Seferis thought he had the gift. And as Durrell grew older, his poetry became less purely lyrical, more experienced, and ever stronger.

Speaking of his own life, Durrell said to Alyn, "I don't have attitudes. I have friendships and I have love. I try to make do with that." And alone in Sommières in his seventies he found friendship and love again with Françoise Kestsman, a Russian-Polish refugee, charming, intellectual, and vital, but so poor she was working in the fields when Durrell met her. Her companionship filled his last years when, having cut out smoking and trying to cut out drinking the French wine he loved, he battled emphysema. Talking to Paul Chutkow, he wryly complained, "Life is no good after forty. I've just turned one hundred and twenty, and I don't like it a bit."

His battle came to an end at seventy-eight on November 7, 1990, as he fell from a stroke. He was cremated immediately, and two days later his ashes were buried beside Claude in the quiet little cemetery next to St. Julien's chapel under a wall covered with dog-rose. The ceremony was kept small by his wishes; seven people were present, but they included Françoise and his daughter Penelope. "Great men always choose the right moment at which to die," he told Alyn, "when everything is ready for their exit."

As a man of letters Durrell was wide-ranging and prolific, both a modernist and a postmodernist, a romantic and a fabulator, and in another sense a classicist too. Not really an expa-triate but one of the new breed of international writers, he was ever attempting to create new molds for old forms and to widen his world. Ultimately, evaluation of his achievement must rest on *The Alexandria Quartet*, his poetry, his evocations of place, and *The Avignon Quintet*. Travelers still will carry his island books on their journeys. *The Avignon Quintet* will continue to challenge interpretation. But the poetry grows stronger with time. And *The Alexandria Quartet* stands, an extraordinary triumph of the likes of *One Hundred Years of Solitude* (1970) and *Wuthering Heights* (1847).

In a very personal statement attributed to Pursewarden in the *Quartet*, he proclaims, "As you get older and want to die more a strange kind of happiness seizes you; you suddenly realize that all art must end in a celebration." *Caesar's Vast Ghost* completes the celebration. The first poem's theme, "So now all time is winding down to die," is sounded again in the magnificent farewell of the last poem:

> Mere time is winding down at last:
> The consenting harvest moon presides. . . .
> A disenfranchised last goodbye,
> > Goodbye.

Bibliographies:

Susan Vander Closter, *Joyce Cary and Lawrence Durrell: A Reference Guide* (Boston: G. K. Hall, 1985);

Grove Koger, "1981-82 Durrell Bibliography," *Deus Loci: The Lawrence Durrell Newsletter*, 7.3 (1984): 25-32;

Alan G. Thomas and James A. Brigham, *Lawrence Durrell: An Illustrated Checklist* (Carbondale: Southern Illinois University Press, 1983).

References:

Michael H. Begnal, *On Miracle Ground: Essays on the Fiction of Lawrence Durrell* (Lewisburg, Pa.: Bucknell University Press, 1990);

Roger Bowen, " 'The Artist at his Papers': Durrell, Egypt, and the Poetry of Exile," *Twentieth Century Literature*, 33.4 (1987): 465-484;

Christopher J. Burns, "Durrell's Heraldic Universe," *Modern Fiction Studies* 13.3 (1967): 375-388;

Michael Cartwright, ed., *Proceedings of the First National Lawrence Durrell Conference* (Kelowna,

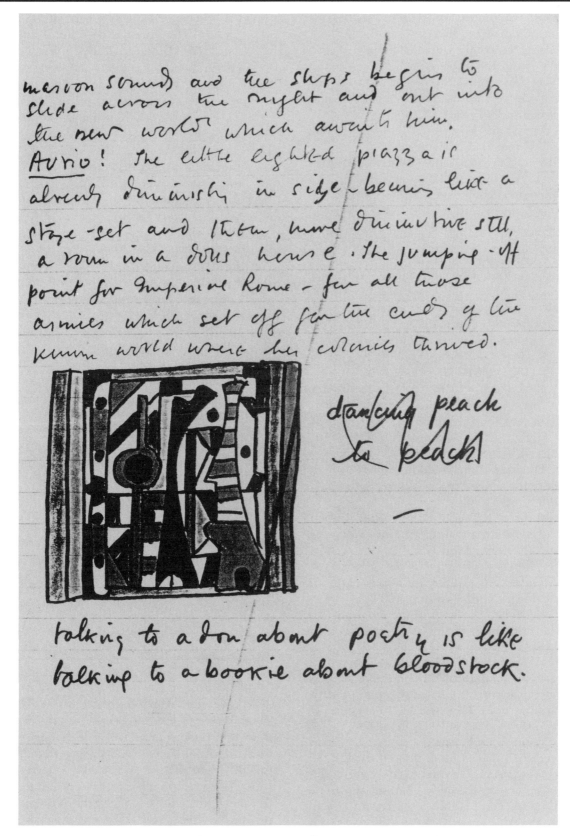

Page from Durrell's Notebook "2" (The Lawrence Durrell Papers Accession II, Special Collections, Morris Library, Southern Illinois University at Carbondale, by permission of the Durrell estate)

British Columbia: *Deus Loci: The Lawrence Durrell Newsletter*, 1982);

Curtis Cate, "Lawrence Durrell," *Atlantic Monthly*, 208 (June 1961): 63-69;

Reed Way Dasenbrock, "Lawrence Durrell and the Modes of Modernism," *Twentieth Century Literature*, 33.4 (1987): 515-527;

Gerald Durrell, *My Family and Other Animals* (London: Rupert Hart-Davis, 1956);

G. S. Fraser, *Lawrence Durrell*, Writers and Their Work 216 (London: Longman, 1970);

Alan Warren Friedman, ed., *Critical Essays on Lawrence Durrell* (Boston: G. K. Hall, 1987);

Friedman, *Lawrence Durrell and the Alexandria Quartet: Art for Love's Sake* (Norman: University of Oklahoma Press, 1970);

Lawrence B. Gamache and Ian S. MacNiven, eds., *The Modernists: Studies in a Literary Phenomenon* (Rutherford, N. J.: Fairleigh Dickinson University Press, 1987);

William L. Godshalk, "Some Sources of Durrell's *Alexandria Quartet*," *Modern Fiction Studies* 13.3 (1967): 361-374;

Jean Paul Hamard, "L'Espace et le temps dans les romans de Lawrence Durrell," *Critique* (Paris), 16.156 (1960): 387-413;

Gilbert Highet, "The Alexandrians of Lawrence Durrell," *Horizon*, 2.4 (1960): 113-118;

Eleanor Hitchins, "The Heraldic Universe in The Alexandria Quartet," *College English*, 24.1 (1962): 56-61;

Christopher G. Katope, "Cafavy and Durrell's The Alexandria Quartet," *Comparative Literature*, 21 (1969): 125-137;

Frank L. Kersnowski, ed., *Into the Labyrinth: Essays on the Art of Lawrence Durrell* (Ann Arbor, Mich.: UMI Research, 1989);

Ian S. MacNiven, "A Room in the House of Art: The Friendship of Anaïs Nin and Lawrence Durrell," *Mosaic*, 11.2 (1978): 37-57;

Lawrence W. Markert, " 'The Pure and Sacred Readjustment of Death': Connections between Lawrence Durrell's *Avignon Quintet* and the Writings of D. H. Lawrence," *Twentieth Century Literature*, 33.4 (1987): 550-564;

Markert and Carol Peirce, eds., *On Miracle Ground II: Second International Lawrence Durrell Conference Proceedings* (Baltimore: The University of Baltimore Monograph Series and *Deus Loci: The Lawrence Durrell Newsletter*, 1984);

J. R. Morrison, "Memory and Light in Lawrence Durrell's *The Revolt of Aphrodite*," *Labrys*, 5 (1979): 141-153;

James R. Nichols, "Lawrence Durrell's *Alexandria Quartet*: The Paradise of Bitter Fruit," *Deus Loci: The Lawrence Durrell Newsletter*, 3.2 (1979): 9-16;

Carol Peirce, " 'Wrinkled Deep in Time': *The Alexandria Quartet* as Many-Layered Palimpsest," *Twentieth Century Literature*, 33.4 (1987): 485-498;

Jane Lagoudis Pinchin, *Alexandria Still: Forster, Durrell, and Cavafy* (Princeton, N. J.: Princeton University Press, 1977);

Nicholas Shrimpton, "The Whodunnit Gnostic-Style," *Sunday Times* (London), 6 November 1983: 41;

Sharon Spencer, "The Ambiguities of Incest in Lawrence Durrell's Heraldic Universe: A Rankian Interpretation," *Twentieth Century Literature*, 33.4 (1987): 436-448;

George Steiner, "Lawrence Durrell: The Baroque Novel," *Yale Review*, 49 (1960) 488-495;

John Unterecker, *Lawrence Durrell*, Columbia Essays on Modern Writers 6 (New York: Columbia University Press, 1964);

Warren Wedin, "The Artist as Narrator in *The Alexandria Quartet*," *Twentieth Century Literature*, 18 (1972): 175-180;

John A. Weigel, *Lawrence Durrell* (New York: Twayne, 1965).

Papers:

Durrell's papers are located in the Morris Library at Southern Illinois University, Carbondale, Illinois. Additional collections are located at the libraries of UCLA and the University of Southern California, Los Angeles, California.

A TRIBUTE

from JEAN FRANCHETTE

Lawrence Durrell once wrote to me: "Thank God, I am not British!" Early in his life the world-famous author of *The Alexandria Quartet* decided not to live in "Pudding Island," as he called Great Britain. Born near Darjeeling in India, he chose to anchor his life around the Mediterranean, the cradle of Civilization. Because Durrell was a Greek, just as he was for that matter, an Elizabethan, stranded from his epoch, Sir Larry of Languedoc.

His last anchorage was in effect to be Languedoc, the troubadour country. Some twenty miles from the Saintes-Maries-de-la-Mer, from 1957 up to his demise in November 1990.

The most important part of his work which will ensure him the admiration of posterity was written in Languedoc. I read *Justine* in 1957, wrote a three-thousand word article about it, the second in the French press. Durrell got it somehow, wrote back, the first of some 150 letters spanning a thirty-three-year-old friendship. Our last encounter was at Easter 1990, just a few days before I left for Georgia to deliver the keynote address at the sixth "On Miracle Ground" conference of the Durrell Society. And I talked to him over the telephone a few days before his death. He was gasping for breath but had time for a joke: "You know, Jean, it's that bloody emphysema. But Emphysema is a Greek goddess, isn't she?"

Lawrence Durrell was not just a great writer, though justice must still be done to his poetry, but one of the dozen English-language writers who shall still be read in two or three centuries hence. He was also a great man, a wonderful, compassionate man, completely devoid of the British stigma of arrogance. He illumined my life. I was privileged to be one of his closest friends. Peace to his shade.

A TRIBUTE

from MICHAEL HAAG

"Capitally, what is this city of ours? What is

resumed in the word Alexandria?" I was sixteen, an impressionable age, and was browsing at the bookrack of a suburban New York drugstore when I read that invitation on the opening page of *Justine*. Forster and Cavafy followed for a start, and I have not stopped reading since. But armchair enquiry was not enough. I went to Alexandria to see for myself; and that should have been enough, you might think, to cure anybody, for as Durrell said, 'There is nothing to *see*!'

But he knew as Plotinus knew that 'to any vision must be brought an eye adapted to what is to be seen.' Durrell has been accused of fancy by those blind to curiosity and insensible to intimation. I thank him for his eye, for in sharing with me his Mediterranean adventure, intellectual and sensate, he opened up my world.

When finally I met him, after I had published in London Forster's *Alexandria* to which he had supplied the introduction, the measure of his influence was my inability to credit that he had written *The Alexandria Quartet*—that anybody could have written it, for I had so long inhabited that unreal city that it seemed my own, which as a city of discovery it was.

And the *real* Alexandria, the one where there is nothing to see? I have been there many times now and know it well enough to say it does not exist. It would be too small a place to hold the friendships I have made there.

Walker Percy

(28 May 1916 - 10 May 1990)

Linda Whitney Hobson

See also the Percy entries in *DLB 2: American Novelists Since World War II* and *DLB Yearbook: 1980.*

BOOKS: *The Moviegoer* (New York: Knopf, 1961; London: Eyre & Spottiswoode, 1963);

The Last Gentleman (New York: Farrar, Straus & Giroux, 1966; London: Eyre & Spottiswoode, 1967);

Love in the Ruins (New York: Farrar, Straus & Giroux, 1971; London: Eyre & Spottiswoode, 1971);

The Message in the Bottle (New York: Farrar, Straus & Giroux, 1975);

Lancelot (New York: Farrar, Straus & Giroux, 1977; London: Secker & Warburg, 1977);

The Second Coming (New York: Farrar, Straus & Giroux, 1980; London: Secker & Warburg, 1981);

Lost in the Cosmos (New York: Farrar, Straus & Giroux, 1983);

The Thanatos Syndrome (New York: Farrar, Straus & Giroux, 1987; London: Andre Deutsch, 1987).

Walker Percy (photograph by Rhoda K. Faust)

The death of Walker Percy on 10 May 1990 in Covington, Louisiana, removed from the literary scene one of its strongest moral voices. During his approximately thirty-year career as a writer, and despite his output of just six novels and two books of nonfiction, Percy became known as the leading philosophical novelist writing in the United States. This reputation was even more striking because of Percy's philosophical-perspective orientation—Catholic existentialism. Percy's intellectual interests combined with his training as a doctor to produce fiction that took as its purpose the diagnosis of the modern human condition. Percy's fiction was personal though not hermetic; his concern radiated out from the individual to the individual's place in society. That engagement with the real world, and Percy's genial and reasoned manner, conferred upon him a moral and intellectual authority rare among writers in the United States.

Walker Percy was born on 28 May 1916 to an established southern family boasting a Spanish land grant of 1776 and a United States senator. He lived with his parents, LeRoy Pratt Percy and Mattie Sue Phinizy Percy, in Birmingham, Alabama, until 1929. After his father committed suicide in 1929, his mother, his two brothers, and Walker—the eldest son—moved to Greenville, Mississippi, to live with his father's cousin, William Alexander Percy, the author of *Lanterns on the Levee* (1941).

After the death of Percy's mother in an automobile accident in 1931, William Alexander Percy adopted the boys. Percy remembered Uncle

Will, as he was known, as "the first man I knew who placed an almost supreme value on art and reading and music." The household was a valuable influence on the impressionable young writer, who began writing poetry and articles for the Greenville High School student newspaper. "Without Uncle Will's influence, I wouldn't have been a writer," Percy affirmed.

During the Depression the Percy house became a standard stopping place for "those making a literary tour of the South." Among others, the psychiatrist Harry Stack Sullivan came and stayed a few weeks, along with people such as the Benéts, Carl Sandburg, and William Faulkner. There was good talk. There were also a thoroughly eclectic library and a fine collection of recorded music.

These years in Greenville not only encouraged Percy's nascent talents as a writer but also provided much raw material for his later work. Once Flannery O'Connor wrote to him after he had sent her a story to read: "That was a good story; why don't you make up another one?" She also told him that "All you have to do to be a writer is live twelve years and write about it." Though Percy said he was not really a very good observer or listener, he took in, maybe peripherally, much of the world, and when he sat down to write, it reappeared, "with good luck and some talent, plus sweating, stinking, sweating blood, practically."

After graduating from high school, Percy studied premed at the University of North Carolina, from which he received his degree in 1937. That course of study might potentially have sidetracked a young writer, but Percy disagreed: "It was a happy decision," he believed, because, paradoxically, a training in premed fitted him for the job of being a writer.

At Chapel Hill he joined a fraternity, "Sat on the porch for four years, drinking and observing the scene" with friends, attended scores of movies, and wrote several articles for the *Carolina Magazine*. He and his friends used to talk often of taking two or three years off to go to Paris or hitchhiking around the country, but they never did it. Of this desire, Percy remarked: "I guess I decided against it, not because my uncle would have opposed it, but because of the Protestant work ethic, you know. You don't just goof off for two years." But despite the camaraderie of his college years, he always felt somewhat a misfit, something of an outsider. The feeling continued when he entered the Columbia University College of

Physicians and Surgeons, from which he received his M.D. in 1941.

As he began working long hours at Columbia-Presbyterian Medical School, and later in the morgue at Bellevue Hospital, Percy became increasingly concerned with this feeling of outsidedness. He himself intending to become a psychiatrist, Percy underwent psychoanalysis five days a week for a period of two years. He liked his psychiatrist, but always felt that he was somehow on the stage in that darkened room while talking to her, that he was supposed to talk even when there was nothing to say. After two years in therapy, Percy left, no worse and no better, determined to look elsewhere than analysis for direction. Despite his active search, over the course of his life, Percy's courage was tested time and again by recurring bouts of depression and feelings of having been abandoned by his parents.

During his internship, he and the other young doctors worked day and night, often without masks or gloves, performing autopsies on "floaters"—bodies the police had dragged from the river—and what they called "five-day cases"—bodies that were put in the icebox, left for five days, and, if unclaimed, considered available for autopsy. Many of these corpses were riddled with tuberculosis. Since Percy was working so hard to learn and did not take the proper precautions "because there wasn't time, and we just took our chances," he contracted the disease and spent the next two years in rural New York sanatoriums, on one occasion occupying the same room that Eugene O'Neill had years before. When a friend, the writer Shelby Foote, went to visit him, he found him "gaunt and pale. He was living the life of a hermit. I worried about him; I wanted him out in the world, near people. But he seemed happy where he was, flat on his back and holding onto those books for dear life."

Those books were what made the difference between a kind of prison sentence for Percy and the escape, for the first time in his life, from the feeling of guilt at being an outsider—one who asks too many questions of life and gets no answers. Percy recalled that:

> It was a truly eerie experience to be laid up with TB during World War II. All hell was busting loose all over the world and I was alone— literally alone in a room for months and saw not a soul except a kind of practical nurse who came in twice a day to bring food. And the strange thing that happened was that it was then that I began to read, for the first time, modern litera-

ture. I began to read Dostoyevsky, and read him and others like Kierkegaard and Camus and Sartre for two years. And I made the most important discovery of my life, artistically. I discovered that my feeling of outsidedness, of abstraction, of distance, alienation, or whatever, was nothing more or less than what the modern writers had been writing about for a hundred years.

The realization of a shared sense of alienation informed his work over the next ten years until 1954, when he began to publish book reviews and articles on philosophy and social anthropology. One of them, "The Man on the Train," is an especially perceptive delineation of the despair of commuting to work each day through impeccable green suburbs, coming home to find one's family, as usual, healthy and attractive, watching several hours of television, sleeping, and waking to begin another well-adjusted but despair-filled day just like the one before and the one to follow.

Percy believed that only a crisis—a heart attack, the news of the death of a president, a hurricane—allows the commuter to "come to himself" and see that he has been sunk in "everydayness," that his talk has been just words filling up the blankness of time. This man cannot learn how to love or how to live a better life just by reading books in the library, as two of Percy's characters, Binx Bolling in *The Moviegoer* (1961) and Allison in *The Second Coming* (1980), try to do. Finally, even the novelist can be of little help. He can dramatize the situation of dislocated postmodern man—man cut adrift from himself—but he has not the authority to be "edifying." The novelist can only show man's predicament indirectly, fictionally, as he perceives it from his own vantage point.

Each person, Percy felt, can only come out of "the despair which does not know that it is despair" by suffering to the point that he has an "epiphany in ordeal. Something happens during ordeal which makes things clearer to the sufferer." Evidently Percy's insights concerning the modern illness had some validity, because he received numerous calls and letters from people who told him, "That's the way it is, and nobody has ever said that before."

Percy's family had been nominally Episcopalian, but this had more to do with aesthetics than faith, he thought, and so after his marriage in 1946 to Mary Bernice Townsend—"Bunt" to her friends and family—the couple, after much discussion and introspection, decided to become

Catholics. Walker and Bunt lived for a year in Sewanee, in the vacation home Uncle Will owned before his death in 1942, and then in New Orleans. Although Percy always found New Orleans intriguing, he discovered in the year he lived there that it was also distracting. In an article published in *Esquire* (April 1980), he admitted that New Orleans is "very much of a place, drenched in its identity, its history, and its rather self-conscious exotica," but that if he decided to come to live in the French Quarter, he would not write but would feel constrained to "turn fey, potter about a patio, and write *feuilletons* and vignettes or catty *romans à clef*, a pleasant enough life but, for me, too seductive."

The Percys had two daughters, Mary Pratt and Ann, and lived a comfortable and supporting life, even when faced with difficulties, as in the case of Ann's deafness. Yet the comfort and love shared by this family was only one side of Percy's life. The other side was filled with waiting and dread for the next bout of writing. Joy had little to do with the process:

> It comes once in a while with good luck. I take great pleasure in writing something either very funny or in writing a good attack on something in our culture—attacking really savagely. The other thing in writing that brings me pleasure is to write a love scene well. Writing is the loneliest goddamn life in the world. It's terrible. It's a miserable life, to tell you the truth.

Despite the anguish of writing, over the last thirty-five years Percy produced six novels, beginning in 1961 with the National Book Award-winning *The Moviegoer*; two books of nonfiction, *The Message in the Bottle* (1975) and *Lost in the Cosmos* (1983); and numerous essays in such publications as *Commonweal*, the *Georgia Review*, *Harper's*, and the *Southern Review*. These essays often concern the South, the difficulty of professing faith within a secular culture, or the responsibilities of the serious novelist in matters of craft and ethics.

Percy also taught writing courses at Loyola University in New Orleans and at Louisiana State University. In addition he was a mentor to many other, younger writers in the South who identified with his struggles and sought excellence in their own works, including Sheila Bosworth, Richard Ford, Josephine Humphreys, James Wilcox, and Chris Wiltz. He read hundreds of manuscripts for the NEA and his PEN-Faulkner committee; went to Rome as an appointed adviser to Pope John Paul II on the state of American culture; traveled with his wife, Bunt, and friends Mr. and Mrs. Shelby Foote; baby-sat his four grandsons in their younger years; avidly despaired—not alone—of Louisiana politics; played golf at the Tchefuncta Country Club in Covington; punctuated his writing sessions by lunch with contemporaries or writer-friends; and always kept a small, bright dog, the latest of which was "Sweet Thing," a corgi whose outsize ears and ego were, by turns, the author's amusement and scourge.

Percy's was a busy and productive life in all these areas, from attending church to firing off letters of outrage to the *Times-Picayune* when he could see that Know-Nothingism or racism had once again manifested itself in the Great State of Louisiana. But though he loved rainy days, his life itself was often clouded by the deaths of his parents in his early adolescence. An inherited predisposition to depression did not help.

He was fascinated with the etiology of despair and alienation, and spent much of his time contemplating in his writing the nature of these maladies. His greatest legacy is, in fact, the questioning of how and why his protagonists and real North Americans and Europeans who have so much can still feel like homeless castaways; to his credit, however, Percy avoids easy scapegoats such as "the banality of late capitalism" or "the waste land." For Percy the problem resides in the individual and must be faced and transformed by the individual in dialogue with other alienated, but still sovereign, individuals.

As a student, a diagnostician, and a displaced person who felt postmodern man had fallen particularly far from the Garden, his mind, soul, and body torn apart, Walker asked many questions to perturb his readers' complacency: "Was this all I had to do [in the face of death], act like a soldier?" "What is the nature of the search? . . . The search is what anyone would undertake if he were not sunk in the everydayness of his own life. This morning, for example, I felt as if I had come to myself on a strange island. And what does such a castaway do: Why he pokes around the neighborhood and he doesn't miss a trick"; "Am I, in my search, a hundred miles ahead of my fellow Americans or a hundred miles behind them?" "What does [the novelist] see in the [postmodern] world which arouses in him the deepest forebodings and at the same time kindles excitement and hope? . . . a new breed of person in whom the potential for catastrophe—and hope—has suddenly escalat-

ed, . . . [bringing] unlimited possibilities for both destruction and liberation, for an absolute loneliness or a rediscovery of community and reconciliation."

All these are valid and subtle questions to ask of experience, but the question which appears most often in Percy's works is a simple "Why?" The flippant cliché "Why not?" does not satisfy as an answer for any of the protagonists in his fiction, reflecting as it does an insipid complacency, which was often the victim of Percy's lacerating satire. Percy's "Why?" deserves a thoughtful response because it means "In a land of material wealth, why are people so lonely, cut off from themselves, from each other, and from the old God, the judge and comforter of His people?" Walker posed this question many times in his writing, invariably as one side of a dialogue.

Community and reconciliation through intersubjectivity were the physical and emotional states the novelist sought, and looking for signs that both states were possible made him a close observer of nature. In *Love in the Ruins* (1971) he called the subject of his scrutiny the "mystery" of the "lovely ordinary world" that a desiring eye might penetrate the world for clues to show that one's term of displacement was just about over. That was the question and mode of response for Walker Percy: "Why?" and "Watch. Listen. Wait." The question and strategy for finding an answer inform each of the novels; the answer itself is, he knew, elusive. Cleanth Brooks suggests that "Percy prefers to let his stories end quietly: a gesture, a minor incident, a brief word that indicates that something of importance has happened, but that the problem of the culture has not thereby been solved and the seeker himself has not reached necessarily a final destination." Flannery O'Connor wrote that "Conversation is the only true theme of any story," and by that measurement Percy has written "true." His conversions are quiet, as Brooks notes, but nonetheless the protagonist has taken a moral stance. And, following Soren Kierkegaard, the implication for the hero is that his conversion is not one for all time; loss of faith and conversion are ebb and flow of quotidian existence. Each of the six conclusions focuses on the moment of the first conversion, the moment he decides what he must do to live out his term of days in good faith. In one of his last letters to me, dated 12 February 1990, Percy wrote, "Who is onto the secret?—that the mystery is to be found in ordinary things in an ordinary room on an ordinary Wednesday afternoon." Percy's

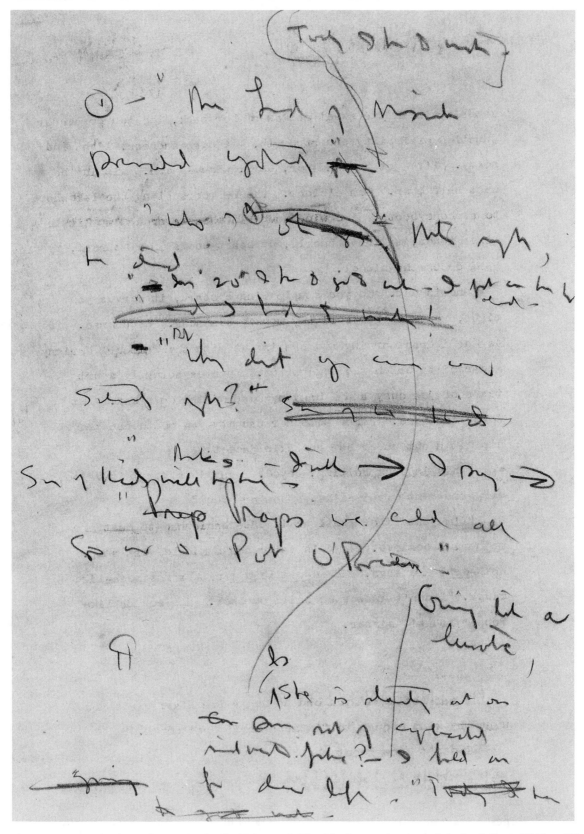

Pages from Percy's manuscript and typescript for his 1961 novel, The Moviegoer *(courtesy of the Louis Round Wilson Library, the University of North Carolina at Chapel Hill, by permission of Mrs. Bunt Percy)*

[263] 204 197

John and noon

hands again in the sweet hollow of her back, the tender tender
junction of frailty and strength, gladness sadness, light and
heavy. I've got to find her, Rory. Now I mean. Within the
next half hour. Ten o'clock. The MG roars along the lakeshore
to a phone booth. The ~~wind and rain whistle~~ around my little
glass tower, my knees buckle, my heart booms in my throat, my fingers drops the nickel.

She is out. Oh you stupid Binx bastard, it serves you
right, you and your solitary monkey business. Of course. It
is Mardi Gras morning and she is out with the Faubourg Marigny
macaroni to watch the Rex parade. My eyes actually spurt
tears of jealousy and I bang my head on the coin box. But
Joyce is there.   Joyce-in-the-window with her naughty-you mouth and her
hip hiked out under her buckskin jacket.

"This is Jack Bolling, Joyce," I say in a Virginia voice,
~~easy and gentlemanly-like~~. "How are you?"

"I'm just fine. Well well Stephanie had to meet her
mother, I believe." Joyce's voice has a Middle West snap.
Moth-_err_, she says, and we-_ull_ we-_ull_ with a business-like
cluck. "~~I don't know when shill be back~~." She sounds like
Pepper Young's sister.

"What about you?"

"What?"

"I was hoping if you had no other immediate plans you
would be kind enough to fix me a Mardi Gras drink."

"~~I don't know about that.~~"

"I wonder if I may be frank with you."

mystical realism, existentialism lightened in tone by Neoplatonism and romanticism, offers a more honest perspective than the better-known scientific method—and perhaps one more vital to the survival of the individual on an ordinary Wednesday afternoon. "Mystical," in that Percy watches for signs of grace and healing, and "realistic," in that he uses reason to see that the healing will occur in time and space, a Percy novel is thereby enriched by detail. God manifests Himself in nature and society, the novels suggest, so one needs to look closely.

The first of Percy's bemused and often confused narrators is Binx Bolling in *The Moviegoer*. Like the later Tom More and Will Barrett, Bolling is a southern aristocrat who has lost the belief in a stable universe. Binx has taken a job as a stockbroker in his uncle's firm and is quietly bound up with seducing his secretaries, making money, and attending movies. Movies are simpering, sentimental affairs, but they seem to be more ordered than life, and Binx is looking for a new order to replace the commonsensical Catholicism of his mother's middle-class family and the impotent stoicism of his dead father's.

The novel is set during the week of Mardi Gras in New Orleans, a few years after the Korean War in which Binx fought and nearly died. Such a crisis as war allows his hero to "come to himself" and begin "a search." While lying wounded in Korea, Binx looked up and saw a hardy dung beetle crawling along. Upon this split-second return to life, Binx determined to use his redeemed life and his inherited "nose for merde" to begin a search, to live authentically—a paraphrase of the ideas Percy absorbed during his convalescence from such writers as Jean-Paul Sartre, Martin Heidegger, Gabriel Marcel, Albert Camus, and Kierkegaard, whose "Knight of Faith" in a secular Christendom is a model for Binx Bolling and later Percy heroes.

But when Binx returns to New Orleans, he forgets the search and turns to mercenary narcissism. Not until he is called to his aunt's Garden District manse from his basement apartment (as in Fyodor Dostoyevski's "Underground Man") to help Aunt Emily persuade her stepdaughter Kate not to commit suicide does Binx face another crisis. In helping Kate, Binx is forced to scrutinize the character of his own life once more. As a result, he makes hard choices so that he and Kate can marry despite their living under the scudding shadow of despair. Issues of middle-class boredom and alienation, the effects of propaganda, enervation of the southern aristocracy, conformity, greed, self-deception, and the death of God contribute to the novel's provocative first-person narration.

Williston (Will) Bibb Barrett, also the scion of a stoical Mississippi family, is the ironical hero of Percy's second novel, *The Last Gentleman* (1966). This third-person, picaresque novel is, until the last few scenes, gently parodic of traditional quest stories; but the novel turns serious as Will witnesses the baptism of a dying boy and the threatened suicide of his mentor, Sutter Vaught. Sutter's plan repeats Will's father's suicide fifteen years earlier. Percy's active social conscience is also seen in segments of the book which deal with political issues of the 1960s: integration of southern universities, white backlash, police brutality, divorce, the changing role of women. However, the strongest impression the novel makes is to depict the boredom and conformity resulting from utilitarian, competitive, agnostic values.

Will Barrett is a young man hungry for relationship and community, for an authentic life, but as he wanders around the United States, ending up in the desert of the Southwest, he sees that the banquet of American culture has been furnished only with plastic airplane food. Will observes and listens carefully, looking for signs, for someone to trust and love, but he finds only the trendy and the narcissistic, mouthing clichés and behaving as though they are before the camera. Impersonations abound; only Jamie Vaught, who is about to die, and Sutter Vaught, who threatens suicide, seem to speak truth to Will. As in *The Moviegoer*, a crisis shocks Will into penetrating the illusory quality of his life. Of his second novel, Percy commented, "Barrett . . . has a passionate pilgrimage that he must follow, and he is looking for a father-figure. His symptoms are ambiguous, however, and he could go in various directions. The ambiguity is deliberate. The reader is free to see him as a sick man among healthy businessmen or as a sane pilgrim in a mad world."

On another occasion Percy recalled that in *The Last Gentleman*, "A good deal of it was satire directed to events happening in the South." Social and political concerns in Percy's next novel, *Love in the Ruins*, are expressed even more forthrightly in satire as caustic as that of Swift or Voltaire. Dr. Thomas More, the antihero, is named for Henry VIII's dissenting lord chancellor who had so secure a concept of self that he would not commit perjury for his king. Playwright Robert

Bolt writes of St. Thomas More's contract with God:

> "More was a very orthodox Catholic and for him an oath was something perfectly specific; it was an invitation to God, an invitation God would not refuse, to act as a witness and to judge; the consequence of perjury was damnation. . . . It may be that a clear sense of self (like More's) can *only* crystallize round something transcendental, in which case our prospects are poor, for we are rightly committed to the rational. I think the paramount gift our thinkers, artists, and . . . men of science should labor to get for us is a sense of selfhood without resort to magic."

Walker Percy created *Love in the Ruins* for just that purpose—to show how Dr. More can be "committed to the rational" yet discover a sense of self as soul in a decadent world of the future (1983) where the individual man or woman is regarded as an organism. In this hostile place, More fights to regain the "lovely ordinary world" and a sense of the numinous in phenomena.

The plot turns on More's invention of the Lapsometer, which, when applied to the forehead, can measure the degree to which the patient has "lapsed" from wholeness. Tom's most serious cases of "angelism-bestialism" are like Sutter Vaught's character in the previous novel: they spend their days theorizing for the government in a techno-industrial park called Fedville, but after work find it impossible to "re-enter" the world except by violent, meaningless sex. Others escape angelism, or theorizing, by drugs, chiefly alcohol, which is More's route. He cannot stand remembering the deaths of his wife and daughter, and he cannot stand the idea of perhaps not getting the Nobel Prize for his invention of the Lapsometer, so he drinks and stumbles fecklessly through his days.

The novel begins north of Lake Pontchartrain during the week of 4 July 1983. More has positioned himself as a sniper near the crucial interstate highway. He has three women holed up in a defunct Howard Johnson's—one blonde, one redhead, and one brunette—as it is the end of the world and he intends to be prepared. Since no one has a clear sense of self anymore—no sense of himself as a child of God with a free will and a relatedness to humanity—man can be anything, which translates into being nothing. All the angry factions of people who fear they are nothing are about to shoot it out in Feliciana Parish, Louisiana, and, by implication, everywhere else.

As More—mad scientist and man of pride—waits for "The shot heard 'round the world" to signal the beginning of the end, he flashes back to tell how this town became so sundered and death-loving. One important part of the flashback concerns Art Immelmann, Percy's figure for Mephistopheles, who tempts More into promising his soul in return for the secret of how to cure, not just diagnose, with the Lapsometer. The power to cure is a temptation to pure power and also, like Faust, to the love of a beautiful woman. The "crisis" of the novel occurs at Fedville, as Immelmann hands out Lapsometers to everyone in the audience gathered to watch Tom demonstrate and cure a patient of his psychic disturbances. Thinking the Lapsometer a toy, the scientists, doctors, and nurses point them at one another, and the whole auditorium is reduced to people acting like beasts or saints. Once they leave the hall, society is doomed, and the rest of the novel is Tom's fight for individuated selfhood now that the world is insane, each person becoming all body or all mind.

Lancelot (1977) continues Percy's theme of the rationalistic self lost in the split between the mind and body: sex is regarded as no restorative to wholeness; only faith suffices. Percy's heroes have been progressively more disturbed in each of the four books; Lancelot Andrews Lamar, a madman named for a seventeenth-century English divine, is another descendant of a stoical southern family in decline. Percy once remarked that in Lancelot he wanted to push Stoicism as far as it would go—and the result is a madman, now incarcerated in a prison-hospital. The time is All Saints' Day one year after Lancelot has blown up Belle Isle, his plantation home, with his wife, Margot, her lover, and two others burned to death inside.

In New Orleans, on this day of tidying gravesites and thinking of the dead, Father John, an old friend of Lancelot's, happens upon the prisoner as the priest makes his counseling visits in the ward. In nine chapters, following Dante's plan for *The Divine Comedy*, Lance tells Percival his infernal tale. Possessed by love for Margot, Lancelot wakes from his sleepy, Miniver Cheevy-like life when he discovers his wife has been unfaithful. He plots revenge immediately and purifies his body in knightly fashion as he goes on a quest for evil. Like Othello, he wants "the ocular proof " of Margot's adulterous sex; in this "sexual-theological" tale, Lancelot is maddened by dealing with people who no longer see sex as a sacred promise—its pleasure inexpressible—between two people for life. To the rationalistic world, sex is just the rubbing together of molecules; being out of step with society drives Lance to obsession and murder. But at the end of this confessional novel, it becomes possible that one who regards married sex as ecstatic, "unspeakable," and sacred could also, by a dialectical movement, turn to God for similar nourishment. In Lancelot's moment of greatest crisis—admitting his "coldness," his murderousness—is the potential for conversion.

In *The Second Coming*, Will Barrett is now a wealthy, retired Wall Street lawyer living in the North Carolina mountains. Percy's fifth novel makes Lancelot's improbable dream of living in the Shenandoah Valley with Anna, a gang-raped New Orleans social worker, a reality for Will. Hamlet-like, Will is haunted by another "old mole," the voice of his father, a suicide, as shown in *The Last Gentleman*. The voice urges Will to kill himself, too, since he is also melancholy and "death-loving." The voice is seductive and asks Will to join him. Will, like Hamlet, wonders whether he can stand up to such a force.

Will gives God one last chance to redeem him; he arms himself with tranquilizers and a flashlight, goes down into a deep mountain cave, and dares God to speak to him as he spoke to Abraham and Jacob. Otherwise he will die. Instead, Will gets an excruciating toothache, the crisis which gives him a chance to stop all his posturing, and runs around in the cave looking for a way out: finding a dentist, not death, is on his mind. What happens, though, is unexpected and spontaneous, and it may be God's answer to him. Will falls through a thin wall of the cave into a greenhouse in which a runaway mental patient, Allison Huger, has been hiding out. She nurses him back to health, and Will is able to fight suicidal tendencies by becoming her lover and a follower of God. Unlike Lancelot Lamar, Will Barrett does not have to choose between death and God once he has failed to understand love: Will Barrett figures out a way to have both God and Allison, the transcendent and immanent. Percy, not easily pleased with his work, liked this novel and his next one the best of his oeuvre. Critics are divided but generally most admire *The Moviegoer* and *Lancelot*.

Percy's sixth and last novel, *The Thanatos Syndrome* (1987), reintroduces Tom More in mythical Feliciana Parish as he returns from a two-year prison term for selling drugs to truckers. Still a

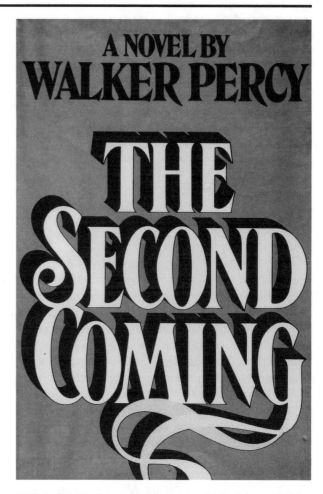

Dust jacket for Percy's 1980 novel, which along with The Thanatos Syndrome *(1987) he regarded as his best work*

psychiatrist, Tom begins noticing that his patients have become as docile as sheep and as lusty as goats. He and his cousin, Dr. Lucy Lipscomb, play detective, and find that for greed and out of sympathy for their irrationality and unhappiness, government scientists at Fedville have injected a potion in the area's drinking water. The chemical effectively robs all citizens of their personalities, their free will, and their "maladaptation" to the social engineers' plan for a utopia in Louisiana: women keep house without complaint and blacks return gladly to the fields, singing decorously as they pick cotton. But Tom and Lucy discover that the power class preaches patriotism as it practices pederasty, the angelism-bestialism split again. As in *Love in the Ruins*, Percy gallops full tilt against the idols of Middle America, and his satire of clichés, trendiness, and narcissistic values is hilariously reflective of what we see and are every day.

Father Rinaldo Smith, who makes a small but corrective appearance in *Love in the Ruins*, here follows an idea Percy learned from Flannery O'Connor. Earlier, Percy explored the motif somewhat in Lancelot's fascist desire to be the leader of a third American Revolution and tell everyone how to live while leaving the weak behind to die. O'Connor, along with Dostoyevski, believed that pity is a dangerous emotion because it leads one to condescend to others and presume to decide for them. Given man's penchant for violence, Percy agrees; Fr. Smith opines that "Tenderness leads to the gas chambers."

Rinaldo Smith runs a hospice in Feliciana where the terminally ill are aided to die with dignity, but the experts at Fedville want to take it over. Fr. Smith predicts that euthanasia and even genocide will result; the drinking water scheme is just the beginning. Like St. Simon Stylites, an early Christian martyr who lived on top of a pole to protest the evildoings of the people below, Fr. Smith barricades himself inside a fire tower in the pine forest to protest government plans to "improve the quality of life." In the priest's intermittent talks there with Tom More, Percy repeats the structure of the dialogues found throughout his novels.

Like a psychomachia, each dialogue—between Binx and Aunt Emily, Will and Sutter, Tom and Art, Lancelot and Percival, Will and the ghost of his father, and Tom and Fr. Smith—is Percy's way of dramatizing the various forms of good and evil extant in America. In fact, as a kind of Isaiah-minus-the-burning-coal, Walker Percy finds his best self-characterization.

Two months after his death, Percy was eulogized by Edward Hoagland in an article on the state of American fiction, "Shhh! Our Writers Are Sleeping! Or Have They Just Fallen into a Deep Moral Coma?" (*Esquire*, July 1990). Hoagland argues that in the grab for lucrative book contracts and the temptation to loaf as writers in residence, many American novelists have become corrupted, losing their toughness of character as rapidly as young Wall Street bond salesmen. Hoagland asks, "Hey, you Fat Cats, and you other guys who write 'experimental' prose but cautiously cling in real life to your professorships, hasn't the group-grope gone on long enough? Hasn't the day dawned to let some fresh air in?"

Hoagland finds these writers so cynical that "no vocabulary, no mind-set existed [in 1989] for digesting the gleeful events in Eastern Europe"

which promised freedoms unheard of a few days ago to millions of people. "Historically," Hoagland writes, chiding such writers as Philip Roth, Norman Mailer, John Barth, and John Updike, "it's been rare for novelists to write so continually about themselves; until 1930 it would have seemed quite absurd." These novelists, he argues, have abrogated their duty to write about and take a moral stand on the many changes taking place in America today: our changing relationships with other peoples; the shrinking and increasingly polluted planet; crime; drugs; racism; AIDS. "Writers in numbers witnessed all this, but forebore to comment for fear of becoming unpopular . . . there has been a feeling lately that to be thought ethical would be an embarrassment."

Only a handful of novelists were "chronicling [this] delirium of change," and Percy heads Hoagland's short list of those writers who address readers who read in order to learn how to live. Hoagland concludes by asking, "Can't we be modern, instead of 'postmodern,' again, even specifying that life of itself is good? From Hawthorne to Nathanael West, we have masterpieces of private vision," but since 1960 writers have "lost that instinct for self-effacement that is a writer's talisman . . . and that precious fluidity" in telling a story that teaches, delights, and moves the reader. Percy fulfills Hoagland's requirement that a valuable book is the product of a life lived honestly and intelligently by a writer who does not "hyperventilate" or "pose for *People*" magazine.

Like Ralph Waldo Emerson, Henry David Thoreau, and Nathaniel Hawthorne, Percy was an ethical writer who exposed an American Vanity Fair but more courageously so since ethics in art was no longer the spirit of the late twentieth century. Humorous, philosophical, satirical, poetic, vituperative, rageful, musing and quizzical by turns, Percy sat—uncomfortable most of the time—high in his own metaphorical fire tower and sounded literary tocsins to wake the forest dwellers from their deep sleep and enable them to live once more related to one another, each sovereign and each searching by means of dialogue.

Bibliographies:

Carol Dana, *Andrew Lytle, Walker Percy, Peter Taylor: A Reference Guide*, edited by Victor Kramer (Boston: G. K. Hall, 1983);

Stuart Wright, *Walker Percy: A Bibliography: 1930-1984* (Westport, Conn.: Meckler, 1986);

Linda Whitney Hobson, *Walker Percy: A Comprehensive Descriptive Bibliography* (New Orleans: Faust, 1988).

Interviews:

Linda Whitney Hobson, "Interview with Walker Percy," *Xavier Review* (1984): 1-19;

Lewis A. Lawson and Victor A. Kramer, eds., *Conversations with Walker Percy* (Jackson: University Press of Mississippi, 1985);

Patrick H. Samway, "An Interview with Walker Percy," *America*, 154 (15 February 1986): 121-123;

Kim Heron, "Technological Hubris," *New York Times Book Review*, 92, 5 April 1987, p. 22;

Phil McCombs, "Century of Thanatos: Walker Percy and His 'Subversive Message,' " *Southern Review*, 24 (Autumn 1988): 808-824;

Wayne King, "Bad Times on the Bayou," *New York Times Magazine*, 11 June 1989, pp. 56-59, 120, 122, 124-125;

Scott Walter, "Nuns, Nazis, and the Poor Old Pope: An Interview with Walker Percy," *Crisis*, 7 (July/August 1989): 12-18.

References:

William Rodney Allen, *Walker Percy: A Southern Wayfarer* (Jackson: University Press of Mississippi, 1986);

Harold Bloom, ed., *Modern Critical Views: Walker Percy* (New York: Chelsea House, 1986);

Robert H. Brinkmeyer, Jr., *Three Catholic Writers of the South* (Jackson: University Press of Mississippi, 1985);

Robert Coles, *Walker Percy: An American Search* (Boston: Little, Brown, 1978);

J. Donald Crowley and Sue Mitchell Crowley, eds., *Walker Percy: Critical Essays* (Boston: G. K. Hall, 1989);

John Edward Hardy, *The Fiction of Walker Percy* (Urbana: University of Illinois Press, 1987);

Linda Whitney Hobson, *Understanding Walker Percy* (Columbia: University of South Carolina Press, 1988);

Lewis A. Lawson, ed., *Following Percy: Essays on Walker Percy's Work* (Troy, N.Y.: Whitson, 1987);

Patricia Lewis Poteat, *Walker Percy and the Old Modern Age: Reflections on Language, Argument, and the Telling of Stories* (Baton Rouge: Louisiana State University Press, 1985);

L. Jerome Taylor, *In Search of Self: Life, Death, and Walker Percy* (Cambridge, Mass.: Cowley, 1986);

Jac Tharpe, *Walker Percy* (Boston: Twayne, 1983);

Tharpe, ed., *Walker Percy: Art and Ethics* (Jackson: University Press of Mississippi, 1980);

Jay Tolson, *Walker Percy: The Making of an American Moralist* (New York: Simon & Schuster, 1990).

Papers:

Walker Percy's papers and manuscripts are in the Southern Historical Collection of the Louis Round Wilson Library, the University of North Carolina at Chapel Hill.

A TRIBUTE

from CLEANTH BROOKS

Walker Percy was one of the most distinguished American novelists of the twentieth century. Though he had planned to become a physician (a major in chemistry at the University of North Carolina and an M.D. at Columbia University), his medical career ended almost as soon as it had begun when he contracted tuberculosis as an intern at Bellevue Hospital.

Percy's turning to fiction was careful and thoughtful and proved to be brilliantly correct. He had the natural talents for a literary career, and his first published novel, *The Moviegoer*, won the National Book Award in 1961.

He followed this work with five other novels and two volumes of nonfiction, the latter concerned with semiotics, observations on contemporary American society, and philosophical and theological disquisitions. Percy loved ideas, his beliefs were powerful and coherent. Rather early he became a Roman Catholic. His views on our culture were special and yet were stated in lively prose that carried conviction.

Though Percy refused to write what he called "The Southern Novel," he possessed a marvelously full and accurate knowledge of his native South—of its people of all classes, of both sexes, and of blacks as well as whites. Moreover, he never forgot that he was a novelist and therefore was not to preach. He must rather render situations in all their particularity and dramatize events in their full emotional power.

He was indeed a sharp and witty commentator on the human scene, a delight to read. But he also had his wisdom to offer to impart. As a man, as a human being, he was generous, kindly, and truly genial.

Literary Awards and Honors Announced in 1990

ACADEMY OF AMERICAN POETS AWARDS

BASSINE CITATION
Allen Grossman.

FELLOW
William Meredith.

LAMONT POETRY SELECTION
Li-Young Lee, *The City in Which I Love You* (BOA).

HAROLD MORTON LANDON TRANSLATION AWARD
Stephen Mitchell, *Variable Directions*, by Dan Pagis (North Point).

PETER I. B. LAVAN YOUNGER POET AWARDS
George Bradley, Jorie Graham, Mary Jo Salter.

WALT WHITMAN AWARD
Elaine Terranova, *The Cult of the Right Hand* (Doubleday).

AMERICAN ACADEMY AND INSTITUTE OF ARTS AND LETTERS AWARDS IN LITERATURE

WITTER BYNNER FOUNDATION POETRY PRIZE
Jacqueline Osherow.

E. M. FORSTER AWARD
Jeanette Winterson.

WILLIAM DEAN HOWELLS MEDAL
E. L. Doctorow, *Billy Bathgate* (Random House).

SUE KAUFMAN PRIZE FOR FIRST FICTION
Allan Gurganus, *Oldest Living Confederate Widow Tells All* (Knopf).

RICHARD AND HINDA ROSENTHAL FOUNDATION AWARD
Daniel Stern, *Twice-Told Tales* (Paris Review Editions).

HAROLD D. VURSELL AWARD
Peter Brown.

MORTON DAUWEN ZABEL AWARD
Paul Auster.

HANS CHRISTIAN ANDERSEN AWARDS

Tormod Haugen, Lisbeth Zwerger.

BANCROFT PRIZES

Neil R. McMillen, *Dark Journey: Black Mississippians in the Age of Jim Crow* (University of Illinois Press).

James H. Merrell, *The Indians' New World: Catawbas and Their Neighbors from European Contact through the Era of Removal* (University of North Carolina Press).

BAY AREA BOOK REVIEWERS ASSOCIATION AWARDS

CHILDREN'S BOOK
Esther Blanc, *Berchick, My Mother's Horse* (Volcano).

FRED CODY MEMORIAL AWARD FOR LIFETIME ACHIEVEMENT
Alice Walker.

FICTION
Amy Tan, *The Joy Luck Club* (Putnam's).

NONFICTION
Robert Easton and Peter Nabokov, *Native American Architecture* (Oxford).

Ronald Takaki, *Strangers from a Different Shore: A History of Asian Americans* (Little, Brown).

POETRY

Adrienne Rich, *Time's Power: Poems 1985-1988* (Norton).

PUBLISHER'S CITATION

Harriet Rohmer and Children's Book Press.

CURTIS G. BENJAMIN AWARD FOR CREATIVE PUBLISHING

Jeremiah Kaplan.

IRMA SIMONTON BLACK AWARD

Robert D. San Souci, *The Talking Eggs*, illustrated by Jerry Pinkney (Dial).

JAMES TAIT BLACK MEMORIAL PRIZES

BIOGRAPHY

Ian Gibson, *Federico Garcia Lorca: A Life* (Faber & Faber).

NOVEL

James Kelman, *A Disaffection* (Secker & Warburg).

BOBBIT PRIZE

James Merrill.

ELMER HOLMES BOBST AWARDS IN ARTS AND LETTERS

EMERGING WRITER IN FICTION
Joe Schall.

EMERGING WRITER IN POETRY
Bruce Murphy.

FICTION
Joyce Carol Oates.

NONFICTION
Susan Sontag.

POETRY
Philip Levine.

BOOKER PRIZE

A. S. Byatt, *Possession* (Chatto & Windus).

BOOTS ROMANTIC NOVEL OF THE YEAR

Reay Tannahill, *Passing Glory* (Century).

BOSTON GLOBE-HORN BOOK AWARDS

FICTION
Jerry Spinelli, *Maniac Magee* (Little, Brown).

NONFICTION
Jean Fritz, *The Great Little Madison* (Putnam's).

PICTURE BOOK
Ed Young. Translator and illustrator, *Lon Po Po: A Red-Riding Hood Story from China* (Philomel).

SPECIAL CITATION FOR CREATIVE EXCELLENCE

Nancy Ekholm Burkert, *Valentine & Orson* (Farrar, Strauss & Giroux).

RANDOLPH CALDECOTT AWARDS

CALDECOTT MEDAL
Lon Po Po: A Red-Riding Hood Story from China, translated and illustrated by Ed Young (Philomel).

CALDECOTT HONOR BOOKS
Bill Peet: An Autobiography, written and illustrated by Bill Peet (Houghton Mifflin).

Color Zoo, written and illustrated by Lois Ehlert (Lippincott).

Hershel and the Hanukkah Goblins, written by Eric Kimmel and illustrated by Tina Schart Hyman (Holiday House).

The Talking Eggs, written by Robert D. San Souci and illustrated by Jerry Pinkney (Dial).

CANADA-AUSTRALIA LITERARY PRIZE

Audrey Thomas.

CAREY-THOMAS PUBLISHING AWARD

Verso.

COMMON WEALTH AWARD OF DISTIN-GUISHED SERVICE TO LITERATURE

Aharon Appelfield.

COMMONWEALTH WRITERS PRIZE

BEST BOOK
Mordecai Richler, *Solomon Gursky Was Here* (Viking).

JOHN DOS PASSOS PRIZE FOR LITERATURE

Paule Marshall.

DOROTHY CANFIELD FISHER AWARD

Amy Erlich, *Where It Stops, Nobody Knows* (Dial).

GOLDEN KITE AWARDS

FICTION
Kirstiana Gregory, *Jenny of the Tetons* (Harcourt Brace Jovanovich / Gulliver).

ILLUSTRATION
Richard Jesse Watson, *Tom Thumb* (Harcourt Brace Jovanovich).

NONFICTION
Judith St. George, *Panama Canal: Gateway to the World* (Putnam's).

THE GOVERNOR GENERAL'S LITERARY AWARDS

CHILDREN'S LITERATURE
(ILLUSTRATION)
Paul Morin, illustrator of *The Orphan Boy*, by Tololwa Marti Mollel (Oxford University Press).

Pierre Pratt, illustrator of *Les Fantaisies de l'oncle Henri*, by Bénédicte Froissart (Annick).

CHILDREN'S LITERATURE
(TEXT)
Michael Bedard, *Redwork* (Lester & Orpen Dennys).

Christine Duchesne, *La Vraie Histoire du chien de Clara Vic* (Editions Québec/Amérique).

DRAMA
Ann-Marie MacDonald, *Goodnight Desdemona (Goodmorning Juliet)* (Coach House Press).

Jovette Marchessault, *Le Voyage magnifique d'Emily Carr* (Leméac).

FICTION
Nino Ricci, *Lives of the Saints* (Cormorant).

Gérald Tougas, *La Mauvaise Foi* (Editions Quebec/Amérique).

NONFICTION
Stephen Clarkson and Christina McCall, *Trudeau and Our Times* (McClelland & Stewart).

Jean-François Lisée, *Dans l'oeil de l'aigle* (Boréal).

POETRY
Margaret Avison, *No Time* (Lancelot).

Jean-Paul Daoust, *Les Cendres bleues* (Les Ecrits des Forges).

TRANSLATION

Jane Brierley, *Yellow-Wolf and Other Tales of the Saint Lawrence*, by Phillipe-Joseph Aubert de Gaspé (Véhicule).

Charlotte and Robert Melançon, *Le Second Rouleau*, by Abraham Moses Klein (Boréal).

DRUE HEINZ LITERATURE PRIZE

Rick Hillis, *Limbo River* (University of Pittsburgh Press).

O. HENRY AWARD

Lance Bertelsen, "San Pietro and the 'Art' of War" (*Southwest Review*, Spring, 1989).

HUGO AWARDS

NOVEL

Dan Simmons, *Hyperion* (Doubleday).

NONFICTION

Alexi Panshin and Cory Panshin, *The World beyond the Hill: Science Fiction and the Quest for Transcendence* (Tarcher).

INGERSOLL PRIZES

T. S. ELIOT AWARD FOR
CREATIVE WRITING

Charles Causley.

RICHARD M. WEAVER AWARD FOR
SCHOLARLY LETTERS

Forrest McDonald.

IOWA SHORT FICTION AWARD

Marly Swark, "A Hole in the Language."

JANET HEIDINGER KAFKA PRIZE FOR FICTION BY AN AMERICAN WOMAN

Marianne Wiggins, *John Dollar* (Harper & Row).

ROBERT F. KENNEDY MEMORIAL BOOK AWARDS

Tracy Kidder, *Among Schoolchildren* (Houghton Mifflin).

Alec Wilkinson, *Big Sugar* (Knopf).

KENYON REVIEW AWARDS

FICTION

Sharon Sheehe Stark.

POETRY

Eleanor Ross Taylor and Charles Simic.

CORETTA SCOTT KING AWARD

Paricia McKissack and Frederick McKissack, *Long Hard Journey: The Story of the Pullman Porter* (Walker).

Nathaniel Talking, *Eloise Greenfield*, illustrated by Jan S. Gilchrist (Black Butterfly Children's Press).

LANNAN LITERARY AWARDS

FICTION

John Hawkes.

NONFICTION

Barry Lopez.

POETRY

Seamus Heaney.

LIBRARY ASSOCIATION MEDALS

BESTERMAN MEDAL

William Ringler, Jr., *Bibliography and Index of English Verse Printed 1476-1558* (Mansell).

CARNEGIE MEDAL

Anne Fine, *Goggle-eyes* (Hamish Hamilton).

KATE GREENAWAY MEDAL

Michael Foreman, *War Boy: A Country Childhood* (Pavilion).

McCOLVIN MEDAL

John Simpson and Edmund Weiner, editors, *The Oxford English Dictionary* (Oxford University Press).

RUTH LILLY POETRY PRIZE

Hayden Carruth.

LOS ANGELES TIMES BOOK PRIZES

BIOGRAPHY

Geoffrey C. Ward, *A First-Class Temperament: The Emergence of Franklin Roosevelt* (Harper & Row).

CURRENT INTEREST

O. B. Hardison, Jr., *Disappearing through the Skylight: Culture and Technology in the Twentieth Century* (Viking/Penguin USA).

FICTION

Edna O'Brien, *Lantern Slides* (Farrar, Straus & Giroux).

HISTORY

Richard Fletcher, *The Quest for El Cid* (Knopf).

ROBERT KIRSCH AWARD

Czeslaw Milosz.

POETRY

John Caddy, *The Color of Mesabi Bones* (Milkweed).

SCIENCE AND TECHNOLOGY

Jane S. Smith, *Patenting the Sun: Polio and the Salk Vaccine* (Morrow).

JOHN D. AND CATHERINE T. MACARTHUR FOUNDATION FELLOWSHIPS

Guy Davenport, Jorie Graham, Patricia Hampl, John Hollander, Thomas Cleveland Holt, Marc Shell, Susan Sontag.

SHIVA NAIPAUL AWARD

Vanessa Juliet Letts.

NATIONAL BOOK AWARDS

FICTION

Charles Johnson, *The Middle Passage* (Atheneum).

MEDAL FOR DISTINGUISHED CONTRIBUTION TO AMERICAN LETTERS

Saul Bellow.

NONFICTION

Ron Chernow, *The House of Morgan: An American Banking Dynasty and the Rise of Modern Finance* (Atlantic Monthly).

NATIONAL BOOK CRITICS CIRCLE AWARDS

BIOGRAPHY / AUTOBIOGRAPHY

Geoffrey C. Ward, *A First Class Temperament: The Emergence of Franklin Roosevelt* (HarperCollins).

CITATION FOR EXCELLENCE IN REVIEWING

Carol Anshaw.

CRITICISM

John Clive, *Not by Fact Alone: Essays on the Writing and Reading of History* (Knopf).

FICTION

E. L. Doctorow, *Billy Bathgate* (Random House).

GENERAL NONFICTION

Michael Dorris, *The Broken Cord* (HarperCollins).

POETRY

Rodney Jones, *Transparent Gestures* (Houghton Mifflin).

IVAN SANDOFF AWARD FOR CONTRIBUTIONS TO AMERICAN PUBLISHING

James Laughlin.

NATIONAL JEWISH BOOK AWARDS

AUTOBIOGRAPHY/MEMOIR

Lucy S. Dawidowicz, *From that Place and Time: A Memoir, 1938-1947* (Norton).

CHILDREN'S LITERATURE
Lois Lowry, *Number the Stars* (Houghton Mifflin).

CHILDREN'S PICTURE BOOK
Esther Silverstein Blanc, *Berchick*, illustrated by Tennessee Dixon (Volcano).

CONTEMPORARY JEWISH LIFE
Riv-Ellen Prell, *Prayer and Community: The Havura in American Judaism* (Wayne State University Press).

FICTION
A. B. Yehoshua, *Five Seasons*, translated by Hillel Halkin (Doubleday).

HOLOCAUST
Abraham Lewin, *A Cup of Tears: A Diary of the Warsaw Ghetto* (Basil Blackwell).

ISRAEL
Harris O. Schoenberg, *A Mandate for Terror: The United Nations and the PLO* (Shapolsky).

JEWISH HISTORY
Eli Lederhendler, *The Road to Modern Jewish Politics* (Oxford University Press).

JEWISH THOUGHT
Marc Saperstein, *Jewish Preaching 1200-1800* (Yale University Press).

SCHOLARSHIP
Jeremy Cohen,*"Be Fertile and Increase, Fill the Earth and Master It": The Ancient and Medieval Career of a Biblical Text* (Cornell University Press).

VISUAL ARTS
David Cohen, editor, *The Jews in America* (Collins).

NEBULA AWARDS

NOVEL
Elizabeth Ann Scarborough, *The Healer's War* (Spectra).

NOVELLA
Lois McMaster Bujold, "The Mountains of Mourning," *Analog* (May 1989).

NOVELETTE
Connie Willis, "At the Rialto," *Omni* (October 1989).

SHORT STORY
Geoffrey A. Landis, "Ripples in the Dirac Sea," *Isaac Asimov's Science Fiction Magazine* (November 1989).

NEUSTADT INTERNATIONAL PRIZE FOR LITERATURE

Tomas Tranströmer.

JOHN NEWBERY AWARDS

NEWBERY MEDAL
Lois Lowry, *Number the Stars* (Houghton Mifflin).

NEWBERY HONOR CITATIONS
Janet Taylor Lisle, *Afternoon of the Elves* (Orchard).

Suzanne Fisher Staples, *Shabanu, Daughter of the Wind* (Knopf).

Gary Paulsen, *The Winter Room* (Orchard).

NOBEL PRIZE FOR LITERATURE

Octavio Paz.

SCOTT O'DELL AWARD FOR HISTORICAL FICTION

Carolyn Reeder, *Shades of Gray* (Macmillan).

PEN LITERARY AWARDS

FAULKNER AWARD FOR FICTION
E. L. Doctorow, *Billy Bathgate* (Random House).

ERNEST HEMINGWAY FOUNDATION AWARD
Mark Richard, *The Ice at the Bottom of the World* (Knopf).

PEN / MARTHA ALBRAND AWARD FOR NONFICTION
Amy Wilentz, *The Rainy Season: Haiti since Duvalier* (Simon & Schuster).

PEN / NELSON ALGREN FICTION AWARD FOR A WORK IN PROGRESS
Kim Edwards, "Sky Juice."

PEN / BOOK-OF-THE-MONTH CLUB TRANSLATION PRIZE
William Weaver, *Foucault's Pendulum* by Umberto Eco (Harcourt Brace Jovanovich).

PEN / JERARD FUND AWARD
Corolyne Wright, "The Road to Isla Negra."

PEN / MALAMUD AWARD FOR EXCELLENCE IN THE SHORT STORY
George Garrett.

RENATO POGGIOLI TRANSLATION AWARD FOR A WORK IN PROGRESS
John Satriano for his translation of Marco Lodoli's *Diario di un millenio che fugge*.

PEN-NEW ENGLAND AWARD FOR LITERARY EXCELLENCE

Stratis Haviaras.

ΦBK'S CHRISTIAN GAUSS AWARD

Evelyn Barish, *Emerson: The Roots of Prophecy* (Princeton University Press).

EDGAR ALLAN POE AWARDS

BEST MYSTERY PLAY
Larry Gelbart, *City of Angels*.

BIOGRAPHICAL/CRITICAL STUDY
Norman Sherry, *The Life of Graham Greene, Volume I: 1904-1939* (Penguin U.S.A.).

FACT CRIME
Jack Olsen, *Doc: The Rape of the Town of Lovell* (Atheneum).

FIRST NOVEL
Susan Wolfe, *The Last Billable Hour* (St. Martin's).

ROBERT L. FISH MEMORIAL AWARD
Connie Holt.

GRAND MASTER
Helen McCloy.

MYSTERY NOVEL
James L. Burke, *Black Cherry Blues* (Little, Brown).

ORIGINAL PAPERBACK
Keith Patterson, *The Rain* (Bantam).

ELLERY QUEEN
Joel Davis.

RAVEN
Carol Brener.

READER OF THE YEAR
Sarah Booth Conroy.

YOUNG ADULT NOVEL
Alane Ferguson, *Show Me the Evidence* (Bradbury).

POETRY SOCIETY OF AMERICA

GEORGE BOGIN MEMORIAL AWARD
John Matthias, *A Gathering of Ways* (Swallow).

MELVILLE CANE AWARD
John Hollander, *Harp Lake* (Knopf).

ALICE FAY DI CASTAGNOLA AWARD
Martha Collins, David Kelly.

GUSTAV DAVIDSON MEMORIAL AWARD
Rhina P. Espaillat.

NORMA FARBER FIRST BOOK AWARD
Lucia Mario Perillo, *Dangerous Life* (Northeastern).

FROST MEDALS
James Laughlin, Denise Levertov.

JOHN MASEFIELD MEMORIAL AWARD
Sophie Cabot Black.

LUCILLE MEDWICK AWARD
Patricia Clark, Carolyn Wright.

SHELLEY MEMORIAL AWARD
Thom Gunn.

WILLIAM CARLOS WILLIAMS AWARD
Ivan Arguelles, *Looking for Mary Lou: Illegal Syntax* (Rock Steady).

ROBERT H. WINNER MEMORIAL AWARD
Carole Oles, Renee Ashley.

PRESENT TENSE/JOEL H. CAVIOR LITERARY AWARDS

BIOGRAPHY/AUTOBIOGRAPHY
Yehuda Nir, *The Lost Childhood* (Harcourt Brace Jovanovich).

CURRENT AFFAIRS
Thomas Friedman, *From Beirut to Jerusalem* (Farrar, Straus & Giroux).

FICTION
Aharon Appelfeld, *For Every Sin* (Grave Weidenfeld).

HISTORY
Yirmiyahu Yovel, *Spinoza and Other Heretics* (Princeton University Press).

JEWISH RELIGIOUS THOUGHT
Marc Saperstein, *Jewish Preaching, 1200-1800* (Yale University Press).

JUVENILE LITERATURE
Eric A. Kimmel and Trina Schart Hyman, *Hershel and the Hanukkah Goblins* (Holiday House).

SPECIAL CITATION FOR LIFETIME ACHIEVEMENT.
Alfred Kazin.

PULITZER PRIZES

BIOGRAPHY
Sebastian de Grazia, *Machiavelli in Hell* (Princeton University Press).

DRAMA
August Wilson, *The Piano Lesson*.

FICTION
Oscar Hijuelos, *The Mambo Kings Play Songs of Love* (Farrar, Straus & Giroux).

GENERAL NONFICTION
Dale Maharidge and Michael Williamson, *And Their Children After Them* (Pantheon).

HISTORY
Stanley Karnow, *In Our Image: America's Empire in the Philippines* (Random House).

POETRY
Charles Simic, *The World Doesn't End* (Harcourt Brace Jovanovich).

REA AWARD FOR THE SHORT STORY

Joyce Carol Oates.

REGINA MEDAL

Virginia Hamilton.

WHITBREAD BOOK OF THE YEAR AWARD

Richard Holmes, *Coleridge, Early Visions* (Hodder & Stoughton).

WHITING AWARD

Lucy Gannon, *Keeping Tom Nice*.

Checklist: Contributions to Literary History and Biography

This checklist is a selection of new books on various aspects of literary and cultural history, including biographies, memoirs, and correspondence of literary people and their associates.

Ackroyd, Peter. *Dickens*. London: Sinclair-Stevenson, 1990.

Aldiss, Brian. *Bury My Heart at W. H. Smith's: A Writing Life*. London: Hodder & Stoughton, 1990.

Amis, Kingsley. *Kingsley Amis: In Life and Letters*. Edited by Dale Salwak. New York: St. Martin's Press, 1990.

Andersen, Hans Christian. *The Diaries of Hans Christian Andersen*. Selected and translated by Patricia L. Conroy and Sven H. Rossel. Seattle: University of Washington Press, 1990.

Anderson, Sherwood. *Sherwood Anderson's Love Letters to Eleanor Copenhaver Anderson*. Edited by Charles E. Modlin. Athens: University of Georgia Press, 1990.

Ansen, Alan. *The Table Talk of W. H. Auden*. New York: Persea Books, 1990.

Austen, Jane. *My Dear Cassandra*. Edited by Penelope Hughes-Hallet. London: Collins & Brown, 1990.

Bair, Deirdre. *Simone de Beauvoir*. New York: Summit Books, 1990.

Belford, Barbara. *Violet: The Story of the Irrepressible Violet Hunt and Her Circle of Lovers and Friends: Ford Madox Ford, H. G. Wells, Somerset Maugham, and Henry James*. New York: Simon & Schuster, 1990.

Bergeen, Laurence. *As Thousands Cheer: The Life of Irving Berlin*. New York: Viking, 1990.

Berry, Wendell. *Harlan Hubbard: Life and Work*. Lexington: University Press of Kentucky, 1990.

Blain, Virginia, with Patricia Clements and Isobel Grundy. *The Feminist Companion to Literature in English: Women Writers from the Middle Ages to the Present*. New Haven: Yale University Press, 1990.

Blishen, Edward. *The Penny World*. London: Sinclair-Stevenson, 1990.

Bowles, Paul. *Two Years Beside the Strait: Tangier Journal 1987-1989*. London: Owen, 1990.

Boyd, Brian. *Vladimir Nabokov: The Russian Years*. Princeton, N.J.: Princeton University Press, 1990.

Brecht, Bertolt. *Letters 1913-1956*. Edited by John Willet, translated by Ralph Manheim. New York: Routledge, 1990.

Browning, Elizabeth Barrett and Robert. *The Brownings' Correspondence*, Volume 6: June 1842 - March 1843; Volume 7: March 1843 - October 1843; Volume 8: October 1843 - May 1844. Edited by Philipp Kelley and Ronald Hudson. Winfield, Kans.: Wedgestone Press, 1990.

Burgess, Anthony. *You've Had Your Time*. London: Heinemann, 1990.

Burney, Fanny. *Early Journals and Letters, Volume 2*. Edited by L. E. Troide. New York: Oxford University Press, 1990.

Canavaggio, Jean. *Cervantes*. Translated by Joseph R. Jones. New York: Norton, 1990.

Carlyle, Jane Welsh and Thomas. *Collected Letters Volumes 16, 17, and 18*. Edited by K. J. Fielding and C. De L. Ryals. Durham, N.C.: Duke University Press, 1990.

Carter, Humphrey. *The Brideshead Generation: Evelyn Waugh and His Friends*. New York: Houghton Mifflin, 1990.

Cassady, Carolyn. *Off the Road: My Years with Cassady, Kerouac, and Ginsberg*. New York: Morrow, 1990.

Caws, Mary Ann. *Women of Bloomsbury: Virginia, Vanessa, and Carrington*. New York: Routledge, 1990.

Chitham, Edward. *A Life of Anne Brontë*. Cambridge, Mass.: Basil Blackwell, 1990.

Clough, Arthur Hugh. *The Oxford Diaries of Arthur Hugh Clough*. Edited by Anthony Kenny. New York: Oxford University Press, 1990.

Coleridge, Samuel Taylor. *The Notebooks of Samuel Taylor Coleridge, Volume 4: 1819-1826*. Edited by Kathleen Coburn and Merton Christensen. Princeton, N.J.: Princeton University Press, 1990.

Coles, Gladys Mary. *Mary Webb*. Mid Glamorgan: Seren Books, 1990.

Conrad, Joseph. *The Collected Letters of Joseph Conrad: Volume 4, 1908-1911*. Edited by Frederick R. Karl and Laurence Davies. New York: Cambridge University Press, 1990.

Cooper, William. *From Early Life*. London: Macmillan, 1990.

Coote, Stephen. *William Morris: His Life and Work*. London: Garamond, 1990.

Cousineau, Phil, ed. *The Hero's Journey: Joseph Campbell on His Life and Work*. San Francisco, Cal.: Harper, 1990.

Davies, Dido. *William Gerhardie: A Biography*. Oxford: Oxford University Press, 1990.

Davies, Russell. *Ronald Searle*. London: Sinclair-Stevenson, 1990.

Deledalle, Gerard. *Charles S. Peirce: An Intellectual Biography*. Philadelphia, Pa: John Benjamins North America, 1990.

Dodd, Valerie A. *George Eliot: An Intellectual Life*. New York: St. Martin's Press, 1990.

Dove, Richard. *He was a German: A Biography of Ernst Toller*. London: Libris, 1990.

Dunn, Jane. *A Very Close Conspiracy: Vanessa Bell and Virginia Woolf*. London: Cape, 1990.

Emerson, Ralph Waldo. *The Letters of Ralph Waldo Emerson, Volume 7: 1807-1844*. Edited by Eleanor M. Tilton. New York: Columbia University Press, 1990.

Ernst, Robert. *Weakness Is a Crime: The Life of Bernarr Macfadden*. Syracuse: Syracuse University Press, 1990.

Farwell, Byron. *Burton: Life of Sir Richard Francis Burton*. London: Penguin, 1990.

Fast, Howard. *Being Red: A Memoir*. Boston, Mass.: Houghton Mifflin, 1990.

Ffinch, Michael. *Cardinal Newman: The Second Spring*. London: Weidenfeld & Nicolson, 1990.

Fiedler, Leslie. *Fiedler on the Roof: Apostle to the Gentiles*. Boston: David R. Godine, 1990.

Fleishman, Lazar. *Boris Pasternak: The Poet and His Politics*. Cambridge, Mass.: Harvard University Press, 1990.

Frank, Katherine. *Emily Brontë: A Chainless Soul*. Boston, Mass.: Houghton Mifflin, 1990.

Gill, Gillian C. *Agatha Christie: The Woman and Her Mysteries*. New York: Free Press, 1990.

Gilley, Sheridan. *Newman and His Age*. London: Darton, Longman & Todd, 1990.

Goethe, Johann Wolfgang von. *Selected Letters from Goethe to Frau von Stein, 1776-1789*. Edited and translated by Robert M. Browning. Columbia, S.C.: Camden House, 1990.

Goodman, Charlotte Margolis. *Jean Stafford: The Savage Heart*. Austin: University of Texas Press, 1990.

Graves, Richard Percival. *Robert Graves: The Years with Laura, 1926-40*. New York: Viking Penguin, 1990.

Griffin, Peter. *Less Than a Treason: Hemingway in Paris*. New York: Oxford University Press, 1990.

Haining, Peter. *Agatha Christie: Murder in Four Acts*. London: Virgin, 1990.

Hardwick, Joan. *An Immodest Violet: The Life of Violet Hunt*. London: Deutsch, 1990.

Hayman, Ronald. *Proust: A Biography*. New York: HarperCollins, 1990.

Hayter, Alethea. *Portrait of a Friendship: Drawn from New Letters of James Russell Lowell to Sybella Lady Lyttelton 1881-1891*. Salisbury: Russell, 1990.

Holmes, Richard. *Coleridge: Early Visions*. New York: Viking, 1990.

Holt, Hazel. *A Lot to Ask: A Life of Barbara Pym*. London: Macmillan, 1990.

Hopkins, Gerard Manley. *Selected Letters*. Edited by Catherine Phillips. New York: Oxford University Press, 1990.

Howe, Irving. *Selected Writings, 1950-1990*. San Diego: Harcourt Brace Jovanovich, 1990.

Ionesco, Eugene. *Fragments of a Journal*. Edited by Jean Stewart. New York: Paragon House, 1990.

James, Henry, and Edith Wharton. *Henry James and Edith Wharton: Letters, 1900-1915*. Edited by Lyall Powers. New York: Grove Weidenfeld, 1990.

Jay, Elisabeth, ed. *The Autobiography of Margaret Oliphant*. New York: Oxford University Press, 1990.

Judd, Alan. *Ford Madox Ford*. London: Collins, 1990.

Jungk, Peter Stephen. *Life Torn by History: Franz Werfel 1890-1945*. New York: Grove Weidenfeld, 1990.

Kaye, M. M. *The Sun in the Morning*. New York: St. Martin's Press, 1990.

Kenney, Catherine. *The Remarkable Case of Dorothy L. Sayers*. Kent, Ohio: Kent State University Press, 1990.

Kent, George E. *A Life of Gwendolyn Brooks*. Lexington: University Press of Kentucky, 1990.

Kesey, Ken. *The Further Inquiry*. With photographs by Ron Bevirt. New York: Viking, 1990.

King, James. *The Last Modern: The Life of Herbert Read*. New York: St. Martin's Press, 1990.

Kipling, Rudyard. *Something of Myself and Other Autobiographical Writings*, revised and enlarged. Edited by Thomas Pinney. New York: Cambridge University Press, 1990.

Kurth, Peter. *American Cassandra: The Life of Dorothy Thompson*. Boston: Little, Brown, 1990.

Lauber, John. *The Inventions of Mark Twain: A Biography*. New York: Hill & Wang, 1990.

Layman, C. H. *Man of Letters: The Early Life and Love-letters of Robert Chambers*. Edinburgh: Edinburgh University Press, 1990.

Layton, Irving, and Robert Creeley. *Irving Layton and Robert Creeley: The Complete Correspondence, 1953-1978*. Edited by Ekbert Faas and Sabrina Reed. Montreal: McGill-Queens University Press, 1990.

Leider, Emily Wortis. *California's Daughter: Gertrude Atherton and Her Times*. Stanford, Cal.: Stanford University Press, 1990.

Leverich, Lyle. *Tom: The Young Tennessee Williams, a Biography*. New York: Grove Weidenfeld, 1990.

Lingeman, Richard R. *Theodore Dreiser. Volume 2: An American Journey 1908-1945*. New York: Putnam's, 1990.

London, Joan. *Jack London and His Daughters*. Berkeley, Cal.: Heyday Books, 1990.

Long, Judith Reick. *Gene Stratton-Porter: Novelist and Naturalist*. Bloomington: Indiana University Press, 1990.

Longsworth, Polly. *The World of Emily Dickinson*. New York: Norton, 1990.

MacAdams, William. *Ben Hecht: A Biography*. New York: Scribners, 1990.

Mann, Golo. *Reminiscences and Reflections: A Youth in Germany*. Translated by Krishna Winston. New York: Norton, 1990.

McKay, F. M. *The Life of James K. Baxter*. New York: Oxford University Press, 1990.

McLellan, David. *Simone Weil: Utopian Pessimist*. New York: Poseidon, 1990.

McLynn, Frank. *Burton: Snow Upon the Desert*. London: John Murray, 1990.

Meyer, Michael. *Not Prince Hamlet*. Oxford: Oxford University Press, 1990.

Meyers, Jeffery. *D. H. Lawrence: A Biography*. New York: Knopf, 1990.

Miller, Henry. *Letters from Henry Miller to Hoki Tokuda Miller*. Compiled by Joyce Howard. London: Robert Hale, 1990.

Miller. *Letters to Emil*. Edited by George Wickes. Manchester: Carcanet, 1990.

Miller, Ruth. *Saul Bellow: A Biography of the Imagination*. New York: St. Martin's Press, 1990.

Molesworth, Charles. *Marianne Moore: A Literary Life*. New York: Atheneum, 1990.

Monk, Ray. *Ludwig Wittgenstein: The Duty of Genius*. New York: Free Press, 1990.

Mullen, Richard. *Anthony Trollope: A Victorian in his World*. London: Duckworth, 1990.

Nash, Ogden. *Loving Letters from Ogden Nash: A Family Album, Volume 1*. Edited by Linell Nash Smith. Boston: Little, Brown, 1990.

Northey, Anthony. *Kafka's Relatives: Their Lives and His Writing*. New Haven, Conn.: Yale University Press, 1990.

Olson, Charles, and Edward Dahlberg. *In Love, In Sorrow: The Complete Correspondence of Charles Olson and Edward Dahlberg*. Edited by Paul Christensen. New York: Paragon House, 1990.

O'Neal, Hank. *"Life Is Painful, Nasty and Short . . . In My Case It Has Only Been Painful and Nasty:" Djuna Barnes, An Informal Memoir 1978-1981*. New York: Paragon House, 1990.

Pasternak, Evgeny. *Pasternak: The Tragic Years, 1930-1960*. London: Collins, 1990.

Pichois, Claude. *Baudelaire*. Translated by G. Robb. London: Hamish Hamilton, 1990.

Du Plessis, Rachel Blau. *The Selected Letters of George Oppen*. Durham, N.C.: Duke University Press, 1990.

Porter, Katherine Anne. *The Letters of Katherine Anne Porter*. Selected and edited by Isabel Bayley. Boston: Atlantic Monthly Press, 1990.

Powys, John Cowper. *The Letters of John Cowper Powys to Ichiro Hara*. Edited by Anthony Head. London: Cecil Woolf, 1990.

Raby, Peter. *The Life of Samuel Butler*. London: Hogarth, 1990.

Reddick, Allen. *The Making of Johnson's Dictionary, 1746-1773*. Cambridge: Cambridge University Press, 1990.

Rice, Edward. *Captain Sir Richard Francis Burton: The Secret Agent Who Made the Pilgrimage to Mecca, Discovered the Kama Sutra, and Brought the Arabian Nights West*. New York: Scribners, 1990.

Richards, I. A. *Selected Letters of I. A. Richards*. Edited by John Constable. New York: Oxford University Press, 1990.

Rollyson, Carl. *Nothing Ever Happens to the Brave: The Story of Martha Gellhorn*. New York: St. Martin's Press, 1990.

Rossetti, William Michael. *Selected Letters of William Michael Rossetti*. Edited by Roger W. Peattie. University Park: Pennsylvania State University, 1990.

Rosslyn, Felicity. *Alexander Pope: A Literary Life*. New York: St. Martin's Press, 1990.

Rudd, Charles A. *Russian Entrepreneur: Publisher Ivan Sytin of Moscow, 1851-1934*. Montreal: McGill-Queen's University Press, 1990.

Shaw, George Bernard, and A. M. Gibbs. *Shaw: Interviews and Recollections*. Iowa City: University of Iowa Press, 1990.

Silesky, Barry. *Ferlinghetti: The Artist in His Time*. New York: Warner, 1990.

Smith, Bruce. *Costly Performances: Tennessee Williams; The Last Stage*. New York: Paragon House, 1990.

Spurling, Hilary. *Paul Scott: A Life*. London: Hutchinson, 1990.

St. John, John. *William Heinemann: A Century of Publishing, 1890-1990*. London: Heinemann, 1990.

Stuart, David. *O. Henry: A Biography of William Sydney Porter*. Chelsea, Mich.: Scarborough House, 1990.

Styron, William. *Darkness Visible: A Memoir of Madness*. New York: Random House, 1990.

Sutherland, John. *Mrs. Humphry Ward: Eminent Victorian, Pre-Eminent Edwardian*. Oxford: Oxford University Press, 1990.

Taylor, Ina. *A Woman of Contradictions: The Life of George Eliot*. New York: Morrow, 1990.

Tennyson, Alfred, Lord. *The Letters of Alfred, Lord Tennyson: Volume III, 1871-1892*. Edited by Cecil Y. Lang and Edgar F. Shannon, Jr. New York: Oxford University Press, 1990.

Thomas, Donald Serell. *Henry Fielding*. London: Weidenfeld & Nicolson, 1990.

Thwaite, Ann. *A. A. Milne: The Man Behind Winnie-the-Pooh*. New York: Random House, 1990.

Tomalin, Claire. *The Invisible Woman: The Story of Nelly Ternan and Charles Dickens*. London: Viking, 1990.

Toth, Emily. *Kate Chopin*. New York: Morrow, 1990.

Toulouse, Teresa, and Andrew H. Delbanco. *The Complete Sermons of Ralph Waldo Emerson, Volume II*. Columbia: University of Missouri Press, 1990.

Twain, Mark. *Mark Twain's Letters, Volume 2: 1867-1868*. Edited by Harriet Elinor Smith and Richard Bucci. Berkeley: University of California Press, 1990.

Twain. *Mark Twain's Own Autobiography: The Chapters from the North American Review*. Madison: University Press of Wisconsin, 1990.

Vanden Heuvel, Katrina. *The Nation, 1965-1990; Selections from the Independent Magazine of Politics and Culture*. New York: Thunder's Mouth Press, 1990.

Vincent, John. *Disraeli*. Oxford: Oxford University Press, 1990.

Webb, Barry. *Edmund Blunden: A Biography*. New Haven, Conn.: Yale University Press, 1990.

Wheen, Francis. *Tom Driberg: His Life and Indiscretions*. London: Chatto & Windus, 1990.

Whitman, Walt. *Selected Letters of Walt Whitman*. Edited by Edwin Haviland Miller. Iowa City: University of Iowa Press, 1990.

Wilhelm, J. J. *Ezra Pound in London and Paris (1908-1925)*. University Park: Pennsylvania State University Press, 1990.

Williams, Tennessee. *Five O'Clock Angel: Letters of Tennessee Williams to Maria St. Just, 1948-1982*. Edited by St. Just. New York: Knopf, 1990.

Wilson, A. N. *C. S. Lewis: A Biography*. New York: Norton, 1990.

Wivel, Ole. *Karen Blixen*. London: Bloomsbury, 1990.

Wodehouse, P. G. *Yours, Plum: The Letters of P. G. Wodehouse*. Edited by Frances Donaldson. London: Hutchinson, 1990.

Woolf, Virginia. *Congenial Spirits: The Selected Letters of Virginia Woolf*. Edited by Joanne Trautmann Banks. San Diego: Harcourt Brace Jovanovich, 1990.

Woolf. *A Moment's Liberty: The Shorter Diary*. Edited by Anne Oliver Bell. San Diego: Harcourt Brace Jovanovich, 1990.

Woolf. *A Passionate Apprentice: The Early Journals, 1897-1909*. Edited by Mitchell A. Leaska. San Diego: Harcourt Brace Jovanovich, 1990.

Yeats, William Butler. *The Collected Letters of W. B. Yeats, Volume III: 1901-1904*. Edited by John Kelly. New York: Oxford University Press, 1990.

Necrology

Louis Althusser—22 October 1990
Evelyn Ames—25 January 1990
Mario Pinto Andrade—26 August 1990
Don Appell—4 May 1990
Reinaldo Arenas—7 December 1990
Colette Audry—20 October 1990
Margot Austin—25 June 1990
John Benedict—23 July 1990
Bruno Bettelheim—13 March 1990
Elisa Bialk—28 February 1990
Joseph Blumenthal—11 July 1990
Florence Bonime—2 October 1990
Edward E. Booher—24 September 1990
Frank P. Bourgin—12 December 1990
Herbert Brodkin—29 October 1990
Anatole Broyard—11 October 1990
William Earl Buckler—25 February 1990
Olive Ann Burns—4 July 1990
Oliver Butterworth—17 September 1990
Howard Cady—5 November 1990
Morley Callaghan—25 August 1990
Bernice Carey—8 February 1990
Josephine Case—8 January 1990
Harry M. Caudill—29 November 1990
Brainard Cheney—15 January 1990
Robert Chesley—5 December 1990
Marquis W. Childs—30 June 1990
John L. Clive—7 January 1990
Carvel Collins—10 April 1990
Alexander T. Colt—2 March 1990
Jack Conroy—28 February 1990
Michael Cooke—11 September 1990
Aaron Copland—2 December 1990
Norman Cousins—39 November 1990
Lester Cowan—21 October 1990
Lawrence Cremin—4 September 1990
Roald Dahl—23 November 1990
Lucy S. Dawidowicz—5 December 1990
Hedley Donovan—13 August 1990
Richard Little Durby—7 August 1990
Lawrence Durrell—7 November 1990
Friedrich Durrenmatt—14 December 1990
Arnard d'Usseau—29 January 1990
Ethyl Eichelberger—11 August? 1990
Fritz Eichenberg—30 November 1990
Harold E. Fey—30 January 1990

Stuart Beroy Flexner—3 December 1990
John Fox—14 August 1990
Pauline Frederick—9 May 1990
John Fuller—7 November 1990
Harold L. Ginsburg—4 October 1990
Maurice Girodias—4 July 1990
Ira Glackens—23 November 1990
Bernard Glemser—3 April 1990
D. B. Hardison—5 August 1990
James D. Hart—23 July 1990
Carolyn Haywood—11 January 1990
Erich Heller—5 November 1990
Jack Iams—27 January 1990
Josephine Johnson—27 February 1990
Louis Jones—25 October 1990
Richard Kain—5 April 1990
Tadeusz Kantor—3 December 1990
Alan Kapelner—3 September 1990
Lawrence Kasha—29 September 1990
Alfred Kouzel—6 September 1990
Samuel Kramer—26 November 1990
Ihsan Abdel Kuddous—11 January 1990
Eric Larrabee—4 December 1990
Lewis Leary—1 May 1990
Larry Lee—5 April 1990
Rosamond Lehmann—12 March 1990
Michel Leiris—30 September 1990
Edmund G. Love—30 August 1990
Alfred Lovell—1 August 1990
Gabriel Mace—23 June 1990
Norman Maclean—2 August 1990
Hugh MacLenran—7 November 1990
Mary Mannes—13 September 1990
Thomas McGrath—20 September 1990
Dennis McIntyre—1 February 1990
Alberto Moravia—26 September 1990
Seth Morgan—17 October 1990
Lilian T. Mowrer—30 September 1990
Malcolm Muggeridge—14 November 1990
Lewis Mumford—26 January 1990
Barney Nagler—22 October 1990
George Nichols III—22 November 1990
Edmund H. North—28 August 1990
Brendan O'Hehir—26 October 1990
William Owens—7 December 1990
William E. Paley—26 October 1990

Walker Percy—10 May 1990
Laurence J. Peter—12 January 1990
Valentin Pikul—17 July (?) 1990
Manuel Puig—22 July 1990
Benjamin L. Reid—30 November 1990
Maurice Richlin—20 November 1990
Lee J. Richmond—17 August 1990
Yannis Ritsos—12 November 1990
Allen Riukin—10 February 1990
Dorothy J. Roberts—27 February 1990
Robert Rodale—20 September 1990
Elliot Roosevelt—27 October 1990
Alma Sioux Scarberry—10 April 1990
Irene Mayer Selznick—10 October 1990
Anya Seton—8 November 1990
Stanley Shapiro—21 July 1990
Kate Simon—4 February 1990
B. F. Skinner—18 August 1990
Dodie Smith—24 November 1990
Carol Sobieski—4 November 1990

Andrew P. Solt—4 November 1990
W. M. Spackman—3 August 1990
Bella Spewack—27 April 1990
Richard Strout—19 August 1990
Phillippe Suopault—11 March 1990
Lola L. Szladits—30 May 1990
A. J. P. Taylor—7 September 1990
Willard Thorp—15 February 1990
Jimmy Van Heusen—7 February 1990
Antoine Vitez—30 April 1990
Matthew Ward—23 June 1990
Charles M. Warren—11 August 1990
Nat Wartels—7 February 1990
Patrick White—30 September 1990
John C. Willey—27 April 1990
Thomas Williams—23 October 1990
Andrew Witwer—22 September 1990
Donald A. Wollheim—2 November 1990
Evarts Ziegler—24 November 1990

Letter from a New Germany

James Hardin
University of South Carolina,
and
Donna Hoffmeister
University of Colorado-Boulder

By all accounts the creation of a united Germany will have as many-sided and profound consequences as those which occurred in France after the French Revolution. The euphoria after the opening of the wall on 9 November 1989 and East German elections on 18 March 1990 was quickly followed by disorientation, skepticism, helplessness, and anxiety. Peter Schneider, who wrote about Germany in the *New York Times Magazine*, summed up the current malaise with this witticism: "the wall is all the Germans have in common." His provocative novel *Der Mauerspringer* (Darmstadt: Luchterhand, 1982; translated by Leigh Hafrey as *The Wall Jumper*, New York: Pantheon, 1983) analyzes the several German walls (conflicting backgrounds, norms, and social values) that prevent a meeting of minds. A variant on a satiric beer hall song of the post-World War I era has also been making the rounds: "Wir wollen unsere Mauer wieder haben." Instead of demanding the return of the kaiser, the refrain is now: "We want our wall back." Unfortunately, these jokes reflect grave conflicts.

The speed of German unification has had repercussions for intellectual life in Germany. The key question is whether Germany's writers and intellectuals can achieve an ideological détente in the face of a bitter controversy that has been reported in the press every week during the last six months. It began with heated attacks on Christa Wolf—a respected East German writer who has often been cited as a contender for the Nobel Prize in Literature—by Frank Schirrmacher in the *Frankfurter Allgemeine Zeitung* on 2 June 1990 and by Ulrich Greiner in *Die Zeit* of 1 June 1990. Wolf, along with other prominent writers—particularly Stefan Heym, Heiner Müller, and Christoph Hein—is being charged with moral complicity in the repressive policies of the East German totalitarian regime. Precisely those members of the creative intelligentsia who reached an accommodation with the SED (the East German Socialist Unity party) while remaining its most outspoken critics are now labeled *Wendehälse* (turncoats). Wolf had managed the almost impossible task of maintaining open channels of communication with the party, with the dissidents, and with her Western readers. Wolf, Walter Jens, Günter de Bruyn, Eduard Goldstücker, Andrzej Szczypiorski, and prominent politicians East and West engaged in a public debate on 13 June at the Third Colloquium in Potsdam organized by Bertelsmann Publishers, but the climate of suspicion and distrust continues. Now almost all the major writers from both Germanies have taken a public position in the controversy, including Volker Braun, Martin Walser, Rainer Kirsch, Peter Härtling, Uwe Friesel, Walter Kempowski, Hans Mayer, Jurek Becker, and Günter Grass. It has been a major event, and because of it the union of the two German PEN Clubs and the two Berlin Academies of Arts has been stymied. Neither Walter Jens, president of the West Berlin Academy of the Arts, nor Heiner Müller, newly elected president of the East Berlin Academy, sees any possibility of a union within the near future.

The publication of Wolf's novella *Was bleibt* (What Remains, Luchterhand)—written in 1979 but not published until June 1990—started the furor. This story, which describes the writer's attempt to cope with overt surveillance by the secret police (*Stasi*), is taken as proof of her alleged opportunism, dishonesty, and lack of concern for the people. It is claimed that if *Was bleibt* had been published in 1979 it might have influenced the course of history. The story's publication now, her critics claim, is merely an embarrassment and the product of a guilty conscience. In the view of Schirrmacher and Greiner it is unprincipled for her to exploit a relatively harmless surveillance when other, less well known people's lives were destroyed by the Communist state.

They further assert that by refusing to speak out against the Stasi and the wall earlier or to comment on the invasions of Czechoslovakia and Afghanistan or about Central European dissidents, she impeded social progress. It has been charged that her hesitation to do so out of fear of aiding the cause of capitalist ideologues is not to her credit. In addition, it is alleged, her talents, like those of other East German writers, have been grossly overestimated because of her special status as a prominent writer of the German Democratic Republic (GDR); she was a state poet, even, some suggest, a lapdog. In part the problem lay in the naïveté of GDR establishment writers, who did not fully understand the repressive nature of Communist power. Writers such as Karl Mickel, Stefan Heym, Christoph Hein, and Stephan Hermlin initially allied themselves with the state apparatus; the move seemed to make sense in the face of the atrocities of Auschwitz and nazism, these writers argue, because the Communist regime could rightly claim that the Communists had been in the opposition during the Hitler era. But by supporting the state these writers inadvertently helped to perpetuate the legacy of fascism. As a variant of the official voice—enabled by power, indebted to power, privileged and courted by power—the writers under scrutiny in the press helped to legitimize the Communist regime.

Other writers, such as Günter Grass, decry the sweeping condemnations and personal vindictiveness voiced by critics such as Schirrmacher and Greiner. The evolution of public discourse as it took shape in GDR literature, they say, is a complicated one, and the literary attacks are actually a part of a hidden West German conservative agenda which, as Christine Schoefer put it in a piece in the *Nation* of 22 October 1990, "is intent not only on doing away with the Communist East but on erasing the history of the G.D.R. and the very idea of socialism itself." She contends that "Wolf is a sacrificial lamb in a larger project: the ideological shaping of unified Germany." The embattled writers object to the tone and tactics of their opponents, which remind them of American-style McCarthyism. Günther Kunert, in an article in the *Frankfurter Allgemeine Zeitung* of 30 June 1990, claims that GDR writers were neither victims nor accomplices but simply defended themselves against a perfidious political system as best they could. Some Western critics, it is claimed elsewhere, idealized GDR dissidents in order to promote their own ideological platform. Lutz

Rathenow, in an article in *Die Welt* of 30 June 1990, claims that an awareness of the subversive activity of such GDR writers as Gert Neumann, Jürgen Fuchs, Gabriele Eckart, Uwe Kolbe, and Stephan Krawczyk is being stifled for ideological reasons also.

Some defenders of GDR writers go so far as to credit them with bringing about the revolution that occurred in East Germany last November. It is pointed out that Christoph Hein, Helga Königsdorf, Christa Wolf, and Stefan Heym participated in the mass demonstrations in Leipzig and Berlin, and that their earlier works depicted the difficulties of life under a totalitarian regime. They helped to weaken official doctrine by criticizing day-to-day life in the GDR, sometimes at great personal cost. Herbert Heckmann reminded his readers, in an article in the *Frankfurter Rundschau* of 30 June 1990, that Christa Wolf's novel *Kindheitsmuster* (Berlin: Aufbau-Verlag, 1976; translated by Ursule Molinaro and Hedwig Rappolt as *A Model Childhood*, New York: Farrar, Straus & Giroux, 1980) depicts the treacherous, seductive powers of state ideology. She may have avoided public controversy as a consequence of her temperament, as Günter Grass says, or she may never have been a political author. Still, as Elizabeth Grotz wrote in *Die Presse*, 7 July 1990, Wolf's works lent courage to her fellow countrymen. Christa Wolf's concern with conscience, authenticity, and individual honesty in all her writings called into question the ideologically closed worldview of the Communist state. Wolf's defenders remind us how often she offended the Communist party establishment. Her novel *Nachdenken über Christa T.* (Halle: Mitteldeutscher Verlag, 1968; translated by Christopher Middleton as *The Quest for Christa T.*, New York: Farrar, Straus & Giroux, 1970), and other such texts as Karl Mickel and Adolf Endler's poetry anthology, *In diesem besseren Land* (In This Better Land, Malle: Mitteldeutscher Verlag, 1966), Ulrich Plenzdorf's *Die neuen Leiden des jungen W.* (Frankfurt: Suhrkamp, 1973; translated by Kenneth P. Wilcox as *The New Sufferings of Young W.*, New York: Ungar, 1979), and the *Unvollendete Geschichte* (Unfinished Story, Frankfurt: Suhrkamp, 1977) by Volker Braun, prepared the way for the revolutionary process. These writers, it is asserted, were greatly admired in the general population because they represented an otherwise forbidden opposition. Plays by Heiner Müller, Volker Braun, and Christoph Hein that focused on Stalinism, the Hitler-Stalin pact, and the purges of the 1930s helped to raise a crucial historical consciousness. Even variations in style provided focal points of resistance on the cultural level. Fragmentation and interrupted sequences, for instance, were a way to criticize state dogma about the inevitable course of history. The fact remains, however, that the intellectuals who signed a petition entitled "Für unser Land" (For Our Country) in December 1989, including Christa Wolf, Helga Schütz, Helga Königsdorf, Sigrid Damm, Daniella Dahn, Gerti Tetzner, Rosemarie Zeplin, Volker Braun, and Stefan Heym, revealed how isolated they were from the true sentiments of an overwhelming majority of the people. The petition called for the continued autonomy of a socialist GDR. The man on the street had other ideas and other intentions.

This separation of intellectual discourse from the world as it suddenly now is has already had far-reaching consequences for many former GDR writers and intellectuals. GDR literature only made sense in the context of the public sphere of East Germany. Seventy-eight East German publishers—all of them state enterprises—produced 6,500 titles and printed 150 million books every year. It is likely that only about ten of these seventy-eight publishing firms will survive in unified Germany. And they will contend with totally different conditions. Because of the pressures of the market economy they will be looking for the kind of trade books that can compete with television. A senior editor of Henschel Publishers predicts that there will be many more popular science books, hobby manuals, and children's books and fewer socially critical literary works. Seventy percent of GDR authors and translators received stipends and subsidies set aside for them in what are called *Kulturfonds*. They will now have to adjust to the business realities of negotiating contracts and tuning in to the tastes of a Western literary market. Many writers were published in the West merely because their works could not be published in the East. Less well known writers will not even have a chance of survival. The most tragic aspect of the impending readjustment is the profound dislocation and disillusionment experienced by those writers who sincerely believed in the ideals of humanistic socialism. Having lost a social context and critical themes, a unique literary function and audience, they have become marginal. Their plays are being performed to half-empty theaters, and they are being lambasted in the press. It will be difficult for many of these writers to carry on the business of earning a living

and even more difficult to cope with their dashed hopes for a humane society which would offer a viable alternative to capitalism.

Other cultural unions are progressing peacefully. Duden Publishers East and West (Bibliographisches Institut Brockhaus AG and Verlag VEB Bibliographisches Institut), publishers that have reigned supreme in their separate spheres in questions of spelling and linguistic usage, have now combined editorial and marketing staffs and plan the joint publication in 1992 of the definitive volume on German spelling. Likewise the East and West Associations of the German Book Trade (Börsenverein) have fused and plan two annual book fairs, one in Leipzig in the spring and one in Frankfurt in the fall. Reclam Publishers in Stuttgart, known for its inexpensive paperbacks, has entered a cooperative arrangement with Reclam of Leipzig to eliminate competition and to strive for mutual projects. The well-known Literaturinstitut Johannes R. Becher in Leipzig, which trained generations of East German authors in the techniques of writing, will continue to exist but now on a fee-paying basis.

Several hundred applications have been made to establish private publishing firms. Bertelsmann is financing the new firm LinksDruck, run by Christoph Links. Autoren-Kolloquium, directed by Harald Müller, will specialize in East German dramatists, using the model of the Frankfurt Verlag der Autoren. Linden Verlag Leipzig, run by Erich Loest's son, will be publishing books by Erich Loest, Günter Grass, and Klaus Staeck. Another of the first private German publishers in the East is Carlsen Rostock GmbH, run by Konrad Reich, who played a significant role in the publishing world under the old regime. As the editor of the respected Hinstorff Publishers, founded in 1831, he fostered the talents of such significant GDR writers as Erich Arendt, Jurek Becker, Fritz Rudolf Fries, Erich Köhler, and Klaus Schlesinger at a time when other choices would have made life easier for him. Reich has great credibility today because of the courage he displayed during the controversy over Wolf Biermann, who catalyzed opposition forces in the GDR with his antiestablishment political poetry and songs. The Communist regime refused him permission to reenter the GDR after a concert tour in the West in 1976. Many analysts of recent events in Germany are of the opinion that the ensuing public protest by GDR writers who sided with Biermann may well have been the event that decisively undermined the East German regime. Over one hundred writers left East Germany for West Berlin or elsewhere in the Federal Republic in the wave of repression which followed. Reich got out of the publishing business altogether when the East German government tried to make him accountable for the protest by the writers he published.

The Biermann affair also gave rise to the alternative literary movement of the 1980s connected with the Prenzlauer Berg region of East Berlin. Included were such writers as Andreas Koziol, Leonhard Lorek, Bernd Igel, Sascha Anderson, Stefan Döring, Uwe Kolbe, Gert Neumann, Rainer Schedlinski, Ulrich Zieger, and Bert Papenfu-Gorek. They expressed protest by means of idiosyncratic style, orthography, and iconography. Only through a radical departure from the norms of literature and syntax could they resist the repressive measures of the government. Many of these writers appeared in an illegal literary magazine called *Mikado: oder Der Kaiser ist nackt* (Mikado, or the Emperor is Naked), which was published by Uwe Kolbe, Lothar Trolle, and Bernd Wagner from 1983 to 1987 under difficult circumstances in a circulation of one hundred copies per issue. In an attempt to retain their iconoclastic image as writers of the counterculture within the new public sphere, these writers have now formed their own publishing firm called Druckhaus Galrev.

Several intriguing literary journals came to life during the last months of the GDR. *Sondeur: Monatsschrift für Kultur und Politik* favors young writers and provocative perspectives, and resembles in appearance the former *Weltbühne*. The April 1990 issue included articles on abortion, pornography, and the former Stasi chief, Markus Wolf. The art journal *Phönix* hopes to attract sophisticated devotees of the arts, and another new journal, *Die Eselsohren*, bills itself as a spiffy, ultramodern review of books.

Many of the established East German journals are also trying to accommodate the changed climate. The respected periodical *Sinn und Form*, for instance, aims to provide a dispassionate, balanced forum for the discussion of the complicity of intellectuals in the totalitarian politics of the GDR. It is bringing to light damaging facts about the prominent "first-generation" East German writers Johannes R. Becher and Anna Seghers and their controversial roles in the cultural politics of the Stalin era. Becker and Seghers, who enjoyed great public respect and influence during the early years of the regime, refused support to

Walter Janke, the head of Aufbau Verlag, when he was sentenced to prison in 1957 during a wave of Stalinist repression. His rehabilitation this year and the publication of his autobiography, *Schwierigkeiten mit der Wahrheit* (Difficulties with the Truth; Reinbeck bei Hamburg: Rowohlt, 1990), captured public attention. The function of writers in public discourse will almost certainly continue to be the favored topic in the year to come.

The reshuffling of Central Europe, as best reflected in the fall of the Berlin Wall, has apparently thus far not brought forth enduring literary works. At the moment there is no lack of critics in Germany who doubt that anyone is producing first-rate literature in the German-speaking world. Grass has never written another work that could be measured against his *Tin Drum* and its sequels, and much of the postmodernist literature of Germany and Austria is so self-absorbed and minimalist that it interests only other artists and cultists.

What links the lesser talents with many of those of the postwar generation who achieved critical and popular acclaim, such as the recently deceased Viennese playwright and novelist Thomas Bernhard, is a bleak vision of society. Bernhard, who died at age fifty-three—bitter, gloomy, and pessimistic to the end—was one of a handful well known outside of Germany and Austria. In a *New Yorker* article of 9 October 1989 John Updike cited a line from Bernhard's last play, *Heldenplatz*, that describes Austria as "a nation of 6.5 million idiots living in a country that is rotting away, falling away, run by the political parties in an unholy alliance with the Catholic Church." Another example of Bernhard as curmudgeon comes from his book *Wittgensteins Neffe* (Frankfurt am Main: Suhrkamp, 1982; translated by David McLintock as *Wittgenstein's Nephew*, New York: Knopf, 1989): "Let us not deceive ourselves: most of the minds we associate with are housed in heads that have little more to offer than overgrown potatoes, stuck on top of whining and tastelessly clad bodies and eking out a pathetic existence that does not even merit our pity." Updike is somehow attracted to Bernhard's stubborn misanthropy, which, as he writes, "almost sinks to the loveable."

In general the most readable German writers are those who have been around for a time. One of them is the novelist and short-story writer Siegfried Lenz, now sixty-four. *Selected Stories of Siegfried Lenz*, edited and translated by Breon

Mitchell (New York: New Directions, 1989), brings together political parables—one treating a German who wishes to learn directly about the realities of the Holocaust—and delightful satires of contemporary German mores, particularly those of academe. Another writer who has achieved continuing popularity with the reading public in the last two decades is Walter Kempowski. Best known for his family chronicle written in reportorial style (and based closely on events in his own life), his most recent and most entertaining novel, *Hundstage* (Munich: Knaus & Albrecht, 1988), is part thriller, part social satire set in present-day Germany. The English translation of the book, which travels better than most German novels, is scheduled for publication, as *Dog Days*, in early 1991 by Camden House.

Another remarkably durable writer is Ernst Jünger (born 1895), a frontline officer in World War I who is best known for his war novel *In Stahlgewittern* (Berlin: E. S. Mittler & Sohn, 1922; translated by B. Creighton as *The Storm of Steel*, Garden City, N.Y.: Doubleday, 1929). This work and his *Der Kampf als inneres Erlebnis* (War as Inner Experience, Berlin: E. S. Mittler & Sohn, 1922), which capture not only the horror of war but also the exhilaration of combat, have made him a controversial figure to this day. It is well known that Goebbels tried—unsuccessfully—to recruit him for the Nazi cause. But it is generally agreed that his 1939 novel *Auf den Marmorklippen* (Hamburg: Hanseatische Verlagsanstalt, 1939; translated by Stuart Hood as *On the Marble Cliffs*, Norfolk, Conn.: New Directions, 1947) about the tyranny of a brutal, anti-intellectual regime is a parable that courageously attacked Hitler's dictatorship. Jünger's continued literary activity has gradually won him the (sometimes grudging) admiration of the German literary establishment, which was skeptical of his turn to cosmopolitan humanism after World War II. But these days he is beginning to be regarded as the good European and grand old man of German letters. The fact that a consensus is emerging is perhaps best indicated by the fact that the new perception of Jünger has even penetrated the academic world. Frank Schirrmacher in the *Frankfurter Allgemeine Zeitung* of 29 March 1990 wrote that a knowledge of Jünger's early works, especially in their relationship to what is now called the "aesthetics of horror," is essential to an understanding of the events of this century. The writer Rolf Hochhuth in *Die Welt* of 28 March 1990 praised Jünger as *the* representative of German contemporary literature, following in the footsteps of Thomas Mann, who died 35 years ago, and of the expressionist poet Gottfried Benn and of Bertolt Brecht. His new book *Die Schere* (Scissors) takes up the theme of the encroachment of death, and yet it is, in Hochhuth's view, a work that looks forward rather than toward closure. Elias Canetti (born 1905) is another major European writer whose formative period lies well before the advent of postmodernism but whose works in English translation—publication was delayed several years in Great Britain at Canetti's insistence—are now revealing a rich intellect and stylist of immense talent. Canetti's single novel, *Die Blendung* (1932; translated as *Auto da Fé*), won him only a small circle of admirers in the 1930s but is now widely lauded as a brilliant existential parable. His greatest contribution, however, may not be that fine work, or his dramas, essays, travel books, and theoretical works, but his multivolume autobiography, *Die gerettete Zunge: Geschichte einer Jugend* (Munich: Hanser, 1977; translated by Joachim Neugroschel as *The Tongue Set Free*, New York: Continuum, 1979); *Die Fackel im Ohr: Lebensgeschichte 1921-1931* (Munich: Hanser, 1980; translated by Neugroschel as *The Torch in My Ear*, New York: Farrar, Straus & Giroux, 1982); and *Das Augenspiel: Lebensgeschichte 1931-1937* (Munich: Hanser, 1985; translated by Ralph Manheim as *The Play of the Eyes*, New York: Farrar, Straus & Giroux, 1986). Canetti is the quintessential intellectual brought up in the humanistic and literary traditions of the Austro-Hungarian Empire, and yet he has lived since 1939 in London. Long appreciated only by specialists and a few writers and intellectuals, he was so obscure a literary figure in 1981, when he won the Nobel Prize for Literature, that the press hardly knew how to categorize him. The *New York Times*, searching for something unique about the man, pointed out that he was "the first Bulgarian to win the prize." The London *Times* said that he was "the first British citizen to win the literature prize since Winston Churchill." In any case, the autobiography shows well why Canetti has emerged as one of the most significant, influential, and *readable* writers of the twentieth century.

Letter from Japan

Kiyohiko Tsuboi
Okayama University
and
Nobuko Tsuboi
Ochanomizu Women's University

Recent Japanese literature reflects the radical changes from the traditional self-conscious, self-exposing "I" stories (watakushishousetu) of post-World War II poverty-stricken society, to the lighter and brighter satirical writing style reflecting the present superficially affluent society.

Western literature has been imported and vigorously translated into Japanese in the past one hundred years since Japan opened her doors to the world. People have been consuming thirstily everything Western, and, after World War II, American civilization poured into Japan. Those who were born after the war and brought up in the modernized or Americanized society are now writing their own stories and translating contemporary American stories as well. Among their main readings are translated American literary works, from Hawthorne's *The Scarlet Letter* to Updike's *Rabbit, Run*. Seventh and eighth graders who have just begun learning English read *The Catcher in the Rye* in translation—not on account of their interest in English language, but because of their interest in the rebellious American boy and the metropolitan atmosphere. Somehow they feel a very close tie to their American counterparts. A noteworthy publication is *Amerika Seishun Shousetsu Tokushu* (Contemporary American Stories), a collection of translated stories of such young American writers as John Fox, Suzan Allen Toth, Tim O'Brien, Ethan Kanin, and Lorrie Moore, published by Shinohosha in 1989. Writers such as Raymond Carver, John Irving, and Peter Taylor have long enjoyed popularity among Japanese youth.

Yasuo Tanaka has been hailed for the materialistic ambience of his novel *Nantonaku Kurisutal* (Crystal Somehow), including lists of brand goods from perfumes to T-shirts, from Christian Dior to Calvin Klein. Haruki Murakami, with his unique sensitivity and peculiar light touch, has been writing book after book, such as *A Wild Sheep Chase*, about young men who find no serious purposes in this materialistic modern world. Murakami, who once declared his attachment to the writings of F. Scott Fitzgerald and translated some of Fitzgerald's essays from *The Crack-Up* into Japanese, has continued by translating contemporary American writers. His recent story "TV People," which appeared in the *New Yorker* (10 November 1990), is the second story by a Japanese writer in the sixty-five-year history of that magazine. It is one of the six stories collected in his *TV People*, published in 1990 by Bungei-shunju in Tokyo. As some observers point out, present Japanese society is quite similar to American society in the 1920s. We have more or less the same social and mental climates as the Jazz Age.

Banana Yoshimoto, daughter of critic Ryumei Yoshimoto, wrote a story called "Merankoria" (Melancholia) for *Kaien* magazine (April 1990), in which she describes the death of a young actress in a minimalistic way. Her best-selling novel *Tsugumi* (Thrush), published in 1989, was made into a movie in 1990.

However, this year's greatest eye-catcher is *Bungakubu Tadano Kyouju* (Professor Tadano of the Literature Department) by Yasutaka Tsutsui, published by Iwanami Shoten, known for publishing classical and serious books. This novel, a satiric portrait of a professor at a university in Tokyo, has attracted the attention not only of academics but of students and common readers as well, and climbed to the top of the best-seller list in a few months. Professor Tadano (meaning "good for nothing" or "no value" in Japanese) is an eccentric and egocentric man of a type often found on university campuses in Japan. Writing caricatures of university professors once considered inviolable, Tsutsui has exposed real life and work in the academic sanctuary. Instead of writing private lives of scholars psychologically in the way old writers have done, he directly reveals faculty meetings and promotion committees, with explanatory notes to the readers. Especially interesting are Tadano's cynical lectures on contemporary literary criticisms. Each chapter contains one of his lectures ranging from New Criticism to Russian formalism to poststructuralism. At the same time he has had an ambition to be a real writer, not a pretentious professor lecturing on writings by others. He writes stories and novels under a pseudonym rather successfully. Finally he wins the most coveted literary prize, but he is destined to be a target of jealous colleagues who have given up hopes of becoming popular writers and are obliged to teach literature at universities only to make a living.

Next Tsutsui published *Tanpenshousetsu Kougi* (Lectures on Short Stories), a collection of his own criticism (Iwanami). His own critical interpretations of short stories are quite orthodox, and he does not make much use of ultramodern literary theories. He discusses stories by Dickens, Hoffmann, Bierce, Twain, Gorki, Mann, Maugham, and others—expounding his position that new writers find new ideas which inevitably create new forms.

In May *Chiryoto* (He Grows Younger Every Second) by Oe Kenzaburo, an already established writer, was published by Iwanami. A science-fictionesque story, *Chiryoto* tells of the exodus from the polluted Earth by a fleet of spaceships to a new planet, leaving the people who chose to stay behind, and of the return to the Earth after ten years. Kenzaburo tells of an apocalyptic world to come; an episode involving a young man called Hikari, who has some sort of mental disadvantage but has a special talent for music (Kenzaburo's own disabled son is named Hikari), chosen to go aboard the ship to survive, is suggestive of his philosophy. Kenzaburo wrote a series of short stories for various magazines in 1990, and it is expected that it will eventually be collected under the title "Shizukana Seikatsu" (A Quiet Life). The narrator, Marchan, lives with his mentally disabled elder brother, Iiyo, and younger brother, Ohchan, who studies French literature at a university. These are stories of the routine life of three children—one mentally disabled—left behind while their writer father, accompanied by their mother, is away in America as a writer in residence, and of the trials and errors of normal people coping with a disabled person, who symbolizes the contemporary world where people have lost their way.

Recently more than ever the problems of disabled persons are drawing attention. At the end of 1989 three volumes of diary, *Wagako Noa* (A Child Called Noah), *Noa no Basho* (A Place For Noah) and *Irainin Noa* (A Client Called Noah), by Josh Greenfeld were translated into Japanese by his novelist wife, Fumiko Kometani, and have aroused great emotional empathy among Japanese readers. Kometani is a writer well-known for her prizewinning story, "Sugikosi no matsuri" (Passover). She received the 1986 Akutagawa Prize, the most prestigious literary award for new writers, and wrote *Taanburuuiido* (Tumbleweed) in 1986 and *Madamu Kyatapila no Wameki* (Cries of Madame Caterpillar) in 1989, both published by Bungeishuju. In these novels she wrote about her mentally disabled son, who is the boy Noah in the diary of Josh Greenfeld. Kometani, who left Japan to study painting in the United States, where she married Greenfeld and bore a mentally disabled son, has an amazing sense of humor. In writing her novels she makes use of the Osaka dialect (which retains some old Japanese flavor and is quite different from the standard Japanese) and makes serious themes entertaining, comical, and even comforting. Another incident attracting attention from intellectuals this year is the refusal of the Japan Writers' Association to accept the membership of Norio Nagayama, a writer who is said to have shot and killed four men and is sentenced to death. While in prison he began writing stories. He had written a story of the innerscape of his mind called "Muchi no Namida" (Tears of Ignorance) in 1971 and *Kibashi* (The Wooden Bridge), a novel, in 1983. In protest against the conservative attitude of the association, Yasutaka Tsutsui, Kenji Nakagami, and Kojin Karatani seceded from the association.

"Shugyoku" (The Gems), a story by Takeshi Kaiko, who died at the end of 1989, was published in the January 1990 issue of *Bungakukai* magazine. This is a story in three parts—the first telling of a young writer's meeting with an old ship's doctor at a bar, the second of his meeting with the proprietor of a Chinese restaurant, and the third of his meeting with a woman. The plotless, talkative story makes use of association and imagination. Kaiko's last novel, *Hana-owaru-Yami* (In the darkness flowers withered), was published by Shincho Sha.

A novel, never published in book form, by the late Junichiro Tanizaki (1886-1965), known for his aesthetic novels such as *Chijin no Ai* (Love of Idiocy) and *Sasame Yuki* (Tokioka Sisters), was found by Chisato Suga, lecturer in modern literature at Kouka Women's College, in April. "Kozou no Yume" (The Dream of Assistant) was written for *Fukuoka Daily* (now *Nishinihon Newspaper*) in 24 serial installments in 1917. In this story the protagonist, an assistant clerk in a liquor store, buys a literary magazine of the naturalist movement, but he thinks beauty is the only truth that can satisfy the human soul. Then he steals money from the store and goes to see a magic show of a beautiful girl. Suda says that, regardless of its literary value, this is one of the novels in which Tanizaki's aesthetic view of the novel is clearly manifested.

In July an unpublished story by Riichi Yokamitsu (1898-1947), found by a member of his family, was published in *Bungei* magazine. The story tells of an ugly man who falls in love with a pretty nurse when he visits his friend in a hospital, but she is taken away by another man. Suffering from the lost love, he himself gets sick and is hospitalized. He bores a hole in the wall and looks into the next room, only to fall from the bed. Since it has the distinct traits of Yokamitsu, such as a persecution mania and a twisted feeling of love, this early apprentice piece is of great value for the study of Yokamitsu's novels.

Also of literary interest was the publication in September 1990 by Chikuma Shobo of *Zoku Meian* (The Sequel to Light and Dark) by Soseki Natsume. *Light and Dark* is Natsume's last novel, unfinished but highly valued for its intricate psychological description of human egos and considered one of the best modern novels in Japan. There have been previous attempts by writers and critics to guess the ending of the novel, but Minae Mizumura's is the first attempt at reconstruction. Her careful study of Natsume's ideas, style, and idiosyncrasies has made this bold sequel worth the reading. Mizamura was born and brought up in Japan until the age of twelve; on account of her father's business she was educated in Boston and France. She has done graduate work on French literature at Yale and has taught Japanese literature at Princeton. She will teach Japanese literature at the University of Michigan in 1991.

The Akutagawa Prize (in memory of Ryunosuke Akutagawa) and the Naoki Prize (in memory of Sanjuugo Naoki) are the two most coveted of Japan's literary awards. The first-place Akutagawa Prize was given to Mieko Takizawa for "Nakobaba-no-iru-machi-de" ("In a town where an old woman called Nekobaba lives").

This is a memoir of a girl who came back to Japan from the United States and is living with her grandmother and aunt next door to an old woman who likes cats (*neko* in Japanese). Her aunt's death triggers her memory of the days she lost her speech. Akira Ohoka, a son of Makoto Ohoka, the poet, shared the prize for his "Hyosou Seikatsu" (A Life in the Surface Structure), a kind of fantasy in which a clerk at a girls' finishing school gets involved in a video experiment of his electronic-maniac friend.

The first-place Naoki Prizes for popular fiction went to Kiyoshi Hosikawa for his "Shoudenshou" (A brief biography of Shoden, Joruri-singer), a story of tragic love in the Edo era, and to Ryo Hara for his "Watashi Ga Koroshita Shojo" (A girl I killed), a hard-boiled mystery of a private detective arrested by mistake for kidnapping.

The Tsubota Joji Prize, in memory of a children's writer, was given to Tamao Ariyoshi, daughter of Sawako Ariyoshi, known for her problem novels. This award was given for her autobiographical account of the relations between the daughter and the well-known writer-mother.

The Yomiuri Newspaper Literary Prizes for novels went to Yuuichi Takai and Yoshikichi Furui; the Yoshikawa Eiji Prize to Hideki Ozaki; the Mystery-Writers Prize to Jo Sasaki; the Kawabata Ysunari Prize (in memory of Kawabata, Nobel laureate) to Tetsuo Miura. The Mishima Yukio Prize was given to Juugi Hisama, and the Yamamoto Shugoro Prize to Jo Sasaki. Oe Kenzaburo was given the Ito Sei Prize for his *Jinsei-no Shinseki* (Relatives of My Life).

Noboru Tsujihara was awarded the second-place Akutagawa Prize in 1990 for his "Mura-no-namae" (The Name of Village). He tells a story of a Japanese young man working for a trading company. Sent to China, he experiences a series of strange, Kafkaesque incidents in a village named Togenkyou (Arcadia).

Tsumao Awasaka was awarded the second-place Naoki Prize for his *Kagekikyou* (A Painter of Coat of Arms), a collection of short stories of a painter and his old love. The Tanizaki Junichiro Prize went to Kyoko Hayashi for her "Yasurakani imawa nemuri tamae" (Please, Sleep in Peace), and the Women Writer Prizes went to Kiyoko Murata for her *Shiroiyama* (White Mountain), published by Bungeishunju, and to Setsuko Tsumura for her *Ryuseiu* (Shootingstar Rain), published by Iwananshoten.

Many writers have been producing stories and novels, but the year 1990 seems the transitional period from the Roaring Eighties to what might be called the Dark Nineties. Science-fiction-like fantasies, satires, metafiction, and minimalistic writings abound, and they certainly represent the not-so-bright undercurrent of Japanese society.

Obituary: Tatsuo Nagai, once called a master of short stories, and Aya Koda, novelist, daughter of Rohan Koda, a novelist famous at the end of the nineteenth century, died this year.

Letter from Khartoum

Ahmed Nimeiri
University of Khartoum

The press reactions to the awarding of the Nobel Prize to Wole Soyinka in 1986 revealed slight familiarity with African literature in the West. The work of the Nobel laureate was known only to those specializing in African literature in academic and literary circles. This obscurity is due, to a great extent, to the fact that African literature, written in or translated into European languages, is a recent phenomenon. Wole Soyinka wrote his first plays in 1958 and 1959. The publication of African authors in the West did not immediately bring the interest and the recognition their work deserved. Often they fell prey to the benevolence of some Western critics who treated every piece of writing by an African as a significant literary work. On the other extreme many readers and critics saw little intrinsic literary merit in the majority of African writing and regarded African literature as important chiefly for historical, anthropological, and sociological reasons. Such readers and critics were looking at African literature from the perspective of Western literary forms and criteria and finding it superficial, deficient, and, at best, "simple."

Western readers did not find African literature readily accessible when it first came to their attention. There were certain barriers to their reading and understanding. First of all, African literature presented a society and a world whose ethnic, cultural, and even geographic characteristics were different from anything Westerners had known. Without some knowledge of the historical and cultural background of the experience depicted by African writers it would be difficult to understand them. The problem was further complicated by the fact that African writers, especially those writing in English, used language differently from British and American writers. The Africans seemed to have an inadequate control of the language or to deliberately change normal usage to suit their purposes. In many cases their language did not read like language as it was used by a European writer.

With the growth of African literature and the study of Africa, this situation changed slightly. There was a larger readership and more recognition of African writers by the time Wole Soyinka was awarded the Nobel Prize, but these changes have been mostly in academic and literary circles. After Soyinka was awarded the Nobel Prize, John W. Kronik, editor of *PMLA*, congratulated "the prescience and good judgment" of the Modern Language Association membership for having recognized Soyinka's significance a year before the Nobel award when it elected him an honorary member of the MLA (*PMLA*, October 1987). By this Kronik illustrates the meagerness of the recognition of Soyinka. But this is not surprising in the case of an author whose work is part of a literature that began to emerge less than half a century ago.

Genuine African literature in European languages—English, French, Portuguese—began to emerge in the late 1940s. But Africans had been writing poetry, folktales, and drama in their own languages—Bantu, Yoruba, and Swahili—since the nineteenth century. They had also written, at the same time, accounts of their native land in the languages they learned from the missionaries. At the beginning of the twentieth century they wrote didactic tales and poems express-ing their Christian faith and allegiance as well as historical romances such as Thomas Mofolo's *Chaka* (written in Sesotho in 1908 and translated into English, but not published until 1925) and E. Casley-Hayford's *Ethiopia Unbound* (1911). This early literature was published by missionary orga-nizations such as the Society for Promoting Chris-tian Knowledge in London, which delayed the publication of *Chaka* because the novel was thought to contain pagan elements.

The new literature emerged with the birth of nationalism and the awakening of a sense of a distinct African identity. The struggle for indepen-dence, the acquisition of education (especially uni-versity education), and the coming into promi-nence of an articulate elite led to the appearance of an African literary expression as well as move-ments and organizations that gave that expres-sion shape and direction. Contemporary African and Caribbean literature in French began as a pro-test against French rule and the French policy of assimilation. The pioneers of this literature, Leo-pold Sedar Senghor and Aimé Césaire, under-took in the 1930s a critical examination of West-ern values and an assessment of African identity. This led them to the formulation of the idea of negritude: the affirmation of African values against Western materialism, and the assertion that African culture has preserved the mystic warmth of life because of its closeness to nature and its contact with the world's ancient rhythm. In November 1947 Allioune Diop, a Senegalese in-tellectual who advocated a debate between Africa and the West in his contacts with French intellectu-als, founded the literary journal *Presence Afri-caine*. The journal was open to all contributors of goodwill (white, yellow, or black) who might be able to help define African originality and to has-ten its introduction into the modern world. It at-tracted the attention of such preeminent French writers as André Gide, Jean-Paul Sartre and Al-bert Camus, as well as the black American Rich-ard Wright and Diop's compatriots Senghor and Césaire. The early issues of the journal included contributions from leading black intellectuals from Africa, the Caribbean, and the Americas as well as opinions and comments from nonblack in-tellectuals. It was first published in French and then, starting in 1957, in English. Since 1965 it has bee published as a bilingual magazine.

Presence Africaine became the leading Afri-can literary and cultural journal by publicizing the new literature from Africa and the Caribbean

and the ideals associated with that literature. A useful impression of this literature is given in an anthology of Negro poetry that Senghor pub-lished in 1948: *Anthologie de la Nouvelle poesie negre et malgache* (published by Presses Univer-sitaires de France in Paris and republished in 1969). Sartre wrote a now-famous introductory essay for the anthology, "Orphee noir" (Black Or-pheus), in which he defines the concept of negri-tude. The anthology and the introductory essay had a great influence on subsequent writing.

Contemporary African literature in English, in its inception, was produced mainly by a genera-tion of graduates of the newly established universi-ties of Africa. The university colleges of Ibadan and Accra were instituted in 1948, and Makerere College in Kampala became a university in 1949. In the 1950s and the 1960s graduates of these col-leges began to produce a significant literature. The University of Ibadan, in particular, was a great influence on Nigerian writers. Many of them studied and taught there, and the univer-sity afforded them a place where they could be close to their native culture and at the same time be open to Western experience.

The development of new literature was influ-enced by the appearance, in 1957, of *Black Or-pheus*, a literary journal edited by Ulli Beier and Janheinz Jahn. Inspired by *Presence Africaine* and the first Congress of African Writers in Paris (1956), the journal aimed to arouse the creative im-pulse in English-speaking Africans. The first issue reflected the virtual absence of indigenous lit-erature in English-speaking West and East Africa. It featured translations of Senghor, Césaire, and Diop, as well as writing by the South African Eze-kiel Mphahlele and the American Langston Hughes. Shortly—beginning with issue number 7—the editorship of the journal was taken over by Wole Soyinka and Ezekiel Mphahlele, and in the 1960s contributions from Anglophone Afric ans—mainly Nigerians—dominated the journal. A second important influence was the establish-ment of the Mbari Club in Ibadan as a meeting place for writers and artists to talk, publish books, and stage art exhibitions. The club, like the journal, published the early work of such writ-ers as Wole Soyinka, Christopher Okigbo, and Dennis Brutus.

In East Africa, the literary review *Transition* was started in Kampala in 1961, and it played an important role in encouraging East African writ-ers. The review was described by one writer as "not merely reporting about Africa or feeling its pulse but . . . charting the directions of its mind." It carried contributions by prominent African politicians such as Julius Nyerere and Kenneth Kaunda as well as such leading African writers as Chinua Achebe, Ezekiel Mphahlele, Okigbo, and Gabriel Okara. The journal also opened its columns to contributions from all over the world.

The pioneering paperback African Writers Series, published in England by Heinemann Educational Books, has had a great influence on the development of African literature. Heinemann published Achebe's novel *Things Fall Apart* in 1958, and in 1962 the series was begun, with Achebe as general editor, with republication of that novel. It was an uncertain beginning, and the series was planned to be part of the educational books aimed at the African market. But it soon became popular and the number of authors it published grew rapidly. By 1989 it had published more than three hundred titles. Many African writers have published all their books in it.

The emergent literature expressed the burgeoning nationalist sentiments. Literary movements, publications, and conferences of Negro writers grew out of meetings that dealt with political and nationalist causes. In 1956 the first Congress of Negro Writers was held in Paris. Many conferences followed, all calling on the African writer to be committed to the cause of African nationalism and to identify with the social needs and political aspirations of the continent. Those conferences usually put forth resolutions and recommendations that, although they helped define a political message, regarded the African experience as essentially the same everywhere on the continent, having its essence in the traditional cultures of Africa. In later conferences, however, beginning with the first Pan-African Festival in 1969, that pattern of thinking changed. Cultural differences within the African experience were acknowledged, and the similarities within this experience were seen to have come more recently as a result of patterns imposed by colonialism. The present rather than the past became the main concern and the unifying factor of the African experience. The later conferences avoided prescriptions, and most of the writers participating in them did not subscribe to ideologies and did not allow their creative efforts to be guided by simple intellectual formulas.

The idea of negritude was rejected by English-speaking African writers and discredited by writers from French-speaking Africa. The conferences, however, continued to insist that nationalism and the struggle for political and cultural freedom were still at the heart of the African creative endeavor. The themes of African literature did not change greatly after African countries gained independence. The demand for freedom, social justice, and equality, the breakdown of the traditional society, the conflict between Africa and the West, and the quest for an African identity have been the main themes of African literature.

With the growth of African literature, the distinctive characteristics of different parts of the continent have come to be clearly reflected in the writing, to such a degree that critics have started to speak of a Nigerian literature and Eastern African literature: Francophone African, Anglophone African, and South African.

Francophone African literature had an earlier beginning than Anglophone African literature. Its pioneers—Leopold Senghor, Leon Damas, as well as the Caribbean Aimé Césaire—began to write and formulate their ideas in the 1930s. They had an early opportunity to be educated in France and they were able to express their opinions through available channels. The idea of negritude was first publicized by a literary magazine in Paris—*Legitime Defense*—in 1932. The French policy of assimilation alienated Africans from their culture and roots, but the Africans used the benefits of education that came with the policy to liberate themselves from the colonial influence.

We tend to think of the first generation of African writers in French as mainly expressing the idea of negritude. We also tend to think of them as being of the same mind. But while those writers had in common their endeavor to discover their cultural identity and express it in a distinctive manner, each had his own individual voice. Leopold Senghor, who was elected the first president of Senegal in 1960, expresses in several collections of poems—*Chants de L'ombre* (1945); *Hosties noires* (1956); *Nocturnes* (1951); and *Poemes* (1964)—themes of negritude in mystical terms. He describes Western civilization as soulless and speaks of its need for African culture to redeem it because African culture has mystic warmth and is closer to nature. Although he maintains that the African world is "intuitive" and "non-intellectual," he shows himself, in his poetry, to be highly intellectual and self-conscious. In this and in other aspects of his poetry he is influenced by his French education and his Roman Catholicism. Translations of Senghor's work in English include: *Selected Poems*, translated by John Reed and Clive Wake (London: Oxford University Press, 1964; New York: Atheneum, 1964); *Prose and Poetry*, selected and translated by Reed and Wake (London: Oxford University Press, 1965); *Nocturnes: Love Poems*, translated by Wake and Reed (London: Heinemann Educational Books, African Writers Series [AWS], no. 71, 1970); and *Selected Poems*, translated by C. Williamson (London: Rex Collins, 1976).

Senghor's associate from Martinique, Aimé Césaire, on the other hand, is less intellectual and more intuitive. There is an element of irrationality in his poetry, which is clear in his long poem and main work, *Cahier d'un retour au pay natal* (1939; translated as *Memorandum on My Martinique*, 1947, and included in his *Collected Poetry*, published by the University of California Press in 1984). He often expresses his negritude in militant political terms as he does in *Un Saison Au Congo* (1966), a play about Patrice Lumumba. Two other Senegalese poets are classed as poets of negritude: Birago Diop and David Diop. Like Senghor, Birago Diop expresses his Africanism in mystic terms and uses Senegalese folklore in his poetry. David Diop wrote the most militant (though often immature) protest poetry of the negritude movement.

The Malagasy poets Jean-Joseph Rabearivelo, Jean-Jacques Rabemanajara, and Flavien Ranaivo made significant contributions to African poetry in French. They used and adapted the traditional poetry of their country and developed a distinctive style of their own. Rabearivelo (1901-1937), who committed suicide, was the most original and gifted of the three. He wrote superb poetry about his personal agony and melancholy. A selection of Rabearivelo's poetry appeared in English as *24 Poems*, translated by Ulli Beier and Gerald Moore (Ibadan: Mbari, 1962).

The only contemporary Francophone poet who equals Rabearivelo in brilliance and gift is the Congolese Gerald Felix Tchicaya U Tam'si. He is less concerned with political and public issues than with his personal suffering, which he expresses in fine lyrical poetry rich in mythological allusions and sexual and religious imagery. He describes his poetry as "spoken poetry, not written poetry." He tries to adapt Bantu oral poetry and create something which has its own laws and logic. U Tam'si's work in English translation includes *Brush Fire*, translated by Sangodare Akanji, pseudonym for Ulli Beier (Ibadan:

Mbari, 1964), and *Poems*, translated by Gerald Moore (London: Heinemann Educational Books, AWS no. 72).

The earliest Francophone African novels were published in the 1920s and 1930s. The Senegalese Bakary Diallo's novel *Force bonte* was published in Paris in 1926; *Doguicimi*, by Paul Hazoume, from Dahomey, in 1935. The first novel praises French colonialism; the second is an apology for colonialism, although it is more subtle and reflects a superior mind. (Both novels have not been translated and are out of print.) The contemporary Francophone novel came of age in the 1950s and has combined two radically different forms: the form of protest and social realism and the ambiguities of the situation of the individual are the main concern. In both cases the predicament of the individual striving to liberate himself from an imposed colonial identity is the central preoccupation.

On the whole the Francophone novel is more complex in its themes and artistry than the more prevalent Anglophone novel (even fewer Francophone novels were written after independence). Without oversimplifying the issues and falling into meaningless critical categorization it may be said that the Cameroonians Ferdinand Oyono and Mongo Beti and the Senegalese Sembene Ousmane are concerned mainly with the political and social implications of colonialism in Africa, and that the Guinean Camera Laye and the Senegalese Cheikh Hamidou Kane, the representatives of the other strain, have focused on the predicament of the individual and his quest for self-knowledge.

While Laye and Kane have written recognized masterpieces and have used the form of the novel skillfully, the novelist of social realism and protest contributed little to the development of the form of the African novel. However, in spite of their often obvious messages, the practitioners of social realism and protest do not force their art to reflect a certain ideology. Their novels are saved from the limitations and narrowness of protest by the writers' effort to be fair and to describe as completely as possible the lives of the poor and the oppressed as well as by their urbane humor.

These qualities are obvious in the novels of Oyono and Beti. Oyono uses satire to attack the French myth of assimilation. His best novels are the first two: *Une Vie de Boy* (1956; translated as *Houseboy*, London: Heinemann, 1961) and *Le Vieux Negre et la medaille* (1957; translated as *The*

Old Man and the Medal, London: Heinemann, 1967). The main characters of the novels live the illusion of assimilation until experience exposes the ugly face of colonialism and they are disillusioned. Oyono's humor, in these novels is an integral part of his criticism of colonialism, and it makes his attack on colonial assimilation effective. Beti's satire is not as sharp as Oyono's but it is an effective part of his message. In his first, and best, three novels, *Le Pauvre Christ de Bomba* (1956; translated as *The Poor Christ of Bomba*, London: Heinemann, 1971), *Mission terminee* (1957; translated as *Mission to Kala*, London: Heinemann, 1958), and *Le Roi Miracule* (1960; translated as *King Lazarus*, London: Heinemann, 1970), he expresses the themes of colonial exploitation and the colonial effort to replace traditional African values with an empty and hypocritical Christianity; the disillusionment of the poor African with white colonial rule and the education and the progress it promises; and the predicament of the cultural half-caste and his alienation from both Africa and the West. The criticism inherent in the satire is seasoned by comedy, which has sometimes seemed to Beti's critics to be sought for its own sake.

Sembene Ousmane is quite a different novelist. He is the most directly political and polemical of all the Francophone novelists. He is not concerned with the cultural impact of colonialism on African life but with more immediate problems such as the political consequences of colonial rule, the suffering and the struggle of the masses, and the corruption and decadence of the postcolonial African society. But in spite of his direct message and obvious politics, Ousmane has produced good art that provides penetrating pictures of poor, ordinary people. He has written many novels (he is also a filmmaker), but his best novel is *Les Bouts de bois de dieu* (1960; translated as *God's Bits of Wood*, New York: Doubleday, 1962; London: Heinemann, 1969), about the strike of railway workers in 1947 and the awakening of political consciousness in ordinary people.

Camara Laye and Cheikh Hamidon Kane are distinguished from other African novelists not only by their themes but also by their ability to use the novel effectively to present African traditional culture. Laye's *Le Regard du Roi* (1954; translated as *Radiance of the King*, London: Collins, 1956; New York: Macmillan, 1970) and Kane's *L'Aventure ambique* (1961; translated as *Ambiguous Adventure*, New York: Walker, 1963; London: Heinemann, 1972) are undoubtedly the two best African novels. Both deal with the confrontation between Africa and Western civilization, but they treat the theme in a complex manner and resolve the conflicts and tensions in ways unparalleled in the African novel.

The hero of *Radiance of the King* is a European who goes in quest of an African king through whom he will achieve personal salvation. Instead of the usual pattern of confrontation, chaos, self-exposure, and final tragedy, the European begins his quest in chaos but ends in understanding and final assimilation in Africa. Laye, in a sense, like Senghor, shows in his comic allegory how African culture could redeem and rejuvenate Western civilization. He wrote other books—*L'enfant noir* (1953; translated as *The African Child*, London: Collins-Fontona Books, 1955, and as *The Dark Child*, New York: Noonday Press, 1954), *Dramouss* (translated as *A Dream of Africa*, London: Collins, 1968), and *Le Maitre de la parole* (1978; translated as *Guardian of the Word*, London: Collins, 1982)—but none of these approaches the level of *Radiance of the King*. Kane's *Ambiguous Adventure* is a philosophical novel that brings out the essential ambiguity of the African's situation: torn between his Africanness and an alien consciousness imposed on him by Western (colonial) culture, Kane explores imaginatively the implications of such a position and shows the impossibility of a facile solution (negritude). What he suggests as a way out of the dilemma—Islamic revelation and mysticism—may not be acceptable or comprehensible to some of his readers, but they are deftly developed in his nearly faultless novel.

Another Francophone writer who deserves attention is Yambo Ouologuem, from Mali. He is a prolific author whose writings include novels, poetry, polemic, pornography, and children's books. Although he has been accused of plagiarism by several writers (among them Graham Greene, who wanted parts of Ouologuem's best-known book, *Le devoir de violence*, deleted or rewritten—a demand which caused a temporary suspension of the circulation of the book), the strength and the literary worth of some of his books are clear. *Le devoir de violence*, published in 1968, was translated as *Bound to Violence* (London: Heinemann, 1971). The novel goes over the history of Africa from the advent of Western colonialism to the present and sees it as a string of acts of violence perpetrated on Africa by the European and Arab colonists and their African followers.

African literature in English was dominated in its beginning by Nigerian writers. In 1952 Amos Tutuola, a Nigerian storekeeper with only six years of primary education and a somewhat poor command of English, had his novel *The Palm-Wine Drinkard* published in London by Faber and Faber. The novel is an extraordinary account of a spiritual adventure written in an English described by critics (including Dylan Thomas, whose review of the book brought it great attention), as "original," "young," and "primitive." It achieved great success in English-speaking countries but embarrassed Nigerians greatly because of what they regarded as its author's poor command of English. European critics viewed it as a remarkable work that combined epic elements with native lore and the children's tall tale. Tutuola published four more novels and a collection of short stories and gradually earned the acceptance of his countrymen, but he lost the admiration of Western critics. He is regarded as the first modern African novelist, and his work is the first to use African materials.

A Tutuola novel has the aspect of a folktale: it consists of a string of tales and episodes rather than the well-developed coherent plot familiar to readers of the traditional Western realistic novel. But the realistic novel was also written at the same time by such writers as Cyprian Ekwensi, T. M. Aluko, and Chinua Achebe. Ekwensi and Aluko wrote novels mainly about urban life. Ekwensi's *People of the City* (London: Heinemann, 1963) and *Jagua Nana* (London: Hutchinson, 1961; Greenwich, Conn.: Fawcett, 1969) are artistically weak and seem to be intended more as entertainment than serious literature, but they give the most realistic pictures of African city life. Aluko wrote satirical novels that portray the conflict between traditional society and the new Western educated professionals who endeavor to modernize African society. His novels, especially the early ones, *One Man, One Wife* (London: Heinemann, 1959), *One Man, One Matchet* (London: Heinemann, 1964), and *Kinsman and Foreman* (London: Heinemann, 1966), are infused with a comic sense that redeems their weakness in plot and characterization.

Ekwensi, Aluko, and other Nigerian novelists are at best minor writers who are more significant in a history of the African novel than for the intrinsic literary merit of their work. The one Nigerian novelist whose work, to some extent, fulfills the claims of serious literature is their contemporary Chinua Achebe. His novels are not fault-less, but they exhibit a craftsmanship rare in the African novel and express intelligently and penetratingly the essential theme of the African novel: the conflict between the traditional and the new. Achebe demonstrates in novel after novel the disruptive and traumatic effect of the encroaching new forms of life. His first novel, *Things Fall Apart* (London: Heinemann, 1958), recounts the downfall of Okonkwo in his Ibo village. *No Longer at Ease* (London: Heinemann, 1960) is about the downfall of Okonkwo's grandson, who succumbs to the prejudices and the pressures of the modern urban milieu. Achebe explores again the breakdown of the traditional society and the failure of traditional values in his third novel, *Arrow of God* (London: Heinemann, 1964), which is set in eastern Nigeria in the 1920s. His fourth novel, *A Man of the People* (London: Heinemann, 1966), is a satire that exposes the corruption of the political system in independent Nigeria and ends in a military coup that anticipates the actual coup of 1966. Since the publication of this novel, Achebe has published a collection of short stories, *Girls at War* (London: Heinemann, 1972), as well as poems, essays, and children's books. But his four novels have secured him a leading position in African literature.

Nigeria also led English-speaking Africa in poetry and drama. One of its outstanding poets is Christopher Okigbo (1932-1967), who was killed fighting on the Biafran side in the Nigerian civil war. Okigbo was a prolific writer with an idiosyncratic style. His two published collections of poetry, *Heavensgate* (Ibadan: Mbari, 1962) and *Limits* (Ibadan: Mbari, 1964), which were republished posthumously along with *Distances* and *Path of Thunder as Labyrinths* (London: Heinemann, 1971; New York: Africana Publishing, 1971), show great sophistication and complexity although the poetry is sometimes obscure.

Other important Nigerian poets—Gabriel Okara, John Pepper Clark, and Wole Soyinka—did not limit themselves to poetry but wrote successfully in other genres. Okara is an original and sensitive poet. Heinemann published his first—and important—novel, *The Voice*, in the African Writers Series in 1964 and his first collection of poems, *The Fisherman's Invocation*, in 1978, though some of his poetry had been previously anthologized. Okara's poetry, like his novel, shows an original use of language. John Pepper Clark is regarded as a better playwright than poet.

Wole Soyinka established himself as a distinguished poet with his first collection, *Idanre and Other Poems* (London: Eyre Methuen, 1967). He also wrote two novels—*The Interpreters* (London: Heinemann, 1965) and *Season of Anomy* (London: Nelson, 1973)—that won critical acclaim. But Soyinka is primarily a playwright. He has been an actor, has written and produced many plays, and has formed two theater companies. Although his plays deal mainly with West Africa and use African materials, Soyinka draws upon the whole human cultural heritage in his works. He has rejected the concept of negritude, with its concentration on Africa to the exclusion of everything else, and its idea of a revival of African culture by means of a return to the glorious African past. His view of life is essentially tragic. He perceives the hubris of the African personality and the heavy cost of achievement and always emphasizes the need for self-awareness.

His early plays—*The Swamp-Dwellers* (1958), *The Lion and the Jewel* (1959), and *The Trials of Brother Jero* (1960)—are farcical works that deal with the encroachment of British colonialization and make fun of teachers and priests while examining their role in the village society. The plays of the 1960s are more complex and deal with the predicament of independent Nigeria and postcolonial Africa. *A Dance in the Forest* (1960), written for the celebrations of Nigerian Independence, expresses a theme that recurs in Soyinka's work: the need to face the realities of African history and culture and to realize that they are as fallible and limited as any human activity.

The Road (1965), a play that bewildered many critics when it was first produced, is highly original in theme, technique, and language. The hero of the play, the Professor, a former lay reader in the church and now the owner of a rundown truck stop, seeks knowledge of death, because it is the way to understand life. But the Professor does not take the proper path to knowledge and is finally defeated and destroyed. Although the play resembles Greek tragedy in its view of man (Soyinka adapted Euripides' *The Bacchae* in 1973) and although it is ridden with metaphysical speculation and language, it is thoroughly African in its atmosphere and use of ritual. Soyinka's other philosophical plays—*The Swamp-Dwellers* and *Strong Breed*—are not as difficult and puzzling as *The Road*. Though they are not topical, they still deal with palpable subjects such as tradition and social responsibility. But the dominant mode in Soyinka's work is satire.

One of his best satirical plays is *Kongi's Harvest*, which opened the first Festival of Negro Art in Dakar in April 1966. The play is an attack on tyranny and dictatorship in postcolonial Africa. The protagonist resembles the then-Ghanaian president Kwame Nkrumah, but Soyinka denied he had any single model in mind and insisted he was only attacking the megalomania of African nationalist politics.

Between August 1967 and October 1969 (during the Biafran War), Soyinka was a political prisoner. He recorded his prison experience in *Poems from Prison* (London: Collins, 1969), which were later revised and included in *A Shuttle in the Crypt* (London: Eyre Methuen, 1972) and in an autobiographical memoir, *The Man Died* (London: Collins, 1972). His traumatic experience during the war undoubtedly inspired *Mad Men and Specialists* (London: Methuen, 1970), a play that exposes the inhumanity of the warmongers. Soyinka described the work as being concerned with "a problem in my country, the betrayal of vocation for the attraction of power in one form or another." During the 1970s and 1980s Soyinka became more concerned with the expression of political ideas. He wrote agitprop plays that commented directly on the political situation in Africa, such as *A Play of Giants* (London: Methuen, 1984), whose characters resemble, only too obviously, the African dictators of the time: Idi Amin and Jean-Bidele Bokassa. The later plays may seem less complex and less subtle than the early ones, but they still give Soyinka's sense of the infinite possibilities in experience and the mind, his rejection of facile solutions to the problems of life, and his intolerance of stupid strictures.

While other English-speaking African countries did not contribute as much to literature as Nigeria, they produced important and, sometimes, original writers. One such writer is the Ghanaian novelist Ayi Kwei Armah, who expresses, in what is perhaps the finest prose style in African literature, a vision of man and society that aligns him with the modernist and postmodernist writers of Western literature. In the five novels he has written to date—*The Beautyful Ones are Not Yet Born* (London: Heinemann, 1968), *Fragments* (London: Heinemann, 1970), *Why Are We So Blest* (London: Heinemann, 1972), *Two Thousand Seasons* (London: Heinemann, 1972), and *The Healers* (London: Heinemann, 1978)—he portrays the political and social corruption in contemporary African society and the alienation of the individual living in that society, as well as the fragmentation of his psyche. Moreover, Armah's novels expose the historical experiences that destroyed and tried to replace the original and pure values of the African past. Armah has been attacked by some African writers, among them Achebe, for writing novels too modern for Africa and for describing states of being that belong to Western civilization and which Africa has, happily, not yet reached.

Another significant West African writer is the Gambian Lenrie Peters. His only novel, *The Second Round* (London: Heinemann, 1965), bothered critics in a similar way to Armah's novels because its concern with Africa is only incidental and limited. He describes emotions and attitudes that could exist anywhere. But Peters is primarily a poet and his verse is directly concerned with the state of contemporary Africa. Peters's poetry has been published by Heinemann. Two volumes have appeared in the African Writers Series: *Satellites*, 1967, and *Selected Poetry*, 1981.

The leading East African writer is the Kenyan novelist (James) Ngũgĩ Wa Thiong'o. Like Achebe, he expresses in his novels the major preoccupations of African literature. But Ngũgĩ is intensely aware of historical processes and chronicles them carefully. His four novels, *Weep Not Child* (1964), *The River Between* (1965), *A Grain of Wheat* (1967), and *Petals of Blood* (1977), were all published by Heinemann in the African Writers Series. They describe the stages of the conflict between Africa and the West: from colonization and exploitation in the first novel, to the struggle for independence carried out by the Mau Mau in the second and third novels, and finally to the replacement of colonialism in independent Africa by a black capitalism allied with and nourished by imperialism in the last novel. Ngũgĩ is a committed writer with a Marxist bias, but his commitment and bias have not affected his novels adversely. In spite of some defects, they are polished works with highly realized characters and scenes, expressing a clear vision of the East African situation.

While Ngũgĩ views the neocolonialism that dominates postindependence Africa as a political and economic force, another talented East African artist—Okot p'Bitek—sees it as a cultural phenomenon. P'Bitek is the most important poet of East Africa, and his work has set the pace and inspired the East African search for a cultural identity. His main concern is the conflict of African culture. He expresses these themes in vigorous language best employed in his long poems *Song of Lawino* (1966) and *Song of Ocul* (1970). (The two poems were republished in the African Writers Series, in one volume, in 1984.)

The current concerns and dilemmas of African life are effectively dealt with in the fiction of the Somali novelist Nuruddin Farah. In the six novels he published between 1970 and 1984—*From a Crooked Rib* (1970), *A Naked Needle* (1976), *Sweet and Sour Milk* (1979), *Sardines* (1981), all part of Heinemann's African Writers Series, and *Close Sesame* (London: Allison & Busby, 1983), and *Maps* (London: Picador, 1984)—Farah gives an honest picture of the new African society. The problems that beset present-day Somalia range from the struggle of women to be free of the domination of men to the political repression and terror and the irresponsible exercise of power that characterize social and political life. With Farah we are completely in contemporary Africa, in a present that has little or no relation to the past. His novels are often topical, but they carry insights and sharp political and historical judgments that go beyond the moment they describe. Three of his novels, *Sweet and Sour Milk*, *Sardines*, and *Close Sesame*, form a trilogy entitled *Variations on the Theme of an African Dictatorship*. Farah, who is now regarded as a major African writer, is distinguished by his mature style and the high quality of his characterization.

South African literature has been conditioned by the special situation of apartheid. Racism in that society and its consequences are the themes of the literature produced by black and colored as well as liberal European South Africans. The black and colored South Africans have the advantage over other Africans of living in an urban milieu, where in spite of the poverty and segregation there are educational opportunities and possibilities for experiencing, first-hand, the realities of the modern world. The race situation in South Africa is not like anywhere else in Africa. The settler colonialism of the Europeans and the discrimination that goes with it are not known to other Africans. The struggle against such a state has produced a literature in which personal predicament and public condition are almost indistinguishable. The autobiography and the short story were the dominant genres in the 1950s and 1960s. Ezekiel Mphahlele, one of the most important South African writers, attributed the prevalence of these genres to the difficulty of writing in the circumstances of oppression. Most South African writers have been in exile, imprisoned, or banned. Besides Mphahlele—who has written an autobiography, *Down Second Avenue* (London: Faber & Faber, 1959), and collections of short stories and essays—the best-known South African writers are Peter Abrahams, Alex La Guma, Dennis Brutus, and Mazisi Kunene. White South African writers are not regarded as African writers, and their work does not normally feature in anthologies and discussions of African literature. This is because they are part of a minority that has refused to assimilate or be assimilated in Africa and that has chosen to live, in Africa, like European colonials. Liberal white South African writers, such as Alan Paton, Laurence van der Post, and Nadine Gordimer, are no exceptions. Although they indict and expose apartheid in their work, they are still members of the white minority, sharing its life and privileges.

Peter Abrahams is South Africa's most prolific novelist. He published his first novel, *Mine Boy*, in 1946 (republished by Heinemann, 1963). It is the story of a young worker and his exposure to the urban life of Johannesburg, a theme that has been developed by many South African writers. In addition to his novels about South Africa, Abrahams has written two novels set outside the country: *A Wreath for Udomo* (1956), set in West Africa with a protagonist whose political career resembles Nkrumah's, and *This Island Now* (1966), set in the Caribbean (both published in London by Faber and Faber).

Alex La Guma wrote short novels in the 1960s and 1970s that are considered brilliant, but his best work is his first short novel, *A Walk in the Night* (1962, republished by Heinemann, 1967). The story is harshly realistic in its description of the horrors of apartheid. Its effectiveness results from La Guma's dispassionate recounting of the details. La Guma, considered one of the most accomplished African short-story writers, has appeared in magazines in Africa, Britain, the United States, South America, Germany, and Sweden. He has also published several short-story collections. In addition he has written three novels: *And a Threefold Cord* (Berlin: Seven Seas Books, 1964), which depicts the struggle for survival of a family and a community in the slums of a South African city; *In the Fog of the Season's End* (London: Heinemann, 1972), a less than fully realized novel of the South African situation; and *Time of the Butcherbird* (Heinemann, 1979), which is set in a tribal area and describes private atrocities and communal anger.

The two outstanding South African poets, Dennis Brutus and Mazisi Kunene, have been exiles whose work is banned in South Africa. Brutus is a mature and sensitive poet whose collections combine love poetry of great tenderness and verse about his prison experience with bitter expressions on the theme of apartheid and the estrangement of South Africans from their own land. *A Simple Lust* (Heinemann, 1972) collects all his poetry published in two previous collections, *Sirens, Knuckles and Boots* (1963) and *Letters to Martha and Other Poems from a South African Prison* (1969), and adds previously uncollected poems. His recent collections of poetry, *Stubborn Hope* (1979), and *Strains* (1981), both published by Heinemann, express his concern, while in exile, with his country and dramatize his own personal conflicts.

Mazisi Kunene writes poetry in his native Zulu and then translates it into English. His poetry is influenced by the Zulu culture that he extols. He has written strong poetry of political dissent but his best poetry is contained in the two ambitious epics *Emperor Shaka the Great* (1979) and *Anthem of the Decade* (1981), in which he sees life from the perspective of Zulu cultural heritage and history.

Between the enthusiastic reception, in the West, of Amos Tutuola's *The Palm-Wine Drinkard* in 1952 and the awarding of the Nobel Prize to Wole Soyinka in 1986, African literature came of age. During this period every African country produced a significant writer or writers who wrote in a European language or whose work was translated into European languages and therefore reached readers outside Africa. Works by African writers have been published by major publishers in Britain (including Oxford University Press, Longmans, Faber and Faber, Heinemann, Methuen, and Macmillan) and France (Gallimard, Julliard, Didier, and Seuil). Major American publishers (Doubleday, Random House, Houghton Mifflin, New American Library, and Little, Brown) and American university presses have reissued the works of major African writers and published for the first time works that became highly successful (Ayi Kwei Armah's great novel *The Beautyful Ones are Not Yet Born* was first published by Houghton Mifflin). African literature has become a recognized academic discipline in many universities all over the world, and African writers have lectured or have been on the staff of major Western universities. In spite of the present limited readership of this literature, the future promises greater visibility and influence.

Letter from London

Nicolette Jones
London, England

The single most significant issue on the British literary scene in the past year—and ever since the late Ayatollah Khomeini's fatwa (death sentence) of 14 February 1989—must be the fate of Indian-born British novelist Salman Rushdie. After a year in hiding, the author of *The Satanic Verses* broke his silence last January, in one of the first issues of the *Independent on Sunday* newspaper, offering a lengthy and elegant defense of the writer's duty to challenge and question. It failed to pacify his detractors, who insisted that it was a further slap in the face of Muslim sensibilities. In February, the playwright Harold Pinter read the text of the Herbert Read Memorial Lecture, written by Rushdie, to an audience at London's Institute of Contemporary Arts. Rushdie's lecture, "Is Nothing Sacred?" (subsequently published as a pamphlet by Granta), made the case for the "little room of literature," the "one place in any society where, within the secrecy of our own heads, we can hear voices talking about everything in every possible way.... Wherever in the world the little room of literature has been closed, sooner or later the walls have come tumbling down." His words, in Pinter's mouth, resonated in a room from which Rushdie was obliged to be absent, and where the presence of security men served as a reminder of the state of siege of the little room of literature.

The British Muslim Action Front continued to bring pressure to extend the nation's blasphemy law to include the Muslim faith. In March, there were calls in the House of Lords for the law to be repealed altogether, including one from the Bishop of Manchester who argued that "God does not need that kind of protection." The question of publishing a British paperback edition of *The Satanic Verses* remains open, although paperbacks have come out in Germany and Norway, and in an American book club edition. Meanwhile demonstrations against the book continue. Last year there were firebombs in bookshops—the book department of Liberty's and Books Etc on Charing Cross Road among them—which caused damage but no casualties.

In April Rushdie gave his first live interview, on Radio 4's *Today* programme, in support of Charter 88, a document that calls for a written British constitution that would eliminate the House of Lords and protect freedom of speech. In June there were half a dozen arrests over attempts to assassinate Rushdie, and two Kuwaitis were deported. In the same month, there were demonstrations in which effigies of the author were burnt. The delay over the paperback has allowed other issues to accumulate around the book, and by May Rushdie had become a bargaining clause in negotiations over the Beirut hostages; in June there were invitations to exchange Britons in Beirut for an assurance that Mr. Rushdie would be deported from Britain.

The possibility of a consortium of publishers bringing out the paperback still exists, but a spokesman for Viking Penguin has said that he believes it would have the disadvantage of being a consortium in name only: all the work of publication and distribution would in fact be done by the hardback publishers. The cost of security since the Ayatollah's death call—which included employees of Viking Penguin—was £1.8 million worldwide in the first year, and Penguin UK budgeted a further £600,000 this year, as well as six figures for legal fees to fight cases unsuccessfully brought against the company under the blasphemy and public order laws. Rushdie's supporters are dismayed that no prosecution has been brought against those who have publicly called for his death, and so incited murder, such as Dr. Kalim Siddiqui of the Muslim Institute.

In August, a Pakistani video, *International Guerrillas*, which depicts Rushdie as a drunken murderer of Muslims, was banned by the British Board of Film Classification. The board resurrected an archaic law of criminal libel to support the ban. When the case was brought to the Video Appeals Committee, however, Rushdie sent a statement opposing this censorship. He argued that it was contrary to the freedom of expression guaranteed in the European convention. The ban was overturned.

Rushdie changed publishers for his next book: a children's novel called *Haroun and the Sea of Stories* was published in September by Granta Books. Granta is one of the new imprints set up in Britain in the last few years, in a countertrend to the conglomeratization of British publishing houses. While the big groups have gotten bigger—with Paul Hamlyn's Octopus group now incorporating the old, established companies of Methuen, Heinemann, Secker and Warburg, as well as its own imprints; and Random Century now including Century Hutchinson, Chatto and Windus, Jonathan Cape, The Bodley Head, and Barrie and Jenkins; and the Penguin Group encompassing Michael Joseph, Hamish Hamilton, and Viking, as well as Penguin—new ventures and breakaway groups have emerged. Granta Books, established by expatriate American Bill Buford, grew out of *Granta Magazine*, a monthly collection of new writing, and was launched, under the Viking Penguin umbrella, in spring 1989. John Berger, Martha Gellhorn, and Nicholson Baker were among the authors who threw in their lot with Buford. And the new managing director, Carolina Michel, came from another young company, Bloomsbury.

Bloomsbury and Headline are the two publishing houses that seemed to set the trend in independent enterprise. Both were formed by individuals who had long experience in older publishing companies. Bloomsbury's Liz Calder was editorial director at Jonathan Cape; managing director Nigel Newton came from Sidgwick and Jackson and marketing director Alan Wherry from Penguin. Headline was formed by a breakaway group from Macdonald. Both now have three years of successful publishing behind them: Bloomsbury with its wide-ranging list from upmarket fiction to reference books, and Headline specializing in popular fiction and blockbusting autobiographies. This year's two most notable newcomers in the same tradition were both formed as a result of disillusionment with corporate publishing. Christopher Sinclair-Stevenson, managing director at Hamish Hamilton, was unhappy with the dictates of the Penguin group money men. He left the company and set up Sinclair-Stevenson Ltd. with £2.4 million of capital from the investment group 3i and the private investments of codirectors who included Tim Waterstone (founder of the bookshop chain) and Lord Rees-Mogg. The first list was launched in September and includes Peter Ackroyd's biography of Charles Dickens, William Boyd's novel *Braz-*

zaville Beach, and new works by Sybille Bedford, J. K. Galbraith, Paul Theroux, and A. N. Wilson. The quality of the list is undisputed, although some contend that Sinclair-Stevenson's flair for the literary is not matched by his commercial sense. The company is believed to have spent £650,000, for instance, on the Dickens biography and a subsequent biography by Ackroyd of William Blake. Paperback rights to Dickens have already gone for £275,000 (to Octopus's Mandarin imprint) and serial rights for £100,000, but there is still ground to make up on so large a sum. Sinclair-Stevenson Ltd. will have to prove to the Penguin group money men and the rest of the world that author-friendly quality publishing can be a commercial success.

Also taking an independent stand is Chapmans Publishers, set up by Ian Chapman, who was chief executive of Collins (before it was bought for £21 million by Rupert Murdoch), and by his wife Majory, Collins's former editorial director. Both opposed the Murdoch purchase and left their jobs when it went through after much unpleasant internal politicking, according to their account. Now, with all the glee of children let out of school early, they launched their first list in August.

The phenomenon of burgeoning independents has been dubbed "unbundling" and is perceived as the aftermath of "mergermania." The takeovers, however, have continued. It is only in the last year that Random Century metamorphosed out of the fusion of the Random House group and Century Hutchinson. And the fusion was not without its casualties. The Bodley Head survives as an imprint, but in little more than name; most of its staff lost their jobs before the new company was rehoused in joint premises.

Since its move, the Random Century group has sprouted a new arm. It has set up a new upmarket paperback imprint, Vintage (also the name of an American imprint at Random House), run by Frances Coady, who was formerly editorial director of Cape. The imprint, with its colorful jackets and night-club launch in September, has a youthful demeanor and includes novels by some of the most noteworthy young writers from both sides of the Atlantic: Jeannette Winterson, Paul Watkins, Deborah Levy, Sebastian Faulks, and Emily Prager. Its nonfiction includes Deirdre Bair's biography of Samuel Beckett; John Pilger's exposé of Australian human rights abuses, *A Secret Country*; and the popularizing work of science in the mold of Stephen

Hawkings's *A Brief History of Time*, Roger Penrose's *The Emperor's New Mind*. Vintage is in some ways the quintessence of various trends: the trend toward designer covers, the rise of the trade paperback, and the changes in the youth market all invite the publication of books like these.

Collins, after its own takeover and loss of the Chapmans, suffered a further loss last March when its chief executive, Sonia Land, resigned. She claimed that in the new transatlantic HarperCollins there was "excessive interference" from the U.S. company in the running of the U.K. business. Her successor, Terry Kitson, formerly ran Collins's Australian and New Zealand operations. However, these defections did not deter the new corporation from doing some more empire-building of its own. In July HarperCollins bought Unwin Hyman, a company that was itself the result of the merger in 1986 of Bell and Hyman with Allen and Unwin. Unwin Hyman has a strong academic list, as well as the women's imprint Pandora and the new-age imprint Mandala, which fits with the Thorsons list Collins acquired in 1989. But Unwin Hyman is most famous as the publisher of the works of J. R. R. Tolkien, author of *The Lord of the Rings*.

Two other smaller independent lists are up for sale. André Deutsch Ltd. has announced that it is seeking a purchaser. The announcement comes only a few years after the retirement of founder André Deutsch, and was made by his former partner, the current chairman Tom Rosenthal. Criticism has been bandied about in the British press of Rosenthal's handling of the firm's financial affairs since Deutsch's departure. The other publisher in search of a buyer is Aurum Press, whose owners, the Really Useful Group, decided to channel off this part of its multiplicitous business interests. There had already been numerous job losses at the company. Aurum's children's book imprint, ABC (Aurum Books for Children), is now functioning separately, however, after a management buyout.

A management buyout was rejected by HarperCollins for its upmarket retail outlet Hatchards, booksellers by appointment to Her Majesty the Queen. In August the prestige premises on Piccadilly were bought by Pentos (the chain that owns the Dillons bookshops) for £10.5 million, thus adding 15,000 square feet of retail space to the Dillons operation. There are some, enamored of the familiar face of London's most traditional bookshop, who are anxious that a Pentos redesign could detract from Hatchards's charm. Pentos, on the other hand, believes it can increase sales at the Piccadilly store, currently running at £6 million, to £10 million.

The acquisition of Hatchards by Pentos draws the bookshop into a controversy that has long simmered in the British book trade. The price of books in Britain is fixed by a trading principle known as the Net Book Agreement, which means that books classified as "net" (the exclusions include many schoolbooks) must be sold for identical prices whatever their outlet. Pentos wishes to cut prices competitively, and break the Net Book Agreement. Publishers are mainly opposed to the abolition, principally because it works to the disadvantage of small independent bookshops, who are not in the strong bargaining position of being able to buy books in very large quantities and therefore to demand extra discounts from publishers. The supporters of the agreement believe its abolition would bring about the demise of small and specialty shops, and therefore decrease the range of books and kinds of service available; it would limit the range of lists of publishers who would not be able to afford to publish specialty and literary texts. Pentos, on the other hand, believes the fixed price is a restrictive trade practice which limits the number of books that can be sold. Pentos discounted certain nonnet titles last Christmas (as it turned out, a rather tame gesture after a year of publicity about its imminent price-slashing), and argued that they sold especially well. Meanwhile, the Publishers' Association threatens to withdraw deliveries to bookshops that break the Net Book Agreement.

Another simmering controversy in the publishing world has had everything to do with the increasing conglomeratization of the industry. The issue is "rights clawback"—the "calling in" of licenses that have long been leased to paperback houses, as they expire, thereby depriving paperback publishers of long-standing authors. In February 1990 Heinemann outbid Collins for a new novel by best-selling author Jack Higgins, called *Cold Harbour*. Collins, Higgins's previous publishers, retaliated for this loss by reclaiming paperback rights in Higgins's previous novels from Pan (Macmillan's paperback arm), in order that they should be paperbacked instead by Collins's own imprint, Fontana. The author objected. This followed a similar move by Octopus, which "clawed back" Wilbur Smith's novels, also from Pan, for its imprint, Mandarin. Such actions are perceived as muscle-flexing by the big boys, who are motivated by money rather than by loyalty to authors, and as a symptom of the passing of the good old days of "gentlemanly" British publishing.

Nineteen ninety was the first year of the "British Book Awards," hosted by the trade journal *Publishing News*, which offered trophies (but no money) to winners in rather random categories such as Best Jacket Design and Best Travel Book. The winners were selected by panels of booksellers, who controversially elected H. R. H. Prince Charles "Author of the Year" for his condemnation of modern architecture, *A Vision of Britain* (Doubleday). Other novel prizewinners were Kazuo Ishiguro's *The Remains of the Day* (the Booker Prize); V. S. Pritchett's *The Careless Widow*

and Other Stories (W. H. Smith Award); and Simon Schama's *Citizens* (the twenty-five-thousand-pound NCR Award). Last year's Whitbread Prize caused a stir when the judges of the Novel Category disagreed over a winner: one belatedly vetoed the announced winner—Alexander Stuart's *The War Zone*—on the grounds of its theme of incest, and the category prize went instead to Lindsay Clarke's *The Chymical Wedding*. (The overall Whitbread Prize went to Richard Holmes's biography of Coleridge.)

Rupert Murdoch, new owner of HarperCollins as well as the News International group, gave £3 million to Oxford University in May to endow a Chair in Language and Communications.

The Year in Drama: London
(31 October 1989 - 1 November 1990)

Matt Wolf
Associated Press
and
Wall Street Journal/Europe

London's commercial theater continued to be all things to all people in the 1989-1990 season, offering blockbuster musicals and downmarket sex farces alongside classics and star vehicles. Of unusual interest, however, was the so-called Broadway-ization of the West End, which was making itself felt. After years of London's ostensible resistance to the sort of overnight flop so common in New York, suddenly productions were folding after a scant two-, three-, or four-week run. The lack of new British writing of broad-based appeal could be sensed as well in the steady stream of imports from New York that made the latter part of the season, in particular, feel like Broadway-upon-Thames.

Still, nothing succeeds like a homegrown smash, and surely the talking point of the season was *Miss Saigon*, the first musical from Alain Boublil and Claude-Michel Schoenberg since *Les Misérables* in 1984. The show opened 20 September 1989, but it remains the town's hottest ticket as of this writing thirteen months later. The musical updates the story of Giacomo Puccini's opera *Madame Butterfly* (1904) to the time of the Vietnam War to tell the tragic tale of Kim, a doomed Vietnamese girl who loves—and loses—the American marine Chris during the fall of Saigon in 1975.

The couple is later reunited in Bangkok, at which point Chris must disclose Kim's existence to his American wife, Ellen. The musical ends tragically, presided over by the scheming "Engineer," the Eurasian pimp acted by Jonathan Pryce, whose performance became the talking point of the year. Indeed, the issue of whether Pryce, a Welshman, should be allowed to repeat his performance in the Broadway version of the show, due to open in April 1991, dominated theatrical news on both sides of the Atlantic. Eventually, both the producer, Cameron Mackintosh, and the American branch of the actors' union, Equity, made the necessary concessions—that Pryce would be allowed to play the Engineer and that Asians would be given every consideration in further casting—to ensure that the show would indeed go on.

Miss Saigon was a surprise loser at the annual Olivier Awards—London's equivalent of the Tony Awards—on 8 April. The top prize went to a long-running rock and roll pastiche, entitled *Return to the Forbidden Planet*, loosely modeled on Shakespeare's *The Tempest*. The prize for best play went to David Hare's *Racing Demon*, the latest state-of-the-nation piece by the author of *Plenty*, *A Map of the World*, and the controversial *The Secret Rapture*, a short-lived Broadway entry in 1989. *Racing Demon* concerns four south London clergymen attempting to come to terms with their own doubts and the realities of Margaret Thatcher's Britain, in a universe where, they feel, God is often silent. The principal doubter, a liberal reverend named Lionel, won the best actor prize for veteran performer Oliver Ford Davies; Michael Bryant, as a homosexual colleague caught up in a smear campaign, was named best supporting performer.

The endlessly prolific Alan Ayckbourn brought to the West End his thirty-sixth play, *Man of the Moment*, one of the author's darkest comedies to date. Directed by Ayckbourn, the play originally starred Michael Gambon as a quintessential British suburbanite, Douglas Beechey, who is brought to a sun-drenched Spanish villa to participate in an English TV program. In Spain he is confronted with the erstwhile criminal-turned-media-celebrity Vic Parks, who, in a bank robbery seventeen years ago, shot in the face and disfigured the employee who ended up becoming Douglas's wife. The play folds discussions of good and evil into its blackly comic view of the world, and it won Gambon the Olivier Award for Comedy Performance of the Year.

Simon Gray, the British author of *Butley*, *Otherwise Engaged*, and *The Common Pursuit*, also returned to the West End this year. His play *Hidden Laughter* stars Felicity Kendal as a middle-class housewife and mother of two married to a philandering publisher, played by Kevin McNally. The play takes its title from T. S. Eliot's poem "Burnt Norton," and is about various lives in crisis, including that of a town vicar, Ronnie (Peter Barkworth), who could be this work's answer to the Reverend Lionel in *Racing Demon*.

Britain's two best-known Howards—Barker and Benton—had a busy year. The former had two plays on simultaneously in January: *Seven Lears*, his so-called prequel to Shakespeare's *King Lear*; and *Scenes from an Execution*, which starred Glenda Jackson as a fiery artist in Renaissance Venice doing battle against the state. Benton meanwhile cowrote, with Tariq Ali, *Moscow Gold*, the last play to be seen at the Royal Shakespeare Company in London before it closed, on 5 November 1990, for four months in a money-saving move. The play, an epic pro-*Glasnost* satire of life in the Soviet Union today, starred English actor David Calder as Mikhail Gorbachev and Sara Kestelman as his wife, Raisa.

Trevor Griffiths, another leading dramatist of the British left, resurfaced at the National with *Piano*, adapted both from Chekhov's *Platonov* and from a Russian film, *Unfinished Piece for Mechanical Piano*. The National later hosted *Dancing at Lughnasa*, the new work from Irishman Brian Friel. The Abbey Theatre staging of this play, about five spinster sisters in County Donegal in 1936, opened in October to possibly the warmest reviews of the season.

Other new plays focused on figures from history. In *Never the Sinner*, American playwright John Logan dramatized the lives of Nathan Leopold and Richard Loeb, the two University of Chicago students who in 1924 murdered a 14-year-old boy. In *Once in a While the Odd Thing Happens*, Paul Godfrey addressed the relationship between composer Benjamin Britten and singer Peter Pears in the years leading up to the premiere of Britten's opera *Peter Grimes* (1945). In *Noel and Gertie*, critic Sheridan Morley expanded his earlier revue about Noel Coward and Gertrude Lawrence. And in *Singer*, Peter Flannery wrote a sweeping play of Thatcher-era Britain, basing his central character on the notorious 1950s slumlord—and concentration camp survivor—Peter Rachman.

Michael Frayn's *Look Look*, a comedy about a theater audience, called it quits after a month, which amazed those who remembered the same author's long-running *Noises Off* and *Benefactors*. A trio of American works lasted a similarly brief time—Jane Stanton Hitchcock's *Vanilla*, a farce about New York social climbers; August Wilson's Pulitzer Prize-winning *Fences*, which proved unable to counter British apathy toward all-black drama on the West End; and A. R. Gurney's *Love Letters*, in which rotating stars played lifelong friends and epistolary partners.

American plays in general were the rule rather than the exception. The season saw the London debuts of such Off-Broadway stalwarts as Charles Ludlam's *The Mystery of Irma Vep*, directed by actress Maria Aitken; Jerry Sterner's *Other People's Money*, starring Maria Aitken; and Barbara Lebow's Holocaust play, *A Shayna Maidel*. The season's most-talked-about American play was Lanford Wilson's Broadway transfer *Burn This*, due to the volatile presence of original leading man, John Malkovich.

Revivals dotted both the commercial and state-subsidized sector. The Peter Hall Company followed *Orpheus Descending* and *The Merchant of Venice* with Ibsen's *The Wild Duck*, which surpassed expectations by turning a profit. The summer also saw the return of Richard Harris to rave reviews as the mad hero of Luigi Pirandello's *Henry IV*. Jerry Hall, the Texan model, generated publicity but sold few tickets as the star of William Inge's *Bus Stop*. Natasha Richardson and Glenda Jackson each tried a hand at two celebrated female roles—Eugene O'Neill's Anna Christie and Bertolt Brecht's Mother Courage, respectively. Joan Collins fulfilled a lifelong ambition to play Amanda in *Private Lives*, and Derek Jacobi geared up for Broadway with the title role in Jean-Paul Sartre's *Kean*.

After that hardy perennial Shakespeare, Henrik Ibsen and Arthur Miller were the playwrights of choice for revival. In addition to *The Wild Duck*, Ibsen was represented with *Peer Gynt* at the National, and the rarely seen *When We Dead Waken*, starring Claire Bloom, at the Almeida. The National honored Arthur Miller's seventy-fifth birthday with back-to-back stagings of *The Crucible* and *After the Fall*. The latter production elicited much attention for being the first to cast a black actress, Josette Simon, in the role of the suicidal Marilyn Monroe figure, Maggie. The Young Vic Theatre produced two Miller plays: an acclaimed revival of *The Price* as well as his first Broadway flop, the 1944 *The Man Who Had All the Luck*.

On the Bardic front, notices were mixed, and commercial presentations of Shakespeare—so popular the previous season with Dustin Hoffman's performance in *Merchant of Venice* and others—seemed to have been forsaken. The Royal Shakespeare Company had a small-scale hit with *Pericles*, directed by the Young Vic's artistic director, David Thacker, alongside main-stage productions of *As You Like It*, *All's Well That Ends*

Well, and film actor Charles Dance in *Coriolanus*. The National in July opened *King Lear*, with Brian Cox, and *Richard III*, with Ian McKellen. Both stagings went on an extensive world tour before returning to London in January 1991.

Other classics on view included Richard Brinsley Sheridan's Restoration romp, *The School for Scandal*, which brought actor John Neville to the National after decades in Canada; Chekhov's *Three Sisters*, starring three Irish sisters—Sinead, Sorcha, and Niamh Cusack—and their father, Cyril; and a pair of Pierre Corneille comedies at the Old Vic: *The Liar* and *The Illusion*. Twenty-five-year-old Cambridge graduate Sam Mendes preceded *Kean* by directing Dion Boucicault's 1847 *London Assurance*, and Ian McKellen preceded his acclaimed portrayal of Richard III by leading a revival of *Bent*, by American writer Martin Sherman.

Musical revivals ranged from *The Rocky Horror Show* and Andrew Lloyd Webber and Don Black's *Song and Dance* (one of Webber's five West End offerings this season) to the Kern/Hammerstein *Show Boat*, the latter in a coproduction of the Royal Shakespeare Company and Opera North, an opera company based in Yorkshire. Several new musicals sank at once: *King*, about Martin Luther King, which arrived amid various accusations from its creators and members of the King family as to whether or not it "trivialized" its subject; and *Bernadette*, Welsh couple Gwyn and Maureen Hughes's musical about Bernadette of Lourdes. The musical *Midas*, director Trevor Nunn, had a rare flop with *The Baker's Wife*, the Joe Stein/Stephen Schwartz musical about infidelity in a French village.

Of longer-lasting appeal was American composer Stephen Sondheim, who was heard from on two major occasions: *Sunday In the Park With George*, his 1985 Pulitzer Prize winner about Georges Seurat, which marked the third musical in the National's history; and *Into the Woods*, his 1987 Broadway hit about the "happily ever after" underside to certain well-known fairy tales. As of this writing, musical hopes for a future blockbuster are pinned on *Children of Eden*, a January 1991 entry composed by Stephen Schwartz and directed by John Caird. But it remains to be seen whether the decade-long British musical invasion of Broadway has peaked with *Miss Saigon*. One fact remains clear: the theater traffic these days is fully two-way.

*West End Chronology: 31 October
1989 - 1 November 1990*

This chronology includes major openings at the Royal Shakespeare Company (abbreviated as RSC) and the Royal National Theatre (abbreviated as NT) as well as a handful of major fringe openings. Following each RSC and NT entry is the auditorium in which the production played. Other abbreviations used here are P play; M musical; SR still running as of 1 November 1990.

1. *A Life in the Theater* (P: Theatre Royal, Haymarket), by David Mamet; starring Denholm Elliott, 31 October - 25 February (transferred to the Strand 13 December).

2. *Salome* (P: NT, Lyttelton), by Oscar Wilde; starring Steven Berkoff, 7 November - 31 March (transferred to the Phoenix 22 January).

3. *The Beaux' Stratagem* (P: NT, Lyttelton), by George Farquhar, 22 November - 20 February.

4. *The Baker's Wife* (M: Phoenix), by Stephen Schwartz and Joe Stein; starring Alun (CQ) Armstrong, 27 November - 6 January.

5. *The Good Person of Sichuan* (P: NT, Olivier), by Bertolt Brecht; starring Fiona Shaw, 28 November - 31 March.

6. *Barnaby and the Old Boys* (P: Vaudeville), by Keith Baxter; starring Jill Gascoine, Keith Baxter, 4 December - 27 January.

7. *The Liar* (P: Old Vic), by Pierre Corneille, 12 December - 24 March.

8. *London Assurance* (P: Theatre Royal, Haymarket), by Dion Boucicault; starring Paul Eddington, 13 December - 10 March.

9. *Treats* (P: Hampstead), by Christopher Hampton; starring Tom Conti, 18 December - February.

10. *Noel and Gertie* (P: Comedy), devised by Sheridan Morley; starring Patricia Hodge, Simon Cadell, 19 December - 16 June.

11. *Seven Lears* (P: Royal Court), by Howard Barker, 5-27 January.

12. *Scenes from an Execution* (P: Almeida), by Howard Barker; starring Glenda Jackson, 9 January - 3 February.

13. *Bent* (P: NT, Lyttelton), by Martin Sherman; starring Ian McKellen, 24 January - 21 April (transferred to the Garrick 6 March).

14. *The Price* (P: Young Vic), by Arthur Miller, 1 February - 24 March.

15. *A Clockwork Orange* (P: RSC, Barbican), by Anthony Burgess with Ron Daniels, 7 February - 26 May (transferred to the Royalty, 23 April).

16. *Racing Demon* (P: NT, Cottesloe), by David Hare; starring Oliver Ford Davies, Michael Bryant, 8 February - SR (transferred to the Olivier 2 August).

17. *Man of the Moment* (P: Globe), by Alan Ayckbourn; starring Michael Gambon, Peter Bowles, 14 February - SR.

18. *When We Dead Waken* (P: Almeida), by Henrik Ibsen; starring Claire Bloom, 20 February - 24 March.

19. *Exchange* (P: Vaudeville), by Yuri Trifonov, translated by Michael Frayn, 22 February - 28 April.

20. *Bus Stop* (P: Lyric), by William Inge; starring Jerry Hall, Shaun Cassidy, 27 February - 6 May.

21. *Peer Gynt* (P: NT, Olivier), by Henrik Ibsen; starring Stephen Moore, 28 February - 24 July.

22. *Sunday In the Park With George* (M: NT, Lyttelton), by Stephen Sondheim and James Lapine; starring Philip Quast, Maria Friedman, 15 March - 16 June.

23. *An Evening With Peter Ustinov* (Solo show: Theatre Royal, Haymarket), starring Peter Ustinov, 21 March - 27 May.

24. *Someone Like You* (M: Strand), by Petula Clark and Dee Shipman; starring Petula Clark, 22 March - 24 April.

25. *The Trackers of Oxyrhynchus* (P: NT, Olivier), by Tony Harrison, 27 March - 10 May.

26. *Singer* (P: RSC, Pit), by Peter Flannery; starring Antony Sher, 28 March - 3 November (transferred to Barbican main stage 7 September).

27. *Never the Sinner* (P: Playhouse), by John Logan; starring Joss Ackland, Julian Glover, 29 March - 19 May.

28. *All's Well That Ends Well* (P: RSC, Barbican), by William Shakespeare, 30 March - 5 June.

29. *Marya* (P: Old Vic), by Isaac Babel, translated by Christopher Hampton, 3 April - 27 May.

30. *Pericles* (P: RSC, Pit), by William Shakespeare, 4 April - 1 November.

31. *Volpone* (P: Almeida), by Ben Jonson; starring Ian McDiarmid, Denis Lawson, 4 April - 5 May.

32. *As You Like It* (P: RSC, Barbican), by William Shakespeare; starring Sophie Thompson, 5 April - 15 September.

33. *Being At Home With Claude* (P: King's Head), by René-Daniel Dubois; starring Lothaire Bluteau, 8 April - 2 June (transferred to the Vaudeville 1 May).

34. *Look Look* (P: Aldwych), by Michael Frayn; starring Stephen Fry, 17 April - 12 May.

35. *King* (M: Piccadilly), by Richard Blackford, Maya Angelou, and Alistair Beaton; starring Simon Estes, Cynthia Haymon, 23 April - 2 June.

36. *The School for Scandal* (P: NT, Olivier), by Richard Brinsley Sheridan; starring John Neville, Jane Asher, Prunella Scales, 24 April - November.

37. *Song and Dance* (M: Shaftesbury), by Andrew Lloyd Webber and Don Black, 25 April - 1 September.

38. *The Duchess of Malfi* (P: RSC, Pit), by Webster; starring Harriet Walter, 1 May - 1 September.

39. *A Shayna Maidel* (P: King's Head), by Barbara Lebow, 1 May - 9 June.

40. *Coriolanus* (P: RSC, Barbican), by Shakespeare; starring Charles Dance, 2 May - 1 September.

41. *Berenice* (P: NT, Cottesloe), by Jean Racine, translated by Neil Bartlett; starring Lindsay Duncan, 9 May - 1 September.

42. *Desire* (P: Almeida), by David Ian, 14 May - 9 June.

43. *Absurd Person Singular* (P: Whitehall), by Alan Ayckbourn, 15 May - SR.

44. *Vanilla* (P: Lyric), by Jane Stanton Hitchcock; starring Sian Phillips, Joanna Lumley, 16 May - 7 July.

45. *The Wild Duck* (P: Phoenix), by Henrik Ibsen; starring Alex Jennings, David Threlfall, 17 May - 11 August.

46. *Henry IV* (P: Wyndham's), by Luigi Pirandello; starring Richard Harris, 23 May - 22 September.

47. *Burn This* (P: Hampstead), by Lanford Wilson; starring John Malkovich, Juliet Stevenson, 29 May - 6 October (transferred to the Lyric 11 July).

48. *The Crucible* (P: NT, Olivier), by Arthur Miller, 30 May - 31 January 1991.

49. *Temptation* (P: Westminster), by Vaclav Havel, 6 June - 14 July.

50. *Gasping* (P: Theatre Royal, Haymarket), by Ben Elton, 7 June - SR.

51. *The Illusion* (P: Old Vic), by Pierre Corneille, 11 June - 28 July.

52. *Hidden Laughter* (P: Vaudeville), by Simon Gray; starring Felicity Kendal, Peter Barkworth, 13 June - SR.

53. *Anna Christie* (P: Young Vic), by Eugene O'Neill; starring Natasha Richardson, 14 June - 14 July.

54. *After the Fall* (P: NT, Cottesloe), by Arthur Miller; starring James Laurenson, Josette Simon, 20 June - 29 December (transferred to the Lyttelton, 29 September).

55. *Bernadette* (M: Dominion), by Gwyn and Maureen Hughes; starring Natalie Wright, 21 June - 14 July.

56. *Mother Courage* (P: Mermaid), by Bertolt Brecht; starring Glenda Jackson, 4 July - 22 September.

57. *Earwig* (P: RSC), Pit), by Paula Milne; starring Lisa Harrow, 12 July - 3 November.

58. *The Rocky Horror Show* (M: Piccadilly), by Richard O'Brien, 15 July - SR.

59. *Three Sisters* (P: Royal Court), by Anton Chekhov; starring Sinead, Sorcha, Niamh, and Cyril Cusack, 19 July - 29 September.

60. *Richard III* (P: NT, Lyttelton), by William Shakespeare; starring Ian McKellen, 25 July - 2 February 1991.

61. *King Lear* (P: NT, Lyttelton), by William Shakespeare; starring Brian Cox, 26 July - 2 February 1991.

62. *Having A Ball* (P: Comedy), by Alan Bleasdale; starring David Ross, 28 August - 10 November.

63. *The Man Who Had All the Luck* (P: Young Vic), by Arthur Miller; starring Iain Glen, 30 July - 1 September.

64. *Barbarians* (P: RSC, Barbican), by Maxim Gorky, 31 July - 30 October.

65. *Show Boat* (M: Palladium), by Jerome Kern and Oscar Hammerstein II, 1 August - 22 September.

66. *A Dream of People* (P: RSC, Pit), by Michael Hastings, 2 August - 30 October.

67. *Kean* (P: Old Vic), by Jean-Paul Sartre; starring Derek Jacobi, 7 August - 24 November.

68. *Piano* (P: NT, Cottesloe), by Trevor Griffiths, 8 August - 19 January 1991.

69. *My Children! My Africa!* (P: NT, Lyttelton), by Athol Fugard; starring John Kani, 5 - 15 September.

70. *The Rehearsal* (P: Almeida), by Jean Anouilh, translated by Jeremy Sams; starring Nicola Pagett, Jonathan Hyde, 13 September - SR (transferred to the Garrick 12 November).

71. *Once in a While the Odd Thing Happens* (P: NT, Cottesloe), by Paul Godfrey, 18 September - 1 December.

72. *Private Lives* (P: Aldwych), by Noel Coward; starring Joan Collins, Keith Baxter, 19 September - SR.

73. *Fences* (P: Garrick), by August Wilson; starring Yaphet Kotto, 24 September - 3 November.

74. *Into the Woods* (M: Phoenix), by Stephen Sondheim and James Lapine; starring Julia McKenzie, Imelda Staunton, 25 September - SR.

75. *Victoria Wood: Up West* (Solo show: Strand), starring Victoria Wood, 25 September - 1 December.

76. *Moscow Gold* (P: RSC, Barbican), by Howard Benton and Tariq Ali; starring David Calder, Sara Kestelman, 26 September - 1 November.

77. *Love Letters* (P: Wyndham's), by A. R. Gurney; starring Stefanie Powers, Robert Wagner, 1 October - 17 November.

78. *Out of Order* (P: Shaftesbury), by Ray Cooney; starring Donald Sinden, Michael Williams, 9 October - SR.

79. *Dancing at Lughnasa* (P: NT, Lyttelton), by Brian Friel, 15 October - 1 January 1991.

80. *Other People's Money* (P: Lyric), by Jerry Sterner; starring Martin Shaw, Maria Aitken, Paul Rogers, 17 October - SR.

81. *Stand up America!* (Comedy revue: Queen's), 22 October - 1 December.

82. *The Mystery of Irma Vep* (P: Ambassadors), by Charles Ludlam; starring Nickolas Grace, Edward Hibbert, 30 October - SR.

83. *Bookends* (P: Apollo), by Keith Waterhouse; starring Sir Michael Hordern, Dinsdale Landen, 31 October - SR.

Contributors

Alida Allison...*San Diego State University*
Leo Balk ....*Garland Publishing Company*
Sarah Barnhill ....*Brevard, North Carolina*
Andrea G. Bell ....*Hunter College*
William Cagle ....*The Lilly Library, Indiana University*
Richard R. Centing..*Ohio State University*
Ron Fortune ....*Illinois State University*
George Garrett ....*University of Virginia*
Ann B. González ....*University of North Carolina at Charlotte*
R. S. Gwynn ....*Lamar University*
James Hardin ....*University of South Carolina*
Mark A. Heberle....................................*University of Hawaii at Manoa*
James W. Hipp ....*Columbia, South Carolina*
Linda Whitney Hobson ....*New Orleans, Louisiana*
Donna Hoffmeister....................................*University of Colorado-Boulder*
Nicolette Jones ....*London, England*
Howard Kissel ....*New York Daily News*
Virginia Lowell Mauck...................................*The Lilly Library, Indiana University*
Joel Myerson...*University of South Carolina*
Ahmed Nimeiri ....*University of Khartoum*
Carol Peirce..*University of Baltimore*
David R. Slavitt..*University of Pennsylvania*
Kiyohiko Tsuboi ....*Okayama University*
Nobuko Tsuboi ....*Ochanomizu Women's University*
John Whalen-Bridge.............................*University of Southern California*
Matt Wolf ....*Associated Press and* Wall Street Journal/Europe

Cumulative Index

Dictionary of Literary Biography, Volumes 1-105
Dictionary of Literary Biography Yearbook, 1980-1990
Dictionary of Literary Biography Documentary Series, Volumes 1-8

Cumulative Index

DLB before number: *Dictionary of Literary Biography,* Volumes 1-105
Y before number: *Dictionary of Literary Biography Yearbook,* 1980-1990
DS before number: *Dictionary of Literary Biography Documentary Series,* Volumes 1-8

A

B

C

D

F

G

H

I

L

Cumulative Index

Q

R

S

Cumulative Index

W

Y

Z

Cumulative Index

(Continued from front endsheets)

80: *Restoration and Eighteenth-Century Dramatists,* First Series, edited by Paula R. Backscheider (1989)

81: *Austrian Fiction Writers, 1875-1913,* edited by James Hardin and Donald G. Daviau (1989)

82: *Chicano Writers,* First Series, edited by Francisco A. Lomelí and Carl R. Shirley (1989)

83: *French Novelists Since 1960,* edited by Catharine Savage Brosman (1989)

84: *Restoration and Eighteenth-Century Dramatists,* Second Series, edited by Paula R. Backscheider (1989)

85: *Austrian Fiction Writers After 1914,* edited by James Hardin and Donald G. Daviau (1989)

86: *American Short-Story Writers, 1910-1945,* First Series, edited by Bobby Ellen Kimbel (1989)

87: *British Mystery and Thriller Writers Since 1940,* First Series, edited by Bernard Benstock and Thomas F. Staley (1989)

88: *Canadian Writers, 1920-1959,* Second Series, edited by W. H. New (1989)

89: *Restoration and Eighteenth-Century Dramatists,* Third Series, edited by Paula R. Backscheider (1989)

90: *German Writers in the Age of Goethe, 1789-1832,* edited by James Hardin and Christoph E. Schweitzer (1989)

91: *American Magazine Journalists, 1900-1960,* First Series, edited by Sam G. Riley (1990)

92: *Canadian Writers, 1890-1920,* edited by W. H. New (1990)

93: *British Romantic Poets, 1789-1832,* First Series, edited by John R. Greenfield (1990)

94: *German Writers in the Age of Goethe: Sturm und Drang to Classicism,* edited by James Hardin and Christoph E. Schweitzer (1990)

95: *Eighteenth-Century British Poets,* First Series, edited by John Sitter (1990)

96: *British Romantic Poets, 1789-1832,* Second Series, edited by John R. Greenfield (1990)

97: *German Writers from the Enlightenment to Sturm und Drang, 1720-1764,* edited by James Hardin and Christoph E. Schweitzer (1990)

98: *Modern British Essayists,* First Series, edited by Robert Beum (1990)

99: *Canadian Writers Before 1890,* edited by W. H. New (1990)

100: *Modern British Essayists,* Second Series, edited by Robert Beum (1990)

101: *British Prose Writers, 1660-1800,* First Series, edited by Donald T. Siebert (1991)

102: *American Short-Story Writers, 1910-1945,* Second Series, edited by Bobby Ellen Kimbel (1991)

103: *American Literary Biographers,* First Series, edited by Steven Serafin (1991)

104: *British Prose Writers, 1660-1800,* Second Series, edited by Donald T. Siebert (1991)

105: *American Poets Since World War II,* Second Series, edited by R. S. Gwynn (1991)

Documentary Series

1: *Sherwood Anderson, Willa Cather, John Dos Passos, Theodore Dreiser, F. Scott Fitzgerald, Ernest Hemingway, Sinclair Lewis,* edited by Margaret A. Van Antwerp (1982)

2: *James Gould Cozzens, James T. Farrell, William Faulkner, John O'Hara, John Steinbeck, Thomas Wolfe, Richard Wright,* edited by Margaret A. Van Antwerp (1982)

3: *Saul Bellow, Jack Kerouac, Norman Mailer, Vladimir Nabokov, John Updike, Kurt Vonnegut,* edited by Mary Bruccoli (1983)

4: *Tennessee Williams,* edited by Margaret A. Van Antwerp and Sally Johns (1984)

5: *American Transcendentalists,* edited by Joel Myerson (1988)

6: *Hardboiled Mystery Writers,* edited by Matthew J. Bruccoli and Richard Layman (1989)

7: *Modern American Poets,* edited by Karen L. Rood (1989)

8: *The Black Aesthetic Movement,* edited by Jeffrey Louis Decker (1991)

Yearbooks

1980, edited by Karen L. Rood, Jean W. Ross, and Richard Ziegfeld (1981)